"Todd Lammle has done it again! Lammle's [*CCNP: Advanced Cisco Router Configuration Study Guide*] is unquestionably better [than other ACRC study guides] for ACRC test preparation....Compared to a 5-day ACRC course which costs $1900 in my area (and likely requires another week or more of study before testing), this book for less than a 50 spot is a staggering bargain. Buy it and spend ample time with it....Todd, my pocketbook thanks you."

A Reader from Amazon.com
Jackson, Mississippi

"[Lammle's *CCNA: Cisco Certified Network Associate Study Guide* is] the best CCNA book on the market! You have to have this book if you are considering taking the CCNA exam. It missed nothing and the review questions at the end of each chapter are right on!"

A reader from Fatbrain.com

"Of the preparation guides available for the Cisco Certified Design Associate exam (640-441), [Lammle's] *CCDA: Cisco Certified Design Associate Study Guide* comes out on top....The author's presentation style uses text to great effect, explaining potentially confusing topics with clear, fact-rich prose that rewards close attention from the reader. There are plenty of helpful conceptual diagrams and flow charts as well....Elaborate solutions to the problems and quick answers to the review questions appear in the back of this book (along with an excellent, extensive glossary)."

David Wall
Amazon.com Editor

"If you are a CCNA candidate, buy it. If you need some review of Cisco essentials, buy it.... If you are a CCNP candidate, the book can build a solid foundation for your CCNP 2.0. [The *CCNA: Cisco Certified Network Associate Study Guide*, Second Edition]."

Watson Chack, Hong Kong
A Reader from Amazon.com

The *CCNA: Cisco Certified Network Associate Study Guide*, Second Edition, has "diagrams, router screen shots, labs, hands-on exercises, practice questions, figures, tables and so much more. You have everything you need to pass this exam first time around. Lammle's attention to detail is what makes this the standout performer of the year."

Michael Woznicki
Technical Instructor and Reviewer

"Buy It. Read It. Pass It. [The *CCNA: Cisco Certified Network Associate Study Guide*, Second Edition]."

Xiang Tang, China
A Reader from Amazon.com

CCNP
Switching
Study Guide

CCNP™ Switching Study Guide

Todd Lammle

Kevin Hales

San Francisco • Paris • Düsseldorf • Soest • London

SYBEX®

Associate Publisher: Neil Edde
Contracts and Licensing Manager: Kristine O'Callaghan
Acquisitions and Developmental Editor: Jill Schlessinger
Editor: Judy Flynn
Production Editor: Shannon Murphy
Technical Editors: Errol Robichaux, Mark Tashiro
Book Designer: Bill Gibson
Graphic Illustrator: Tony Jonick
Electronic Publishing Specialist: Nila Nichols
Proofreaders: Laurie O'Connell, Erika Donald, Nanette Duffy, Laura Schattschneider, Camera Obscura
Indexer: Jerilyn Sproston
CD Coordinator: Kara Eve Schwartz
CD Technician: Keith McNeil
Cover Designer: Archer Design
Cover Photographer: Tony Stone Images

Copyright © 2001 SYBEX Inc., 1151 Marina Village Parkway, Alameda, CA 94501. World rights reserved. No part of this publication may be stored in a retrieval system, transmitted, or reproduced in any way, including but not limited to photocopy, photograph, magnetic, or other record, without the prior agreement and written permission of the publisher.

Library of Congress Card Number: 00-106238

ISBN: 0-7821-2711-8

SYBEX and the SYBEX logo are trademarks of SYBEX Inc. in the USA and other countries.

The CD interface was created using Macromedia Director, © 1994, 1997-1999 Macromedia Inc. For more information on Macromedia and Macromedia Director, visit http://www.macromedia.com

This study guide and/or material is not sponsored by, endorsed by or affiliated with Cisco Systems, Inc. Cisco®, Cisco Systems®, CCDA™, CCNA™, CCDP™, CCNP™, CCIE™, CCSI™, the Cisco Systems logo and the CCIE logo are trademarks or registered trademarks of Cisco Systems, Inc. in the United States and certain other countries. All other trademarks are trademarks of their respective owners.

TRADEMARKS: SYBEX has attempted throughout this book to distinguish proprietary trademarks from descriptive terms by following the capitalization style used by the manufacturer.

The author and publisher have made their best efforts to prepare this book, and the content is based upon final release software whenever possible. Portions of the manuscript may be based upon pre-release versions supplied by software manufacturer(s). The author and the publisher make no representation or warranties of any kind with regard to the completeness or accuracy of the contents herein and accept no liability of any kind including but not limited to performance, merchantability, fitness for any particular purpose, or any losses or damages of any kind caused or alleged to be caused directly or indirectly from this book.

Manufactured in the United States of America

10 9 8 7 6 5 4 3

Software License Agreement: Terms and Conditions

The media and/or any online materials accompanying this book that are available now or in the future contain programs and/or text files (the "Software") to be used in connection with the book. SYBEX hereby grants to you a license to use the Software, subject to the terms that follow. Your purchase, acceptance, or use of the Software will constitute your acceptance of such terms.

The Software compilation is the property of SYBEX unless otherwise indicated and is protected by copyright to SYBEX or other copyright owner(s) as indicated in the media files (the "Owner(s)"). You are hereby granted a single-user license to use the Software for your personal, noncommercial use only. You may not reproduce, sell, distribute, publish, circulate, or commercially exploit the Software, or any portion thereof, without the written consent of SYBEX and the specific copyright owner(s) of any component software included on this media.

In the event that the Software or components include specific license requirements or end-user agreements, statements of condition, disclaimers, limitations or warranties ("End-User License"), those End-User Licenses supersede the terms and conditions herein as to that particular Software component. Your purchase, acceptance, or use of the Software will constitute your acceptance of such End-User Licenses.

By purchase, use or acceptance of the Software you further agree to comply with all export laws and regulations of the United States as such laws and regulations may exist from time to time.

Reusable Code in This Book

The authors created reusable code in this publication expressly for reuse for readers. Sybex grants readers permission to reuse for any purpose the code found in this publication or its accompanying CD-ROM so long as all three authors are attributed in any application containing the reusable code, and the code itself is never sold or commercially exploited as a stand-alone product.

Software Support

Components of the supplemental Software and any offers associated with them may be supported by the specific Owner(s) of that material but they are not supported by SYBEX. Information regarding any available support may be obtained from the Owner(s) using the information provided in the appropriate read.me files or listed elsewhere on the media.

Should the manufacturer(s) or other Owner(s) cease to offer support or decline to honor any offer, SYBEX bears no responsibility. This notice concerning support for the Software is provided for your information only. SYBEX is not the agent or principal of the Owner(s), and SYBEX is in no way responsible for providing any support for the Software, nor is it liable or responsible for any support provided, or not provided, by the Owner(s).

Warranty

SYBEX warrants the enclosed media to be free of physical defects for a period of ninety (90) days after purchase. The Software is not available from SYBEX in any other form or media than that enclosed herein or posted to www.sybex.com. If you discover a defect in the media during this warranty period, you may obtain a replacement of identical format at no charge by sending the defective media, postage prepaid, with proof of purchase to:

SYBEX Inc.
Customer Service Department
1151 Marina Village Parkway
Alameda, CA 94501
(510) 523-8233
Fax: (510) 523-2373
e-mail: info@sybex.com
WEB: HTTP://WWW.SYBEX.COM

After the 90-day period, you can obtain replacement media of identical format by sending us the defective disk, proof of purchase, and a check or money order for $10, payable to SYBEX.

Disclaimer

SYBEX makes no warranty or representation, either expressed or implied, with respect to the Software or its contents, quality, performance, merchantability, or fitness for a particular purpose. In no event will SYBEX, its distributors, or dealers be liable to you or any other party for direct, indirect, special, incidental, consequential, or other damages arising out of the use of or inability to use the Software or its contents even if advised of the possibility of such damage. In the event that the Software includes an online update feature, SYBEX further disclaims any obligation to provide this feature for any specific duration other than the initial posting. The exclusion of implied warranties is not permitted by some states. Therefore, the above exclusion may not apply to you. This warranty provides you with specific legal rights; there may be other rights that you may have that vary from state to state. The pricing of the book with the Software by SYBEX reflects the allocation of risk and limitations on liability contained in this agreement of Terms and Conditions.

Shareware Distribution

This Software may contain various programs that are distributed as shareware. Copyright laws apply to both shareware and ordinary commercial software, and the copyright Owner(s) retains all rights. If you try a shareware program and continue using it, you are expected to register it. Individual programs differ on details of trial periods, registration, and payment. Please observe the requirements stated in appropriate files.

Copy Protection

The Software in whole or in part may or may not be copy-protected or encrypted. However, in all cases, reselling or redistributing these files without authorization is expressly forbidden except as specifically provided for by the Owner(s) therein.

To my new friends at learnit.com. You're all awesome!
Todd Lammle

To Claudia, Christopher, and Clarissa—the balance in my life.
Kevin Hales

Acknowledgments

We would all be millionaires if we could bottle Jill Schlessinger's energy and great attitude. This project owes her a debt of gratitude. Thanks to Kevin Hales for hanging in there and adding the great material needed to make this book the best.

Todd Lammle

I would like to acknowledge the great support my wife has been. Again, thanks to Todd Lammle for including me on this project. A great deal of gratitude for all those at Sybex, especially Jill Schlessinger and Shannon Murphy.

Kevin Hales

We would both like to thank all the folks associated with Sybex who helped get this book on the shelves. Judy Flynn was a superb editor. This book would be a stack of typewritten pages without the layout finesse of Nila Nichols. Tony Jonick magically transformed sketches into works of art. Thanks to technical editors Errol Robichaux and Mark Tashiro for being our watchdogs. Finally, our other watchdogs are the proofreaders: thanks to Laurie O'Connell, Erika Donald, Nanette Duffy, Camera Obscura, and Laura Schattschneider.

Contents at a Glance

Introduction			*xviii*
Assessment Test			*xxxiv*
Chapter	**1**	The Campus Network	1
Chapter	**2**	Connecting the Switch Block	51
Chapter	**3**	VLANs	99
Chapter	**4**	Layer 2 Switching and the Spanning Tree Protocol (STP)	149
Chapter	**5**	Using Spanning Tree with VLANs	181
Chapter	**6**	Inter-VLAN Routing	225
Chapter	**7**	Multi-Layer Switching (MLS)	263
Chapter	**8**	Hot Standby Routing Protocol (HSRP)	305
Chapter	**9**	Multicast	339
Chapter	**10**	Configuring Multicast	385
Chapter	**11**	Access Policies	423
Appendix	**A**	Practice Exam	465
Appendix	**B**	Commands Used in This Book	487
Appendix	**C**	Internet Multicast Addresses	499
Glossary			525
Index			*607*

Contents

Introduction   *xviii*

Assessment Test   *xxxiv*

Chapter 1   **The Campus Network**   **1**

    Campus Internetworks   3
    Looking Backwards at Traditional Campus Networks   4
        Performance Problems and Solutions   4
    The New Campus Model   10
        Network Services   11
    Switching Technologies   12
        Open Systems Interconnection (OSI) Model   12
        Layer 2 Switching   15
        Routing   17
        Layer 3 Switching   18
        Layer 4 Switching   19
        Multi-Layer Switching (MLS)   19
    The Cisco Hierarchical Model   20
        Three-Layer Hierarchical Model   21
    Cisco Catalyst Products   25
        Access Layer Switches   25
        Distribution Layer Switches   26
        Core Layer Switches   26
    The Building Block   27
        Switch Block   28
        Core Block   29
        Scaling Layer 2 Backbones   32
        Scaling Layer 3 Backbones   34
    Summary   35
        Key Terms   36
    Written Lab   36
        Lab 1.1: Switching Definitions   36

	Lab 1.2: Cisco's Three-Layer Model	37
	Lab 1.3: Theory	38
Review Questions		39
Answers to Written Lab		45
	Answers to Lab 1.1	45
	Answers to Lab 1.2	46
	Answers to Lab 1.3	46
Answers to Review Questions		48

Chapter 2 Connecting the Switch Block   51

Cable Media	52
The Background of IEEE Ethernet	53
Switched Ethernet	54
Using Ethernet Media in Your Internetwork	55
10BaseT	55
FastEthernet	56
Gigabit Ethernet	59
Connecting and Logging In to a Switch	61
Cabling the Switch Block Devices	62
Cisco IOS- and Set-Based Commands	65
Summary	81
Key Terms	82
Commands Used in This Chapter	83
Written Lab	85
Hands-On Lab	86
Review Questions	90
Answers to Written Lab	96
Answers to Review Questions	97

Chapter 3 VLANs   99

The Benefits of Virtual LANs	101
Broadcast Control	101
Security	102
Flexibility and Scalability	103
The Collapsed Backbone and the VLAN	103

Scaling the Switch Block	105
Defining VLAN Boundaries	106
VLAN Memberships	107
Configuring Static VLANs	108
Identifying VLANs	112
Frame Tagging	113
VLAN Identification Methods	114
Trunking	116
Configuring Trunk Ports	117
Clearing VLANs from Trunk Links	119
Verifying Trunk Links	120
VLAN Trunk Protocol (VTP)	121
VTP Modes of Operation	122
VTP Advertisements	123
Configuration Revision Number	126
Configuring VTP	126
Adding to a VTP Domain	131
VTP Pruning	132
Summary	133
Key Terms	133
Commands Used in This Chapter	134
Written Lab	135
Hands-On Lab	136
Review Questions	140
Answers to Written Lab	146
Answers to Review Questions	147

Chapter 4   Layer 2 Switching and the Spanning Tree Protocol (STP)   149

Layer 2 LAN Switching	150
Three Switch Functions at Layer 2	151
Spanning Tree Operation	156
Selecting the Root Bridge	158
Selecting the Designated Port	159
Spanning Tree Port States	160
Spanning Tree Example	162

	LAN Switch Types	163
	Store-and-Forward	164
	Cut-Through (Real Time)	164
	FragmentFree (Modified Cut-Through)	164
	Configuring Spanning Tree	165
	Summary	168
	Key Terms	168
	Commands Used in This Chapter	169
	Written Lab	170
	Review Questions	171
	Answers to Written Lab	177
	Answers to Review Questions	178
Chapter 5	**Using Spanning Tree with VLANs**	**181**
	Cisco and IEEE 802.1q Committee	182
	Per-VLAN Spanning Tree (PVST)	183
	Common Spanning Tree (CST)	184
	Per-VLAN Spanning Tree+ (PVST+)	184
	Scaling the Spanning Tree Protocol	185
	Determining the Root	186
	Configuring the Root	186
	Setting the Port Cost	191
	Setting the Port Priority	193
	Changing the STP Timers	197
	Redundant Links with STP	199
	Parallel Fast EtherChannel Links	199
	EtherChannel Guidelines	200
	Configuring EtherChannel	200
	Port Aggregation Protocol (PAgP)	204
	PortFast	205
	PortFast Configuration	205
	UplinkFast	206
	UplinkFast Configuration	207
	BackboneFast	209
	Configuring and Verifying BackboneFast	209

		Summary	210
		Key Terms	210
		Commands Used in This Chapter	211
		Written Lab	213
		Hands-On Lab	214
		Review Questions	217
		Answers to Written Lab	222
		Answers to Review Questions	223
Chapter	6	**Inter-VLAN Routing**	**225**
		Routing between VLANs	226
		Multiple Links	227
		A Single Trunked Link	228
		Route Switch Modules (RSMs)	229
		Inter-Switch Link Routing	230
		Configuring ISL	230
		Summary	238
		Key Terms	238
		Commands Used in This Chapter	239
		Written Lab	240
		Hands-On Lab	241
		Lab 6.1: External Inter-VLAN Routing	241
		Lab 6.2: Internal Inter-VLAN Routing	252
		Review Questions	254
		Answers to Written Lab	260
		Answers to Review Questions	261
Chapter	7	**Multi-Layer Switching (MLS)**	**263**
		Fundamentals of MLS	264
		MLS Requirements	266
		MLS Procedures	266
		MLSP Discovery	268
		XTAGs	269
		MLS Cache	270
		Disabling MLS	275

	MLS-RP Configuration	276
	Enabling MLS	276
	VTP Domain Assignments	277
	VLAN Assignments	279
	Interface Configurations	279
	MSA Management Interface	280
	Verifying the MLS Configuration	281
	Access Lists	283
	Configuring the MLS Engine	283
	Enabling MLS on the MLS-SE	284
	Cache Entries	284
	Displaying the MLS Cache Entries	287
	Removing MLS Cache Entries	288
	Acceptable MLS Topologies	288
	Summary	290
	Key Terms	291
	Commands Used in This Chapter	291
	Written Lab	293
	Hands-On Lab	294
	Review Questions	296
	Answers to Written Lab	301
	Answers to Review Questions	302
Chapter 8	**Hot Standby Routing Protocol (HSRP)**	**305**
	Fault-Tolerant Routing	307
	Proxy ARP	307
	Dynamic Routing Protocols	312
	ICMP Router Discovery Protocol (IRDP)	313
	HSRP	313
	Configuring HSRP	314
	Active Router Properties	317
	HSRP Tracking	318
	HSRP with Multiple Destinations	319
	HSRP with Multiple Groups	320

Summary		321
Key Terms		322
Commands Used in This Chapter		322
Written Lab		324
Hands-On Lab		325
Review Questions		331
Answers to Written Lab		336
Answers to Review Questions		337

Chapter 9 Multicast — 339

Multicast Overview	340
Unicast	341
Broadcast	342
Multicast	343
Multicast Addressing	345
Mapping IP Multicast to Ethernet	346
Managing Multicast in an Internetwork	350
Subscribing and Maintaining Groups	351
Internet Group Management Protocol Version 1 (IGMPv1)	352
Internet Group Management Protocol Version 2 (IGMPv2)	355
Cisco Group Management Protocol (CGMP)	357
Routing Multicast Traffic	358
Distribution Trees	359
Managing Multicast Delivery	363
Time to Live (TTL)	364
Routing Protocols	365
Sparse Mode Routing Protocols	372
Summary	375
Key Terms	376
Review Questions	377
Answers to Review Questions	382

Chapter 10 Configuring Multicast — 385

Planning and Preparing for Using IP Multicast	387
End-to-End IP Multicast	388

	Configuring IP Multicast Routing	388
	Enabling IP Multicast Routing	389
	Enabling PIM on an Interface	391
	Configuring a Rendezvous Point	395
	Configuring TTL	398
	Joining a Multicast Group	399
	Changing the IGMP Version	402
	Enabling CGMP	402
	Summary	404
	Key Terms	404
	Commands Used in This Chapter	405
	Written Lab	407
	Hands-On Lab	408
	Review Questions	414
	Answers to Written Lab	420
	Answers to Review Questions	421
Chapter 11	**Access Policies**	**423**
	Definition of an Access Policy	424
	Applying Policies to the Hierarchical Model	425
	Managing Network Devices	426
	Physical Security	426
	Passwords	427
	Privileged Levels	438
	Banners	441
	Limiting VTY Access	442
	Controlling HTTP Access	443
	Access Layer Policy	444
	Managing the MAC Address Table	444
	Distribution Layer Policy	447
	Access Lists	447
	Route Filtering	452
	Summary	453
	Key Terms	454
	Commands Used in This Chapter	454

		Written Lab	456
		Review Questions	457
		Answers to Written Lab	462
		Answers to Review Questions	463
Appendix	A	**Practice Exam**	**465**
		Answers to Practice Exam	481
Appendix	B	**Commands Used in This Book**	**487**
Appendix	C	**Internet Multicast Addresses**	**499**
Glossary			**525**
Index			*607*

Introduction

The new Cisco certifications reach beyond the popular certifications, such as the MCSE and CNE, to provide you with an indispensable factor in understanding today's network—insight into the Cisco world of internetworking. This book is intended to help you continue on your exciting new path toward obtaining CCNP and CCIE certification. Before reading this book, you should have at least read Sybex's *CCNA: Cisco Certified Network Associate Study Guide*. Although you can take the Cisco tests in any order, you should pass the CCNA exam before pursuing your CCNP. Many questions in the CCNP Switching exam (640-504) are built upon the CCNA material. However, we have done everything possible to make sure you can pass the 640-504 exam by reading this book and practicing with Cisco routers.

Cisco—A Brief History

A lot of readers may already be familiar with Cisco and what they do. However, those of you who are new to the field, just coming in fresh from your MCSE, or those of you who have maybe 10 or more years in the field but wish to brush up on the new technology, may appreciate a little background on Cisco.

In the early 1980s, Len and Sandy Bosack, a married couple who worked in different computer departments at Stanford University, were having trouble getting their individual systems to communicate (like many married people). So in their living room they created a gateway server that made it easier for their disparate computers in two different departments to communicate using the IP protocol. In 1984, they founded cisco Systems (notice the small c) with a small commercial gateway server product that changed networking forever. Some people think the name was intended to be San Francisco Systems but the paper got ripped on the way to the incorporation lawyers—who knows? In 1992, the company name was changed to Cisco Systems, Inc.

The first product the company marketed was called the Advanced Gateway Server (AGS). Then came the Mid-Range Gateway Server (MGS), the Compact Gateway Server (CGS), the Integrated Gateway Server (IGS), and the AGS+. Cisco calls these "the old alphabet soup products."

In 1993, Cisco came out with the amazing 4000 router and then created the even more amazing 7000, 2000, and 3000 series routers. These are still around and evolving (almost daily, it seems).

Cisco has since become an unrivaled worldwide leader in networking for the Internet. Its networking solutions can easily connect users who work from diverse devices on disparate networks. Cisco products make it simple for people to access and transfer information without regard to differences in time, place, or platform.

In the big picture, Cisco provides end-to-end networking solutions that customers can use to build an efficient, unified information infrastructure of their own or to connect to someone else's. This is an important piece in the Internet/networking-industry puzzle because a common architecture that delivers consistent network services to all users is now a functional imperative. Because Cisco offers such a broad range of networking and Internet services and capabilities, users who need to access their local network or the Internet regularly can do so unhindered, making Cisco's wares indispensable.

Cisco answers this need with a wide range of hardware products that form information networks using the Cisco Internetwork Operating System (IOS) software. This software provides network services, paving the way for networked technical support and professional services to maintain and optimize all network operations.

Along with the Cisco IOS, one of the services Cisco created to help support the vast amount of hardware it has engineered is the Cisco Certified Internetwork Expert (CCIE) program, which was designed specifically to equip people to effectively manage the vast quantity of installed Cisco networks. The business plan is simple: If you want to sell more Cisco equipment and install more Cisco networks, ensure that the networks you install run properly.

However, having a fabulous product line isn't all it takes to guarantee the huge success that Cisco enjoys—lots of companies with great products are now defunct. If you have complicated products designed to solve complicated problems, you need knowledgeable people who are fully capable of installing, managing, and troubleshooting them. That part isn't easy, so Cisco began the CCIE program to equip people to support these complicated networks. This program, known colloquially as the Doctorate of Networking, has also been successful, primarily due to its extreme difficulty. Cisco continuously monitors the CCIE program, changing it as it sees fit, to make sure that it remains pertinent and accurately reflects the demands of today's internetworking business environments.

Building upon the highly successful CCIE program, Cisco Career Certifications permit you to become certified at various levels of technical proficiency, spanning the disciplines of network design and support. So whether you're beginning a career, changing careers, securing your present position, or seeking to refine and promote your position, this is the book for you!

Cisco's Network Support Certifications

Cisco has created new certifications that will help you get the coveted CCIE, as well as aid prospective employers in measuring skill levels. Before these new certifications, you took only one test and were then faced with the lab, which made it difficult to succeed. With these new certifications, which add a better approach to preparing for that almighty lab, Cisco has opened doors that few were allowed through before. So, what are these new certifications, and how do they help you get your CCIE?

Cisco Certified Network Associate (CCNA) 2.0

The CCNA certification is the first in the new line of Cisco certifications and is a precursor to all current Cisco certifications. With the new certification programs, Cisco has created a stepping-stone approach to CCIE certification. Now you can become a Cisco Certified Network Associate for the meager cost of Sybex's CCNA: *Cisco Certified Network Associate Study Guide*, plus $100 for the test. And you don't have to stop there—you can continue with your studies and achieve a higher certification called the Cisco Certified Network Professional (CCNP). Someone with a CCNP has all the skills and knowledge needed to attempt the CCIE lab. However, because no textbook can take the place of practical experience, we'll discuss what else you need to be ready for the CCIE lab shortly.

> **NOTE** Check www.routersim.com for a cost-effective Cisco router simulator.

Cisco Certified Network Professional (CCNP) 2.0

Cisco Certified Network Professional (CCNP), Cisco's new certification, has opened up many opportunities for those individuals wishing to become Cisco-certified but lacking the training, the expertise, or the bucks to pass the notorious and often failed two-day Cisco torture lab. The new Cisco certifications will truly provide exciting new opportunities for the CNE and MCSE who are unsure of how to advance to a higher level.

So, you're thinking, "Great, what do I do after passing the CCNA exam?" Well, if you want to become a CCIE in Routing and Switching (the most popular certification), understand that there's more than one path to that much-coveted CCIE certification. The first way is to continue studying and become a Cisco Certified Network Professional (CCNP), which means four more tests, in addition to the CCNA certification.

The CCNP program will prepare you to understand and comprehensively tackle the internetworking issues of today and beyond—and it is not limited to the Cisco world. You will undergo an immense metamorphosis, vastly increasing your knowledge and skills through the process of obtaining these certifications.

> **NOTE** Todd Lammle offers a hands-on Cisco seminar (www.lammle.com) that provides two Cisco courses in one week of training. The Cisco CCNA/CCNP/CCDP seminars include CCNA/CCDA, Routing/Support, and Remote Access/Switching. Each course is six days long, and every student receives two routers and a switch to configure. Todd Lammle now offers a new three-day CCNA to help the busy professional.

Although you don't need to be a CCNP or even a CCNA to take the CCIE lab, it's extremely helpful if you already have these certifications.

What Skills Do You Need to Become a CCNP?

Cisco demands a certain level of proficiency for its CCNP certification. In addition to mastering the skills required for the CCNA, you should have the following skills for the CCNP:

- Installing, configuring, operating, and troubleshooting complex routed LAN, routed WAN, and switched LAN networks, along with dial-access services

- Understanding complex networks, such as IP, IGRP, IPX, Async Routing, AppleTalk, extended access lists, IP RIP, route redistribution, IPX RIP, route summarization, OSPF, VLSM, BGP, serial, IGRP, Frame Relay, ISDN, ISL, X.25, DDR, PSTN, PPP, VLANs, Ethernet, ATM LAN Emulation (LANE), access lists, 802.10, FDDI, and transparent and translational bridging

To meet the CCNP requirements, you must be able to perform the following:

- Install and/or configure a network to increase bandwidth, quicken network response times, and improve reliability and quality of service.
- Maximize performance through campus LANs, routed WANs, and remote access.
- Improve network security.
- Create a global intranet.
- Provide access security to campus switches and routers.
- Provide increased switching and routing bandwidth—end-to-end resiliency services.
- Provide custom queuing and routed priority services.

How Do You Become a CCNP?

After becoming a CCNA, you must take four exams to get your CCNP 2.0:

Exam 640-503: Routing   This exam continues to build on the fundamentals learned in the CCNA course. It focuses on large multiprotocol internetworks and how to manage them with access lists, queuing, tunneling, route distribution, router maps, BGP, OSPF, and route summarization. The forthcoming *CCNP: Routing Study Guide* covers all the exam objectives.

Exam 640-504: Switching   This exam tests your knowledge of the 1900 and 5000 series of Catalyst switches. This book, *CCNP: Switching Study Guide*, covers all the objectives you need to understand to pass the Switching exam.

Exam 640-505: Remote Access   This exam tests your knowledge of installing, configuring, monitoring, and troubleshooting Cisco ISDN and dial-up access products. You must understand PPP, ISDN, Frame Relay, and authentication. The new Sybex *CCNP: Remote Access Study Guide* covers all the exam objectives.

Exam 640-506: Support   This exam tests you on the Cisco IOS troubleshooting information available. You must be able to troubleshoot Ethernet and Token Ring LANs, IP, IPX, and AppleTalk networks, as well as ISDN, PPP, and Frame Relay networks. The new Sybex *CCNP: Support Study Guide* covers all the exam objectives.

> **Note:** If you hate tests, you can take fewer of them by signing up for the CCNA exam and the Support exam and then taking just one more long exam called the Foundation R/S exam (640-509). Doing this also gives you your CCNP—but beware, it's a really long test that fuses all the material listed previously into one exam. Good luck! However, by taking this exam, you get three tests for the price of two, which saves you $100 (if you pass). Some people think it's easier to take the Foundation R/S exam because you can leverage the areas in which you would score higher against the areas in which you wouldn't.

> **Tip:** Remember that test objectives and tests can change at any time without notice. Always check the Cisco Web site (www.cisco.com) for the most up-to-date information.

Cisco Certified Internetwork Expert (CCIE)

You've become a CCNP, and now you fix your sights on getting your Cisco Certified Internetwork Expert (CCIE) in Routing and Switching—what do you do next? Cisco recommends that before you take the lab, you take test 640-025: Cisco Internetwork Design (CID) and the Cisco authorized course called Installing and Maintaining Cisco Routers (IMCR). By the way, no Prometric test for IMCR exists at the time of this writing, and Cisco recommends a *minimum* of two years of on-the-job experience before taking the CCIE lab. After jumping those hurdles, you then have to pass the CCIE-R/S Exam Qualification (exam 350-001) before taking the actual lab.

To become a CCIE, Cisco recommends the following:

1. Attend all the recommended courses at an authorized Cisco training center and pony up around $15,000–$20,000, depending on your corporate discount.

2. Pass the Drake/Prometric exam ($200 per exam—so hopefully you'll pass it the first time).

3. Pass the two-day, hands-on lab at Cisco. This costs $1,000 per lab, which many people fail two or more times. (Some never make it through!) Also, you might just need to add travel costs to that $1,000 because you can currently take the exam only in San Jose, California; Research Triangle Park, North Carolina; Sydney, Australia; Halifax, Nova Scotia; Tokyo, Japan; or Brussels, Belgium. Cisco is adding new sites for the CCIE lab; it is best to check the Cisco Web site for the most up-to-date information.

What Skills Do You Need to Become a CCIE?

The CCIE Routing and Switching exam includes the advanced technical skills that are required to maintain optimum network performance and reliability, as well as advanced skills in supporting diverse networks that use disparate technologies. CCIEs just don't have problems getting jobs; these experts are basically inundated with offers to work for six-figure salaries! But that's because it isn't easy to attain the level of capability that is mandatory for Cisco's CCIE. For example, a CCIE must have the following skills down pat:

- Installing, configuring, operating, and troubleshooting complex routed LAN, routed WAN, switched LAN, and ATM LANE networks, along with dial-access services

- Diagnosing and resolving network faults

- Using packet/frame analysis and Cisco debugging tools

- Documenting and reporting the problem-solving processes used

- Having general LAN/WAN knowledge, including data encapsulation and layering; windowing and flow control and their relation to delay; error detection and recovery; link-state, distance vector, and switching algorithms; management, monitoring, and fault isolation

- Having knowledge of a variety of corporate technologies—including major services provided by Desktop, WAN, and Internet groups—as well as the functions, addressing structures, and routing, switching, and bridging implications of each of their protocols

- Having knowledge of Cisco-specific technologies, including router/switch platforms, architectures, and applications; communication servers; protocol translation and applications; configuration commands and system/network impact; and LAN/WAN interfaces, capabilities, and applications

- Designing, configuring, installing, and verifying voice-over-IP and voice-over-ATM networks

> **NOTE** Check www.netfix.com for a great price on used Cisco gear that can help you build a home lab.

Cisco's Network Design Certifications

In addition to the network support certifications, Cisco has created another certification track for network designers. The two certifications within this track are the Cisco Certified Design Associate (CCDA) and Cisco Certified Design Professional (CCDP) certifications. If you're reaching for the CCIE stars, we highly recommend the CCNP and CCDP certifications before attempting the lab (or attempting to advance your career). Preparing for these certifications will give you the knowledge to design routed LAN, routed WAN, and switched LAN and ATM LANE networks.

Cisco Certified Design Associate (CCDA)

To become a CCDA, you must pass the DCN (Designing Cisco Networks) test (640-441). To pass this test, you must understand how to do the following:

- Design simple routed LAN, routed WAN, and switched LAN and ATM LANE networks.
- Use Network-layer addressing.
- Filter with access lists.
- Use and propagate VLANs.
- Size networks.

> Sybex's *CCDA: Cisco Certified Design Associate Study Guide* is the most cost-effective way to study for and pass your CCDA exam.

Cisco Certified Design Professional (CCDP) 2.0

If you're already a CCNP and want to get your CCDP, you can simply take the CID 640-025 test. If you're not yet a CCNP, however, you must take the CCDA, CCNA, Routing, Switching, Remote Access, and CID exams.

CCDP certification skills include the following:

- Designing complex routed LAN, routed WAN, and switched LAN and ATM LANE networks
- Building upon the base level of the CCDA technical knowledge

CCDPs must also demonstrate proficiency in the following:

- Network-layer addressing in a hierarchical environment
- Traffic management with access lists
- Hierarchical network design
- VLAN use and propagation
- Performance considerations: required hardware and software; switching engines; memory, cost, and minimization

What Does This Book Cover?

This book covers everything you need to pass the CCNP Switching exam. The following list describes what you will learn in each chapter:

- Chapter 1 describes the traditional campus network model and moves into the new emerging campus model. Layer 2, 3, and 4 switching is also discussed. In addition, this chapter discusses the Cisco three-layer model, the Cisco switching product line, and how to build switch and core blocks.

- Chapter 2 describes the various Ethernet media types and how to log in and configure both a set-based and IOS-based Cisco Catalyst switch.

- Chapter 3 covers VLANs—how they work and how to configure them in a Cisco internetwork. Trunking and VLAN Trunk Protocol (VTP) will be described and implemented.

- Chapter 4 will give you an in-depth look at the Spanning Tree Protocol (STP), its timers, and how to configure STP in a switch.

- Chapter 5 shows you how to configure STP timers and includes a discussion of root bridge selection. Redundant links with STP will also be covered.

- Chapter 6 covers Inter-Switch Link (ISL) routing. Both internal route processors and external route processors are covered, as well as how to configure both internal and external route processors to connect multiple VLANs.

- Chapter 7 will provide the fundamentals of multi-layer switching on both internal and external route processors. In addition to covering IP routing with MLS, we'll show you how to configure the MLS engine.

- Chapter 8 gives you an extensive discussion of Hot Standby Routing Protocol (HSRP). The chapter provides HSRP as a solution to IP default gateway issues. Configuring HSRP is also covered.

- Chapter 9 covers the background of multicast addresses and how to translate from a layer 3 address to a layer 2 multicast address. Chapter 9 also covers IGMP and CGMP.

- Chapter 10 is about configuring multicast in a Cisco internetwork. Enabling multicast, joining a multicast group, and enabling CGMP are also covered.

- Chapter 11 ends this book by talking about access policies, how to create them, and how to implement them.

- Appendix A is a practice exam (see "How to Use This Book" later in this introduction for more on the practice exam).

- Appendix B includes all of the commands used in this book along with explanations of each command and how they are used with both access layer and distribution layer switches.

- Appendix C is a list of all multicast addresses as listed in RFC 1112. It also includes a list of all the assigned multicast addresses.

Each chapter begins with a list of the topics covered related to the CCNP Switching test, so make sure to read them over before working through the chapter. In addition, each chapter ends with review questions specifically designed to help you retain the knowledge presented. To really nail down your skills, read each question carefully, and if possible, work through the chapters' hands-on labs.

Where Do You Take the Exams?

You may take the exams at any of the more than 800 Sylvan Prometric Authorized Testing Centers around the world. For the location of a testing center near you, call (800) 755-3926. Outside the United States and Canada, contact your local Sylvan Prometric Registration Center.

To register for a Cisco Certified Network Professional exam:

1. Determine the number of the exam you want to take. (The Switching exam number is 640-504.)

2. Register with the nearest Sylvan Prometric Registration Center. At this point, you will be asked to pay in advance for the exam. At the time of this writing, the exams are $100 each and must be taken within one year of payment. You can schedule an exam up to six weeks in advance or as soon as one working day prior to the day you wish to take it. If something comes up and you need to cancel or reschedule your exam appointment, contact Sylvan Prometric at least 24 hours in advance. Same-day registration isn't available for the Cisco tests.

3. When you schedule the exam, you'll get instructions regarding all appointment and cancellation procedures, the ID requirements, and information about the testing-center location.

Tips for Taking Your CCNP Exam

The CCNP Switching test contains about 70 questions to be completed in 90 minutes. However, the number of exam questions and time may vary.

Many questions on the exam have answer choices that at first glance look identical—especially the syntax questions! Remember to read through the choices carefully because "close enough" doesn't cut it. If you get commands in the wrong order or forget one measly character, you'll get the question wrong. So, to practice, do the hands-on exercises at the end of the chapters over and over again until they feel natural to you.

Unlike Microsoft or Novell tests, the exam has answer choices that are syntactically similar—although some syntax is dead wrong, it is usually just *subtly* wrong. Some other syntax choices may be right, but they're shown in the wrong order. Cisco does split hairs, and they're not at all averse to giving you classic trick questions. Here's an example:

`access-list 101 deny ip any eq 23` denies Telnet access to all systems.

This question looks correct because most people refer to the port number (23) and think, "Yes, that's the port used for Telnet." The catch is that you can't filter IP on port numbers (only TCP and UDP).

Also, never forget that the right answer is the Cisco answer. In many cases, more than one appropriate answer is presented, but the *correct* answer is the one that Cisco recommends.

Here are some general tips for exam success:

- Arrive early at the exam center, so you can relax and review your study materials.

- Read the questions *carefully*. Don't just jump to conclusions. Make sure you're clear about *exactly* what each question asks.

- Don't leave any questions unanswered. They count against you.

- When answering multiple-choice questions that you're unsure about, use the process of elimination to get rid of the obviously incorrect answers first. Doing this greatly improves your odds if you need to make an educated guess.

- You can no longer move forward and backward through the Cisco exams (except the CCIE written exam and the CCDA exam), so double-check your answer before moving to the next question.

After you complete an exam, you'll get immediate, online notification of your pass or fail status, a printed Examination Score Report that indicates your pass or fail status, and your exam results by section. (The test administrator will give you the printed score report.) Test scores are automatically forwarded to Cisco within five working days after you take the test, so you don't need to send your score to them. If you pass the exam, you'll receive confirmation from Cisco, typically within two to four weeks.

How to Use This Book

This book can provide a solid foundation for the serious effort of preparing for the Cisco Certified Network Professional Switching exam. To best benefit from this book, use the following study method:

1. Take the assessment test immediately following this introduction. (The answers are at the end of the test.) Carefully read over the explanations for any question you get wrong, and note which chapters the material comes from. This information should help you plan your study strategy.

2. Study each chapter carefully, making sure you fully understand the information and the test objectives listed at the beginning of each chapter. Pay extra close attention to any chapter where you missed questions in the assessment test.

3. Complete all hands-on exercises in the chapter, referring to the chapter so that you understand the reason for each step you take. If you do not have Cisco equipment available, make sure to study the examples carefully. Also, check www.routersim.com for a router simulator.

4. Answer the review questions related to each chapter. (The answers appear at the end of the chapter, after the review questions.) Note the questions that confuse you, and study those sections of the book again.

5. Take the practice exam in Appendix A. The answers appear at the end of the exam.

6. Try your hand at the bonus practice exam that is included on the CD that comes with this book. The questions in this exam appear only on the CD. This will give you a complete overview of what you can expect to see on the real thing.

7. Use the products on the CD included with this book. The electronic flashcards, the Boson Software utilities, and the EdgeTest exam preparation software have all been specifically picked to help you study for and pass your exam. Study on the road with the *CCNP: Switching Study Guide* electronic book in PDF, and be sure to test yourself with the electronic flashcards.

> The electronic flashcards can be used on your Windows computer or on your Palm device.

8. Make sure to read the "Key Terms" and "Commands in This Chapter" lists at the end of the chapters. Appendix B includes all the commands used in the book, including explanations for each command.

To learn all the material covered in this book, you'll have to apply yourself regularly and with discipline. Try to set aside the same time period every day to study, and select a comfortable and quiet place to do so. If you work hard, you will be surprised at how quickly you learn this material. All the best!

What's on the CD?

We worked hard to provide some really great tools on the CD to help you with your certification process. All of the following tools should be loaded on your workstation when you're studying for the test.

The EdgeTest for Cisco Switching Test Preparation Software

Provided by EdgeTek Learning Systems, the test preparation software prepares you to successfully pass the Switching exam. In this test engine you will find all the questions from the book, plus an additional bonus practice exam that appears exclusively on the CD. You can take the assessment test, test yourself by chapter, take the practice exam that appears in the book or on the CD, or take an exam randomly generated from any of the questions.

> To find more test-simulation software for all Cisco and NT exams, look for the exam link on www.lammle.com.

Electronic Flashcards for PC and Palm Devices

To prepare for the exam, you can read this book, study the review questions at the end of each chapter, and work through the practice exams included in the book and on the CD. But wait, there's more! Test yourself with the flashcards included on the CD. If you can get through these difficult questions and understand the answers, you'll know you're ready for the CCNP Switching exam.

The flashcards include more than 150 questions specifically written to hit you hard and make sure you are ready for the exam. Between the review questions, practice exams, and flashcards, you'll be more than prepared for the exam.

The *Dictionary of Networking* and the *CCNP: Switching Study Guide* in PDF

Sybex offers the Cisco Certification books on CD so you can read them on your PC or laptop. The *Dictionary of Networking* and the *CCNP: Switching Study Guide* are in Adobe Acrobat format. Acrobat Reader 4 with Search is also included on the CD. This will be helpful to readers who travel and don't want to carry a book, as well as to readers who prefer reading from their computer.

Boson Software Utilities

Boson Software is an impressive company: They provide many free services to help you, the student. Boson has the best Cisco exam preparation questions on the market at a very nice price. On this book's CD, they have provided the following:

- IP Subnetter
- eeSuperPing
- System-Logging
- Wildcard Mask Checker
- Router GetPass

CCNA Virtual Lab AVI Demo Files

The *CCNA Virtual Lab e-trainer* provides a router and switch simulator to help you gain hands-on experience without having to buy expensive Cisco gear. The demos are AVI files that you can play in RealPlayer, which is included on the CD. The files will help you gain an understanding of the product features and the labs that the routers and switches can perform. Read more about the *CCNA Virtual Lab e-trainer* at www.sybex.com/cgi-bin/rd_bookpg.pl?2728back.html. You can upgrade this product at www.routersim.com.

How to Contact the Authors

You can reach Todd Lammle through GlobalNet Training Solutions, Inc. (www.lammle.com)—his training and systems integration company in Colorado—or e-mail him at todd@lammle.com.

You can e-mail Kevin Hales at kb7dfs@yahoo.com.

Assessment Test

1. Transparent bridging uses which protocol to stop network loops on layer 2 switched networks?

   A. IP routing

   B. STP

   C. VSTP

   D. UplinkFast Bridging

2. Choose the three components that make MLS implementation possible.

   A. MLS-CP

   B. MLSP

   C. MLS-SE

   D. MLS-RP

3. Why would you configure VTP version 2 on your network? (Choose all that apply.)

   A. You need to support Token Ring VLANs.

   B. To correct TLV errors.

   C. You want to forward VTP domain messages without the switches checking the version.

   D. You have all Cisco switches.

4. If you want to see the virtual IP address used on an HSRP router, which command should you use?

   A. `show hsrp status`

   B. `show hsrp standby address`

   C. `show standby`

   D. `show hsrp address`

5. Which is the proper syntax for enabling IP multicast on a router?

    A. `multicast ip routing`

    B. `ip-multicast routing`

    C. `ip multicast-routing`

    D. `ip mroute cache`

6. Which of the following are true regarding the blocking state of an STP switch port? (Choose all that apply.)

    A. Blocking ports do not forward any frames.

    B. Blocking ports listen for BPDUs.

    C. Blocking ports forward all frames.

    D. Blocking ports do not listen for BPDUs.

7. Choose the correct definition of an XTAG.

    A. A value assigned to each packet to assign it to an MLS flow

    B. A value assigned by the router to each MLS-SE in the layer 2 network

    C. A value assigned by each MLS-SE for each MLS-RP in the layer 2 network

    D. A value assigned by the NFFC or PFC to identify each flow

8. What Cisco Catalyst switches provide distribution layer functions? (Choose all that apply.)

    A. 1900

    B. 2926G

    C. 5000

    D. 6000

    E. 8500

9. Which is used to find the hardware address of a router if none is specified in the workstation's configuration?

   A. HSRP

   B. IP addressing

   C. IP ARP

   D. Proxy ARP

10. What would you type at a 1900 console prompt to see the transmit and receive statistics of VTP?

    A. show vtp stat

    B. show stat

    C. sh vtp domain

    D. sh int e0/9

11. If you wanted to configure VLAN 6 on an internal route processor with an IP address of 10.1.1.1/24, which of the following commands would you use?

    A. set vlan6 ip address 10.1.1.1 255.255.255.0

    B. config t, vlan6 ip address 10.1.1.1 255.255.255.0

    C. int vlan 6, ip address 10.1.1.1 255.255.255.0

    D. set int vlan6, ip address 10.1.1.1 255.255.255.0

12. Which is the correct multicast MAC address if it is mapped from the multicast IP address 224.127.45.254?

    A. 01-00-5e-7f-2d-fe

    B. 01-00-5e-7e-2d-fe

    C. 00-00-e0-7f-2d-fe

    D. 01-00-e0-7f-2d-fe

13. Which of the following describes local VLAN services?

   A. Users do not cross layer 3 devices and the network services are in the same broadcast domain as the users. This type of traffic never crosses the backbone.

   B. Users cross the backbone to log in to servers for file and print services.

   C. Users would have to cross a layer 3 device to communicate with the network services, but they might not have to cross the backbone.

   D. Layer 3 switches or routers are required in this scenario because the services must be close to the core and would probably be based in their own subnet.

14. What command do you use to add an access list to an HTTP server running on a router?

   A. `access-class`

   B. `access-group`

   C. `vty access-list`

   D. `http access-list`

15. Which of the following protocols is used to determine the locations of data loops and the election of a root bridge?

   A. STP

   B. VSTP

   C. BPDU

   D. BackboneFast

16. What is the syntax for configuring a router to be an RP Mapping Agent?

    A. `ip multicast mapping-agent scope`

    B. `ip pim send-rp-discovery scope`

    C. `ip rp-mapping-agent scope`

    D. `ip auto-rp mapping-agent scope`

17. Which of the following is an IEEE standard for frame tagging?

    A. ISL

    B. 802.3z

    C. 802.1q

    D. 802.3u

18. How do you set the enable mode password on a 5000 series switch?

    A. `set sco password todd`

    B. `set user password todd`

    C. `set password todd`

    D. `set enablepass`

    E. `set enable password todd`

19. Which of the following is true?

    A. You are required to assign a password to an RSM interface CLI.

    B. You must perform a `no shutdown` command for every subinterface on an external route processor.

    C. You must perform a `no shutdown` command for every VLAN on an internal route processor.

    D. You can use a 2500 series router for ISL routing.

20. Which version of IGMP is the Cisco proprietary version?

   A. IGMPv1

   B. IGMPv2

   C. CGMP

   D. None

21. If you wanted to set a default route on a 5000 series switch, which of the following commands would you use?

   A. `route add 0.0.0.0 0.0.0.0 172.16.1.1`

   B. `set route default 0.0.0.0 172.16.1.1`

   C. `set route default 172.16.1.1`

   D. `set route 0.0.0.0 0.0.0.0 172.16.1.1`

22. Which of the following is a type of access policy that you can apply at the distribution layer? (Choose all that apply.)

   A. Port security

   B. Access lists

   C. Distribute lists

   D. Physical security

23. Which of the following defines remote VLAN services?

   A. Users do not cross layer 3 devices, and the network services are in the same broadcast domain as the users. This type of traffic never crosses the backbone.

   B. Users only cross layer 2 devices to find the network file and print services needed to perform their job function.

   C. Users would have to cross a layer 3 device to communicate with the network services, but they might not have to cross the backbone.

   D. Layer 3 switches or routers are required in this scenario because the services must be close to the core and would probably be based in their own subnet.

24. If you want to clear the VTP prune eligibility from all VLANs except VLAN 2, what command would you type in on a set-based switch?

   A. `delete pruneeligible 3, 4, 5, etc...`

   B. `delete vtp pruneeligible 1, 3-1005`

   C. `clear vtp pruneeligible 3-1005`

   D. `clear vtp pruneeligible 1, 3-1005`

25. Which of the following devices is responsible for rewriting a layer 3 switched packet? (Choose all that apply.)

   A. Multilayer Switch Feature Card (MSFC)

   B. Route Switch Module (RSM)

   C. NetFlow Feature Card (NFFC)

   D. Policy Feature Card (PFC)

26. What command do you use to add an access list to a VTY line?

   A. `access-class`

   B. `access-group`

   C. `vty access-list`

   D. `http access-list`

27. If you wanted to have a 5000 switch supervisor module in a VLAN other than the default of VLAN 1, what should you type in?

   A. `set int slo 3`

   B. `set int sc0 2`

   C. `set sco2 3`

   D. `set vlan management 2`

28. What does a switch do with a multicast frame received on an interface?

    A. Forwards the switch to the first available link

    B. Drops the frame

    C. Floods the network with the frame looking for the device

    D. Sends back a message to the originating station asking for a name resolution

29. Choose the effects of configuring PIM SM on an interface.

    A. Enabling IGMP

    B. Enabling CGMP

    C. Enabling IGMP and CGMP

    D. Enabling Auto-RP

30. Choose the three basic steps in establishing a shortcut cache (MLS cache) entry.

    A. Identification of the MLS-RP

    B. Identification of the MLS-SE

    C. Identification of a candidate packet

    D. Identification of an enable packet

    E. Identification of ISL trunking

31. What is the default VLAN on all switches?

    A. VLAN 64

    B. VLAN 1005

    C. VLAN 1

    D. VLAN 10

32. Which of the following is a type of access policy that you can apply at the access layer?

A. Port security

B. Access lists

C. Distribute lists

D. Physical security

33. Which of the following is true regarding the Cisco 2926G switch?

A. Provides an enterprise solution for up to 96 users and up to 36 Gigabit Ethernet ports for servers

B. Supports a large number of connections and also supports an internal route processor module

C. Only uses an external router processor like a 4000 or 7000 series router

D. Also recommended for use at the core layer

34. How many bits are available for mapping a layer 3 IP address to a multicast MAC address?

A. 16

B. 32

C. 23

D. 24

35. What command will set the enable mode password on a 1900 switch?

A. `1900EN(config)#enable password level 1 todd`

B. `1900EN(config)#enable password level 15 todd`

C. `1900EN#set enable password todd`

D. `1900EN(Config)#enable password todd`

36. What does the PVST protocol provide?

   A. One instance of spanning tree per network

   B. One instance of STP per VLAN

   C. Port Aggregation Protocol support

   D. Routing between VLANs

37. If you want to see the standby virtual MAC address used on an HSRP router, which command could you use?

   A. `show standby`

   B. `show hsrp standby address`

   C. `show hsrp status`

   D. `show hsrp address`

38. Which of the following are examples of out-of-band management? (Choose all that apply.)

   A. Console port

   B. VTY line

   C. Auxiliary port

   D. Telnet

39. Which of the following IP address ranges is the valid multicast address range?

   A. 127.0.0.0–127.255.255.255

   B. 223.0.0.1–237.255.255.255

   C. 224.0.0.1–239.0.0.0

   D. 224.0.0.0–239.255.255.255

40. Which of the following defines enterprise services?

  A. Users do not cross layer 3 devices, and the network services are in the same broadcast domain as the users. This type of traffic never crosses the backbone.

  B. No layer 3 switches or devices are used in this network.

  C. The users would have to cross a layer 3 device to communicate with the network services, but they might not have to cross the backbone.

  D. Layer 3 switches or routers are required in this scenario because the services must be close to the core and would probably be based in their own subnet.

41. What is the default LAN switch type for the 1900 switch?

  A. FastForward

  B. Cut-through

  C. LANSwitch type 1

  D. FragmentFree

  E. Store-and-forward

42. Which is true regarding IRDP?

  A. It can be used only on Ethernet LANs.

  B. It is used to update ARP caches on workstations.

  C. IRDP works only with Unix devices.

  D. It uses ICMP to send update messages to clients regarding the default gateway address.

43. What type of cable must you use to connect between two switch uplink ports?

  A. Straight

  B. Rolled

  C. Cross-over

  D. Fiber

44. Which LAN switch methods have a fixed latency time? (Choose all that apply.)

   A. Cut-through

   B. Store-and-forward

   C. FragmentCheck

   D. FragmentFree

45. Which of the following are true regarding an RSFC card? (Choose all that apply.)

   A. Passwords are required to be set on the RSFC card.

   B. The RSFC takes one slot in a 5000 series chassis.

   C. The RSFC is a daughter card for the Supervisor Engine II G and Supervisor III G cards.

   D. The RSFC is a fully functioning router running the Cisco IOS.

46. Which of the following is used to provide fault-tolerant routing? (Choose all that apply.)

   A. Proxy ARP

   B. IP ARP

   C. RIP

   D. IRDP

   E. HSRP

47. How do you set the usermode password on a 5000 switch?

   A. `set sco password todd`

   B. `set user password todd`

   C. `set password`

   D. `set enable password todd`

48. Which of the following is a Cisco proprietary protocol?

   A. IP

   B. ICMP

   C. HSRP

   D. Proxy ARP

49. When will a switch update its VTP database?

   A. Every 60 seconds.

   B. When a switch receives an advertisement that has a higher revision number, the switch will overwrite the database in NVRAM with the new database being advertised.

   C. When a switch broadcasts an advertisement that has a lower revision number, the switch will overwrite the database in NVRAM with the new database being advertised.

   D. When a switch receives an advertisement that has the same revision number, the switch will overwrite the database in NVRAM with the new database being advertised.

50. What is the typical time a switch port will go from blocking to forwarding state?

   A. 5 seconds

   B. 50 seconds

   C. 10 seconds

   D. 100 seconds

51. Which topology scenario(s) support Multi-Layer Switching (MLS)? (Choose all that apply.)

   A. Router on a stick

   B. Multiple switches connected via ISL trunks with only one switch connected to a router

   C. Multiple switches connected to a router

   D. Multiple routers connected to one switch

52. Which of the following commands is used to view the configuration of an RSM?

   A. `sh vlan`

   B. `show config`

   C. `sho run`

   D. `sh port` *slot/type*

53. To configure a root bridge on a set-based switch, what command would be used?

   A. `set spanning tree backup`

   B. `set spantree secondary`

   C. `set spantree root`

   D. `spanning tree 2`

Answers to Assessment Test

1. B. The Spanning Tree Protocol was designed to help stop networks loops that can happen with transparent bridge networks running redundant links. See Chapter 5 for more information.

2. B, C, D. MLSP is the routing protocol for MLS, MLS-SE is the switching engine, and MLS-RP is the route processor. MLS-CP is an invalid answer. See Chapter 7 for more information.

3. A, B, C. If you have Token Ring, you would want to run VTP version 2. For more information, see Chapter 3.

4. C. To see both the virtual IP address and the virtual hardware address used by HSRP, use the `show standby` command. See Chapter 8 for more information on HSRP.

5. C. The first two are not valid commands. `Ip mroute cache` allows the interface to use fast switching or other types of interface switching for multicast traffic. See Chapter 10 for more information.

6. A, B. When a port is in blocking state, no frames are forwarded. This is used to stop network loops. However, the blocked port will listen for BPDUs received on the port. For more information on STP, see Chapter 4.

7. C. XTAG values are locally significant values that are assigned by the Multilayer Switching Switching Engine (MLS-SE) to keep track of the Multilayer Switching Route Processors (MLS-RPs) in the network. See Chapter 7 for more information.

8. B, C, D. The 2926G, 5000 series, and 6000 series were specifically designed to provide distribution layer functions. See Chapter 1 for more information on the distribution layer and the Cisco switches designed to run at the distribution layer.

9. D. Proxy ARP will send an ARP broadcast for every packet sent on a device if the default gateway is set the same as the workstation's IP address. Proxy ARP, running on the router, will forward these frames if necessary. See Chapter 8 for more information on Proxy ARP.

10. A. The command `show vtp stat` is used to see VTP updates being sent and received on your switch. For more information, see Chapter 3.

11. C. The command `interface vlan #` is used to create a VLAN interface. The IP address of the interface is then configured with the `ip address` command. See Chapter 6 for more information on internal and external route processors.

12. A. 23 bits allows us to use the 127 value in the second octet. The MAC prefix is always 01-00-5e. See Chapter 9 for more information.

13. A. Local VLAN services are network services that are located in the same VLAN as the user trying to access them. Packets will not pass through a layer 3 device. See Chapter 1 for more information.

14. A. Use the `ip http access-class number` command to set an access list on an HTTP server. See Chapter 11 for more information on HTTP servers.

15. C. Bridge Protocol Data Units are sent out every two seconds by default and provide information to switches throughout the internetwork. This includes finding redundant links, electing the root bridge, monitoring the links in the spanning tree, and notifying other switches in the network about link failures. See Chapter 5 for more information.

16. B. The router uses PIM to distribute RP information to multicast routers. The other syntax options are not valid. See Chapter 10 for more information.

17. C. Cisco's propriety version of frame tagging is ISL. However, if you do not have all Cisco switches, the IEEE 802.1q version would be used. For more information, see Chapter 3.

Answers to Assessment Test

18. **D.** The command `set enablepass` will set the password on a 5000 series switch. See Chapter 2 for more information on configuring the 5000 series of switches.

19. **C.** An external route processor configured with subinterfaces does not need a shutdown performed on each subinterface, only the main interface. However, an internal route processor must have a `no shutdown` command performed under every VLAN interface. See Chapter 6 for more information on internal and external route processors.

20. **D.** CGMP is not a version of IGMP. It was developed by Cisco Systems, but it was never an additional version of IGMP. See Chapter 9 for more information.

21. **C.** The command `set route default` and the command `set route 0.0.0.0` are the same command and can be used to set a default gateway on a 5000 series switch. See Chapter 6 for more information on configuring a 5000 series switch.

22. **B, C.** The distribution layer security can include access lists. Distribute lists are access lists that you can use to filter routing tables. See Chapter 11 for more information on access policies.

23. **C.** To communicate to another VLAN, packets must cross a layer 3 device. See Chapter 1 for more information on local and remote VLAN services.

24. **C.** You cannot turn off Pruneeligible for VLAN 1, which makes C the only correct answer. For more information, see Chapter 3.

25. **C, D.** The Multilayer Switch Feature Card (MSFC) is a Route Processor (RP) and does not perform the rewrites for MLS packets. The same goes for the Route Switch Module (RSM). The NetFlow Feature Card (NFFC) and the Policy Feature Card (PFC) are responsible for the MLS packet rewrite. See Chapter 7 for more information.

26. **A.** Use the `access-class number in/out` command to set an access list on a VTY line. See Chapter 11 for more information on access lists.

27. B. The set command `set int sc0 vlan#` changes the default VLAN for the supervisor module to the specified VLAN. See Chapter 2 for more information.

28. C. The switch will flood the network with the frame looking for the device. For more information on LAN switching, see Chapter 4.

29. A. Adding the PIM configuration to the interface enables only Internet Group Management Protocol (IGMP) in addition to PIM. Auto-RP and Cisco Group Management Protocol (CGMP) must be configured separately. See Chapter 10 for more information.

30. A, C, D. The Multilayer Switching Switching Engine (MLS-SE) needs to know three things to create an entry: the Multilayer Switching Route Processor (MLS-RP), a candidate packet, and an enable packet. See Chapter 7 for more information.

31. C. VLAN 1 is a default VLAN and used for management by default. See Chapter 5 for more information.

32. A, D. Physical security of switches is one of the most important access policies you can create at the access layer. Stopping users from plugging into any port on a switch is part of port security. See Chapter 11 for more information on access policies.

33. C. The 2926G is not capable of handling an internal route processor. See Chapter 1 for more information regarding the 2926G switch.

34. C. Due to the prefix length and the high order bit already in use in the multicast MAC address, only 23 bits are left for mapping. See Chapter 9 for more information.

35. B. The command to set the enable password on a 1900 switch is `enable password level 15 password`. See Chapter 2 for more information.

36. B. The Cisco proprietary protocol Per-VLAN Spanning Tree (PVST) uses a separate instance of spanning tree for each and every VLAN. See Chapter 5 for more information.

Answers to Assessment Test

37. **A.** To see both the virtual IP address and the virtual hardware address used by HSRP, use the `show standby` command. See Chapter 8 for more information on HSRP.

38. **A, C.** Connecting to the console port or auxiliary port is out-of-band management because you are not accessing the equipment from within the network. See Chapter 11 for more information on in-band and out-of-band management.

39. **D.** A is a Class B address. 223.0.0.1 does not have the proper mask. C is within the valid range, but it is not all-inclusive. See Chapter 9 for more information.

40. **D.** Enterprise services are defined as services that are provided to all users on the internetwork. See Chapter 1 for more information.

41. **D.** The 1900 defaults to FragmentFree, but it can be changed to store-and-forward. For more information on LAN switch types, see Chapter 4.

42. **D.** Internet Control Message Protocol (ICMP) is used by ICMP Router Discovery Protocol (IRDP) to update clients dynamically about default gateways. See Chapter 8 for more information regarding IRDP.

43. **C.** A cross-over cable is used to connect switches to switches and hubs to hubs. See Chapter 2 for more information on the Catalyst 5000 configuration.

44. **A, D.** Cut-through and FragmentFree always read only a fixed amount of a frame. For more information on LAN switch types, see Chapter 4.

45. **C, D.** The Route Switch Feature Card (RSFC) is a daughter card used on a supervisor II and III card to provide a fully functioning router IOS. See Chapter 6 for more information on internal and external route processors.

46. A, C, D, E. Proxy ARP, dynamic routing protocols (RIP, for example), IRDP, and HSRP are used to provide fault tolerance in routed networks. See Chapter 8 for more information on HSRP.

47. C. The set command `set password` sets the usermode password on a 5000 series switch. See Chapter 2 for more information on configuring the 5000 series of switches.

48. C. Hot Standby Routing Protocol (HSRP) is a Cisco proprietary protocol used for allowing redundant connections. See Chapter 8 for more information on HSRP.

49. B. Only when a VTP update is received with a higher data VTP revision number will a switch update its VTP database. For more information, see Chapter 3.

50. B. Fifty seconds is the default time for changing from blocking to forwarding state. This is to allow enough time for all switches to update their STP database. For more information on STP, see Chapter 4.

51. A, B, D. The router on a stick is the typical and simplest topology for Multi-Layer Switching (MLS). Multiple switches connected to each other can use MLS if only one switch is connected to the router. Multiple routers can be connected to one switch as long as each router only has one link to the switch. See Chapter 7 for more information.

52. C. The RSM commands are the same for any Cisco IOS router, and the `show running-config` is used to view the current configuration. See Chapter 6 for more information on internal and external route processors.

53. C. The `set spantree root` command allows you to configure a root bridge. See Chapter 5 for more information.

Chapter 1

The Campus Network

THE CCNP EXAM TOPICS COVERED IN THIS CHAPTER INCLUDE THE FOLLOWING:

- ✓ Traditional campus internetworks
- ✓ The difference between the 80/20 rule and the 20/80 rule
- ✓ The new campus internetwork model
- ✓ Understanding the details of switching technologies
- ✓ The differences between layer 2 switching, layer 3 switching, routing, layer 4 switching, and multi-layer switching
- ✓ The three layers in the Cisco hierarchical model
- ✓ The different Cisco switch solutions available at the access layer
- ✓ The different Cisco switch solutions available at the distribution layer
- ✓ The different Cisco switch solutions available at the core layer
- ✓ The differences between a switch block and core block

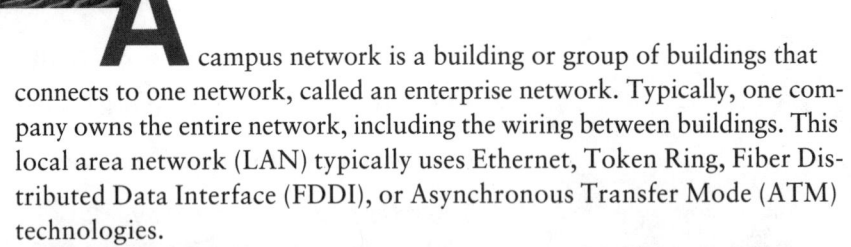

A campus network is a building or group of buildings that connects to one network, called an enterprise network. Typically, one company owns the entire network, including the wiring between buildings. This local area network (LAN) typically uses Ethernet, Token Ring, Fiber Distributed Data Interface (FDDI), or Asynchronous Transfer Mode (ATM) technologies.

The main challenge for network administrators is to make the campus network run efficiently and effectively. To do this, they must understand current campus networks as well as the new emerging campus networks. Therefore, in this chapter, you will learn about current and future requirements of campus internetworks. We'll explain the limitations of traditional campus networks as well as the benefits of the emerging campus designs. You will learn how to choose from among the new generation of Cisco switches to maximize the performance of your networks. Understanding how to design for the emerging campus networks is not only critical to your success on the Switching exam, it's also critical for implementing production networks.

As part of the instruction in network design, we'll discuss the specifics of technologies, including how to implement Ethernet and the differences between layer 2, layer 3, and layer 4 switching technologies. In particular, you will learn how to implement FastEthernet, Gigabit Ethernet, Fast EtherChannel, and Multi-Layer Switching (MLS) in the emerging campus designs. This will help you learn how to design, implement, and maintain an efficient and effective internetwork.

Finally, you will learn about the Cisco hierarchical model, which is covered in all the Cisco courses. In particular, you will learn which catalyst switches can—and should—be implemented at each layer of the Cisco model. And you will learn how to design networks based on switch and core blocks.

This chapter, then, will provide you with a thorough overview of campus network design (past, present, and future) and teach you how, as a network administrator, to choose the most appropriate technology for a particular network's needs. This will allow you to configure and design your network now, with the future in mind.

Campus Internetworks

It doesn't seem that terribly long ago that the mainframe ruled the world and the PC was just used to placate some users. However, in their arrogance, mainframe administrators never really took the PC seriously, and like rock 'n' roll naysayers, they said it would never last. Maybe they were right after all—at least in a way. In the last year or two, server farms have replaced distributed servers in the field.

In the last 15 years we have seen operators and managers of the mainframe either looking for other work or taking huge pay cuts. Their elitism exacerbated the slap in the face when people with no previous computer experience were suddenly making twice their salary after passing a few key certification exams.

Mainframes were not necessarily discarded, they just became huge storage areas for data and databases. The NetWare and NT server took over as a file/print server and soon started running most other programs and applications as well.

The last 20 years have witnessed the birth of the LAN and the growth of WANs and the Internet. So where are networks headed in the twenty-first century? Are we still going to see file and print servers at all branch locations? Are all workstations just going to connect to the Internet with ISPs to separate the data, voice, and other multimedia applications?

Looking Backwards at Traditional Campus Networks

In the 1990s, the traditional campus network started as one LAN and grew and grew until segmentation needed to take place just to keep the network up and running. In this era of rapid expansion, response time was secondary to just making sure the network was functioning.

And by looking at the technology, you can see why keeping the network running was such a challenge. Typical campus networks ran on 10BaseT or 10Base2 (thinnet). As a result, the network was one large collision domain—not to mention even one large broadcast domain. Despite these limitations, Ethernet was used because it was scalable, effective, and somewhat inexpensive compared to other options. ARCnet was used in some networks, but Ethernet and ARCnet are not compatible, and the networks became two separate entities. ARCnet soon became history.

Because a campus network can easily span many buildings, bridges were used to connect the buildings together; this broke up the collision domains, but the network was still one large broadcast domain. More and more users were attached to the hubs used in the network, and soon the performance of the network was considered extremely slow.

Performance Problems and Solutions

Availability and performance are the major problems with traditional campus networks. Bandwidth helps compound these problems. The three performance problems in traditional campus networks included collisions, broadcasts and multicasts, and bandwidth.

Collisions

A campus network typically started as one large collision domain, so all devices could see and also collide with each other. If a host had to broadcast, then all other devices had to listen, even though they themselves were trying to transmit. And if a device were to jabber (malfunction), it could almost bring the entire network down.

Because routers didn't really become cost effective until the late 1980s, bridges were used to break up collision domains, but the network was still one large broadcast domain and the broadcast problems still existed. However, bridges did break up the collision domain, and that was an improvement. Bridges also solved distance-limitation problems because they usually had repeater functions built into the electronics and/or they could break up the physical segment.

Bandwidth

The *bandwidth* of a segment is measured by the amount of data that can be transmitted at any given time. Think of bandwidth as a water hose; the amount of water that can go through the hose depends on different elements:

- Pressure
- Distance

The pressure is the current and the bandwidth is the size of the hose. If you have a hose that is only 1/4 inch in diameter, you won't get much water through it regardless of the current or the size of the pump on the transmitting end.

Another issue is distance. The longer the hose, the more the water pressure drops. You can put a repeater in the middle of the hose and reamplify the pressure of the line, which would help, but you need to understand that all lines (and hoses) have degradation of the signal, which means that the pressure drops off the farther the signal goes down the line. For the remote end to understand digital signaling, the pressure must stay at a minimum value. If it drops below this minimum value, the remote end will not be able to receive the data. In other words, the far end of the hose would just drip water instead of flow. You can't water your crops with drips of water; you need a constant water flow.

The solution to bandwidth issues is maintaining your distance limitations and designing your network with proper segmentation of switches and routers. Congestion on a segment happens when too many devices are trying to use the same bandwidth. By properly segmenting the network, you can eliminate some of the bandwidth issues. You never will have enough bandwidth for your users; you'll just have to accept that fact. However, you can always make it better.

Broadcasts and Multicasts

Remember that all protocols have broadcasts built in as a feature, but some protocols can really cause problems if not configured correctly. Some protocols that, by default, can cause problems if not correctly implemented are Internet Protocol (IP), Address Resolution Protocol (ARP), Network Basic Input Output System (NetBIOS), Internetworking Packet eXchange (IPX), Service Advertising Protocol (SAP), and Routing Information Protocol (RIP). However, remember that there are features built into the Cisco router Internetworking Operating System (IOS) that, if correctly designed and implemented, can alleviate these problems. Packet filtering, queuing, and choosing the correct routing protocols are some examples of how Cisco routers can eliminate some broadcast problems.

Multicast traffic can also cause problems if not configured correctly. Multicasts are broadcasts that are destined for a specific or defined group of users. If you have large multicast groups or a bandwidth-intensive application like Cisco's IPTV application, multicast traffic can consume most of the network bandwidth and resources.

To solve broadcast issues, create network segmentation with bridges, routers, and switches. However, understand that you'll move the bottleneck to the routers, which break up the broadcast domains. Routers process each packet that is transmitted on the network, which can cause the bottleneck if an enormous amount of traffic is generated.

Virtual LANs (VLANs) are a solution as well, but VLANs are just broadcast domains with boundaries created by routers. A VLAN is a group of devices on different network segments defined as a broadcast domain by the network administrator. The benefit of VLANs is that physical location is no longer a factor for determining the port into which you would plug a device into the network. You can plug a device into any switch port, and the network administrator gives that port a VLAN assignment. Remember that routers or layer 3 switches must be used for different VLANs to communicate.

The 80/20 Rule

The traditional campus network placed users and groups in the same physical location. If a new salesperson was hired, they had to sit in the same physical location as the other sales personal and be connected to the same physical network segment in order to share network resources. Any deviation from this caused major headaches for the network administrators. Figure 1.1 shows the traditional 80/20 network.

FIGURE 1.1 A traditional 80/20 network

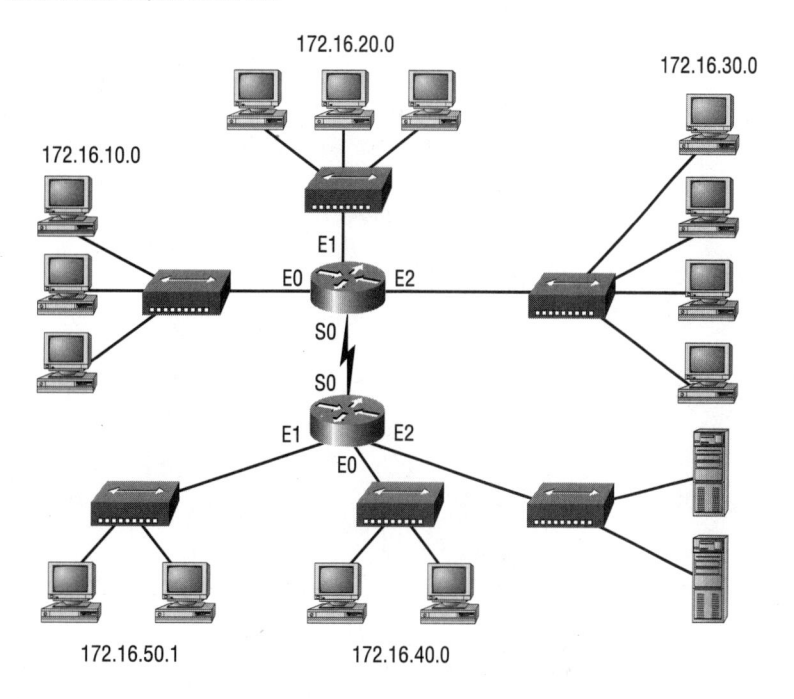

The rule that needed to be followed in this type of network was called the *80/20 rule* because 80 percent of the users' traffic was supposed to remain on the local network segment and only 20 percent or less was supposed to cross the routers or bridges to the other network segments. If more than 20 percent of the traffic crossed the network segmentation devices, performance issues arose.

Because network administrators are responsible for the network design and implementation, network performance was improved in the 80/20 network by making sure all of the network resources for the users were contained within their own network segment. The resources include network servers, printers, shared directories, software programs, and applications.

The New 20/80 Rule

With new Web-based applications and computing, any PC can be a subscriber or publisher at any time. Also, because businesses are pulling servers from remote locations and creating server farms (sounds like a mainframe, doesn't it?) to centralize network services for security, reduced cost, and administration, the old 80/20 rule is obsolete and could not possibly work in this environment. All traffic must now traverse the campus backbone, which means we now have a *20/80 rule* in effect. Twenty percent of what the user performs on the network is local, whereas up to 80 percent crosses the network segmentation points to get to network services. Figure 1.2 shows the new 20/80 rule network.

FIGURE 1.2 A 20/80 network

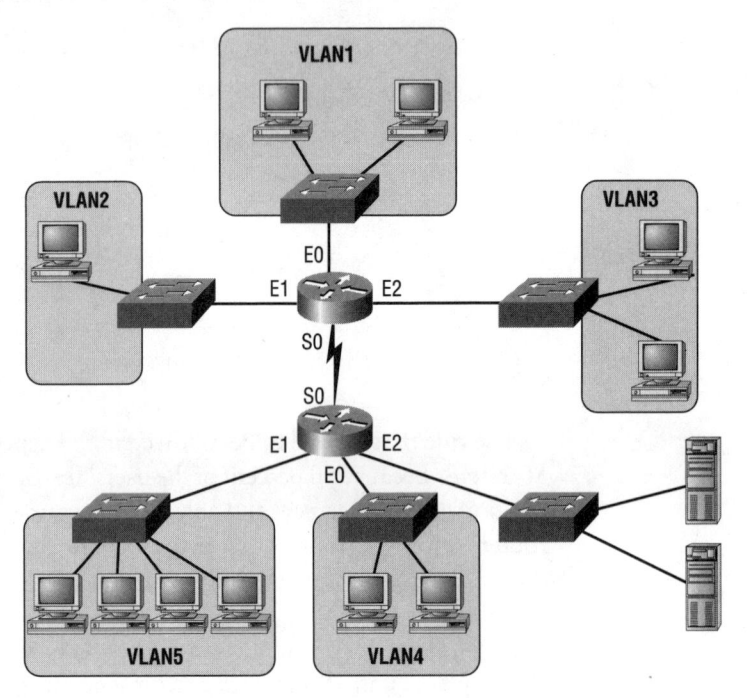

The problem with the 20/80 rule is not the network wiring and topology as much as it is the routers themselves. They must be able to handle an enormous amount of packets quickly and efficiently at wire speed. This is probably where we should be talking about how great Cisco routers are and how our networks would be nothing without them. We'll get to that later in this chapter—trust me.

Virtual LANs

With this new 20/80 rule, more and more users need to cross broadcast domains (VLANs), and this puts the burden on routing, or layer 3 switching. By using VLANs within the new campus model, you can control traffic patterns and control user access easier than in the traditional campus network. Virtual LANs break up broadcast domains by using either a router or switch that can perform layer 3 functions. Figure 1.3 shows how VLANs are created and might look in an internetwork.

FIGURE 1.3 VLANs break up broadcast domains in a switched internetwork.

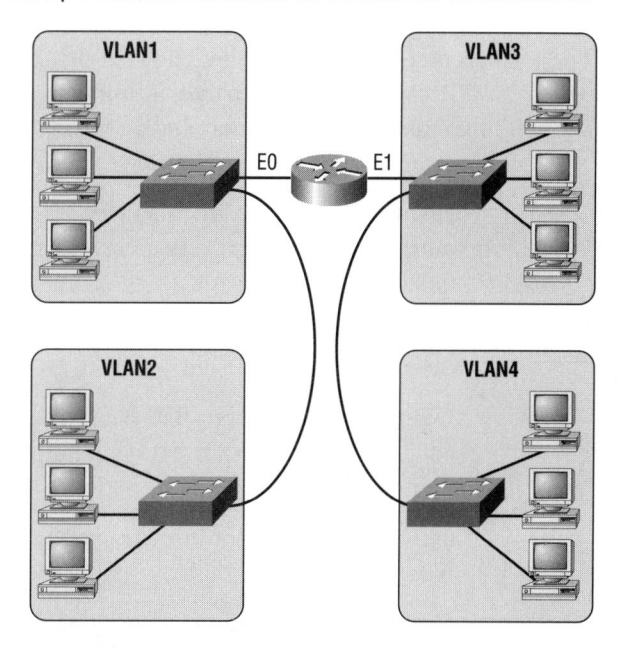

Chapter 3 includes detailed information about VLANs and how to configure them in an internetwork. It is imperative that you understand VLANs because the traditional way of building the campus network is being redesigned and VLANs are a large factor in building the new campus model.

The New Campus Model

The changes in customer network requirements—in combination with the problems with collision, bandwidth, and broadcasts—have necessitated a new network campus design. Higher user demands and complex applications force the network designers to think more about traffic patterns instead of solving a typical isolated department issue. We can no longer just think about creating subnets and putting different departments into each subnet. We need to create a network that makes everyone capable of reaching all network services easily. Server farms, where all enterprise servers are located in one physical location, really take a toll on the existing network infrastructure and make the way we used to design networks obsolete. We must pay attention to traffic patterns and how to solve bandwidth issues. This can be accomplished with higher-end routing and switching techniques.

Because of the new bandwidth-intensive applications, video and audio to the desktop, as well as more and more work being performed on the Internet, the new campus model must be able to perform the following:

Fast Convergence   When a network change takes place, the network must be able to adapt very quickly to new changes and keep data moving quickly.

Deterministic paths   Users must be able to gain access to a certain area of the network without fail.

Deterministic failover   The network design must have provisions that make sure the network stays up and running even if a link fails.

Scalable size and throughput   As users and new devices are added to the network, the network infrastructure must be able to handle the new increase in traffic.

Centralized applications   Enterprise applications accessed by all users must be available to support all users on the internetwork.

The new 20/80 rule   Instead of 80 percent of the users' traffic staying on the local network, 80 percent of the traffic will now cross the backbone and only 20 percent will stay on the local network.

Multiprotocol support Campus networks must support multiple protocols, both routed and routing protocols. Routed protocols are used to send user data through the internetwork (for example, IP or IPX). Routing protocols are used to send network updates between routers, which will in turn update their routing tables. Examples of routing protocols include RIP, Enhanced Interior Gateway Routing Protocol (EIGRP), and Open Shortest Path First (OSPF).

Multicasting Multicasting is sending a broadcast to a defined subnet or group of users. Users can be placed in multicast groups, for example, for videoconferencing.

Network Services

The new campus model provides remote services quickly and easily to all users. The users have no idea where the resources are located in the internetwork, nor should they. There are three types of network services, which are created and defined by the administrator and should appear to the users as local services:

- Local services
- Remote services
- Enterprise services

Local Services

Local services are network services that are located on the same subnet or network as the users accessing them. Users do not cross layer 3 devices and the network services are in the same broadcast domain as the users. This type of traffic never crosses the backbone.

Remote Services

Remote services are close to users but not on the same network or subnet as the users. The users would have to cross a layer 3 device to communicate with the network services. However, they might not have to cross the backbone.

Enterprise Services

Enterprise services are defined as services that are provided to all users on the internetwork. Layer 3 switches or routers are required in this scenario because an enterprise service must be close to the core and would probably be based in its own subnet. Examples of these services include Internet access, e-mail, and possibly videoconferencing. When servers that host enterprise services are placed close to the backbone, all users would be the same distance from the servers, but all user data would have to cross the backbone to get to the services.

Switching Technologies

Switching technologies are crucial to the new network design. Because the prices on layer 2 switching have been dropping dramatically, it is easier to justify the cost of buying switches for your entire network. This doesn't mean that every business can afford switch ports for all users, but it does allow for a cost-effective upgrade solution when the time comes.

To understand switching technologies and how routers and switches work together, you must understand the Open Systems Interconnection (OSI) model. This section will give you a general overview of the OSI model and the devices that are specified at each layer.

> **NOTE** For more detailed information about the OSI model, please see *CCNA: Cisco Certified Network Associate Study Guide*, by Todd Lammle (Sybex, 2000). You'll need a basic understanding of the OSI model to fully understand discussions in which it is included throughout the rest of the book.

Open Systems Interconnection (OSI) Model

As you probably already know, the OSI model has seven layers, each of which specifies functions that allow data to be transmitted from host to host on an internetwork. Figure 1.4 shows the OSI model and the functions of each layer.

FIGURE 1.4 The OSI model and the layer functions

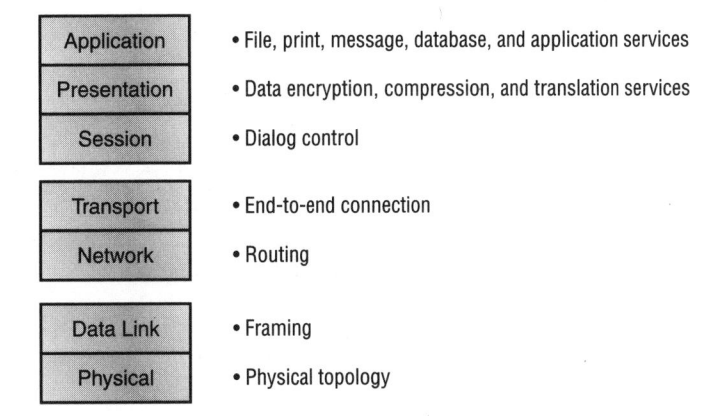

Application	• File, print, message, database, and application services
Presentation	• Data encryption, compression, and translation services
Session	• Dialog control
Transport	• End-to-end connection
Network	• Routing
Data Link	• Framing
Physical	• Physical topology

The OSI model is the cornerstone for application developers to write and create networked applications that run on an internetwork. What is important to network engineers and technicians is the encapsulation of data as it is transmitted on a network.

Data Encapsulation

Data encapsulation is the process by which the information in a protocol is wrapped, or contained, in the data section of another protocol. In the OSI reference model, each layer encapsulates the layer immediately above it as the data flows down the protocol stack.

The logical communication that happens at each layer of the OSI reference model doesn't involve many physical connections because the information each protocol needs to send is encapsulated in the layer of protocol information beneath it. This encapsulation produces a set of data called a packet (see Figure 1.5).

Chapter 1 · The Campus Network

FIGURE 1.5 Data encapsulation at each layer of the OSI reference model

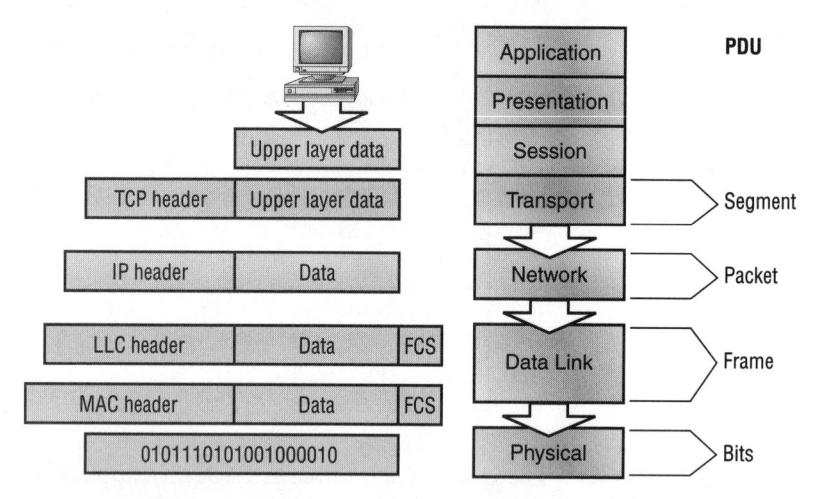

Looking at Figure 1.5, you can follow the data down through the model as it's encapsulated at each layer of the OSI reference model. Cisco courses typically focus only on layers 2–4.

Each layer communicates only with its peer layer on the receiving host, and they exchange Protocol Data Units (PDUs). The PDUs are attached to the data at each layer as it traverses down the model and is read only by its peer on the receiving side. Each layer has a specific name for the PDU, as shown in Table 1.1.

TABLE 1.1 OSI Encapsulation

OSI Layer	Name of Protocol Data Units (PDUs)
Transport	Segment
Network	Packet
Data Link	Frames
Physical	Bits

Starting at the Application layer, data is converted for transmission on the network, then encapsulated in Presentation layer information. When the Presentation layer receives this information, it looks like generic data. The Presentation layer hands the data to the Session layer, which is responsible for synchronizing the session with the destination host.

The Session layer then passes this data to the Transport layer, which transports the data from the source host to the destination host in a reliable fashion. But before this happens, the Network layer adds routing information to the packet. It then passes the packet on to the Data Link layer for framing and for connection to the Physical layer. The Physical layer sends the data as 1s and 0s to the destination host across fiber or copper wiring. Finally, when the destination host receives the 1s and 0s, the data passes back up through the model, one layer at a time. The data is de-encapsulated at each of the OSI model's peer layers.

At a transmitting device, the data encapsulation method is as follows:

1. User information is converted to data for transmission on the network.

2. Data is converted to segments at the Transport layer, and a reliable session is possibly set up.

3. Segments are converted to packets or datagrams at the Network layer, and routing information is added to the PDU.

4. Packets or datagrams are converted to frames at the Data Link layer, and hardware addresses are used to communicate with local hosts on the network medium.

5. Frames are converted to bits, and 1s and 0s are encoded within the digital signal.

Now that you have a sense of the OSI model and how routers and switches work together, it is time to turn our attention to the specifics of each layer of switching technology.

Layer 2 Switching

Layer 2 switching is hardware based, which means it uses the Media Access Control (MAC) address from the host's network interface cards (NICs) to filter the network. Switches use Application-Specific Integrated Circuits

(ASICs) to build and maintain filter tables. It is OK to think of a layer 2 switch as a multiport bridge.

Layer 2 switching provides the following:

- Hardware-based bridging (MAC)
- Wire speed
- High speed
- Low latency
- Low cost

Layer 2 switching is so efficient because there is no modification to the data packet, only to the frame encapsulation of the packet, and only when the data packet is passing through dissimilar media (such as from Ethernet to FDDI).

Use layer 2 switching for workgroup connectivity and network segmentation (breaking up collision domains). This allows you to create a flatter network design and one with more network segments than traditional 10BaseT shared networks.

Layer 2 switching has helped develop new components in the network infrastructure:

Server farms Servers are no longer distributed to physical locations because virtual LANs can be created to create broadcast domains in a switched internetwork. This means that all servers can be placed in a central location, yet a certain server can still be part of a workgroup in a remote branch, for example.

Intranets Allows organization-wide client/server communications based on a Web technology.

These new technologies are allowing more data to flow off of local subnets and onto a routed network, where a router's performance can become the bottleneck.

Limitations of Layer 2 Switching

Layer 2 switches have the same limitations as bridge networks. Remember that bridges are good if you design the network by the 80/20 rule: users spend 80 percent of their time on their local segment.

Bridged networks break up collision domains, but the network is still one large broadcast domain. Similarly, layer 2 switches (bridges) cannot break up broadcast domains, which can cause performance issues and limits the size of your network. Broadcast and multicasts, along with the slow convergence of spanning tree, can cause major problems as the network grows. Because of these problems, layer 2 switches cannot completely replace routers in the internetwork.

Routing

We want to explain how routing works and how routers work in an internetwork before discussing layer 3 switching in the next section. Routers and layer 3 switches are similar in concept but not design. In this section, we'll discuss routers and what they provide in an internetwork today.

Routers break up collision domains like bridges do. In addition, routers also break up broadcast/multicast domains.

The benefits of routing include:

- Break up of broadcast domains
- Multicast control
- Optimal path determination
- Traffic management
- Logical (layer 3) addressing
- Security

Routers provide optimal path determination because the router examines each and every packet that enters an interface and improves network segmentation by forwarding data packets to only a known destination network. Routers are not interested in hosts, only networks. If a router does not know about a remote network to which a packet is destined, it will just drop the packet and not forward it. Because of this packet examination, traffic management is obtained.

The Network layer of the OSI model defines a virtual—or logical—network address. Hosts and routers use these addresses to send information from host to host within an internetwork. Every network interface must have a logical address, typically an IP address.

Security can be obtained by a router reading the packet header information and reading filters defined by the network administrator (access lists).

Layer 3 Switching

The only difference between a layer 3 switch and a router is the way the administrator creates the physical implementation. Also, traditional routers use microprocessors to make forwarding decisions, and the switch performs only hardware-based packet switching. However, some traditional routers can have other hardware functions as well in some of the higher-end models. Layer 3 switches can be placed anywhere in the network because they handle high-performance LAN traffic and can cost-effectively replace routers.

Layer 3 switching is all hardware-based packet forwarding, and all packet forwarding is handled by hardware ASICs. Layer 3 switches really are no different functionally than a traditional router and perform the same functions, which are listed here:

- Determine paths based on logical addressing
- Run layer 3 checksums (on header only)
- Use Time to Live (TTL)
- Process and responds to any option information
- Can update Simple Network Management Protocol (SNMP) managers with Management Information Base (MIB) information
- Provide Security

The benefits of layer 3 switching include the following:

- Hardware-based packet forwarding
- High-performance packet switching
- High-speed scalability
- Low latency
- Lower per-port cost
- Flow accounting
- Security
- Quality of service (QoS)

> **NOTE:** The Cisco 12000 Gigabit Switch router (GSR) performs (layer 3 switching) by using a crossbar switch matrix, but all in the Catalyst family of switches use ASIC switching.

Layer 4 Switching

Layer 4 switching is considered a hardware-based layer 3 switching technology that can also consider the application used (for example, Telnet or FTP). Layer 4 switching provides additional routing above layer 3 by using the port numbers found in the Transport layer header to make routing decisions. These port numbers are found in Request for Comments (RFC) 1700 and reference the upper-layer protocol, program, or application.

Layer 4 information has been used to help make routing decisions for quite a while. For example, extended access lists can filter packets based on layer 4 port numbers. Another example is accounting information gathered by NetFlow switching in Cisco's higher-end routers.

The largest benefit of layer 4 switching is that the network administrator can configure a layer 4 switch to prioritize data traffic by application, which means a QoS can be defined for each user. For example, a number of users can be defined as a Video group and be assigned more priority, or bandwidth, based on the need for videoconferencing.

However, because users can be part of many groups and run many applications, the layer 4 switches must be able to provide a huge filter table or response time would suffer. This filter table must be much larger than any layer 2 or 3 switch. A layer 2 switch might have a filter table only as large as the number of users connected to the network, maybe even less if some hubs are used within the switched fabric. However, a layer 4 switch might have five or six entries for each and every device connected to the network! If the layer 4 switch does not have a filter table that includes all the information, the switch will not be able to produce wire-speed results.

Multi-Layer Switching (MLS)

Multi-layer switching combines layer 2, 3, and 4 switching technologies and provides high-speed scalability with low latency. It accomplishes this high combination of high-speed scalability with low latency by using huge filter tables based on the criteria designed by the network administrator.

Multi-layer switching can move traffic at wire speed and also provide layer 3 routing, which can remove the bottleneck from the network routers. This technology is based on the idea of route once, switch many.

Multi-layer switching can make routing/switching decisions based on the following:

- MAC source/destination address in a Data Link frame
- IP source/destination address in the Network layer header
- Protocol filed in the Network layer header
- Port source/destination numbers in the Transport layer header

There is no performance difference between a layer 3 and a layer 4 switch because the routing/switching is all hardware based.

> **NOTE** MLS will be discussed in more detail in Chapter 8.

It is important that you have an understanding of the different OSI layers and what they provide before continuing on to the Cisco three-layer hierarchical model.

The Cisco Hierarchical Model

Most of us learned about hierarchy early in life. Anyone with older siblings learned what it was like to be at the bottom of the hierarchy! Regardless of where you were first exposed to hierarchy, most of us experience it in many aspects of our lives. *Hierarchy* helps us to understand where things belong, how things fit together, and what functions go where. It brings order and understandability to otherwise complex models. If you want a pay raise, hierarchy dictates that you ask your boss, not your subordinate. That is the person whose role it is to grant (or deny) your request.

Hierarchy has many of the same benefits in network design that it has in other areas. When used properly in network design, it makes networks more predictable. It helps us to define and expect at which levels of the hierarchy we should perform certain functions. You would ask your boss, not your subordinate, for a raise because of their positions in the business hierarchy. The hierarchy requires that you ask someone at a higher level than yours. Likewise, you can use tools like access lists at certain levels in hierarchical networks and you must avoid them at others.

Let's face it, large networks can be extremely complicated, with multiple protocols, detailed configurations, and diverse technologies. Hierarchy helps us to summarize a complex collection of details into an understandable model. Then, as specific configurations are needed, the model dictates the appropriate manner for them to be applied.

Three-Layer Hierarchical Model

The Cisco hierarchical model is used to help you design a scalable, reliable, cost-effective hierarchical internetwork. Cisco defines three layers of hierarchy, as shown in Figure 1.6, each with specific functionality.

FIGURE 1.6 The Cisco hierarchical model

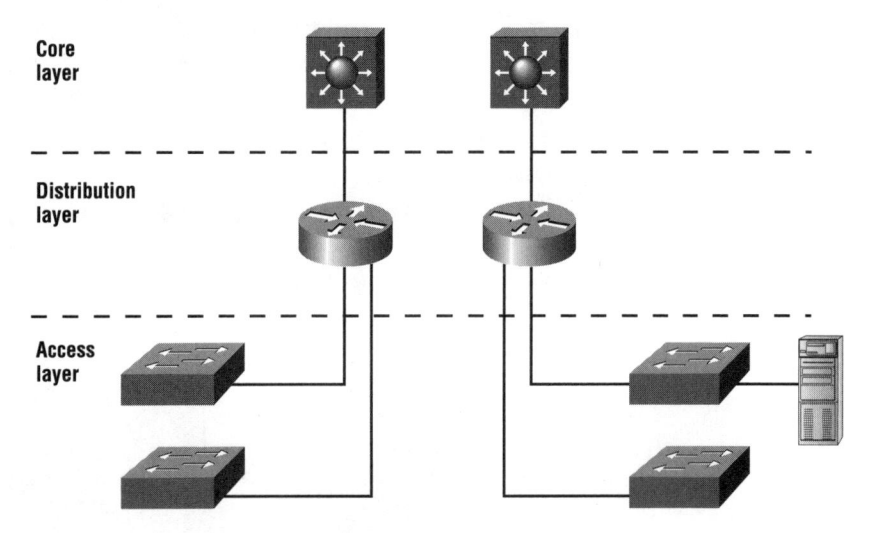

The three layers are as follows:

- Core
- Distribution
- Access

Each layer has specific responsibilities. Remember, however, that the three layers are logical and not necessarily physical. Three layers do not necessarily mean three separate devices. Consider the OSI model, another logical hierarchy. The seven layers describe functions but not necessarily protocols, right? Sometimes a protocol maps to more than one layer of the OSI model, and sometimes multiple protocols communicate within a single layer. In the same way, when you build physical implementations of hierarchical networks, you may have many devices in a single layer, or you might have a single device performing functions at two layers. The definition of the layers is logical, not physical.

Before we examine these layers and their functions, consider a common hierarchical design as shown in Figure 1.7. The phrase "keep local traffic local" has almost become a cliché in the networking world. However, the underlying concept has merit. Hierarchical design lends itself perfectly to fulfilling this concept. Now, let's take a closer look at each of the layers.

FIGURE 1.7 A hierarchical network design

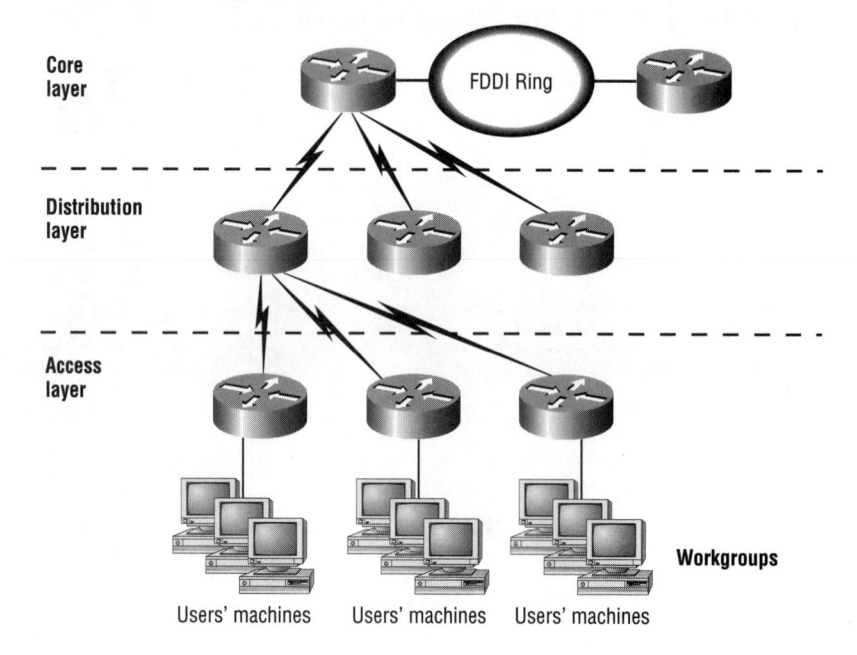

Core Layer

The *core layer* is literally the core of the network. At the top of the hierarchy, the core layer is responsible for transporting large amounts of traffic both reliably and quickly. The only purpose of the core layer of the network is to switch traffic as quickly as possible. The traffic transported across the core is common to a majority of users. However, remember that user data is processed at the distribution layer, and the distribution layer forwards the requests to the core, if needed.

If there is a failure in the core, *every single* user can be affected. Therefore, fault tolerance at this layer is an issue. The core is likely to see large volumes of traffic, so speed and latency are driving concerns here. Given the function of the core, we can now look at some design specifics to consider. Let's start with some things you know you don't want to do:

- Don't do anything to slow down traffic. This includes using access lists, routing between virtual local area networks (VLANs), and packet filtering.

- Don't support workgroup access here.

- Avoid expanding the core when the internetwork grows (i.e., adding routers). If performance becomes an issue in the core, give preference to upgrades over expansion.

Now, there are a few things that you want to make sure to get done as you design the core:

- Design the core for high reliability. Consider data-link technologies that facilitate both speed and redundancy, such as FDDI, FastEthernet (with redundant links), or even ATM.

- Design with speed in mind. The core should have very little latency.

- Select routing protocols with lower convergence times. Fast and redundant data-link connectivity is no help if your routing tables are shot!

Distribution Layer

The *distribution layer* is sometimes referred to as the workgroup layer and is the communication point between the access layer and the core. The primary function of the distribution layer is to provide routing, filtering, and

WAN access and to determine how packets can access the core, if needed. The distribution layer must determine the fastest way that user requests are serviced (for example, how a file request is forwarded to a server). After the distribution layer determines the best path, it forwards the request to the core layer. The core layer is then responsible for quickly transporting the request to the correct service.

The distribution layer is the place to implement policies for the network. Here, you can exercise considerable flexibility in defining network operation. There are several items that generally should be done at the distribution layer:

- Implement tools such as access lists, packet filtering, and queuing.
- Implement security and network policies, including address translation and firewalls.
- Redistribute between routing protocols, including static routing.
- Route between VLANs and other workgroup support functions.
- Define broadcast and multicast domains.

Things to avoid at the distribution layer are limited to those functions that exclusively belong to one of the other layers.

Access Layer

The *access layer* controls user and workgroup access to internetwork resources. The access layer is sometimes referred to as the desktop layer. The network resources that most users need will be available locally. Any traffic for remote services is handled by the distribution layer. The following functions should be included at this layer:

- Continued (from distribution layer) access control and policies.
- Creation of separate collision domains (segmentation).
- Workgroup connectivity to the distribution layer.
- Technologies such as dial-on-demand routing (DDR) and Ethernet switching are frequently seen here in the access layer. Static routing (instead of dynamic routing protocols) is seen here as well.

As already noted, three separate levels do not have to imply three separate routers. It could be fewer, or it could be more. Remember that this is a *layered* approach.

Cisco Catalyst Products

Understanding the campus size and traffic is an important factor in network design. A large campus is defined as several or many colocated buildings, and a medium campus is one or more colocated buildings. Small campus networks have only one building.

By understanding your campus size, you can choose Cisco products that will fit your business needs and grow with your company. Cisco switches are produced to fit neatly within its three-layer model. This helps you decide which equipment to use for your network efficiently and quickly.

Access Layer Switches

The access layer, as you already know, is where users gain access to the internetwork. The switches deployed at this layer must be able to handle connecting individual desktop devices to the internetwork.

The Cisco solutions at the access layer include the following:

1900/2800   Provide switched 10Mbps to the desktop or to 10BaseT hubs in small to medium campus networks.

2900   Provides 10/100Mbps switched access for up to 50 users and gigabit speeds for servers and uplinks.

4000   Provides a 10/100/1000Mbps advanced high-performance enterprise solution for up to 96 users and up to 36 Gigabit Ethernet ports for servers.

5000/5500   Used in large campuses to provide access for more than 250 users. The Catalyst 5000 series supports 10/100/1000Mbps Ethernet switching.

Distribution Layer Switches

As discussed earlier, the primary function of the distribution layer is to provide routing, filtering, and WAN access and to determine how packets can access the core, if needed.

Distribution layer switches are the aggregation point for multiple access switches and must be capable of handling large amounts of traffic from these access layer devices. The distribution layer switches must also be able to participate in multi-layer switching (MLS) and be able to handle a route processor.

The Cisco switches that provide these functions are as follows:

2926G A robust switch that uses an external router processor like a 4000 or 7000 series router.

5000/5500 The most effective distribution layer switch, it can support a large amount of connections and also an internal route processor module called a Route Switch Module (RSM). It can switch process up to 176KBps.

6000 The Catalyst 6000 can provide up to 384 10/100 Ethernet connections, 192 100FX FastEthernet connections, and 130 Gigabit Ethernet ports.

Core Layer Switches

The core layer must be efficient and do nothing to slow down packets as they traverse the backbone. The following switches are recommended for use in the core:

5000/5500 The 5000 is a great distribution layer switch, and the 5500 is a great core layer switch. The Catalyst 5000 series of switches includes the 5000, 5002, 5500, 5505, and 5509. All of the 5000 series switches use the same cards and modules, which makes them cost effective and provides protection for your investment.

6500 The Catalyst 6500 series switches are designed to address the need for gigabit port density, high availability, and multi-layer switching for the core layer backbone and server-aggregation environments. These switches use the Cisco IOS to utilize the high speeds of the ASICs, which allows the delivery of wire-speed traffic management services end to end.

8500 The Cisco Catalyst 8500 is a core layer switch that provides high-performance switching. The Catalyst 8500 uses Application-Specific Integrated Circuits (ASICs) to provide multiple-layer protocol support including Internet Protocol (IP), IP multicast, bridging, Asynchronous Transfer Mode (ATM) switching, and CiscoAssure policy-enabled Quality of Service (QoS).

All of these switches provide wire-speed multicast forwarding, routing, and Protocol Independent Multicast (PIM) for scalable multicast routing. These switches are perfect for providing the high bandwidth and performance needed for a core router. The 6500 and 8500 switches can aggregate multiprotocol traffic from multiple remote wiring closets and workgroup switches.

The Building Block

Remember the saying "Everything I need to know I learned in kindergarten"? Well, it appears to be true. Cisco has determined that if you follow the hierarchical model they have designed, it promotes a building block approach to network design. If you did well with building blocks in your younger years, you can just apply that same technique to building large, multimillion-dollar networks. Kind of makes you glad it's someone else's money you're playing with, doesn't it?

In all seriousness, Cisco has determined some fundamental campus elements that help you build network building blocks:

Switch blocks Access layer switches connected to the distribution layer devices

Core blocks Support of multiple switch blocks connected together with possibly 5500, 6500, or 8500 switches.

Within these fundamental elements, there are three contributing variables:

Server blocks Groups of network servers on a single subnet

WAN blocks Multiple connections to an ISP or multiple ISPs

Mainframe blocks Centralized services to which the enterprise network is responsible for providing complete access

By understanding how these work, you can build large, expensive networks with confidence (using someone else's money).

Switch Block

The *switch block* is a combination of layer 2 switches and layer 3 routers. The layer 2 switches connect users in the wiring closet into the access layer and provide 10 or 100Mbps dedicated connections; 1900/2820 and 2900 Catalyst switches can be used in the switch block.

From here, the access layer switches will connect into one or more distribution layer switches, which will be the central connection point for all switches coming from the wiring closets. The distribution layer device is either a switch with an external router or a multi-layer switch. The distribution layer switch will then provide layer 3 routing functions, if needed.

The distribution layer router will prevent broadcast storms that could happen on an access layer switch from propagating throughout the entire internetwork. The broadcast storm would be isolated to only the access layer switch in which the problem exists.

Switch Block Size

To understand how large a switch block can be, you must understand the traffic types and the size and number of workgroups that will be using them. The number of switches that can collapse from the access layer to the distribution layer depend on the following:

- Traffic patterns
- Routers at the distribution layer
- Number of users connected to the access layer switches
- Distance VLANs must traverse the network
- Spanning tree domain size

If routers at the distribution layer become the bottleneck in the network (which means the CPU processing is too intensive), the switch block has grown too large. Also, if too many broadcasts or multicast traffic slow down the switches and routers, your switch blocks have grown too large.

> **NOTE** A large number of users does not determine whether the switch block is too large, the amount of traffic going across the network does.

Core Block

If you have two or more switch blocks, the Cisco rule of thumb states that you need a *core block*. No routing is performed at the core, only transferring of data. It is a pass-through for the switch block, the server block, and the Internet. Figure 1.8 shows a possible core block.

FIGURE 1.8 The core block

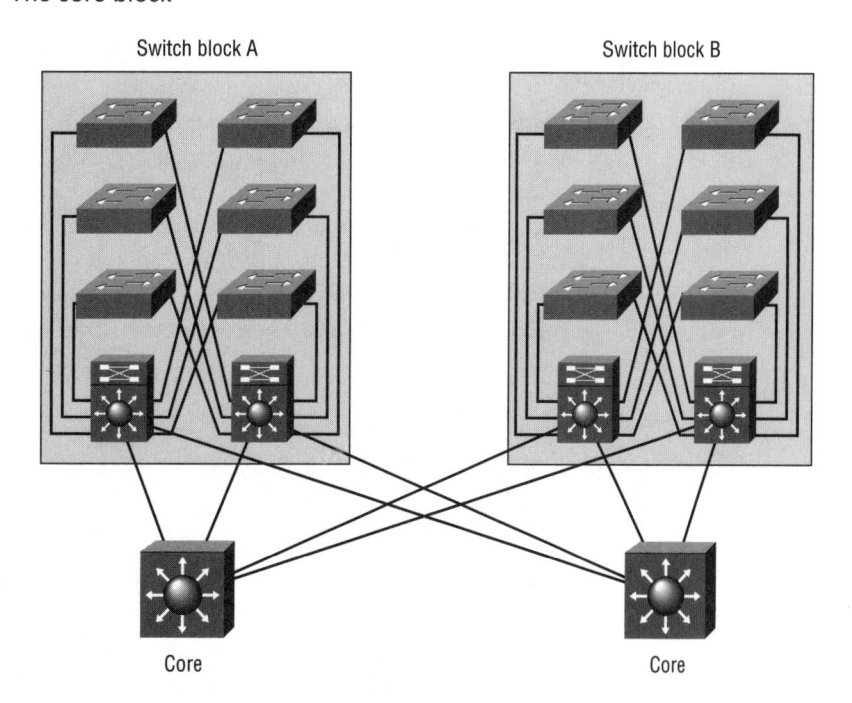

The core is responsible for transferring data to and from the switch blocks as quickly as possible. You can build a fast core with a frame, packet, or cell (ATM) network technology. The Switching exam is based on an Ethernet core network.

Typically, you would only have one subnet configured on the core network. However, for redundancy and load balancing, you could have two or more subnets configured.

Switches can trunk on a certain port or ports. This means that a port on a switch can be a member of more than one VLAN at the same time. However, the distribution layer will handle the routing and trunking for VLANs, and the core is only a pass-through once the routing has been performed. Because of this, core links will not carry multiple subnets per link, the distribution layer will.

A Cisco 6500 or 8500 switch is recommended at the core, and even though only one of those switches might be sufficient to handle the traffic, Cisco recommends two switches for redundancy and load balancing. You could consider a 5500 Catalyst switch if you don't need the power of the 6500 or the 8500.

Collapsed Core

A *collapsed core* is defined as one switch performing both core and distribution layer functions. The collapsed core is typically found in a small network; however, the functions of the core and distribution layer are still distinct.

Redundant links between the distribution layer and the access layer switches and between each access layer switch may support more than one VLAN. The distribution layer routing is the termination for all ports.

Figure 1.9 shows a collapsed core network design.

FIGURE 1.9 Collapsed core

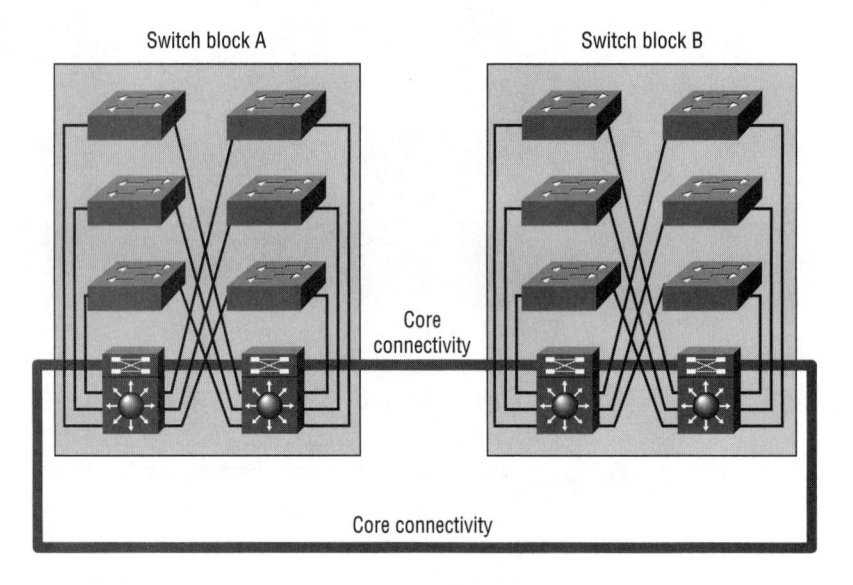

In a collapsed core network, Spanning Tree Protocol (STP) blocks the redundant links to prevent loops. Hot Standby Routing Protocol (HSRP) can provide redundancy in the distribution layer routing. It can keep core connectivity if the primary routing process fails.

> **NOTE** HSRP is covered in Chapter 8.

Dual Core

If you have more than two switch blocks and need redundant connections between the core and distribution layer, you need to create a dual core. Figure 1.10 shows a possible dual core configuration. Each connection would be a separate subnet.

FIGURE 1.10 Dual core configuration

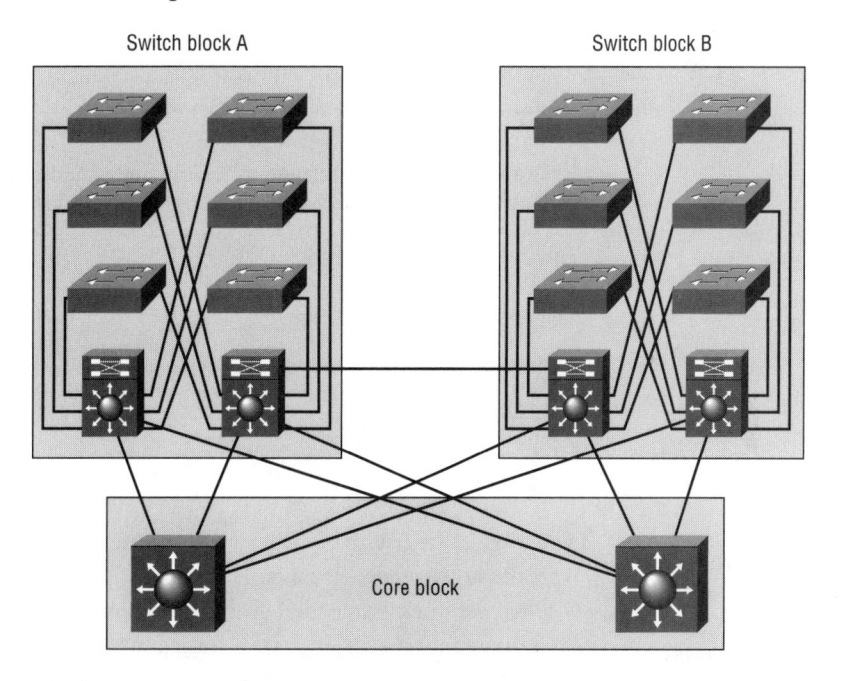

In Figure 1.10, you can see that each switch block is redundantly connected to each of the two core blocks. The distribution layer routers already have links to each subnet in the routing tables, provided by the layer 3 routing protocols. If a failure on a core switch takes place, convergence time will not be an issue. HSRP can be used to provide quick cutover between the cores. Notice that there is no redundancy between the two core networks, so STP will not be used on the core.

Core Size

Routing protocols are the main factor in determining the size of your core. This is because routers, or any layer 3 device, isolate the core. Routers send updates to other routers, and as the network grows, so do these updates, so it takes longer to converge, or have all the routers update. Because at least one of the routers will connect to the Internet, it's possible that there will be more updates throughout the internetwork.

The routing protocol dictates the size of the distribution layer devices that can communicate to the core. Table 1.2 shows a few of the more popular routing protocols and the number of blocks each routing protocol supports. Remember that this includes all blocks, including server, mainframe, and WAN.

TABLE 1.2 Blocks Supported by Routing Protocol

Routing Protocol	Max Number of Peers	Number of Subnet Links to the Core	Max Number of Supported Blocks
OSPF	50	2	25
EIGRP	50	2	25
RIP	30	2	15

Scaling Layer 2 Backbones

Typically, layer 2 switches are in the remote closets and represent the access layer, the layer where users gain access to the internetwork. Ethernet switched networks scale well in this environment, where the layer 2 switches then connect into a larger, more robust layer 3 switch representing the distribution layer. The layer 3 device is then connected into a layer 2 device representing the core. Because routing is not necessarily recommended in a classic design model at the core, the model then looks like Table 1.3.

TABLE 1.3 Classic Design Model

Access ➤	Distribution ➤	Core
Layer 2 switch	Layer 3 switch	Layer 2 switch

Spanning Tree Protocol (STP)

Chapters 4 and 5 details the Spanning Tree Protocol (STP), but some discussion is necessary here. STP is used by layer 2 bridges to stop network loops in networks that have more than one physical link to the same network. There is a limit to the number of links in a layer 2 switched backbone that needs to be taken into account. As you increase the number of core switches, the problem becomes that the number of links to distribution links must increase also, for redundancy reasons. If the core is running the Spanning Tree Protocol, then it can compromise the high-performance connectivity between switch blocks. The best design on the core is to have two switches without STP running. You can do this only by having a core without links between the core switches. This is demonstrated in Figure 1.11.

FIGURE 1.11 Layer 2 backbone scaling without STP

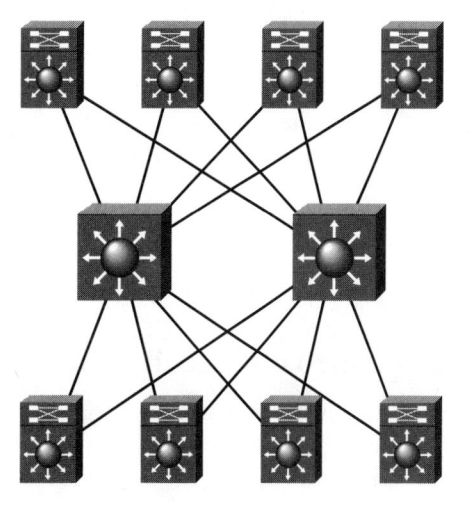

Figure 1.11 shows redundancy between the core and distribution layer without spanning tree loops. This is accomplished by not having the two

core switches linked together. However, each distribution layer 3 switch has a connection to each core switch. This means that each layer 3 switch has two equal-cost paths to every other router in the campus network.

Scaling Layer 3 Backbones

As discussed in "Scaling Layer 2 Backbones," you'll typically find layer 2 switches connecting to layer 3 switches, which connect to the core with the layer 2 switches. However, it is possible that some networks might have layer 2/layer 3/layer 3 designs (layer 2 connecting to layer 3 connecting to layer 3). But this is not cheap, even if you're using someone else's money. There is always some type of network budget, and you need to have good reason to spend the type of money needed to build layer 3 switches into the core.

There are three reasons you would implement layer 3 switches into the core:

- Fast convergence
- Automatic load balancing
- Eliminate peering problems

Fast Convergence

If you have only layer 2 devices at the core layer, the STP will be used to stop network loops if there is more than one connection between core devices. The STP has a convergence time of over 50 seconds, and if the network is large, this can cause an enormous amount of problems if it has just one link failure.

STP is not implemented in the core if you have layer 3 devices. Routing protocols, which have a much faster convergence time than STP, are used to maintain the network.

Automatic Load Balancing

If you provide layer 3 devices in the core, the routing protocols can load balance with multiple equal-cost links. This is not possible with layer 3 devices only at the distribution layer because you would have to selectively choose the root for utilizing more than one path.

Eliminate Peering Problems

Because routing is typically performed in the distribution layer devices, each distribution layer device must have reachability information about each of the other distribution layer devices. These layer 3 devices use routing protocols to maintain the state and reachability information about neighbor routers. This means that each distribution device becomes a peer with every other distribution layer device, and scalability becomes an issue because every device has to keep information for every other device.

If your layer 3 devices are located in the core, you can create a hierarchy, and the distribution layer devices will no longer be peer to each other's distribution device. This is typical in an environment in which there are more than 100 switch blocks.

Summary

In this chapter, you learned about switches and the different models available from Cisco. It is imperative that you understand the different models and what they are used for in the Cisco hierarchical design.

The past and future requirements of campus internetworks are an important part of your studies for your Cisco Switching exam. We discussed the current campus designs as well as how to implement FastEthernet, Gigabit Ethernet, Fast EtherChannel, and Multi-Layer Switching (MLS) in the emerging campus designs.

We also discussed the differences between layer 2, layer 3, and layer 4 switching technologies. You learned about the Cisco three-layer model and the different catalyst switches that can be implemented at each layer of the Cisco model.

The chapter ended with a discussion of the switch and core blocks, which are based on the Cisco three-layer model, and how to design networks based on this model.

Key Terms

Before you take the exam, be sure you're familiar with the following terms:

20/80 rule	distribution layer
80/20 rule	enterprise services
access layer	hierarchy
bandwidth	local services
collapsed core	multi-layer switching
core block	remote services
core layer	switch block
data encapsulation	

Written Lab

In this section, you will complete the following written labs:

- Switching Definitions
- Cisco's Three-Layer Model
- Switching Theory

Lab 1.1: Switching Definitions

In the following table, the first column contains definitions of different types of switching. Fill in the second column with the number or numbers of the correct switching technology.

1. Layer 2 switching
2. Layer 3 switching
3. Layer 4 switching
4. Multi-layer switching

Definition	Switch
Based on route once, switch many	
Enables prioritization based on specific applications	
Creates security using source or destination addresses and port numbers	
Can use NetFlow switching	
Allows you to create flatter networks	
Builds filtering table based on application port numbers	
Communicates with peer layers in a different system with packets	
Reads the TCP and UDP port fields for filter and forwarding information	
Uses access lists to control traffic	
Uses hardware-based routing	
Uses hardware-based bridging	
Uses an ASIC to handle frame forwarding	
Provides both layer 2 and layer 3 functions	

Lab 1.2: Cisco's Three-Layer Model

Options 1, 2, and 3 are the layers in the Cisco three-layer model. Match the functions to the correct layer.

1. Access layer
2. Distribution layer
3. Core layer

Function	Layer
Routes traffic between VLANs	
Uses collision domains	
Uses broadcast domains	

Function	Layer
Uses access lists	
Provides end users with access to the network	
Communicates between the switch blocks and to the enterprise servers	
Switches traffic as quickly as possible	

Lab 1.3: Theory

1. Which device is used to break up broadcast domains?

2. Which device is used to break up collision domains?

3. What are the four methods of encapsulating user data through the OSI model?

4. Which Cisco layer is used to pass traffic as quickly as possible?

5. What is the Protocol Data Unit (PDU) used at the Transport layer?

6. What is the PDU used at the Network layer?

7. Which Cisco layer is used to break up collision domains?

8. Which OSI layer creates frames by encapsulating packets with a header and trailer?

9. What devices can provide multicast control and security?

10. What breaks up broadcast domains in a layer 2 switched network?

Review Questions

1. You work for a large company that needs to connect four buildings with a high-speed, high-bandwidth backbone. They are all on the same city block and fiber already connects between the buildings. There are multiple departments in each building and all run multiple protocols. The company already owns Cisco Catalyst 6000 series switches, which you can use for the distribution layer. What switch should you use for the core layer?

   A. 2900

   B. 4000

   C. 6500

   D. 8500

2. You need to install a large switched network for a company that has already defined its business requirements to be gigabit speed data transfer, high availability, and ISL routing to the server farms for all 300 users. What switch would you install for the distribution layer?

   A. 2900 with gigabit uplinks

   B. 4000 series

   C. 6000 series with a 16-port gigabit module

   D. 8500 series with gigabit uplinks

3. You just have been hired as a consultant for a small company that has users distributed across many floors in the same buildings. Servers for the company are all located on the first floor, and 30 users access them from various parts of the building. What switch would you install for the access layer connection?

   A. 1900 series

   B. 5000 series

   C. 6000 series

   D. 8000 series

4. You have just been promoted to network manager (congratulations!) for a large company and you need to connect 4 switch blocks that each contains 1,500 users. You want to control broadcast domains at the switch blocks and use ISL to route between them. What switch would you purchase for the distribution layer?

   A. 1900 with gigabit links

   B. 4000 with gigabit VLAN

   C. 5500 with RSM module

   D. Catalyst 6000 with 16-port gigabit module

5. Which layer must be efficient and do nothing to slow down packets as they traverse the backbone?

   A. Access

   B. Distribute

   C. Distribution

   D. Backbone

   E. Core

6. Which of the following switches are recommended for use in the core? (Choose all that apply.)

   A. 4000

   B. 5000

   C. 6500

   D. 8500

7. Which of the following is the main factor in determining the size of your core?

   A. Routing protocols

   B. Routed protocols

   C. IP broadcasts

   D. ARPs

   E. ICMP Redirects

   F. Number of distribution layer switches

8. The number of switches that can collapse from the access layer to the distribution layer depends on _____ . (Choose all that apply.)

   A. Traffic patterns

   B. Routers at the distribution layer

   C. Number of users connecting to the core layer

   D. Amount of users connected to the access layer switches

   E. Number of distribution layer switches

   F. Distance VLANs must traverse the network

   G. Spanning tree domain size

9. Which of the following is generally performed at the distribution layer? (Choose all that apply.)

   A. Breaking up of collision domains

   B. No packet filtering

   C. Access lists, packet filtering, and queuing.

   D. Routing between VLANs

10. Which of the following is also generally performed at the distribution layer? (Choose all that apply.)

   A. Broadcast and multicast domain definition

   B. Security and network policies

   C. Redistribution between routing protocols

   D. User access to the network

11. Which of the following is true regarding the access layer? (Choose all that apply.)

   A. This is where users gain access to the internetwork.

   B. The switches deployed at this layer must be able to handle connecting individual desktop devices to the internetwork.

   C. It is the aggregation point for multiple access switches.

   D. It can participate in MLS and handle a router processor.

12. Which of the following series of switches are suggested for use at the access layer? (Choose all that apply.)

   A. 1900/2800

   B. 2900

   C. 4000

   D. 5000

   E. 6000

   F. 8000

13. Which of the following Cisco switches provides a 10/100/1000Mbps advanced high-performance enterprise solution for up to 96 users and up to 36 Gigabit Ethernet ports for servers?

   A. 2926G

   B. 4000 series

   C. 6000 series

   D. 8000 series

14. Which of the following switches provides 10/100Mbps switched access for up to 50 users and gigabit speeds for servers and uplinks?

   A. 1900

   B. 2900

   C. 4000

   D. 6000

   E. 8000

15. Which of the following switches provides switched 10Mbps to the desktop or to 10BaseT hubs in small to medium campus networks?

   A. 1900/2800

   B. 2926G

   C. 4000 series

   D. 6000 series

16. Which layer of switching makes no modification of the data packet?

   A. Layer 2

   B. Layer 3

   C. Layer 4

   D. MLS

17. Layer 2 switching is _____ . (Choose all that apply.)

   A. Software based

   B. Hardware based

   C. Wire speed

   D. Asymmetrical

   E. Filtering using ASICs

18. Which Cisco switch can provide up to 384 10/100 Ethernet connections, 192 100FX FastEthernet connections, and 130 Gigabit Ethernet ports?

    A. 1900EN XL

    B. 2926G

    C. 4000

    D. 6000

19. Which of the following describes Cisco Catalyst 5000 series switches?

    A. Provide an enterprise solution for up to 96 users and up to 36 Gigabit Ethernet ports for servers.

    B. Support a large amount of connections and also support an internal route processor module.

    C. Only use an external router processor like a 4000 or 7000 series router.

    D. The 5000 series is the Catalyst low-end model.

20. Which of the following is true regarding the distribution layer switches? (Choose all that apply.)

    A. The distribution layer is the aggregation point for multiple access switches.

    B. This is where users gain access to the internetwork.

    C. The switches deployed at this layer must be able to handle connecting individual desktop devices to the internetwork.

    D. The distribution layer can participate in MLS and handle a router processor.

Answers to Written Lab

Answers to Lab 1.1

Definition	Numbered Answer
Based on route once, switch many	4
Enables prioritization based on specific applications	3
Creates security using source or destination addresses and port numbers.	3
Can use NetFlow switching	2, 3
Allows you to create flatter networks	1
Builds filtering table based on application port numbers	2, 3
Communicates with peer layers in a different system with packets	2
Reads the TCP and UDP port fields for filter and forwarding information	3
Uses access lists to control traffic	2, 3
Uses hardware-based routing	2
Uses hardware-based bridging	1
Uses an ASIC to handle frame forwarding	1
Provides both layer 2 and layer 3 functions	4

Answers to Lab 1.2

Definition	Layer
Routes traffic between VLANs	2
Uses collision domains	1
Uses broadcast domains	2
Uses access lists	2
Provides end users with access to the network	1
Communicates between the switch blocks and to the enterprise servers	3
Switches traffic as quickly as possible	3

Answers to Lab 1.3

1. A layer 3 device, usually a router. Layer 2 devices do not break up broadcast domains.

2. A layer 2 device, typically a switch. Although routers break up both collision domains and broadcast domains, layer 2 switches are primarily used to break up collision domains.

3. Segment, packet, frame, bits. It is important to understand the question. This question asked for the encapsulation methods, which means how data is encapsulated as user data goes from the Application layer down to the Physical layer.

4. The core layer should have no packet manipulation, if possible.

5. Port or socket. TCP uses port numbers. IPX uses sockets.

6. A packet or datagram is the PDU used at the Network layer.

7. Access layer. Remember, the distribution layer is used to break up broadcast domains and the access layer is used to break up collision domains.

8. Data Link. Data is encapsulated with header and trailer information at the Data Link layer.

9. Routers or layer 3 devices are the only devices that control broadcasts and provide packet filtering

10. Virtual LANs. These are configured on the layer 2 switches and layer 3 devices provide a means for moving traffic between the VLANs.

Answers to Review Questions

1. **D.** A Cisco 6500 or 8500 switch is recommended at the core, and even though only one of those switches might be sufficient to handle the traffic, Cisco recommends two switches for redundancy and load balancing. You could consider a 5500 Catalyst switch if you don't need the power of the 6500 or the 8500. Because the customer is using 6500 at the distribution layer, you should use 8500s as the core switches. D is the best answer.

2. **C.** The Catalyst 6000 can provide up to 384 10/100 Ethernet connections, 192 100FX FastEthernet connections, and 130 Gigabit Ethernet ports. Because there are 300 users, the 6000 series would be a good fit. The 8500 is a recommended core switch, and the question asks for an access layer/distribution layer solution.

3. **A.** A 5000 series switch may be overkill for the needs of the company. Because the question involves a small company and no growth was specified, the 1900 would be the most cost-effective solution.

4. **C.** The 5500 can use a Route Switch Module (RSM) to provide layer 3 services to the internetwork. It also can provide a large amount of ports per switch.

5. **E.** The core layer should be designed to connect distribution layer devices. No packet manipulation should occur at this layer.

6. **C, D.** The core layer needs very fast switches to move data as quickly as possible between distribution layer devices.

7. **A.** Routing protocols are protocols that are used to update routers with network information. Routed protocols are used to send user data through an internetwork.

8. **A, B, D, F, G.** Traffic patterns, the amount of routers, the number of users connected into access layer switches, distance, and spanning tree size are all factors that contribute to the amount of switches that can collapse from the access layer to the distribution layer.

9. **C, D.** The distribution layer performs routing, which breaks up broadcast domains. Routers can be configured with access lists, packet filters, and queuing.

10. **A, B, C.** The distribution layer performs routing, which breaks up broadcast domains by default. Security can be performed as well as network policies implemented. Routing protocols can be redistributed with most Cisco routers.

11. **A, B.** The access layer breaks up collision domains and connects the access layer to the internetwork by connecting to the distribution layer.

12. **A, B, C, D.** Any switches from the 1900 series to the 5000 series can work at the access layer. The 5000 and above are used at the distribution layer and the core layer.

13. **B.** The Cisco 4000 series was created for high performance, up to 36 gigabit ports, and 96-user connectivity.

14. **B.** The 1900 is fixed 10 or 100Mbps ports and cannot handle gigabit speeds. The 2900 is the lowest model to handle gigabit speeds for up to 50 users maximum.

15. **A.** The 1900 is a low-end model that provides 10Mbps switched networking with up to 24 ports.

16. **A.** The Data Link layer (layer 2) encapsulates the packet but does not make any changes to it.

17. **B, C, E.** Layer 2 switching is considered hardware based because it uses an ASIC chip to make filtering decisions. It is also considered wire speed because no modification to the data packet takes place.

18. **D.** The Cisco Catalyst 6000 series provides up to 384 10/100 Mbps Ethernet ports for user connectivity. It can also provide 192 100Mbps FastEthernet fiber uplinks and 130 Gigabit Ethernet ports.

19. **B.** The 5000 series Catalyst switches are the mainstay of the Cisco workforce. They can provide a very large amount of connections and use an internal Route Switch Module (RSM) to run a fast router on the back plane of the switch.

20. **A, D.** The distribution layer connects the access layer devices, performs routing, and can provide multi-layer switching.

Chapter 2

Connecting the Switch Block

THE CCNP EXAM TOPICS COVERED IN THIS CHAPTER INCLUDE THE FOLLOWING:

- ✓ Cable media and the IEEE
- ✓ The differences and benefits of 10BaseT, FastEthernet, and Gigabit Ethernet
- ✓ Connecting and logging in to a set-based switch and an IOS-based switch
- ✓ Setting the hostname, interface descriptions, passwords, and IP addresses of a set-based switch and an IOS-based switch
- ✓ Configuring the duplex and speed of switch interfaces
- ✓ Verifying IP connectivity
- ✓ Deleting the set-based and IOS-based switch configurations

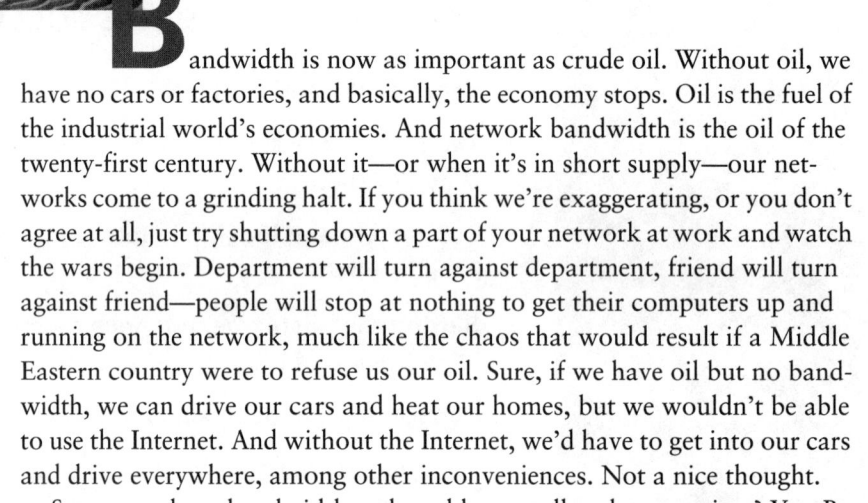

Bandwidth is now as important as crude oil. Without oil, we have no cars or factories, and basically, the economy stops. Oil is the fuel of the industrial world's economies. And network bandwidth is the oil of the twenty-first century. Without it—or when it's in short supply—our networks come to a grinding halt. If you think we're exaggerating, or you don't agree at all, just try shutting down a part of your network at work and watch the wars begin. Department will turn against department, friend will turn against friend—people will stop at nothing to get their computers up and running on the network, much like the chaos that would result if a Middle Eastern country were to refuse us our oil. Sure, if we have oil but no bandwidth, we can drive our cars and heat our homes, but we wouldn't be able to use the Internet. And without the Internet, we'd have to get into our cars and drive everywhere, among other inconveniences. Not a nice thought.

So, can we have bandwidth and world peace all at the same time? Yes. By creating a sound, hierarchical network that follows the Cisco three-layer model, you too can be a Nobel laureate at home and on the job.

This chapter will help you understand the different *contention media* available. Contention networks are first come, first served, or what we call Ethernet. This course covers only contention media because it runs at least 50 percent of the networks in the world, if not much more.

Cable Media

To know when and how to use the different kinds of cable media, you need to understand what users *do* on the corporate network. The way to find this information is to ask questions. After that, you can use monitoring equipment to really see what is going on inside the network cabling. Before you deploy an application on a corporate network, carefully consider bandwidth requirements as well as latency issues. More and more users need to compete for bandwidth on the network because of bandwidth-consuming applications. Although layer 2 switches break up collision domains and certainly help a congested network if correctly designed and installed, you must also understand the different cable media types available and where to use each type for maximum efficiency. That's where this chapter comes in.

In this chapter, we'll teach you the basics of Ethernet networking and how to use the various flavors of Ethernet networking in your access, distribution, and core networks. After you have learned about the different Ethernet cable media types, you'll learn how to log in and configure both a set-based switch and an IOS-based switch. The chapter will end with hands-on labs in which you'll connect the switches together and configure them.

The Background of IEEE Ethernet

In 1980, the Digital, Intel, and Xerox (DIX) consortium created the original Ethernet. Predictably, Ethernet_II followed and was released in 1984. The standards-setting organization Institute of Electrical and Electronics Engineers (IEEE) termed this the 802 project. The 802 project was initially divided into three groups:

- The High Level Interface (HILI) became the 802.1 committee and was responsible for high-level internetworking protocols and management.

- The Logical Link Control (LLC) group became the 802.2 committee and focused on end-to-end link connectivity and the interface between the higher layers and the medium-access-dependant layers.

- The Data Link and Medium Access Control (DLMAC) group became responsible for the medium-access protocols. The DLMAC ended up splitting into three different committees:
    - 802.3 for Ethernet
    - 802.4 for Token Bus
    - 802.5 for Token Ring

DEC, Intel, and Xerox pushed Ethernet, while Burroughs, Concord Data Systems, Honeywell, Western Digital, and later, General Motors and Boeing, pushed 802.4. IBM took on 802.5.

The IEEE then created the 802.3 subcommittee to come up with an Ethernet standard that happens to be almost identical to the Ethernet_II version of Ethernet. The two differ only in their descriptions of the Data Link layer. Ethernet_II has a Type field, whereas 802.3 has a Length field. Even so, they're both common in their Physical layer specifications, MAC addressing, and understanding of the LLC layer's responsibilities.

> **NOTE** See *CCNA: Cisco Certified Network Associate Study Guide* by Todd Lammle (Sybex, 2000) for a detailed explanation of Ethernet frame types.

Ethernet_II and 802.3 both define a bus-topology LAN at 10Mbps, and the cabling defined in these standards are identical:

10Base2/Thinnet   Segments up to 185 meters using RG58 coax at 50 ohms.

10Base5/Thicknet   Segments up to 500 meters using RG8 or 11 at 50 ohms.

10BaseT/UTP   All hosts connect using unshielded twisted-pair (UTP) cable to a central device (a hub or switch). Category 3 UTP is specified to 10Mbps, category 5 to 100Mbps, category 6 to 155Mbps, and category 7 to 1Gbps.

Switched Ethernet

Ethernet is the most popular type of network in the world and will continue to be so. It is important to understand how hubs and switches work within an Ethernet internetwork.

By using *switched Ethernet* in layer 2 of your network, you no longer have to share bandwidth with the different departments in the corporation. With hubs, all devices have to share the same bandwidth, which can cause havoc in today's networks.

Remember that layer 2 switches break up collision domains, but the network is still one large broadcast domain. Switched Ethernet has replaced shared hubs in the networking world because each connection from a host to the switch is its own collision domain. Remember that, with shared hubs, the network was one large collision domain and one large broadcast domain, whereas layer 2 switches break up collision domains on each port, but all ports are still considered, by default, to be in one large broadcast domain. Only virtual LANs, covered in Chapter 3, break up broadcast domains in a layer 2 switched network.

Switched Ethernet is a good way to dynamically allocate dedicated 10, 100, and 1000Mbps connections to each user. By also running full-duplex Ethernet, you can theoretically double the throughput on each link. In the next sections, we'll discuss how Ethernet is used in your internetwork, the differences between the Ethernet types, and half- and full-duplex.

Using Ethernet Media in Your Internetwork

In this section, you'll learn the difference between the Ethernet media types and how to use them in your internetworks. We'll cover the following Ethernet types:

- 10BaseT
- FastEthernet
- Gigabit Ethernet

10BaseT

10BaseT stands for 10 million bits per second (Mbps), baseband technology, twisted-pair. This Ethernet technology has the highest install base of any network in the world. It runs the Carrier Sense Multiple Access/Collision Detection (CSMA/CD) protocol and, if correctly installed, is an efficient network. However, if it gets too large and the network is not segmented correctly, problems occur. It is important to understand collision and broadcast domains and how to correctly design the network with switches and routers.

Use 10BaseT at the Access Layer

10BaseT Ethernet is typically used only at the access layer, and even then, FastEthernet (100BaseT) is quickly replacing it as the prices for 100BaseT continue to drop. It would be poor design to place 10BaseT at the distribution or core layers. You need transits that are much faster than 10BaseT at these layers.

Distance

The distance that 10BaseT can run and be within specification is 100 meters (330 feet). The 100 meters includes the following:

- Five meters from the switch to the patch panel
- Ninety meters from the patch panel to the office punch-down block
- Five meters from the punch-down block to the desktop connection

This doesn't mean that you can't really run more then 100 meters on a cable run; it just is not guaranteed to work.

FastEthernet

FastEthernet is 10 times faster than 10Mbps Ethernet. The great thing about FastEthernet is that, like 10BaseT, it is still based on the Carrier Sense Multiple Access/Collision Detection (CSMA/CD) signaling. What this means is that you can run 10BaseT and 100BaseT on the same network without any problems. What a nice upgrade path this type of network can give you. You can put all your servers on 10BaseT and upgrade only the clients to 100BaseT if you need to. However, you can't really even buy a PC that doesn't have a 10/100 Ethernet card in it anymore, so you really don't need to worry about compatibility and speed issues from the user's perspective.

Use FastEthernet at All Three Layers

FastEthernet works great at all layers of the hierarchical model. It can be used to give high performance to PCs and other hosts at the access layer, provide connectivity from the access layer to the distribution layer switches, and connect the distribution layer switches to the core network. Connecting a server block to the core layer would need, at a minimum, FastEthernet or maybe even Gigabit Ethernet.

IEEE Specifications for FastEthernet

There are two different specifications for FastEthernet, but the IEEE 802.3u is the most popular. The 802.3u specification is 100Mbps over category 3 or 5, twisted-pair (typically just category 5 or 5 plus is used for FastEthernet). The second Ethernet specification, called 802.12, used a different signaling technique, which was more efficient than the CSMA/CD access method. The

IEEE passed both methods in June 1995, but because 802.3 Ethernet had such a strong name in the industry, 802.12, also called Demand Priority Access Method (DPAM), has virtually disappeared from the market. As with the Macintosh and NetWare operating systems, it doesn't mean anything if you have a better product; it only matters how you market it.

The IEEE 802.3u committee can be summarized as follows:

- Provide seamless integration with the installed base
- Provide 100BaseT at only two times the cost (or less) of 10BaseT
- Increase aggregate bandwidth
- Provide multiple-vendor standardization and operability
- Provide time-bounded delivery

Media Independent Interface (MII)

FastEthernet requires a different interface than 10BaseT Ethernet. 10Mbps Ethernet used the Attachment Unit Interface (AUI) to connect Ethernet segments together. This provided a decoupling of the MAC layer from the different requirements of the various Physical layer topologies, which allowed the MAC to remain constant but meant the Physical layer could support any existing and new technologies. However, the AUI interface could not support 100Mbps Ethernet because of the high frequencies involved. 100BaseT needed a new interface, and the MII provides it.

100BaseT actually created a new subinterface between the Physical layer and the Data Link layer called the Reconciliation Sublayer (RS). The RS maps the 1s and 0s to the MII interface. The MII uses a nibble, which is defined as 4 bits. AUI used only 1 bit at a time. Data transfers across the MII at one nibble per clock cycle, which is 25MHz. 10Mbps uses a 2.5MHz clock.

Full-Duplex Ethernet and FastEthernet

Full-duplex Ethernet can both transmit and receive simultaneously and uses point-to-point connections. It is typically referred to as collision free because it doesn't share bandwidth with any other devices. Frames sent by two nodes cannot collide because there are physically separate transmit and receive circuits between the nodes.

Use Full-Duplex Ethernet in the Distribution Layer

Because users typically use client/server applications using read/write asymmetrical traffic, the best performance for full-duplex would be in the distribution layer, not necessarily in the access layer.

Full-Duplex with Flow Control was created to avoid packets being dropped if the buffers on an interface fill up before all packets can be processed. However, some vendors might not interoperate, and the buffering might have to be handled by upper-layer protocols instead.

Auto-Negotiation

Auto-negotiation is a process that allows clients and switches to agree on a link capability. This is used to determine the link speed as well as the duplex being used. The auto-negotiation process uses priorities to set the link configuration. Obviously, if both a client and switch port can use 100Mbps, full-duplex connectivity, that would be the highest-priority ranking, whereas half-duplex, 10Mbps Ethernet is the lowest ranking.

You need to understand that the auto-negotiation protocols do not work that well and you would be better off to configure the switch and NICs to run in a dedicated mode instead of letting the clients and switches auto-negotiate. Later in this chapter, we'll show you how to configure your switches with both the speed and duplex options.

Distance

FastEthernet does have some drawbacks. It uses the same singing techniques as 10Mbps Ethernet, so it has the same distance constraints. In addition, 10Mbps Ethernet can use up to four repeaters, whereas FastEthernet can use only one or two, depending on the type of repeater. Table 2.1 shows a comparison of FastEthernet technologies.

TABLE 2.1 Comparison of FastEthernet Technologies

Technology	Wiring Category	Distance
100BaseTX	Category 5 UTP wiring, category 6 and 7 is now available. Category 6 is sometimes referred to as cat 5 plus. Two-pair wiring.	100 meters
100BaseT4	Four-pair wiring, using UTP category 3, 4, or 5.	100 meters
100BaseFX	Multi-Mode Fiber (MMF) with 62.5-micron fiber-optic core with a 125-micron outer cladding (62.5/125).	400 meters

Gigabit Ethernet

In the corporate market, *Gigabit Ethernet* is the new hot thing. What is so great about Gigabit is that it can use the same network that your 10 and 100Mbps Ethernet now use. You certainly do have to worry about distance constraints, but what a difference it can make in just a server farm alone!

Just think how nice it would be to have all your servers connected to Ethernet switches with Gigabit Ethernet and all your users using 100BaseT switched connections. Of course, all your switches would connect with Gigabit links as well. Add the hot xDSL to connect to the Internet and you have more bandwidth than you ever could have imagined just a few years ago. Will it be enough bandwidth a few years from now? Probably not. If you have the bandwidth, users will find a way to use it.

Use Gigabit Ethernet in the Switch, Core, and Server Blocks

Gigabit Ethernet can work in the switch block, the core block, and your server blocks:

Switch block You can use Gigabit Ethernet between the access layer switches and the distribution layer switches. Gigabit is not typically connected to end users, but that can change quickly.

Core block You can use Gigabit Ethernet to connect distribution layer switches in each building to the core switches.

Server block By placing a Gigabit switch in the server block, you can effectively connect your high-performance servers to the network with gigabit speeds. However, remember that, unless the server is tremendously fast, you might not notice a difference in speeds from FastEthernet because the server processing can become the bottleneck. Time to throw out your Pentium 90 servers.

Protocol Architecture

Gigabit Ethernet became an IEEE 802.3 standard in the summer of 1998. The standard was called 802.3z. Gigabit uses Ethernet framing the same way 10BaseT and FastEthernet does. This means that, not only is it fast, it can run on the same network as older Ethernet technology, which provides a nice migration plan. The goal of the IEEE 802.3z was to maintain compatibility to the 10Mb/s and 100Mb/s existing Ethernet network. They needed to provide a seamless operation to forward frames between segments running at different speeds. The committee kept the minimum and maximum frame lengths the same. However, they needed to change the CSMA/CD for half-duplex operation from its 512-bit times to help the distance that Gigabit Ethernet could run.

Will Gigabit ever run to the desktop? Maybe. People said that FastEthernet would never run to the desktop when it came out, but it's now common. If Gigabit is run to the desktop, however, it's hard to imagine what we'll need to run the backbone with. 1000BaseT to the rescue! Yes, 10 Gigabit Ethernet is just around the corner!

Comparing 10BaseT, FastEthernet, and Gigabit Ethernet

There are some major differences between FastEthernet and Gigabit Ethernet. FastEthernet uses the Media Independent Interface (MII), and Gigabit uses the Gigabit Media Independent Interface (GMII). 10BaseT used the Attachment Unit Interface, or AUI. A new interface was designed to help FastEthernet scale to 100Mbps, and this interface was redesigned for Gigabit Ethernet. The GMII uses an 8-bit data path instead of the 4-bit path that FastEthernet MII uses. The clocking must operate at 125MHz to achieve the 1Gb/s data rate.

Time Slots

Because Ethernet networks are sensitive to the round-trip-delay constraint of CSMA/CD, time slots are extremely important. Remember that in 10BaseT and 100BaseT, the time slots were 512-bit times. However, this is not feasible for Gigabit because the time slot would be only 20 meters in length. To make Gigabit useable on a network, the time slots were extended to 512 bytes (4096-bit times!). However, the operation of full-duplex Ethernet was not changed at all. Table 2.2 compares the new Gigabit Ethernet technologies.

TABLE 2.2 Comparison of Gigabit Ethernet Technologies

Technology	Wiring Category	Cable Distance
1000BaseCX	Copper shielded twisted-pair	25 meters
1000BaseT	Copper category 5, four-pair wiring, UTP	100 meters
1000BaseSX	MMF using 62.5 and 50-micron core, uses a 780-nanometer laser	260 meters
1000BaseLX	Single-mode fiber that uses a 9-micron core, 1300-nanometer laser	3 km up to 10 km

Connecting and Logging In to a Switch

In this section, you will learn about two different types of switches Cisco sells: the Catalyst 1900, which is IOS based, and the Catalyst 5000, which is set based. The Catalyst 1900 switch can now use a command-line interface (CLI) and the Cisco Internetworking Operating System (IOS) runs on the switch. This makes configuring the switch very similar to how you would configure a router. The 5000 series is still set based, which means you use the command **set** to configure the router. Throughout the rest of this book, we'll show you commands on both types of switches.

There are two types of operating systems that run on Cisco switches:

IOS based   You can configure the switch from a command-line interface (CLI) that is very similar to the one used on Cisco routers. Catalyst 1900, 2820, and 2900 switches can be used with an IOS-based CLI, although they can be set with a menu system as well.

Set based   Uses older, set-based CLI configuration commands. The Cisco switches that use the set-based CLI are the 2926 series, the 1948G, the 4000, the 5000, and the 6000 series.

It's time to be introduced to the 1900 and 5000 series of Catalyst switches. Why the 1900? Cisco uses it on the exams, of course, and it allows you to run a CLI with IOS-based commands on a less-expensive switch than you would need to use with the 5000 series. The 1900 switches are great for home offices or other small offices where you can get 10Mbps switched ports with 100Mbps uplinks at a decent price. It sure beats shared hubs!

Cabling the Switch Block Devices

You can physically connect to a Cisco Catalyst switch by connecting either to the console port or an Ethernet port, just as you would with a router.

Connecting to the Console Port

The 1900 and 5000 series switches both have a console connector. However, the 5000 series switch has a console connector that uses only an RS-232-type connector, which will come with the switch when purchased. The 1900 switch, on the other hand, has a console port on the back, which is an RJ-45 port. Both console cables are rolled cables.

> **NOTE**   1924 switches use a null-modem cable for the console port.

After you connect to the console port, you need to start a terminal emulation program like Hyperterm in Windows. The settings are as follows:

- 9600 BPS
- 8 data bits
- No parity
- 1 stop bits
- No flow control

WARNING: Do not connect an Ethernet cable, ISDN, or live telephone line into the console port. These things can damage the electronics of the switch.

Connecting to an Ethernet Port

The Catalyst 1900/2800 series switches have fixed port types. They are not modular like the 5000 series switches. The 1900/2800 switches use only 10BaseT ports for workstations and 100BaseT or FX for uplinks. Each switch has either 12 (model 1912) or 24 (model 1924) 10BaseT switch ports with 2 FastEthernet uplinks. The 100BaseTX ports are referred to as ports A and B. We have connected servers into these ports and are able to run 100Mbps. Works great for a small network. To connect the ports to another switch as an uplink, you must use a crossover cable. It would be nice if there were a button for this function, but there isn't.

The Catalyst 5000 switches can run either 10 or 100Mbps on any port, depending on the type of cards you buy. The supervisor cards always take the first slot and have two 100BaseTX or FX ports for uplinks. All devices connected into either the 1900/2800 or 5000 series switches must be within 100 meters (330 feet) of the switch port.

NOTE: When connecting devices like workstations, servers, printers, and routers to the switch, you must use a straight-through cable. Use a crossover cable to connect between switches.

When a device is connected to a port, the port status LED light comes on and stays on. If the light does not come on, the other end might be off or there might be a cable problem. Also, if a light comes on and off, an auto-speed and duplex problem is possible. We'll show you how to check that in the next section.

5000 Switch Startup

The 5000 series switch loads the software image from flash, then asks you to enter a password, even if there isn't one set. Press Enter, and then you will see a Console > prompt. At this point, you can enter enable mode and configure the switch using set commands:

```
BOOTROM Version 5.1(2), Dated Apr 26 1999 10:41:04
BOOT date: 08/02/02 BOOT time: 08:49:03
Uncompressing NMP image.  This will take a minute...
Downloading epld sram device please wait ...
Programming successful for Altera 10K10 SRAM EPLD
Updating epld flash version from 0000 to 0600

Cisco Systems Console

Enter password: [press return here]
1997 Mar 22 22:22:56 %SYS-5-MOD_OK:Module 1 is online
1997 Mar 22 22:23:06 %SYS-5-MOD_OK:Module 2 is online

Console>
```

1900 Switch Startup

When you connect to the 1900 console, the menu below appears. By pressing K, you can use the command-line interface, and M will allow you to configure the switch through a menu system. The I option allows you to configure the IP configuration of the switch (this can also be accomplished through the menu or CLI at any time). Once the IP configuration is set, the I selection no longer appears:

```
1 user(s) now active on Management Console.

        User Interface Menu

    [M] Menus
    [K] Command Line
    [I] IP Configuration

Enter Selection:  K

        CLI session with the switch is open.
        To end the CLI session, enter [Exit].

    >
```

Cisco IOS- and Set-Based Commands

In this section, you'll learn how to configure the basics on both types of switches. Specifically, you'll learn how to do the following:

- Set the passwords
- Set the hostname
- Configure the IP address and subnet mask
- Identify the interfaces
- Set a description on the interfaces
- Configure the port speed
- Define the port duplex
- Verify the configuration

Setting the Passwords

The first thing you should do is configure the passwords. You don't want unauthorized users connecting to the switch. You can set both the usermode and privileged mode passwords, just as you can with a router. However, you use different commands.

As with any Cisco router, the login (usermode) password can be used to verify authorization of the switch, including telnet and the console port. The enable password is used to allow access to the switch so the configuration can be viewed or changed.

NOTE The passwords cannot be less than four characters or more than eight. They are not case sensitive.

5000 Series Set-Based Switch

To configure the two passwords on a 5000 series switch, use the command `set password` for the usermode password and the command `set enablepass` for the enable password:

```
1997 Mar 21 06:31:54 %SYS-5-MOD_OK:Module 1 is online
1997 Mar 21 06:31:54 %SYS-5-MOD_OK:Module 2 is online
```

```
Console> en

Enter password:
Console> (enable) set password ?
Usage: set password
Console> (enable) set password [press enter]
Enter old password:
Enter new password:
Retype new password:
Password changed.
```

When you see the "Enter old password" prompt, you can leave it blank and press Enter if you don't have a password set. The output for the "Enter new password" prompt doesn't show on the console screen. If you want to clear the usermode (login) password, type in the old password and then just press Enter when you're asked for a new password.

To set the enable password, use the command set enablepass, then press Enter:

```
Console> (enable) set enablepass
Enter old password:
Enter new password:
Retype new password:
Password changed.
Console> (enable)
```

You can type **exit** at this point to log out of the switch completely, which will allow you to test your new passwords.

1900 IOS-Based Switch

Even though the 1900 switch is a CLI running an IOS, the commands for the usermode and enable mode passwords are different than they are for a router. You use the command enable password, which is the same, but you choose different access levels, which is optional on a Cisco router but not on the 1900 switch. The enable secret password can be set as well, and it supercedes the enable password level 15. The telnet password is set by setting either the enable password level 15 or the enable secret password.

Press K to enter CLI mode, and then enter enable mode and global configuration mode by using the `config t` command:

```
1 user(s) now active on Management Console.

        User Interface Menu

    [M] Menus
    [K] Command Line
    [I] IP Configuration

Enter Selection: K

        CLI session with the switch is open.
        To end the CLI session, enter [Exit].
```

#config t
```
Enter configuration commands, one per line.  End with CNTL/Z
```
(config)#**enable password ?**
```
  level  Set exec level password
```
(config)#**enable password level ?**
```
  <1-15>  Level number
```

To enter the usermode password, use level number 1. To enter the enable mode password, use level mode 15:

(config)#**enable password level 1 todd**
(config)#**enable password level 15 sanfran**
(config)#**enable secret cisco**
(config)#**exit**
#exit
```
CLI session with the switch is now closed.
Press any key to continue.
Catalyst 1900 Management Console
Copyright (c) Cisco Systems, Inc.  1993-1998
All rights reserved.
Enterprise Edition Software
```

```
Ethernet Address:        00-30-80-CC-7D-00
PCA Number:              73-3122-04
PCA Serial Number:       FAB033725XG
Model Number:            WS-C1912-A
System Serial Number:    FAB0339T01M
Power Supply S/N:        PHI031801CF
PCB Serial Number:       FAB033725XG,73-3122-04
------------------------------------------------
1 user(s) now active on Management Console.
        User Interface Menu
    [M] Menus
    [K] Command Line
Enter Selection:  K
Enter password:  ****
        CLI session with the switch is open.
        To end the CLI session, enter [Exit].
>en
Enter password:  ****
#
```

Notice that the program prompted for a usermode password, which was the level 1 password entered. The enable password was the enable secret password set, which superceded the enable password level 15.

Setting the Hostname

The hostname on a switch, as well as on a router, is only locally significant. This means that it doesn't have any function on the network or for name resolution whatsoever. However, it is helpful to set a hostname on a switch so you can identify the switch when connecting to it. A good rule of thumb is to name the switch after the location it is serving.

5000 Series Set-Based Switch

To set the hostname on a 5000 series switch, use the set prompt command:

```
Cisco Systems Console              Thu Mar 21 1997, 06:31:54

Enter password:
```

```
Console> en
Enter password:
Console> (enable) set prompt Todd5000
Todd5000 (enable) set prompt Todd5000>
Todd5000> (enable)
```

Because the location is his office, Todd5000 works for Todd. Notice that the first command used did not include a > prompt. We like to see that prompt, but you have to choose it. On a router, you can change the prompt, but the default is always a > prompt.

1900 IOS-Based Switch

The 1900 switch command to set the hostname is exactly as it is with any router. You use the hostname command (remember, it is one word):

```
1 user(s) now active on Management Console.

        User Interface Menu

      [M] Menus
      [K] Command Line
      [I] IP Configuration
Enter Selection: K
Enter password: ****
        CLI session with the switch is open.
        To end the CLI session, enter [Exit].
>en
Enter password: ****
#config t
Enter configuration commands, one per line.  End with CNTL/Z
(config)#hostname Todd1900EN
Todd1900EN(config)#
```

Setting the IP Information

You do not have to set any IP configuration on the switch to make it work. You can just plug in devices and they should start working, as they do on a hub.

IP address information is set so that you can either manage the switch via Telnet or other management software or configure the switch with different VLANs and other network functions.

5000 Series Set-Based Switch

To set the IP address information on a 5000 series switch, configure the supervisor engine that is plugged into slot one of every switch. This is called the *in-band* logical interface. Use the command set interface sc0:

```
Todd5000> (enable) set int sc0 172.16.10.17 255.255.255.0
Interface sc0 IP address and netmask set.
```

By default, the switch is configured for VLAN 1, which can be seen by using the show interface command. Notice also that the broadcast address for the subnet shows up and that you can change that by entering it with the set int sc0 command (but we can think of only one reason you would want to change that—to mess with the people in your MIS department):

```
Todd5000> (enable) sh int
sl0: flags=51<UP,POINTOPOINT,RUNNING>
   slip 0.0.0.0 dest 0.0.0.0
sc0: flags=63<UP,BROADCAST,RUNNING>
 vlan 1 inet 172.16.10.17 netmask 255.255.255.0 broadcast 172.16.10.255
Todd5000> (enable)
```

If you wanted to have the switch in a different VLAN, instead of the default VLAN 1, you can use the set int sc0 command:

```
Todd5000> (enable) set int sc0 2
Interface sc0 vlan set.
Todd5000> (enable) sh int
sl0: flags=51<UP,POINTOPOINT,RUNNING>
   slip 0.0.0.0 dest 0.0.0.0
sc0: flags=63<UP,BROADCAST,RUNNING>
 vlan 2 inet 172.16.10.11 netmask 255.255.255.0 broadcast 172.16.10.255
Todd5000> (enable)
```

Cisco recommends that you use the VLAN 1 for management of the switch device and then create other VLANs for users. In other words, they don't recommend what we just showed you.

1900 IOS-Based Switch

To set the IP configuration on a 1900 switch, use the command **ip address**. By typing the command **show ip**, you can see the configuration (by default, nothing is set):

```
Todd1900EN#sh ip
IP Address: 0.0.0.0
Subnet Mask: 0.0.0.0
Default Gateway: 0.0.0.0
Management VLAN:   1
Domain name:
Name server 1: 0.0.0.0
Name server 2: 0.0.0.0
HTTP server : Enabled
HTTP port :   80
RIP : Enabled
```

The default gateway should also be set, and the command is **ip default-gateway**:

```
Todd1900EN#config t
Enter configuration commands, one per line.  End with CNTL/Z
Todd1900EN(config)#ip address 172.16.10.16 255.255.255.0
Todd1900EN(config)#ip default-gateway 172.16.10.1
Todd1900EN(config)#

Todd1900EN#sh ip
IP Address: 172.16.10.16
Subnet Mask: 255.255.255.0
Default Gateway: 172.16.10.1
Management VLAN:   1
Domain name:
Name server 1: 0.0.0.0
```

```
                Name server 2: 0.0.0.0
                HTTP server : Enabled
                HTTP port :  80
                RIP : Enabled
                Todd1900EN#
```

Switch Interfaces

It is important to understand how to access switch ports. The 5000 series uses the `slot/port` command. The 1900 series of switches uses the `type slot/port` command.

5000 Series Set-Based Switch

You can use the `show` command to view port statistics on a 5000 switch. Notice that, by default, the duplex and speed of the port are both set to auto. Also, typically the ports on a 2900, 4000, 5000, and 6000 series switch may be enabled, but it might be necessary to configure the ports so that they can be enabled with the `set port enable` command. You can turn off any port with the `set port disable` command:

```
Todd5000> (enable) show port ?
Usage: show port
       show port <mod_num>
       show port <mod_num/port_num>
Todd5000> (enable) show port 2/1
 Port  Name     Status   Vlan   Level      Duplex Speed Type
 ----- -------- -------- ------ ---------- ------ ----- ------------
 2/1            connect  2      normal     auto   auto  10/100BaseTX

Todd5000> (enable) set port disable 2/1
Port 2/1 disabled.
       Todd5000> (enable) sh port 2/1
 Port  Name     Status     Vlan   Level  Duplex Speed Type
 ----- -------- ---------- ------ ------ ------ ----- -----
 2/1            disabled   1      normal auto   auto  10/100BaseTX

Todd5000> (enable) set port enable 2/1
Port 2/1 enabled.
```

```
Todd5000> (enable) sh port 2/1
Port  Name     Status     Vlan       Level    Duplex  Speed Type
----- ------   ---------  ---------- --------- ------  ----- ------
2/1            connect    1          normal    auto    auto  10/100BaseTX
```

> **NOTE:** The command show config displays the complete current configuration of the set-based switch.

1900 IOS-Based Switch

The 1900 switch takes the type slot/port command with either the interface command or the show command. The interface command allows you to set interface-specific configurations. The 1900 switch has only one slot, zero (0):

```
Todd1900EN#config t
Enter configuration commands, one per line.  End with CNTL/Z
Todd1900EN(config)#int ethernet ?
  <0-0>  IEEE 802.3
Todd1900EN(config)#int ethernet 0?
  /
Todd1900EN(config)#int ethernet 0/?
  <1-25>  IEEE 802.3
Todd1900EN(config)#int ethernet 0/1
Todd1900EN(config-if)#?
Interface configuration commands:
  cdp          Cdp interface subcommands
  description  Interface specific description
  duplex       Configure duplex operation
  exit         Exit from interface configuration mode
  help         Description of the interactive help system
  no           Negate a command or set its defaults
  port         Perform switch port configuration
  shutdown     Shutdown the selected interface
```

spantree	Spanning tree subsystem
vlan-membership	VLAN membership configuration

You can switch between interfaces by using the `int e 0/#` command. Notice that we demonstrate below commands with spaces or without—it makes no difference.

To configure the two FastEthernet ports, the command is `interface fastethernet 0\#`. You cannot go to the FastEthernet ports from the 10BaseT ports without typing **exit** to go back one level:

```
Todd1900EN(config-if)#int e 0/2
Todd1900EN(config-if)#int e0/3
Todd1900EN(config-if)#exit

Todd1900EN(config)#int fastEthernet ?
  <0-0>  FastEthernet IEEE 802.3
Todd1900EN(config)#int fastEthernet 0/?
  <26-27>  FastEthernet IEEE 802.3
Todd1900EN(config)#int fastEthernet 0/26
Todd1900EN(config-if)#int fast 0/27
Todd1900EN(config-if)# [control+Z]
```

You can view the ports with the `show interface` command:

```
Todd1900EN#sh int e0/1
Ethernet 0/1 is Suspended-no-linkbeat
Hardware is Built-in 10Base-T
Address is 0030.80CC.7D01
MTU 1500 bytes, BW 10000 Kbits
802.1d STP State:  Forwarding      Forward Transitions:  1
[output cut]
 Todd1900EN#sh int f0/26
FastEthernet 0/26 is Suspended-no-linkbeat
Hardware is Built-in 100Base-TX
Address is 0030.80CC.7D1A
MTU 1500 bytes, BW 100000 Kbits
802.1d STP State:  Blocking        Forward Transitions:  0
[output cut]
```

Configuring Interface Descriptions

You can set a description on an interface, which will allow you to administratively set a name for each interface. As with the hostname, the descriptions are only locally significant.

5000 Series Set-Based Switch

To set a description with the 5000 switch, use the set port name slot/port command. Spaces are allowed. You can set a name up to 21 characters long:

```
Todd5000> (enable) set port name 2/1 Sales Printer
Port 2/1 name set.
Todd5000> (enable) sh port 2/1
Port  Name             Status      Vlan Level  Duplex Speed Type
----- ---------------- ----------  ---- ------ ------ ----- -----
2/1   Sales Printer    notconnect  2    normal auto   auto  10/100BaseTX
```

1900 IOS-Based Switch

For the 1900 series switch, use the description command. You cannot use spaces with the description command, but you can use underlining if you need to:

```
Todd1900EN#config t
Enter configuration commands, one per line.  End with CNTL/Z
Todd1900EN(config)#int e0/1
Todd1900EN(config-if)#description Finance_VLAN
Todd1900EN(config-if)#int f0/26
Todd1900EN(config-if)#description trunk_to_Building_4
Todd1900EN(config-if)#
```

You can view the descriptions with either the show interface command or the show running-config command:

```
Todd1900EN#sh int e0/1
Ethernet 0/1 is Suspended-no-linkbeat
Hardware is Built-in 10Base-T
Address is 0030.80CC.7D01
MTU 1500 bytes, BW 10000 Kbits
```

```
                802.1d STP State:   Forwarding      Forward Transitions:  1
                Port monitoring: Disabled
                Unknown unicast flooding: Enabled
                Unregistered multicast flooding: Enabled
                Description: Finance_VLAN
                Duplex setting: Half duplex
                Back pressure: Disabled

                Todd1900EN#sh run
                Building configuration...

                Current configuration:
                hostname "Todd1900EN"
                !
                ip address 172.16.10.16 255.255.255.0
                ip default-gateway 172.16.10.1
                !
                interface Ethernet 0/1

                   description "Finance_VLAN"
                !
                [output cut]
```

Configuring the Port Speed and Duplex

By default, all 10/100 ports on the 5000 series switch are set to auto-detect the speed and duplex of the port. However, the 1900 switch has only 12 or 24 10BaseT ports, which cannot be changed. It comes with one or two FastEthernet ports, which allows you to change the duplex only. The 2820 series has 24 10BaseT ports and 2 modular slots for FastEthernet.

5000 Series Set-Based Switch

Because the ports on a 10/100 card are auto-detect, you don't have to necessarily set the speed and duplex. However, there are situations where the auto-detect does not work correctly, and by setting the speed and duplex, you can stabilize the link:

```
Todd5000> (enable) set port speed 2/1 ?
Usage: set port speed <mod_num/port_num> <4|10|16|100|auto>
```

```
Todd5000> (enable) set port speed 2/1 100
Port(s) 2/1 speed set to 100Mbps.
```

If you set the port speed to auto, both the speed and duplex are set to auto-negotiate the link. You can't set the duplex without first setting the speed:

```
Todd5000> (enable) set port duplex 2/1 ?
Usage: set port duplex <mod_num/port_num> <full|half>
Todd5000> (enable) set port duplex 2/1 full
Port(s) 2/1 set to full-duplex.
Todd5000> (enable) ^C
```

Notice that the command Ctrl+C was used in the preceding code. This is a break sequence used on both types of switches.

You can view the duplex and speed with the show port command:

```
Todd5000> (enable) sh port 2/1
Port  Name            Status       Vlan    Level  Duplex Speed Type
----- --------------- ------------ ------- ------ ------ ----- ----
 2/1  Sales Printer   notconnect   2       normal full   100   10/100BaseTX
```

1900 IOS-Based Switch

You can set only the duplex on the 1900 switch because the ports are all fixed speeds. Use the duplex command in interface configuration:

```
Todd1900EN(config)#int f0/26
Todd1900EN(config-if)#duplex ?
    auto               Enable auto duplex configuration
    full               Force full duplex operation
    full-flow-control  Force full duplex with flow control
    half               Force half duplex operation
Todd1900EN(config-if)#duplex full
```

Table 2.3 shows the different duplex options available on the 1900/2800 and 2900XL switches.

TABLE 2.3 Duplex Options

Parameter	Definition
Auto	Sets the port to auto-negotiation mode, which is the default for all 100BaseTX ports
Full	Forces the 10 or 100Mbps ports into full-duplex mode.
Full-flow-control	Works only with 100BaseTX ports; uses flow control so buffers won't overflow
Half	Default for 10BaseT ports, forces the ports to work only in half-duplex mode

Use the `show interface` command to view the duplex configuration:

```
Todd1900EN#sh int f0/26
FastEthernet 0/26 is Suspended-no-linkbeat
Hardware is Built-in 100Base-TX
Address is 0030.80CC.7D1A
MTU 1500 bytes, BW 100000 Kbits
802.1d STP State: Blocking     Forward Transitions: 0
Port monitoring: Disabled
Unknown unicast flooding: Enabled
Unregistered multicast flooding: Enabled
Description: trunk_to_Building_4
Duplex setting: Full duplex
Back pressure: Disabled
```

Verifying IP Connectivity

It is important to test the switch IP configuration. You can, of course, use the Ping program, as well as Telnet. The 5000 series also allows you to use the traceroute command.

5000 Series Set-Based Switch

Use the IP utilities Ping, Telnet, and traceroute to test the switch in the network:

```
Todd5000> (enable) ping 172.16.10.10
172.16.10.10 is alive
Todd5000> (enable) telnet ?
Usage: telnet <host> [port]
       (host is IP alias or IP address in dot notation:
a.b.c.d)
Todd5000> (enable) traceroute
Usage: traceroute [-n] [-w wait] [-i initial_ttl] [-m max_
ttl]
       [-p dest_port] [-q nqueries] [-t tos] host [data_
size]
(wait = 1..300, initial_ttl = 1..255, max_ttl = 1..255
dest_port = 1..65535, nqueries = 1..1000, tos = 0..255
data_size = 0..1420, host is IP alias or IP address in
dot notation: a.b.c.d)
```

> **NOTE** You can use the keystrokes Ctrl+Shift+6, then x, as an escape sequence.

1900 IOS-Based Switch

You can use the Ping program, and you can telnet into the 1900 switch. However, you cannot telnet from the 1900 switch or use traceroute:

```
Todd1900EN#ping 172.16.10.10
Sending 5, 100-byte ICMP Echos to 172.16.10.10, time out
is 2 seconds:
!!!!!
Success rate is 100 percent (5/5), round-trip min/avg/max
0/2/10/ ms
Todd1900EN#telnet
                ^
% Invalid input detected at '^' marker.
```

Erasing the Switch Configuration

The switches automatically copy their configuration to NVRAM. You can delete the configurations if you want to start over.

5000 Series Set-Based Switch

To delete the configurations stored in non-volatile RAM (NVRAM) on the 5000 series switch, use the `clear config all` command. The `erase all` command will delete the contents of flash without warning! Be careful. Here is the code:

```
Todd5000> (enable) clear config ?
Usage: clear config all
       clear config <mod_num>
       clear config rmon
       clear config extendedrmon
Todd5000> (enable) clear config all
This command will clear all configuration in NVRAM.
This command will cause ifIndex to be reassigned on the
next system startup.
Do you want to continue (y/n) [n]? y
........
................
System configuration cleared.
```

To delete the contents of flash, use the `erase all` command:

```
Todd5000> (enable) erase all
FLASH on Catalyst:
Type            Address             Location
Intel 28F016    20000000            NMP (P3) 8MB SIM

Erasing flash sector...
Todd5000> (enable)
Todd5000> (enable) sh flash

File      Version         Sector    Size     Built
-------   -------------   -------   ------   ------
```

Notice that when you type **erase all** and press Enter, it just starts erasing the flash and you can't break out of it. By doing a `show flash` command, you can see that the contents of flash are now empty. You might not want to try this on your production switches. You can use the `copy tftp flash` command to reload the software.

1900 IOS-Based Switch

To delete the contents of NVRAM on a 1900 switch, use the `delete NVRAM` command. VLAN Trunk Protocol configuration is not deleted by using `delete VRAM` because it has its own NVRAM. You need to use the command `delete vtp` to clear the VTP configuration:

```
Todd1900EN#delete ?
  nvram  NVRAM configuration
  vtp    Reset VTP configuration to defaults
Todd1900EN#delete nvram
This command resets the switch with factory defaults.  All
system parameters will revert to their default factory
settings.  All static and dynamic addresses will be
removed.
Reset system with factory defaults, [Y]es or [N]o? Yes
```

Summary

This chapter covered the different types of Ethernet you can use in an internetwork as well as the distance each type of Ethernet media can run. It's important to remember what you learned here.

Remember that the distance that 10BaseT can run and be within specification is 100 meters (330 feet). The 100 meters includes the following:

- Five meters from the switch to the patch panel
- Ninety meters from the patch panel to the office punch-down block
- Five meters from the punch-down block to the desktop connection

For FastEthernet, the specifications for each type are as follows:

100BaseTX Category 5 UTP wiring; category 6 and 7 is now available. Category 6 is sometimes referred to as cat 5 plus. Two-pair wiring. 100 meters.

100BaseT4 Four-pair wiring, using UTP category 3, 4, or 5. 100 meters.

100BaseFX Multi-Mode Fiber (MMF) with 62.5-micron fiber-optic core with a 125-micron outer cladding (62.5/125). 400 meters.

For Gigabit Ethernet, the specifications for each type are as follows:

1000BaseCX Copper shielded twisted-pair, 25 meters.

1000BaseT Copper category 5, four-pair wiring, UTP 100 meters.

1000BaseSX MMF using 62.5 and 50-micron core, uses a 780-nanometer laser, up to 260 meters.

1000BaseLX Single-mode fiber that uses a 9-micron core, 1300-nanometer laser. From 3 km up to 10 km.

We showed you how to configure both a set-based switch and a command-line interface (CLI) switch. And we showed you how to set hostnames and passwords. Finally, you learned how to configure an IP address on each switch and how to verify the configuration.

Key Terms

Before you take the exam, be sure you're familiar with the following terms:

10BaseT

contention media

FastEthernet

Gigabit Ethernet

in-band

switched Ethernet

Commands Used in This Chapter

Access Layer Switch Commands (1900 Series in This Chapter)	Meaning
`hostname`	Assigns a name to the Catalyst 1900 or 2800 series switch
`ip address`	Assigns an IP address to the 1900 or 2820 switch
`interface ethernet module/port`	Used to identify or set parameters on an interface on the 1900 or 2820 switch
`duplex`	Sets the duplex of an interface, with half- or full-duplex
`show run`	Displays the running-config of the 1900 and 2820 switch
`interface fastethernet module/port`	Displays or changes parameters on the two available FastEthernet interfaces
`enable password level`	Sets the usermode (level 1) and the enable password (level 15) of the switch
`shutdown`	Disables a particular interface
Ctrl+Shift+6, then x	Used as an escape sequence

Distribution Layer Switch Commands (5000 Series in This Chapter)	Meaning
Ctrl+C	Used as a break sequence
`set prompt`	Assigns a name to the Catalyst switch

Distribution Layer Switch Commands (5000 Series in This Chapter)	Meaning
`set interface sco`	Assigns an IP address to the management interface of the set-based switch
`set password`	Sets the usermode password
`set enablepass`	Sets the enable password
`set port speed`	Sets the speed of a port
`set port duplex`	Sets the duplex of a port
`show config`	Shows the current configuration of the switch
Ctrl+Shift+6, then x	Used as an escape sequence

Written Lab

1. 100BaseFX is a point-to-point Ethernet topology that can run up to ___ meters.

2. 1000BaseSX uses a 780-meter laser that can run a distance of ___ meters.

3. 100BaseT can run a total distance of ___ meters.

4. What command will set port 3 on card 2 of a 5000 series switch to full duplex?

5. What command will allow you to view the speed and duplex of port 6 on card 3 of a 5000 switch?

6. What command will show you the IP address of a 1900 switch?

7. How do you set the IP address on a 5000 series switch to 172.16.10.17 255.255.255.0?

8. What command sets the enable password on a 5000 series switch?

9. What three IP commands can be used to test network connectivity of a device?

10. What type of Ethernet topology is suggested at the core layer?

Hands-On Lab

This lab will provide step-by-step instructions for configuring both access layer and distribution layer switches. You'll use a 1900 switch for the access layer and a 5000 series switch for the distribution layer. Figure 2.1 will provide the network diagram that will be configured in this lab.

FIGURE 2.1 Access layer to distribution layer configuration

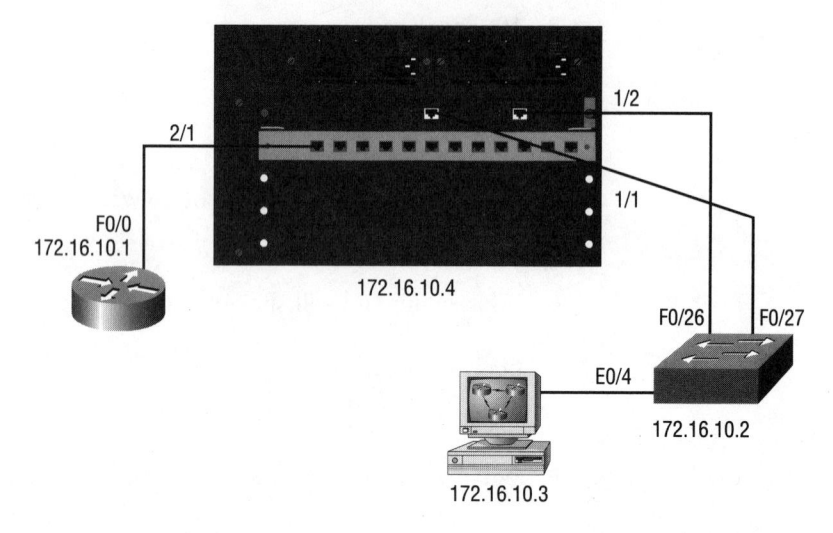

1. Configure the access layer switch by going to the console and pressing K to enter the CLI.

2. Assign the usermode password:

   enable
   config t
   enable password level 1 cisco

3. Assign the enable password:

   enable password level 15 sanfran

4. (Optional) Assign the enable secret, which will override the enable password:

   enable secret todd

5. Set the hostname of the switch:

   config t
   hostname 1900A

6. Set the IP address of the switch:

   config t
   ip address 172.16.10.2 255.255.255.0

7. Set the default gateway for the switch:

   config t
   ip default-gateway 172.16.10.1

8. Set interface 4 to run in full duplex:

   config t
   int Ethernet 0/4
   duplex full

9. Set the description of the interface to Management PC:

   config t
   int e0/4
   description Management_PC

10. Type the command to view the current configuration:

    show running-config

11. Verify the IP configuration of the switch:

    show ip

12. Verify the configuration of interface 4:

    show int e0/4

13. Configure the interface to full-duplex and add a description of Link to 5000A:

    config t (if needed)
    int fa 0/27
    duplex full
    description Link_To_5000a

14. Configure interface F0/26 to connect to the FastEthernet port 1/2 of the 5000 switch. Set the description and duplex as well:

    Int fa0/26
    Duplex full
    Description Another_Link_to_5000a

15. Move your console cable to the 5000 series distribution switch. Set the hostname to be 5000A:

    en
    set prompt 5000A>

16. Set the usermode and enable passwords:

    (examples)

    set password cisco
    set enablepass sanfran

17. Set the IP address of the 5000A switch:

    set int sc0 172.16.10.4 255.255.255.0

18. Configure the port speed and duplex of the connection to the access layer switch:

    set port duplex 1/1 full
    set port speed 1/1 100

19. Set the description of port 1/1 to Link to Access Layer:

    set port name 1/1 Link to Access Layer

20. Set port 1/2 as the second connection to the access layer switch:

    ```
    Set port duplex 1/2 full
    Set port speed 1/2 100
    Set port name 1/2 Another Link to Access Layer
    ```

21. Type the command to view port 1/1:

    ```
    show port 1/1
    ```

22. Type the command to view the configuration of the 5000 switch:

    ```
    show config
    ```

23. Test the connections by pinging all devices.

Review Questions

1. Which of the following is true about full-duplex Ethernet?

   A. Full-duplex Ethernet can both transmit and receive simultaneously and use point-to-multipoint connections.

   B. Full-duplex Ethernet can both transmit and receive simultaneously and use point-to-point connections.

   C. Full-duplex Ethernet can only transmit simultaneously and uses point-to-multipoint connections.

   D. Full-duplex Ethernet can only receive simultaneously and uses point-to-point connections.

2. Which of the following is *not* true regarding the 1900 switch?

   A. You can ping from a 1900 switch if configured.

   B. You can ping to a 1900 switch if configured.

   C. You can telnet to a 1900 switch if configured.

   D. You can telnet from a 1900 switch if configured.

3. What command sets interface e0/10 on a 1900 switch to run full-duplex Ethernet?

   A. `full duplex on`

   B. `duplex on`

   C. `duplex full`

   D. `full-duplex`

   E. `set duplex on full`

4. Which command sets a 1900 switch interface to communicate so its buffers will not overflow on a congested link?

   A. `flow on`

   B. `duplex flow control`

   C. `duplex full-flow-control`

   D. `full duplex-flow`

5. If port 2 on card 3 on a 5000 series switch were disabled, what command would enable this interface?

   A. `set enable port 3/2`

   B. `set port enable 3/2`

   C. `set port enable 2/3`

   D. `set enable port 2/3`

6. If you wanted to verify the duplex on a 1900 switch, port 26, what command should you use?

   A. `show port 26`

   B. `show int 26`

   C. `show int e0/26`

   D. `show int f0/26`

   E. `show int g0/26`

   F. `show int h0/26`

7. What is the command to set port 4 on card 3 to full duplex on a 5000 series switch?

   A. `port duplex full 4/3`

   B. `set port duplex 3/4 full`

   C. `set port duplex 4/3 full`

   D. `duplex full`

8. What command would you use to set a description of the Sales printer on card 2, int 3 for a 5000 switch?

   A. `set port name 2/3 Sales Printer`

   B. `set port name 2/3 Sales_Printer`

   C. `description Sales Printer`

   D. `description Sales_printer`

9. If you wanted to set the hostname on a 5000 series switch to Cat5k>, what command would you use?

   A. `host name cat5k`

   B. `hostname cat5k`

   C. `set prompt cat5k`

   D. `set prompt cat5k>`

10. What is the distance you can run a MMF, 62.5-micron Gigabit Ethernet cable?

    A. 400 meters

    B. 25 meters

    C. 260 meters

    D. 3 km

    E. 10 km

11. What is the distance a single-mode, 9-micron Gigabit that uses a 1300-nanometer laser can run?

    A. 400 meters

    B. 25 meters

    C. 260 meters

    D. Up to 10km

12. What is the distance you can run a MMF with 62.5-micron fiber-optic core with a 125-micron outer cladding (62.5/125) using FastEthernet?

    A. 25 meters

    B. 400 meters

    C. 260 meters

    D. 3 km

13. What is the distance you can run, and stay in spec, from a patch panel to a switch using 10BaseT?

    A. 5 meters

    B. 25 meters

    C. 90 meters

    D. 100 meters

    E. 330 feet

14. If you wanted to set port 3 on card 2 on a 5000 switch to run only 100Mbps, what command would you use?

    A. `set port speed 100 2/3`

    B. `port speed 100 3/2`

    C. `set port duplex 2/3 100`

    D. `set port speed 2/3 100`

15. Which of the following is true regarding a port status light on a switch?

    A. It is used to see if a loop has occurred on the network.

    B. It is used to identify RTS signaling.

    C. When a device is connected to a port, the port status LED light comes on and stays on.

    D. When a device is connected to a port, the port status LED light comes on, then goes off.

16. If you want to delete the startup-config on a 1900 switch, what command do you use?

    A. erase startup-config

    B. delete startup-config

    C. delete nvram

    D. delete startup

17. If you want to delete the configuration on a 5000 series switch, what command do you use?

    A. clear config all

    B. clear nvram

    C. delete nvram

    D. erase startup

18. What command would you use to identify port 3 on a 1900 switch to be Finance Server?

    A. int e0/3, description Finance Server

    B. int e0/3, description Finance_ Server

    C. set port name e0/3 Finance server

    D. set port name e0/3 Finance_Server

19. What is the IEEE specification for FastEthernet?

    A. 802.3

    B. 802.2

    C. 802.3u

    D. 802.3z

20. What is the IEEE specification for Gigabit Ethernet?

   A. 802.3

   B. 802.2

   C. 802.3u

   D. 802.3z

Answers to Written Lab

1. 400
2. 260
3. 100
4. `set port duplex 2/3 full`
5. `show port 3/6`
6. `show ip`
7. `set int sc0 172.16.10.17 255.255.255.0`
8. `set enablepass`
9. ping, telnet, and traceroute
10. FastEthernet or Gigabit Ethernet

Answers to Review Questions

1. **B.** Full-duplex Ethernet uses a point-to-point connection between the transmitter of the transmitting station and the receiver of the receiving station.

2. **D.** You cannot telnet from a 1900 switch console. You can telnet into the switch. You can ping to a 1900 switch and from a 1900 switch console.

3. **C.** The privileged command `duplex full` sets the duplex of a 1900 interface.

4. **C.** You can use the command `duplex full-flow-control` on a 1900 switch interface so flow control will be used on that particular interface.

5. **B.** The 5000 series of switches uses the `set` commands. To set a parameter on a certain interface, use the `set port` command. To enable a port that has been disabled, use the command `set port enable slot/port`.

6. **D.** The 1900 switch command-line interface uses the `show interface slot/port` command, the same as any router that has modular interface cards.

7. **B.** The 5000 uses the `set port` command to change interface parameters. The `set port duplex slot/port` command is used to set the duplex of a particular port.

8. **A.** Unlike the 1900, you do not need to add an underscore when you add a description on an interface with the 5000 series switch. The `set port` command is used to change port parameters, and `set port name slot/port description` is used to identify the port to an administrator. A is the best answer.

9. **D.** Use the command `set prompt` to set the hostname on a 5000 series switch.

10. C. The maximum distance a Multi-Mode Fiber, 62.5-micron Gigabit Ethernet link can run is 260 meters.

11. D. Cisco supports up to 10 km for a 1300-nanometer laser run using 9-micron Gigabit Ethernet.

12. B. FastEthernet point-to-point fiber runs can go a maximum distance of 400 meters.

13. A. Although everyone breaks this rule, the specifications state that the patch panel to switch can only be 5 meters.

14. D. The `set port` command sets the parameters for individual ports. The `set port speed port/slot speed` command sets the port speed on a 10/100 port.

15. C. If a device is correctly connected to a port, and the device is powered on, the port light emitting diode (LED) will come on and stay on.

16. C. The command `delete nvram` sets the configuration on a 1900 switch to the factory defaults.

17. A. The command that allows you to delete the configuration on a 5000 series switch is `clear config all`.

18. B. With the 1900 switch, you must use underscores between words. No spaces are allowed in the description of an interface.

19. C. The IEEE committee for FastEthernet is 802.3u.

20. D. The IEEE specification for Gigabit Ethernet is 802.3z.

Chapter 3

VLANs

THE CCNP EXAM OBJECTIVES COVERED IN THIS CHAPTER INCLUDE THE FOLLOWING:

- ✓ Describing VLANs
- ✓ Defining the difference between local and end-to-end VLANs
- ✓ Configuring static VLANs on both set-based and IOS-based Catalyst switches
- ✓ Describing and configuring Virtual Trunk Protocol on both set-based and IOS-based switches
- ✓ Describing and configuring trunking on both set-based and IOS-based switches
- ✓ Frame tagging and the different VLAN identification methods

A virtual local area network (VLAN) is a logical grouping of network users and resources connected to administratively defined ports on a layer 2 switch. By creating VLANs, you are able to create smaller broadcast domains within a switch by assigning different ports in the switch to different subnetworks. A VLAN is treated as its own subnet or broadcast domain. This means that when frames are broadcast, they are switched between ports only within the same VLAN.

Using virtual LANs, you're no longer confined to creating workgroups by physical locations. VLANs can be organized by location, function, department, or even the application or protocol used, regardless of where the resources or users are located.

In this chapter, you'll learn about the following:

- What a VLAN is.
- How to configure VLANs on both set-based and IOS-based switches.
- VLAN trunking and VLAN Trunk Protocol (VTP) configurations.
  - Trunking allows you to pass information about more than one VLAN on the same link.
  - VTP is used to send VLAN configuration information between switches.
- Frame tagging and identification methods.
  - Identification methods both encapsulate a frame and insert a new field in a frame to identify it as it traverses a switched internetwork fabric.

The Benefits of Virtual LANs

Remember that layer 2 switches break up collision domains and that only routers can break up broadcast domains. However, virtual LANs can be used to break up broadcast domains in layer 2 switched networks. Routers are still needed in a layer 2 virtual LAN switched internetwork to allow the different VLANs to communicate with each other.

There are many benefits to creating VLANs in your internetwork. Remember that in a layer 2 switched network, the network is a *flat network*, as shown in Figure 3.1. Every broadcast packet transmitted is seen by every device on the network, regardless of whether the device needs to receive the data or not.

FIGURE 3.1 A flat network structure

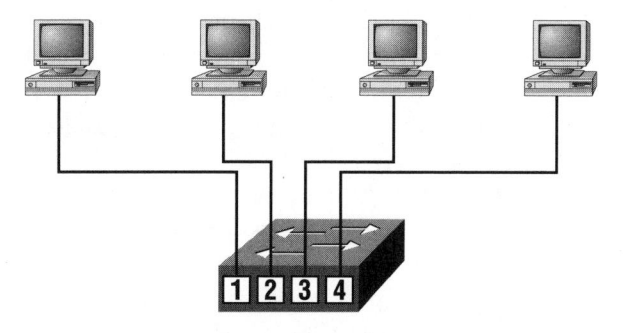

- Each segment has its own collision domain.
- All segments are in the same broadcast domain.

In a flat network, your only security consists of passwords, and all users can see all devices. You cannot stop devices from broadcasting or users from trying to respond to broadcasts. Your security consists of passwords on the servers and other devices.

By creating VLANs, you can solve many of the problems associated with layer 2 switching.

Broadcast Control

Broadcasts occur in every protocol, but how often they occur depends upon the protocol, the application(s) running on the internetwork, and how these services are used. VLANs can define smaller broadcast domains, which means that it is possible to stop application broadcasts to segments that do not use the application.

Although some older applications have been rewritten to reduce their bandwidth needs, there is a new generation of applications that are bandwidth greedy, consuming all they can find. These are multimedia applications that use broadcasts and multicasts extensively. Faulty equipment, inadequate segmentation, and poorly designed firewalls can also add to the problems of broadcast-intensive applications.

These bandwidth-gobbling applications have added a new factor to network design because broadcasts can propagate through the switched network. Routers, by default, send broadcasts only within the originating network, but layer 2 switches forward broadcasts to all segments. This is called a flat network because it is one broadcast domain.

As an administrator, you must make sure the network is properly segmented to keep problems on one segment from propagating through the internetwork. The most effective way of doing this is through switching and routing. Since switches have become more cost effective, a lot of companies are replacing the hub-and-router flat network with a pure switched network and VLANs. The largest benefit gained from switches with defined VLANs is that all devices in a VLAN are members of the same broadcast domain and receive all broadcasts. The broadcasts, by default, are filtered from all ports that are on a switch and are not members of the same VLAN.

To stop broadcasts from propagating through the entire internetwork, either a router, layer 3 switches, or Route Switch Modules (RSMs) must be used in conjunction with switches to provide connections between networks (VLANs).

Security

In a flat internetwork, security is implemented by connecting hubs and switches together with routers. Security is then maintained at the router, but this causes three serious security problems:

- Anyone connecting to the physical network has access to the network resources on that physical LAN.

- A user can plug a network analyzer into the hub and see all the traffic in that network.

- Users can join a workgroup by just plugging their workstation into the existing hub.

By using VLANs and creating multiple broadcast groups, administrators now have control over each port and user. Users can no longer just plug their workstation into any switch port and have access to network resources. The administrator controls each port and whatever resources it is allowed to use.

Because groups can be created according to the network resources a user requires, switches can be configured to inform a network management station of any unauthorized access to network resources. If inter-VLAN communication needs to take place, restrictions on a router can also be implemented. Restrictions can also be placed on hardware addresses, protocols, and applications.

Flexibility and Scalability

VLANs also add more flexibility to your network by limiting or adding only the users you want in the broadcast domain regardless of their physical location. Layer 2 switches read frames only for filtering; they do not look at the Network layer protocol. This can cause a switch to forward all broadcasts. However, by creating VLANs, you are essentially creating separate broadcast domains. Broadcasts sent out from a node in one VLAN will not be forwarded to ports configured in a different VLAN. By assigning switch ports or users to VLAN groups on a switch—or group of connected switches (called a *switch-fabric*)—you have the flexibility to add only the users you want in the broadcast domain regardless of their physical location. This can stop broadcast storms caused by a faulty network interface card (NIC) or an application from propagating throughout the entire internetwork.

When a VLAN gets too big, you can create more VLANs to keep the broadcasts from consuming too much bandwidth. The fewer users in a VLAN, the fewer are affected by broadcasts.

The Collapsed Backbone and the VLAN

To understand how a VLAN looks to a switch, it's helpful to begin by first looking at a traditional collapsed backbone. Figure 3.2 shows a collapsed backbone created by connecting physical LANs to a router.

FIGURE 3.2 Physical LANs connected to a router

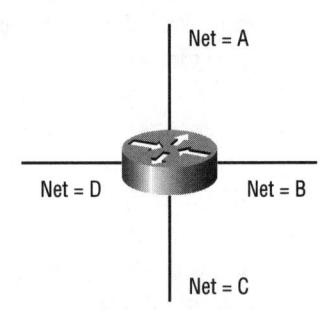

Each network is attached to the router, and each network has its own logical network number. Each node attached to a particular physical network must match that network number to be able to communicate on the internetwork. Now let's look at what a switch accomplishes. Figure 3.3 shows how switches remove the physical boundary.

FIGURE 3.3 Switches remove the physical boundary.

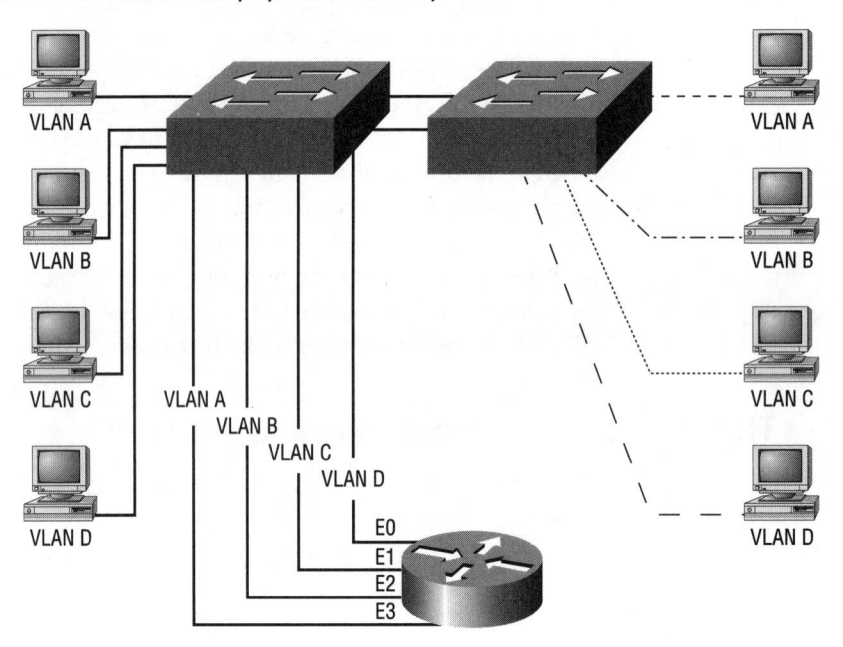

Switches create greater flexibility and scalability than routers can by themselves because they define the network VLANs and VLAN port assignments. You can group users into communities of interest, which are known as VLAN organizations.

Because of switches, we don't need routers anymore, right? Wrong. In Figure 3.3, notice that there are four VLANs, or broadcast domains. The nodes within each VLAN can communicate with each other but not with any other VLAN or node in another VLAN. When configured in a VLAN, the nodes think they are actually in a collapsed backbone, as in Figure 3.2. What do these hosts in Figure 3.2 need to do in order to communicate to a node or host on a different network? They need to go through the router, or other layer 3 device, just as they do when they are configured for VLAN communication, as shown in Figure 3.3. Communication between VLANs, just as in physical networks, must go through a layer 3 device.

Scaling the Switch Block

First introduced in Chapter 1, switch blocks represent a switch or group of switches providing access to users. These switches then connect to distribution layer switches, which in turn handle routing issues and VLAN distribution.

To understand how many VLANs can be configured in a switch block, you must understand the following factors:

- Traffic patterns
- Applications used
- Network management
- Group commonality
- IP addressing scheme

Cisco recommends a one-to-one ratio between VLANs and subnets. For example, if you have 2,000 users in a building, then you must understand how they are broken up by subnets to create your VLANs. If you had 1,000 users in a subnet, which is ridiculous, you would create only 2 VLANs. If you had only 100 users in a subnet, you would create around 20 VLANs or more.

It is actually better to create your broadcast domain groups (VLANs), then create a subnet mask that fits the need. That is not always possible, and you usually have to create VLANs around an already configured network.

> **NOTE:** VLANs should not extend past the distribution switch on to the core.

Defining VLAN Boundaries

When building the switch block, you need to understand two basic methods for defining the VLAN boundaries:

- End-to-end VLANs
- Local VLANs

End-to-End VLANs

End-to-end VLANs are VLANs that span the switch-fabric from end to end; all switches in end-to-end VLANs understand about all configured VLANs. End-to-end VLANs are configured to allow membership based on function, project, department, and so on.

The best feature of end-to-end VLANs is that users can be placed in a VLAN regardless of their physical location. The administrator defines the port the user is connected to as a VLAN member. If the user moves, the administrator defines their new port as a member of their existing VLAN. In accordance with the 80/20 rule, the goal of an administrator in defining end-to-end VLANs is to maintain 80 percent of the network traffic as local, or within the VLAN. Only 20 percent or less should extend outside the VLAN.

Local VLANs

Local VLANs are configured by physical location and not by function, project, department, and so on as with end-to-end VLANs. Local VLANs are used in corporations that have centralized server and mainframe blocks because end-to-end VLANs are difficult to maintain in this situation. In other words, when the 80/20 rule becomes the 20/80 rule, end-to-end VLANs are more difficult to maintain, and so you will want to use a local VLAN.

In contrast to end-to-end VLANs, local VLANs are configured by geographic location; these locations can be a building or just a closet in a building, depending on switch size. Geographically configured VLANs are designed around the fact that the business or corporation is using centralized resources, such as a server farm. The users will spend most of their time utilizing these centralized resources and 20 percent or less on the local VLAN. From what you have read in this book so far, you must be thinking that 80 percent of the traffic is crossing a layer 3 device. That doesn't sound efficient, does it?

Because layer 3 devices are becoming faster and faster, you must design a geographic VLAN with a fast layer 3 device (or devices). The benefit of this design is that it will give the users a deterministic, consistent method of getting to resources. However, you cannot create this design with a lower-end layer 3 model. This is not for the poor.

VLAN Memberships

Once your VLANs are created, you need to assign switch ports to them. There are two types of VLAN port configurations: static and dynamic. A static VLAN requires less work initially but is more difficult for an administrator to maintain. A dynamic VLAN, on the other hand, takes more work up front but is easier to maintain.

Static VLANs

In a *static VLAN*, the administrator assigns switch ports to the VLAN, and the association does not change until the administrator changes the port assignment. This is the typical way of creating VLANs, and it is the most secure. This type of VLAN configuration is easy to set up and monitor, working well in a network where the movement of users within the network is maintained by basically just locking the network closet doors. Using network management software to configure the ports can be helpful but is not mandatory.

Dynamic VLANs

If the administrator wants to do a little more work up front and assign all devices' hardware addresses into a database, hosts in an internetwork can be assigned VLAN assignments dynamically. Using intelligent management software, you can enable hardware (MAC) addresses, protocols, or even applications to create *dynamic VLANs*.

For example, suppose MAC addresses have been entered into a centralized VLAN management application. If a node is then attached to an unassigned switch port, the VLAN management database can look up the hardware address and assign and configure the switch port to the correct VLAN. This can make management and configuration easier for the administrator. If a user moves, the switch will automatically assign them into the correct VLAN. However, more administration is needed initially to set up the database.

Cisco administrators can use the VLAN Management Policy Server (VMPS) service to set up a database of MAC addresses that can be used for dynamic addressing of VLANs. VMPS is a MAC-address-to-VLAN mapping database.

Configuring Static VLANs

The Cisco Switching exam is interested only in static VLAN configuration. We'll show you how to configure VLANs on a Catalyst 5000 switch as well as a Catalyst 1900 switch.

It is important to understand the difference between the Catalyst 5000 series VLAN configuration and the IOS-based VLAN configuration.

Catalyst 5000 Series

To configure VLANs on a Catalyst 5000 switch, use the `set vlan [vlan#] [name]` command. Then, after your VLANs are configured, assign the ports to each VLAN:

```
Todd5000> (enable) set vlan 2 name Sales
Vlan 2 configuration successful
```

After the VLAN is configured, use the `set vlan number slot/ports` command:

```
Todd5000> (enable) set vlan 2 2/1-2
VLAN   Mod/Ports
----   -----------------------
2      1/1-2
       2/1-2


Please configure additional information for VLAN 2.
Todd5000> (enable)
```

The additional information the switch wants you to configure is the VLAN Trunk Protocol (VTP) information. (VTP and trunking is covered in more detail at the end of this chapter, where we will continue with the 5000 switch VLAN configuration.) The 5000 series switch allows you to configure as many ports as you wish to a VLAN at one time. However, the 1900 switch allows you to configure only one interface at a time to a VLAN.

Catalyst 1900 Series

On the 1900 series switch, choose K from the initial user interface menu to get into IOS configuration:

```
1 user(s) now active on Management Console.

    User Interface Menu

   [M] Menus
   [K] Command Line
   [I] IP Configuration

Enter Selection: K

    CLI session with the switch is open.
    To end the CLI session, enter [Exit].
```

To configure VLANs on an IOS-based switch, use the vlan [vlan#] name [vlan name] command:

```
>en
#config t
Enter configuration commands, one per line.  End with CNTL/Z
(config)#hostname 1900EN
1900EN(config)#vlan 2 name sales
1900EN(config)#vlan 3 name marketing
1900EN(config)#vlan 4 name mis
1900EN(config)#exit
```

Note: Remember that a created VLAN is unused until it is mapped to a switch port or ports and that all ports are always in VLAN 1 unless set otherwise.

After you create the VLANs that you want, you use the `show vlan` command to see the configured VLANs. However, notice that, by default, all ports on the switch are in VLAN 1. To change that, you need to go to each interface and tell it what VLAN to be a part of:

```
1900EN#sh vlan

VLAN Name              Status     Ports
-------------------------------------------
1    default           Enabled    1-12, AUI, A, B
2    sales             Enabled
3    marketing         Enabled
4    mis               Enabled
1002 fddi-default      Suspended
1003 token-ring-defau  Suspended
1004 fddinet-default   Suspended
1005 trnet-default     Suspended
-------------------------------------------

VLAN Type       SAID   MTU  Parent RingNo BridgeNo Stp  Trans1 Trans2
---------------------------------------------------------------------
1    Ethernet   100001 1500 0      0      0        Unkn 1002   1003
2    Ethernet   100002 1500 0      1      1        Unkn 0      0
3    Ethernet   100003 1500 0      1      1        Unkn 0      0
4    Ethernet   100004 1500 0      1      1        Unkn 0      0
1002 FDDI       101002 1500 0      0      0        Unkn 1      1003
1003 Token-Ring 101003 1500 1005   1      0        Unkn 1      1002

--More--
1004 FDDI-Net       101004 1500 0      0      1        IEEE 0      0
1005 Token-Ring-Net 101005 1500 0      0      1        IEEE 0      0
---------------------------------------------------------------------
```

You can configure each port to be in a VLAN by using the **vlan-membership** command. You can only configure VLANs port by port (there is no command to assign more than one port to a VLAN at a time):

```
1900EN#config t
Enter configuration commands, one per line.  End with CNTL/Z
1900EN(config)#int e0/2
1900EN(config-if)#v?
vlan-membership
1900EN(config-if)#vlan-membership ?
  dynamic  Set VLAN membership type as dynamic
  static   Set VLAN membership type as static
1900EN(config-if)#vlan-membership static ?
  <1-1005>  ISL VLAN index
1900EN(config-if)#vlan-membership static 2
1900EN(config-if)#int e0/4
1900EN(config-if)#vlan-membership static 3
1900EN(config-if)#int e0/5
1900EN(config-if)#vlan-membership static 4
1900EN(config-if)#exit
1900EN(config)#exit
```

Now, type **show vlan** again to see the ports assigned to each VLAN:

```
1900EN#sh vlan

VLAN Name              Status      Ports
---------------------------------------------
1    default           Enabled     1, 3, 6-12, AUI, A, B
2    sales             Enabled     2
3    marketing         Enabled     4
4    mis               Enabled     5
1002 fddi-default      Suspended
1003 token-ring-defau  Suspended
1004 fddinet-default   Suspended
1005 trnet-default     Suspended
---------------------------------------------
```

```
VLAN Type          SAID    MTU   Parent RingNo BridgeNo Stp  Trans1 Trans2
---------------------------------------------------------------------------
1    Ethernet      100001  1500  0      0      0        Unkn 1002   1003
2    Ethernet      100002  1500  0      1      1        Unkn 0      0
3    Ethernet      100003  1500  0      1      1        Unkn 0      0
4    Ethernet      100004  1500  0      1      1        Unkn 0      0
1002 FDDI          101002  1500  0      0      0        Unkn 1      1003
1003 Token-Ring    101003  1500  1005   1      0        Unkn 1      1002
1004 FDDI-Net      101004  1500  0      0      1        IEEE 0      0
1005 Token-Ring-Net 101005 1500  0      0      1        IEEE 0      0
---------------------------------------------------------------------------
```

You could also just type **show vlan #** to gather information about only one VLAN at a time:

```
1900EN#sh vlan 2

VLAN Name                Status    Ports
----------------------------------------
2    sales               Enabled   2
----------------------------------------

VLAN Type     SAID    MTU   Parent RingNo BridgeNo Stp  Trans1 Trans2
---------------------------------------------------------------------
2    Ethernet 100002  1500  0      1      1        Unkn 0      0
---------------------------------------------------------------------
1900EN#
```

Identifying VLANs

VLANs can span multiple connected switches, which Cisco calls a switch-fabric. Switches within the switch-fabric must keep track of frames as they are received on the switch ports, and they must keep track of the VLAN they belong to as the frames traverse the switch-fabric. Frame tagging performs this function. Switches can then direct frames to the appropriate port.

There are two different types of links in a switched environment:

Access link   An *access link* is a link that is part of only one VLAN and referred to as the native VLAN of the port. Any device attached to an access link is unaware of a VLAN membership. This device just assumes it is part of a broadcast domain, with no understanding of the physical network. Switches remove any VLAN information from the frame before it is sent to an access link device. Access link devices cannot communicate with devices outside of their VLAN unless the packet is routed through a router.

Trunk link   Trunks can carry multiple VLANs. Originally named after the trunks of the telephone system, which carries multiple telephone conversations, *trunk links* are used to connect switches to other switches, to routers, or even to servers. Trunked links are supported on FastEthernet or Gigabit Ethernet only. To identify the VLAN that a frame belongs to, Cisco switches support two different identification techniques: Inter-Switch Link (ISL) and 802.1q. Trunk links are used to transport VLANs between devices and can be configured to transport all VLANs or just a few VLANs. Trunk links still have a native VLAN, and that VLAN is used if the trunk link fails.

Frame Tagging

The switch in an internetwork needs a way to keep track of users and frames as they travel the switch-fabric and VLANs. Frame identification (*frame tagging*) uniquely assigns a user-defined ID to each frame. This is sometimes referred to as a VLAN ID or color.

Cisco created frame tagging to be used when a frame traverses a trunked link. The VLAN tag is removed before the frame exits trunked links. Each switch that the frame reaches must identify the VLAN ID, then make a determination on what to do with the frame based on the filter table. If the frame reaches a switch that has another trunked link, the frame will be forwarded out the trunk link port. Once the frame reaches an exit to an access link, the switch removes the VLAN identifier. The end device will receive the frames without having to understand the VLAN identification.

If you are using NetFlow switching hardware on your Cisco switches, this will allow devices on different VLANs to communicate after taking just the first packet through the router. This means that communication can occur from port to port on a switch, rather than port to router to port, when traversing VLANs.

VLAN Identification Methods

To keep track of frames traversing a switch-fabric, VLAN identification is used to identify which frames belong to which VLAN. There are multiple trunking methods:

Inter-Switch Link (ISL)   Proprietary to Cisco switches, it is used for FastEthernet and Gigabit Ethernet links only. Can be used on switch ports and router interfaces as well as server interface cards to trunk a server. Server trunking is good if you are creating functional VLANs and don't want to break the 80/20 rule. The server that is trunked is part of all VLANs (broadcast domains) simultaneously. The users do not have to cross a layer 3 device to access a company shared server.

IEEE 802.1q   Created by the IEEE as a standard method of frame tagging. It actually inserts a field into the frame to identify the VLAN.

LAN Emulation (LANE)   Used to communicate with multiple VLANs over ATM.

802.10 (FDDI)   Used to send VLAN information over FDDI. Uses a SAID field in the frame header to identify the VLAN. This is proprietary to Cisco devices.

> The Cisco Switching exam covers only the ISL and 802.1q methods of VLAN identification.

Inter-Switch Link Protocol (ISL)

Inter-Switch Link Protocol (ISL) is a way of explicitly tagging VLAN information onto an Ethernet frame. This tagging information allows VLANs to be multiplexed over a trunk link through an external encapsulation method. By running ISL, you can interconnect multiple switches and still maintain VLAN information as traffic travels between switches on trunk links.

Cisco created the ISL protocol, and therefore ISL is proprietary in nature to Cisco devices only. If you need a nonproprietary VLAN protocol, use the 802.1q, which is covered next in this chapter.

ISL is an external tagging process, which mean the original frame is not altered but instead is encapsulated with a new 26-byte ISL header. It also adds a second frame check sequence (FCS) field at the end of the frame. Because the frame is encapsulated with information, only ISL-aware devices can read the frame. Also, the size of the frame can be up to 1,522 bytes long.

On multi-VLAN (trunk) ports, each frame is tagged as it enters the switch. ISL network interface cards (NICs) allow servers to send and receive frames tagged with multiple VLANs so the frames can traverse multiple VLANs without going though a router, which reduces latency. This technology can also be used with probes and certain network analyzers. In addition, it makes it easy for users to attach to servers quickly and efficiently without going through a router every time they need to communicate with a resource. Administrators can use the ISL technology to simultaneously include file servers in multiple VLANs, for example.

It is important to understand that ISL VLAN information is added to a frame only if the frame is forwarded out a port configured as a trunk link. The ISL encapsulation is removed from the frame if the frame is forwarded out an access link.

Standard for Virtual Bridged Local Area Networks (IEEE 802.1q)

Unlike ISL, which uses an external tagging process and encapsulates a frame with a new ISL encapsulation, 802.1q uses an internal tagging process by modifying the existing internal Ethernet frame. To access both links and trunk links, the frame looks as if it is just a standard Ethernet frame because it is not encapsulated with VLAN information. The VLAN information is added to a field within the frame itself.

Like ISL, the purpose of 802.1q is to carry the traffic of more than one subnet down a single cable. 802.1q tags the frame in a standard VLAN format, which allows for the VLAN implementations of multiple vendors. The standard tag allows for an open architecture and standard services for VLANs and a standard for protocols in the provision of these services. Because adding VLAN information to a frame affects the frame length, two committees were created to deal with this issue: 802.3ac and 802.1q.

The VLAN frame format defined in both the 802.1q and 802.3ac is a 4-byte field that is inserted between the original Ethernet frame Source address field and the Type or Length field. The CRC of the frame must be recomputed whenever the VLAN information is inserted or removed from the frame. The Ethernet frame size can now be up to 1,522 bytes if a tag is inserted.

The VLAN Tag Protocol Identifier (TPID) is globally assigned and uses an EtherType field value of 0x81-00. The Tag Control Information (TCI) is a 16-bit value and has three fields contained within:

User Priority   A 3-bit field used to assign up to eight layers of priority. The highest priority is 0, and 7 is the lowest (specified in 802.1q).

Canonical Format Indicator (CFI)   A 1-bit field that is always a 0 if running an 802.3 frame. This field was originally designed to be used for Token Ring VLANs, but it was never implemented except for some proprietary Token Ring LANs.

VLAN ID (VID)   The actual VLAN number the frame is assigned upon entering the switch (12 bits). The reserved VLAN IDs are as follows:

0x0-00   Null, or no VLAN ID, which is used when only priority information is sent

0x0-01   Default VLAN value of all switches

0x-F-FF   Reserved

Because Ethernet frames cannot exceed 1,518 bytes and ISL and 802.1q frames can be up to 1,522 bytes, the switch may record the frame as a baby giant frame.

Trunking

Trunk links are point-to-point, 100 or 1000Mbps links between two switches, between a switch and a router, or between a switch and a server. Trunked links carry the traffic of multiple VLANs, from 1 to 1,005 at a time. You cannot run trunked links on 10Mbps links.

Cisco switches use the Dynamic Trunking Protocol (DTP) to manage trunk negation in the Catalyst switch engine software release 4.2 or later, using either ISL or 802.1q. DTP is a point-to-point protocol and was created to send trunk information across 802.1q trunks. Dynamic ISL (DISL) was used to support trunk negation on ISL links only before DTP was released in software release 4.1, and before DISL, auto-negotiation of trunk links was not allowed.

Configuring Trunk Ports

This section will show you how to configure trunked links on both the 5000 series and 1900 series switches.

5000 Switch

To configure a trunk on a 5000 series switch, use the `set trunk` command, and on the IOS-based switch, use the `trunk on` command:

```
Console> (enable) set trunk 2/12 ?
Usage: set trunk <mod_num/port_num>
[on|off|desirable|auto|nonegotiate] [vlans] [trunk_type]
(vlans = 1..1005 An example of vlans is 2-10,1005)
        (trunk_type = isl,dot1q,dot10,lane,negotiate)

Console> (enable) set trunk 2/12 on isl
Port(s) 2/12 trunk mode set to on.
Port(s) 2/12 trunk type set to isl.
Console> (enable) 1997 Mar 21 06:31:54
%DTP-5-TRUNKPORTON:Port 2/12 has become k
```

Port 2/12 has become a trunk port using ISL encapsulation. Notice that we did not specify the VLANs to trunk. By default, all VLANs would be trunked. Take a look at a configuration in which we specified the VLANs to use:

```
Console> (enable) set trunk 2/12 on 1-5 isl
Adding vlans 1-5 to allowed list.
Please use the 'clear trunk' command to remove
vlans from allowed list.
Port(s) 2/12 allowed vlans modified to 1-1005.
Port(s) 2/12 trunk mode set to on.
Port(s) 2/12 trunk type set to isl.
```

Notice that, even though we told the switch to just use VLANs 1–5, it added 1–1005 by default. To remove VLANs from a trunk port, use the `clear VLAN` command. We'll do that in a minute.

We need to explain the different options for turning up a trunk port:

On The switch port is a permanent trunk port regardless of the other end. If you use the on state, you must specify the frame tagging method because it will not negotiate with the other end.

Off The port becomes a permanent non-trunk link.

Desirable The port you want to trunk becomes a trunk port only if the neighbor port is a trunk port set to on, desirable, or auto.

Auto The port wants to become a trunk port but becomes a trunk only if the neighbor port asked the port to be a trunk. This is the default for all ports. However, because auto switch ports will never ask (they only respond to trunk requests), two ports will never become a trunk if they are both set to auto.

Nonegotiate Makes a port a permanent trunk port, but the port does not use DTP frames for communication. If you're having DTP problems with a switch port connected to a non-switch device, then use the nonegotiate command when using the set trunk command. This will allow the port to be trunked, but you won't be sent any DTP frames.

1900 Switch

The 1900 switch has the same options but runs only the DISL encapsulation method:

```
1900EN#config t
Enter configuration commands, one per line.
End with CNTL/Z
1900EN(config)#int f0/26
1900EN(config-if)#trunk ?
  auto          Set DISL state to AUTO
  desirable     Set DISL state to DESIRABLE
  nonegotiate   Set DISL state to NONEGOTIATE
  off           Set DISL state to OFF
  on            Set DISL state to ON
1900EN(config-if)#trunk auto
```

Clearing VLANs from Trunk Links

As demonstrated in the preceding sections, all VLANs are configured on a trunk link unless cleared by an administrator. If you want a trunk link to not carry VLAN information because you want to stop broadcasts on a certain VLAN from traversing the trunk link, or because you want to stop topology change information from being sent across a link where a VLAN is not supported, use the `clear trunk` command.

This section will show you how to clear VLANs from trunked links on both the 5000 and 1900 series of switches.

5000 Series

The command to clear a VLAN from a trunked link is `clear trunk slot/port vlans`. Here is an example:

```
Console> (enable) clear trunk 2/12 5-1005
Removing Vlan(s) 5-1005 from allowed list.
Port 1/2 allowed vlans modified to 1-4
```

1900 Switch

To delete VLANs from a trunk port on a 1900, use the interface `no trunk-vlan` command:

```
1900EN(config-if)#no trunk-vlan ?
  <1-1005>   ISL VLAN index
1900EN(config-if)#no trunk-vlan 5
1900EN(config-if)#
```

Per Cisco documentation, you can clear up to 10 VLANs at once. The syntax is `no trunk-vlan <vlan-list>`. The VLANS must be separated by spaces. Typically, you wouldn't clear more than a few VLANs anyway, because functionally, it makes no difference if they are turned on or not. If you have security, broadcast, or routing update issues, you need to consider clearing VLANs from a trunked link.

Verifying Trunk Links

To verify your trunk ports, use the `show trunk` command. If you have more than one port trunking and want to see statistics on only one trunk port, you can use the `show trunk [port_number]` command:

```
Console> (enable) sh trunk 2/12
Port      Mode           Encapsulation   Status         Native vlan
--------  -------------  --------------  -------------  -----------
 2/12     on             isl             trunking       1

Port      Vlans allowed on trunk
--------  ---------------------------------------------------------
 2/12     1-4

Port      Vlans allowed and active in management domain
--------  ---------------------------------------------------------
 2/12     1

Port      Vlans in spanning tree forwarding state and not pruned
--------  ---------------------------------------------------------
 2/12     1
Console> (enable)
```

On the 1900 switch, it is the same command, but it can be run only on FastEthernet ports 26 and 27. For some reason, when the `show trunk` command is used, the IOS calls these ports A and B:

```
1900EN#sh trunk ?
  A    Trunk A
  B    Trunk B
1900EN#sh trunk a
DISL state: Auto, Trunking: On, Encapsulation type: ISL

1900EN#sh trunk ?
  A    Trunk A
  B    Trunk B
1900EN#sh trunk a ?
```

```
  allowed-vlans    Display allowed vlans
  joined-vlans     Display joined vlans
  joining-vlans    Display joining vlans
  prune-eligible   Display pruning eligible vlans
  <cr>
1900EN#sh trunk a allowed-vlans
1-4, 6-1004
1900EN#
```

VLAN Trunk Protocol (VTP)

VLAN Trunk Protocol (VTP) was created by Cisco to manage all the configured VLANs across a switched internetwork and to maintain consistency throughout the network. VTP allows an administrator to add, delete, and rename VLANs, and these changes would then be propagated to all switches.

VTP provides the following benefits to a switched network:

- Consistent configuration of VLANs across all switches in the network
- Allowing VLANs to be trunked over mixed networks, like Ethernet to ATM LANE or FDDI
- Accurate tracking and monitoring of VLANs
- Dynamic reporting when VLANs are added to all switches
- Plug-and-play VLAN adding to the switched network

To allow VTP to manage your VLANs across the network, you must first create a VTP server. All servers that need to share VLAN information must use the same domain name, and a switch can be in only one domain at a time. This means that a switch can share VTP domain information only with switches configured in the same VTP domain.

A VTP domain can be used if you have more than one switch connected in a network. If all switches in your network are in only one VLAN, then VTP doesn't need to be used. VTP information is sent between switches via a trunk port between the switches.

Switches advertise VTP management domain information as well as a configuration revision number and all known VLANs with any specific parameters.

You can configure switches to forward VTP information through trunk ports but not accept information updates nor update their VTP database. This is called VTP transparent mode.

You can set up a VTP domain with security by adding passwords, but remember that every switch must be set up with the same password, which may be difficult. However, if you are having problems with users adding switches to your VTP domain, then a password can be used.

Switches detect the additional VLANs within a VTP advertisement and then prepare to receive information on their trunk ports with the newly defined VLAN in tow. The information would be VLAN ID, 802.10 SAID fields, or LANE information. Updates are sent out as revision numbers that are notification +1. Anytime a switch sees a higher revision number, it knows the information it receives is more current and will overwrite the current database with the new one.

Do you remember the `clear config all` command we talked about in Chapter 2? Well, guess what? It really doesn't "clear all" after all. It seems that VTP has its own NVRAM, which mean that VTP information as well as the revision number would still be present if you perform a `clear config all` and think that the configuration is gone. You can clear the revision number by power-cycling the switch.

VTP Modes of Operation

There are three different modes of operation within a VTP domain: server, client, and transparent. Figure 3.4 shows the three VTP modes.

FIGURE 3.4 VTP modes

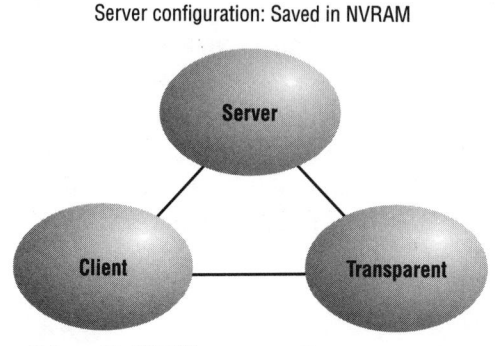

Server configuration: Saved in NVRAM

Server

Client

Transparent

Client configuration: Not saved in NVRAM

Transparent configuration: Saved in NVRAM

Server

VTP server mode is the default for all Catalyst switches. You need at least one server in your VTP domain to propagate VLAN information throughout the domain. The following must be completed within server mode:

- Create, add, or delete VLANs on a VTP domain.
- Change VTP information. Any change made to a switch in server mode is advertised to the entire VTP domain.

Client

VTP clients receive information from VTP servers and send and receive updates, but they cannot make any changes. No ports on a client switch can be added to a new VLAN before the VTP server notifies the client switch about the new VLAN. If you want a switch to become a server, first make it a client so that it receives all the correct VLAN information, then change it to a server.

Transparent

VTP transparent switches do not participate in the VTP domain, but they will still forward VTP advertisements through the configured trunk links. However, for a transparent switch to advertise the VLAN information out the configured trunk links, VTP version 2 must be used. If not, the switch will not forward anything. VTP transparent switches can add and delete VLANs because they keep their own database and do not share it with other switches. Transparent switches are considered locally significant.

VTP Advertisements

Once the different types of VTP switches are defined, the switches can start advertising VTP information between them. VTP switches advertise information they know about only on their trunk ports. They advertise the following:

- Management domain name
- Configuration revision number
- VLANs the switch knows about
- Parameters for each VLAN

The switches use multicast addresses so all neighbor devices receive the frames. A VTP server creates new VLANs, and that information is propagated through the VTP domain.

Figure 3.5 shows the three different VTP advertisements: client, summary, and subset.

FIGURE 3.5 VTP advertisement content

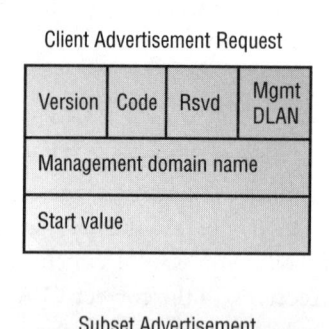

Client Advertisement Request

Version	Code	Rsvd	Mgmt DLAN
Management domain name			
Start value			

Summary Advertisement

Version code follows mgmtDLAN
Management domain name
Config revision number
Updater identity
Updater timestamp
MD5 digest

Subset Advertisement

Version	Code	Seq-num	Mgmt DLAN
Managmt domain name			
Config revision			
VLAN-info field I			
VLAN info field N			

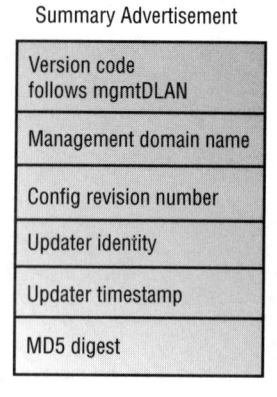

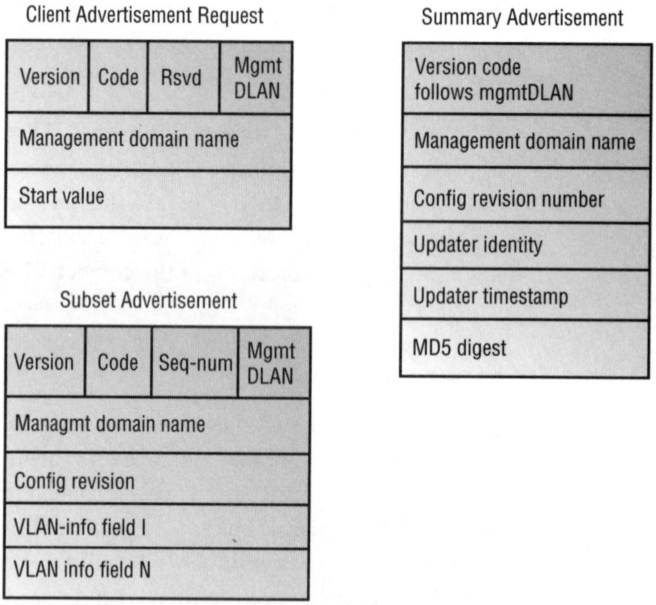

The three different types of messages are as follows:

Client requests   Clients can send requests for VLAN information to a server. Servers will respond with both summary and subset advertisements.

Summary   These advertisements are sent out every 300 seconds on VLAN 1 and every time a change occurs.

Subset   These advertisements are VLAN specific and contain details about each VLAN.

The summary advertisements can contain the following information:

Management domain name   The switch that receives this advertisement must have the name that's in this field or the update is ignored.

Configuration revision number   Receiving switches use this to identify whether the update is newer than the one they have in their database.

Updater identity   The name of the switch from which the update is sent.

Updater timestamp   May or may not be used.

MD5Digest   The key sent with update when a password is assigned to the domain. If the key doesn't match, the update is ignored.

The subset advertisements contain specific information about a VLAN. Once an administrator adds, deletes, or renames a VLAN, the switches are notified that they are about to receive a VLAN update on their trunk links via the VLAN-info field 1. Figure 3.6 shows the VTP subset advertisement inside this field.

FIGURE 3.6   Subset advertisement

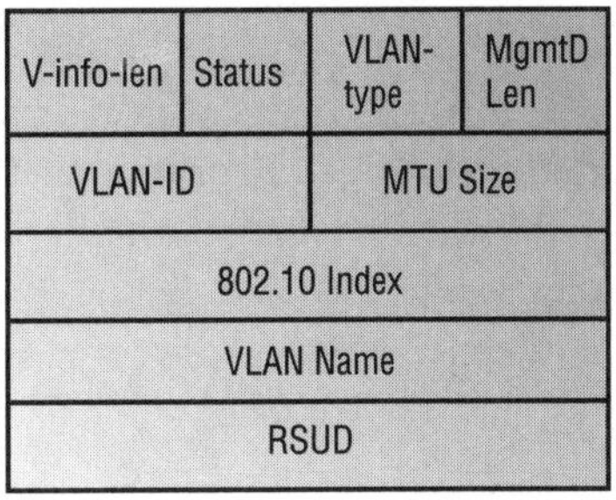

V-info-len	Status	VLAN-type	MgmtD Len
VLAN-ID		MTU Size	
802.10 Index			
VLAN Name			
RSUD			

The following list includes some of the information that is advertised and distributed in the VLAN-info field 1:

VLAN ID   Either ISL or 802.1q

802.10   SAID field that identifies the VLAN ID in FDDI

VTP   VTP domain name and revision number

MTU   Maximum transmission size for each VLAN

Configuration Revision Number

The revision number is the most important piece in the VTP advertisement. Figure 3.7 shows an example of how a revision number is used in an advertisement.

FIGURE 3.7 VTP revision number

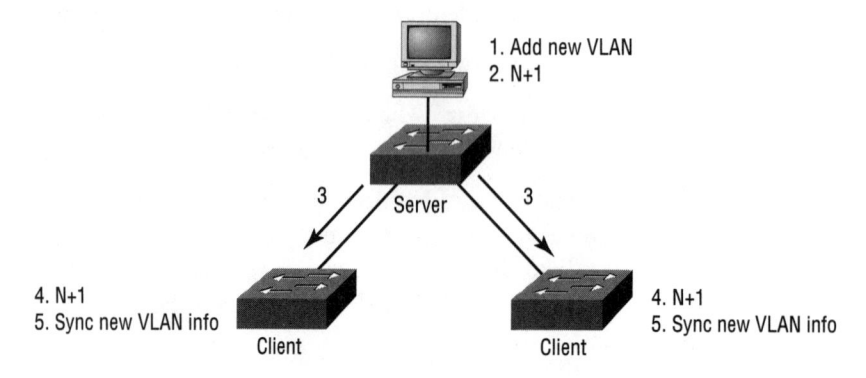

```
                    1. Add new VLAN
                    2. N+1
                       Server
           3                    3
4. N+1                                  4. N+1
5. Sync new VLAN info                   5. Sync new VLAN info
       Client                Client

VTP advertisements are sent every five
minutes or whenever there is a change.
```

Figure 3.7 shows a configuration revision number as N. As a database is modified, the VTP server increments the revision number by 1. The VTP server then advertises the database with the new configuration revision number.

When a switch receives an advertisement that has a higher revision number, then the switches will overwrite the database in NVRAM with the new database being advertised.

Configuring VTP

There are several options that you need to be aware of before attempting to configure the VTP domain:

1. Consider the revision number of the VTP you will run.

2. Decide if the switch is going to be a member of an already existing domain or if you are creating a new one. To add it to an existing domain, find the domain name and password, if used.

3. Choose the VTP mode for each switch in the internetwork.

Configure the VTP Version

There are two different versions of VTP that are configurable on Cisco switches. Version 1 is the default VTP version on all switches and is typically used. No VTP version configuration is needed if you will be running version 1. Version 1 and version 2 are not compatible, so it is an all-or-nothing configuration for your switches. However, if all of your switches are VTP version 2 compatible, changing one switch changes all of them. Be careful if you are not sure if all of your switches are version 2 compatible.

You would configure version 2 for the following reasons:

Token Ring VLAN support In order to run Token Ring, you must run version 2 of the VTP protocol. This means that all switches must be capable of running version 2.

TLV support Unrecognized type-length-value (TLV) support. If a VTP advertisement is received and has an unrecognized type-length-value, the version 2 VTP switches will still propagate the changes through their trunk links.

Transparent mode Switches can run in transparent mode, which means that they will only forward messages and advertisements, not add them to their own database. In version 1, the switch will check the domain name and version before forwarding, but in version 2, the switches will forward VTP messages without checking the version.

Consistency checks Consistency checks are run when an administrator enters new information in the switches, either with the CLI or other management software. If information is received by an advertisement or read from NVRAM, a consistency check is not run. A switch will check the digest on a VTP message, and if it is correct, no consistency check will be made.

To configure VTP version 2, use the set vtp v2 enable command:

```
Console> (enable) set vtp v2 enable
This command will enable the version 2 function
in the entire management domain.
All devices in the management domain should
be version2-capable before enabling.
Do you want to continue (y/n) [n]? y
VTP domain  modified
Console> (enable)
```

The 1900 switch only uses VTP version 1. There are no configuration options for VTP versions:

```
1900EN(config)#vtp ?
  client        VTP client
  domain        Set VTP domain name
  password      Set VTP password
  pruning       VTP pruning
  server        VTP server
  transparent   VTP transparent
  trap          VTP trap
```

Configure the Domain

After you decide which version to run, set the VTP domain name and password on the first switch. The VTP name can be up to 32 characters long. On the 5000, you can set the VTP domain password (the password is a minimum of 8 characters with a maximum of 64):

```
Console> (enable) set vtp domain ?
Usage: set vtp [domain <name>] [mode <mode>]
              [passwd <passwd>]
              [pruning <enable|disable>]
              [v2 <enable|disable>]
       (mode = client|server|transparent
        Use passwd '0' to clear vtp password)
Usage: set vtp pruneeligible <vlans>
       (vlans = 2..1000
        An example of vlans is 2-10,1000)
Console> (enable) set vtp domain Globalnet
VTP domain Globalnet modified
Console> (enable)
```

On the 1900, you don't have a VTP password option:

```
1900EN(config)#vtp domain ?
  WORD  Name of the VTP management domain
1900EN(config)#vtp domain Globalnet ?
  client       VTP client
```

```
  pruning      VTP pruning
  server       VTP server
  transparent  VTP transparent
  trap         VTP trap
  <cr>
1900EN(config)#vtp domain Globalnet
1900EN(config)#
```

Configure the VTP Mode

Create your first switch as a server, and then create the connected switches as clients, or whatever you decided to configure them as. You don't have to do this as a separate command as we did; you can configure the VTP information in one line, including passwords, modes, and versions:

```
Console> (enable) set vtp domain
Usage: set vtp [domain <name>] [mode <mode>]
[passwd <passwd>]pruning <enable|disable>]
[v2 <enable|disable>
(mode = client|server|transparent
        Use passwd '0' to clear vtp password)
Usage: set vtp pruneeligible <vlans>
        (vlans = 2..1000
         An example of vlans is 2-10,1000)
Console> (enable) set vtp domain Globalnet mode server
VTP domain Globalnet modified
```

On the 1900, use the `vtp client` command:

```
1900EN(config)#vtp ?
  client       VTP client
  domain       Set VTP domain name
  password     Set VTP password
  pruning      VTP pruning
  server       VTP server
  transparent  VTP transparent
  trap         VTP trap
1900EN(config)#vtp client ?
```

```
             pruning    VTP pruning
             trap       VTP trap
             <cr>
         1900EN(config)#vtp client
```

Verifying the VTP Configuration

You can verify the VTP domain information by using the commands show vtp domain and show vtp statistics. However, you cannot run a show vtp domain command on a 1900.

The show VTP domain command will show you the domain name, mode, and pruning information:

```
Console> (enable) sh vtp domain
Domain Name              Domain Index VTP Version Local Mode  Password
--------------------     ------------ ----------- ----------
Globalnet        1               2           server
Vlan-count Max-vlan-storage Config Revision Notifications
---------- ---------------- --------------- -------------
5          1023             1               disabled

Last Updater     V2 Mode   Pruning  PruneEligible on Vlans
---------------  --------  -------- ------------------------
172.16.10.14     disabled  disabled 2-1000
Console> (enable)
```

5000 Series

The show VTP statistics command shows a summary of VTP advertisement messages sent and received. It also will show configuration errors if detected:

```
Console> (enable) sh vtp stat
VTP statistics:
summary advts received           0
subset  advts received           0
request advts received           0
summary advts transmitted        5
```

```
subset  advts transmitted         2
request advts transmitted         0
No of config revision errors      0
No of config digest errors        0
VTP pruning statistics:
Trunk      Join Transmitted   Join Received   Summary advts received from
                                              non-pruning-capable device
--------   ----------------   -------------   ----------------------------
 2/12      0                  0               0
Console> (enable)
```

1900 Series

Here is an example of the same command run on the 1900 switch:

```
1900EN#sh vtp stat
              Receive Statistics                     Transmit Statistics
        ---------------------------------     ------------------------------
Summary Adverts                      0        Summary Adverts              0
Subset Adverts                       0        Subset Adverts               0
Advert Requests                      0        Advert Requests             56
Configuration Errors:
   Revision Errors                   0
   Digest Errors                     0
VTP Pruning Statistics:
Port    Join Received    Join Transmitted   Summary Adverts received
                                            with no pruning support
----    -------------    ----------------   -------------------------
 A      0                0                  0
 B      0                0                  0
             1900EN#
```

Adding to a VTP Domain

You need to be careful when adding a new switch into an existing domain. If a switch is inserted into the domain and has incorrect VLAN information, the result could be a VTP database propagated throughout the internetwork with false information.

Before inserting a switch, make sure that you follow these thee steps:

1. Perform a `clear config all` to remove any existing VLAN configuration on a set-based switch. On the 1900, use the `delete NVRAM` command.

2. Power-cycle the switch to clear the VTP NVRAM.

3. Configure the switch to perform the mode of VTP that it will participate in. Cisco's rule of thumb is that you create several VTP servers in the domain, with all the other switches set to client mode.

VTP Pruning

To preserve bandwidth, you can configure the VTP to reduce the amount of broadcasts, multicasts, and other unicast packets. This is called *VTP pruning*. VTP restricts broadcasts to only trunk links that must have the information. If a trunk link does not need the broadcasts, the information is not sent. VTP pruning is disabled by default on all switches.

For example, if a switch does not have any ports configured for VLAN 5 and a broadcast is sent throughout VLAN 5, the broadcast would not traverse the trunk link going to the switch without any VLAN 5 members.

Enabling pruning on a VTP server enables pruning for the entire domain, and by default, VLANs 2 through 1005 are eligible for pruning. VLAN 1 can never prune.

Use the following command to set VLANs to be eligible for pruning:

```
Console> (enable) set vtp pruneeligible ?
Usage: set vtp [domain <name>] [mode <mode>]
[passwd <passwd>] [pruning <enable|disable>]
[v2 <enable|disable> (mode = client|server|transparent
       Use passwd '0' to clear vtp password)
Usage: set vtp pruneeligible <vlans>
       (vlans = 2..1000
         An example of vlans is 2-10,1000)
Console> (enable) set vtp pruneeligible 2
Vlans 2-1000 eligible for pruning on this device.
VTP domain Globalnet modified.
```

Notice, once again, that when you enable a VLAN for pruning, by default, it configures all of the VLANs. Use the following command to clear the unwanted VLANs:

```
Console> (enable) clear vtp pruneeligible 3-1005
Vlans 1,3-1005 will not be pruned on this device.
VTP domain Globalnet modified.
Console> (enable)
```

To verify the pruned state of a trunk port, use the `show trunk` command.

Summary

In this chapter, you learned how to break up broadcast domains in layer 2 switched networks: by creating virtual LANs. When you create VLANs, you are able to create smaller broadcast domains within a switch by assigning different ports in the switch to different subnetworks.

We showed you how to configure VLANs on both set-based and IOS-based switches. It is important to understand how to configure VLANs on both types of switch as well as how to set the configuration of VLANs on individual interfaces.

We also showed you how to configure trunking between links on an access layer switch and a distribution layer switch, where trunking allows you to send information about multiple VLANs down one link, in contrast to an access link that only can send information about one VLAN.

The chapter ended with a discussion of VLAN Trunk Protocol (VTP), which really doesn't have much to do with trunking other than the fact that VTP information is sent down trunked links only. VTP is used to update all switches in the internetwork with VLAN information.

Key Terms

Before you take the exam, be sure you're familiar with the following terms:

access link   *local VLANs*

dynamic VLANs   *static VLAN*

end-to-end VLANs   *switch-fabric*

flat network   *trunk links*

frame tagging   *VTP pruning*

Commands Used in This Chapter

Access Layer Switch Commands (1900 Switch in This Book)	Meaning
interface	Used to select an interface
trunk	Turns trunking on or off of interface fa0/26 and fa0/27
no trunk-vlan	Removes VLANs from a trunked link
vlan	Sets VLAN information
vlan-membership	Sets an interface to a VLAN
vtp name	Configures the VTP domain name
vtp mode	Changes the VTP mode to server, transparent, or client
vtp password	Sets an optional vtp password
show vtp	Shows the switches' VTP configuration

Distribution Layer switch command (5000 Series in This Book)	Meaning
set vlan	Creates a VLAN and also assigns port to a VLAN
set trunk	Configures trunking on a port
clear trunk	Clears VLANs from a trunked port
set vtp domain	Sets the VTP domain name
set vtp mode	Sets the VTP mode of the switch
set vtp passwd	Sets the optional VTP password
show vlan	Shows the configured VLANs
show vtp domain	Shows the VTP domain configurations

Written Lab

Answer the following questions by writing out the answer.

1. What command will create VLAN 35 on a 5000 series switch named Sales using ports 5 through 9 on card 3?

2. What command will set the VTP domain name to Acme and the switch to a VTP client on a set-based switch?

3. What command would you use on a 1900 switch and a set-based switch to see the configured VLANs?

4. What type of frame tagging places a VLAN identifier into the frame header?

5. What type of frame tagging encapsulates the frame with VLAN information?

6. What protocol handles the negotiation of trunked links?

7. How do you configure trunking on a set-based switch, port 1/1, using ISL tagging?

8. What command would you use to clear VLANs 10 through 14 from the trunked link 1/1 on a 5000 switch?

9. What command will display the VTP statistics on a 5000 series switch?

10. If the VTP domain is already configured, how would you set a VTP password on a 5000 switch to cisco?

Hands-On Lab

In this lab, you will continue to configure the network used in the hands-on lab in Chapter 2. This lab will configure the network with VTP domain information and trunking. Figure 3.8 is a review of the lab we are configuring.

FIGURE 3.8 Switched internetwork for hands-on lab

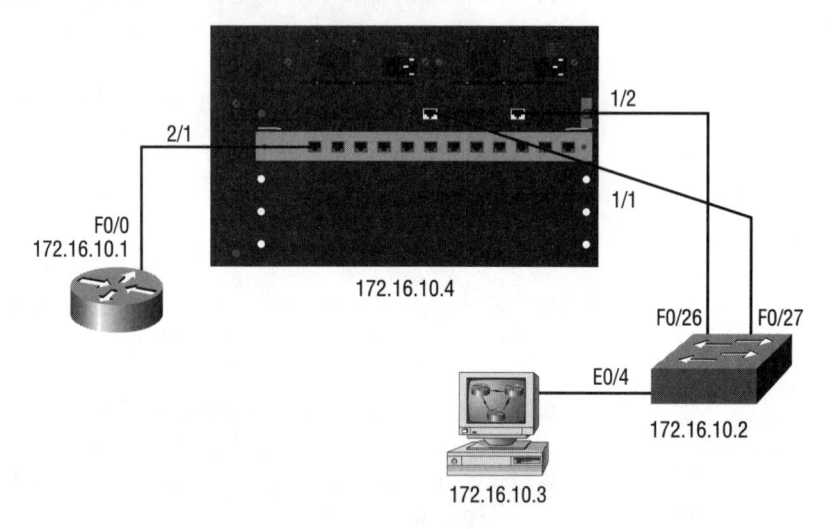

1. Start with the 5000 series switch and configure the VTP domain as Routersim:

set vtp domain Routersim

2. The default VTP mode is server, which is what you want the 5000 series switch to be. The 1900 switch will be a VTP client. Create three VLANs on the 5000 series switch:

   - VLAN 1 is the default; it will be used for management.
   - VLAN 2 will be the Sales VLAN and will use IP network 172.16.20.0. Ports 1 and 2 on card 2 will be used.

- VLAN 3 will be the Mrkt VLAN and will use IP network 172.16.30.0. Ports 3 and 4 on card 2 will be used.
- VLAN 4 will be the Accnt VLAN and will use IP network 172.16.40.0. Ports 5 and 6 on card 2 will be used.

Here is the configuration:

Set vlan 2 name Sales
Set vlan 3 name Mrkt
Set vlan 4 name Accnt
Set vlan 2 2/1-2
Set vlan 3 2/3-4
Set vlan 4 2/5-6

3. Type in the commands to verify the VLAN configuration and VTP configuration:

show vtp
show vlan

4. Because you want VLAN information to be propagated to the 1900 switch, a trunked link needs to be configured between both the switches. Set the trunked link on port 1/1 and port 1/2 of the 5000 switch. These are your connections to the access layer switch (1900A). Remember that the 1900 switch can use only ISL trunking, so the 5000 needs to be configured with ISL trunking:

set trunk 1/1 on isl
set trunk 1/2 on isl

5. Type the command to view the trunked link:

show trunk 1/1
show trunk 1/2

6. Connect to the 1900 switch and set the VTP domain name:

config t
vtp domain Routersim

7. Set the VTP mode to client:

vtp mode client

8. Before any VLAN information will be propagated through the internetwork, you need to make both interface f0/26 and f0/27 a trunked link:

   Config t
   Int f0/27
   Trunk on
   Int f0/26
   Trunk on

9. Verify that the trunked link is working:

   show trunk a
   show trunk b

10. Ping the 5000 series switch:

    ping 172.16.10.4

11. Now verify that you have received VLAN information from the 5000 series switch:

    show vlan

    You should see all configured VLANs.

12. Once you have the trunked link working and have received the VLAN information, you can assign VLANs to individual ports on the switch. Assign ports 1 and 2 to VLAN 2, ports 3 and 4 to VLAN 3, and ports 5 and 6 to VLAN 4:

    Config t
    Int e0/1
    Vlan-membership static 2
    Int e0/2
    Vlan-membership static 2
    Int e0/3
    Vlan-membership static 3
    Int e0/4
    Vlan-membership static 3
    Int e0/5
    Vlan-membership static 4
    Int e0/6
    Vlan-membership static 4

13. Verify the configuration:

    Show vlan-membership
    Show vlan

Review Questions

1. Which of the following is a true statement regarding VLANs?

   A. You must have at least two VLANs defined in every Cisco switched network.

   B. All VLANs are configured at the access layer and extend to the distribution layer.

   C. VLANs should extend past the distribution switch on to the core.

   D. VLANs should not extend past the distribution switch on to the core.

2. If you want to configure ports 3/1-12 to be part of VLAN 3, which command is valid on a set-based switch?

   A. `console> (enable) set vlan 3 2/1, 2/2, 2/3, etc.`

   B. `console> (config) vlan 3 set port 3/1-12`

   C. `console> (enable) set vlan 3 3/1-12`

   D. `console>  set vlan 3 3/1-12`

   E. `console>vlan membership 3 3/1-12`

3. What are the two ways that an administrator can configure VLAN memberships?

   A. DHCP server

   B. Static

   C. Dynamic

   D. VTP database

4. How are local VLANs configured?

   A. By geographic location

   B. By function

   C. By application

   D. Doesn't matter

5. If you want to verify the VTP configured information on a set-based switch, which of the following commands would you use?

   A. `sh vtp domain`

   B. `sh domain`

   C. `set vtp domain output`

   D. `sho vtp info`

6. What size frames are possible with ISL and 802.1q frames?

   A. 1,518

   B. 1,522

   C. 4,202

   D. 8,190

7. What is true regarding the Canonical Format Indicator (CFI)? (Choose all that apply.)

   A. It is a 1-bit field that is always a 0 if running an 802.3 frame.

   B. The CFI field was originally designed to be used for Token Ring VLANs, but it was never implemented except for some proprietary Token Ring LANs.

   C. It is not used on any switch but the 5000 series.

   D. It is used with FDDI trunk ports only.

8. Regarding 802.1q, what is the TPID EtherType field always set to?

   A. 17

   B. 6

   C. 0x81-00

   D. 0x2102

9. How are dynamic VLANs configured?

    A. Statically

    B. By an administrator

    C. Using a DHCP server

    D. Using VLAN Management Policy Server

10. If you want to completely clear all configurations on a 1900 switch, what two commands must you type in?

    A. `clear config`

    B. `delete nvram`

    C. `delete vtp`

    D. `delete start`

11. What do VTP switches advertise on their trunk ports? (Choose all that apply.)

    A. Management domain name

    B. Configuration revision number

    C. VLAN identifiers configured on Cisco routers

    D. VLANs the switch knows about

    E. Parameters for each VLAN

    F. CDP information

12. Which of the following is true regarding VTP?

    A. VTP pruning is enabled by default on all switches.

    B. VTP pruning is disabled by default on all switches.

    C. You can run VTP pruning only on 5000 or higher switches.

    D. VTP pruning is configured on all switches by default if it is configured on just one switch.

13. Which of the following Cisco standards encapsulates a frame and even adds a new FCS field?

    A. ISL

    B. 802.1q

    C. 802.3z

    D. 802.3u

14. What does setting the VTP mode to transparent accomplish?

    A. Transparent mode will only forward messages and advertisements, not add them to their own database.

    B. Transparent mode will forward messages and advertisements and add them to their own database.

    C. Transparent mode will not forward messages and advertisements.

    D. Transparent mode makes a switch dynamically secure.

15. Which of the following IEEE standards actually inserts a field into a frame to identify VLANs on a trunked link?

    A. ISL

    B. 802.3z

    C. 802.1q

    D. 802.3u

16. How long can a VTP domain name be on a 5000 series switch?

    A. The VTP name can be up to 23 characters.

    B. The VTP name can be up to 32 characters.

    C. The VTP name can be up to 48 characters.

    D. The VTP name can be up to 80 characters.

17. If you want to view the trunk status on port 27 of a 1900 switch, which command would you use?

   A. show port 27

   B. show trunk

   C. show trunk B

   D. show trunk f0/27

   E. show trunk e0/27

18. VTP provides which of the following benefits to a switched network? (Choose all that apply.)

   A. Multiple broadcast domains in VLAN 1

   B. Management of all switches and routers in an internetwork

   C. Consistent configuration of VLANs across all switches in the network

   D. Allowing VLANs to be trunked over mixed networks, like Ethernet to ATM LANE or FDDI.

   E. Tracking and monitoring of VLANs accurately

   F. Dynamic reporting of added VLANs to all switches

   G. Plug-and-play VLAN adding

   H. Plug-and-play configuration

19. Which of the following is true regarding VTP?

   A. Changing the VTP version on one switch changes all of the switches in a domain.

   B. If you change the VTP version on one switch, you must change the version on all switches.

   C. VTP is on by default with a domain name of Cisco on all Cisco switches.

   D. All switches are VTP clients by default.

20. Which of the following is true regarding trunked links?

   A. They are configured on by default on all switch ports.

   B. They work only with a type of Ethernet network and not with Token Ring, FDDI, or ATM.

   C. You can set trunk links on any 10, 100, and 1000Mbps ports.

   D. You must clear the unwanted VLANs by hand.

Answers to Written Lab

1. set vlan 35 name Sales
   set vlan 35 3/5-9
2. set vtp domain Acme mode client
3. show vlan
4. 802.1q
5. ISL
6. Dynamic Trunk Protocol (DTP)
7. set trunk 1/1 on isl
8. clear trunk 1/1 10-14
9. show vtp stat
10. set vtp passwd cisco

Answers to Review Questions

1. **D.** VLANs should not pass through the distribution layer. The distribution layer devices should route between VLANs.

2. **C.** The set-based switches can configure multiple ports to be part of a VLAN at the same time. The command is `set vlan # slot/ports`.

3. **B, C.** Static VLANs are set port by port on each interface or port. Dynamic VLANs can be assigned to devices via a server.

4. **A.** Local VLANs are created by location—for example, an access closet.

5. **A.** The command `show vtp domain` will provide the server's VTP mode and the domain name.

6. **B.** ISL encapsulates frames with another frame encapsulation type. This means that a data frame can extend past the regular frame size of 1,518 bytes up to 1,522 bytes.

7. **A, B.** The CFI field is not used often, and only in proprietary Token Ring LANs. It will always be a 0 unless a programmer specifically programs it to be different.

8. **C.** The EtherType file will always be a 0x81-00 when 802.1q frame tagging is used.

9. **D.** A VLAN Management Policy Server (VMPS) must be configured with the hardware addresses of all devices on your internetwork. Then the server is allowed to hand out VLAN assignments configured by the administrator into the VMPS database.

10. **B, C.** The command `delete nvram` deletes the configuration of the switch but not the VTP configuration. To delete the VTP information configured on the switch, use the `delete vtp` command.

11. A, B, D, E.   VLAN Trunk Protocol is used to update switches within a domain about configured VLANs. This includes the management domain name and configuration revision number so that receiving switches know if new VLAN information (including configured parameters) has been added to the VTP database and all of the VLANs the switch knows about.

12. B.   VTP pruning stops VLAN information from traversing a trunked link if it would be discarded on the remote end because no VLANs are configured on the switch.

13. A.   Inter-Switch Link (ISL) encapsulates a new header and trailer to an existing data frame.

14. A.   VTP transparent switches do not update their VTP database with VLAN information received on trunked links. However, they will forward these updates.

15. C.   802.1q does not encapsulate a data frame as ISL does. Instead, it puts a new field into the existing frame to identify the VLAN the packet belongs to.

16. B.   VTP domain names can be up to 32 characters and must be the same on all switches with which you want to share VLAN information.

17. C.   The 1900 switches use port A to reference interface 0/26 and B to reference interface 0/27.

18. B, C, D, E, F, G, H.   VTP does not have anything to do with breaking up or configuring broadcast domains. All answers except A are correct.

19. A.   If you change the VTP version on one switch, all other switches will be changed automatically if they support the new version.

20. D.   Trunked links, by default, are assigned to forward all VLANs. You must delete these by hand if you don't want all VLANs to be sent down a trunked link.

Chapter 4

Layer 2 Switching and the Spanning Tree Protocol (STP)

THE CCNP EXAM OBJECTIVES COVERED IN THIS CHAPTER INCLUDE THE FOLLOWING:

- ✓ Layer 2 LAN switching
- ✓ The three distinct functions of layer 2 switching: address filtering, forward/filter decision, and loop avoidance
- ✓ The Spanning Tree Protocol
- ✓ Configuring the Spanning Tree Protocol
- ✓ Determining the root bridge

In this chapter, we'll explore the three distinct functions of layer 2 switching: address filtering, forward/filter decision, and loop avoidance. We will probe the issue of loop avoidance in depth and discuss how the Spanning Tree Protocol (STP) works to stop network loops from occurring on your layer 2 network.

It is very important to have a clear understanding of the Spanning Tree Protocol. This chapter will continue the discussion of layer 2 switching started in Chapter 1. We'll discuss how network loops occur in a layer 2 network and then provide an introduction to STP, the different components of STP, and how to configure STP on layer 2 switched networks. By the end of this chapter, you will know how to use the STP to stop network loops, broadcast storms, and multiple frame copies. In Chapter 5, we'll continue discussing STP and provide the more complex and advanced configurations used with it.

It is typical these days to create a network with redundant links. This provides consistent network availability when a network outage occurs on one link. However, loop avoidance is needed, and STP provides this function. It is possible to load-balance over the redundant links as well; we'll cover load-balancing in Chapter 5.

Layer 2 LAN Switching

You can think of layer 2 switches as bridges with more ports. Remember from Chapter 1 that *layer 2 switching* is hardware based, which means it uses the *Media Access Control (MAC) address* from the hosts' network interface cards (NICs) to filter the network. You should also remember how switches use *Application-Specific Integrated Circuits (ASICs)* to build and maintain filter tables.

However, as shown in Table 4.1, there are some differences between bridges and switches that you should be aware of:

- Bridges are considered software based, and switches are hardware based because they use an ASIC's chip to help make filtering decisions.
- Bridges can have only one spanning-tree instance per bridge, and switches can have many. (Spanning tree is covered later in this chapter.)
- Bridges can have only up to 16 ports, whereas a switch can have hundreds.

TABLE 4.1 Comparison of Bridges and Switches

	Bridges	Switches
Filtering	Software based	Hardware based
Spanning tree numbers	One spanning tree instance	Many spanning tree instances
Ports	16 ports maximum	Hundreds of ports available

You probably won't go out and buy a bridge, but it's important to understand how bridges are designed and maintained because layer 2 switches function in a similar fashion.

Three Switch Functions at Layer 2

There are three distinct functions of layer 2 switching:

Address learning Layer 2 switches and bridges remember the source hardware address of each frame received on an interface and enter it into a MAC database.

Forward/filter decision When a frame is received on an interface, the switch looks at the destination hardware address and looks up the exit interface in the MAC database.

Loop avoidance If multiple connections between switches are created for redundancy, network loops can occur. STP is used to stop network loops and allow redundancy.

152 Chapter 4 · Layer 2 Switching and the Spanning Tree Protocol (STP)

These functions of the layer 2 switch—address learning, forward and filtering decisions, and loop avoidance—are discussed in detail in the following sections.

Address Learning

The layer 2 switch is responsible for address learning. When a switch is powered on, the MAC filtering table is empty. When a device transmits and a frame is received on an interface, the switch takes the source address and places it in the MAC filter table. It remembers what interface the device is located on. The switch has no choice but to flood the network with this frame because it has no idea where the destination device is located.

If a device answers and sends a frame back, then the switch will take the source address from that frame, place the MAC address in the database, and associate this address with the interface on which the frame was received. Because the switch now has two MAC addresses in the filtering table, the devices can now make a point-to-point connection and the frames will be forwarded only between the two devices. This is what makes layer 2 switches better than hubs. In a hub network, all frames are forwarded out all ports every time.

Figure 4.1 shows the procedures for building a MAC database.

FIGURE 4.1 How switches learn hosts' locations

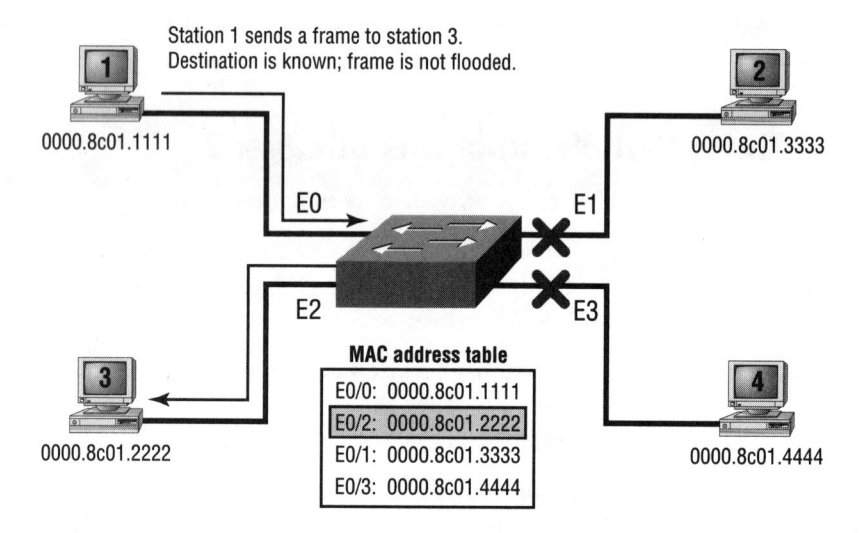

In the figure, there are four hosts attached to a switch. The switch has nothing in the MAC address table when it is powered on. The figure shows the switch's MAC filter table after each device has communicated with the switch. The following steps show how the table is propagated:

1. Station 1 sends a frame to station 3. Station 1 has a MAC address of 0000.8c01.1111. Station 3 has a MAC address of 0000.8c01.2222.

2. The switch receives the frame on Ethernet interface 0/0 and places the source address in the MAC address table.

3. Because the destination address is not in the MAC database, the frame is forwarded out all interfaces.

4. Station 3 receives the frame and responds to station 1. The switch receives this frame on interface E0/2 and places the source hardware address in the MAC database.

5. Station 1 and station 3 can now make a point-to-point connection and only the two devices will receive the frames. Stations 2 and 4 will not see the frames.

If the two devices do not communicate with the switch again within a certain time limit, the switch will flush the entries from the database to keep the database as current as possible.

Forward/Filter Decision

The layer 2 switch also uses the MAC filter table to both forward and filter frames received on the switch. When a frame arrives at a switch interface, the destination hardware address is compared to the forward/filter MAC database. If the destination hardware address is known and listed in the database, the frame is sent out only on the correct exit interface. The switch does not transmit the frame out of any interface except for the destination interface. This preserves bandwidth on the other network segments. This is called frame filtering.

If the destination hardware address is not listed in the MAC database, the frame is broadcasted out all active interfaces except the interface on which the frame was received. If a device answers the broadcast, the MAC database is updated with the device location (interface).

Broadcast and Multicast Frames

Remember that layer 2 switches forward all *broadcasts* by default. The forwarding/filtering decision is not used in a broadcast situation because broadcast and multicast frames do not have a destination hardware address specified. The source address will always be the hardware address of the device transmitting the frame, and the destination address either will be all 1s (broadcast), or it will be a combination of the network or subnet address specified and all 1s for the host address (multicast). For example, a broadcast and multicast in binary would be as shown in Table 4.2.

TABLE 4.2 Broadcast and Multicast Example

	Binary	Decimal
Broadcast	11111111.11111111.11111111.11111111	255.255.255.255
Multicast	10101100.00010000.11111111.11111111	172.16.255.255

> **NOTE:** Even though we have given you an example of a multicast address, the term *multicast* is most commonly used with regard to multicasting groups using the class D IP address space.

Notice that the broadcast is all 1s and the multicast is not. They are both a type of broadcast, except that multicasts send the frame to only a certain network or subnet and all hosts within that network or subnet, whereas a broadcast of all 1s sends the frame to all networks and all hosts.

When a switch receives these types of frames, the frames are then quickly flooded out all active ports of the switch by default. To have broadcasts and multicasts forwarded out only a limited amount of administratively assigned ports, you create virtual LANs (VLANs), which were discussed in Chapter 3.

Loop Avoidance

Finally, the layer 2 switch is responsible for *loop avoidance*. It's a good idea to use redundant links between switches. They help stop complete network failures if one link fails. Even though redundant links are extremely helpful, they cause more problems than they solve. In the following sections, we'll discuss some of the most serious problems:

- Broadcast storms
- Multiple frame copies
- Multiple loops

Broadcast Storms

If no loop avoidance schemes are put in place, the switches will flood broadcasts endlessly throughout the internetwork. This is sometimes referred to as a broadcast storm. Figure 4.2 shows how a broadcast may be propagated throughout the network.

FIGURE 4.2 Broadcast storms

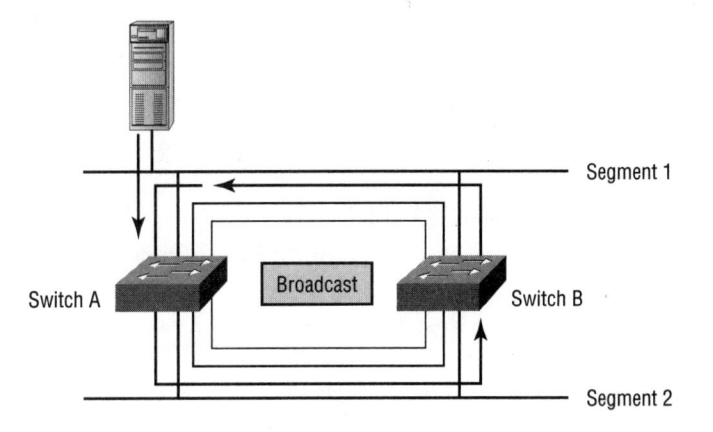

Multiple Frame Copies

Another problem is that a device can receive multiple copies of the same frame because the frame can arrive from different segments at the same time. Figure 4.3 shows how multiple frames can arrive from multiple segments simultaneously.

FIGURE 4.3 Multiple frame copies

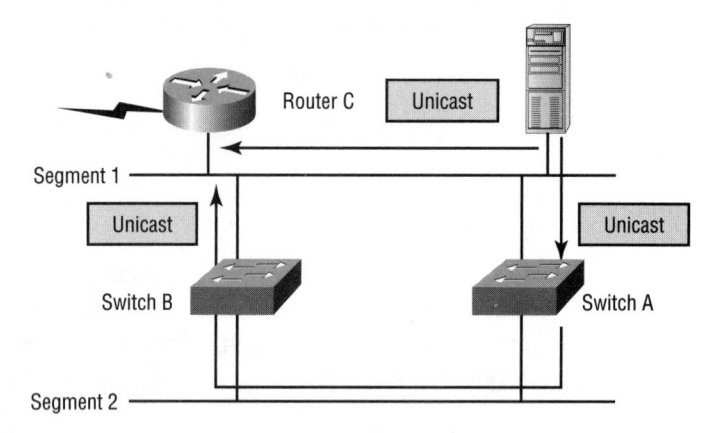

The MAC address filter table will be confused about where a device is located because the switch can receive the frame from more than one link. It is possible that the switch can't forward a frame because it is constantly updating the MAC filter table with source hardware address locations. This is called thrashing the MAC table.

Multiple Loops

One of the biggest problems is multiple loops generating throughout an internetwork. This means that loops can occur within other loops. If a broadcast storm were to then occur, the network would not be able to perform packet switching.

To solve these three problems, the Spanning Tree Protocol was developed.

Spanning Tree Operation

In layer 3 devices, which are typically routers, the routing protocols are responsible for making sure routing loops do not occur in the network. What is used to make sure network loops do not occur in layer 2 switched networks? This is the job of the *Spanning Tree Protocol (STP)*.

Digital Equipment Corporation (DEC), which was purchased and is now called Compaq, was the original creator of STP. The IEEE then created its version of STP called 802.1d. By default, all Cisco switches run the IEEE 802.1d version of STP, which is not compatible with the DEC version.

The big picture is that STP stops network loops from occurring on your layer 2 network (bridges or switches). STP is constantly monitoring the network to find all links and make sure loops do not occur by shutting down redundant links.

The Spanning Tree Protocol executes an algorithm called the spanning-tree algorithm. This algorithm chooses a reference point in the network and calculates the redundant paths to that reference point. After it finds all the links in the network, the spanning-tree algorithm chooses one path on which to forward frames and shuts down the other redundant links to stop any network loops from occurring in the network. It does this by electing a root bridge that will decide on the network topology.

There can be only one *root bridge* in any given network. The root bridge ports are called designated ports, and designated ports operate in what is called forwarding state. Forwarding state ports send and receive traffic.

If you have other switches in your network, as shown in Figure 4.4, they are called nonroot bridges. However, the port that has the lowest cost to the root bridge is called a root port and sends and receives traffic. The cost is determined by the bandwidth of a link.

FIGURE 4.4 Spanning tree operations

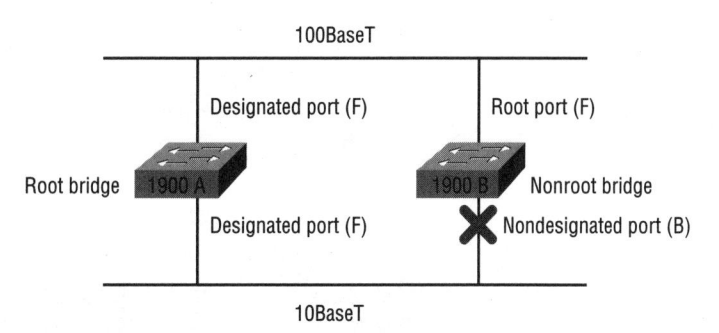

Ports that are determined to have the lowest-cost path to the root bridge are called the *designated ports*. The other port or ports on the bridge are considered *nondesignated ports* and will not send or receive traffic. This is called blocking mode.

Selecting the Root Bridge

Switches or bridges running STP exchange information with what are called *Bridge Protocol Data Units (BPDUs)*. BPDUs are used to send configuration messages using multicast frames. The bridge ID of each device is sent to other devices using BPDUs.

The *bridge ID* is used to determine the root bridge in the network and to determine the root port. The bridge ID is 8 bytes long and includes the priority and the MAC address of the device. The priority on all devices running the IEEE STP version is 32768 by default.

To determine the root bridge, combine the priority of the bridge and the MAC address. If two switches or bridges have the same priority value, then the MAC address is used to determine which has the lowest ID.

For example, if two switches, A and B, both use the default priority of 32768, the MAC address will be used. If switch A's MAC address is 0000.0c00.1111.1111 and switch B's MAC address is 0000.0c00.2222.2222, switch A would become the root bridge.

The network analyzer output below shows a BPDU broadcasted on a network. BPDUs are sent out every two seconds by default. That may seem like a lot of overhead, but remember that this is only a layer 2 frame, with no layer 3 information in the packet:

```
Flags:          0x80    802.3
Status:         0x00
Packet Length:64
Timestamp:      19:33:18.726314 02/28/2000
```
802.3 Header
```
Destination:    01:80:c2:00:00:00
Source:         00:b0:64:75:6b:c3
LLC Length:     38
```
802.2 Logical Link Control (LLC) Header
```
Dest. SAP:      0x42    802.1 Bridge Spanning Tree
Source SAP:     0x42    802.1 Bridge Spanning Tree
Command:        0x03    Unnumbered Information
```
802.1 - Bridge Spanning Tree
```
Protocol Identifier:  0
Protocol Version ID:  0
Message Type:         0   Configuration Message
Flags:                %00000000
```

```
Root Priority/ID:      0x8000  / 00:b0:64:75:6b:c0
Cost Of Path To Root:  0x00000000  (0)
Bridge Priority/ID:    0x8000  / 00:b0:64:75:6b:c0
Port Priority/ID:      0x80   / 0x03
```
Message Age: 0/256 seconds
  (*exactly 0seconds*)
Maximum Age: 5120/256
  seconds (*exactly 20seconds*)
Hello Time: 512/256 seconds
  (*exactly 2seconds*)
Forward Delay: 3840/256
  seconds (*exactly 15seconds*)
Extra bytes (Padding):
  ....   00 00 00 00 00 00 00 00
Frame Check Sequence: 0x2e006400

Notice the cost of path to root. It is zero because this switch is actually the root bridge. We'll discuss path costs in more detail in the next section, "Selecting the Designated Port."

The network analyzer output above also shows the BPDU timers, which are used to prevent bridging loops because the timers determine how long it will take the spanning tree to converge after a failure.

BPDUs are susceptible to propagation delays, which happen because of packet length, switch processing, bandwidth, and utilization problems. This can create an unstable network because temporary loops might occur in the network when BPDUs are not received on time to the remote switches in the network. The STP uses timers to force ports to wait for the correct topology information.

As you can see in the output, the hello time is exactly 2 seconds, the maximum age is exactly 20 seconds, and the forward delay is exactly 15 seconds.

Selecting the Designated Port

After you have selected the root bridge, all switches must become buddies with the root bridge. Each switch listens to BPDU on all active ports, and if more than one BPDU is received, the switch knows it has a redundant link to the root bridge. The switch has to determine which port will become the root port and which port will be put into blocking state.

To determine the port that will be used to communicate with the root bridge, the path cost is determined. The STP cost is an accumulated total path cost based on the bandwidth of the links. Table 4.3 shows the typical costs associated with the different Ethernet networks.

TABLE 4.3 STP Link Cost

Speed	New IEEE Cost	Original IEEE Cost
10Gbps	2	1
1Gbps	4	1
100Mbps	19	10
10Mbps	100	100

The IEEE 802.1d specification has recently been revised to handle the new higher-speed links, hence the different costs shown in Table 4.3.

Once the cost is determined for all links to the root bridge, the switch will decide which port has the lowest cost. The lowest cost port is put into forwarding, and the other ports are placed in blocking mode. If there are equal-cost paths, the port with the lowest port ID will be put into the forwarding state.

Spanning Tree Port States

The ports on a bridge or switch running the STP can transition through four different states:

Blocking Won't forward frames; listens to BPDU. All ports are in blocking state by default when the switch is powered on.

Listening Listens to BPDUs to make sure no loops occur on the network before passing data frames.

Learning Learns MAC addresses and builds a filter table, but does not forward frames.

Forwarding Bridge port is able to send and receive data. A port will never be placed in forwarding state unless there are no redundant links or the port determines that it has the best path to the root bridge.

An administrator can put a port in disabled state, or if a failure with the port occurs, the switch will put it into disabled state.

Typically, switch ports are in either blocking or forwarding state. A forwarding port is a port that has been determined to have the lowest cost to the root bridge. However, if the network has a topology change because of a failed link, or the administrator adds a new switch to the network, the ports on a switch will be in listening and learning states.

Blocking ports are used to prevent network loops. Once a switch determines the best path to the root bridge, all other ports will be in blocking state. Blocked ports will still receive BPDUs.

If a switch determines that a blocked port should now be the designated port, it will go to listening state. It will check all BPDUs heard to make sure that it won't create a loop once the port goes to forwarding state.

Figure 4.5 shows the default STP timers and their operation within STP.

FIGURE 4.5 STP default timers

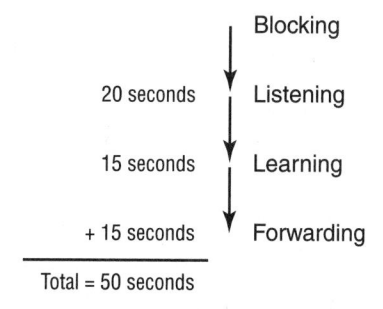

```
                          | Blocking
                          ▼
          20 seconds      | Listening
                          ▼
          15 seconds      | Learning
                          ▼
         + 15 seconds     | Forwarding
         ─────────────
         Total = 50 seconds
```

Notice the time from blocking to forwarding. Blocking to listening is 20 seconds. Listening to learning is another 15 seconds. Learning to forwarding is 15 seconds, for a total of 50 seconds. However, the switch could go to disabled if the port is administratively shut down or the port has a failure.

Convergence

Convergence occurs when bridges and switches have transitioned to either the forwarding or blocking state. No data is forwarded during this time. Convergence is important in making sure that all devices have the same database.

The problem with convergence is the time it takes for all devices to update. Before data can start to be forwarded, all devices must be updated.

The time it usually takes to go from blocking to forwarding state is 50 seconds. Changing the default STP timers is not recommended, but the timers can be adjusted if they need to be. The time it takes to transition a port from the listening state to the learning state or from the learning state to the forwarding state is called the forward delay.

Spanning Tree Example

In Figure 4.6, the three switches all have the same priority of 32768. However, notice the MAC address of each switch. By looking at the priority and MAC addresses of each switch, you should be able to determine the root bridge.

FIGURE 4.6 Spanning tree example

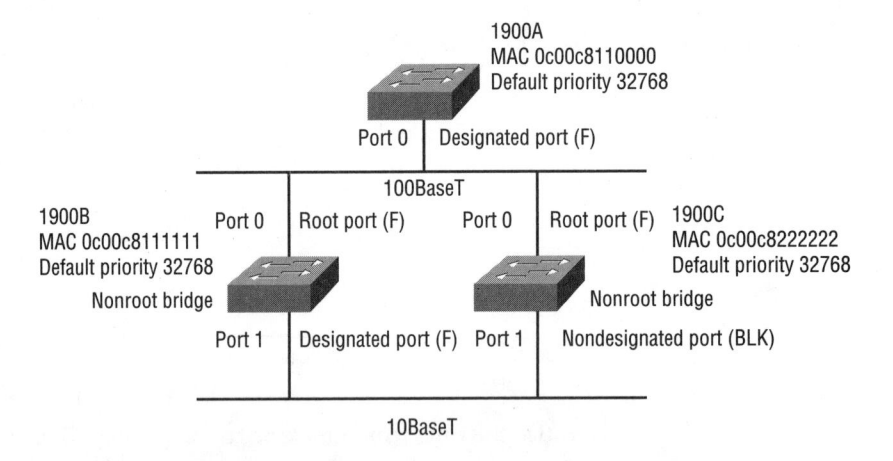

```
                                    1900A
                                    MAC 0c00c8110000
                                    Default priority 32768

                        Port 0 | Designated port (F)
                              100BaseT
1900B          Port 0  Root port (F)   Port 0  Root port (F)  1900C
MAC 0c00c8111111                                              MAC 0c00c8222222
Default priority 32768                                        Default priority 32768
Nonroot bridge                                                Nonroot bridge
               Port 1  Designated port (F)  Port 1  Nondesignated port (BLK)
                              10BaseT
```

Because 1900A has the lowest MAC address and all three switches use the default priority, 1900A will be the root bridge.

To determine the root ports on switches 1900B and 1900C, you need to look at the cost of the link connecting the switches. Because the connection from both switches to the root switch is from port 0 using a 100Mbps link, that has the best cost and both switches' root port will then be port 0.

Use the bridge ID to determine the designated ports on the switches. The root bridge always has all ports as designated. However, because both 1900B and 1900C have the same cost to the root bridge, the designated port will be on switch 1900B because it has the lowest bridge ID. Because 1900B has been determined to have the designated port, switch 1900C will put port 1 in blocking state to stop any network loop from occurring.

LAN Switch Types

LAN switching is used to forward or filter frames based on their hardware destination. However, there are three different methods in which frames can be forwarded or filtered. Each method has its advantages and disadvantages, and by understanding the different LAN switch methods available, you can make smart switching decisions.

There are three switching modes:

Store-and-forward With the *store-and-forward* mode, the complete data frame is received on the switch's buffer, a cyclic redundancy check (CRC) is run, and then the destination address is looked up in the MAC filter table.

Cut-through With the *cut-through* mode, the switch waits for only the destination hardware address to be received and then looks up the destination address in the MAC filter table.

FragmentFree *FragmentFree* is the default mode for the Catalyst 1900 switch; it is sometimes referred to as modified cut-through. Checks the first 64 bytes of a frame for fragmentation (because of possible collisions) before forwarding the frame.

Figure 4.7 shows the different points where the switching mode takes place in the frame. The different switching modes are discussed in detail in the following sections.

FIGURE 4.7 Different switching modes within a frame

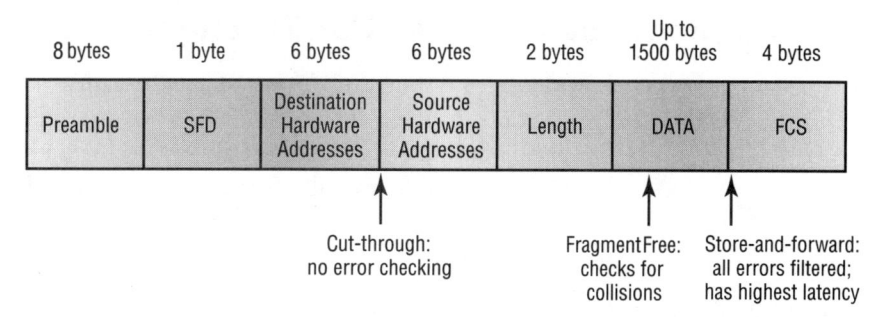

8 bytes	1 byte	6 bytes	6 bytes	2 bytes	Up to 1500 bytes	4 bytes
Preamble	SFD	Destination Hardware Addresses	Source Hardware Addresses	Length	DATA	FCS

Cut-through: no error checking

FragmentFree: checks for collisions

Store-and-forward: all errors filtered; has highest latency

Store-and-Forward

Store-and-forward switching is one of three primary types of LAN switching. With the store-and-forward switching method, the LAN switch copies the entire frame onto its onboard buffers and computes the cyclic redundancy check (CRC). Because it copies the entire frame, latency through the switch varies with frame length.

The frame is discarded if it contains a CRC error, if it's too short (less than 64 bytes including the CRC), or if it's too long (more than 1,518 bytes including the CRC). If the frame doesn't contain any errors, the LAN switch looks up the destination hardware address in its forwarding or switching table and determines the outgoing interface. It then forwards the frame toward its destination. This is the mode used by the Catalyst 5000 series switches, and it cannot be modified on the switch.

Cut-Through (Real Time)

Cut-through switching is the other main type of LAN switching. With this method, the LAN switch copies only the destination address (the first 6 bytes following the preamble) onto its onboard buffers. It then looks up the hardware destination address in the MAC switching table, determines the outgoing interface, and forwards the frame toward its destination. A cut-through switch provides reduced latency because it begins to forward the frame as soon as it reads the destination address and determines the outgoing interface.

Some switches can be configured to perform cut-through switching on a per-port basis until a user-defined error threshold is reached. At that point, they automatically change over to store-and-forward mode so they will stop forwarding the errors. When the error rate on the port falls below the threshold, the port automatically changes back to cut-through mode.

FragmentFree (Modified Cut-Through)

FragmentFree is a modified form of cut-through switching in which the switch waits for the collision window (64 bytes) to pass before forwarding. If a packet has an error, it almost always occurs within the first 64 bytes. FragmentFree mode provides better error checking than the cut-through mode, with practically no increase in latency. This is the default switching method for the 1900 switches.

Configuring Spanning Tree

The configuration of spanning tree is pretty simple unless you want to change your timers or add multiple spanning tree instances; then it can get complex. The timers and more advanced configurations are covered in Chapter 5.

STP is enabled on all Cisco switches by default. However, you may want to change your spanning tree configuration to have many spanning tree instances. This means that each VLAN can be its own spanning tree. This is known as Per-VLAN spanning tree.

To enable or disable spanning tree on a set-based switch, use the set spantree [parameter] command. This is performed on a VLAN-by-VLAN basis rather than a port-by-port configuration:

```
Todd5000> (enable) set spantree disable 1-1005
Spantrees 1-1005 disabled.

Todd5000> (enable) set spantree enable 1-1005
Spantrees 1-1005 enabled.
```

The above configuration shows the disabling of spanning tree on an individual VLAN basis. To enable spanning tree on an individual VLAN basis, use set spantree enable [VLAN(s)]. Cisco recommends that you do not disable spanning tree on a switch, particularly on uplinks where a loop can occur.

> **NOTE** On a chassis with a Supervisor Engine III or III F with a NFFC or NFFC II, you cannot enable spanning tree on a per-VLAN basis. You must enable spanning tree on every VLAN using the set spantree enable all command.

To enable or disable spanning tree on a Cisco IOS-based switch, use the spantree command or the no spantree command. The configuration below shows how to enable and disable spanning tree on a 1900 switch:

```
1900A#config t
Enter configuration commands, one per line.  End with CNTL/Z
1900A(config)#spantree ?
  <1-1005>  ISL VLAN index
```

```
1900A(config)#no spantree 1
1900A#sh span 1
Error: STP is not enabled for VLAN 1

1900A#config t
Enter configuration commands, one per line.  End with CNTL/Z
1900A(config)#span 1
1900A#sh span 1
VLAN1 is executing the IEEE compatible Spanning Tree Protocol
   Bridge Identifier has priority 32768, address 0030.80CC.7B40
   Configured hello time 2, max age 20, forward delay 15
   Current root has priority 32768, address 0030.80CC.7B40
   Root port is N/A, cost of root path is 0
   Topology change flag not set, detected flag not set
   Topology changes 0, last topology change occurred 0d00h00m00s ago
   Times:  hold 1, topology change 8960
           hello 2, max age 20, forward delay 15
   Timers: hello 2, topology change 35, notification 2
 Port Ethernet 0/1 of VLAN1 is Forwarding
   [output cut]
```

Notice in the above output that the no spantree 1 command turned off spanning tree for VLAN 1. Typing spantree 1 (span 1 for short) turned the Spanning Tree Protocol back on for VLAN 1. The show spantree 1 command displays the STP information for VLAN 1. Notice that the bridge ID, MAC address, and timers are displayed.

To see the spanning tree configuration and whether it is active on a Catalyst 5000 set-based switch, use the show spantree command as shown here:

```
Todd5000> (enable) show spantree
VLAN 1
Spanning tree enabled
Spanning tree type          ieee
```

```
Designated Root              00-e0-34-88-fc-00
Designated Root Priority     32768
Designated Root Cost         0
Designated Root Port         1/0
Root Max Age   20 sec     Hello Time 2  sec    Forward Delay 15 sec

Bridge ID MAC ADDR           00-e0-34-88-fc-00
Bridge ID Priority           32768
Bridge Max Age 20 sec     Hello Time 2  sec    Forward Delay 15 sec

Port  Vlan  Port-State      Cost   Priority Fast-Start Group-Method
----  ----  --------------  -----  -------- ---------- -----
1/1   1     forwarding       19      32      disabled
1/2   1     not-connected    19      32      disabled
2/1   1     not-connected   100      32      disabled
2/2   1     not-connected   100      32      disabled
2/3   1     not-connected   100      32      disabled
2/4   1     not-connected   100      32      disabled
2/5   1     not-connected   100      32      disabled
--More--
```

By default, the show spantree command provides information about VLAN 1. You can gather spanning tree information about other VLANs by using the show spantree [vlan #] command.

The show spantree command will provide you with the following information:

Designated Root The MAC address of the root bridge.

Designated Root Priority The priority of the root bridge. All bridges have a default of 32768.

Designated Root Cost The cost of the shortest path to the root bridge.

Designated Root Port The port that is chosen as the lowest cost to the root bridge.

Root Timers The timers received from the root bridge.

Bridge ID MAC Address This bridge's ID. This plus the Bridge Priority make up the Bridge ID.

Bridge ID Priority   The priority set; the bridge output above is using the default of 32768.

Bridge Timers   The timers used by this bridge.

Ports in the Spanning Tree   Not all available ports are displayed in the output above. However, this field does show all ports participating in this spanning tree. It also shows whether they are forwarding or not.

Summary

This chapter covered layer 2 switching. You learned how redundant links can be used to provide redundancy in a network but also how they can cause problems.

The Spanning Tree Protocol was discussed at length, including how it can be used to stop network loops, broadcast storms, and multiple frame copies.

We discussed STP configuration and showed you some examples. However, we showed you only how to turn spanning tree off and on. In Chapter 5, we'll show you how to use STP to create complex configurations on the switch.

Key Terms

Before you take the exam, be sure you're familiar with the following terms:

Application-Specific Integrated Circuits (ASICs)	*layer 2 switching*
bridge ID	*loop avoidance*
Bridge Protocol Data Units (BPDUs)	*Media Access Control (MAC) address*
broadcasts	*nondesignated ports*
cut-through	*root bridge*
designated ports	*Spanning Tree Protocol (STP)*
FragmentFree	*store-and-forward*

Commands Used in This Chapter

Access Layer Switch Commands (1900 Switch in This Book)	Meaning
spantree	Turns on spanning tree for a VLAN
no spantree	Turns off spanning tree for a VLAN
show spantree	Used to view spanning tree information on a VLAN

Distribution Layer Switch Commands (5000 Switch in This Book)	Meaning
set spantree	Turns spanning tree off or on for a VLAN
show spantree	Used to view spanning tree information on a VLAN

Written Lab

Write out the answers to the following questions.

1. What command will show you whether a port is in forwarding mode?

2. What command would you use to disable spanning tree for VLAN 5 on a set-based switch?

3. What command will enable spanning tree for VLAN 6 on a 1900 switch?

4. What is a switch's priority by default?

5. What is used to determine a bridge ID?

6. What is the hello time of BPDU?

7. What is the amount of time it would take a switch port to go from blocking state to forwarding state?

8. What are the four states of a bridge port?

9. What are the two parameters used to determine which port will be forwarding data and which ports will be blocking on a switch with redundant links?

10. True/False: A bridge must forward all broadcasts out all ports except for the port that initially received the broadcast.

Review Questions

1. Which LAN switch method runs a CRC on every frame?
   A. Cut-through
   B. Store-and-forward
   C. FragmentCheck
   D. FragmentFree

2. Which LAN switch type checks only the hardware address before forwarding a frame?
   A. Cut-through
   B. Store-and-forward
   C. FragmentCheck
   D. FragmentFree

3. What is true regarding the STP blocked state of a port? (Choose all that apply.)
   A. No frames are transmitted or received on the blocked port.
   B. BPDUs are sent and received on the blocked port.
   C. BPDUs are still received on the blocked port.
   D. Frames are sent or received on the blocked port.

4. Layer 2 switching provides which of the following? (Choose all that apply.)
   A. Hardware-based bridging (MAC)
   B. Wire speed
   C. High latency
   D. High cost

5. What is used to determine the root bridge in a network? (Choose all that apply.)

    A. Priority

    B. Cost of the links attached to the switch

    C. MAC address

    D. IP address

6. What is used to determine the designated port on a bridge?

    A. Priority

    B. Cost of the links attached to the switch

    C. MAC address

    D. IP address

7. What are the four port states of an STP switch?

    A. Learning

    B. Learned

    C. Listened

    D. Heard

    E. Listening

    F. Forwarding

    G. Forwarded

    H. Blocking

    I. Gathering

8. What are the three distinct functions of layer 2 switching?

   A. Address learning
   B. Routing
   C. Forward and filtering
   D. Creating network loops
   E. Loop avoidance
   F. IP addressing

9. Which of the following is true regarding BPDUs?

   A. BPDUs are used to send configuration messages using IP packets.
   B. BPDUs are used to send configuration messages using multicast frames.
   C. BPDUs are used to set the cost of STP links.
   D. BPDUs are used to set the bridge ID of a switch.

10. If a switch determines that a blocked port should now be the designated port, what state will the port go into?

    A. Unblocked
    B. Forwarding
    C. Listening
    D. Listened
    E. Learning
    F. Learned

11. What is the difference between a bridge and a layer 2 switch? (Choose all that apply.)

   A. There can be only one spanning tree instance per bridge.

   B. There can be many different spanning tree instances per switch.

   C. There can be many spanning tree instances per bridge.

   D. There can be only one spanning tree instance per switch.

12. What is the difference between a bridge and a layer 2 switch? (Choose all that apply.)

   A. Switches are software based.

   B. Bridges are hardware based.

   C. Switches are hardware based.

   D. Bridges are software based.

13. What does a switch do when a frame is received on an interface and the destination hardware address is unknown or not in the filter table?

   A. Forwards the switch to the first available link

   B. Drops the frame

   C. Floods the network with the frame looking for the device

   D. Sends back a message to the originating station asking for a name resolution

14. Which LAN switch type waits for the collision window to pass before looking up the destination hardware address in the MAC filter table and forwarding the frame?

   A. Cut-through

   B. Store-and-forward

   C. FragmentCheck

   D. FragmentFree

15. What is the default LAN switch type on a 1900 switch?

   A. Cut-through

   B. Store-and-forward

   C. FragmentCheck

   D. FragmentFree

16. How is the bridge ID of a switch communicated to neighbor switches?

   A. IP routing

   B. STP

   C. During the four STP states of a switch

   D. Bridge Protocol Data Units

   E. Broadcasts during convergence times

17. How is the root port on a switch determined?

   A. The switch determines the highest cost of a link to the root bridge.

   B. The switch determines the lowest cost of a link to the root bridge.

   C. By sending and receiving BPDUs between switches. The fastest BPDU transfer rate on an interface becomes the root port.

   D. The root bridge will broadcast the bridge ID, and the receiving bridge will determine what interface this broadcast was received on and make this interface the root port.

18. How many root bridges are allowed in a network?

   A. 10

   B. 1

   C. 1 for each switch

   D. 20

19. What could happen on a network if no loop avoidance schemes are put in place?

   A. Faster convergence times.

   B. Broadcast storms.

   C. Multiple frame copies.

   D. IP routing will cause flapping on a serial link.

20. What is the default priority of STP on a switch?

   A. 32768

   B. 3276

   C. 100

   D. 10

   E. 1

Answers to Written Lab

1. `show spantree`. This command will display the spanning tree information of a VLAN and all the ports' participation in STP.

2. `set spantree disable 5`. The `set spantree` command is used to enable or disable spanning tree for a VLAN.

3. `spantree 6`. This command is used to turn on spanning tree for a VLAN. You can disable STP for an interface with the `no spantree` command.

4. 32768. This is the default priority on all switches and bridges.

5. Bridge priority and then MAC address. If the priorities of the switches are set the same, the MAC address would be used to determine the bridge ID.

6. Two seconds. Every two seconds, BPDUs are sent out all forwarding ports.

7. Fifty seconds. From blocking to listening is 20 seconds. From listening to learning is 15 seconds, and from learning to forwarding is another 15 seconds.

8. Blocking, listening, learning, forwarding. Each state is used to stop network loops from occurring on redundant links.

9. The path cost and port ID are used to determine the designated port and nondesignated ports.

10. True. Bridges forward all frames that are received and are broadcasts or are not in the filter table.

Answers to Review Questions

1. **B.** Store-and-forward LAN switching checks every frame for CRC errors. It has the highest latency of any LAN switch type.

2. **A.** The cut-through method does no error checking and has the lowest latency of the three LAN switch types. Cut-through checks only the hardware destination address before forwarding the frame.

3. **A, C.** BPDUs are still received on a blocked port, but no forwarding of frames and BPDUs are allowed.

4. **A, B.** Layer 2 switching uses ASICs to provide frame filtering and is considered hardware based. Layer 2 switching also provides wire-speed frame transfers, with low latency.

5. **A, C.** Layer 2 devices running the STP use the priority and MAC address to determine the root bridge in a network.

6. **B.** For switches to determine the designated ports, the cost of the links attached to the switch is used.

7. **A, E, F, H.** The four states are blocking, listening, learning, and forwarding. Disabled is a fifth state.

8. **A, C, E.** Layer 2 features include address learning, forward and filtering of the network, and loop avoidance.

9. **B.** Bridge Protocol Data Units are used to send configuration messages to neighbor switches. This includes the bridge IDs.

10. **C.** A blocked port will always listen for BPDUs to make sure that a loop will not occur when the port is put into forwarding state.

11. **A, B.** Unlike a bridge, a switch can have many different spanning tree instances. Bridges can only have one.

12. **C, D.** Bridges are considered software based and switches are considered hardware based.

13. C. Switches forward all frames that have an unknown destination address. If a device answers the frame, the switch will update the MAC address table to reflect the location of the device.

14. D. FragmentFree looks at the first 64 bytes of a frame to make sure a collision has not occurred. It is sometimes referred to as modified cut-through.

15. D. By default, 1900 switches use the FragmentFree LAN switch type. The 1900 can use the store-and-forward method.

16. D. The bridge ID is sent via a multicast frame inside a BPDU update.

17. B. Root ports are determined by using the lowest cost of a link to the root bridge.

18. B. Only one root bridge can be used in any network.

19. B, C. Broadcast storms and multiple frame copies are typically found in a network that has multiple links to remote locations without some type of loop avoidance scheme.

20. A. The default priorities on all switches are 32768.

Chapter 5

Using Spanning Tree with VLANs

THE CCNP EXAM TOPICS COVERED IN THIS CHAPTER INCLUDE THE FOLLOWING:

- ✓ Describing the Spanning Tree Protocol
- ✓ Understanding the different types of STP used with VLANs
- ✓ Determining the STP root bridge
- ✓ Configuring STP
- ✓ Setting STP port priorities
- ✓ Setting the VLAN port priorities
- ✓ Changing the STP timers

Redundancy is the ability to provide an immediate backup solution to a fault in the network that might otherwise cause a network or component service outage. When you're building a redundant network—which is a network with redundant power, hardware, links, and other network-critical components—network loops can occur. The Spanning Tree Protocol (STP) was created to overcome the problems associated with transparent bridging at layer 2.

This chapter will focus on providing link redundancy by using STP and the IEEE 802.1d algorithm used to support STP. The Spanning Tree Protocol uses timers to make the network stable. You'll learn how to manage the different STP timers to maximize the efficiency of your network.

Cisco and IEEE 802.1q Committee

Cisco and the IEEE do not see everything eye-to-eye when it comes to using spanning tree and VLANs. Per-VLAN Spanning Tree (PVST) is a Cisco proprietary implementation of STP. PVST uses Inter-Switch Link (ISL) routing and runs a separate instance of STP for each and every VLAN.

The IEEE uses what is called Common Spanning Tree (CST), which is defined with IEEE 802.1q. The IEEE 802.1q defines one spanning tree instance for all VLANs.

There is one more implementation of STP, and that is called PVST+. Because it ends with a plus sign, it must be better, right? Well, maybe. What it does is allow CST information to be passed into PVST. Cisco thinks it would be easier if you just had all Cisco switches; then you wouldn't even have to think about this issue.

The following list includes a brief explanation of each STP implementation:

Per-VLAN Spanning Tree (PVST)   Default for Cisco switches, it runs a separate instance of spanning tree for each VLAN. Makes smaller STP for easier convergence.

Common Spanning Tree (CST)   The 802.1q standard, it runs one large STP on the entire network regardless of the amount of VLANs. Problems with convergence can occur in large networks.

Per-VLAN Spanning Tree+ (PVST+)   Allows Cisco switches to communicate with CST switches.

In the following sections, we'll go into more detail about each type of STP implementation and its use with VLANs.

Per-VLAN Spanning Tree (PVST)

The STP protocol does not scale well with large switched networks. In large switched networks, there can be delays in receiving Bridge Protocol Data Units (BPDUs). These delays can cause instability in the STP database. Delays in larger switched networks can also cause convergence time problems, which means that the network will not be forwarding frames.

To solve late BPDU and convergence issues, Cisco created a separate instance of *Per-VLAN Spanning Tree (PVST)*. It basically makes smaller STP implementations, which is easier for the switches to manage. Also, with PVST, each VLAN has a unique Spanning Tree Protocol topology for its root, port cost, path cost, and priority.

By running PVST, you still provide a loop-free network, but it is based within each VLAN. The benefits of having a PVST are listed here:

- It reduces the STP recalculation time when the switched network is converging.
- The spanning tree topology is smaller.
- It makes the switched network easier to scale.
- Recovery is faster than with a large network with one STP instance.
- It allows administrative control of forwarding paths on a subnet basis.

However, there are some disadvantages of using a spanning-tree-per-instance implementation:

- The utilization on the switch is a factor because it needs to manage all the STP instances.
- You must take into consideration that the trunk links have to support all the VLAN STP information as well.

Common Spanning Tree (CST)

The IEEE 802.1q is referred to as the *Common Spanning Tree (CST)*. It is also called the Mono-Spanning Tree because it uses only one spanning tree instance regardless of the size of the switched layer 2 network.

The CST runs on all VLANs by default, and all switches are involved in the election process to find the root bridge. The switches then form an association with that root bridge. Typically, using CST does not allow for optimization of the root bridge placement.

There are some advantages to CST. With one STP instance, there are fewer BPDUs consuming bandwidth. Because there is only one instance of STP in the network, there is less STP processing performed by the switches.

However, the disadvantages typically outweigh the advantages in a larger network. With a single root bridge, the path that has been calculated as the best cost to the root bridge might not be the most efficient for some users to send their data. Another disadvantage with CST is that the STP topology increases in size to make sure all ports in the network are found. This can cause delays in the updates and convergence times if the network topology is too large.

Per-VLAN Spanning Tree+ (PVST+)

Per-VLAN Spanning Tree+ (PVST+) is an extension of the PVST standard. Starting with the Catalyst software 4.1 or later, PVST+ is supported on Cisco Catalyst switches. This allows Cisco switches to support the IEEE 802.1q standard. Basically, the PVST+ extension of the PVST protocol provides support for links across an IEEE 802.1q CST region.

PVST+ also supports the Cisco default PVST and adds checking mechanisms to make sure there are no configuration problems on trunked ports and VLAN IDs across switches. PVST+ is plug-and-play compatible with PVST with no configuration necessary. In order to provide support for the

IEEE 802.1q standard, Cisco's existing PVST has been modified with additional features enabling it to support a link across the IEEE 802.1q Common Spanning Tree region.

PVST+ includes features such as the following:

- Provides notification of inconsistencies related to port trunking or VLAN identification across the switches.

- Adds mechanisms to ensure that there is no unknown configuration.

- Tunnels PVST BPDUs through the 802.1q VLAN region as multicast data.

- Provides compatibility with IEEE 802.1q's CST and Cisco's PVST protocols.

- Interoperates with 802.1q-compliant switches using CST through 802.1q trunking. A CST BPDU is transmitted or received with an IEEE standard bridge group MAC address.

- Blocks ports that receive inconsistent BPDUs in order to prevent forwarding loops.

- Notifies users via syslog messages about all inconsistencies.

Scaling the Spanning Tree Protocol

The STP prevents loops in layer 2 switched networks and is basically plug-and-play. However, it may be advantageous to change some of the default timers and settings to create a more stable environment.

In this section, we'll discuss how to scale the STP protocol on a large, switched internetwork. It is important to understand how to provide proper placement of the root bridge to create an optimal topology. If the root bridge is automatically chosen through an election, which is the default, the actual path the frames may take might not be the most efficient. The administrator can then change the root placement, which allows for a possibly more optimal path. However, you can cause more damage as well, but hopefully you'll have thought out your network design before making any changes.

To change the root placement, you need to do the following:

- Determine the root device.

- Configure the device.

- Set the port priorities.
- Set the VLAN port priorities.
- Change the STP timers.

Determining the Root

Determining the root device is the most important decision that you make when configuring the STP protocol on your network. If you place the root in the wrong place in your network, it will be difficult to scale the network, and really, that is what you are trying to do: create a scalable layer 2 switched internetwork.

However, by placing the root switch as close as possible to the center of your network, more optimal and deterministic paths can be easily chosen. You can choose the root bridge and secondary and backup bridges as well. Secondary bridges are very important for network stability in case the root bridge fails.

Because the root bridge should be close to the center of the network, the device will typically be a distribution layer switch and not an access layer switch.

After the root bridge has been chosen and configured, all the connected switches must determine the best path to the root bridge. The STP uses several different costs in determining the best path to the root bridge:

- Port cost
- Path cost
- Port priority

When a BPDU is sent out a switch port, the BPDU is assigned a port cost. The path cost is then determined by the sum of all of the port costs. The STP will first look at the path cost to figure out the forwarding and blocking ports. If the path costs are equal on two or more links to the root bridge, the port ID is used to determine the root port. The port with the lowest port ID is determined to be the forwarding port. You can change the port ID on a switch by changing the port priority, but Cisco doesn't recommend this. However, we'll show you how to do it later in this section (so you can have some fun on a rainy Saturday).

Configuring the Root

After you choose the best switch to become your root bridge, you can use the Cisco command-line interface (CLI) to configure the STP parameters in a switched network.

Scaling the Spanning Tree Protocol

The command to configure the Spanning Tree Protocol (STP) is `set spantree`. The following switch output (from our Catalyst 5000) shows the different command parameters you can use when configuring the Spanning Tree Protocol. We are interested in the `set spantree root` and `set spantree secondary` commands at this point:

```
Todd5000> (enable) set spantree ?
Set spantree commands:
-----------------------------------------------------------------
set spantree backbonefast        Enable or disable fast convergence
set spantree disable             Disable spanning tree
set spantree enable              Enable spanning tree
set spantree fwddelay            Set spantree forward delay
set spantree hello               Set spantree hello interval
set spantree help                Show this message
set spantree maxage              Set spantree max aging time
set spantree multicast-address   Set multicast address type for trbrf's
set spantree portcost            Set spantree port cost
set spantree portfast            Set spantree port fast start
set spantree portpri             Set spantree port priority
set spantree portstate           Set spantree logical port state
set spantree portvlancost        Set spantree port cost per vlan
set spantree portvlanpri         Set spantree port vlan priority
set spantree priority            Set spantree priority
set spantree root                Set switch as primary or secondary root
set spantree uplinkfast          Enable or disable uplinkfast groups
Todd5000> (enable)
```

The `set spantree root` command sets the primary root bridge for a specific VLAN, or even for all your VLANs. The `set spantree root secondary` command allows you to configure a backup root bridge.

In the following switch output, notice the options that are available with the `set spantree root` command:

```
Todd5000> (enable) set spantree root ?
Usage: set spantree root [secondary] <vlans> [dia <network_diameter>]
                         [hello <hello_time>]
       (vlans = 1..1005, network_diameter = 2..7, hello_time = 1..10)
```

Table 5.1 shows the different parameters available with the `set spantree` command and their definitions.

TABLE 5.1 set spantree Parameters

Parameter	Definition
root	Designation to change the switch to the root switch. The `set spantree root` command changes the bridge priority from 32768 to 8192.
secondary	Designation to change the switch to a secondary root switch if the primary fails. This automatically changes the bridge priority from a default of 32768 to 16384.
VLAN_List	Optional command that changes the STP parameters on a specified VLAN. If no VLAN is specified, then it changes only VLAN 1 by default. You can change the parameters for VLANs 1–1005.
dia <network diameter>	Another optional command that specifies the maximum number of bridges between any two points where end stations attach. You can set these parameters from 2 to 7. Figure the network diameter by starting at the root bridge and counting the number of bridges in the VLAN. The root bridge is 1, so if you have only one more switch, set the network diameter to 2. This changes the timers in the VLAN to reflect the new diameter.
hello <hello time>	Optional command that specifies in seconds the duration between configuration messages from the root switch. You can set this anywhere from 1 to 10 seconds (2 is the default).

The following switch output is an example of using the `set spantree root` command:

```
Todd5000> (enable) set spantree root 1-4 dia 2
VLANs 1-2 bridge priority set to 8192.
VLANs 1-2 bridge max aging time set to 10.
VLANs 1-2 bridge hello time set to 2.
VLANs 1-2 bridge forward delay set to 7.
Switch is now the root switch for active VLANs 1-4.
Todd5000> (enable)
```

The `set spantree root` command tells the switch to change the bridge priority to 8192, which will automatically change the switch to the root bridge. The 1-4 represents the VLANs for which the STP will change the parameters, and the `dia 2` is the network diameter. To figure the network diameter, we just counted the number of switches from the root, including the root bridge, which in our example equaled 2.

Notice the output after the command. The bridge priority was changed to 8192, max age time to 10, hello time is still 2 seconds, and the forward delay was set to 7 seconds. If the network diameter is set, the STP will set the timers to what it would consider efficient for that size network.

You can verify your STP configuration with the `show spantree` command. If you type the command **show spantree** with no parameters, it will show you the spanning tree configuration for all VLANs. You can type **show spantree vlan** to see the parameters for just a particular VLAN. The following switch output shows the spanning tree information for VLAN 1:

```
Todd5000> (enable) sh spantree 1
VLAN 1
Spanning tree enabled
Spanning tree type            ieee

Designated Root               00-e0-34-88-fc-00
Designated Root Priority      8192
Designated Root Cost          0
Designated Root Port          1/0
Root Max Age   10 sec    Hello Time 2  sec   Forward Delay 7  sec

Bridge ID MAC ADDR            00-e0-34-88-fc-00
Bridge ID Priority            8192
```

```
Bridge Max Age 10 sec     Hello Time 2  sec    Forward Delay 7  sec

Port      Vlan  Port-State        Cost    Priority  Fast-Start
--------  ----  --------------    -----   --------  ----------
 1/1       1    forwarding         19        32     disabled
 1/2       1    forwarding         19        32     disabled
 2/1       1    not-connected     100        32     disabled
 2/2       1    not-connected     100        32     disabled
 2/3       1    not-connected     100        32     disabled
 2/4       1    not-connected     100        32     disabled
 2/5       1    not-connected     100        32     disabled
--More--
```

Notice that the bridge IP priority is set to 8192; the designated root and bridge IP MAC ADDR is the same because this is the root bridge. The Port-States are both 19, which is the default for 100Mbps. Because both ports are in forwarding state, the 1900 switch must have one of its FastEthernet ports in blocking mode. Let's take a look by using the show spantree command on the 1900 CLI:

```
Port FastEthernet 0/26 of VLAN1 is Blocking
    Port path cost 10, Port priority 128
    Designated root has priority 8192, address
    00E0.3488.FC00
    Designated bridge has priority 8192, address
    00E0.3488.FC00
    Designated port is 2, path cost 0
    Timers: message age 10, forward delay 7, hold 1

Port FastEthernet 0/27 of VLAN1 is Forwarding
    Port path cost 10, Port priority 128
    Designated root has priority 8192, address
    00E0.3488.FC00
    Designated bridge has priority 8192, address
    00E0.3488.FC00
    Designated port is 1, path cost 0
    Timers: message age 10, forward delay 7, hold 1
```

Notice that port f0/26 is in blocking mode and port f0/27 is in forwarding mode. If we want port f0/26 to be in forwarding mode and f0/27 in blocking mode, we can set the port costs to help the switch determine the best path to use. Note that we are not saying you should do this; we just wanted to show you how.

Setting the Port Cost

The parameters in this next set are used to allow the network administrator to influence the path that spanning tree chooses when setting the port priority, port cost, and path cost.

Cisco does not recommend changing these settings unless it's absolutely necessary. However, the best way to get a good understanding of how the STP works is by changing the defaults. We do not recommend trying any of this on a production network unless you have permission from the network manager and they understand that you can bring the network down.

By changing the port cost, you can change the port ID, which means it can be a more desirable port to the STP protocol. Remember that STP only uses the port ID if there is more than one path to the root bridge and they are equal cost. Path cost is the sum of the costs between a switch and the root bridge. The STP calculates the path cost based on the media speed of the links between the switch and the port cost of each port forwarding the frames. In our lab, both links are 100Mbps, so the port ID is important and will be used.

To change the path used between a switch and the root bridge, first calculate the current path cost. Then change the port cost of the port you want to use, making sure that you keep in mind the alternate paths if the primary path fails before making any changes to your switch. Remember that ports with a lower port cost are more likely to be chosen; this doesn't mean they always will be chosen.

To change the port cost of a port on a 5000 series switch, use the **set spantree portcost** command:

```
Todd5000> (enable) set spantree portcost ?
Usage: set spantree portcost <mod_num/port_num> <cost>
       set spantree portcost <trcrf> <cost>
       (cost = 1..65535)
```

The parameters to set the cost of a port are the module and port number and the cost you want to configure. The following example shows how to set the port cost on port 1/1 to 10 from the default of 19:

```
Todd5000> (enable) set spantree portcost 1/1 10
Spantree port 1/1 path cost set to 10.
```

You would verify the change with the `show spantree` command. However, because both ports are in forwarding mode, the command shown above will not change the switch's STP parameters. Notice in the following switch output that both ports are forwarding, but the costs of the ports are different:

```
Port       Vlan  Port-State      Cost    Priority  Fast-Start
---------  ----  -------------   -----   --------  ----------
1/1        1     forwarding      10      32        disabled
1/2        1     forwarding      19      32        disabled
```

Remember that a root switch will be forwarding on all active ports, so the port IDs are irrelevant to the switch. However, the 1900 must then choose a port to perform blocking on the interface with the lowest cost.

To change the port cost on a 1900 CLI-based switch, use the `spantree cost` interface command. The cost values can be any number from 1 to 65535; however, you cannot make it less than the path cost of both links. For example, notice in the following switch output that we tried to set port f0/26 to a lower number than the default of 10. The switch would not allow us to do that because both f0/26 and f0/27 are running the default of 10. What we need to do is to raise the port priority of the port we don't want STP to use for forwarding. Notice that we changed the cost of port f0/27 to 20. This should make the f0/26 port a more desirable path:

```
1900A#config t
Enter configuration commands, one per line.  End with
  CNTL/Z
1900A(config)#int f0/26
1900A(config-if)#spantree cost 5
Error: Option 1 path cost should be greater
       than or equal to option 2 path cost 10
1900A(config-if)#int f0/27
1900A(config-if)#spantree cost 20
1900A(config-if)#
```

To verify the port priorities, use the `show spantree` command:

```
Port FastEthernet 0/26 of VLAN1 is Forwarding
   Port path cost 10, Port priority 128
   Designated root has priority 8192, address
   00E0.3488.FC00
```

```
        Designated bridge has priority 8192, address
        00E0.3488.FC00
        Designated port is 2, path cost 0
        Timers: message age 10, forward delay 7, hold 1

    Port FastEthernet 0/27 of VLAN1 is Blocking
        Port path cost 20, Port priority 128
        Designated root has priority 8192, address
        00E0.3488.FC00
        Designated bridge has priority 8192, address
        00E0.3488.FC00
        Designated port is 1, path cost 0
        Timers: message age 10, forward delay 7, hold 1
    1900A#
```

In the preceding switch output, notice that port 0/26 is now forwarding and port f0/27 is now blocking. In the output, the port path cost is 10 for f0/26 and 20 for f0/27. This is a pretty simple and straightforward configuration, and our network never went down. However, caution should be used when changing the port costs in a real production network because you can cause havoc in a network if the configuration is not thought out carefully.

Setting the Port Priority

Another option you can use to help the switch determine the path selection that STP uses in your network is to set the port priorities. Remember, this only influences STP; it doesn't demand that STP do anything. However, between setting the port cost and priority, STP should always make your path selection.

The port priority and port cost configurations work similarly. The port with the lowest port priority will forward frames for all VLANs. The command to set a port priority is `set spantree portpri`:

```
Todd5000> (enable) set spantree portpri ?
Usage: set spantree portpri <mod_num/port_num> <priority>
       set spantree portpri <trcrf> <trcrf_priority>
       (priority = 0..63, trcrf_priority = 0..7)
Todd5000> (enable)
```

The possible port priority range is from 0 to 63, where the default is 32. If all ports have the same priority, then the port with the lowest port number will forward frames. For example, 2/1 is lower than 2/2. In the following example, the 5000 switch priority for port 1/1 is set to 20:

```
Todd5000> (enable) set spantree portpri 1/1 20
Bridge port 1/1 port priority set to 20.
Todd5000> (enable)
```

Once you change your port priority, you can verify the configuration with the show spantree 1/1 command:

```
Todd5000> (enable) sh spantree 1/1
Port      Vlan  Port-State     Cost  Priority  Fast-Start
--------- ----  -------------- ----- --------  ----------
 1/1      1     forwarding      10     20      disabled
 1/1      2     forwarding      10     20      disabled
 1/1      3     forwarding      10     20      disabled
 1/1      4     forwarding      10     20      disabled
 1/1      1003  not-connected   10     20      disabled
 1/1      1005  not-connected   10      4      disabled
Todd5000> (enable)
```

Notice that, because port 1/1 is a trunked port, all VLAN priorities were changed on that port. Also notice in the following output that the priority is 20 for 1/1, but the default of 32 is set for 1/2:

```
Todd5000> (enable)Sh spantree
[output cut]
Port      Vlan  Port-State     Cost  Priority  Fast-Start
--------- ----  -------------- ----- --------  ----------
 1/1      1     forwarding      10     20      disabled
 1/2      1     forwarding      19     32      disabled
```

You can go one step further and set the port priority on a per-VLAN basis. The port with the lowest priority will forward frames for the VLAN for which you've set the priority. Again, if all the ports have the same priority, the lowest port number wins and begins forwarding frames.

There is an advantage to setting the port priority per VLAN. If you have a network with parallel paths, STP will stop at least one link from forwarding frames so a network loop will not occur. All traffic would then have to travel over only the one link. However, by changing the port priority for a specific group of VLANs, you can distribute the VLANs across the two links.

To change the priority of STP for a certain VLAN or group of VLANs, use the set spantree portvlanpri command:

```
Todd5000> (enable) set spantree portvlanpri ?
Usage: set spantree portvlanpri <mod_num/port_num>
<priority> [vlans] (priority = 0..63)
Todd5000> (enable)
```

The priority can be set for each VLAN from 0 to 63. In the following example, we'll set port 1/1 to forward only VLANs 1 and 2 and port 1/2 to forward VLANs 3 and 4:

```
Todd5000> (enable) set spantree portvlanpri 1/1 16 1-2
Port 1/1 vlans 1-2 using portpri 16.
Port 1/1 vlans 3-1004 using portpri 20.
Port 1/1 vlans 1005 using portpri 4.


Todd5000> (enable) set spantree portvlanpri 1/2 16 3-4
Port 1/2 vlans 1-2,5-1004 using portpri 32.
Port 1/2 vlans 3-4 using portpri 16.
Port 1/2 vlans 1005 using portpri 4.
Todd5000> (enable)
```

The switch output above displays the VLAN priority information. We set both VLAN port priorities to 16. Notice that for VLANs 1–4, the priority is 16. However, on port 1/1, all the other VLANs are listed as having a port priority of 20 because that is what we set the port priority to earlier in this chapter. On port 1/2, the switch thinks all the other ports have a port priority of 32, except for VLAN 1005, which becomes a default priority of 4.

You can view the changes by using the show spantree slot/port command, as shown below:

```
Todd5000> (enable) sh spantree 1/1
Port      Vlan Port-State      Cost   Priority Fast-Start
--------- ---- --------------- ----- -------- ----------
 1/1        1  forwarding        10         16 disabled
 1/1        2  forwarding        10         16 disabled
 1/1        3  forwarding        10         20 disabled
 1/1        4  forwarding        10         20 disabled
 1/1     1003  not-connected     10         20 disabled
```

```
   1/1      1005  not-connected   10        4    disabled
```

```
Todd5000> (enable) sh spantree 1/2
Port      Vlan  Port-State      Cost  Priority  Fast-Start
--------- ----  --------------  ----- --------  ----------
1/2       1     forwarding      19    32        disabled
1/2       2     forwarding      19    32        disabled
1/2       3     forwarding      19    16        disabled
1/2       4     forwarding      19    16        disabled
1/2       1003  not-connected   19    32        disabled
1/2       1005  not-connected   19     4        disabled
Todd5000> (enable)
```

We want to set the VLAN port priority on the 1900 switch now. Notice in the following switch output that f0/26 is in forwarding mode and f0/27 is blocking. Remember that we changed the port cost to 20 for f0/27, which makes port f0/26 more desirable to the switch:

```
Port FastEthernet 0/26 of VLAN1 is Forwarding
   Port path cost 10, Port priority 128
   Designated root has priority 8192, address
   00E0.3488.FC00
   Designated bridge has priority 8192, address
   00E0.3488.FC00
   Designated port is 2, path cost 0
   Timers: message age 10, forward delay 7, hold 1
Port FastEthernet 0/27 of VLAN1 is Blocking
   Port path cost 20, Port priority 128
   Designated root has priority 8192, address
   00E0.3488.FC00
   Designated bridge has priority 8192, address
   00E0.3488.FC00
   Designated port is 1, path cost 0
   Timers: message age 10, forward delay 7, hold 1
```

You can change the priority of the port, but not the VLAN priority as you can with the 5000 series switch. The command is `spantree priority`:

```
1900A#config t
1900A(config-if)#int f0/27
1900A(config-if)#spantree priority 16
1900A(config-if)#
```

Once the priority is set, use the `show spantree [vlan]` command to see the port priority. Notice that, because both ports are equal 100Mbps ports, the switch will use the path cost to determine the forwarding or root port. The priority won't be used unless the path costs are the same. If both ports have the same priority, the interface f0/26 will be used because it is a lower port number:

```
1900A# sh spantree 1
[output cut]
Port FastEthernet 0/26 of VLAN1 is Forwarding
   Port path cost 10, Port priority 128
   Designated root has priority 8192, address
   00E0.3488.FC00
   Designated bridge has priority 8192, address
   00E0.3488.FC00
   Designated port is 2, path cost 0
   Timers: message age 10, forward delay 7, hold 1
Port FastEthernet 0/27 of VLAN1 is Blocking
   Port path cost 20, Port priority 16
   Designated root has priority 8192, address
   00E0.3488.FC00
   Designated bridge has priority 8192, address
   00E0.3488.FC00
   Designated port is 1, path cost 0
   Timers: message age 10, forward delay 7, hold 1
1900A#
```

By changing either the port priority or the port cost, you can basically just persuade the switch to use your chosen paths. However, there are some miscellaneous other STP variables that you can change. We'll discuss those next.

Changing the STP Timers

The timers are important in an STP network to stop network loops from occurring. The different timers are used to give the network time to update the correct topology information to all the switches and also to determine the whereabouts of all the redundant links.

The problem with the STP timers is that, if a link goes down, it can take up to 50 seconds for the backup link to take over forwarding frames. This is a convergence problem that can be addressed when instability is occurring in the network. The following timers can be changed:

fwddlay   This interval indicates how long it takes for a port to move from listening to learning state and then from learning to forwarding state. The default is 15 seconds, but it can be changed to anywhere from 4 to 30 seconds. If you set this too low, the switch won't be allowed ample time to make sure no loops will occur before setting a port in forwarding mode. The following switch output shows how to set the fwddelay to 10 seconds:

```
Todd5000> (enable) set spantree fwddelay ?
Usage: set spantree fwddelay <delay> [vlans]
       (delay = 4..30 seconds, vlan = 1..1005)
Todd5000> (enable) set spantree fwddelay 10
Spantree 1 forward delay set to 10 seconds.
```

hello   This is the time interval for sending BPDUs from the root switch. It is set to 2 seconds by default; you would think it couldn't be set any lower, but it can. You can set it to 1 second to actually double the amount of BPDUs sent out that must be lost before triggering an unwanted convergence in the network. However, it doubles the CPU load and processing load as well. The following switch output shows how to change the BPDU timers to 1 second:

```
Todd5000> (enable) set spantree hello ?
Usage: set spantree hello <interval> [vlans]
       (interval = 1..10, vlan = 1..1005)
Todd5000> (enable) set spantree hello 1
Spantree 1 hello time set to 1 seconds.
```

maxage   The maxage is the amount of time that a switch will hold BPDU information. If a new BPDU is not received before the maxage expires, then the BPDU is discarded and is considered invalid. The default is 20 seconds; it can be set to as low as 6 seconds. However, network instability will happen if too many BPDUs are discarded because this timer is set too low. The following output shows how to change the maxage of a BPDU to 30 seconds:

```
Todd5000> (enable) set spantree maxage ?
Usage: set spantree maxage <agingtime> [vlans]
       (agingtime = 6..40, vlan = 1..1005)
Todd5000> (enable) set spantree maxage 30
Spantree 1 max aging time set to 30 seconds.
Todd5000> (enable)
```

We have been discussing redundant links and STP, but most of the discussion has been about how to make STP run efficiently, and that is by making the nonroot port a blocking port. We discussed load balancing only when we showed you how to set the port priority on a per-VLAN basis. However, that really wasn't load balancing to the degree that is possible with a Cisco switched network. In the next section, we'll cover the most efficient ways of dealing with redundant links in a large, switched internetwork.

Redundant Links with STP

Fast EtherChannel and *Gigabit EtherChannel* allow high-speed redundant links in a spanning tree environment by allowing dual parallel links to be treated as though they were one link. Cisco Fast EtherChannel technology uses the standards-based 802.3 Full-Duplex Fast Ethernet to provide a reliable high-speed solution for the campus network backbone. Fast EtherChannel can scale bandwidth within the campus, providing full-duplex bandwidth at wire speeds of 200Mbps to 800Mbps. It provides high bandwidth, load sharing, and redundancy of links in a switched internetwork.

Broadcast traffic, as well as unicast and multicast traffic, is distributed equally across the links in the channel. Fast EtherChannel also provides redundancy in the event of a link failure. If a link is lost in a Fast EtherChannel network, traffic is rerouted to one of the other links in just a few milliseconds, making the convergence transparent to the user.

Parallel Fast EtherChannel Links

Fast EtherChannel uses load distribution to share the links in a bundle, which is a group of FastEthernet or Gigabit Ethernet links managed by the Fast EtherChannel process. Should one link in the bundle fail, the Ethernet Bundle Controller (EBC) informs the Enhanced Address Recognition Logic (EARL) ASIC of the failure, and the EARL in turn ages out all addresses learned on that link. The EBC and the EARL use hardware to recalculate the source and destination address pair on a different link.

The convergence time is sometimes referred to as the failover time, which is the time it takes for the new address to be relearned—about 10 microseconds. Windowing flow control techniques can make this process a touch longer, but that depends on the particular application in use. The key is not having the application time out, and the failover time is fast enough to stop the time-out from happening.

EtherChannel Guidelines

EtherChannel does not work under certain circumstances. This is to ensure that no network loops will occur if the bundle comes up. There are certain guidelines to follow when configuring EtherChannel technology:

- All ports must be in the same VLAN or they must all be trunk ports.
- All ports must be configured as the same trunk mode if trunking is used.
- When trunking is used, all ports must be configured with the same VLAN range. If it is not the same, packets will be dropped and the ports will not form a channel when set to the auto or desirable mode.
- All ports must be configured with the same speed and duplex settings.
- If broadcast limits are configured on the ports, configure the limits for all the ports or packets may be dropped.
- The ports cannot be configured in a channel as dynamic VLAN ports.
- Port security must be disabled on channeled ports.
- All ports must be enabled in the channel. If you disable a port, a link failure occurs.

Configuring EtherChannel

To create an EtherChannel bundle, use the `set port channel` command. You must first make sure that all the conditions for EtherChannel have been met.

Notice the switch output when we try to configure the ports on our 5000 switch as a bundle to the 1900 switch:

```
Todd5000> (enable) set port channel 1/1-2 on
Mismatch in trunk mode.
Mismatch in port duplex.
Mismatch in STP port priority.
Failed to set port(s) 1/1-2 channel mode to on.
Todd5000> (enable)
```

There is a mismatch in trunking, duplex, and STP port priority. All of the ports must be configured the same for EtherChannel to work.

To view the configuration of a port, use the `show port capability slot/port` command:

```
Todd5000> (enable) sh port cap 1/1
Model                   WS-X5509
Port                    1/1
Type                    100BaseTX
Speed                   100
Duplex                  half,full
Trunk encap type        ISL
Trunk mode              on,off,desirable,auto,nonegotiate
Channel                 1/1-2
Broadcast suppression   percentage(0-100)
Flow control            no
Security                yes
Membership              static,dynamic
Fast start              yes
Rewrite                 no
Todd5000> (enable)
```

The preceding output shows the card model number and the configuration of the port. The easiest way for us to make sure all the ports we want to channel are configured the same is to just clear the configuration. We're not suggesting that you just clear your config whenever any problems come up, but the configuration we created in this chapter is pretty extensive, and it's just easier to just clear it out of the switch to perform the next function:

```
Todd5000> (enable) clear config all
This command will clear all configuration in NVRAM.
This command will cause ifIndex to be reassigned on the
next system startup.
Do you want to continue (y/n) [n]? y
........
................
System configuration cleared.
Console> (enable)
```

Remember that you need to reset the switch after erasing the configuration to clear the configuration. We need to reconfigure the switch with an IP address and trunking on ports 1/1 and 1/2. Now, we're also going to delete the configuration on the 1900 so we then will have both switches back to our STP default:

```
1900A#delete nvram
This command resets the switch with factory defaults.  All system
parameters will revert to their default factory settings.  All
static and dynamic addresses will be removed.
Reset system with factory defaults, [Y]es or [N]o? Yes
```

Now that we have both the switches back to their default configurations, we'll just configure the IP addresses and turn on trunking on ports 1/1 and 1/2 of the 5000 and ports 0/26 and 0/27 of the 1900:

```
#config t
(config)#hostname 1900A
1900A(config)#ip address 172.16.10.2 255.255.255.0
1900A(config)#ip default-gateway 172.16.10.1
1900A(config)#int f0/26
1900A(config-if)#trunk on
1900A(config-if)#int f0/27
1900A(config-if)#trunk on

Console> (enable) set prompt Todd5000>
Todd5000> (enable) set int sc0 172.16.10.4 255.255.255.0
Interface sc0 IP address and netmask set.
Todd5000> (enable) set trunk 1/1 on
Port(s) 1/1 trunk mode set to on.
Todd5000> (enable) set trunk 1/2 on
Port(s) 1/2 trunk mode set to on.
Todd5000> (enable)
```

To verify that the ports are trunking, use the `show trunk` command:

```
Todd5000> (enable) sh trunk
Port      Mode           Encapsulation   Status       Native vlan
--------  -------------  --------------  ----------   -------
1/1       on             isl             trunking     1
1/2       on             isl             trunking     1
```

Let's try to configure EtherChannel between the switches again:

```
Todd5000> (enable) set port channel 1/1-2 on
Port(s) 1/1-2 channel mode set to on.
Todd5000> (enable) 1997 Jul 25 23:08:20 %PAGP-5-PORTFROMSTP:Port
    1/1 left bridge  port 1/1
1997 Jul 25 23:08:20 %PAGP-5-PORTFROMSTP:Port 1/2 left bridge
    port 1/2
1997 Jul 25 23:08:20 %PAGP-5-PORTTOSTP:Port 1/1 joined bridge
    port 1/1-2
1997 Jul 25 23:08:21 %PAGP-5-PORTTOSTP:Port 1/2 joined bridge
    port 1/1-2
```

To verify the EtherChannel bundle, use the `show port channel` command:

```
Todd5000> (enable) sh port channel
Port  Status      Channel   Channel    Neighbor   Neighbor
                  mode      status     device     port
-----  ----------  --------  ---------  ---------  ----------
1/1   errdisable  on        channel
1/2   errdisable  on        channel
-----  ----------  --------  ---------  ---------  ----------
Todd5000> (enable)
```

You can see that the status is error disabled and that no neighbors are found. This is because we still need to configure Fast EtherChannel on the 1900 switch. If this were a remote switch, you would lose contact with the switch and have to go to the site and console into the switch to configure EtherChannel. You should configure the remote site first; then you will lose contact with it until you configure the local switch bundle.

To configure the EtherChannel bundle on a 1900 switch, use the `port-channel mode` command:

```
1900A(config)#port-channel mode ?
    auto       Set Fast EtherChannel mode to AUTO
    desirable  Set Fast EtherChannel mode to DESIRABLE
    off        Set Fast EtherChannel mode to OFF
    on         Set Fast EtherChannel mode to ON
1900A(config)#port-channel mode on
```

That is all you can configure on the 1900. The switch will look for the neighbor device ID and neighbor group capability that are the same and form the connections into a channel. In this case, ports 0/26 and 0/27 are connected to the same device ID (hostname). By using the command **show spantree 1**, you can see that ports 0/26 and 0/27 are now one port:

```
1900A#show spantree 1
[output cut]
Port PortChannel of VLAN1 is Forwarding
   Port path cost 10, Port priority 128
   Designated root has priority 32768, address
   0030.80CC.7B40
   Designated bridge has priority 32768, address
   0030.80CC.7B40
   Designated port is 26, path cost 0
   Timers: message age 20, forward delay 15, hold 1
```

Ports 0/26 and 0/27 are now just listed as Port PortChannel. To verify the EtherChannel on the 5000 series switch, use the **show port channel** command:

```
Todd5000> (enable) sh port channel
Port  Status      Channel    Channel     Neighbor            Neighbor
                  mode       status      device              port
----- ---------- ---------- ----------- ------------------- ----------
1/1   connected   on         channel     cisco 1900  1900A   A
1/2   connected   on         channel     cisco 1900  1900A   B
----- ---------- ---------- ----------- ------------------- ----------
Todd5000> (enable)
```

The preceding switch output shows the port numbers, status, mode, channel status, neighbor device, and neighbor port ID. Our EtherChannel is working!

Port Aggregation Protocol (PAgP)

The Port Aggregation Protocol (PAgP) is used to add more features to the EtherChannel technology. This protocol is used to learn the capabilities of the neighbors' EtherChannel ports. By doing this, it allows the switches to connect via Fast EtherChannel automatically.

The PAgP protocol groups the ports that have the same neighbor device ID and neighbor group capability into a channel. This channel is then added to the Spanning Tree Protocol as a single bridge port.

For PAgP to work, all the ports must be configured with static VLANs, not dynamic, and all the ports must also be in the same VLAN or be configured as trunk ports. All ports must be the same speed and duplex as well. In other words, all the ports must be configured the same or PAgP will not work.

If an EtherChannel bundle is already working and you make a change on a port, all ports in that bundle are changed to match the port. If you change the speed or duplex of one port, all ports will then run that speed or duplex.

PortFast

By default, the Spanning Tree Protocol (STP) runs on all ports on a switch. Because most of the ports connect to workstations, printers, servers, routers, and so on, it's basically a waste of resources for these point-to-point ports to be running the Spanning Tree Protocol. When a device, let's say a workstation, powers up, it takes up to 50 seconds before the switch will forward data on the port because the STP is making sure no loops are going to occur when the port is in forwarding mode. Not only is this a waste of time (because a loop will not occur with point-to-point links), but some protocols or applications could time out.

PortFast is used to make a point-to-point port almost immediately enter into forwarding state by decreasing the time of the listening and learning states. This is very helpful for switch ports that have workstations or servers attached because these devices will connect immediately instead of waiting for the STP to converge. If you connect a hub to a port configured with PortFast and then accidentally connect another port into the switch from the hub, you will have a network loop and STP will not stop it. It is important to make sure that PortFast is used only on point-to-point links connected only to workstations or servers.

PortFast Configuration

To configure PortFast on a switch, use the `set spantree portfast` command. The following switch output shows how to configure ports 2/1-12 with PortFast:

```
Todd5000> (enable) set spantree portfast ?
Usage: set spantree portfast <mod_num/port_num> <enable|disable>
       set spantree portfast <trcrf> <enable|disable>

Todd5000> (enable) set spantree portfast 2/1-12 enable
```

```
Warning: Spantree port fast start should only be enabled on ports
         connected to a single host. Connecting hubs,
         concentrators, switches, bridges, etc. to a fast start
         port can cause temporary spanning tree loops. Use with
         caution.
Spantree ports 2/1-12 fast start enabled.
Todd5000> (enable)
```

Notice the nice warning received on the switch console when PortFast was turned on. Also notice that we were able to turn on all 12 ports of our 10/100 card.

To configure PortFast on a 1900 switch, use the `spantree start-forwarding` command:

```
1900A#config t
1900A(config)#int e0/1
1900A(config-if)#spantree start-forwarding
1900A(config-if)#
```

This must be configured on each port you want to run PortFast.

UplinkFast

UplinkFast is used to minimize network downtime by ensuring that network loops do not occur when the network topology changes. The problem is that STP convergence time is very time-consuming, so network loops can occur when the convergence is taking place. UplinkFast can reduce the convergence time during a link failure or a topology change.

Another problem with STP and the convergence time is that some hosts will not be available for communication during the convergence time because STP has disabled ports on a switch during convergence. The key is decreased convergence time, which UplinkFast was developed to provide.

UplinkFast allows a blocked port on a switch to begin forwarding frames immediately when a link failure is detected. For the switch to change a port from blocking to forwarding mode, UplinkFast must have direct knowledge of the link failure.

In order to utilize UplinkFast, several criteria must be met. First, UplinkFast must be enabled on the switch. The switch must have at least one blocked port, and the failure must be on the root port. If the failure is not on a root port, UplinkFast will ignore it and normal STP functions will occur.

When a link fault occurs on the primary root link, UplinkFast transitions the blocked port to a forwarding state. UplinkFast changes the port without passing through the listening and learning phases, which allows the switch to skip the normal convergence time and start forwarding in about 3 to 4 seconds instead of the normal 50 seconds.

Cisco has designed UplinkFast to work with its access layer switches, not its core switches, because the switch running UplinkFast must not be the root bridge.

UplinkFast Configuration

When configuring UplinkFast, remember that all VLANs on the switch are affected and that you cannot configure UplinkFast on individual VLANs.

To configure UplinkFast on a set-based switch, use the `set spantree uplinkfast` command:

```
Todd5000> (enable) set spantree uplinkfast ?
Usage: set spantree uplinkfast <enable> [rate <station_update_rate>]
       [all-protocols <off|on>]
       set spantree uplinkfast <disable>
```

The options are really just enable or disable. However, the station update rate value is the number of multicast packets transmitted per 100 milliseconds (by default, it is set to 15 packets per millisecond). It is not recommended that you change this value.

The switch will provide you with an output describing what the command changed on the switch, as shown here:

```
Todd5000> (enable) set spantree uplinkfast enable
VLANs 1-1005 bridge priority set to 49152.
The port cost and portvlancost of all ports set to above 3000.
Station update rate set to 15 packets/100ms.
uplinkfast all-protocols field set to off.
uplinkfast enabled for bridge.
Todd5000> (enable)
```

The VLAN priorities are automatically changed to 49152 and the port costs are set to above 3000. These are changed to make it unlikely that the switch will become the root switch.

You can verify the UplinkFast configuration with the `show spantree uplinkfast` command:

```
Todd5000> (enable) show spantree uplinkfast
Station update rate set to 15 packets/100ms.
uplinkfast all-protocols field set to off.

VLAN            port list
-------------------------------------------------
1               1/1(fwd)
2               1/1(fwd)
3               1/1(fwd)
4               1/1(fwd)
Todd5000> (enable)
```

Notice that all four VLANs are changed and that we were not asked which VLANs to run UplinkFast on.

To configure UplinkFast on a 1900 switch, use the command `uplink-fast` in global configuration mode:

```
1900A#config t
1900A(config)#uplink-fast
1900A(config)#exit
```

To verify that UplinkFast is configured and running, use the commands `show uplink-fast` and `show uplink-fast statistics`:

```
1900A#show uplink-fast
  Uplink fast                              Enabled
  Uplink fast frame generation rate        15

1900A#show uplink-fast statistics
  Uplink fast Transitions                  0
  Uplink fast Station Learning Frames      0
1900A#
```

The default frame generation rate is 15, which is displayed with the `show uplink-fast` command. The next command used to help STP maintain a consistent network is BackboneFast.

BackboneFast

Sometimes a switch may receive from a designated switch a BPDU that identifies the root bridge and the designated bridge as the same switch. This shouldn't happen, and the BPDU is then considered inferior.

BPDUs are considered inferior when a link from the designated switch has lost its link to the root bridge. The designated switch transmits the BPDUs with the information that it is now the root bridge as well as the designated bridge. The receiving switch will ignore the inferior BPDU for the maxage time.

After receiving inferior BPDUs, the receiving switch will try to determine if there is an alternate path to the root bridge. If the port that the inferior BPDUs are received on is already in blocking mode, then the root port and other blocked ports on the switch become alternate paths to the root bridge. However, if the inferior BPDUs are received on a root port, then all presently blocking ports become the alternate paths to the root bridge. Also, if the inferior BPDUs are received on a root port and there are no other blocking ports on the switch, the receiving switch assumes that the link to the root bridge is down and the maximum aging time expires, which turns the switch into the root switch.

If the switch finds an alternate path to the root bridge, it will use this new alternate path. This new path, and any other alternate paths, will be used to send a Root Link Query BPDU. By turning on BackboneFast, the Root Link Query BPDUs are sent out as soon as an inferior BPDU is received. This basically can enable faster convergence in the event of a backbone link failure.

Configuring and Verifying BackboneFast

Configuring BackboneFast is pretty easy, but it sounds difficult, which is the cool part about this command. You turn it on with the set spantree backbonefast command. Here is an example of this command being enabled:

```
Todd5000> (enable) set spantree backbonefast
Usage: set spantree backbonefast <enable|disable>

Todd5000> (enable) set spantree backbonefast enable
Backbonefast enabled for all VLANs
```

Notice in the preceding switch output that BackboneFast is enabled for all VLANs and it must be enabled on all switches in your network to function. To verify that it is running on a switch, use the show spantree backbonefast command:

```
Todd5000> (enable) sh spantree backbonefast
Backbonefast is enabled.
Todd5000> (enable)
```

The above command shows that BackboneFast is enabled. That's all there is to it.

Summary

This chapter covered the detailed Spanning Tree Protocol information you need to be successful in the day-to-day maintenance of a layer 2 switched internetwork. Specifically, we covered the following:

- Cisco and the IEEE 802.1q committee
- Scaling the STP protocol
- Redundant links with STP
- Parallel FastEthernet links
- EtherChannel guidelines
- Port Aggregation Protocol
- PortFast
- UplinkFast
- BackboneFast

Key Terms

Before you take the exam, be sure you're familiar with the following terms:

Common Spanning Tree (CST)

Fast EtherChannel

Gigabit EtherChannel

Per-VLAN Spanning Tree (PVST)

Per-VLAN Spanning Tree+ (PVST+)

Commands Used in This Chapter

Access Layer Switch Commands (1900 Switch in This Book)	Meaning
`show spantree`	Displays the spanning tree information
`spantree start-forwarding`	Enables PortFast on an interface
`spantree cost`	Configures a cost for an interface
`spantree priority`	Configures the priority for an interface
`uplink-fast`	Turns on UplinkFast for the switch
`show uplink-fast`	Shows the UplinkFast parameters
`port-channel mode`	Enables an EtherChannel bundle
`show uplink-fast statistics`	Shows the UplinkFast statistics

Distribution Layer Switch Commands (5000 Switch in This Book)	Meaning
`set spantree root`	Makes a set-based switch a root bridge
`set port channel`	Creates an EtherChannel bundle
`show port channel`	Shows the status of an EtherChannel bundle
`show spantree`	Shows the state of the STP per VLAN
`set spantree portcost`	Sets the STP port cost
`set spantree portpri`	Sets the STP port priority
`set spantree portvlanpri`	Configures links to forward only certain VLANs

Distribution Layer Switch Commands (5000 Switch in This Book)	Meaning
`set spantree fwddelay`	Changes the forward delay time on a switch
`set spantree hello`	Changes the BPDU hello time on a switch
`set spantree maxage`	Sets how long a BPDU that is received will stay valid until another BPDU is received
`sh port capabilities`	Shows the configuration of individual ports
`set spantree portfast`	Enables PortFast on a port
`set spantree uplinkfast`	Enables UplinkFast on a port
`show spantree uplinkfast`	Shows the UplinkFast parameters and statistics
`set spantree backbonefast`	Enables BackboneFast for a switch

Written Lab

Write out the answers to the following questions:

1. Write the command to set a switch to the root for VLANs 50–1000 with four switches in the internetwork on a 5000 series switch.

2. What command will show you the port cost and priority for VLAN 1 on a set-based switch?

3. Write the command to set the port cost on a 5000 switch port 2/1 to 10 from the default of 19.

4. Write the command to set the switch priority for port 1/1 to 20.

5. Once you change your port priority, you can verify the configuration with which command?

6. Write the command to set port 1/1 priority on a set-based switch to 16 for VLANs 1 and 2 only.

7. Write the command to turn on PortFast on ports 2/1-12 on a set-based switch.

8. Write the command to set UplinkFast on a set-based switch to on.

9. Write the command to create an EtherChannel bundle on a set-based switch using port 1/1-2.

10. Write the command to change the fwddelay to 10 seconds on a set-based switch.

Hands-On Lab

In this lab, you'll test PortFast and UplinkFast on the network, then you'll configure the 5000 series switch as an STP root and add EtherChannel between the 5000 and 1900 switch. Figure 5.1 shows the network configuration used in this lab. Make sure the configurations of your switches are deleted and the default STP configuration is on both switches.

FIGURE 5.1 Network diagram for the hands-on lab

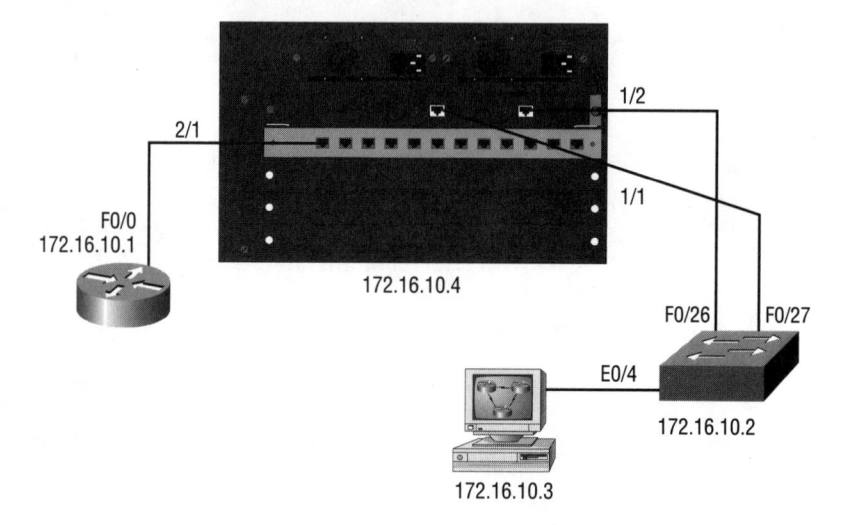

Configure both the 5000 series switch and the 1900 switch with the labs from Chapters 2 and 3. Each switch should have the hostname, interface descriptions, passwords, VTP domain information, and VLANs configured and trunked links on. Test by pinging from the workstation to the 1900 and 5000 switch.

1. Remember that PortFast is disabled on all ports of a switch by default. By turning on PortFast, you can start forwarding up to 50 seconds sooner when bringing up a device. To test this, connect your workstation into interface e0/4 of the 1900 switch and then from the DOS prompt of your workstation, ping the 5000 series switch.

   ```
   Ping -t 172.16.10.4
   ```

2. The –t will keep the ping running. Go to the 1900 switch and perform a **shut** and **no shut** on int e0/4, then notice how long it takes before the pings resume. This could be up to 50 seconds (although, if you have a small network, it may resume faster).

3. Leave the pings running. Go to int e0/4 and type **spantree start-forwarding**, which turns on PortFast for that port.

4. Go to the 1900 switch and perform a **shut**, then a **no shut** on e0/4. The pings will time out but should resume after only a few seconds.

5. Leave the Ping program running. Type **show spantree 1** and notice which port is forwarding and which port is blocking.

6. Leave the Ping program running. Perform a **shutdown** on the forwarding interface. Notice that the pings have timed out, but they should resume after a few seconds.

7. Type **show spantree 1** and notice which port is forwarding.

8. Perform a **no shutdown** on the port you originally shut down. Notice that the pings have timed out again, but the pings should resume after a few moments.

9. Turn on UplinkFast on your 1900 forwarding port by typing **uplink-fast** from global configuration mode.

10. Perform steps 5 through 8 again and notice that the ping's time-out and resume cycle was shorter. UplinkFast demonstrated an almost immediate transition to the second trunk link when the forwarding link was shut down.

11. Configure the 5000 series switch as the STP root switch by typing **set spantree root 1-4 dia 2** from the enable mode of the switch. The diameter of the network is determined by counting the switches connected to the root, including the root, which in this case is 2. The VLANs configured are 1–4.

12. Verify the configuration by typing **show spantree 1**. Notice the root designation.

13. Make sure your links are trunked by typing **show trunk** on the 5000 series switch.

14. Go to the 1900 and verify the forwarding port. Change the cost of the forwarding port to 20, which should make the blocked port the forwarding port. Type **spantree cost 20** from interface configuration of the forwarding port.

15. Verify the configuration with the **show spantree** command and notice that the blocked port is now forwarding and the forwarding port has been changed to blocked. Also notice the port costs.

16. Set the port priority on the forwarding port as well, to make sure that STP always uses this port to forward, by typing **spantree priority 64** from interface configuration, which is half of the 128 default interface priority.

17. Verify the configuration with the **show spantree** command.

18. Create an EtherChannel bundle between your two switches, but before you do, make sure your port configurations are exactly the same. Change the 1900 switch back to the default configuration. Type **spantree cost 10** and **spantree priority 128** from interface configuration mode. Also, set the duplex of the links to full duplex on both the 1900 and 5000. Set the 5000 to be 100Mbps as well.

19. From the 1900 interface configuration mode, type **duplex full** on both ports.

20. From the 5000 series switch, type **set port speed 100** and **set port duplex full** from port 1/1 and 1/2.

21. Set the EtherChannel bundle to on for the 1900 switch by typing **port-channel mode on** from global configuration mode.

22. From the 5000 series switch, turn on EtherChannel by typing **set port channel 1/1-2 on**.

23. Verify the EtherChannel bundle by typing **show port channel**.

Review Questions

1. The Spanning Tree Protocol was created to overcome the problems of what type of bridging?

    A. Source route bridging

    B. Shorter path bridging

    C. Transparent bridging

    D. UplinkFast bridging

2. Bridge Protocol Data Units (BPDUs) are responsible for providing information for which four services in a spanning tree?

    A. Determining the locations of data loops

    B. Electing a root bridge

    C. Monitoring the spanning tree

    D. Deciding the manufacturer's MAC address on a physical interface

    E. Notifying other switches of network changes

3. On what VLAN are Bridge Protocol Data Units (BPDUs) sent by default?

    A. VLAN 64

    B. VLAN 1005

    C. VLAN 1

    D. VLAN 10

4. Which of the following provides for a separate instance of Spanning Tree Protocol for every VLAN?

    A. Common Spanning Tree (CST)

    B. Spanning Tree Algorithm (STA)

    C. Port Aggregation Protocol (PAgP)

    D. Per-VLAN Spanning Tree (PVST)

5. To configure a backup root bridge on a set-based switch, what command would be used?

   A. `set spanning tree backup`

   B. `set spantree secondary`

   C. `set spantree root secondary`

   D. `spanning tree 2`

6. How many VLANs can be configured to support Spanning Tree Protocol on the 1900 switch?

   A. 1,005

   B. 10

   C. 512

   D. 64

7. Which of the following would change the VLAN port priority on an IOS command-based switch to a value of 16?

   A. `spantree priority 16`

   B. `set spantree priority 16`

   C. `config spantree priority 16`

   D. `change spantree pri 16`

8. When setting the VLAN port priority, what are the available values you can use?

   A. 0–63

   B. 1–64

   C. 0–255

   D. 1–1005

9. When you're using EtherChannel on your switches and a link failure occurs, what controlling device notifies the EARL of the failure?

   A. SAMBA

   B. CPU

   C. EBC

   D. SAINT

10. From which of the following can PAgP form a bundle?

    A. Only statically assigned VLAN ports

    B. Dynamically assigned VLAN ports

    C. Dynamically and statically assigned VLAN ports

    D. Ports using different duplex types

11. What will the STP use to choose a forwarding port if the port costs are equal on a switch?

    A. Port ID

    B. MAC address

    C. Bridge name

    D. Hello timer

12. What is used to make a point-to-point port enter almost immediately into forwarding state by decreasing the time of the listening and learning states?

    A. PortUp

    B. PortFast

    C. Priority

    D. BackboneFast

13. What protocol sends Root Link Query BPDUs upon receiving an inferior BPDU?

    A. PortUp

    B. PortFast

    C. Priority

    D. BackboneFast

14. Which of the following commands is used to create a bundle on a 5000 series switch?

    A. `port set channel`

    B. `set port channel`

    C. `etherchannel on`

    D. `set bundle slot/port`

15. Which of the following commands is used to turn on BackboneFast?

    A. `set port channel backbonefast`

    B. `set spantree backbonefast on`

    C. `set spantree backbonefast enable`

    D. `set bundle enable slot/port`

16. Which of the following is true regarding PVST+? (Choose all that apply.)

    A. It is a Cisco proprietary protocol.

    B. It adds checking mechanisms to make sure there are not configuration problems on trunked ports and VLAN IDs across switches.

    C. It is set on a port-by-port basis.

    D. It allows Cisco switches to support the IEEE 802.1q standard.

17. What is the IEEE implementation of the STP?

   A. CST

   B. PVST

   C. PVST+

   D. 802.1u

18. How many spanning tree instances are defined with the PVST protocol running on a switch with six VLANs configured?

   A. 1,005

   B. 1

   C. 6

   D. 64

19. How many spanning tree instances are defined with the CST protocol running on a switch with six VLANs configured?

   A. 1,005

   B. 1

   C. 6

   D. 64

20. Which three of the following can STP use to determine the best path to the root bridge?

   A. STP protocol

   B. Port cost

   C. Path cost

   D. Bridge priority

   E. Port priority

Answers to Written Lab

1. `set spantree root 50-1000 dia 4`
2. `show spantree 1`
3. `set spantree portcost 2/1 10`
4. `set spantree portpri 1/1 20`
5. `show spantree 1/1`
6. `set spantree portvlanpri 1/1 16 1-2`
7. `set spantree portfast 2/1-12 enable`
8. `set spantree uplinkfast enable`
9. `set port channel 1/1-2 on`
10. `set spantree fwddelay 10`

Answers to Review Questions

1. **C.** The Spanning Tree Protocol was designed to help stop networks loops that can happen with transparent bridge networks running redundant links.

2. **A, B, C, E.** The Bridge Protocol Data Units are sent out every 2 seconds by default and provide information to switches throughout the internetwork. This includes finding redundant links, electing the root bridge, monitoring the links in the spanning tree, and notifying other switches in the network about link failures.

3. **C.** VLAN 1 is a default VLAN and used for management by default.

4. **D.** The Cisco proprietary protocol Per-VLAN Spanning Tree (PVST) uses a separate instance of spanning tree for each and every VLAN.

5. **C.** The `set spantree root secondary` command allows you to configure a backup root bridge.

6. **D.** The 1900 switch can support up to 1,005 VLANs but only up to 64 STP instances.

7. **A.** On an IOS-based switch, a 1900 for example, use the `spantree priority 16` from interface configuration to change the port priority.

8. **A.** A priority from 0 to 63 can be set for each VLAN.

9. **C.** Should one link in the bundle fail, the Ethernet Bundle Controller (EBC) informs the Enhanced Address Recognition Logic (EARL) ASIC of the failure, and the EARL in turn ages out all addresses learned on that link.

10. **A.** PAgP bundled ports must all be configured the same, including the duplex and speed. Also, dynamic VLANs will not work, so VLANs must be assigned statically or they all must be trunked ports.

11. **A.** The switch will use the port ID to find the best forwarding port if the link costs are equal.

12. **B.** PortFast is used to put a blocked port into forwarding state immediately upon a boot up of a point-to-point device such as a workstation or server.

13. **D.** When BackboneFast is turned on, the Root Link Query BPDUs are sent out as soon as an inferior BPDU is received. This basically can enable faster convergence in the event of a backbone link failure.

14. **B.** The command `set port channel [slot/port] [on/off]` is used to create an EtherChannel bundle.

15. **C.** To enable BackboneFast on a switch, use the `set spantree backbonefast enable` command, which turns the protocol on for every VLAN.

16. **A, B, D.** PVST is proprietary to Cisco and PVST+ is an extension of PVST. PVST+ allows non-PVST information to be accepted and received into PVST, adds configuration checking, and allows Cisco switches to support 802.1q.

17. **A.** The IEEE uses what is called Common Spanning Tree (CST), which is defined with IEEE 802.1q. The IEEE 802.1q defines one spanning tree instance for all VLANs.

18. **C.** The PVST protocol defines one instance of STP per VLAN.

19. **B.** The CST protocol defines one instance of STP per network regardless of the amount of VLANs configured.

20. **B, C, E.** The port cost, path cost, and port priority are used to determine the best path to the root bridge.

Chapter 6

Inter-VLAN Routing

THE CCNP EXAM TOPICS COVERED IN THIS CHAPTER INCLUDE THE FOLLOWING:

- ✓ Inter-VLAN routing issues and solutions
- ✓ Configuring inter-VLAN routing
- ✓ Configuring internal route processors
- ✓ Configuring external route processors

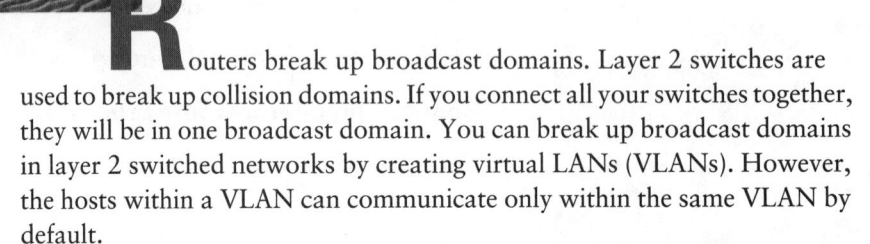

Routers break up broadcast domains. Layer 2 switches are used to break up collision domains. If you connect all your switches together, they will be in one broadcast domain. You can break up broadcast domains in layer 2 switched networks by creating virtual LANs (VLANs). However, the hosts within a VLAN can communicate only within the same VLAN by default.

For devices in one VLAN to communicate with devices in a different VLAN, they must be routed through a layer 3 device. This is called *inter-VLAN* routing. You can perform inter-VLAN routing with internal route processors in a layer 2 switch or with an external router called an *external route processor*.

In this chapter, we will cover both internal route processors, known as Route Switch Modules (RSMs), and external route processors and how to configure them for inter-VLAN configuration.

Routing between VLANs

A VLAN's main job is to keep local traffic local, which it does very well. We have already mentioned in this book that you cannot communicate between VLANs without a router (layer 3 device), so understanding the configuration of VLANs and understanding routing go hand in hand.

Route processors provide the communication that hosts need between VLANs. However, if you are using local VLANs (see Chapter 3 for a thorough explanation), you want to design your networks so at least 80 percent of the users' traffic does not cross over into another VLAN. Therefore, you should design the network so that the users have access to local servers and other needed resources to prevent excessive packets from crossing the route processor.

VLANs should be configured one for one with IP subnet designs. What this means is that you need to create a subnet mask for your network, then design your VLANs around the subnet design. For example, if you have engineering, marketing, sales, and support departments, you will typically—not always, but typically—create a subnet for each department, making sure you have room for growth. You would then create a VLAN for each department. In Chapter 3, we discussed the difference between local and end-to-end VLANs. Regardless of the type of VLAN you configure, each of these types would associate with a subnet.

Each device within a VLAN would have a default gateway of the inter-VLAN device connected to its LAN. The inter-VLAN device would then route any packets with a destination not on the local network.

Before configuring routing between your VLANs, you need to understand the type of data sharing that is needed. By understanding the user and business needs, you can design the network with load balancing and/or redundant links if needed.

There are basically three options that you can choose from:

- Multiple links
- A single trunked link
- Route Switch Module (RSM)

Multiple Links

You can configure your VLANs to communicate by connecting a router interface into a switch port that is configured for each VLAN. Each workstation in the VLAN would have its default gateway configured for this router interface. Figure 6.1 shows how this might look in an internetwork.

FIGURE 6.1 Routers with multiple links

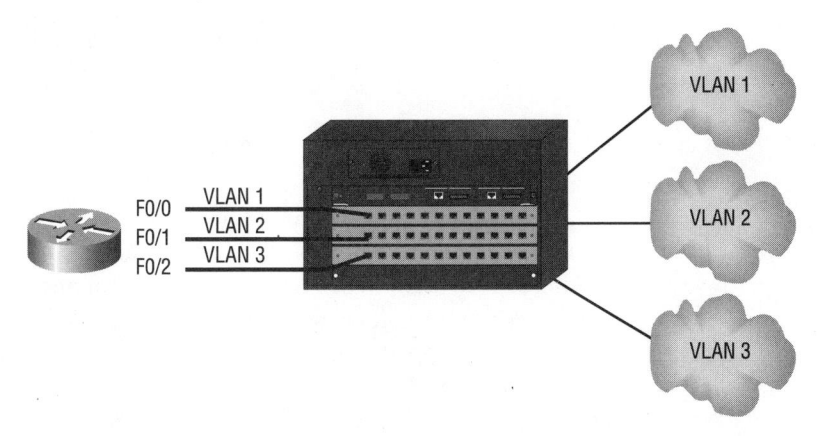

This is not a bad solution, but it does not scale well when you have over four or so VLANs. It depends on the type of router you have. For every VLAN, you need to have a router interface (typically FastEthernet or Gigabit Ethernet) so a larger, more expensive router can have more interfaces without being saturated.

The more VLANs you have, the more router interfaces you have to purchase with the router. Also, you should have a fast router like a high-end (at least a 4700 or 7000 series) router that can route quickly so the router does not become a bottleneck. Cost then becomes the issue with multiple links.

A Single Trunked Link

Another possible solution to routing between VLANs is creating a trunked link on a switch and then using a frame tagging protocol such as ISL or 802.1q (which are used to identify frames as they traverse FastEthernet and Gigabit Ethernet links) on the router. Cisco calls this solution "router on a stick."

Figure 6.2 shows how the internetwork might look with a single trunked link for all VLANs.

FIGURE 6.2 Single trunked link for all VLANs

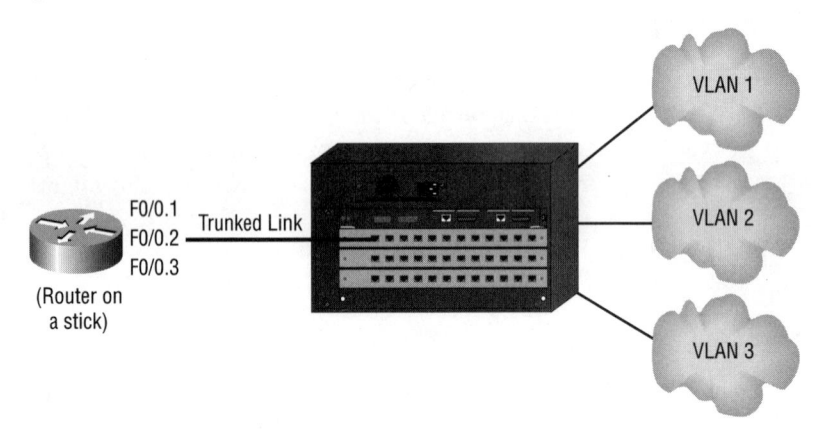

This solution uses only one router interface on the router, but it also puts all the traffic on one interface. You really have to have a fast router to do this. Also, to even perform this function, you need at minimum a FastEthernet interface on a 2600 series router. ISL does not work on 10BaseT interfaces, nor would you want to run this on 10BaseT because it is processor and bandwidth intensive.

There are some really nice high-end routers that provide multi-layer switching by communicating to a NetFlow Feature Card (NFFC) in the Cisco Catalyst 5000 series of switches. The routers must have the IOS versions of 11.3.4 or later and run the MultiLayer Switch Protocol (MLSP). The routers that support this are the 7500, 7200, 4500, and 4700 series of routers.

Route Switch Modules (RSMs)

Route Switch Modules (RSMs) are also called *internal route processors* because the processing of layer 3 packets is internal to a switch. You need to add an RSM to a layer 2 device—for example, a 5000 Catalyst switch—to be able to provide switching of layer 3 packets without a router.

An RSM makes layer 2 switches a multi-layer switch and can integrate layer 2 and layer 3 functionality in a single box. The 5000 series uses the RSM or a *Route Switch Feature Card (RSFC)*, and the 6000 series uses the Multilayer Switch Module (MSM) to perform this function. The RSM, RSFC, and MSM are configured in exactly the same way on the switch.

The RSM is a module plugged directly into the switch, which runs the Cisco IOS in order to perform inter-VLAN communication. The 5000 series switch sees the RSM as a single trunked port and a single MAC address. In other words, it appears as a router on a stick to the switch. The RSM interface to the switch is through VLAN 0 and VLAN 1. VLAN 0 is not accessible to the administrator. The RSM uses two channels, and VLAN 0 maps to channel 0, which supports communication between the RSM and the Catalyst 5000 series default VLAN (VLAN 1). VLAN 1 maps to channel 1. The MAC address assigned to the RSM is from the Programmable Read Only Memory (PROM) on the line communication processor (LCP). This MAC address is used to identify the slot of the RSM and for diagnostics. The MAC addresses for VLAN 1 are assigned from a PROM that contains 512 MAC addresses. All routing interfaces except VLAN 0 use the base MAC address.

The RSFC is a daughter card for the Supervisor Engine II G and Supervisor III G cards. The RSFC is a fully functioning router running the Cisco IOS.

The MSM uses four full-duplex Gigabit Ethernet interfaces to connect to the switch and looks like an external router to the switch. These four interfaces can be four separate links for four different VLANs, or they can be trunked and configured as one load-balanced link running EtherChannel and ISL or 802.1q. Subinterfaces are then used to configure each VLAN.

Inter-Switch Link Routing

The best solution to inter-VLAN routing is to provide a Gigabit Ethernet router interface for each VLAN. However, we have found that this can be cost prohibitive. What if you have 500 VLANs? Can you really afford a router with 500 Gigabit Ethernet ports? That would be an interesting configuration.

Cisco to the rescue! You can use either one FastEthernet or one Gigabit Ethernet interface for all your VLANs. Cisco has created the proprietary protocol Inter-Switch Link (ISL) to allow routing between VLANs with only one Ethernet interface. To run ISL, you need to have two VLAN-capable FastEthernet or Gigabit Ethernet devices, such as a Cisco 5000 switch and a 7000 series router.

Remember from Chapter 3 that ISL is a way of explicitly tagging VLAN information onto an Ethernet frame? This tagging information allows VLANs to be multiplexed over a trunk link through an external encapsulation method. By running ISL, you can interconnect multiple switches and still maintain VLAN information as traffic travels between switches on trunk links.

Configuring ISL

You can configure inter-VLAN routing with either an external router or an internal route processor that can be placed in a slot of a Catalyst switch. In this section, we'll take a look at both options.

External

An external layer 3 device can be used to provide routing between VLANs. You can use almost any router to perform this function, but FastEthernet or Gigabit Ethernet is suggested. If you have many small VLANs that perform at least 80 percent or more of their network function on the local VLAN, then you can probably get away with a 10Mbps Ethernet connection into each VLAN. Still, you should get FastEthernet if you can.

The external router can be configured to have one Ethernet interface for each VLAN, or you can use trunking protocols like ISL or 802.1q to configure one FastEthernet or Gigabit Ethernet for all the VLANs that use subinterfaces. These subinterfaces give you an extremely flexible solution for providing routing between VLANs. To perform ISL routing on a single interface, the interface must be at least a FastEthernet interface that supports ISL routing. The Cisco 2600 is the least expensive router that can perform this function.

To configure ISL routing on a single interface, you must configure subinterfaces. These are configured by using the *type int.subinterface_number* command. Here is an example on a 2600 router with a FastEthernet interface:

```
Router#config t
Enter configuration commands, one per line.  End with CNTL/Z.
Router(config)#int f0/0.?
  <0-4294967295>  FastEthernet interface number

Router(config)#int f0/0.1
Router(config-subif)#
```

Notice the amount of subinterfaces available (4.2 billion). You can choose any number that feels good because they are only locally significant to the router. However, we usually like to choose the VLAN number for ease of administration. Notice that the prompt on the router is now telling you that you are configuring a subinterface (`config-subif`).

Once you configure the subinterface number you want, you then need to define the type of encapsulation you are going to use. Here is an example of the different types of trunking protocols you can use:

```
Router(config-subif)#encap ?
  dot1Q   IEEE 802.1Q Virtual LAN
  isl     Inter Switch Link - Virtual LAN encapsulation
  sde     IEEE 802.10 Virtual LAN - Secure Data Exchange
  tr-isl  Token Ring Inter Switch Link - Virtual LAN  encapsulation
```

You're not done yet. You need to tell the subinterface which VLAN it is a member of, and you provide this information on the same line as the encapsulation command. Here is an example:

```
Router(config-subif)#encap isl ?
  <1-1000>  Virtual LAN Identifier.
```

Notice that you can configure the subinterface to be a part of any VLAN up to 1000. The dot1q encapsulation is for the IEEE standard 802.1q trunking. ISL is for ISL encapsulation.

After you choose the interface and encapsulation type and VLAN number, configure the IP address this subinterface is a member of. The complete configuration would look like this:

```
Router#config t
Enter configuration commands, one per line.  End with CNTL/Z.
Router(config)#int f0/0.1
Router(config-subif)#encap isl 1
Router(config-subif)#ip address 172.16.10.1 255.255.255.0
```

The above configuration is for subinterface f0/0.1 to VLAN 1. You would create a subinterface for each VLAN. You can verify your configuration with the `show running-config` command:

```
!
interface FastEthernet0/0.1
 encapsulation isl 1
 ip address 172.16.10.1 255.255.255.0
!
```

Internal

If you do not have an external router or if you have many VLANs, you should use a Route Switch Module (RSM) or Route Switch Feature Card (RSFC) to provide the layer 3 routing for your 5000 series switch.

The first thing you need to type in is the `show module` command so you can see the RSM. Notice in the switch output below that the 5000 switch has an RSFC in slot 1, but it is in module 15. This information will allow you to connect and configure the internal route processor:

```
Todd5000> (enable) sh module
Mod Slot Ports Module-Type              Model         Status
--- ---- ----- ------------------------ ------------- --------
1   1    2     1000BaseX Supervisor IIIG WS-X5550     ok
15  1    1     Route Switch Feature Card WS-F5541     ok
2   2    24    10/100BaseTX Ethernet    WS-X5225R     ok
3   3    2     UTP OC-3 Dual-Phy ATM    WS-X5156      ok
13  13         ASP/SRP

Mod Module-Name         Serial-Num
--- ------------------- -------------------
1                       00014364176
15                      14452699
2                       00017581709
3                       00014173130

Mod MAC-Address(es)                          Hw     Fw      Sw
--- ---------------------------------------- ------ ------- -----------
1   00-b0-c2-b2-d0-00 to 00-b0-c2-b2-d3-ff  1.1    5.1(1)  5.2(1)
15  00-30-f2-c8-11-00 to 00-30-f2-c8-11-3f  1.0    12.0(3c)W5 12.0(3c)W5(8a),
2   00-30-7b-36-2b-50 to 00-30-7b-36-2b-67  3.3    4.3(1)  5.2(1)
3   00-10-7b-42-e7-da                       2.4    1.3     11.3(8)WA4(11a)3.2(13)
```

Not only does the command `show module` provide the module and slot that each card is in, it provides the serial number and the modules' MAC addresses. Once you find the module number, you can then connect to that module using the `session` command. Here is an example:

```
Todd5000> (enable)
Todd5000> (enable) session 15
Trying Router-15...
Connected to Router-15.
Escape character is '^]'.
```

Chapter 6 · Inter-VLAN Routing

You are now connected to the internal route processor and can continue to configure the device like any other router. Notice in the router output below that we set the hostname and routing protocol as well:

```
Router>
Router>ena
Router#
Router#config t
Enter configuration commands, one per line.  End with CNTL/Z.
Router(config)#hostname ToddRSM
ToddRSM(config)#router eigrp 10
ToddRSM(config-router)#netw 172.16.0.0
```

As we mentioned, the route processor looks like any Cisco router, which is a really nice feature. It's just as important to configure the routing protocols on this device as it is to configure them on any other router.

Before we continue with configuring VLANs on the internal route processor, let's take a look at another 5000 series switch that has a Route Switch Module:

```
Todd5000> (enable) sh module
Mod  Module-Name   Ports  Module-Type            Model      Serial-Num  Status
---  -----------   -----  ---------------------  ---------  ----------  -------
1                  2      100BaseTX Supervisor   WS-X5509   005147178   ok
2                  12     10/100BaseTX Ethernet  WS-X5213A  005153813   ok
4                         Route Switch Ext Port
5                  1      Route Switch           WS-X5304   018465234   ok

Mod  MAC-Address(es)                            Hw   Fw          Sw
---  ----------------------------------------   ---  ----------  --------
1    00-e0-34-88-fc-00 to 00-e0-34-88-ff-ff     1.8  5.1(2)      4.5(5)
2    00-e0-1e-11-73-64 to 00-e0-1e-11-73-6f     1.1  1.4         4.5(5)
5    00-e0-1e-90-d2-bc to 00-e0-1e-90-d2-bd     7.6  20.14       11.3(8)WA4(11)

Mod  Sub-Type  Sub-Model  Sub-Serial  Sub-Hw
---  --------  ---------  ----------  ------
1    EARL 1+   WS-F5511   0005059935  1.1
```

Notice that the RSM on the 5000 series is in module 5. To configure the RSM, we would type **session 5**, as shown below:

```
Todd5000> (enable) session 5
Trying Router-5...
Connected to Router-5.
Escape character is '^]'.
```

```
Router>en
Router#
```

Once we have entered the CLI of the RSM, you can see that the Router# prompt appears just as it does on the RSFC. They are configured exactly the same.

Creating VLANs on an RSM

Instead of creating subinterfaces as you would with an external router, you configure each VLAN with the int vlan # command. Here is an example of how to configure the processor to route between three VLANs:

```
ToddRSM#config t
ToddRSM(config)#int vlan 1
ToddRSM(config-if)#ip address 172.16.1.1 255.255.255.0
ToddRSM(config-if)#int vlan 2
ToddRSM(config-if)#ip address 172.16.2.1 255.255.255.0
ToddRSM(config-if)#int vlan 3
ToddRSM(config-if)#ip address 172.16.3.1 255.255.255.0
ToddRSM(config-if)#no shut
```

The interesting part of the configuration is the necessary no shutdown command for each VLAN interface. Notice in the configuration above that we only performed a no shut on interface vlan 3. Take a look at the output of interface vlan 2:

```
ToddRSM#sh int vlan 2
Vlan2 is administratively down, line protocol is down
   Hardware is Cat5k RP Virtual Ethernet, address is
0030.f2c8.1138 (bia 0030.f2c8.1138)
```

It is important to think of each VLAN interface as a separate interface that needs an `IP address` and a `no shutdown` performed, just as with any other router interface.

You can then verify your configuration with the `show running-config` command:

```
ToddRSM#sh run
Current configuration:
!
version 12.0
service timestamps debug uptime
service timestamps log uptime
no service password-encryption
!
hostname ToddRSM
!
interface Vlan1
 ip address 172.16.1.1 255.255.255.0
!
interface Vlan2
 ip address 172.16.2.1 255.255.255.0
!
interface Vlan3
 ip address 172.16.3.1 255.255.255.0
!
router eigrp 10
 network 172.16.0.0
```

To view the routing table on the internal processor, use the `show ip route` command:

```
ToddRSM#sh ip route
Codes: C - connected, S - static, I - IGRP, R - RIP, M -
[output cut]
Gateway of last resort is not set

     172.16.0.0/24 is subnetted, 3 subnets
C       172.16.3.0 is directly connected, Vlan3
```

```
C        172.16.2.0 is directly connected, Vlan2
C        172.16.1.0 is directly connected, Vlan1
C    127.0.0.0/8 is directly connected, Vlan0
ToddRSM#
```

OK, the most interesting part about the difference between the RSM and an external router is the presence of VLAN0. Notice in the show ip route output above that VLAN0 is connected via 127.0.0.0/8, which is a diagnostic IP address. Remember that VLAN0 cannot be accessed by an administrator and is used to provide support for the communication between the RSM and the Catalyst 5000 switch.

Assigning MAC Addresses to VLAN Interfaces

The RSM uses only one global MAC address for all VLAN interfaces on the device. If you want to assign a specific MAC address to a VLAN interface, use the mac-address command. You may want to configure this option to enhance the operation of the RSM interface. Here is an example:

```
ToddRSM#config t
ToddRSM(config)#int vlan 2
ToddRSM(config-if)#mac-address 4004.0144.0011
ToddRSM(config-if)#exit
ToddRSM(config)#exit
ToddRSM#sh run
[oputput cut]
interface Vlan2
 mac-address 4004.0144.0011
 ip address 172.16.2.1 255.255.255.0
```

Defining a Default Gateway

One thing to keep in mind before configuring ISL on your switches is that the switches must be configured correctly with an IP address, subnet mask, and default gateway. Understand that this has nothing to do with routing because the switches work only at layer 2. However, the switches need to communicate with IP through the network. Remember that this will not affect data that is passing through the switch. You can think of layer 2 switches as being just like any host on the network. To be able to send packets off the local network, you need to have a default gateway configured.

To configure a default gateway on a 5000 series switch, use the `set ip route` command:

```
Todd5000> (enable) set ip route 0.0.0.0 172.16.1.1
Route added.
```

You can also use the command `set ip route default 172.16.1.1`, which will configure the route the same as the `set ip route 0.0.0.0 172.16.1.1` will.

> **NOTE:** The 1900 switch `default-gateway` command was covered in Chapter 2.

Summary

In this chapter, we described inter-VLAN routing issues and solutions. Because routers are needed to allow hosts on different networks to communicate, you also need to remember that a layer 3 device, either an external router or an internal route processor, is needed to allow inter-VLAN communication.

We discussed both internal route processors, known as Route Switch Modules (RSMs), and external route processors and showed you how to use them for inter-VLAN configuration.

Key Terms

Before you take the exam, be sure you're familiar with the following terms:

external route processor

internal route processors

inter-VLAN routing

Route Switch Feature Card (RSFC)

Route Switch Modules (RSMs)

Commands Used in This Chapter

This chapter showed how to configure only a distribution layer switch, so there is no listing for the access layer commands.

Commands	Meaning
`session`	Connects the CLI to a session on a route processor module
`set ip route`	Configures a default route on a set-based switch
`show config`	Shows the configuration of the 5000 series switch
`show module`	Shows the module and numbers of cards in the switch
`interface vlan`	Enables interface configuration mode for the specified VLAN interface
`mac-address`	Sets a specific MAC address on an interface

Written Lab

Complete this lab by writing out the answers to the following questions.

1. Write the command to configure ISL routing for VLAN 1 with an IP address of 172.16.10.0 on FastEthernet interface 0/0.

2. Write the command to view the different type of cards in a 5000 series switch.

3. Write the command to connect to an RSM module in slot 3.

4. Write the command to configure two VLANs on an RSM. VLAN 1 has an IP address of 172.16.1.1, and VLAN 2 has an IP address of 172.16.2.1.

5. Write the command to set a hardware address on the VLAN 2 interface of 4004.0144.0011.

6. What type of link is needed to run ISL routing on a FastEthernet interface?

7. What is the IEEE version of ISL?

8. True/False: You can assign a MAC address to a VLAN ISL interface.

9. How many VLANs can you create with subinterfaces on a FastEthernet interface?

10. What command would you use to see the configuration on a Catalyst 5000 switch?

Hands-On Lab

In this lab, you will configure a 5000 series switch, two 1900 switches, and one 2621 router to provide ISL routing between VLANs.

This section will provide two labs:

Lab 6.1 External Inter-VLAN Routing

Lab 6.2 Internal Inter-VLAN Routing

In both of the labs, refer to Figure 6.3 for configuring inter-VLAN communication.

FIGURE 6.3 Configuring inter-VLAN communication for hands-on lab

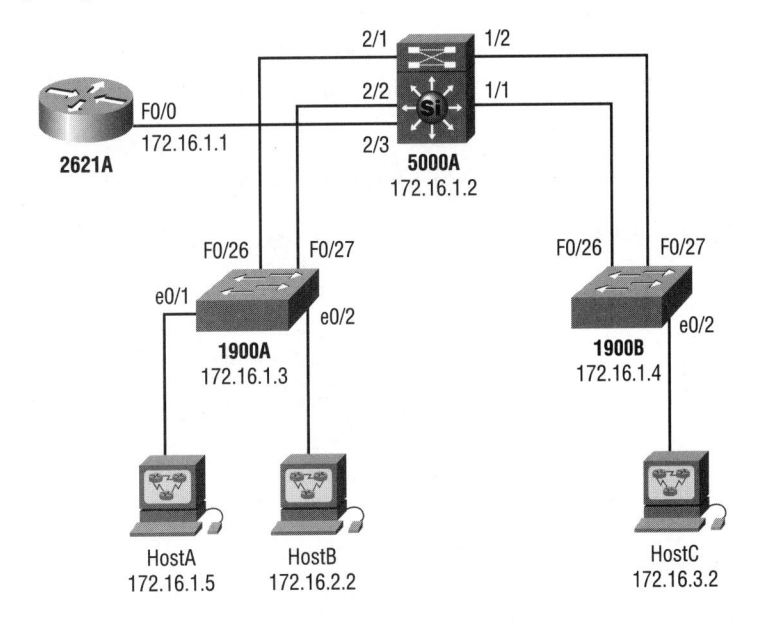

Lab 6.1: External Inter-VLAN Routing

In this first lab, you'll configure the 2621 with ISL routing. You'll start with configuring the two 1900 switches, then the 5000 switch, and then the 2621 router.

Configuring the 1900A Switch

1. Plug into the 1900A console port and press k to enter the CLI.

2. Enter privileged mode by typing **enable**.

3. Enter configuration mode and set the hostname.

   #config t
   (config)#**hostname 1900A**

4. Set the usermode and privilege mode passwords.

   1900A(config)#**enable password level 1 cisco**
   1900A(config)#**enable secret todd**

5. Set the IP address of the switch by using the IP address assigned in Figure 6.3. Set the default gateway address by using the interface f0/0 of the 2621 as the gateway.

   1900A(config)#**ip address 172.16.1.3 255.255.255.0**
   1900A(config)#**ip default-gateway 172.16.1.1**

6. Verify the IP configuration on the switch by typing **show ip**.

7. Set the VTP domain to SwitchSim and then make the switch a VTP client so that when you set the VLANs on the 5000 switch, the 1900A switch will automatically be updated with VLAN information.

   1900A(config)#**vtp domain SwitchSim**
   1900A(config)#**vtp client**

8. Set the FastEthernet interfaces to trunk on so that all VLAN information will be sent down both links from the 5000 series switch.

   1900A(config)#**int f0/26**
   1900A(config-if)#**trunk on**
   1900A(config-if)#**int f0/27**
   1900Aconfig-if)#**trunk on**

9. Configure the FastEthernet connection to the 5000 series switch to be full duplex.

   1900A(config)#**int f0/26**
   1900A(config-if)#**duplex full**
   1900A(config-if)#**int f0/27**
   1900A(config-if)#**duplex full**

Configuring the 1900B Switch

1. Plug into the 1900B switch console port and press k to enter the CLI.

2. Enter privileged mode by typing **enable**.

3. Enter configuration mode and set the hostname.

   #**config t**
   (config)#**hostname 1900B**

4. Set the usermode and privilege mode passwords.

   1900B(config)#**enable password level 1 cisco**
   1900B(config)#**enable secret todd**

5. Set the IP address of the switch by using the IP address assigned in Figure 6.3. Set the default gateway address by using the interface f0/0 of the 2621 as the gateway.

   1900B(config)#**ip address 172.16.1.4 255.255.255.0**
   1900B(config)#**ip default-gateway 172.16.1.1**

6. Verify the IP configuration on the switch by typing **show ip**.

7. Set the VTP domain to Routersim and then make the switch a VTP client so that when you set the VLANs on the 5000 switch, the 1900B switch will automatically be updated with VLAN information.

   1900B(config)#**vtp domain SwitchSim**
   1900B(config)#**vtp client**

8. Set the FastEthernet interfaces to trunk on so that all VLAN information will be sent down both links from the 5000 series switch.

   1900B(config)#**int f0/26**
   1900B(config-if)#**trunk on**
   1900B(config-if)#**int f0/27**
   1900B(config-if)#**trunk on**

9. Configure the FastEthernet connection to the 5000 series switch to be full duplex.

   ```
   1900B(config)#int f0/26
   1900B(config-if)#duplex full
   1900B(config-if)#int f0/27
   1900B(config-if)#duplex full
   ```

10. Set the ports to configure an EtherChannel bundle when the 5000 series is configured. This can be run only on the supervisor card or a specific EtherChannel card. EtherChannel will be run only on the 1900B connection to the 5000 switch.

    ```
    1900B(config-if)#port-channel mode on
    ```

Configuring the 5000 Series Switch

1. Connect your console cable to the 5000 series switch and press Enter. Press Enter at the password prompt, then again at the password prompt, type **enable** and press Enter.

2. Set the hostname of the switch.

   ```
   #(enable)set prompt Cat5000>
   ```

3. Set the usermode and privilege mode passwords.

   ```
   Cat5000>(enable)set password [press enter]
   Enter old password: [press enter]
   Enter new password: [this doesn't show]
   Retype new password: [this doesn't show]
   Password changed.
   Cat5000> (enable)set enablepass
   Enter old password:[press enter]
   Enter new password: [this doesn't show]
   Retype new password: [this doesn't shoow]
   Password changed.
   Cat5000> (enable)
   ```

4. Set the IP address and default gateway of the switch.

   Cat5000>(enable)**set int sc0 172.16.1.2 255.255.255.0**
   Cat5000>(enable)**set route default 172.16.1.1**

5. Verify this configuration by typing **show int**.

6. Set the VTP domain name to SwitchSim.

   Cat5000>(enable)**set vtp domain SwitchSim**

7. Set all ports connected to the 1900 switches as 100Mbps and full duplex. The two ports on the supervisor engine are labeled 1/1 and 1/2 and only run in 100Mbps, so only the duplex can be set on those ports.

   Cat5000> (enable) **set port duplex 1/1 full**
   Port(s) 1/1-2 set to full-duplex.
   Cat5000> (enable) **set port duplex 1/2 full**
   Port(s) 1/1-2 set to full-duplex.
   Cat5000> (enable) **set port speed 2/1 100**
   Port(s) 2/1 speed set to 100Mbps.
   Cat5000> (enable) **set port speed 2/2 100**
   Port(s) 2/2 speed set to 100Mbps.
   Cat5000> (enable) **set port duplex 2/1 full**
   Port(s) 2/1 set to full-duplex.
   Cat5000> (enable) **set port duplex 2/2 full**
   Port(s) 2/2 set to full-duplex.
   Cat5000> (enable)

8. It is possible that the ports on the 5000 may have been disabled because of mismatched port configurations between the 1900 and 5000. Type the command **show port slot/port** to see the status. If it is disabled, use the **set port enable slot/port** command.

   Cat5000> (enable) **set port enable 1/1**
   Port 1/1 enabled.

9. Configure trunking on all ports connected to the 1900A and 1900B switches.

   ```
   Cat5000> (enable) set trunk 2/1 on isl
   Port(s) 2/1 trunk mode set to on.
   Port(s) 2/1 trunk type set to isl.
   Cat5000> (enable) set trunk 2/2 on isl
   Port(s) 2/2 trunk mode set to on.
   Port(s) 2/2 trunk type set to isl.
   Cat5000> (enable) set trunk 1/1 on isl
   Port(s) 1/1-2 trunk mode set to on.
   Port(s) 1/1-2 trunk type set to isl.
   Cat5000> (enable) set trunk 1/2 on isl
   Port(s) 1/1-2 trunk mode set to on.
   Port(s) 1/1-2 trunk type set to isl.
   ```

10. Verify that the trunk ports are working by typing **show trunk**.

    ```
    Cat5000>(enable)show trunk
    Port      Mode          Encapsulation  Status     Native vlan
    --------  ------------  -------------  ---------  -----------
    1/1       on            isl            trunking   1
    1/2       on            isl            trunking   1
    2/1       on            isl            trunking   1
    2/2       on            isl            trunking   1
    5/1       on            isl            trunking   1
    ```

    [output cut]

11. Configure EtherChannel on both ports connected to the 1900B switch.

    ```
    Cat5000> (enable) set port channel 1/1-2 on
    Port(s) 1/1-2 channel mode set to on.
    ```

12. Verify that the EtherChannel is working by typing **show channel**.

```
Cat5000> (enable) show port channel
Port  Status      Channel   Channel    Neighbor         Neighbor
                  mode      status     device           port
----- ----------  --------  ---------- ---------------  -----
1/1   connected   on        channel    cisco 1900 1900B A
1/2   connected   on        channel    cisco 1900 1900B B
----- ----------  --------  ---------- ---------------  -----
Cat5000> (enable)
```

13. At this point, the three switches should be up and working and you should be able to ping all devices in the 172.16.1.0 network.

```
Cat5000> (enable) ping 172.16.1.3
172.16.1.3 is alive
Cat5000> (enable) ping 172.16.1.4
172.16.1.4 is alive
```

Configuring VLANs

Because the 5000 series switch is a VTP server and the two 1900 switches are VTP clients, you can configure VLANs on just the 5000 series switch and the 5000 switch will automatically update the VTP NVRAM on the 1900 switches.

1. On the 5000 series switch console, create two new VLANs.

VLAN 2: Sales

VLAN 3: Admin

```
Cat5000> (enable) set vlan 2 name Sales
Vlan 2 configuration successful
Cat5000> (enable) set vlan 3 name Admin
Vlan 3 configuration successful
Cat5000>(enable)
```

2. Type the command **show vlan** to view the configured VLANs on the switch.

```
Cat5000>(enable)sh vlan
VLAN Name                   Status    IfIndex  Mod/Ports, Vlans
---- ----------------       --------  -------  ----------------
1    default                active    5        2/3-12
2    Sales                  active    10
3    Admin                  active    11
1002 fddi-default           active    6
1003 token-ring-default     active    9
1004 fddinet-default        active    7
1005 trnet-default          active    8        1003
[output cut]
```

3. Verify that VTP is up and running correctly by telneting into 1900A and 1900B and typing **show vlan**. The same VLANs should appear if VTP if working properly. If not, verify that you spelled the VTP domain the same on all switches.

4. Configure HostA to be in VLAN 1, HostB to be in VLAN 2, and HostC to be in VLAN 3.

```
1900A#config t
Enter configuration commands, one per line.  End with CNTL/Z
1900A(config)#int e0/1
1900A(config-if)#vlan-membership static 1
1900A(config-if)#int e0/2
1900A(config-if)#vlan-membership static 2

1900B#config t
Enter configuration commands, one per line.  End with CNTL/Z
1900B(config)#int e0/2
1900B(config-if)#vlan-membership static 3
```

5. Type the **show vlan** command on the 1900B switch and verify that e0/2 is a member of VLAN 3. Type the same command on 1900A and verify that e0/1 is a member of VLAN 1 and e0/2 is a member of VLAN 2.

   ```
   1900B#sh vlan
   VLAN Name                         Status      Ports
   ---------------------------------------------------
   1    default                      Enabled     1, 3-12, AUI, A, B
   2    Sales                        Enabled
   3    Admin                        Enabled     2
   [output cut]
   1900A#sh vlan
   VLAN Name                         Status      Ports
   ---------------------------------------------------
   1    default                      Enabled     1, 3-12, AUI, A, B
   2    Sales                        Enabled     2
   3    Admin                        Enabled
   [output cut]
   ```

6. Configure each host with the following IP addresses:

   HostA: 172.16.1.5/24 default gateway 172.16.1.1

   HostB: 172.16.2.2/24 default gateway 172.16.2.1

   HostC: 172.16.3.2/24 default gateway 172.16.3.1

7. Try pinging from host to host. This should fail. However, you should be able to ping from HostA to all switches in the network, and all switches should be able to ping to HostA because they are all in the same VLAN. To allow hosts in different VLANs to communicate, you need to configure inter-VLAN routing.

Configuring the 2621 Router

The 2621 router will provide the inter-VLAN routing and allow the hosts to communicate with each other.

1. Go to the privilege mode of the router and enter global configuration mode.

   ```
   Router>ena
   Router#config t
   Router(config)#
   ```

2. Set the hostname and passwords on the 2621 router.

   ```
   Router(config)#hostname 2621A
   2621A(config)#enable secret todd
   2621A(config)#line con 0
   2621A(Config-line)login
   2621A(config-line)password console
   2621A(config)#line vty 0 4
   2621A(Config-line)login
   2621A(config-line)password telnet
   ```

3. Configure the FastEthernet interface to run ISL routing for all three VLANs.

   ```
   2621A(config-line)#exit
   2621A(config)#int f0/0.1
   2621A(config-subif)#encap isl 1
   2621A(config-subif)#ip address 172.16.1.1 255.255.255.0
   2621A(config-subif)#int f0/0.2
   2621A(config-subif)#encap isl 2
   2621A(config-subif)#ip address 172.16.2.1 255.255.255.0
   2621A(config-subif)#int f0/0.3
   2621A(config-subif)#encap isl 3
   2621A(config-subif)#ip address 172.16.3.1 255.255.255.0
   2621A(config-subif)#int f0/0
   2621A(config-if)#no shut
   2621A(config-if)#
   ```

4. Before this will work, you need to set the port on the 5000 to trunk mode. Go to the 5000 switch and configure the port.

   ```
   Cat5000> (enable) set trunk 2/3 on
   Port(s) 2/3 trunk mode set to on.
   Cat5000> (enable)
   ```

5. Test the configuration by pinging to all devices from the router.

   ```
   2621A#ping 172.16.3.2
   Type escape sequence to abort.
   Sending 5, 100-byte ICMP Echos to 172.16.3.2, timeout
      is 2 seconds:
   .!!!!
   Success rate is 80 percent (4/5), round-trip min/avg/
      max = 1/1/4 ms
   2621A#ping 172.16.1.3
   Type escape sequence to abort.
   Sending 5, 100-byte ICMP Echos to 172.16.1.3, timeout
      is 2 seconds:
   .!!!!
   Success rate is 80 percent (4/5), round-trip min/avg/
      max = 4/5/8 ms
   2621A#ping 172.16.2.2
   Type escape sequence to abort.
   Sending 5, 100-byte ICMP Echos to 172.16.2.2, timeout
      is 2 seconds:
   .!!!!
   Success rate is 80 percent (4/5), round-trip min/avg/
      max = 4/5/8 ms
   2621A#ping 172.16.1.5
   Type escape sequence to abort.
   Sending 5, 100-byte ICMP Echos to 172.16.2.2, timeout
      is 2 seconds:
   .!!!!
   Success rate is 80 percent (4/5), round-trip min/avg/
      max = 4/5/8 ms
   2621A#ping 172.16.1.4
   Type escape sequence to abort.
   Sending 5, 100-byte ICMP Echos to 172.16.2.2, timeout
      is 2 seconds:
   .!!!!
   ```

```
    Success rate is 80 percent (4/5), round-trip min/avg/
       max = 4/5/8 ms
2621A#
```

The reason for the 80% success rate is that the IP hosts have not communicated before and the first ping timed out waiting for the ARP protocol to resolve the hardware addresses of each device.

6. Verify that all hosts can communicate by pinging from host to host.

Lab 6.2: Internal Inter-VLAN Routing

In this second lab, you'll configure the RSM in the 5000 switch for inter-VLAN routing using ISL. The 1900s will be configured first, then the 5000s. The 2621 router will not be needed in this lab.

1. Unplug the 2621 router from the 5000 series switch. The hosts should no longer be able to ping each other.

2. Configure the RSM on the 5000 series switch to provide inter-VLAN routing. Use the **show module** command to view the RSM card location.

```
Cat5000> (enable) sh module
Mod Module-Name  Ports Module-Type        Model      Serial-Num Status
--- ------------ ----- ------------------ ---------- ---------- ------
1                2     100BaseTX Supervisor WS-X5509  005147178  ok
2                12    10/100BaseTX Ethernet WS-X5213A 005153813 ok
4                      Route Switch Ext Port
5                1     Route Switch       WS-X5304   018465234  ok
```

3. Connect to the RSM through the 5000 console.

```
Cat5000> (enable) session 5
Trying Router-5...
Connected to Router-5.
Escape character is '^]'.

Router>
```

4. Configure three VLAN interfaces, one for each VLAN configured in the switched internetwork.

   ```
   Router>en
   Router#config t
   Enter configuration commands, one per line.  End with CNTL/Z.
   Router(config)#hostname 5000RSM
   5000RSM(config)#int vlan 1
   5000RSM(config-if)#ip address 172.16.1.1 255.255.255.0
   5000RSM(config-if)#no shut
   5000RSM(config-if)#int vlan 2
   5000RSM(config-if)#ip address 172.16.2.1 255.255.255.0
   5000RSM(config-if)#no shut
   5000RSM(config-if)#int vlan 3
   5000RSM(config-if)#ip address 172.16.3.1 255.255.255.0
   5000RSM(config-if)#no shut
   ```

5. Verify that the RSM is working by pinging between hosts.

Review Questions

1. What command is used to connect to an RSM from a set-based switch CLI?

   A. `connect`

   B. `telnet`

   C. `session`

   D. `module`

2. What command will show you the hardware address of each card in a 5000 series switch?

   A. `sh cards`

   B. `show session`

   C. `show version`

   D. `show module`

3. What command is used to set a virtual hardware address on a VLAN interface?

   A. `mac-address` *mac-address*

   B. `config mac` *slot/port mac-address*

   C. `set vlan mac-address` *mac-address*

   D. `set mac` *mac-address*

4. What are the two types of frame tagging encapsulation methods used with Fast and Gigabit Ethernet trunk links?

   A. dot1q

   B. sde

   C. isl

   D. tr-isl

5. What are the two options you can consider when you need to have inter-VLAN communication and you have only an external router?

   A. One router interface for every switch in the internetwork

   B. One router interface for every single VLAN

   C. Two router interfaces for every switch in the internetwork

   D. One router interface into one switch port running a trunking protocol

6. What is the correct configuration for a subinterface on a modular router?

   A. `int 10.f0/0`

   B. `int fa0/0.3980`

   C. `faste 0/0 subinterface 3`

   D. `set int f0/0.1`

7. Which of the following is true regarding layer 2 switches? (Choose all that apply.)

   A. They break up collision domains by default.

   B. They break up broadcast domains by default.

   C. They provide inter-VLAN routing by default.

   D. An external route processor can be attached to the backplane of the switch to provide inter-VLAN routing.

8. What are the types of internal route processors that can be used with Catalyst switches? (Choose all that apply.)

   A. FRM

   B. RSM

   C. MSM

   D. RSFC

9. Which of the following is true regarding the configuration between the different internal route processors?

   A. The 6000 series internal processors use the `set` commands.

   B. The 5000 series internal processors use the same Cisco IOS commands a 1900 switch uses.

   C. The 8500 series of switches do not support internal route processors.

   D. There is no difference in the configuration between the different internal route processors.

10. Which two commands can be used to set a default route on a 5000 series switch to 172.16.1.1?

    A. `route add 0.0.0.0 0.0.0.0 172.16.1.1`

    B. `set route default 0.0.0.0 172.16.1.1`

    C. `set route default 172.16.1.1`

    D. `set route 0.0.0.0 172.16.1.1`

11. Which of the following is used to configure VLAN 1 on an internal route processor with an IP address of 208.211.78.200/28?

    A. `set vlan1 ip address 208.21.78.200 255.255.255.240`

    B. `config t, vlan1 ip address 208.21.78.200 255.255.255.240`

    C. `int vlan 1, ip address 208.211.78.200 255.255.255.240`

    D. `set int vlan1, ip address 208.211.78.200 255.255.255.224`

12. Which of the following is true?

    A. You are required to assign a password to an RSM interface CLI.

    B. You must perform a `no shutdown` command for every subinterface on an external route processor.

    C. You must perform a `no shutdown` command for every VLAN on an internal route processor.

    D. You can use a 2500 series router for ISL routing.

13. Which of the following internal route processors is a daughter card?

    A. RSM

    B. RSFM

    C. RSFC

    D. MSM

14. If you wanted to view the VLAN configuration of an RSM card, which command would you use?

    A. `sh vlan`

    B. `show config`

    C. `sho run`

    D. `sh port slot/type`

15. To view the routing table on the internal processor, use the _____ command.

    A. `show routing protocol`

    B. `show vlan`

    C. `show config`

    D. `show ip route`

258 Chapter 6 · Inter-VLAN Routing

16. If you assigned a virtual hardware address to VLAN 2 on an internal route processor, how do you view this configuration? (Choose all that apply.)

    A. `show virtual address`

    B. `show vlan 2`

    C. `show inter vlan 2`

    D. `show run`

17. Which command will display the BIA address of a VLAN on an internal route processor?

    A. `show virtual address`

    B. `show vlan 2`

    C. `show inter vlan 2`

    D. `show run`

18. What type of link must be used on a switch port if you are running ISL on an external router interface?

    A. Access

    B. Trunk

    C. Virtual

    D. Ethernet

19. Which of the following will set VLAN 3 to run ISL on an external route processor with one FastEthernet interface?

    A. `(config)#encap isl vlan3`

    B. `(config)#encap vlan3 isl`

    C. `(config-if)#encap isl 3`

    D. `(config-if)encap 3 isl`

20. Which of the following is used to provide support for the communication between the RSM and the Catalyst 5000 switch?

   A. ISL

   B. VLAN 1

   C. VLAN 0

   D. 127.0.0.1/8

Answers to Written Lab

1. Router#**config t**
   Enter configuration commands, one per line. End with CNTL/Z.
   Router(config)#**int f0/0.1**
   Router(config-subif)#**encap isl 1**
   Router(config-subif)#**ip address 172.16.10.1 255.255.255.0**

2. show module

3. session 3

4. ToddRSM#**config t**
   ToddRSM(config)#**int vlan 1**
   ToddRSM(config-if)#**ip address 172.16.1.1 255.255.255.0**
   ToddRSM(config-if)#**no shut**
   ToddRSM(config-if)#**int vlan 2**
   ToddRSM(config-if)#**ip address 172.16.2.1 255.255.255.0**
   ToddRSM(config-if)#**no shut**

5. ToddRSM#**config t**
   ToddRSM(config)#**int vlan 2**
   ToddRSM(config-if)#**mac-address 4004.0144.0011**

6. Trunk

7. 802.1q

8. True

9. 1000

10. show config

Answers to Review Questions

1. **C.** The `session` command is used to create a session from the switch CLI to the RSM CLI.

2. **D.** The `show module` command displays the type of cards in each slot, the hardware address, and serial number of each card.

3. **A.** The command `mac-address` *mac-address* is used under the `interface vlan #` command to set a virtual MAC address to a VLAN interface.

4. **A, C.** The frame tagging encapsulation methods are dot1q and isl. Dot1q is the IEEE standard for frame tagging between disparate systems. ISL is a Cisco proprietary Fast and Gigabit Ethernet frame tagging method.

5. **B, D.** If you have an external router, you certainly can have a router interface for every single VLAN. However, you can also have only one Fast or Gigabit Ethernet interface connected into a switch running a trunking protocol that will provide inter-VLAN routing.

6. **B.** You can create subinterfaces on a FastEthernet or Gigabit Ethernet modular interface by using the *type slot/port.subinterface_number* command.

7. **A.** Layer 2 switches break up only collision domains by default. A layer 3 device is needed for inter-VLAN routing. An external route processor cannot attach to the backplane of a switch, only into a switch port.

8. **B, C, D.** The 5000 series uses the RSM or a Route Switch Feature Card (RSFC), and the 6000 series uses the Multilayer Switch Module (MSM).

9. **D.** There is absolutely no difference in the configuration of the different types of internal route processors.

10. C, D. The command `set route default` and the command `set route 0.0.0.0` are the same command and can be used to set a default gateway on a 5000 series switch.

11. C. The command `interface vlan #` is used to create a VLAN interface. The IP address of the interface is then configured with the `ip address` command.

12. C. An external route processor configured with subinterfaces does not need a shutdown performed on each subinterface, only the main interface. However, an internal route processor must have a `no shutdown` command performed under every VLAN interface.

13. C. The Route Switch Feature Card (RSFC) is a daughter card for the Supervisor Engine II G and Supervisor III G cards. The RSFC is a fully functioning router running the Cisco IOS.

14. C. The RSM commands are the same as they are for any Cisco IOS router, and the `show running-config` is used to view the current configuration.

15. D. To view the routing table on the internal processor, use the `show ip route` command, just as you would with any IOS-based router.

16. C, D. The command `show interface vlan #` and the `show running-config` command will display the virtual hardware address of an interface if set.

17. C. The command `show interface vlan #` will show both the virtual MAC address if set and the burned-in address (BIA) of the VLAN interface.

18. B. A switch port must be configured with a trunking protocol to run ISL inter-VLAN communication to a single router interface.

19. C. The subinterface command `encapsulation type vlan` is used to set the VLAN ID and encapsulation method on a subinterface.

20. C. VLAN 0, which cannot be accessed by an administrator, is used to provide support for the communication between the RSM and the Catalyst 5000 switch.

Chapter 7

Multi-Layer Switching (MLS)

THE CCNP EXAM TOPICS COVERED IN THIS CHAPTER INCLUDE THE FOLLOWING:

- ✓ MLS overview
- ✓ MLS functionality
- ✓ MLS features
- ✓ MLS implementation

In this chapter, we'll discuss *Multi-Layer Switching (MLS)*, which is part of the Bridging/Switching group of topics outlined by Cisco for the Switching exam (640-504).

Why MLS? Why do you need layer 3 switching when you have layer 3 routing? The answer to both of these questions is simple: enhanced performance. Why do you implement any features on any piece of Cisco equipment? To increase performance and take advantage of the robust feature set provided by Cisco.

Fundamentals of MLS

You have undoubtedly heard of the term *"router on a stick."* Figure 7.1 depicts the router on a stick architecture. As you can see from the diagram, there are multiple hosts using two separate VLAN assignments. One segment is running on VLAN10, and the other segment is running on VLAN50. Both VLANs, or segments, are connected to the same switch. The switch is then connected to a router. Here we show an external router, but an RSM provides the same functionality, just internally.

FIGURE 7.1 Router on a stick diagram

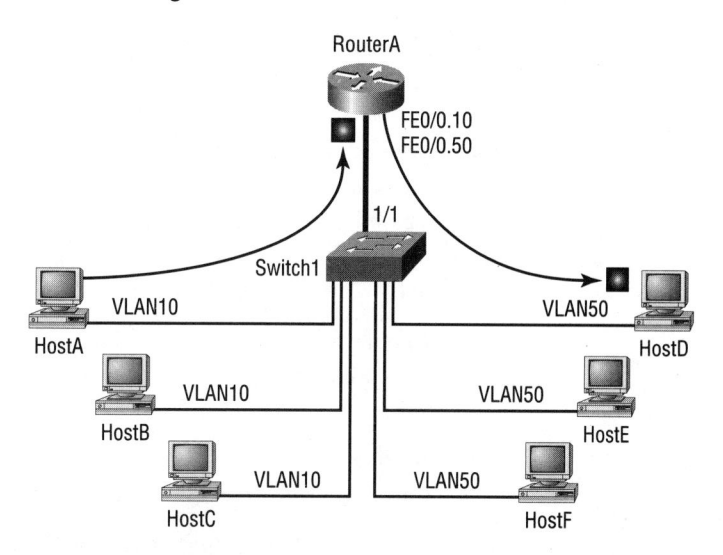

By now you understand that for HostA on VLAN10 to communicate to HostD on VLAN50, packets must be routed through RouterA. Because of the VLAN assignments, the switch must send the packet to the router on interface FE0/0.10. The router knows that the route to the network assigned to VLAN50 is through interface FE0/0.50. The packet is then sent back to the switch and forwarded to Host D.

Now back to our original question. Why use MLS? You can see from the diagram in Figure 7.1 that it very inefficient to have to use a router, or *Route Switch Module (RSM)*, to move a packet from HostA to HostD when they are connected to the same device. MLS is used to bypass the router on subsequent packets of the same flow. A *flow* is created by using packet header information—Inter-Switch Link (ISL), layer 2, and layer 3 headers. There are several fields within a packet that make it unique:

- Source and destination IP addresses
- Source and destination MAC addresses
- Type of Service (TOS)
- Protocol type (i.e., HTTP, FTP, ICMP, etc.)

These are just some of the characteristics of a packet that can be used to establish a flow. A flow is defined by using a specified set of these attributes.

MLS Requirements

Cisco Catalyst switches require additional hardware to see the packet header information. Catalyst 5000 switches use the *NetFlow Feature Card (NFFC)* to gather this information and cache it. Catalyst 6000 series switches use the *Multilayer Switch Feature Card (MSFC)* and the *Policy Feature Card (PFC)* to gather and cache header information. There is a detailed process, which will be discussed later in the chapter, that allows switches to establish flows.

MLS requires three components to function in any network (we have already briefly discussed two of them):

- *Multilayer Switching Protocol (MLSP)* is a protocol that runs on the router and allows it to communicate to the MLS-SE regarding topology or security changes.

- *Multilayer Switching Route Processor (MLS-RP)* can be an MLS-capable router or an RSM installed in the switch.

- *Multilayer Switching Switching Engine (MLS-SE)* is an MLS-capable switch (a 5000 with an NFFC or a 6000 with an MSFC and PFC).

Now that you have a basic understanding of what MLS does and what is required for MLS to function in a network, let's get into the nitty-gritty of how it works.

MLS Procedures

We discussed the three required components of MLS. It is important to understand how they work together to enable layer 3 switching. Let's look at a sample network topology that will support MLS. Figure 7.2 shows a simple architecture of a router and a switch with two connected hosts on the switch. Again, the hosts have different VLAN assignments, requiring the router's intervention to route packets. Notice that the figure depicts the main interface with two subinterfaces, FE0/0.2 and FE0/0.3.

FIGURE 7.2   MLS example topology

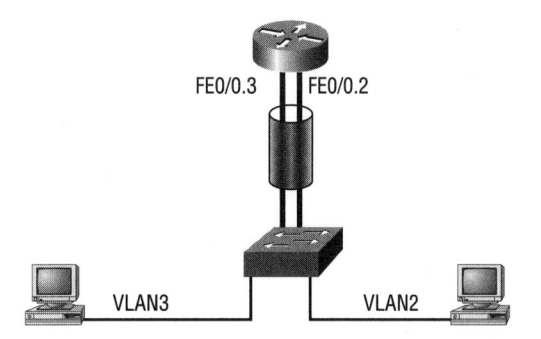

MLS follows a four-step process to establish the layer 3 switching functionality. These four steps can then be broken down into more detailed processes. The four steps required to enable MLS are as follows:

MLSP discovery   The MLS-RP uses MLSP to send hello packets out all interfaces to discover MLS-SE and establish MLS-RP/MLS-SE neighbor relationships.

Identification of candidate packets   The NFFC or PFC watches incoming packets and creates partial cache entries for them, thus identifying the packets as potential candidates for a flow, or candidate packets.

Identification of enable packets   The NFFC or PFC watches packets coming from the MLS-RP and tries to match them with candidate packet entries. If matches are made, the packets are tagged as enable packets and a shortcut forwarding entry is made in the CAM table.

Subsequent flow packets are layer 3 switched   Incoming packets are compared against CAM table entries. If the packets match the flow criteria, they are rewritten by the NFFC or PFC, then sent to the corresponding exit port for the flow.

The preceding list is an overview of the steps that must take place before packets can be switched at layer 3. We'll discuss each step in detail in the following sections.

MLSP Discovery

Switches, NFFCs or PFCs specifically, need routers to perform the initial route table lookup and the packet rewrite. This dependency requires that MLS adjacencies are established between the switch and the router. This is accomplished using the MLSP protocol.

Initially, the router, or MLS-RP, sends hello packets containing all of the MAC addresses and VLANs configured for use on the router. These messages are sent every 15 seconds to a layer 2 multicast address of 01-00-0C-DD-DD-DD. The intended recipients of these hello packets are the MLS-SE devices on the network.

When an MLS-SE receives the information, it makes an entry in the CAM table of all the MLS-RP devices in the layer 2 network. Layer 2 is mentioned because MLS-SE devices are not concerned with devices that are not directly connected to layer 2 devices, such as switches. Figure 7.3 depicts the MLSP discovery process.

FIGURE 7.3 MLSP discovery

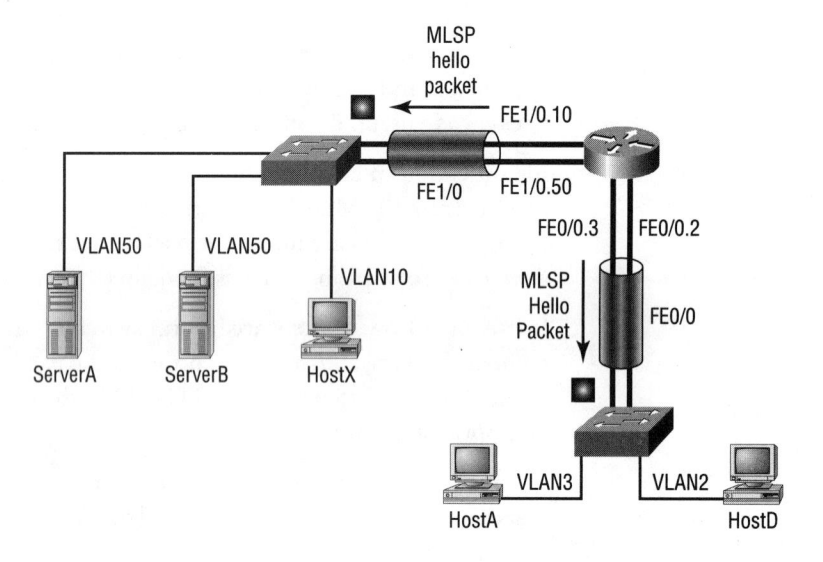

Part of the information that is stored in the CAM table once an MLSP hello packet is received is an ID called an XTAG. The next section describes the significance and purpose of the XTAG.

XTAGs

Simply put, an *XTAG* is a unique identifier that MLS-SEs (switches) use to keep track of the MLS-RPs in the network. All of the MAC addresses and VLANs in use on the MLS-RP are associated to the XTAG value in the CAM table.

The following output is from a Catalyst 6509 with an MSFC and PFC card. The **show mls** command was issued to provide the output:

```
Switch1> (enable) sho mls
Total packets switched = 4294967295
Total Active MLS entries = 85
IP Multilayer switching aging time = 256 seconds
IP Multilayer switching fast aging time = 0 seconds, packet
threshold = 0
IP Current flow mask is Destination flow
Active IP MLS entries = 85
Netflow Data Export version: 7
Netflow Data Export disabled
Netflow Data Export port/host is not configured.
Total packets exported = 0

IP MSFC ID         Module XTAG MAC                Vlans
---------------    ------ ---- -----------------  ----------
172.16.100.5       15     1    00-d0-bc-e3-70-b1  2,3

IPX Multilayer switching aging time = 256 seconds
IPX flow mask is Destination flow
IPX max hop is 0
Active IPX MLS entries = 0

IPX MSFC ID        Module XTAG MAC                Vlans
---------------    ------ ---- -----------------  ----------
172.16.100.5       15     1    -                  -

Switch1> (enable)
```

You can clearly see that the MFSC has been assigned the XTAG value of 1. The MFSC receives the assignment because the MFSC acts as the MLS-RP. In this example, only one MAC address is associated with XTAG 1. However, there are two VLANs associated with it.

MLS Cache

Once MLS-SEs have established CAM entries for MLS-RPs, the switch is ready to start scanning packets and creating cache entries. This was described previously as identification of candidate and enable packets.

The cache entries are made in order to maintain flow data. Flow data allows the MLS-SE to rewrite the packets with the new source and destination MAC address and then forward the packets. All this is done without sending the packets to the router for a route lookup and to be rewritten.

Cache entries happen in two steps:

- Candidate packet entries
- Enable packet entries

After these entries have been made in the MLS-SE, subsequent packets are matched against existing flow entries and dealt with accordingly.

Identifying Candidate Packets

The process of identifying *candidate packets* is quite simple. As has already been established, the MLS-SE has MAC address entries for any and all interfaces that come from the MLS-RP. Using this information, the MLS-SE starts watching for incoming frames destined for any MLS-RP-related MAC addresses.

An incoming frame will match one of the following three criteria:

- Not destined for an MLS-RP MAC address
- Destined for an MLS-RP MAC address, but no cache entry exists for this flow
- Destined for an MLS-RP MAC address, but a cache entry already exists for this flow

Different actions will be taken by the MLS-SE, depending on which criteria match. We will discuss the first one right now. The others will be addressed in the following sections.

If the incoming frame is not destined for a MAC address associated with the MLS-RP, no cache entry is made. No cache entry is made because MLS is used to avoid additional route lookups. If the frame is destined to another MAC address in the CAM table, the frame is layer 2 switched.

Let's move on to discuss the processes for identifying and acting on the next two criteria. First we'll discuss what happens when an entry already exists. Then we'll cover the details of the cache entry process for a candidate packet. Figure 7.4 depicts the occurrence of a candidate packet.

FIGURE 7.4 Candidate packet

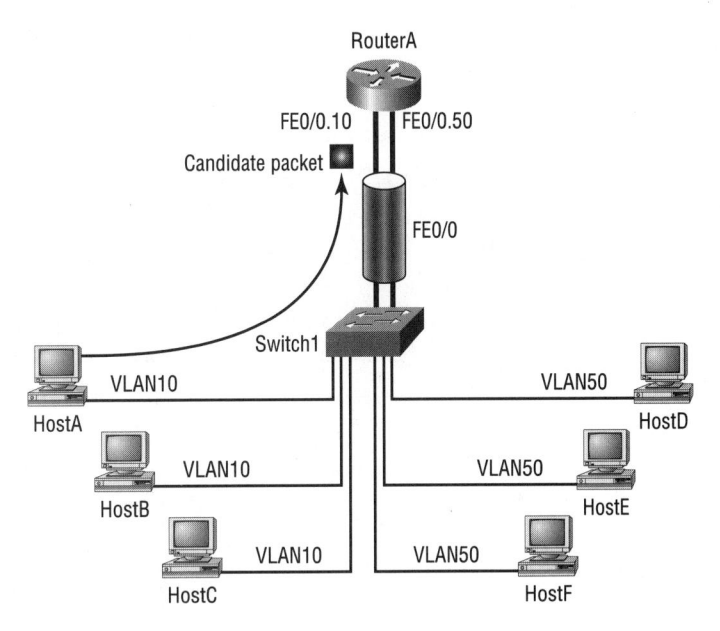

Cache Entry Exists

When frames enter the switch destined for an MLS-RP MAC address, the MLS-SE checks to see if a cache entry has been made that matches the attributes of the current packet.

As was mentioned briefly previously, each frame has distinguishing characteristics or attributes that allow the MLS-SE to categorize a packet into a flow. The MLS-SE uses these attributes to pattern match. If an incoming packet has the same attributes as an established flow cache entry, the packet is layer 3– or shortcut-switched.

No Cache Entry

When a qualified (destined for an MLS-RP MAC address) incoming frame is compared against the cache and fails (no match is found), a cache entry is made. At this point, the packet is tagged as a candidate packet.

Once the cache entry is made, the packet is forwarded to the router (MLS-RP) for normal processing. Here the router performs the route lookup, rewrites the layer 2 header, and sends the packet out the next-hop interface, whichever it may be.

The state of the MLS cache is only partial at this stage. A complete flow cache has not been established because the MLS-SE has only seen a packet come in and be forwarded to the router. It still needs to see something that it can tag as an enable packet come back from the router.

Identifying Enable Packets

Enable packets are the missing piece of the flow cache puzzle. Just as the MLS-SE watched all incoming frames destined for the MLS-RP MAC addresses, it also watches all of the packets coming from the MLS-RP.

It watches these packets hoping for a match with the candidate packet cache entry. If it can make the match, the packet is tagged as an enable packet and the remaining elements of the flow cache are completed in the CAM table. Figure 7.5 depicts the occurrence of an enable packet.

FIGURE 7.5 Enable packet

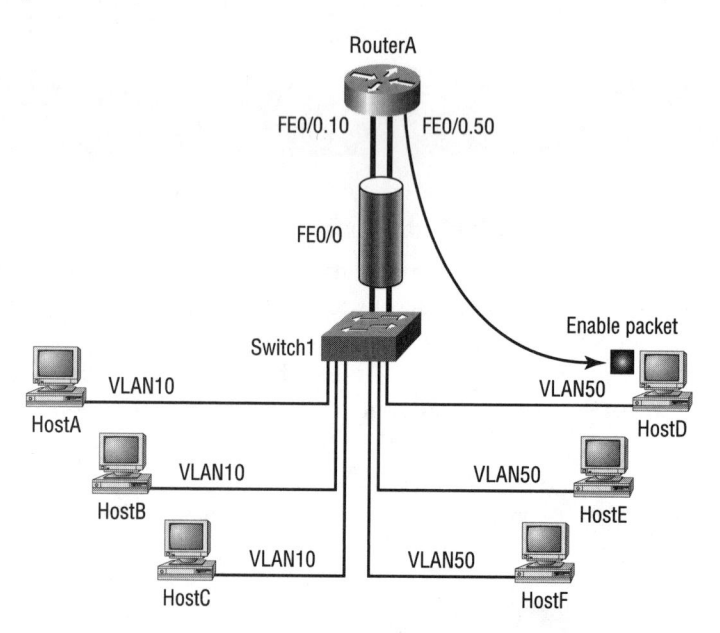

The match is made using the following criteria:

- The source MAC address is from an MLS-RP.
- The destination IP matches the destination IP of a candidate packet.
- The source MAC address is associated to the same XTAG value as the candidate packet's destination MAC address.

If all three of these criteria are met, the MLS-SE completes the shortcut cache entry.

Frame Modification

It is important to understand that this shortcut switching occurs at layer 3. The layer 2 frame is rewritten by the switch. Normally, a router (layer 3 device) would rewrite the frame with the necessary information. A rewrite consists of changing the VLAN assignment, the source and destination MAC addresses, and the checksums. The MLS-SE can also modify the TTL, checksums, TOS, and encapsulation

Because MLS packets are no longer sent to the router, the MLS-SE must perform the rewrite function. When it changes the source and destination MAC address, the MLS-SE uses the MAC address of the MLS-RP for the source, and it changes the destination MAC to the MAC of the directly connected host. Through this procedure, the frame appears to the destination host as if it had come through the router. Figure 7.6 depicts the differences between the incoming frame and the exiting frame.

FIGURE 7.6 Frame modification

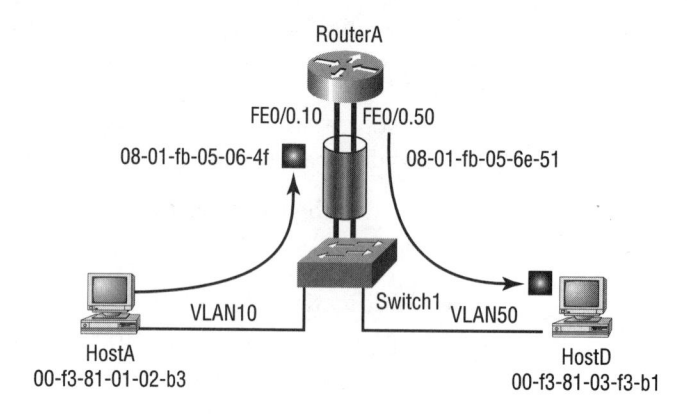

RouterA
FE0/0.10 — 08-01-fb-05-06-4f
FE0/0.50 — 08-01-fb-05-6e-51

Switch1

HostA — VLAN10 — 00-f3-81-01-02-b3
HostD — VLAN50 — 00-f3-81-03-f3-b1

Initial Header Information

ISL header		Ethernet header	
10	08-01-fb-05-06-4f	00-f3-81-01-02-b3	

↑ VLAN assignment value ↑ Destination MAC ↑ Source MAC

ISL header		Ethernet header	
50	00-f3-81-03-f3-b1	08-01-fb-05-6e-51	

↑ VLAN assignment value ↑ Destination MAC ↑ Source MAC

Subsequent Packets

Once the candidate and enable packets have been identified and a shortcut, or flow cache, has been established, subsequent packets are forwarded by the switch to the destination without the use of the router. Because the MLS-SE has the capability to rewrite the frames, it can make the necessary modifications and forward the frame directly to the destination host.

The MLS-SE stores the necessary information in cache, such as the source and destination IP addresses, the source and destination MAC addresses, and the MLS-RP-related MAC addresses. Using this information, the MLS-SE is then capable of identifying packets belonging to a specific flow, rewriting the frame, and forwarding the packets to the proper destination.

Disabling MLS

There is a right way and a wrong way (not necessarily wrong, just unwanted) to disable MLS on a router or switch. Both methods will be discussed here.

The Right Way

The normal, and correct, way to disable MLS depends on the equipment you are using. Disabling MLS on a router can be paralleled with disabling MLS on an MSFC for a 6500 series switch. The command is even the same: `no mls rp ip` issued from the interface on either the router or the MSFC. To disable it completely, you can issue the same command from the global configuration mode. The consequences of this action vary depending on the system on which it is issued. When the command is issued on the router, the router alone disables MLS. When it's issued on an MSFC, MLS is disabled on the MSFC and the switch itself.

That's why there is a difference when different switches are used. When you're using a 5000 series switch, MLS is disabled by default. However, on a 6000 series switch, MLS is enabled by default. To disable MLS on a 5000 series switch, use the `set mls disable` command. On a 6000 series, MLS should be disabled by issuing the `no ip mls` command on the MSFC.

The Wrong Way

There are several ways to inadvertently disable MLS on switches. Some are temporary, and others are permanent. Here is a list of MSFC/router commands that can disable MLS:

- `no ip routing`
- `ip security`
- `ip tcp compression-connections`
- `ip tcp header-compression`
- `clear ip route`

By disabling IP routing on the MSFC or router, you automatically disable MLS. IP security disables MLS on the interface to which the command is applied. The same results occur with the IP TCP compression commands. Finally, the `clear ip route` command simply clears the MLS cache entries and the flow caches must be reestablished.

MLS-RP Configuration

To fully enable MLS, you must properly configure all participating devices. This section covers the different configurations and settings that must be executed on the MLS-RP. Remember, the MLS-RP can be an external router, an RSM on a 5000 series switch, or an MSFC on a 6000 series switch.

We will start with the most basic and essential commands, then move on to management commands that can be used for verification and troubleshooting if necessary.

Enabling MLS

This is the first and foremost command that must be configured on the MLS-RP. It should be entered in as a global configuration. Because methods differ between external routers and the MSFC for the 6000 series switches, both will be discussed.

External Router

For external routers. The command is `mls rp ip`. Here is an example:

```
RouterA#conf t
Enter configuration commands, one per line.  End with CNTL/Z.
RouterA(config)#mls rp  ip
RouterA(config)#^Z
RouterA#

!
ip subnet-zero
mls rp ip
!
```

MSFC

The command is still issued as a global command on the MSFC. However, the syntax is slightly different. MLS is on by default on the MFSC, but if you need to issue the command, the syntax is `mls ip`.

This command is required for MLS to operate on the MLS-RP. The following sections discuss optional configuration settings. These options will depend on the existing layer 2 network and configuration. All of the remaining sections, except "Verifying the MLS Configuration," apply only to external routers.

VTP Domain Assignments

If a router interface is connected to a switch that is a VTP server or client, assigning the VLAN Trunk Protocol (VTP) domain is also a necessary step for MLS to work properly. It is very important to note that this step should be executed before any further MLS interface-specific commands are entered.

Verifying the VTP Domain

First you should verify which VTP domain the interface belongs to. This is done with the `show vtp domain` command from the switch. You can also obtain this information by looking at the switch configuration. Here are the two examples:

```
switch1> sho vtp domain
Domain Name    Domain Index  VTP Version  Local Mode  Password
-----------    ------------  -----------  ----------
test           1             2            server      -

Vlan-count  Max-vlan-storage  Config Revision  Notifications
----------  ----------------  ---------------  -------------
7           1023              2                disabled

Last Updater    V2 Mode   Pruning   PruneEligible on Vlans
-------------   -------   -------   ----------------------
172.16.10.1     disabled  disabled  2-1000
switch1>
```

Chapter 7 · Multi-Layer Switching (MLS)

```
switch1> (enable) wr t
.....
.........
.........
.........
.........
..
-- ommitted text --
!
#vtp
set vtp domain test
set vtp mode server
```

VTP Interface Configuration

Once you have the VTP domain name, you are ready to assign the router interface to that VTP domain. This is done with the execution of the command `mls rp vtp-domain [domain-name]` on the specified interface.

Here is an example:

```
RouterA#conf t
Enter configuration commands, one per line.  End with CNTL/Z.
RouterA(config)#interface fastethernet 4/0
RouterA(config-if)#mls rp vtp-domain test
RouterA(config-if)#^Z
RouterA#


!
interface FastEthernet4/0
 ip address 172.16.10.1 255.255.255.0
 no ip directed-broadcast
 no ip route-cache
 no ip mroute-cache
 mls rp vtp-domain test
!
```

VLAN Assignments

This command is used only if an external router's interface is not using ISL or 802.1q encapsulation. (RSMs and MSFCs use logical VLAN interfaces.) An example may be when a router has two physical interfaces connected to the same switch, each to a different VLAN. This scenario doesn't require that the router be aware of VLAN assignments.

If you wish to enable MLS on interfaces that are not encapsulated, you can issue the `mls rp vlan-id [vlan-id-number]` command to assign a VLAN to the interface. Here is an example:

```
RouterA#conf t
Enter configuration commands, one per line.  End with CNTL/Z.
RouterA(config)#interface fastethernet 4/0
RouterA(config-if)#mls rp vlan-id 10
RouterA(config-if)#^Z
RouterA#


!
interface FastEthernet4/0
 ip address 172.16.10.1 255.255.255.0
 no ip directed-broadcast
 no ip route-cache
 no ip mroute-cache
 mls rp vtp-domain web-ut
 mls rp vlan-id 10
!
```

Interface Configurations

Once VTP and VLAN assignments have been made, you can finally enable MLS on the interface. This is done with the same command that was used to globally enable MLS, `mls rp ip`. Here is an example:

```
RouterA#conf t
Enter configuration commands, one per line.  End with CNTL/Z.
RouterA(config)#interface fastethernet 4/0
```

```
RouterA(config-if)#mls rp ip
RouterA(config-if)#^Z
RouterA#


!
interface FastEthernet4/0
 ip address 172.16.10.1 255.255.255.0
 no ip directed-broadcast
 no ip route-cache
 no ip mroute-cache
 mls rp vtp-domain web-ut
 mls rp vlan-id 10
 mls rp ip
!
```

MSA Management Interface

You may remember that we discussed that there were three components to MLS. The third component was MLSP. Well, in order for MLS to function between a switch and a router, MLSP must be able to communicate between both devices.

This requirement makes this next configuration step essential for MLS functionality. At least one interface on the router that is connected to the same switch must be enabled as the management interface. This indicates which interface is going to allow MLSP exchanges.

Another requirement is that there be at least one management interface per VLAN on the switch. To specify a router interface as a management interface, issue the `mls rp management-interface` command on the specified interface. Here is an example of the syntax for the command:

```
RouterA#conf t
Enter configuration commands, one per line.  End with CNTL/Z.
RouterA(config)#interface fastethernet 4/0
RouterA(config-if)#mls rp management-interface
RouterA(config-if)#^Z
RouterA#
```

Verifying the MLS Configuration

Once all of the pieces have been configured, you may issue the `show mls rp` command to view the MLS status and information on the router. There are two options in correlation with the main command. All three commands are shown here:

`show mls rp`   Provides global MLS information

`show mls rp interface`   Provides interface-specific MLS information

`show mls rp vtp-domain`   Provides MLS information for the VTP domain

Here is an example of the global command:

```
RouterA#show mls rp
multilayer switching is globally enabled
mls id is 0010.a6a9.3400
mls ip address 172.16.21.4
mls flow mask is destination-ip
number of domains configured for mls 1

vlan domain name: test
    current flow mask: destination-ip
    current sequence number: 3041454903
    current/maximum retry count: 0/10
    current domain state: no-change
    current/next global purge: false/false
    current/next purge count: 0/0
    domain uptime: 00:34:35
    keepalive timer expires in 4 seconds
    retry timer not running
    change timer not running
    fcp subblock count = 1

    1 management interface(s) currently defined:
        vlan 10 on FastEthernet4/0
```

```
                    1 mac-vlan(s) configured for multi-layer switching:

                      mac 0010.a6a9.3470
                        vlan id(s)
                        10

                    router currently aware of following 1 switch(es):
                      switch id 00-e0-4e-2d-43-ef
```

RouterA#

Here is an example of the interface option:

RouterA#**show mls rp interface fastethernet 4/0**
```
mls active on FastEthernet4/0, domain test
interface FastEthernet4/0 is a management interface
RouterA#
```

These are the show commands, and as with any IOS, there are debugging opportunities. Table 7.1 provides a summary of the debug commands available for MLS troubleshooting.

TABLE 7.1 MLS Debug Command Summary

Command	Description
all	Performs all MLS debugging
error	Displays information on MLS errors
events	Displays information from MLS events
ip	Displays IP MLS events
locator	Displays MLS Locator information
packets	Displays information for all MLS packets
verbose packets	Displays information on all MLS verbose packets

Access Lists

Access control lists (ACLs) throw an interesting twist into MLS configuration and operation. There are some definite caveats when trying to use MLS and ACLs at the same time.

Until IOS release 12.0(2), inbound access lists were not supported. If a router interface had an inbound access list applied, MLS was disabled. With versions after 12.0(2), inbound access lists are supported.

Outbound ACLs are a little more problematic. Although they have always been supported, application thereof causes the MLS cache to clear and reestablish. Also, outbound lists utilizing the following functions will disable MLS on the interface to which they are applied:

- TOS
- Established
- Log
- Precedence

Configuring the MLS Engine

Switch configuration is very simple. MLS is on by default for both the 6000 and 2926G and for the 5000s with RSMs and NFFC cards in them. The only time that it is necessary to perform configuration tasks on the MLS-SE is when you want to change specific MLS attributes or when the device requires configuration. Here are some examples:

- Using an external router
- Changing the MLS cache aging timers
- Enabling NDE (NetFlow Data Export)

Each of these topics will be addressed in the following sections.

Enabling MLS on the MLS-SE

As mentioned, the only time you need to actually enable MLS on the MLS-SE is when it has been disabled or on a system on which MLS is off by default.

To enable MLS on the MLS-SE, issue the command **set mls enable**. Here is an example:

```
Switch2> (enable) set mls enable
Multilayer switching is enabled
Switch2> (enable)
```

Cache Entries

MLS entry or shortcut cache exists on the NFFC for the 5000 series switches and on the PFC for 6000 series switches. The purpose for the cache is consistent across all platforms. The cache is a layer 3 switching table. It maintains the flow information that facilitates MLS.

Here is a sample of a layer 3 cache table:

```
Switch1> (enable) sho mls entry
Dest-IP    Source-IP  Prot DstPrt SrcPrt Dest-Mac          Vlan EDst ESrc DPort SPort
Stat-Pkts  Stat-Bytes Uptime     Age
---------------  --------------- ----- ------ ------ ----------------- ----
---- ---- ------ ------ ---------- ----------- -------- --------
MSFC 10.10.100.5 (Module 15):
172.16.10.1   -              -        -       -        00-30-96-2d-24-20 188   ARPA
ARPA 2/7      2/6      870          157785         00:05:29 00:00:27
172.16.55.115 -              -        -       -        00-30-96-2d-24-20 188
ARPA ARPA 2/7 2/6      2407         642886         00:00:39 00:00:00
172.16.96.101 -              -        -       -        00-d0-bc-f3-69-44 4
ARPA ARPA 2/2 2/7      2710         2200670        00:12:23 00:00:00
172.16.8.35   -              -        -       -        00-d0-bc-f3-66-9c 180
ARPA ARPA 3/7 3/3      76634        24951932       00:24:31 00:00:00
172.16.8.17   -              -        -       -        00-30-96-2d-24-20 188
ARPA ARPA 2/7 2/6      81752        26599352       00:18:32 00:00:00
172.16.8.102  -              -        -       -        00-30-96-2d-24-20 188
ARPA ARPA 2/7 2/6      313          148298         00:00:24 00:00:22
```

Cache entries are kept while the flow is active. Once the flow no longer receives traffic, the cache entry gets aged out and removed from the layer 3 cache on the NFFC or PFC. This attribute can be modified and adjusted. The following sections describe how this can be done.

Modifying the Cache Aging Time

A layer 3 cache entry will remain in cache for 256 seconds after the last packet for the flow has passed through the switch. This is the default value. The value can be changed to different values depending on your needs as a network administrator.

The syntax is `set mls agingtime` *agingtime*, where *agingtime* is a value of seconds. The value is a multiple of 8. The valid range is from 8 to 2032. If the value specified is not a multiple of 8, the nearest multiple will be used. Here is an example:

```
Switch2> (enable) set mls agingtime 125
Multilayer switching aging time set to 128
Switch2> (enable)
```

Modifying Fast Aging Time

When the layer 3 cache grows greater than 32K in size, there is an increased possibility that the PFC or NFFC will not be able to perform all layer 3 switching, causing some packets to be forwarded to the router. To aid in maintaining a layer 3 cache smaller than 32K, you can enable and adjust fast aging times

Because some flows can be very short, you can enable packet thresholds that can be used in correlation with the fast aging time to quickly age out these entries. Both of these attributes are thresholds. When you set the fast aging time, you specify the amount of time for which *n* number of packets (defined by the packet threshold) must have used the cache entry.

When a flow is initialized, the switch must see a number of packets equal to or greater than the packet threshold set within the time specified by the fast aging time. If this criterion isn't met, the cache entry is aged out immediately.

Valid values for the fast aging time are 32, 64, 96, and 128. Valid values for the packet threshold are 0, 1, 3, 7, 15, 31, and 63. Let's do an example so we can understand how this works.

Say you configured a fast aging time of 64 seconds and the packet threshold to 31 packets using the `set mls agingtime fast 64 31` command on the switch. This is telling the MLS-SE that a layer 3 cache entry has 64 seconds in which 31 packets or more must utilize the entry. If this doesn't happen, the cache entry is removed.

The actual syntax for the command is `set mls agingtime fast fastagingtime pkt-threshold`. An example configuration follows:

```
Switch2> (enable) set mls agingtime fast 64 31
Multilayer switching fast aging time set to 64 seconds for
entries with no more than 31 packets switched.
Switch2> (enable)
```

Verifying the Configuration

MLS-SE configuration settings can be seen by using the `show mls ip` command. The command provides information regarding the aging time, fast aging time, and packet threshold values. In addition, it gives summary statistics for the type of flow mask and MLS entries. Finally, it provides details about the MLS-RP, including XTAG, MAC, and VLAN values. Here is an example:

```
Switch1> sho mls ip
IP Multilayer switching aging time = 256 seconds
IP Multilayer switching fast aging time = 0 seconds, packet threshold = 0
IP Current flow mask is Destination flow
Active IP MLS entries = 87
Netflow Data Export version: 7
Netflow Data Export disabled
Netflow Data Export port/host is not configured.
Total packets exported = 0

IP MSFC ID         Module XTAG MAC               Vlans
---------------    ------ ---- ----------------- -----------------
172.16.10.1        15     1    00-d0-bc-f4-81-c0 10,100
Switch1>
```

Displaying the MLS Cache Entries

There are several different methods of viewing MLS cache entries. The base command is show mls entry. However, there are many options available to customize the output of this basic command.

If you are on a switch and issue the help command for show mls entry, this is what you get.

```
Switch1> (enable) sho mls entry ?
Usage: show mls entry [mod] [long|short]
       show mls entry ip [mod] [destination <ip_addr_spec>]
                [source <ip_addr_spec>] [protocol <protocol>]
                [src-port <src_port>] [dst-port <dst_port>]
[short|long]
       show mls entry ipx [mod] [destination <ipx_addr_spec>]
[short|long]
    (mod = 15 or 16
      ip_addr_spec = ip_addr|ip_addr/netmask|ip_addr/maskbit
(maskbit: 0..32)
      protocol = 1..255|ip|ipinip|icmp|igmp|tcp|udp
      src_port, dst_port = 1..65535|dns|ftp|smtp|telnet|x|www
      ipx_addr_spec = dest_net.dest_node|dest_net/mask)
Switch1> (enable)
```

As you can see, there are quite a few different options. This command, with the options shown, allows the administrator to view very general information or very specific information. To get an idea of what can be generated from this command, let's review the options.

You can show MLS entries based on the module. The long and short options modify the output in different ways. Long displays the information all on one line, and short displays the information using carriage returns. It is impossible to give an example due to the formatting limitations in this book.

More specific information can be obtained by specifying an IP address or port information. By specifying options, you can refine your output. Instead of getting pages and pages of cache entries, you get entries that match your criteria.

Removing MLS Cache Entries

If you do not want to wait for aging times to expire, or if you want to clear the cache immediately, you can issue the `clear mls entry` command. This command also has options that allow the network administrator to clear specific cache entries instead of the entire table.

The syntax of the command is as follows:

```
clear mls entry destination ip-addr-spec source ip-addr-spec flow protocol src_port dst_port [all]
```

The use of the `all` option keyword causes all MLS cache entries to be removed. If you use specific IP addresses, ports, or protocols, specific cache entries can be removed.

Acceptable MLS Topologies

There are few topologies that support MLS. Due to the nature of MLS, only certain system topologies will allow candidate and enable packets to transit the router and switch properly. If both candidate and enable packets cannot be identified, no complete flow cache entry can be made. Acceptable topologies include the following:

Router on a stick   This includes one router (internal RSM/MSFC or external) and one switch. See Figure 7.7.

Multiple switches, one router   This is acceptable if only one switch connects to the router and the switches are connected via an ISL trunk. See Figure 7.8

Two routers, one switch   This works, but it requires more work for the MLS-SE. The packet must be rewritten twice to account for the hops across two routers. It also requires the candidate and enable packets to be identified for each router. See Figure 7.9

Acceptable MLS Topologies **289**

FIGURE 7.7 Router on a stick

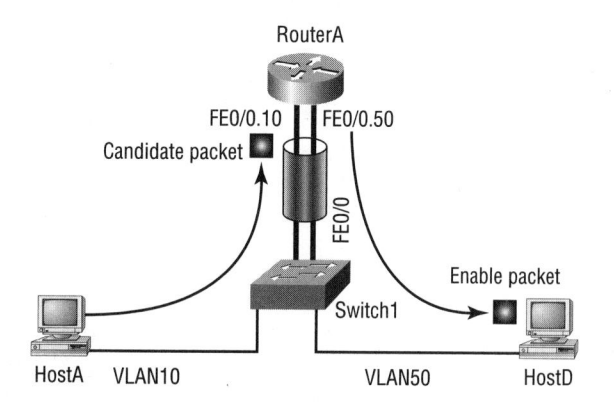

FIGURE 7.8 Multiple switches, one router

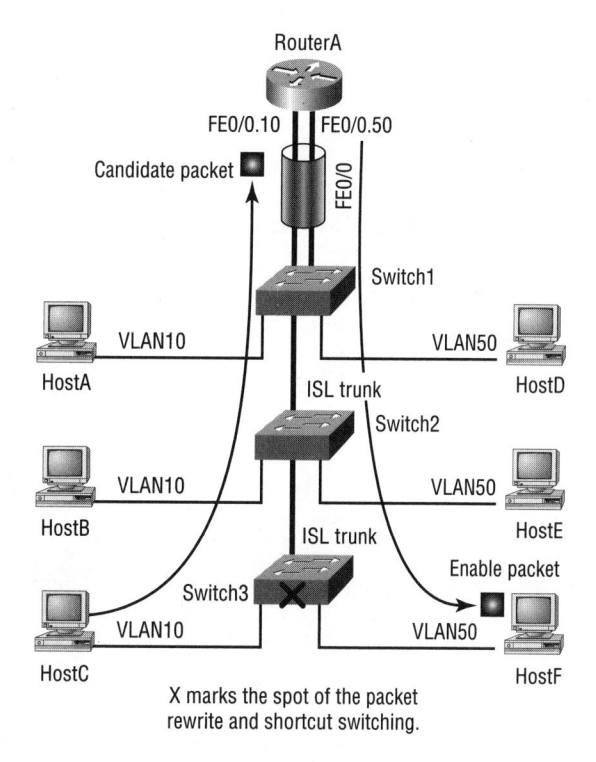

FIGURE 7.9 Single switch, two routers

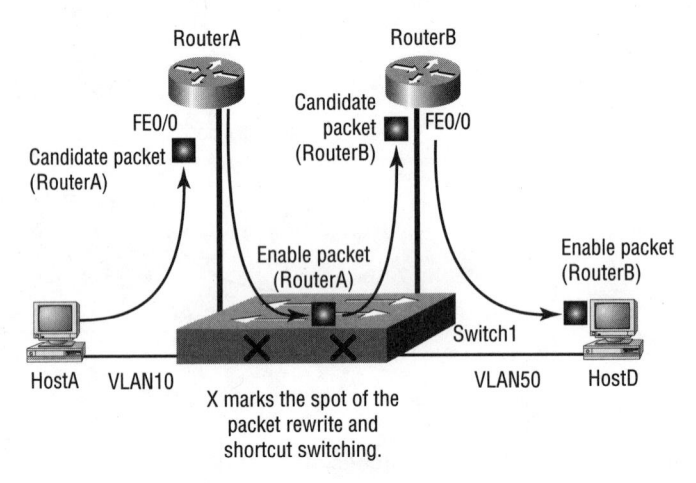

Summary

You have learned a great deal in this chapter. It is important that you understand the fundamentals of MLS as well as the different platforms that support it.

The fact that MLS is supported on multiple platforms shouldn't be of much concern. However, implementation and configuration syntax depend greatly on the equipment and topology being deployed.

To summarize, in this chapter you learned the following:

- The fundamentals of MLS: layer 3 switching
- Components of MLS
- System and topology requirements
- Candidate and enable packet identification processes
- Layer 3 cache entry properties
- MLS configuration on multiple platforms

Key Terms

Before you take the exam, be sure you're familiar with the following terms:

candidate packets

enable packets

flow

Multilayer Switch Feature Card (MSFC)

Multi-Layer Switching (MLS)

Multilayer Switching Protocol (MLSP)

Multilayer Switching Route Processor (MLS-RP)

Multilayer Switching Switching Engine (MLS-SE)

NetFlow Feature Card (NFFC)

Policy Feature Card (PFC)

Route Switch Module (RSM)

router on a stick

XTAG

Commands Used in This Chapter

The following table provides a summary of the commands used in this chapter. There were no access layer switches used in this chapter, so the table is based on a distribution switch.

Command	Meaning
show mls	Shows MLS information on a switch.
mls rp ip	Enables MLS on an external router, both global and interface specific.
set mls enable	Enables MLS on Catalyst switches. For most switches, this is set to on by default.
show vtp domain	Provides VTP domain information on the switch.

Command	Meaning
mls rp vtp-domain [*domain-name*]	Assigns the interface to the VTP domain.
mls rp vlan-id [*vlan-id-number*]	Assigns the interface the proper VLAN number.
mls rp management-interface	Assigns the interface to the MLS-RP. This allows MLSP updates to use this interface.
show mls rp	Provides global MLS information.
show mls rp interface	Provides interface-specific MLS information.
show mls rp vtp-domain	Provides MLS information for the VTP domain.
show mls entry	Provides MLS entry data on the MLS-SE.
set mls agingtime *agingtime*	Sets the MLS agingtime value to the specified value.
set mls agingtime fast *fastagingtime pkt-threshold*	Allows the fast aging time and packet threshold to be set.
clear mls entry destination *ip-addr-spec* source *ip-addr-spec* flow *protocol src_port dst_port* [all]	Allows all MLS entries to be cleared in addition to allowing specific entries to be terminated.

Written Lab

Write out the answers to the following questions.

1. Write the command that enables MLS globally on an external router.

2. Write the command that will assign the VTP domain to the external router's interface. Use *cisco* as the VTP domain name

3. Write the command that will assign VLAN 5 to the interface.

4. Write the command that will configure an external router interface to allow MLSP packets across it.

5. Write the command that will show you MLS information on a switch.

6. Write the command that will show you the XTAG information on a switch.

7. Write the command that will display all of the layer 3 cache entries.

8. Write the command that will display a layer 3 cache entry based on the destination IP address of 172.16.10.100.

9. Write the command to clear all MLS cache entries.

10. Write the command that sets the fast aging time to 64 and the packet threshold to 63.

Hands-On Lab

Refer to Figure 7.10 for the topology of this lab. This lab will use the simplest architecture: router on a stick using a Catalyst 5000 and an external router (7200 series).

FIGURE 7.10 Lab topology

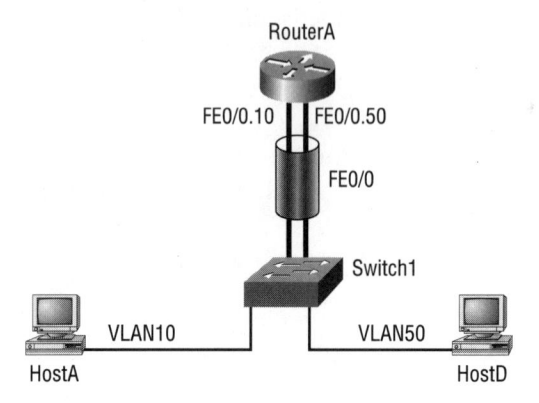

1. Assume that RouterA does not have MLS enabled. You may assume that the subinterfaces are running ISL and have VLAN assignments. Switch1 is a VTP server for the sybex domain. Configure MLS to work on RouterA.

   Answer:

   RouterA#**conf t**
   Enter configuration commands, one per line. End with CNTL/Z.

```
RouterA(config)#mls rp ip
RouterA(config)#interface fastethernet 4/0
RouterA(config-subif)#mls rp vtp-domain sybex
RouterA(config-subif)#interface fastethernet4/0.50
RouterA(config-subif)#mls rp management-interface
RouterA(config-subif)#mls rp ip
RouterA(config-subif)#interface fastethernet4/0.10
RouterA(config-subif)#mls rp ip
RouterA(config-subif)#^Z
RouterA#
```

2. The aging timers need to be adjusted to be shorter than the default of 256 seconds. Make the new value 128. In addition to changing the aging timers, add a command that will help keep the layer 3 cache size under 32K. To do this, use values of agingtimer = 64 and packet-threshold = 31.

    Answer:

    ```
    Switch1> (enable) set mls agingtime 128
    Multilayer switching aging time set to 128
    Switch1> (enable) set mls agingtime fast 64 31
    Multilayer switching fast aging time set to 64 seconds
    for entries with no more than 31 packets switched.
    Switch1> (enable)
    ```

3. Verify MLS status on the switch and router. Provide samples of the MLS entries and XTAG values.

    Answer: Results will vary on this answer; here are the commands that should be issued:

    - show mls (executed on the switch)
    - show mls rp (executed on the router)
    - show mls entry (executed on the router)

Review Questions

1. Which of the following is one of the three components of MLS? (Choose one.)

   A. MFSC

   B. PCF

   C. MLS-P

   D. MLSP

2. Which of the following is one of the three components of MLS? (Choose one.)

   A. MLS

   B. MLS-SW

   C. MLS-ES

   D. MLS-SE

3. Which of the following is one of the three components of MLS? (Choose one.)

   A. RP

   B. RSP

   C. MLS-RP

   D. MLS-MSFC

4. Which of the following describes the router on a stick topology? (Choose all that apply.)

   A. A router connected to a switch with coax

   B. A single external router connected to a single switch

   C. A single internal router (RSM/MSFC) installed in a switch

   D. A switch with an RSM/MSFC connected to an external router

5. Which of the following elements are *not* used to create a flow or shortcut cache entry? (Choose all that apply.)

   A. TOS

   B. Protocol

   C. CRC

   D. Payload

   E. Source MAC

   F. Destination MAC

   G. Destination IP

6. Which answer best describes the MLSP discovery process? (Choose one.)

   A. The MLS-SE sends hello packets to the multicast address 01-00-0C-DD-DD-DD. MLS-RPs then respond to these hello packets.

   B. The MLS-RP sends hello packets to the multicast address 01-00-0C-DD-DD-DD. MLS-SEs then respond to these hello packets.

   C. The MLS-RP sends hello packets to the multicast address 01-00-0C-DD-DD-DD. MLS-SEs then record the hello packet information.

   D. The MLS-SE sends hello packets to the multicast address 01-00-0C-DD-DD-DD. MLS-RPs then record the hello packet information.

7. What is the XTAG used for, and what is its significance?

   A. XTAG is a numerical value assigned by the MLS-SE to identify an MLS-RP. It must be unique throughout the VTP domain.

   B. XTAG is a numerical value assigned by the MLS-SE to identify an MLS-RP. It is locally significant.

   C. The XTAG is the MLS-RP router ID and is used to uniquely identify the MLS-RP to the MLS-SE. It is a unique value throughout the layer 2 network.

   D. The XTAG is the MLS-SE ID and is used to identify each MLS-SE in the layer 2 network. Therefore, it must be unique across all switches.

8. Which of the following commands will display XTAG information on a switch?

    A. show mls entry

    B. show mls statistics

    C. show mls

    D. show mls rp ip

9. What are the two prerequisites before a complete shortcut entry may be entered into cache?

    A. Identification of the MLS-SE

    B. Identification of the candidate packet

    C. Identification of the MLS topology

    D. Identification of the enable packet

10. Which of the following criteria qualify a packet as a candidate packet?

    A. Any incoming packet that is destined to a MAC address associated with the MLS-RP

    B. Incoming packets sourcing from 224.0.0.1 and destined for the MAC address of the MLS-SE

    C. Incoming packets sourcing a MAC address associated with the MLS-RP

    D. Outbound packets destined for a remote host

11. Which of the following criteria qualify a packet as an enable packet? (Choose all that apply.)

    A. The packet is sourced from an MLS-RP MAC address.

    B. The XTAG value matches the candidate packet XTAG value.

    C. The destination MAC address is the same as the corresponding candidate packet's source MAC address.

    D. The destination IP address matches the destination IP of the corresponding candidate packet.

12. Which component or device performs the frame rewrite? (Choose all that apply.)

   A. PFC

   B. MSFC

   C. RSM

   D. NFFC

13. Which of the following fields can be rewritten by the MLS-SE? (Choose all that apply.)

   A. ISL header

   B. DEST MAC

   C. Source MAC

   D. Destination IP address

14. Which of the following fields can be rewritten by the MLS-SE? (Choose all that apply.)

   A. Source IP address

   B. TOS

   C. CRC

   D. Payload

15. At what MLS cache size does the probability of involving the router increase dramatically?

   A. 8K

   B. 64K

   C. 32K

   D. 128K

   E. 256K

16. What commands can inadvertently disable MLS on a router or interface? (Choose all that apply.)

    A. `no ip routing`

    B. `ip security`

    C. `ip access-group access-list-number [in|out]`

    D. `no tcp-small-servers`

17. What commands may inadvertently disable MLS on a router or an MLS-configured interface.

    A. `clear ip route`

    B. `ip tcp header-compression`

    C. `route-map`

    D. `ip router rip`

18. Which of the following commands will enable MLS on an MSFC?

    A. `set mls ip enable`

    B. `set mls enable`

    C. `mls rp ip`

    D. `mls ip`

19. Which of the following commands will enable MLS on an external router?

    A. `set mls ip enable`

    B. `set mls enable`

    C. `mls rp ip`

    D. `mls ip`

20. When must you configure the VTP domain on an interface of an external router?

    A. Always

    B. When it uses ISL encapsulation

    C. When it doesn't use ISL or 802.1q encapsulation

    D. When it is connected to a VTP server or client

Answers to Written Lab

1. `mls rp ip`
2. `mls rp vtp-domain cisco`
3. `mls rp vlan-id 5`
4. `mls rp management-interface`
5. `show mls`
6. `show mls`
7. `show mls entry`
8. `show mls entry ip destination 172.16.10.100`
9. `clear mls entry destination all`
10. `set mls agingtime fast 64 63`

Answers to Review Questions

1. **D.** MLSP is the proper acronym for Multilayer Switching Protocol. MFSC should be MSFC; PCF should be PFC.

2. **D.** Multilayer Switching Switching Engine is the name of the component. The proper acronym is provided by D.

3. **C.** MLS-RP represents the broad spectrum of route processors. RP, RSP, and MSFC are all types of route processors.

4. **B, C.** The topology name comes from the original look of an external router connected to a switch. With the implementation of RSM/MSFC, the same functional topology is achieved in the same chassis. The media connection type does not define the topology.

5. **C, D.** CRC can vary from packet to packet and is used for error checking. The payload is also unique for each packet. Flows are established using packet similarities.

6. **C.** The key to this question is twofold. The MLS-RP is the only device that sends hello packets. Because the packets are sent to a multicast address, the MLS-RP doesn't require a response from the switch. The MLS-RP doesn't need to establish an actual connection with the switch.

7. **B.** XTAGs are used by the MLS-SE to identify each MLS-RP connected to the layer 2 network. Each switch can utilize the same XTAG values; they are only used locally.

8. **C.** The `show mls rp ip` command is used on routers and doesn't provide XTAG information. Neither do any of the other switch commands.

9. **B, D.** Both packets must be identified to complete the shortcut entry.

10. A. Incoming packets must be destined to a MAC address that is associated to the MLS-RP via the XTAG value. If the packet is not destined for this address, the packet is not tagged as a candidate packet.

11. A, B, D. Enable packets have more criteria to match than do candidate packets. Because the destination MAC address is different for every hop, there is no way that a packet could match using the destination MAC address and still use MLS.

12. A, D. MFSC and RSMs are layer 3 devices that are used in Catalyst switches. Pattern matching and frame rewrites are done by the NFFC and PFC.

13. A, B, C. Although the rewrite engine can modify some fields in the IP header, it does not change the IP addresses.

14. B, C. The MLS-SE has to rewrite the CRC because it changes the values for the SMAC and DMAC. It calculates a new CRC for the new frame.

15. C. Once the MLS cache size is above 32K, chances are that the MLS-SE will not be able to shortcut-switch all flows and packets will be sent to the router.

16. A, B. There are other commands as well that may inadvertently disable MLS, but access lists no longer do. They can cause the cache to be cleared, but now, since IOS 12.0(2), inbound as well as outbound access lists are supported and do not disable MLS.

17. B. Using header compression disables MLS on the configured interface. `Clear ip route` is not a correct answer because it temporarily clears the cache, but it doesn't disable MLS.

18. D. The `mls rp ip` command is used on an external router, the first command is invalid, and `set mls enable` is used to enable MLS on a 5000 series switch.

19. C. The `mls ip` syntax is only used on the MSFC. The first command is invalid, and `set mls enable` is used to enable MLS on a 5000 series switch.

20. D. Internal routers such as RSMs or MSFCs don't require a VTP domain configuration. However, external routers that have connections to VTP servers or clients must configure the interface for the VTP domain.

Chapter 8

Hot Standby Routing Protocol (HSRP)

THE CCNP EXAM TOPICS COVERED IN THIS CHAPTER INCLUDE THE FOLLOWING:

- ✓ Fault-tolerant routing
- ✓ HSRP
- ✓ Configuring HSRP
- ✓ Setting the active routing properties
- ✓ Configuring HSRP tracking
- ✓ Configuring HSRP with multiple groups

LAN segments are very reliable when compared to their wide area counterparts. However, failure occurs on these segments as well, making fault tolerance an important issue. The most well-known fault-tolerance mechanism on a LAN consists of the dual rings encountered in Fiber Distributed Data Interface (FDDI) networks. This FDDI technique occurs at the Physical layer of the OSI model.

In this chapter, you will learn about fault-tolerance methods that occur beyond the Physical layer—in particular, fault tolerance that occurs at the Data Link and Network layers of the OSI model. The types of fault tolerance covered here include Proxy Address Resolution Protocol (ARP), Internet Control Message Protocol (ICMP), ICMP Router Discovery Protocol (IRDP), dynamic routing protocols, and the Hot Standby Routing Protocol (HSRP).

The *Hot Standby Routing Protocol (HSRP)* is a proprietary protocol developed by Cisco to support fault tolerance on multi-access media. This protocol provides high network availability and transparent network topology changes.

The specifications for HSRP were published in March 1998 as RFC 2281. A month later, the open standards implementation, called the Virtual Router Redundancy Protocol (VRRP), was published in RFC 2338. VRRP and HSRP perform the same essential function.

The purpose of HSRP is to allow hosts to appear to use a single router and still maintain connectivity, even if the actual next hop router (default gateway) they are using fails. This is accomplished by creating a virtual router and having the physical routers communicate in such a way that the virtual router is always available.

Fault-Tolerant Routing

The problem with IP routing is the default gateway configuration on a workstation. When a host is configured with a default gateway, it will always use that address to send packets out of the local network. If the router that is assigned to the default gateway goes down, the host is down to the outside world until the default gateway is fixed.

There are a few solutions, one being HSRP, of course. However, let's take a look at the other options:

- Proxy ARP
- Enabling dynamic routing protocols on the hosts
- IRDP
- HSRP

Proxy ARP

Proxy Address Resolution Protocol (Proxy ARP) is a variation of the ARP protocol in which an intermediate device, such as a router, sends an ARP response on behalf of an end node to the requesting host. Proxy ARP has been defined and referenced in many RFCs.

This technology once had a strong following, and one benefit is that it can lessen bandwidth use on slow-speed WAN links. As networks grew, however, Proxy ARP did not scale with them.

In this section, you will learn about the origin, implementation, and advantages and disadvantages of Proxy ARP.

The Origin of Proxy ARP

Originally, Proxy ARP was designed for dial-up connections, such as the example shown in Figure 8.1. You could give the dial-in machine an address taken from the subnet of the local LAN without having to create a new subnet. This conserved a substantial amount of address space.

FIGURE 8.1 Proxy ARP for dial-up connections

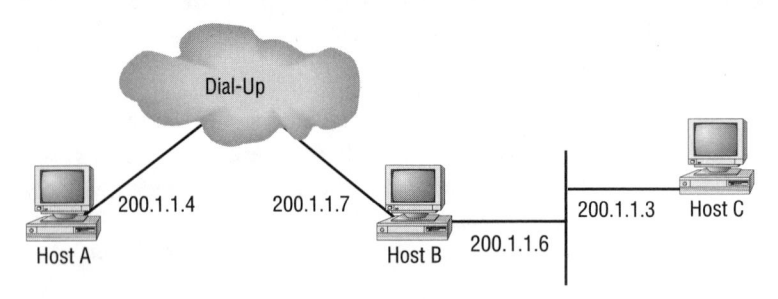

First, you should review how Proxy ARP typically functions in dial-up environments. In the example shown in Figure 8.1, when Host C wants to send a packet to Host A, it assumes that Host A is on the same segment. When Host C sends a broadcast ARP for 200.1.1.4, Host B will reply with its own MAC address. Host C will send packets that are destined for Host A to Host B's MAC address. Host B will then forward them to A. This style of Proxy ARP is still prevalent in dial-up environments.

Implementing Proxy ARP with Routers

Proxy ARP with routers works similarly to the example in Figure 8.1, but it can be configured to provide some fault tolerance. Let's consider Figure 8.2 and how Proxy ARP could be used in this example.

FIGURE 8.2 Proxy ARP with routers

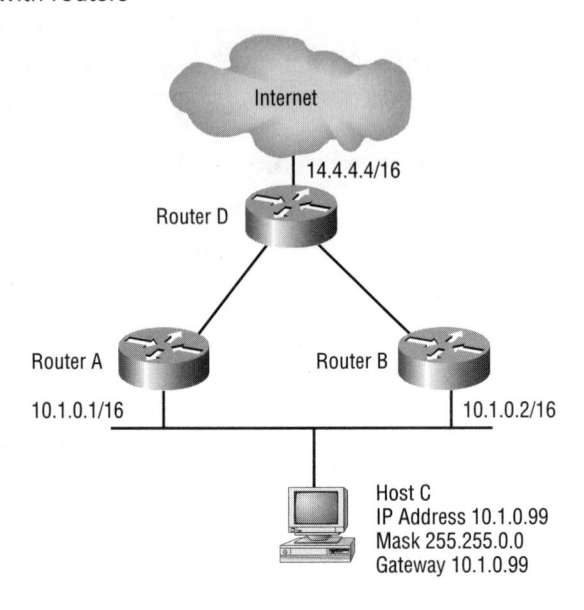

Host C has an IP address of 10.1.0.99 and a default gateway of 10.1.0.99. Note that the IP address and default gateway should be the same when clients are configured in a Proxy ARP environment. Host C will use ARP for every single IP address to which it wants to connect, regardless of whether it is on the local segment.

Enabling Proxy ARP on Cisco Routers

Proxy ARP is enabled on Cisco routers by default, as displayed in the results of the following show ip interface command:

```
RouterA#show ip interface ethernet 0
Ethernet0 is up, line protocol is up
  Internet address is 10.1.0.1/16
  Broadcast address is 255.255.255.255
  Address determined by setup command
  MTU is 1500 bytes
  Helper address is not set
  Directed broadcast forwarding is disabled
  Multicast reserved groups joined: 224.0.0.9
  Outgoing access list is not set
  Inbound  access list is not set
  Proxy ARP is enabled
  Security level is default
  Split horizon is enabled
  ICMP redirects are always sent
  ICMP unreachables are always sent
  ICMP mask replies are never sent
  IP fast switching is enabled
  IP fast switching on the same interface is disabled
  IP Null turbo vector
  IP multicast fast switching is disabled
  IP multicast distributed fast switching is disabled
  Router Discovery is disabled
  IP output packet accounting is disabled
  IP access violation accounting is disabled
  TCP/IP header compression is disabled
  Probe proxy name replies are disabled
```

```
                        Policy routing is disabled
                        Network address translation is disabled
                        Web Cache Redirect is disabled
                        BGP Policy Mapping is disabled
            RouterA#
```

If you need to enable Proxy ARP on an interface because you had disabled it, use the `ip proxy arp` command at interface level:

```
RouterA#conf t
RouterA(config)#interface ethernet 0
RouterA(config-if)#ip proxy-arp
RouterA(config-if)#^Z
```

Disabling Proxy ARP on Cisco Routers

Proxy ARP can also be disabled on the router by using the `no ip proxy-arp` command, as shown here:

```
RouterA#conf t
RouterA(config)#interface ethernet 0
RouterA(config-if)#no ip proxy-arp
RouterA(config-if)#^Z
```

Going back to the example in Figure 8.2, when Host C tries to connect to any IP address, it sends out an ARP request. Both Router A and Router B reply to this broadcast with their own MAC addresses. Host C accepts the first response that it receives and places an entry into the local ARP table. The entry will stay in the ARP table until it expires, which can be from minutes to hours, depending on the operating system.

> **NOTE:** Cisco routers default to four-hour ARP time-out.

In this example, when Host C tries to ping 14.4.4.4, it gets the following results:

```
C:\>ping 14.4.4.4

Pinging 14.4.4.4 with 32 bytes of data:
```

```
Reply from 14.4.4.4: bytes=32 time=8ms TTL=255
Reply from 14.4.4.4: bytes=32 time=3ms TTL=255
Reply from 14.4.4.4: bytes=32 time=3ms TTL=255
Reply from 14.4.4.4: bytes=32 time=3ms TTL=255

Ping statistics for 14.4.4.4:
    Packets: Sent = 4, Received = 4, Lost = 0 (0% loss),
Approximate round trip times in milli-seconds:
    Minimum = 3ms, Maximum =  8ms, Average =  4ms
```

Use the `arp -a` command to view the ARP cache on a Windows machine:

```
C:\>arp -a

Interface: 10.1.0.99 on Interface 0x1000002
  Internet Address      Physical Address       Type
  10.1.0.1              00-50-73-07-92-9c      dynamic
  10.1.0.2              00-50-73-07-c7-0b      dynamic
  14.4.4.4              00-50-73-07-c7-0b      dynamic

C:\>
```

Notice that the MAC address for 10.1.0.2 and 14.4.4.4 are the same. Router A and Router B both replied; however, Router B's packet arrived first.

You can observe the exchange on the router as shown in this output:

```
RouterB#
IP ARP: rcvd req src 10.1.0.99 0040.0526.d7ee, dst
14.4.4.4 Ethernet0
IP ARP: sent rep src 14.4.4.4 0050.7307.c70b,
            dst 10.1.0.99 0040.0526.d7ee Ethernet0
```

Now let's assume that Router B's Ethernet0 fails and Host C attempts to ping 14.4.4.4 again. Host C still has Router B's MAC address in the ARP table for getting to 14.4.4.4. The ping will fail. Now when Host C tries to ping 14.4.4.4, it gets the following results:

```
C:\>ping 14.4.4.4

Pinging 14.4.4.4 with 32 bytes of data:
```

```
Request timed out.
Request timed out.
Request timed out.
Request timed out.
C:\>
```

In this example, Host C's ARP time-out value is set to 6 minutes. After the time expires, Host C will again be able to reach 14.4.4.4. However, Host C has immediate access via Router A to any IP address it has not yet cached.

Advantages and Disadvantages of Proxy ARP

Proxy ARP offers a number of advantages and disadvantages. Among the benefits are the following:

- No need to configure clients with a gateway
- Load balancing, although this is somewhat random
- Immediate fault tolerance for addresses not recently contacted

There are also several drawbacks to Proxy ARP:

- A lot of broadcast traffic
- Must wait for ARP cache to time out in the event of failure
- No control over which router is primary and secondary

Proxy ARP does provide some fault tolerance on a multi-access segment, but it does not give the control administrators desire. A more robust and flexible method is needed. In response to this need, Cisco developed the Hot Standby Routing Protocol (HSRP).

Dynamic Routing Protocols

Another solution to the IP default gateway problem is to run dynamic routing protocols on all the hosts. The end-station host will then maintain a table of which routers have a path to the remote network they need. Of course, all your hosts on a network must be able to support dynamic routing. Both Unix workstations and Windows NT workstations support IP RIP, for example. However, the workstations will be slow to converge and have a tremendous overhead of processing and memory.

ICMP Router Discovery Protocol (IRDP)

A third solution to the IP default gateway problem is *ICMP Router Discovery Protocol (IRDP)*. This will allow hosts to use the *Internet Control Message Protocol (ICMP)* to find a new path when the primary router becomes unavailable.

IRDP is an extension of the ICMP protocol and not a dynamic routing protocol. This ICMP extension allows routers to advertise default routes to end stations. This saves processing on the end stations because they don't need to run routing protocols and no configuration of hosts by an administrator is required. However, they need to run the IRDP daemon. You can find an IRDP daemon on the Cisco FTP site (`ftp.cisco.com`).

Hosts running the IRDP daemon listen for the IRDP hello messages, which are sent out from a router as multicast packets. The hello messages are sent out every 7 to 10 minutes, with a holdtime of 30 minutes.

The problem with this topology is that it is very broadcast intensive. IRDP is not as broadcast intensive as routing protocols running on the workstations, but it still uses broadcasts to communicate to the router.

HSRP

Hot Standby Routing Protocol (HSRP) can solve the default gateway problems we listed earlier. HSRP will enable end stations to continue to communicate through the network if a router fails without placing excessive broadcasts on a network.

HSRP works by creating a single virtual standby router that really is a set of at least two routers or more. To the workstations, it appears that the virtual router is just one router interface. If a router fails in the group, another router will automatically assume the function of the default router. There is a drawback to all this, and maybe you have already figured it out. You need more than one router to run HSRP. So, although it doesn't have the broadcast problems the solutions we mentioned earlier in this chapter have, it does cost money.

What HSRP does is create a Hot Standby router group with a lead router that services all packets that are sent to the Hot Standby address. All of the other routers in the group monitor the lead router, and if the lead router fails, then a standby router inherits both the lead position and the Hot Standby group address.

HSRP defines six states in which an HSRP router may run:

Initial   All routers begin in this state when configured with HSRP. HSRP is not running on the router yet because the interface configured with HSRP is not up and active yet.

Learn   The router is in the learn state when it has not heard from the active router. It does not know the active router and does not know the IP address of the virtual router

Listen   The router enters the listen state after it hears from the active router and knows the IP virtual address. This router is not the active or standby router.

Speak   After a router learns the IP address of the virtual router, the router will enter the speak state. It will actively participate in the election of the active and standby router. It sends hello messages to the active router.

Standby   This state means the router will become the active router if the active router fails. There must one active router in the HSRP group.

Active   This state tells the router to forward packets, which are sent to the virtual IP address. There must be one active router in the HSRP group.

Configuring HSRP

Configuring HSRP is pretty simple. We'll show you more difficult configurations of HSRP that you can use in larger internetworks later in this chapter. But for now, let's consider the simple example shown in Figure 8.3. Here there is a virtual router with the IP address of 10.1.0.200. All clients on that Ethernet segment configure that IP address as their default gateway.

FIGURE 8.3 HSRP with two routers

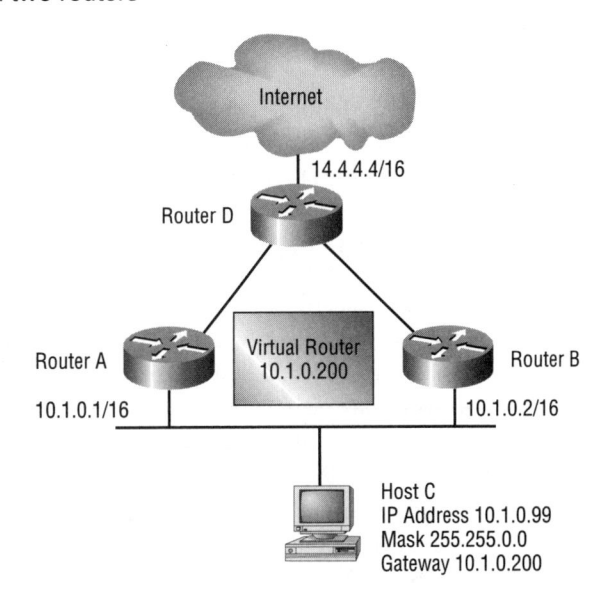

Enabling HSRP on the router requires minimal configuration. In the example shown in Figures 8.3, we want Routers A and B to create a virtual router with the IP address of 10.1.0.200.

To do this, use the following commands:

```
RouterB#conf t
Router(config)#int f0/0
RouterB(config-if)#standby 1 ip 10.1.0.200
RouterB(config-if)#^Z
00:03:31: %STANDBY-6-STATECHANGE: Standby: 1: FastEthernet0/0 state Speak-> Standby
00:03:31: %STANDBY-6-STATECHANGE: Standby: 1: FastEthernet0/0 state Standby-> Active
```

When workstations ARP for the hardware address of 10.1.0.200, the virtual address will be given. All routers will use this virtual address to give to workstations. You verify the HSRP configuration with the show standby command:

```
RouterB#show standby
Ethernet0 - Group 1
```

```
       Local state is Standby, priority 100
       Hellotime 3 holdtime 10
       Next hello sent in 00:00:01.628
       Hot standby IP address is 10.1.0.200 configured
       Active router is 10.1.0.1 expires in 00:00:09
       Standby router is local
       Standby virtual mac address is 0000.0c07.ac01
RouterB#
```

You can also see the virtual router address by looking at the ARP table on a router. Remember that the Address Resolution Protocol (ARP) is used to find a hardware (MAC) address from a known IP address. Once the ARP protocol has resolved an IP address to a hardware address, the hardware address is placed in the ARP cache for four hours. The next time the router needs to communicate to a device connected on a LAN that is connected to a router interface, the router will look in the ARP cache for the hardware address. This makes the resolution faster than it would be if a broadcast were sent every time. The command to see the ARP table is show ip arp. Here is an example:

```
Router#sh ip arp
Protocol  Address     Age (min)  Hardware Addr   Type  Interface
Internet  10.1.0.200     -       0000.0c07.ac01  ARPA  FastEthernet0/0
Router#
```

Notice that the address 10.1.0.200 is in the ARP table and is resolved to a hardware address. The router's F0/0 interface is configured with the IP address, hence the dash (-) in the minute column. The 0000.0c is the Cisco vendor code. The 07.ac is the HSRP Well-Known Virtual MAC Address. The 01 is the HSRP group number.

After both routers have been configured, they begin transmitting hello packets every three seconds to the multicast address 224.0.0.2. This is shown in the output below:

```
SB1:Ethernet0 Hello out 10.1.0.2 Standby pri 100 hel 3 hol
10 ip 10.1.0.200
SB1:Ethernet0 Hello in 10.1.0.1 Active pri 100 hel 3 hol
10 ip 10.1.0.200
```

If the standby router stops receiving hellos from the active router, it will then start answering for the virtual IP address, thinking the active router is down.

Active Router Properties

The first router configured will become the active router. The active router is the router currently forwarding packets for the virtual router. The standby router is the primary backup router.

The Priority option set on the router controls which router will be the active router when the election occurs. The default priority on a router is 100, and the router with the highest priority wins the election. However, if a router with a lower priority is the active router and a router with a higher priority joins the group, an election will not occur unless the Preempt option is set. If the Preempt option is set, then the new router will force an election. If the new router wins, it becomes the active router. This process is called a *coup*.

The router output below shows this process:

```
RouterB#conf t
RouterB(config)#int ethernet 0
RouterB(config-if)#standby 1 priority 110
RouterB(config-if)#standby 1 preempt
17:44:30: %STANDBY-6-STATECHANGE: Standby: 1: Ethernet0
state Standby     -> Active
RouterB(config-if)#^Z
RouterB#sh standby
Ethernet0 - Group 1
  Local state is Active, priority 110, may preempt
  Hellotime 3 holdtime 10
  Next hello sent in 00:00:01.288
  Hot standby IP address is 10.1.0.200 configured
  Active router is local
  Standby router is 10.1.0.1 expires in 00:00:09
  Standby virtual mac address is 0000.0c07.ac01
RouterB#
```

Additional properties can be set to control the virtual address of the router: the Hello interval, which is 3 seconds by default, and the Hold interval, which is 10 seconds by default. If Router B did not transmit any hellos for 10 seconds, Router A would become the active router.

HSRP Tracking

The next problem addressed by HSRP is the failing of other interfaces besides the one running HSRP. In the example shown in Figure 8.3, for instance, if Router B's WAN connection should fail, you would want Router A to become the active router. You can accomplish this by HSRP tracking.

You can configure Router B so that if the WAN interface fails, Router B will reduce its priority by a set amount. The default amount is 10. Take a look at this sample to see how it is done:

```
RouterB#conf t
RouterB(config)#int ethernet 0
RouterB(config-if)#standby 1 track serial 0 50
RouterB(config-if)#exit
RouterB(config)#int serial 0
RouterB(config-if)#shutdown
%LINEPROTO-5-UPDOWN: Line protocol on Interface Serial0,
changed state to down
SB1: Ethernet0 Priority was 110 now 60, configured as 110
SB1:Ethernet0 Hello out 10.1.0.2 Active pri 60 hel 3 hol
10 ip 10.1.0.200
SB1:Ethernet0 Coup in 10.1.0.1 Standby pri 100 hel 3 hol
10 ip 10.1.0.200
18:01:37: %STANDBY-6-STATECHANGE: Standby: 1: Ethernet0
state Active     -> Speak
SB1:Ethernet0 Resign out 10.1.0.2 Speak pri 60 hel 3 hol
10 ip 10.1.0.200
SB1:Ethernet0 Hello out 10.1.0.2 Speak pri 60 hel 3 hol 10
ip 10.1.0.200
SB1:Ethernet0 Hello in 10.1.0.1 Active pri 100 hel 3 hol
10 ip 10.1.0.200
```

Let's consider what happened in the preceding sample. Router B was configured to track interface serial 0. If interface serial 0 goes down, then Router B should reduce the standby priority by 50. When serial 0 is shut down, the priority drops from 110 to 60. Router A, which must be configured to Preempt, becomes the active router (a coup) because it has a priority of 100. As you can see in the following output, Router B is now the standby router:

```
RouterB#show standby
Ethernet0 - Group 1
  Local state is Standby, priority 60, may preempt
```

```
          Hellotime 3 holdtime 10
          Next hello sent in 00:00:01.172
          Hot standby IP address is 10.1.0.200 configured
          Active router is 10.1.0.1 expires in 00:00:08
          Standby router is local
          Standby virtual mac address is 0000.0c07.ac01
          Tracking interface states for 1 interface, 0 up:
            Down Serial0 Priority decrement: 50
        RouterB#
```

HSRP with Multiple Destinations

HSRP has provisions for more complex scenarios involving multiple routers and multiple destinations. Consider three routers on a LAN segment providing connectivity to two different locations, as shown in Figure 8.4.

FIGURE 8.4 HSRP with multiple destinations

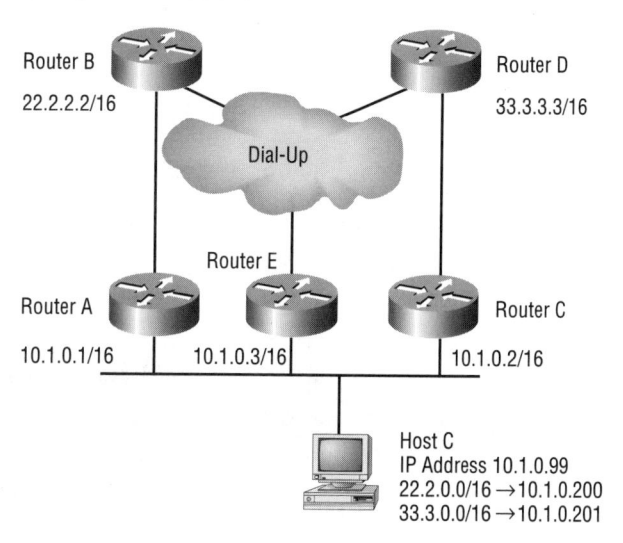

As you can see in this figure, Router A is directly connected and the primary link to the 22.2.0.0/16 network, and Router C is directly connected and the primary link to the 33.3.0.0/16 network. In the event that Router A fails, Router E can establish a link to the 22.2.0.0/16 network. In the event that Router C fails, Router E can establish a link to the 33.3.0.0/16 network. Notice that the gateway addresses are virtual so that the workstation is not stuck using one default gateway address. This stops the administrators from having to reconfigure the workstation's IP configuration if a router fails.

HSRP with Multiple Groups

HSRP uses the concept of groups to allow for just about any combination of router and backup topologies that you can imagine. Generally, you will create one HSRP group per destination. In this example (as shown in Figure 8.5), you will create two HSRP groups.

FIGURE 8.5 HSRP with multiple groups

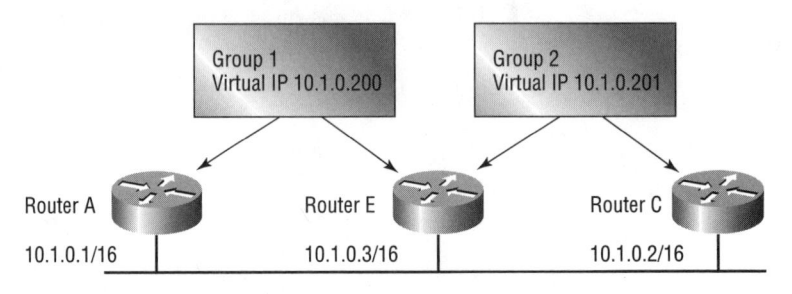

This shows the process of creating two HSRP groups:

```
RouterE#conf t
RouterE(config)#interface ethernet 0
RouterE(config-if)#standby 1 ip 10.1.0.200
RouterE(config-if)#standby 1 preempt
RouterE(config-if)#standby 1 priority 90
RouterE(config-if)#standby 1 authentication dallas
RouterE(config-if)#standby 2 ip 10.1.0.201
RouterE(config-if)#standby 2 preempt
RouterE(config-if)#standby 2 priority 90
RouterE(config-if)#standby 2 authentication clearwater
RouterE(config-if)#
```

Router E is made a member of both Group 1 and Group 2. The lower priority of 90 ensures that Routers A and C will be the primary routers. The authentication key is not really for security because it is transmitted in the packet. The key helps prevent against incorrect configuration.

HSRP also provides support protocols other than IP, including AppleTalk, Banyan Vines, Novell IPX, DECnet, and XNS. This provides a complete solution to providing fault tolerance on multi-access media.

Once you have HSRP configured, you can troubleshoot and monitor HSRP with the show standby and debug standby commands. Because we have already looked at the show standby command, we'll demonstrate only the debug standby command:

```
Router#debug standby
Hot standby protocol debugging is on
Router#
00:15:32: SB1:FastEthernet0/0 Hello out 10.1.0.200 Active pri 100
hel 3 hol 10 ip 10.1.0.200
00:15:35: SB1:FastEthernet0/0 Hello out 10.1.0.200 Active pri 100
hel 3 hol 10 ip 10.1.0.200
00:15:38: SB1:FastEthernet0/0 Hello out 10.1.0.200 Active pri 100
hel 3 hol 10 ip 10.1.0.200
```

Notice that the hello is sent out 10.1.0.200 and is the active router with a priority of 100. The hello time is shown as 3 seconds with a holdtime of 10 seconds.

Summary

In this chapter, we discussed the different ways you can configure your network to support redundant connections—specifically, default gateways.

The types of fault tolerance that we covered included Proxy Address Resolution Protocol (Proxy ARP), Internet Control Message Protocol (ICMP), ICMP Router Discovery Protocol (IRDP), dynamic routing protocols, and the Hot Standby Routing Protocol (HSRP).

We showed you how to configure HSRP and implement it in an internetwork using Cisco routers.

Key Terms

Before you take the exam, be sure you're familiar with the following terms:

Hot Standby Routing Protocol (HSRP)

ICMP Router Discovery Protocol (IRDP)

Internet Control Message Protocol (ICMP)

Proxy Address Resolution Protocol (Proxy ARP)

Commands Used in This Chapter

Because this chapter was not based on layer 2 distribution and access layer switches, only one table of commands is supplied.

Commands	Meaning
`show ip interface ethernet 0`	Shows the IP configuration of Ethernet 0, including whether Proxy ARP is configured and if access lists are set on the interface
`ip proxy-arp`	Enables the interface for Proxy ARP (on by default)
`no ip proxy-arp`	Disables Proxy ARP on an interface
`standby`	Sets an interface to be part of an HSRP group
`show standby`	Shows the HSRP configuration of an interface
`show ip arp`	Shows the IP addresses that have been resolved to a hardware address
`standby 1 priority`	Sets the priority of HSRP on an interface

Commands	Meaning
standby 1 preempt	Sets the interface to force an election if a router joins the HSRP group with a higher priority than the other routers in the group
standby 1 track serial 0 50	Tells HSRP to monitor a connected serial link that is not running HSRP
standby 1 authentication	Does not provide authentication, only checks that correct information is received
debug standby	Allows you to monitor and verify the HSRP group

Written Lab

Complete this lab by writing out the answers to the following questions:

1. Write the command that will allow you to view the table that holds the IP-to-MAC addresses resolved on a router.

2. Write the command to enable HSRP on an FE0/0 interface using a group number of 2, IP address of 1.1.1.1.

3. Write the command that will force an election if a new router joins the HSRP group 2 with a higher priority than the active router.

4. Write the command to change the priority to 110.

5. Write the command to set the router to track serial 0 and set the router priority to decrement by 50 if it fails.

6. Write the command to view the virtual address of an HSRP group.

7. What command can you type on the router to view the hellos being sent and received on an HSRP interface?

8. The router enters the _____ state after it hears from the active router and knows the virtual IP address.

9. This state means the router will become the active router if the active router fails.

10. The default priority on a router is _____ .

Hands-On Lab

In this lab, you'll use Figure 8.6 as a network diagram to configure HSRP. Notice that we have added another router to the network. This will allow you to run the HSRP protocol as a redundancy method.

FIGURE 8.6 Chapter 8 hands-on lab

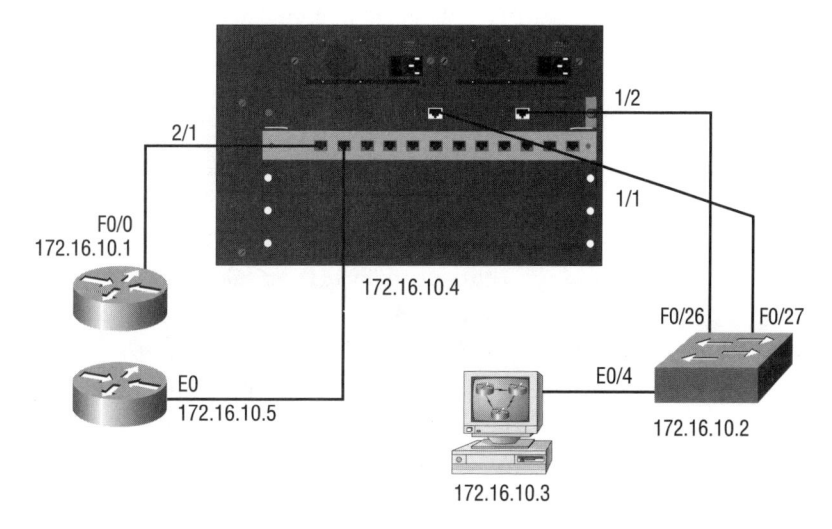

1. Check your connections to make sure both your routers are connected to the switch.

2. Configure the 2501A with an IP address of 172.16.10.5 on the ethernet interface 0.

3. Ping the 2501A from the 5000 switch and from the 2621A router.

4. From the 2621A console, create a standby group 1 with an IP address of 172.16.10.50 in FastEthernet 0/0.

   ```
   2621A(config-if)#int f0/0
   2621A(config-if)#ip address 172.16.10.1 255.255.255.0
   2621A(config-if)#no shut
   2621A(config-if)#standby 1 ip 172.16.10.50
   2621A(config-if)#
   ```

5. On the console of the 2501A router, create the standby group 1 with the virtual IP address of 172.16.10.50.

   2501A(config)#**int e0**
   2501A(config-if)#**ip address 172.16.10.5 255.255.255.0**
   2501A(config-if)#**no shut**
   2501A(config-if)#**standby 1 ip 172.16.10.50**

6. Type the show standby command on both routers to view the HSRP information.

   ```
   2621A#sh stan
   FastEthernet0/0 - Group 1
     Local state is Active, priority 100
     Hellotime 3 holdtime 10
     Next hello sent in 00:00:01.104
     Hot standby IP address is 172.16.10.50 configured
     Active router is local
     Standby router is 172.16.10.5 expires in 00:00:09
     Standby virtual mac address is 0000.0c07.ac01
   2621A#


   2501A#sh stand
   Ethernet0 - Group 1
     Local state is Standby, priority 100
     Hellotime 3 holdtime 10
     Next hello sent in 00:00:00.586
     Hot standby IP address is 172.16.10.50 configured
     Active router is 172.16.10.1 expires in 00:00:09
     Standby router is local
     Standby virtual mac address is 0000.0c07.ac01
   2501A#
   ```

7. Notice that the 2621A router is the active router (local) and that 2501A is the standby. This is because the 2621A router was configured first. Both have a priority of 100, hello time of 3 seconds, and holdtime of 10 seconds.

8. Type the debug standby command on the 2621A router to view the hello messages being sent and received on the router's F0/0 interface.

```
2621A#debug stand
Hot standby protocol debugging is on
2621A#
00:16:48: SB1:FastEthernet0/0 Hello in 172.16.10.5
Standby pri 100 hel 3 hol 10
ip 172.16.10.50
00:16:51: SB1:FastEthernet0/0 Hello out 172.16.10.1
Active pri 100 hel 3 hol 10
ip 172.16.10.50
00:16:51: SB1:FastEthernet0/0 Hello in 172.16.10.5
Standby pri 100 hel 3 hol 10
ip 172.16.10.50
00:16:53: SB1:FastEthernet0/0 Hello out 172.16.10.1
Active pri 100 hel 3 hol 10
ip 172.16.10.50
00:16:54: SB1:FastEthernet0/0 Hello in 172.16.10.5
Standby pri 100 hel 3 hol 10
ip 172.16.10.50
2621#un all
All possible debugging has been turned off
2621A#
```

9. Notice that the hello is from 172.16.10.5 and is announcing itself as a standby router with a priority of 100, a hello time of 3 seconds, and a holdtime of 10 seconds. Also notice that the 2621A router is sending out the same information, except that it is advertising itself as the active router.

10. Run the `debug standby` command on the 2501A router and view the information.

   ```
   2501A#debug stand
   00:05:13: SB1:Ethernet0 Hello out 172.16.10.5 Standby pri 100 hel 3 hol 10 ip 172.16.10.50
   00:05:14: SB1:Ethernet0 Hello in 172.16.10.1 Active pri 100 hel 3 hol 10 ip 172.16.10.50
   00:05:16: SB1:Ethernet0 Hello out 172.16.10.5 Standby pri 100 hel 3 hol 10 ip 172.16.10.50
   00:05:17: SB1:Ethernet0 Hello in 172.16.10.1 Active pri 100 hel 3 hol 10 ip 172.16.10.50
   2501A#un all
   All possible debugging has been turned off
   RouterC#
   ```

11. Notice that the 2501A router is transmitting standby router information and receiving active router hellos.

12. Unplug the cable for the 2621A router and turn on debugging on the 2501A router.

   ```
   2501A#debug stand
   Hot standby protocol debugging is on
   RouterC#
   00:06:06: SB1:Ethernet0 Hello out 172.16.10.5 Standby pri 100 hel 3 hol 10 ip 172.16.10.50
   00:06:07: %STANDBY-6-STATECHANGE: Standby: 1: Ethernet0 state Standby   -> Active
   00:06:07: SB1:Ethernet0 Hello out 172.16.10.5 Active pri 100 hel 3 hol 10 ip 172.16.10.50
   00:06:07: SB1: Ethernet0 changing MAC address to 0000.0c07.ac01
   ```

13. Notice that when the cable to the 2621A router was unplugged, the state change took place. The 2501A router is now the active router. Notice that the Ethernet MAC address is changed to the virtual MAC address.

14. Plug the cable to the 2621A router back in and notice that the 2621A router does not become the active router. Run `debug stand` on the 2501A router to see this.

    ```
    00:06:54: SB1:Ethernet0 Hello out 172.16.10.5 Active
    pri 100 hel 3 hol 10 ip 172
    .16.10.50
    00:06:57: SB1:Ethernet0 Hello in 172.16.10.1 Speak pri
    100 hel 3 hol 10 ip 172.1
    6.10.50
    00:06:57: SB1:Ethernet0 Hello out 172.16.10.5 Active
    pri 100 hel 3 ho
    ```

15. Even though the 2621A router has sent and received a hello, it is in speak state and did not cause a reelection because the priorities are the same. You want the 2621A to be the active router because it is running FastEthernet, so change the priority of the router so it's higher and make it force an election. In addition, to make an HSRP router force an election, you must also add the `preempt` command or it won't work.

    ```
    2621A#config t
    Enter configuration commands, one per line.  End with CNTL/Z.
    2621A(config)#int f0/0
    2621A(config-if)#stand 1 prio 150
    2621A(config-if)#stand 1 preempt
    2621A(config-if)#^Z
    2621A#debug stand
    00:23:26: %SYS-5-CONFIG_I: Configured from console by console
    Hot standby protocol debugging is on
    2621A#
    00:23:26: %STANDBY-6-STATECHANGE: Standby: 1:
    ```

```
FastEthernet0/0 state Standby
-> Active

00:23:29: SB1:FastEthernet0/0 Hello in 172.16.10.5
Speak pri 100 hel 3 hol 10 ip
 172.16.10.50
00:23:29: SB1:FastEthernet0/0 Hello out 172.16.10.1
Active pri 150 hel 3 hol 10
ip 172.16.10.50
```

16. Type the show standby command to view the HSRP configuration. Notice that the priority is 150 and it may preempt.

```
2621A#sh stand
FastEthernet0/0 - Group 1
  Local state is Active, priority 150, may preempt
  Hellotime 3 holdtime 10
  Next hello sent in 00:00:01.930
  Hot standby IP address is 172.16.10.50 configured
  Active router is local
  Standby router is 172.16.10.5 expires in 00:00:08
  Standby virtual mac address is 0000.0c07.ac01
2621A#
```

Review Questions

1. What state would an HSRP router be in if it was answering for the virtual IP address?

   A. Active

   B. Passive

   C. Initial

   D. Standby

2. What state would an HSRP router be in if it was listening for hellos from the router that is answering the virtual IP address and will take over if that router fails?

   A. Active

   B. Passive

   C. Initial

   D. Standby

3. What state is an HSRP router in when it first boots and does not know the virtual IP address?

   A. Active

   B. Passive

   C. Initial

   D. Standby

4. Which two of the following will help you monitor and troubleshoot HSRP?

   A. `sh active`

   B. `show standby`

   C. `debug standby`

   D. `debug all`

5. What is the default priority of an HSRP router?

   A. 10

   B. 100

   C. 1000

   D. 1

6. Which of the following commands is correct for assigning interface ethernet 0 to HSRP group 3?

   A. router(config)#standby 3 1.1.1.1

   B. router(config-if)#standby 3 1.1.1.1

   C. router(config)#standby 3 ip 1.1.1.1

   D. router(config-if)#standby 3 ip 1.1.1.1

7. If you are running HSRP on FastEthernet 0/1 and you want to monitor serial 0, which is on the same router but is not running HSRP, which of the following commands will allow the router to drop the priority on the HSRP router so that the serial interface can be used on the standby router if serial 0 drops on the active router?

   A. standby f0/0 to s0

   B. standby 1 track serial 0 50

   C. standby f0/0 serial 0 55

   D. standby s0 f0/0 50

8. If you want to change the priority of an HSRP interface from the default to 110, which of the following commands would you use?

   A. standby 1 priority 110

   B. standby priority group 110

   C. standby group priority 110

   D. int e0, group priority 110

9. Which command will you use to force an election if a router with a higher HSRP priority joins HSRP group 1?

   A. `standby election on`

   B. `standby priority 1`

   C. `standby preempt 1`

   D. `standby 1 preempt`

10. If you use the command `standby 1 authentication denver`, which of the following statements is then true?

    A. Only routers sending packets to Denver can use the HSRP protocol.

    B. Only routers in the router group named Denver can use HSRP.

    C. Each router in the network must use the password Denver to use HSRP.

    D. The Denver authentication is used to make sure packets are sent with correct information; no authentication actually takes place.

11. What protocols can be used with HSRP?

    A. IP

    B. TCP

    C. AppleTalk

    D. DECnet

    E. Banyan

    F. IPX

12. After a router learns the virtual IP address, the router will enter the _____ state.

    A. Active

    B. Passive

    C. Speak

    D. Listen

    E. Standby

13. What is the minimum number of routers that need to be in an active state within an HSRP group?

    A. One

    B. Two

    C. Three

    D. All routers in the network

14. Which command is used to see the cache on a router that stores the IP-to-Ethernet translations?

    A. `show arp cache`

    B. `show ip arp`

    C. `show cache`

    D. `show arp cache`

15. Which is true regarding Proxy ARP?

    A. It is used to find the hardware address of a Token Ring device.

    B. It is used only with Ethernet.

    C. It is used to find an IP address of a remote device.

    D. It is used to find the hardware address of a router if none is specified in the workstation's configuration.

16. Which of the following is used to provide fault-tolerant routing? (Choose all that apply.)

    A. Proxy ARP

    B. IP ARP

    C. RIP

    D. IRDP

    E. HSRP

17. Which is true regarding IRDP?

    A. The broadcasts are sent out every interface every 30 seconds.

    B. The hello messages are sent out every 7 to 10 minutes, with a hold-time of 30 minutes.

    C. IRDP works only with Unix devices.

    D. IRDP hello messages are sent out every 60 seconds with a holdtime of 7 to 10 minutes.

18. Which of the following commands is used to see the virtual IP address of the HSRP active router?

    A. `show hsrp status`

    B. `show hsrp standby address`

    C. `show standby`

    D. `show hsrp address`

19. Which of the following is true regarding HSRP?

    A. It is a Cisco proprietary protocol.

    B. It can be used on routers and switches.

    C. It is an industry-standard protocol.

    D. It can be used only with Cisco 7000 series routers.

20. What command will show you the standby virtual MAC address?

    A. `show hsrp status`

    B. `show hsrp standby address`

    C. `show standby`

    D. `show hsrp address`

Answers to Written Lab

1. show ip arp
2. int f0/0
   standby 2 ip 1.1.1.1
3. Standby 2 preempt
4. standby 2 priority 110
5. standby 1 track serial 0 50
6. show standby
7. debug standby
8. Listen
9. Standby
10. 100

Answers to Review Questions

1. A. A router that is in the active state answers the ARP request for the virtual IP address.

2. D. The HSRP standby state means that a router will not answer for the virtual IP address unless the active router goes down.

3. C. An HSRP router will come up into initial state upon bootup and then listens for the active router to provide the virtual IP address.

4. B, C. The `show standby` and `debug standby` are used to check the virtual IP address, the virtual MAC address, and the hellos sent and received.

5. B. The default priority of an HSRP router is 100. To configure a router with a higher priority, you would set it at 150, for example.

6. D. The interface command `standby [group] [protocol] [virtual ip address]` is used to create a standby group.

7. B. The `standby [group] track [interface] [new priority]` command is used to keep an eye on an interface other than the interface running HSRP.

8. A. The `standby [group] priority [new priority]` command is used to change an interface to a new HSRP priority.

9. D. The `standby [group] preempt` command must be used to tell a router that a new election must be held if a new HSRP interface joins the group with a higher priority. If you do not use the `preempt` command, an election will not be held.

10. D. The authentication command does not provide authentication; it makes the router interface running HSRP check to make sure that the packets contain the correct information and are not corrupted.

11. A, C, D, E, F. HSRP allows most protocols including IP, AppleTalk, Banyan Vines, Novell IPX, DECnet, and XNS.

12. D. An HSRP router will enter the listen state after the virtual IP address is known.

13. A. You can have only one router answering for the virtual IP address at a time.

14. B. The command `show ip arp` will display the contents of the ARP cache. The entries are valid for four hours by default.

15. D. If you set the default gateway on a Windows device to the same address as the workstation's IP address, the workstation will arp for every device as if it were local. A router running the Proxy ARP protocol will forward those requests if necessary.

16. A, C, D, E. Proxy ARP, dynamic routing protocols running on hosts (RIP, for example), IRDP, and HSRP are used to provide fault tolerance in routed networks.

17. B. Routers send IRDP multicasts to IRDP hosts every 7 to 10 minutes. The hosts will hold this information up to 30 minutes.

18. C. The `show standby` command will display the virtual IP address, the virtual MAC address, and the IP address of the active and standby routers.

19. A. HSRP was developed by Cisco and only works with the Cisco IOS.

20. C. The `show standby` command will display the virtual IP address, the virtual MAC address, and the IP address of the active and standby routers.

Chapter 9

Multicast

THE CCNP EXAM TOPICS COVERED IN THIS CHAPTER INCLUDE THE FOLLOWING:

- ✓ Overview of multicast
- ✓ Multicast addressing
- ✓ Managing multicast in an internetwork
- ✓ Routing multicast traffic

Just as blue, green, and red are the primary colors, unicast, multicast, and broadcast are the primary forms of communication on networks.

Today's Web and enterprise applications are directed to larger audiences on the network than ever before, causing increased bandwidth requirements. This increased demand on bandwidth can be accommodated with as little cost increase as possible by using multicast. For example, voice and video are being sourced for larger and larger audiences. One-on-one communications can overwhelm both servers and network resources. Unlike unicast and broadcast, however, multicast services can eliminate this problem.

This chapter will help you understand the differences in unicast, broadcast, and multicast communication methods and when each should be used. Unicast is an excellent method of point-to-point communication, whereas broadcast traffic is imperative for many systems and protocols to work on a network. Multicast comes in as a bridge between these two communication extremes by efficiently allowing point-to-multipoint data forwarding. It is imperative that you understand how multicast addressing spans both layer 3 and layer 2 of the OSI model. You will also learn about the protocols and tools used to implement and control multicast traffic on your network. As with any service that runs on your network, you must understand the resources needed and the implications of enabling multicast.

Multicast Overview

Just as blue, green, and red are different and each has its own place within the spectrum of visible light, unicast, broadcast, and multicast are different in that each is used to achieve a specific purpose or fulfill requirements of a specific part of the communication spectrum. It is important to know where each falls within the spectrum as well as the potential applications.

RFC 1112 discusses multicast and goes into great detail about host extensions and multicast groups. In addition to address assignment for multicast applications and hosts, protocol methods and procedures are discussed. For example, it covers the methods by which hosts join and leave multicast groups, and it also covers group advertisements and multicast forwarding.

Unicast

Unicast is used for direct host-to-host communication. When the layer 3 Protocol Data Unit (PDU, or packet) is formed, two layer 3 IP addresses are added to the IP header. These are the source and destination IP addresses. They specify a particular originating and receiving host. After the layer 3 PDU is formed, it is passed to layer 2 to create the layer 2 PDU, or frame. The frame consists of all of the previous layers' headers in addition to the layer 2 header. With an Ethernet frame, for example, the two 48-bit source and destination MAC addresses are specified in the layer 2 header. Other protocols such as IEEE 802.5 (Token Ring) and FDDI also have headers that contain specific host source and destination addresses.

Unicast communication is used when two hosts need only to exchange data with one another and are not concerned with sharing the data with everyone. A MAC address must *uniquely* identify a host. No two MAC addresses are the same. Therefore, unicast capitalizes on the unique MAC address for each host. With the specific address, any source host should be able to contact the destination host without confusion.

One of the caveats to unicast communication is that the source host must know or be able to learn what every destination MAC is for every station it wishes to communicate with. This may not be done on a host-by-host basis. The normal operation is that the host has a default gateway assigned for use when the logical destination address does not reside on the same subnet as the source host. Figure 9.1 depicts how unicast traffic works on the same subnet.

FIGURE 9.1 Unicast communication

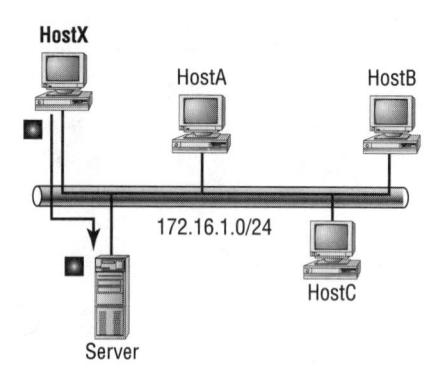

The unicast process, then, is a two-way communication. These two hosts are interested only in communicating with one another. So what happens when one host wants to talk to multiple hosts or all of the hosts on the same network segment? That is where broadcast communications come in.

Broadcast

Now that you have a good understanding of unicast, we can discuss the principle of broadcast communication on networks. Whereas unicast messages target a single host on a network (unicast communication can be compared to sending an e-mail to a friend; the mail is addressed to the friend, and it is sent from you), *broadcast* messages are meant to reach all hosts on a broadcast domain. Figure 9.2 depicts a broadcast message sent from HostX to all machines within the same broadcast domain.

FIGURE 9.2 Broadcast message on a network

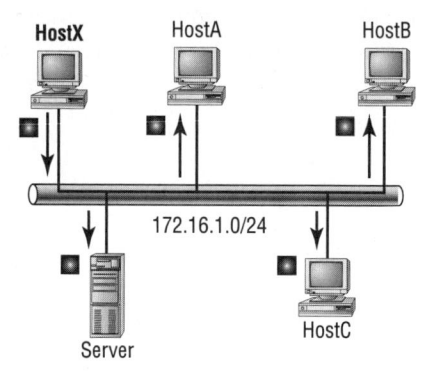

A good example of a broadcast message is an Address Resolution Protocol (ARP) request. When a host has a packet destined for a logical address that is not located on the same network, the host must ARP for the default gateway's MAC address so it can create the layer 2 frame and in turn send the datagram to the router. The MAC address is obtained via an ARP request. The ARP request is a broadcast message sent to all devices in the broadcast domain. The router will be the device that responds to the broadcast message, whereas other stations will evaluate the frame but not respond.

This brings up another good point. Broadcasts can cause problems on networks. Because the broadcast frame is addressed to include every host, every host must process the frame. CPU interruption occurs so that the frame may be processed. This interruption affects other applications that are running on the host. When unicast frames are seen by a router, a quick check is made to identify whether the frame is intended for the host or not. If it isn't, the frame is discarded.

Multicast

Multicast is a different beast entirely. At first glance, it appears to be a hybrid of unicast and broadcast communication, but that isn't quite accurate. Multicast does allow point-to-multipoint communication, which is similar to broadcasts, but it happens in a different manner. The crux of *multicast* is that it allows multiple recipients to receive messages without flooding the messages to all hosts on a broadcast domain.

Multicast works by sending messages or data to IP *multicast group* addresses. Routers then forward copies of the packet out every interface that has hosts *subscribed* to that group address. This is where multicast differs from broadcast messages. With unicast communication, copies of packets are sent only to subscribed hosts.

The difference between multicast and unicast is comparable to the difference between mailing lists and SPAM. You subscribe to a mailing list when you want to receive mail from a specific group regarding specific information—for example, a Cisco User Group mailing list. You expect to get only messages from other members of the group regarding topics related to the user group. In contrast, SPAM is unsolicited mail that arrives in your inbox. You aren't expecting it from the sender, nor are you likely to be interested in the content.

Chapter 9 · Multicast

Multicast works in much the same way as a mailing list. You (as a user) or an application will *subscribe* to a specific IP multicast group to become a member. Once you're a member of the group, IP multicast packets containing the group address in the destination field in the header will arrive at your host and be processed. If the host isn't subscribed to the group, it will not process packets addressed to that group. Refer to Figure 9.3 for a visual reference on how multicast works.

FIGURE 9.3 Multicast communication

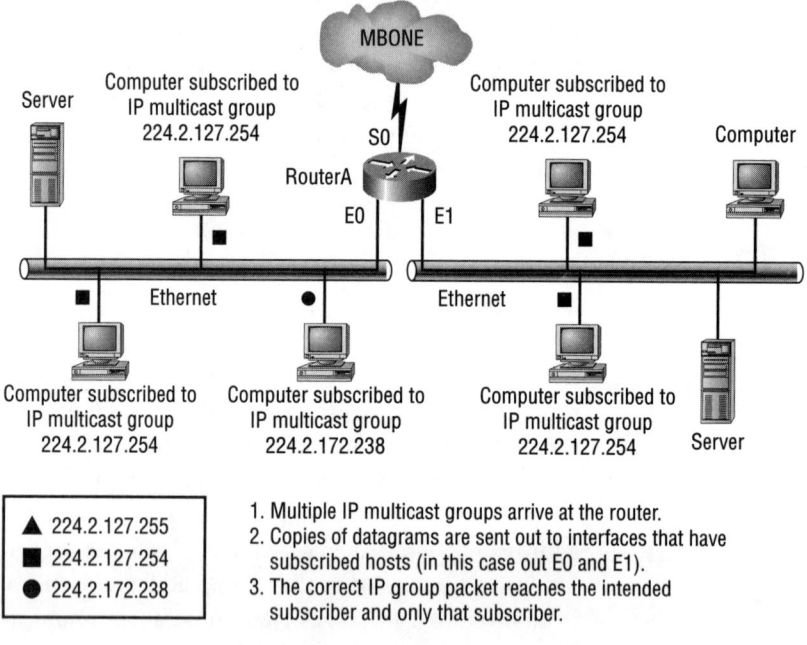

1. Multiple IP multicast groups arrive at the router.
2. Copies of datagrams are sent out to interfaces that have subscribed hosts (in this case out E0 and E1).
3. The correct IP group packet reaches the intended subscriber and only that subscriber.

Note: The router did not forward packets belonging to 224.2.127.255.

The key to multicast is the addressing structure. This is key because all communication is based on addressing. In unicast communication, there is a unique address for every host on a network. With broadcast communication, a global address that all hosts will respond to is used. Multicast uses addressing that only some hosts will respond to. The next section will cover multicast addressing in detail.

Multicast Addressing

Just as with mailing lists, there are several different groups that users or applications can subscribe to. The range of multicast addresses starts with 224.0.0.0 and goes through 239.255.255.255. As you can see, this range of addresses falls within IP Class D address space based on classful IP assignment. This is denoted by the fact that the first four bits in the first octet are 1110. Just as with regular IP addresses, there are some addresses that can be assigned and there are ranges of reserved addresses.

It is important to recognize that the reserved addresses are categorized. Table 9.1 depicts some of the reserved addresses and their corresponding categories. For a full listing of these assignments, you can go to **www.isi.edu/in-notes/iana/assignments/multicast-addresses**.

TABLE 9.1 IP Multicast Reserved Addresses

Address	Purpose	Reserved Category
224.0.0.0–224.0.0.18	Use by network protocols	Local-link
224.0.0.1	All hosts	Local-link
224.0.0.2	All routers	Local-link
224.0.0.19–224.0.0.255	Unassigned	Local-link
224.0.1.0–224.0.1.255	Multicast Applications	Misc. Applications
224.0.1.1	NTP	Misc Applications
224.0.1.8	NIS+	Misc Applications
224.0.1.39	Cisco-RP-Announce	Misc Applications
224.0.1.40	Cisco-RP-Discovery	Misc Applications

TABLE 9.1 IP Multicast Reserved Addresses *(continued)*

Address	Purpose	Reserved Category
224.0.1.80–224.0.1.255	Unassigned	Misc Applications
239.0.0.0–239.255.255.255	Private multicast domain	Administratively Scoped

Each address range is managed by the Internet Address Number Authority (IANA). Due to the limited amount of multicast addresses, there are very strict requirements for new assignments within this address space. The 239.0.0.0–239.255.255.255 range is equivalent in purpose to the private networks defined by RFC 1918.

The difference between the IP multicast ranges of 224.0.0.0–224.0.0.255 and 224.0.1.0–224.0.1.255 is that addresses in the first range will not be forwarded by an IP router. Both ranges of addresses are used by applications and network protocols. The first group, classified as local-link, is meant to remain local to the subnet or broadcast domain on which the system resides. The second group is a global address that can be routed and forwarded across multiple IP routers.

Mapping IP Multicast to Ethernet

Multicast addressing began on MAC addresses. Growth needs required that there be a way to use multicast across routers instead of limiting it to the physical segment where hosts were located. In regular unicast, MAC addresses are layer 2 addresses, and in order for the local host to reach remote hosts, layer 3 logical IP addresses are used to route data to the destination. Once the packet reaches the remote subnet, the Address Resolution Protocol (ARP) is used to find the MAC address of the host. By using an existing ARP table, or via an ARP request, the MAC address that is associated to the layer 3 IP address is found and the packet is forwarded to the destination host.

IP multicast generates a MAC address based on the layer 3 IP multicast address. The MAC frame has a standard prefix of 24 bits. This prefix, 01-00-5e, is used for all Ethernet multicast addresses. This leaves another 24 bits for use in creating the multicast MAC address. When the MAC address is generated, the 25th bit (or high order bit) is set to 0 and then the last 23 bits of the IP address are mapped in to the remaining 23 bits of the MAC address. Figure 9.4 depicts how this looks.

FIGURE 9.4 IP multicast mapped to MAC multicast

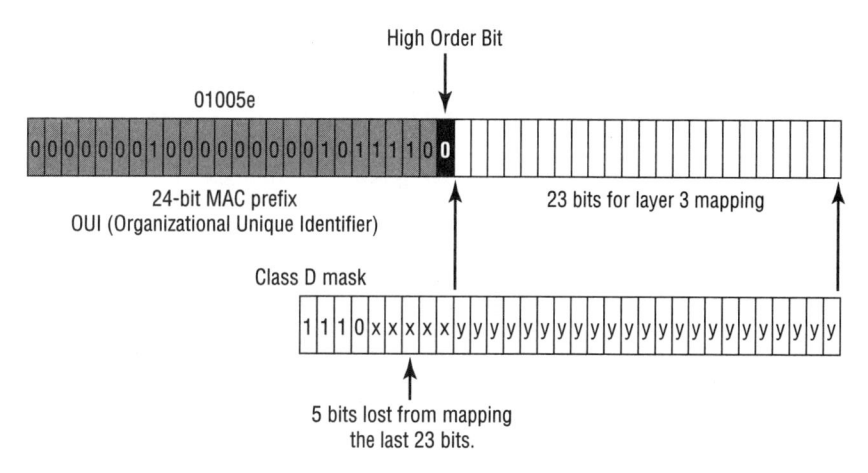

Let's look at some examples for mapping layer 3 multicast addresses to layer 2 multicast addresses. A local IP multicast address is 224.0.0.1. Refer to Figure 9.5 to see how this is mapped. The conversion from binary to hex reveals the MAC multicast address. The prefix was 01-00-5e. The last 23 bits, including the high order bit, give you 00-00-01. Put them together and you get 01-00-5e-00-00-01 as the MAC address.

FIGURE 9.5 Example #1 for mapping IP multicast to MAC multicast addresses

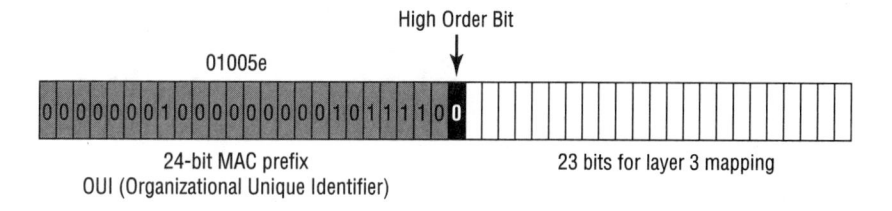

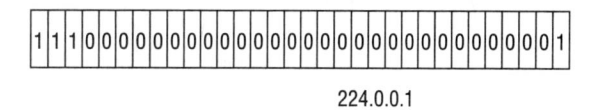

Now let's try one a little bit harder. Suppose, for example, you have the IP multicast address of 225.1.25.2 (follow along with Figure 9.6). Part of the 225 octet falls within the Class D mask. However, there is one bit that is not masked. By looking carefully at the location of the bit, you will see that it is part of five lost bits and is not mapped to the layer 2 MAC multicast address.

FIGURE 9.6 Example #2 for mapping IP multicast to MAC multicast addresses

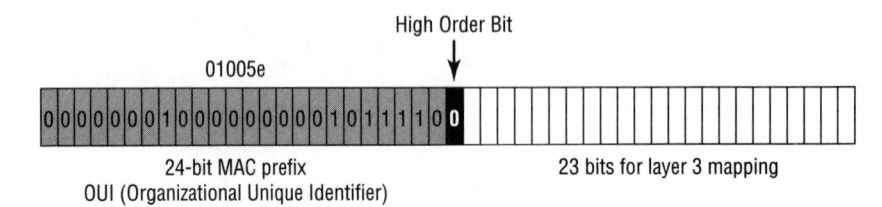

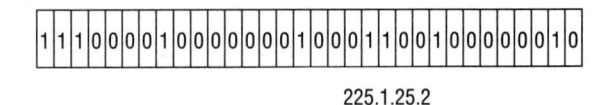

Do the conversion of the octets from decimal into binary so you can get a clear picture of what the last 23 bits are. Here you would see the following address (the last 23 bits are indicated with the bold font): 11100001.00000001.00011001.00000010. Also, as you can see, Figure 9.6 depicts the last 23 bits that are mapped into the free spaces of the multicast MAC address. After the mapping has occurred in binary, convert the binary value to hex and you will have the new MAC multicast address.

After you do the math and map the last 23 bits, the MAC address becomes 01-00-5e-01-19-02. The easiest way to map layer 3 to layer 2 manually is to do the math and make the binary conversion so you can see what the last 23 bits of the layer 3 IP address are. Once you have that number, all you have to do is insert it into the MAC address and then calculate the remaining 3 hex octet values. The first three octets will always be the same, 01-00-5e.

It is important that you spend time studying this procedure and the steps needed to convert a layer 3 IP multicast address to a layer 2 MAC multicast address.

There is one last method of determining the last 23 bits, but this method will work only on some addresses. Keep in mind that the highest value you can get in the second octet is 127 and still have it be included in the 23 bits that will map to the MAC address. You know that the last 2 octets (3 and 4) will map no matter what. So you will have 7 bits from the second octet and a total of 16 bits from the last 2 octets for a total of 23 bits. Once your value goes above 127 in the second octet, you will have to break down the octet into binary so you can see the values of the first 7 fields.

Layer 3 to Layer 2 Overlap

After you have done a few of these conversions, you'll notice, or maybe you already have, that there is a problem with this conversion scheme. By not using all available bits for a Class D address, you cannot get an accurate map of layer 3 to layer 2 addresses. If you look at properties of a Class D address, you will see that the high order bit lies in the first octet and is in the 16's value position. This leaves 28 bits for host specification. However, by using only 23 bits of the layer 3 IP address, you leave 5 bits out of the mapping. This causes an overlap of 2^5, or 32 layer 3 addresses for every 1 layer 2 address. With a ratio of 32:1, you can expect to see a significant amount of address ambiguity. It is safe to say that any IP addresses that have the same values in the last 23 bits will map to the same MAC multicast address.

For example, 224.0.1.1 and 225.128.1.1 map to the same MAC address. Figure 9.7 shows why this is true. You can see that the bits that differ between 224.0.1.1 and 225.128.1.1 are all within the lost 5 bits. The last 23 bits are equivalent.

FIGURE 9.7 Multicast addressing overlap

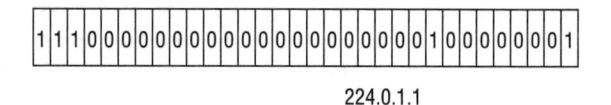

224.0.1.1

225.128.1.1

Final MAC multicast address
01-00-5e-00-01-01

The impact that this may have can be significant. This overlap creates a window for multiple multicast groups' data to be forwarded to and processed by machines that didn't intentionally subscribe to the multiple groups. To give another example, a machine that subscribes to a multicast group 224.2.127.254 would be given a MAC address of 01-00-5e-02-7f-fe. This host will also process packets that come from multicast group 225.2.127.254 because the layer 2 MAC address is identical.

The problem this creates is that the end host must now process packets from both multicast groups even though it is only interested in data from 224.2.127.254. This causes unwanted overhead and processor interrupts on the host machine.

Managing Multicast in an Internetwork

As a user on the network, you can understand that SPAM is not something that is managed by a systems administrator, whereas valid mailing lists require maintenance to keep a current list of valid subscribers. The same can be said of multicast. Reverting a little to the differences between broadcast and multicast communication, one of the major differences that we discussed is that broadcast traffic goes to all hosts on a subnet, whereas multicast traffic only goes to the hosts that request it. The distinguishing factor that puts multicast traffic so far ahead of broadcast traffic in utility is the ability to specify which multiple hosts will receive the transmission.

This isn't done magically; it doesn't know who and where the recipients are just because it's multicast traffic. As with any application, protocols are needed to make things happen. Multicast works on the basis of host subscription to groups.

Several methods and protocols have been developed and implemented to facilitate multicast functionality within the internetwork:

- Subscribing groups
- Maintenance groups
- Joining groups
- Leaving groups

Each of these protocols and methods is used for specific tasks or to achieve specific results within the multicast environment.

We will now look at these protocols and learn just where they fit in and what they are needed for. We will begin with the most important, subscription and group maintenance, and then move on to enhancements for multicast deployment and distribution.

Subscribing and Maintaining Groups

For multicast traffic to reach a host, that host must be running an application that sends a request to a multicast-enabled router informing the router that it wishes to receive data belonging to the specified multicast group. If this request were to never take place, the router wouldn't be aware that the host was waiting for data for the specified group.

As an overview, a multicast-enabled router receives all group advertisements and routes. It listens on all interfaces, waiting for a request from a host to forward multicast group traffic. Once a host on an interface makes a request to become a member of a group, the interface activates the requested group on itself and only on itself. While the host is a member, multicast data will be forwarded to that interface and any host subscribed to the group will receive the data.

That was a simple overview; now let's look at how this is accomplished in more detail. We will start by discussing three major host subscription protocols:

- IGMPv1
- IGMPv2
- CGMP

The differences among them will become apparent as we get further into the discussion.

Internet Group Management Protocol Version 1 (IGMPv1)

As the name indicates, *Internet Group Management Protocol version 1 (IGMPv1)* was the first version of the protocol. It was a result of RFC 1112. The purpose of this protocol is to allow hosts to subscribe to or join specified multicast groups. By subscribing to groups, the hosts are thereby enabled to receive multicast data forwarded from the router.

IGMP has several processes that it executes to manage multicast group subscription and maintenance. We will discuss them in greater detail so you can get an understanding of what happens.

IGMPv1 Processes

Three processes are employed by version 1 of IGMP:

- Query
- Joining
- Leaving

These processes are the means by which multicast group membership is maintained. The first two processes are functional processes, whereas the Leaving process is more of a time-out than a formal request. Each process is defined in detail in the following sections.

Membership Query Process

One important process is the *IGMP Query process*, which is kindred to a keepalive procedure. Because the router needs to keep tabs on which multicast groups need to remain active or be made active or inactive, it sends a

Membership Query out each interface. The query is directed to the reserved address of 224.0.0.1, to which all multicast hosts will answer.

Once the request is received, the hosts report back with their group subscription information. Once a specific group has been reported to the router, subsequent reports for the same group coming from different hosts will be suppressed. This is done because only one host on a subnet/VLAN needs to request membership for the router to activate that group on the interface. Once active on the router interface, any host on that segment wanting to receive data for that specific group will receive it. Figure 9.8 depicts how this process works.

FIGURE 9.8 IGMPv1 Query routine

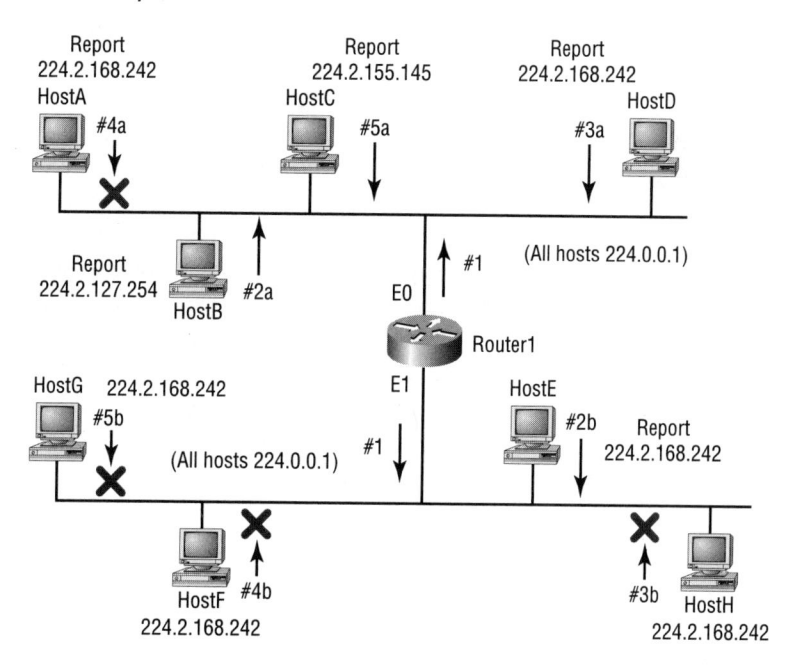

You can follow the numbers indicated in the figure. First, the query to 224.0.0.1 is sent, and subsequently, the hosts begin to report back. The first host to respond (#2a) is HostB, requesting data for the multicast group 224.2.127.254. HostD responds next (#3a) with a request for the group 224.2.168.242. The next host to reply is HostA (#4a). However, because the report from HostD was already multicast to the 224.2.168.242 group, HostA heard the report and suppressed its own report to the group.

The protocol is smart enough to understand that once one host has reported, more hosts need to report as well. This helps prevent unwanted and unnecessary bandwidth and processor utilization.

HostC (#5a) responds with a different group number, 224.2.155.145. Once all of the hosts have responded to the query, Router1 can maintain activity for these groups on interface E0.

Notice that this description applies to interface E0 on Router1. Simultaneously, a multicast flood to 224.0.0.1 was sent out interface E1 as well. The first host to respond on this segment is HostE (#2b), and it is reporting membership to 224.2.168.242. Notice that this report was not suppressed, even though HostD had already multicast a report to this group. The router queries the local All hosts address 224.0.0.1, which is not forwarded by the router. That is why the same query is sent out all interfaces on the router. Now that HostE has multicast to the group for that segment, none of the other hosts on the E1 segment will report due to the fact that they are all members of the 224.2.168.242 group.

Joining Process

The other processes are joining and leaving multicast groups. Both of these processes are quite simple and straightforward. You understand how interfaces are maintained in an active state through Membership Queries. The query process only runs every 60 seconds. If a host wants to join a multicast group outside the Membership Query interval, it may simply send an unsolicited report to the multicast router stating that it wants to receive data for the specified multicast group. Figure 9.9 depicts how this occurs. This is known as the *IGMP Join process*.

FIGURE 9.9 Unsolicited join requests

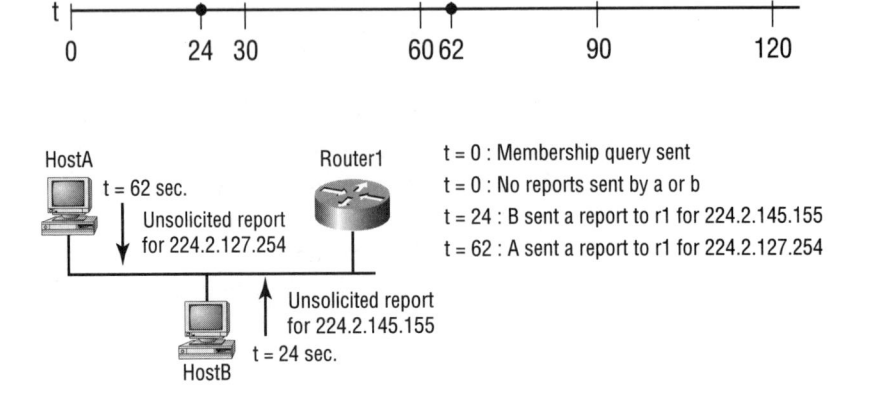

HostA
t = 62 sec.
Unsolicited report for 224.2.127.254

HostB
Unsolicited report for 224.2.145.155
t = 24 sec.

Router1

t = 0 : Membership query sent
t = 0 : No reports sent by a or b
t = 24 : B sent a report to r1 for 224.2.145.155
t = 62 : A sent a report to r1 for 224.2.127.254

Leaving Process

Withdrawal from a group is not initiated by the host as one would imagine. The router hosts a timer that is reset every time a response is received from a host on the subnet. The timer runs for 3 minutes, which is equivalent to 3 Membership Query cycles (every 60 seconds). If the timer expires and no response is received from the hosts on the interface, the router disables multicast forwarding on that interface.

Internet Group Management Protocol Version 2 (IGMPv2)

As with any software revision, things are made better. Defined by RFC 2236, *Internet Group Management Protocol version 2 (IGMPv2)* provides the same functionality as version 1 did, but with a few enhancements:

- The Leave process in version 2 was included to avoid long time-outs that are experienced in version 1.
- There are two Query forms, General and Group.
- Network traffic is less bursty due to new timing mechanisms.

In the following sections, these enhancements will be discussed.

IGMPv2 Processes

It is important to be aware of issues when both versions of IGMP are present on the network. Version 2 provides backward compatibility with version 1, but the functionality of version 2 is lost when it's operating with version 1 devices. A version 2 host has to use version 1 frame formats when talking with a version 1 router. The same applies when a version 2 router tries to communicate with a version 1 host; it must use the version 1 format.

General and Group-Specific Query Processes

One enhancement that was made to IGMPv2 processes was the creation of a new query type. The Membership Query, as it was called in IGMPv1, was renamed General Queries, and the new type is Group-Specific Query. The new query type is used to query a specific multicast group (kind of obvious from the name). The overall procedure is the same as it is in IGMPv1.

When multiple IGMPv1 routers existed on the same segment, a multicast routing protocol made the decision as to which of all the multicast routers would perform the Membership Queries. Now, the decision is made using a feature added to IGMPv2. This feature is known as the Querier Election Process.

The frame for the query was changed to enable a Maximum Response Time that allows the hosts on the segment more time to respond to the query. This reduces the bursty traffic on the network.

IGMPv2 Leave Process

IGMPv2 implemented the capability for hosts to remove themselves from the multicast group immediately (in a matter of seconds) instead of having to wait up to three minutes. The process is known as the *IGMP Leave process*. The two new additions of the Leave and Group-Specific messages work together to allow a host to remove itself from the multicast group immediately without interrupting the state of the interface on the multicast router.

Figure 9.10 depicts how the IGMPv2 Leave process works. First, HostA sends a Leave message to the All multicast routers address (224.0.0.2) expressing the intent to withdraw from the multicast group. Because Router1 doesn't know how many hosts on the segment belong to group 224.2.155.145, it must send a Group-Specific Query to see if there are any hosts that remain members of the group. If no responses are received, the router disables multicast forwarding out of the interface for the 224.2.155.145 group. If any hosts respond to the query, the router leaves the interface status quo. In the figure, you can see that HostB responds because it is still participating in the group 224.2.155.145. Hence, the interface is left active for that group.

FIGURE 9.10 IGMPv2 Leave process

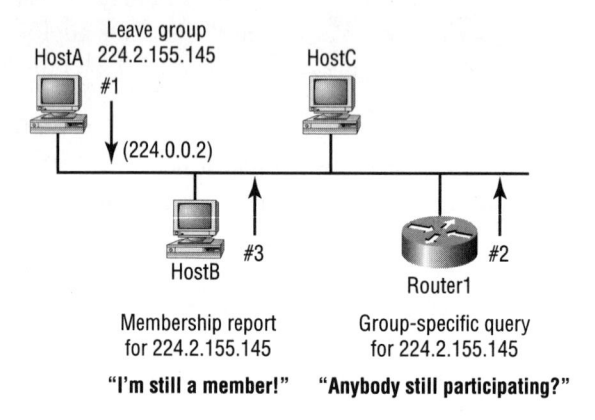

Cisco Group Management Protocol (CGMP)

We have discussed IGMPv1 and IGMPv2, which are open standard protocols for host membership of multicast groups. When running multicast at layer 2, things get a little complicated for the switch. It doesn't know which packets are membership report messages or which are actual multicast group data packets because all of them have the same MAC address. *Cisco Group Management Protocol (CGMP)* was implemented to fill this void. It runs on both routers and switches.

The key feature of CGMP is that it uses two MAC addresses:

Group Destination Address (GDA)   The GDA is the multicast group address mapped to the MAC multicast address.

Unicast Source Address (USA)   The USA is the unicast MAC address of the host. It allows the host to send multicast membership reports to the multicast router—the multicast router can also be a Route Switch Module (RSM) or Multilayer Switch Feature Card (MSFC)—and still tell the switch which port needs to receive the multicast data using the USA.

In addition to being able to make port assignments on the switch, CGMP also handles the interface assignment on the router. If a switch doesn't have any ports that need to receive multicast data, CGMP will inform the router that it doesn't need to forward multicast group data out the router interface.

CGMP Processes

CGMP uses many of the same processes IGMP uses. The main difference is that CGMP is used between the router and switch. When switches are involved, the IGMP requests must be translated to CGMP and passed on to the switch. These processes include the following:

- CGMP Join process
- Switch host management
- CGMP Leave process

CGMP Join

Hosts do not use CGMP; only the switches and routers that the host connects to use it. When a host sends an IGMP report (membership report) advertising membership of a multicast group, the message is forwarded to the router (i.e., an actual multicast router, RSM, or an MSFC) for processing. The router sees the request and processes it accordingly. The multicast group is set up, and the two MAC addresses are generated. The router then gives the switch the CGMP message. With the CGMP message, the switch can assign the multicast group to the port of the requesting host. You can see the entire process in Figure 9.11.

FIGURE 9.11 CGMP Join process

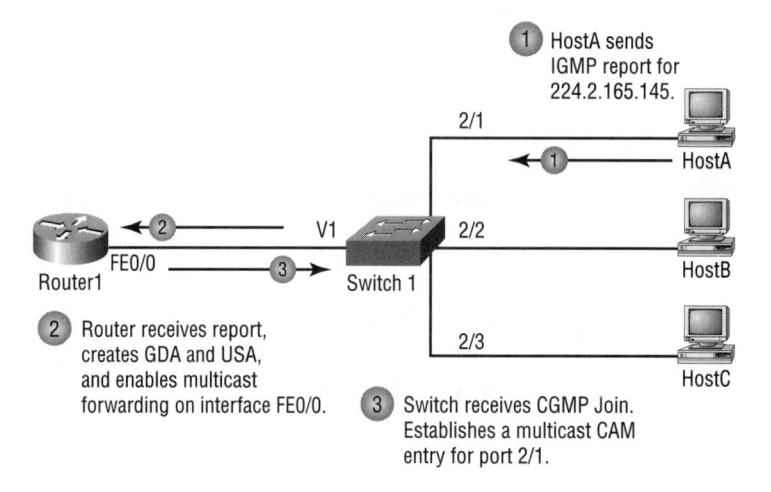

```
1  HostA sends IGMP report for 224.2.165.145.
2  Router receives report, creates GDA and USA, and enables multicast forwarding on interface FE0/0.
3  Switch receives CGMP Join. Establishes a multicast CAM entry for port 2/1.
```

Host Management

Host management is performed by the router. The router continues to receive IGMP messages from the host. Then the router converts the message into a CGMP message and forwards it to the switch. The switch then performs the port maintenance as directed by the router. This process is followed for the multiple types of message that the host can generate.

The CGMP Leave process is done in the same manner. The router receives the request and then informs the switch that the multicast group address needs to be removed from the Content Addressable Memory (CAM) table for the host's port.

Routing Multicast Traffic

Up to this point, we have been discussing the host side of multicast. You have learned how hosts interact with switches and routers to join multicast groups and receive the traffic. It is now time to move on to discuss how multicast traffic travels across the Internet (or intranet) from a source on a remote network to a local router and host.

Unicast data uses routing protocols to accomplish the task of getting data to and from remote destinations. Multicast does the same, but it goes about it in a somewhat different manner. Unicast relies on routing tables. Multicast uses a sort of spanning tree system to distribute its data. The following sections describe the tree structures that can be implemented to allow multicast routing. In addition to trees, several different protocol methods can be used to achieve the desired implementation of multicast.

Distribution Trees

Two types of trees exist in multicast:

Source trees *Source trees* use the architecture of the source of the multicast traffic as the root of the tree.

Shared trees *Shared trees* use an architecture in which multiple sources share a common rendezvous point.

Each of these methods is effective and allows sourced multicast data to reach an arbitrary number of recipients of the multicast group. Let's discuss each of them in detail.

Source Tree

Source trees use special notation. This notation is used in what becomes a multicast route table. Unicast route tables use the destination address and next hop information to establish a topology for forwarding information. Here is a sample from a unicast routing table:

```
B    210.70.150.0/24 [20/0] via 208.124.237.10, 3d08h
B    192.5.192.0/24 [20/0] via 208.124.237.10, 2w1d
B    193.219.28.0/24 [20/0] via 208.124.237.10, 1d03h
B    136.142.0.0/16 [20/0] via 208.124.237.10, 3d07h
B    202.213.23.0/24 [20/0] via 208.124.237.10, 1w2d
     202.246.53.0/24 is variably subnetted, 2 subnets, 2 masks
B       202.246.53.0/24 [20/0] via 208.124.237.10, 1w2d
B       202.246.53.60/32 [20/0] via 208.124.237.10, 1w2d
```

Multicast route tables are somewhat different. Here is a sample of a multicast table. Notice that the notation is different. Instead of having the destination address listed and then the next hop to get to the destination, source tree uses the notation of (S, G). This notation specifies the source host's IP address and the multicast group address for which it is sourcing information. Let's take the first one, for example. This is seen as (198.32.163.74, 224.2.243.55), which means that the source host is 198.32.163.74 and it is sourcing traffic for the multicast group 224.2.243.55:

```
(198.32.163.74, 224.2.243.55), 00:01:04/00:01:55, flags: PT
  Incoming interface: POS1/0/0, RPF nbr 208.124.237.10, Mbgp
  Outgoing interface list: Null
(198.32.163.74, 224.2.213.101), 00:02:06/00:00:53, flags: PT
  Incoming interface: POS1/0/0, RPF nbr 208.124.237.10, Mbgp
  Outgoing interface list: Null
(195.134.100.102, 224.2.127.254), 00:00:28/00:02:31, flags: CLM
  Incoming interface: POS1/0/0, RPF nbr 208.124.237.10, Mbgp
  Outgoing interface list:
    FastEthernet4/0/0, Forward/Sparse, 00:00:28/00:02:54
    FastEthernet4/1/0, Forward/Sparse, 00:00:28/00:02:31
(207.98.103.221, 224.2.127.254), 00:00:40/00:02:19, flags: CLM
  Incoming interface: POS1/0/0, RPF nbr 208.124.237.10, Mbgp
  Outgoing interface list:
    FastEthernet4/0/0, Forward/Sparse, 00:00:41/00:02:53
    FastEthernet4/1/0, Forward/Sparse, 00:00:41/00:02:19
(128.39.2.23, 224.2.127.254), 00:04:43/00:02:06, flags: CLMT
  Incoming interface: POS1/0/0, RPF nbr 208.124.237.10, Mbgp
  Outgoing interface list:
    FastEthernet4/0/0, Forward/Sparse, 00:04:43/00:02:43
    FastEthernet4/1/0, Forward/Sparse, 00:04:43/00:03:07
(129.237.25.152, 224.2.177.155), 00:17:58/00:03:29, flags: MT
  Incoming interface: POS1/0/0, RPF nbr 208.124.237.10, Mbgp
  Outgoing interface list:
    FastEthernet4/0/0, Forward/Sparse, 00:17:58/00:02:44
```

Figure 9.12 gives you a good picture of how source trees work.

FIGURE 9.12 Source tree forwarding

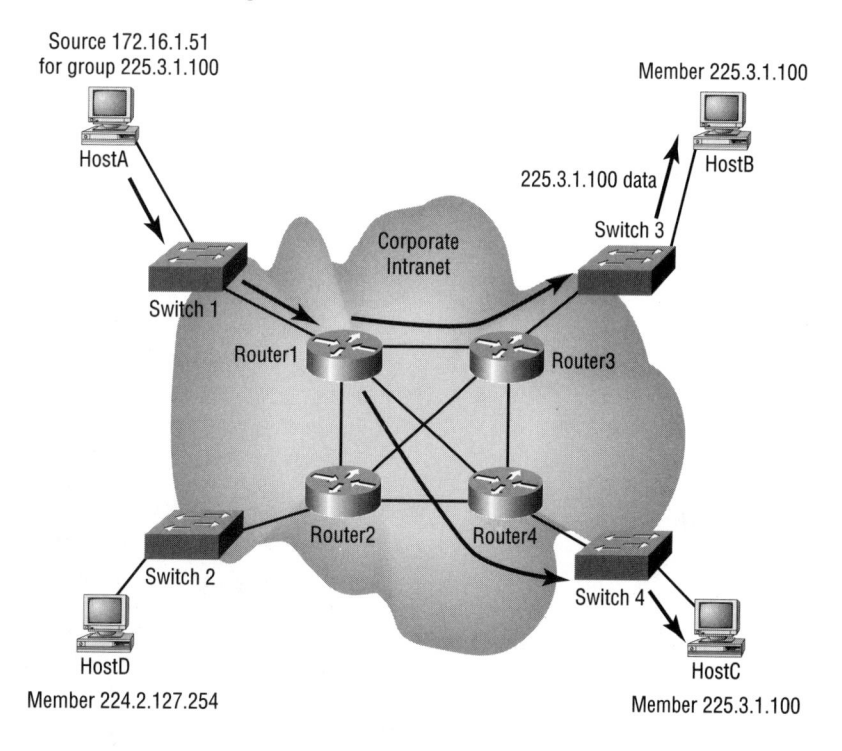

Also notice in the drawing that the shortest path to the receivers was chosen. This is known as choosing the shortest path tree (SPT). You can see from the preceding output that there are three sources for the same group of 224.2.127.254. This indicates that there are three SPT groups shown here: (195.134.100.102, 224.2.127.254), (207.98.103.221, 224.2.127.254), and (128.39.2.23, 224.2.127.254). Each of these sources has its own shortest path tree to the receivers.

Shared Tree

There are two types of shared tree distribution:

- Unidirectional
- Bidirectional

They both work a little differently than source tree distribution. Shared tree architecture lies in the characteristic that there may be multiple sources for one multicast group. Instead of each individual source creating its own SPT and distributing the data apart from the other sources, a shared root is designated. Multiple sources for a multicast group forward their data to a shared root or rendezvous point (RP). The rendezvous point then follows SPT to forward the data to the members of the group. Figure 9.13 depicts how the shared tree distribution works.

FIGURE 9.13   Shared tree forwarding

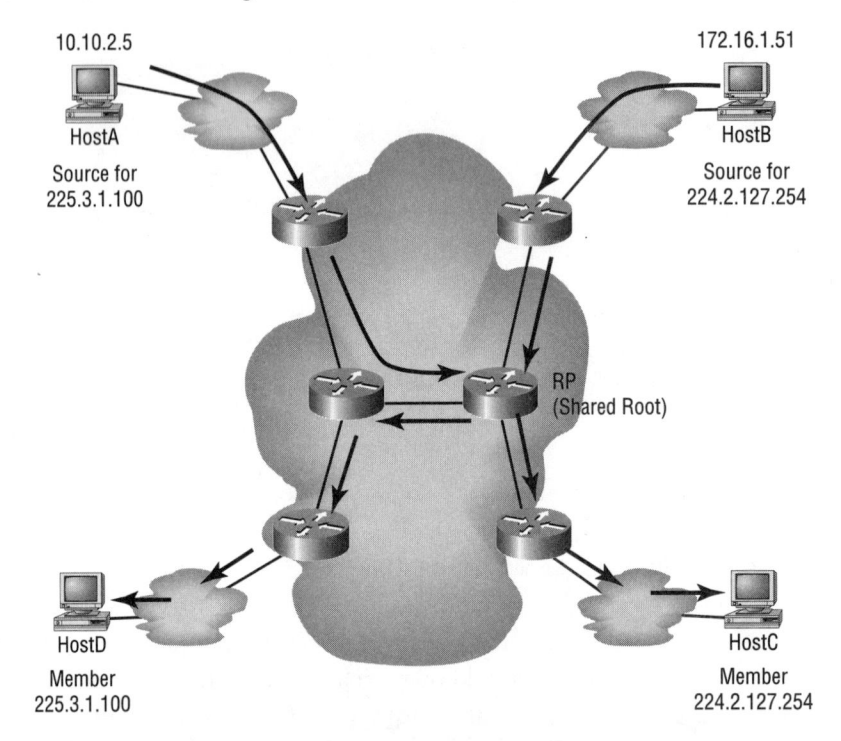

Unidirectional Shared Tree Distribution

Unidirectional shared tree distribution operates as shown in Figure 9.13. All recipients of a multicast group receive the data from a rendezvous point (RP) no matter where they are located in the network.

Bidirectional Shared Tree Distribution

Bidirectional shared tree distribution operates somewhat differently. If a receiver lives upstream from the RP, it can receive data directly from the upstream source. Figure 9.14 depicts how this works. As you can see, HostA is a source for group 224.2.127.254 and HostB is a receiver of that same group. In a bidirectional shared tree, data goes directly from HostA to HostB without having to come from the RP.

FIGURE 9.14 Bidirectional shared tree

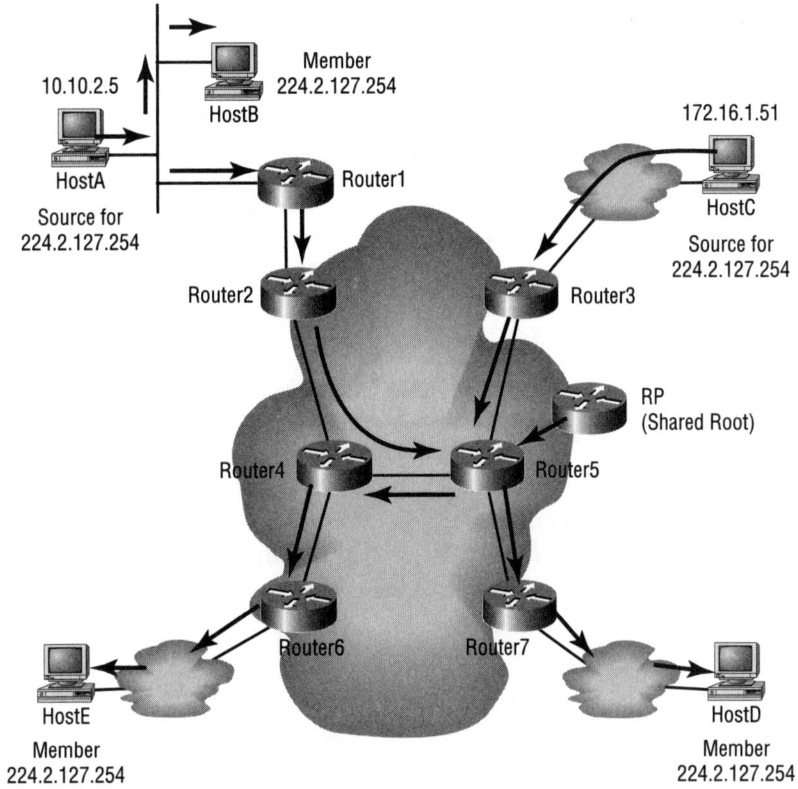

Managing Multicast Delivery

Even though the tree distributions explain how source information is managed, we must now discuss how the actual data delivery is managed. There are several methods of making sure that delivery is as efficient as possible. The ones that will be discussed here are Reverse Path Forwarding (RPF), Time-to-Live (TTL) attributes, and routing protocols.

RPF works in tandem with the routing protocols, but it will be described briefly here. As you have seen in the figures, specifically Figures 9.13 and 9.14, the traffic goes only to the multicast group receivers. We also broached the fact that bidirectional distribution eliminates the need to forward data upstream. You may ask, "How do you define *upstream*?" It is easy to clarify. By means of the routing protocols, routers are aware of which interface leads to the source(s) of the multicast group. That interface is considered *upstream*.

The Reverse Path Forwarding process is based on the upstream information. When it receives an incoming multicast packet, the router verifies that the packet came in on an interface that leads back to the source. The router forwards the packet if the verification is positive, otherwise the packet is discarded. This check stops potential loops. To avoid increased overhead on the router's processor, a multicast forwarding cache is implemented for the RPF lookups.

Time to Live (TTL)

You can also control the delivery of IP multicast packets through the TTL counter and TTL thresholds. The Time-to-Live counter is decremented by one every time the packet hops a router. Once the TTL counter is set to zero, the packet is discarded.

Thresholds are used to achieve higher granularity and greater control within one's own network. Thresholds are applied to specified interfaces of multicast-enabled routers. The router compares the threshold value of the multicast packet with the value specified in the interface configuration. If the TTL value of the packet is greater than or equal to the TTL threshold configured for the interface, the packet will be forwarded through that interface.

TTL thresholds allow network administrators to bound their network and limit the distribution of multicast packets beyond the boundaries. This is accomplished by setting high values for outbound external interfaces. The maximum value for the TTL threshold is 255. Refer to Figure 9.15 to see how network boundaries can be set to limit distribution of multicast traffic.

FIGURE 9.15 TTL threshold utilization

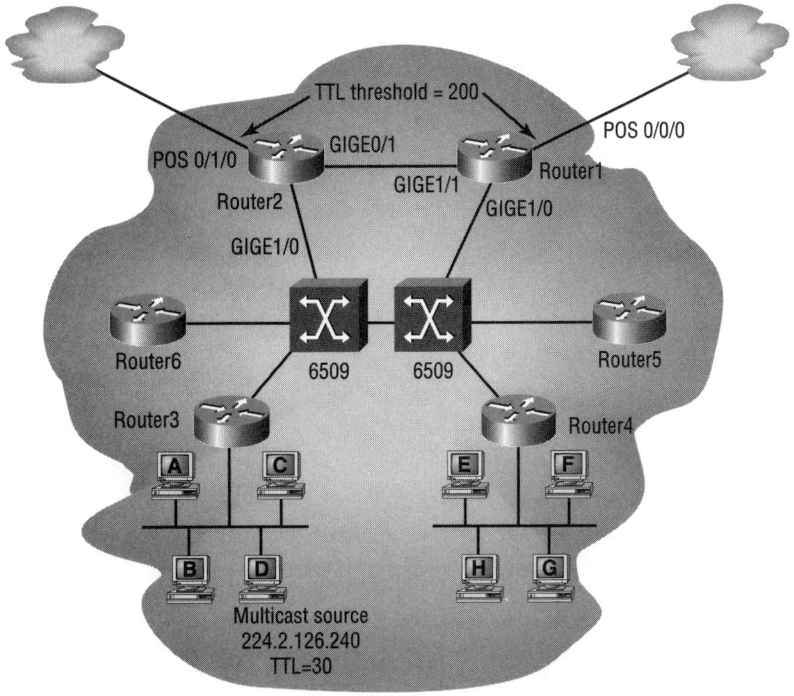

The multicast source initially sets the TTL value for the multicast packet and then forwards it on throughout the network. In this scenario, the TTL threshold values have been set to 200 on both of the exiting POS interfaces. The initial TTL value has been set to 30 by the application. There are three to four router hops to get out of the campus network. Router3 will decrement by one, leaving a TTL value of 29; the Catalyst 6509's MSFC will decrement by one as well, leaving the value set to 28. Once the packet gets to Router2 or Router1, the value will be 27 or 26 respectively. Both of these values are less than the TTL threshold of 200, which means Router1 and Router2 will drop any outbound multicast packets.

Routing Protocols

We now need to turn our attention to the variety of multicast routing protocols. Unicast has several routing protocols that build route tables that enable layer 3 devices such as routers and some switches to forward unicast

366 Chapter 9 • Multicast

data to the next hop toward its final
some of the methods that multicast, i
data. Similar to unicast, multicast has
ing distance vector and link state pro

Protocols are used to enhance the
tion data is distributed and to optimiz
This section will cover Distance Vect
(DVMRP), Multicast Open Shortest
pendent Multicast (PIM).

Distance Vector Multicast Routing Protocol (DVMRP)

Distance Vector Multicast Routing Protocol (DVMRP) has achieved widespread use in the multicast world. A few years ago, you may have often heard the term "DVMRP Tunnel" used when discussing the implementation of multicast feeds from an ISP or a feed from the MBONE. As the name indicates, this protocol uses a distance vector algorithm. It uses several of the features that other distance vector protocols (such as RIP) implement. Some of these features are a 32 max hop-count, poison reverse, and 60-second route updates. It also allows for IP classless masking of addresses.

Just as with other routing protocols, DVMRP-enabled routers must establish adjacencies in order to share route information. Once the adjacency is established, the DVMRP route table is created. Route information is exchanged via route reports. It is important to remember that the DVMRP route table is stored separately from the unicast routing table. The DVMRP route table is more like a unicast route table than the multicast route table that was shown earlier in this chapter. A DVMRP table contains the layer 3 IP network of the multicast source and the next hop toward the source.

Because the DVMRP table has this form, it works perfectly in conjunction with source tree distribution, as discussed earlier. Using the information in the DVMRP table, the tree for the source can be established. In addition, the router uses this information to perform the Reverse Path Forwarding check to verify that the multicast data coming into the interface is coming in an interface that leads back to the source of the data. DVMRP uses SPT for its multicast forwarding.

Figure 9.16 gives a description of how DVMRP works. You can see that not every router in the network is a DVMRP router. You should also notice that the adjacencies are established over tunnel interfaces. DVMRP information is tunneled through an IP network. On either end of the tunnel, information is learned and exchanged to build a multicast forwarding database or route table.

FIGURE 9.16 DVMRP tunnels

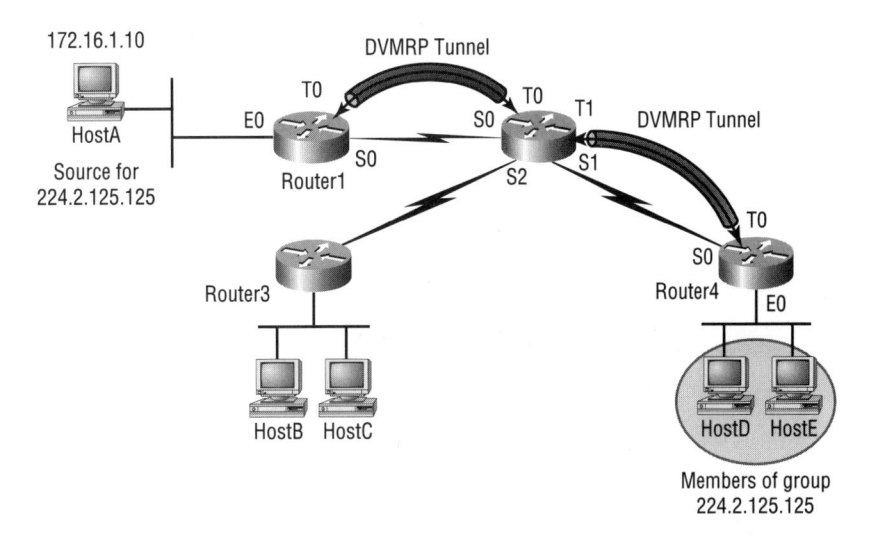

Multicast Open Shortest Path First (MOSPF)

Now we will concentrate on *Multicast Open Shortest Path First (MOSPF)*, which is a link state protocol. OSPFv2 includes some changes to allow multicast to be enabled on OSPF-enabled routers. This eliminates the need for tunnels like those used for DVMRP.

To completely understand the full functionality of MOSPF, you must have a good understanding of OSPF itself. However, here we will attempt to cover only the basic functionality of MOSPF, so you should be fine with just a basic understanding of OSPF.

> For more on the OSPF, see *CCNP: Advanced Cisco Router Configuration* by Todd Lammle, Kevin Hales, and Don Porter (Sybex, 1999).

MOSPF's basic functionality lies within a single OSPF area. Things get more complicated as you route multicast traffic to other areas (inter-area routing) or to other autonomous systems (inter-AS routing). This additional complication requires more knowledge of OSPF routing. We will briefly discuss how this is accomplished in MOSPF, but most detail will be given regarding MOSPF intra-area routing.

Intra-Area MOSPF

OSPF route information is shared via different Link State Advertisement (LSA) types. LSAs are flooded throughout an area to give all OSPF-enabled routers a logical image of the network topology. When changes are made to the topology, new LSAs are flooded to propagate the change.

In addition to the unicast-routing LSA types, in OSPFv2 there is a special multicast LSA for flooding multicast group information throughout the area. This additional LSA type required some modification to the OSPF frame format.

Here is where you need to understand a little about OSPF. Multicast LSA flooding is done by the Designated Router (DR) when there are multiple routers connected to a multi-access media, such as Ethernet. On point-to-point connections, there are no DR and Backup Designated Router (BDR). Look at the following code from a Cisco router running OSPF over point-to-point circuits.

```
Neighbor ID     Pri   State       Dead Time   Address       Interface
172.16.1.2      1     FULL/  -    00:00:31    172.16.1.2    Serial3/0
192.168.1.2     1     FULL/  -    00:00:39    192.168.1.2   Serial3/1
```

On a multi-access network, the DR must be multicast enabled; that is, running MOSPF. If there are any non-MOSPF routers on the same network, their OSPF priority must be lowered so none of them become the DR. If a non-MOSPF router were to become the DR, it would not be able to forward the multicast LSA to the other routers on the segment.

Inside the OSPF area, updates are sent describing which links have active multicast members on them so that the multicast data can be forwarded to those interfaces. MOSPF also uses (S, G) notation and calculates the SPT using the Dijkstra algorithm. You must also understand that an SPT is created for each source in the network.

Inter-Area and Inter-AS MOSPF

When discussing the difference between intra-area and inter-area MOSPF, you must remember that all areas connect through Area 0, the backbone. In large networks, having full multicast tables in addition to all the unicast tables flow across Area 0 would cause a great deal of overhead and possibly latency.

Unicast OSPF uses a Summary LSA to inform the routers in Area 0 about the networks and topology in an adjacent area. This task is performed by the area's ABR (Area Border Router). The ABR summarizes all the information about the area and then passes it on to the backbone (Area 0) routers in a summary LSA. The same is done for the multicast topology. The ABR summarizes which multicast groups are active and which groups have sources within the area. This information is then sent to the backbone routers.

In addition to summarizing multicast group information, the ABR is responsible for the actual forwarding of multicast group traffic into and out of the area. Each area has an ABR that performs these two functions within an OSPF network.

OSPF implements Autonomous System Border Routers to be the bridges between different Autonomous Systems. These routers perform much the same as an ABR but must be able to communicate with non-OSPF speaking devices. Multicast group information and data is forwarded and received by the Multicast Autonomous Border Router (MASBR). Because MOSPF runs natively within OSPF, there must be a method or protocol by which the multicast information can be taken from MOSPF and communicated to the external AS. Historically, DVRMP has provided this bridge.

PIM DM

We briefly mentioned *Protocol Independent Multicast (PIM)* previously. Now we will dedicate some time to learning how it is used in conjunction with the other multicast routing protocols. Although *PIM dense mode (PIM DM)* maintains several functions, the ones that will be discussed here are flooding, pruning, and grafting.

PIM is considered "protocol independent" because it actually uses the unicast route table for RPF and multicast forwarding. PIM DM understands classless subnet masking and uses it when the router is running an IP classless unicast protocol.

PIM DM routers establish neighbor relationships with other routers running PIM DM. It uses these neighbors to establish an SPT and forward multicast data throughout the network. The SPT created by PIM DM is based on source tree distribution.

Flooding

When a multicast source begins to transmit data, PIM runs the RPF using the unicast route table to verify that the interface leads toward the source. It then forwards the data to all PIM neighbors. Those PIM neighbors then forward the data to their PIM neighbors. This happens throughout the network whether there are group members on the router or not. This is why it is considered *flooding*.

When multiple, equal-cost links exist, the router with the highest IP address is elected to be the incoming interface (used for RPF). Every router runs the RPF when it receives the multicast data.

Figure 9.17 depicts the initial multicast flooding in a PIM DM network. You can see that the data is forwarded to every PIM neighbor throughout the network. Once a PIM neighbor does the RPF calculation, the router will then forward the data to interfaces that have active members of the group.

FIGURE 9.17 PIM DM flooding

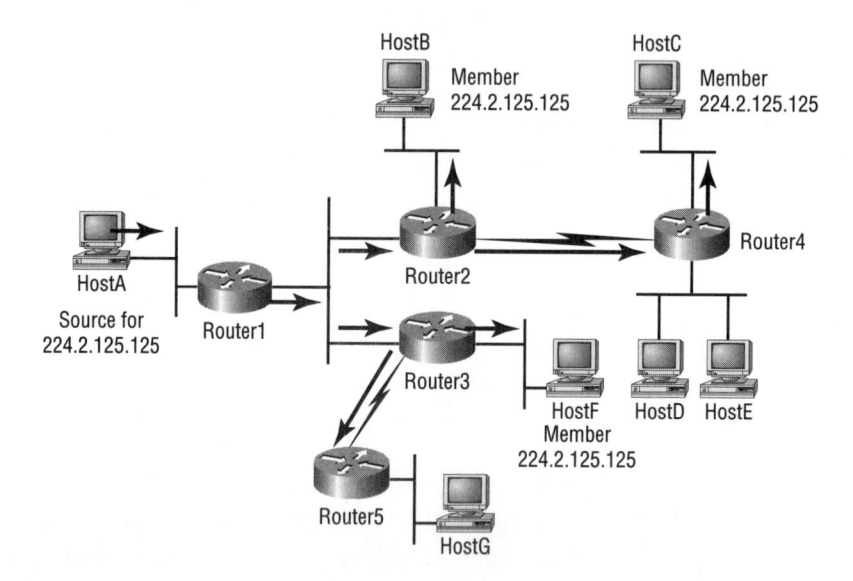

Pruning

After the initial flooding through the PIM neighbors, pruning starts. *Pruning* is the act of trimming down the SPT. Because the data has been forwarded to every router, regardless of group membership, the routers must now prune back the distribution of the multicast data to routers that actually have active group members connected.

Figure 9.18 shows the pruning action that occurs for the PIM DM routers that don't have active group members. Router5 does not have any active group members, so it sends a prune message to Router3. Even though

Router4 has a network that does not have members, it does have an interface that does, so it will not send a prune message.

FIGURE 9.18 PIM DM pruning

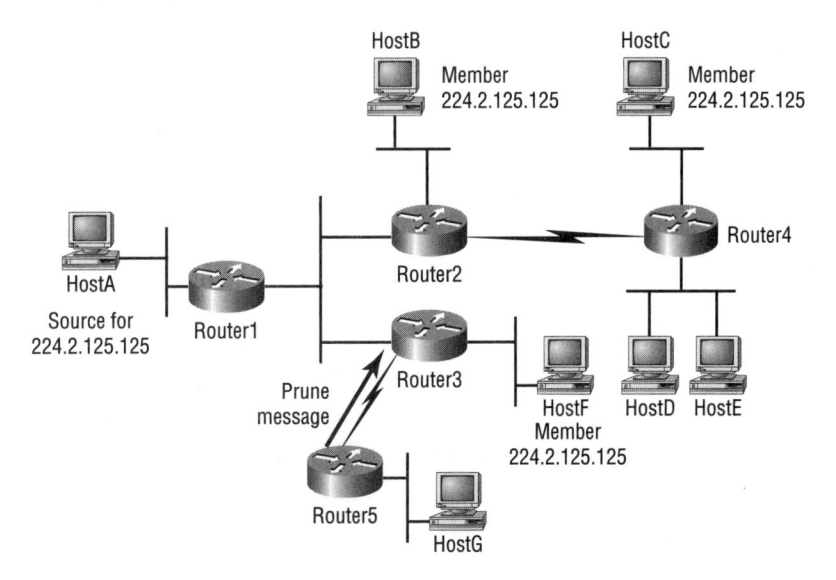

There are four criteria that merit a prune message being sent by a router:

- The incoming interface fails the RPF check.

- There are no directly connected active group members and no PIM neighbors (considered a leaf router because it has no downstream PIM neighbors).

- A point-to-point non-leaf router receives a prune request from a neighbor.

- A LAN non-leaf router receives a prune request from another router and no other router on the segment overrides the prune request.

If any of these criteria are met, a prune request is sent to the PIM neighbor and the SPT is pruned back.

Grafting

PIM DM is also ready to forward multicast data once a previously inactive interface becomes active. This is done through the process of *grafting*. When a host sends an IGMP group membership report to the router, the router then sends a Graft message to the nearest upstream PIM neighbor. Once this message is acknowledged, multicast data begins to be forwarded to the router and on to the host. Figure 9.19 depicts the grafting process.

FIGURE 9.19 PIM DM grafting

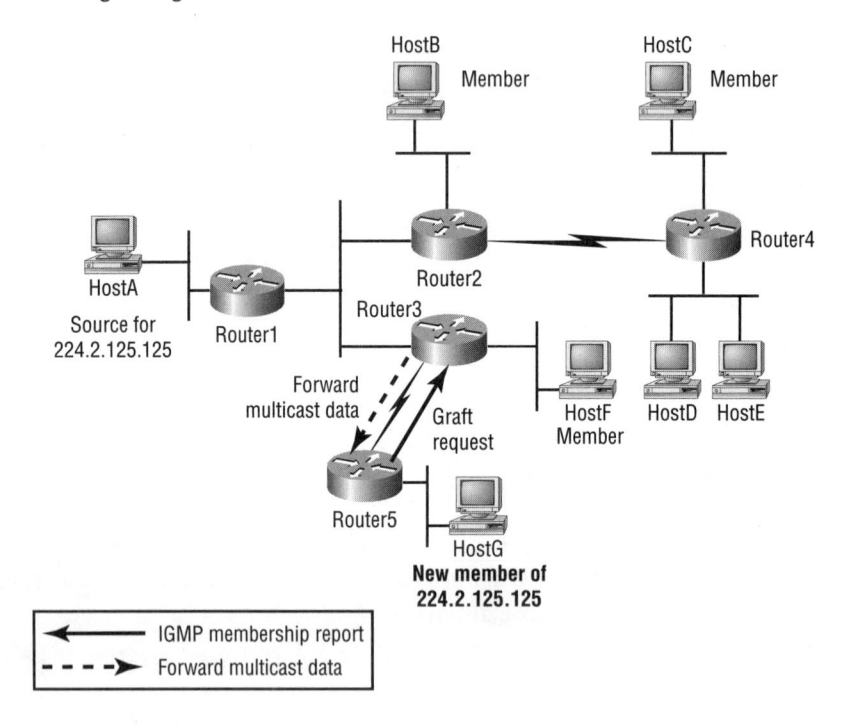

Sparse Mode Routing Protocols

Sparse mode protocols use shared tree distribution as their forwarding methods. This is done to create a more efficient method of multicast distribution. There are two sparse mode protocols that will be discussed in this section:

- Core-based trees (CBT)
- Protocol Independent Multicast sparse mode (PIM SM)

Core-Based

When we discussed shared trees, you learned that there were two types, unidirectional and bidirectional. CBT utilizes the bidirectional method for its multicast data distribution. Because CBT uses a shared tree system, it designates a *core* router that is used as the root of the tree, allowing data to flow up or down the tree.

Data forwarding in a CBT multicast system is similar to the shared tree distribution covered earlier. If a source to a multicast group sends multicast data to the CBT-enabled router, the router then forwards the data out all interfaces that are included in the tree, not just the interface that leads to the core router. In this manner, data flows up and down the tree. Once the data gets to the core router, the core router then forwards the information to the other routers that are in the tree. Figure 9.20 depicts this process.

FIGURE 9.20 CBT data distribution

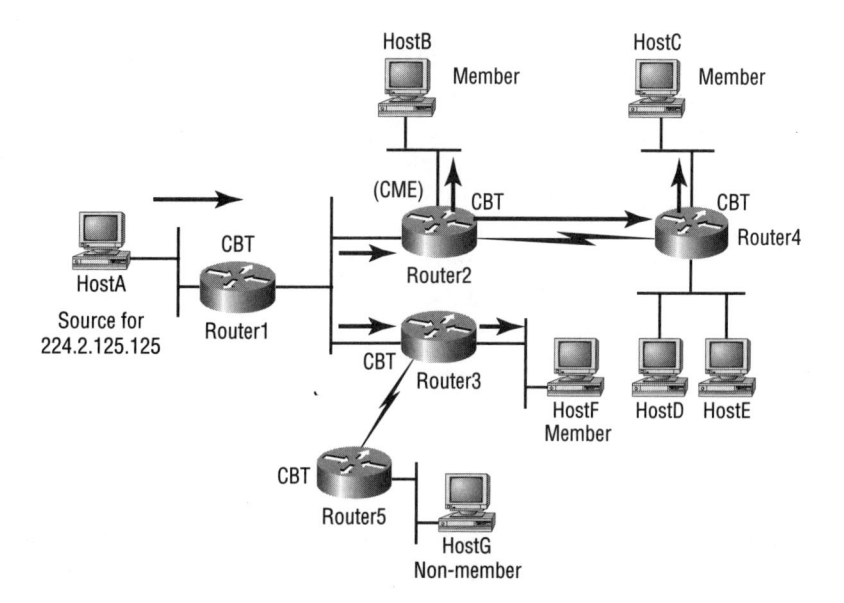

It is important to see the difference between this sparse mode method and the dense mode method. In sparse mode operation, routers are members of the tree only if they have active members directly connected. Dense mode operates on the initial premise that all PIM neighbors have active members directly connected. The tree changes when the directly connected routers request to be pruned from the tree.

A CBT router may become part of the tree once a host sends an IGMP Membership Record to the directly connected router. The router then sends a join tree request to the *core* router. If the request reaches a CBT tree member first, that router will add the *leaf* router to the tree and begin forwarding multicast data.

Pruning the tree is done much the same way. Once there are no more active members on a router's interfaces, the router will send a prune request to the upstream router. The answering router will remove the interface from the forwarding cache if it is on a point-to-point circuit, or it will wait for a timer to expire it if is on a shared access network. The timer gives enough time for other CBT routers on the segment to override the prune request.

PIM SM

PIM sparse mode (PIM SM) also uses the architecture of shared tree distribution. There is an RP (rendezvous point) router that acts as the root of the shared tree. Unlike CBT, however, PIM SM uses the unidirectional shared tree distribution mechanism. Because PIM SM uses the unidirectional method, all multicast sources for any group must register with the RP of the shared tree. This enables the RP and other routers to establish the RPT, or RP tree (synonymous with SPT in source tree distribution).

Just as with CBT, PIM SM routers join the shared tree when they are notified via IGMP that a host requests membership of a multicast group. If the existing group entry (*, G) does not already exist in the router's table, it is created and the join tree request is sent to the next hop toward the RP. The next router receives the request. Based on whether or not it has an exiting entry for (*, G), two things can happen:

- If an entry for (*, G) exists, the router simply adds the interface to the shared tree and no further join requests are sent toward the RP.

- If an entry for (*, G) does not exist, the router creates an entry for the (*, G) group and adds the link to the forwarding cache. In addition to doing this, the router sends its own join request toward the RP.

This happens until the join request reaches a router that already has the (*, G) entry or a join request reaches the RP.

The next facet of PIM SM is the shared tree pruning. With PIM SM, pruning turns out to be just the opposite of the explicit Join mechanism used to construct the shared tree.

When a member leaves a group, it does so via IGMP. When it happens to be the last member on a segment, the router removes the interface from the forwarding cache entry and then sends a prune request toward the RP of the shared tree. If there is another router with active members connected to the router requesting the prune, it is removed from the outgoing interface list and no additional Prune messages are sent to the RP. See Figure 9.21 for a visual description.

FIGURE 9.21 PIM SM pruning

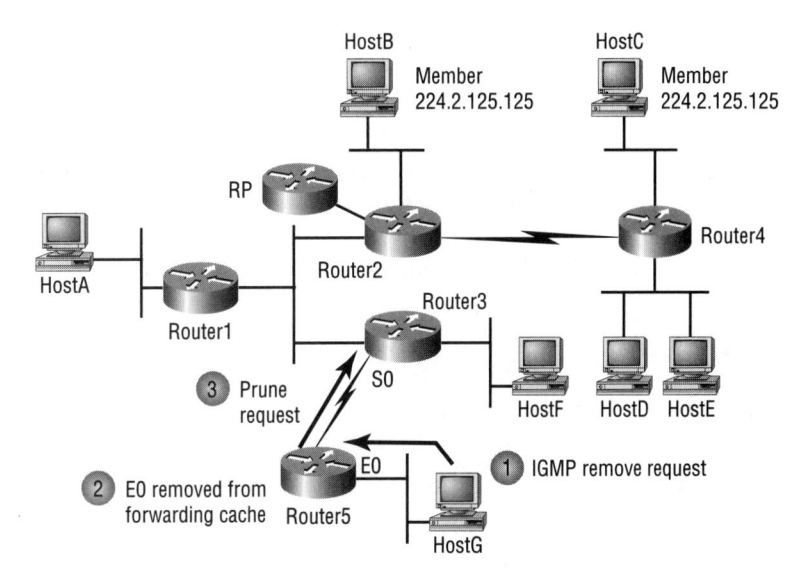

Router5 receives an IGMP message requesting the removal of HostG from the group. Because HostG was the last active member of the group, the (*, G) entry is set to null 0 and a prune request is sent by Router5 to Router3. When Router3 receives the request, it removes the link for interface S0 from the forwarding table. Because HostF is a directly connected active member of the group, the entry for (*, G) is not null 0, so no prune request is sent to Router2 (the RP for this example).

If HostF were not active, the entry for (*, G) would have been set to null 0 also and a prune request would have been sent to the RP.

Summary

In this chapter, we described the many different facets of IP multicast. We started out with an overview of multicast and compared it with unicast and broadcast communications. We then discussed how IP addresses were designated as multicast addresses. You learned how to convert them to layer 2 MAC addresses also.

The implementation of multicast can have significant impact on a network. This merited the topics regarding managing multicast distribution. Once you understood the basics of multicast and how hosts and sources participate, we were able to move on and cover topics regarding the different types of routing protocols that were made for multicast routing. Finally, we discussed PIM-DM, PIM-SM, and CBT. These are independent protocols that use tree distribution to manage multicast data delivery in a network.

Because this chapter focused on theory instead of configuration, there were no commands introduced. Therefore, this chapter doesn't include a table of commands, nor does it include a written lab and hands-on lab. You'll learn more about configuring multicast in Chapter 10.

Key Terms

Before you take the exam, be sure you're familiar with the following terms:

bidirectional shared tree	multicast
broadcast	multicast group
Cisco Group Management Protocol (CGMP)	Multicast Open Shortest Path First (MOSPF)
Distance Vector Multicast Routing Protocol (DVMRP)	PIM dense mode (PIM DM)
flooding	PIM sparse mode (PIM SM)
grafting	Protocol Independent Multicast (PIM)
IGMP Join process	Pruning
IGMP Leave process	shared trees
IGMP Query process	source trees
Internet Group Management Protocol version 1 (IGMPv1)	unicast
Internet Group Management Protocol version 2 (IGMPv2)	unidirectional shared tree

Review Questions

1. Which of the following is the valid range of IP multicast addresses?

    A. 223.0.0.0–239.255.255.255

    B. 224.0.0.0–225.255.255.255

    C. 224.0.0.0–239.0.0.0

    D. 224.0.0.0–239.255.255.255

2. Which of the following addresses is within the range of valid IP multicast addresses? (Choose all that apply.)

    A. 242.127.1.1

    B. 224.0.0.1

    C. 239.255.255.254

    D. 225.128.1.1

3. What is the main difference between broadcast and multicast communications?

    A. Multicast data is distributed to subscribed hosts on specific groups.

    B. Broadcast data is distributed to subscribed hosts on specific groups.

    C. Multicast data uses unicast route tables to flood the network instead of using the network's broadcast address.

    D. There really is no difference.

4. What is the purpose of the reserved IP multicast address 224.0.0.1?

    A. All MOSPF routers

    B. All multicast routers

    C. All hosts

    D. All CGMP-enabled hosts

5. What is the purpose of the reserved IP multicast address 224.0.0.2?

    A. All DVMRP routers

    B. All routers

    C. All hosts

    D. All CGMP-enabled routers

6. What is the MAC prefix (first 24 bits) that identifies a multicast MAC address?

    A. 01-00-5E

    B. 01-00-5F

    C. FF-FF-FF

    D. 01-00-50

7. How many bits of the layer 3 IP address are used to map to the layer 2 MAC address?

    A. 24

    B. 22

    C. 25

    D. 23

8. How many layer 3 IP addresses can be represented by the same layer 2 MAC address?

    A. 1

    B. 23

    C. 32

    D. 24

9. What is the layer 2 MAC address for the layer 3 IP address 224.2.127.254?

   A. 01-00-5E-02-7E-FF

   B. 01-00-5E-02-7F-FE

   C. 01-00-5E-00-7E-FF

   D. 01-00-5E-00-7F-FE

10. What is the layer 2 MAC address for the layer 3 IP address 224.224.155.155?

    A. 01-00-5E-70-9B-9B

    B. 01-00-5E-40-9B-9B

    C. 01-00-5E-60-9B-9B

    D. 01-00-5E-30-9B-9B

11. What is the layer 2 MAC address for the layer 3 IP address 224.215.145.230?

    A. 01-00-5E-57-91-E6

    B. 01-00-5E-D7-91-E6

    C. 01-00-5E-5B-91-E6

    D. 01-00-5E-55-91-E6

12. Which of the following protocols can hosts use to subscribe to a multicast group? (Choose all that apply.)

    A. IBMP

    B. IGMPv1

    C. IGMPv2

    D. CGMP

    E. DVMRP

    F. MOSPF

    G. PIM (DM/SM)

    H. CBT

13. Why do Cisco Catalyst switches use CGMP instead of just using IGMP?

    A. Cisco's proprietary code is easier to compile into IOS.

    B. Cisco catalysts don't understand IGMP packets.

    C. Routers need switches to translate IGMP requests into CGMP requests in order to process them.

    D. Catalysts can't distinguish between membership report packets and actual multicast data packets.

14. How does a host connected to a Catalyst switch subscribe to a multicast group? (Choose all that apply.)

    A. It sends an IGMP request directly to the sc0 interface on the switch.

    B. It sends an IGMP membership report to the router.

    C. It sends a CGMP membership report to the router.

    D. It sends a CGMP membership report to the switch.

    E. The router converts the CGMP to IGMP and forwards it to the switch for processing.

    F. The router converts the IGMP membership request to a CGMP join request and forwards it to the switch for processing.

15. What two address values does CGMP use compared to IGMP?

    A. CGMP utilizes the USA and GDA.

    B. CGMP utilizes the MAC address and IP address.

    C. CGMP utilizes the GSA and UDA.

    D. CGMP uses the MAC address and switch port.

16. What are the two types of distribution trees?

    A. RP trees

    B. Multicast trees

    C. Shared root trees

    D. Source root trees

17. What are two types of shared root tree distributions?

    A. Unidirectional

    B. Unicast

    C. Multidirectional

    D. Bidirectional

18. What multicast attribute can be applied to multicast router interfaces to limit the scope of multicast group and data distribution?

    A. TTY

    B. IP access lists

    C. TTL thresholds

    D. Multicast disabled on the router

19. How does PIM DM differ from PIM SM? (Choose all that apply.)

    A. PIM DM assumes that all PIM neighbors have active members directly connected and initially forwards multicast data out every interface.

    B. PIM SM requires an explicit join from a router before the router is added to the shared tree.

    C. PIM DM is based on a source root tree distribution mechanism.

    D. PIM SM is based on bidirectional shared root tree distribution.

20. How does CBT differ from PIM SM?

    A. CBT uses unidirectional shared root tree distribution.

    B. CBT uses bidirectional shared root tree distribution.

    C. CBT routers are only included in the tree when there are active hosts directly connected.

    D. PIM SM uses the unicast route table to verify the RPF.

Answers to Review Questions

1. **D.** The valid range of IP addresses for multicast start at 224.0.0.0. Anything lower than that is not within the specified range. The range continues until 239.255.255.255, which specifies the entire Class D network. That makes D the correct answer.

2. **B, C, D.** The first response is outside of the valid range for IP multicast addresses. The other choices are valid host addresses within the range.

3. **A.** Broadcast communications use the broadcast IP or MAC address to communicate information to all hosts. Multicast data is sent only to hosts that subscribe to groups that are active on the network.

4. **C.** IANA reserved the address 224.0.0.1 for all multicast hosts on a local segment. This address is not routed or forwarded by routers.

5. **B.** IANA reserved the address 224.0.0.2 to indicate all local multicast routers. Again, this address is not forwarded by any routers in the network.

6. **A.** The first 24 bits of a MAC address were assigned the value of 0x01005e for all multicast addresses. The other values do not designate a multicast MAC address.

7. **D.** Because only one half of one OEM was allocated for individual multicast MAC addresses, only 23 bits transfer from the layer 3 IP address.

8. **C.** Due to the lost 5 bits in the mapping, a value of 2^5 is left ambiguous.

9. **B.** The MAC prefix is 01-00-5E. You know you don't have to worry about the lost bits because the second octet of the IP address is less than 127. Therefore, the value is 02. The last two octets are mapped with no problem.

10. **C.** Again, the MAC prefix is 01-00-5E. Now that the second octet is greater than 127, you need to remember that it is possible that the value in the high order bit will be discarded. In this case, it was discarded, which leaves a binary value of 1100000 that needs to be converted to hex. In turn, that leaves 60 as the value for the fourth octet of the MAC address.

11. **A.** Again, the MAC prefix is 01-00-5E. Now that the second octet is greater than 127, you need to remember that it is possible that the value in the high order bit will be discarded. In this case, it was, which leaves a binary value of 1010111 that needs to be converted to hex. In turn, that leaves 57 as the value for the fourth octet of the MAC address.

12. **B, C.** CGMP is Cisco's proprietary version of IGMP. IBMP is not a valid protocol. The other protocols are for routing purposes and group management within a network.

13. **D.** Because IGMP is an overloaded protocol, the switches cannot distinguish between membership report packets and normal IGMP packets containing data. The router must run CGMP in order to translate the IGMP requests received from the hosts into something the switch can process.

14. **B, F.** There is a little more detail involved than just these two steps, but the host can speak only IGMP, and it sends its requests directly to the router. The router must then communicate with the switch to activate the port.

15. **A.** The USA is the Unicast Source Address (the unique MAC address of the machine), and the GDA is the Group Destination Address (the newly mapped layer 2 multicast MAC address). By using these two values, the switch knows which port to make a CAM entry for.

16. **C, D.** Multicast trees don't exist. Some protocols that are based in shared root trees can create RPTs (or RP trees) that are parallel to the shortest path tree, but this is a flavor of shared root tree distribution.

17. A, D. We are discussing multicast in this chapter, so unicast is not a valid answer. Because there are only two directions on a tree, the correct answers are bidirectional and unidirectional.

18. C. TTY is a telecommunications term, and IP access lists are not multicast attributes. TTL thresholds are used to compare against the TTL value of a multicast packet. Disabling multicast on the router works, but it isn't necessarily an attribute.

19. A, B, C. The problem with D is that PIM SM is based on unidirectional shared root tree distribution.

20. B. Answers C and D are actually similarities between the two protocols. PIM SM uses unidirectional shared root tree distribution.

Chapter 10

Configuring Multicast

THE CCNP EXAM TOPICS COVERED IN THIS CHAPTER INCLUDE THE FOLLOWING:

- ✓ IP multicast
- ✓ IP multicast configuration
- ✓ Routing

This chapter will cover the steps and syntax for configuring IP multicast on Cisco routers and switches. There will be several new commands seen in this chapter. Learning about multicast and actually getting it working on a network are two different things. By the time you finish this chapter, questions, and lab, you will be thoroughly familiar with multicast and its implementation. Pay attention to small details that would normally seem unimportant. They are usually the key to a successful implementation of an IP multicast network.

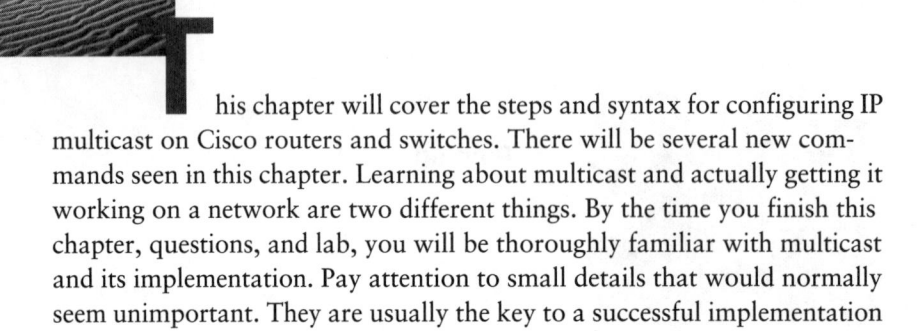

First you will need to understand how to deploy an IP multicast network. Once you have a plan in place, you can move on to actually configuring equipment. Not only do the routers have to be IP multicast enabled, but you must enable a multicast protocol on every interface that you want to be able to forward multicast traffic.

An IP multicast network won't work too well without a couple of (or at least one) rendezvous points (RPs), so you'll have to configure them as well. Then, in order to keep your multicast local to the enterprise network, you'll need to configure the Time to Live (TTL) thresholds on your external interfaces.

After the routers have been configured, you can concentrate on the hosts. Of course, we won't discuss host configuration in this chapter, but we will get down and enable Cisco Group Management Protocol (CGMP) on the routers and switches, so once the hosts are configured, the network will be available.

Planning and Preparing for Using IP Multicast

As you learned in Chapter 9, multicast networks behave differently than unicast networks. It is important to keep this in mind when planning the deployment of an IP multicast network. There are several factors that should be taken into consideration, including bandwidth implications, multicast applications, application requirements, user requirements, the location of the recipients, required equipment, cost, and most importantly, what multicast source(s) will be used.

All of these factors require attention and planning for a successful deployment of IP multicast throughout the network. You must also think upside down when thinking about multicast routing. As was discussed in the preceding chapter, distribution trees are built based on the position of the root (source) of the tree. Therefore, when planning the routing for the multicast network, you must know where your sources or RPs will be located.

By taking the time to plan and prepare for a multicast deployment, you will avoid headaches later on. You must become familiar with the customer's requirements as well as the impact multicast will have on the existing network.

There are many methods of implementing multicast on a network. Commonly, institutions will want to connect with the Multicast Backbone (MBONE) multicast sessions; therefore, they must implement multicast through a Distance Vector Multicast Routing Protocol (DVMRP) tunnel or with Multicast Border Gateway Protocol (MBGP). If the multicast source is within the network and meant to stay within the confines of the network, other design issues come into play. It is important that you understand what each multicast routing protocol brings to the table when it comes to operational functionality.

By better understanding the many protocols and possible implementations of multicast, you will be able to better plan and prepare for its deployment. With so many options, there is bound to be a solution for almost any requirement. Through understanding requirements, and through preparing and planning, you can successfully implement an IP multicast network.

End-to-End IP Multicast

Part of deploying multicast is the determination of how much of the network should be multicast enabled. This is an important decision because it directly affects many aspects of multicast implementation. To strategically place the *rendezvous points (RPs)*, you must know where all of the multicast leaf routers will be. Knowing an approximate number of potential multicast subscribers can have an impact on which protocols are run in the network to allow efficient multicast forwarding and routing.

The decision to use end-to-end deployment can be based on the applications that will be used or the intent of multicast implementation. If you are enabling multicast for a corporate application, you would need to enable multicast on every interface on every router throughout the enterprise. However, if you need to provide access to only the MBONE for the engineering department, or some other department within the organization, perhaps the most efficient method would not include end-to-end configuration and deployment.

It is important to keep in mind that the state of technology is dynamic. Today, you might receive a request from a single department for multicast access. Before jumping on the project and planning for just that department, consider that in the near future, it is likely that other departments will also request access. Applications that will require end-to-end multicast capability may be purchased or integrated into the enterprise. It is far better to plan an end-to-end deployment and initially activate only the routers and interfaces that are needed than to plan your implementation on a limited initial activation. It will be easier to "build it right the first time" than to try to come back and work around or rebuild a poor IP multicast deployment.

Configuring IP Multicast Routing

When configuring multicast, keep in mind that there are many different options and protocols that may be configured. This is why it is so important that you have previously prepared and planned for the actual configuration. It isn't something that you can just sit down and throw together (not without a lot of problems anyway).

Configuring routers for IP multicast is different than enabling CGMP on switches. You must also remember that switches do not understand Internet

Group Management Protocol (IGMP) and that you will need to enable CGMP on switches and routers for hosts to be able to subscribe to a multicast group.

This section of the chapter covers the basics of configuring multicast on routers and switches. It also covers the configuration of rendezvous points. This is a very important task because without a rendezvous point, you will not be able to send or receive multicast packets across a network. We will also cover the individual interface configurations on routers. CGMP processes will be discussed in a little more detail than in the preceding chapter.

It is best to prepare a configuration task list before setting out to actually configure a group of routers. The configuration list should be specific to the device that will be configured. That fact makes it hard to present a set list of configuration tasks that would apply to all scenarios. However, there are definitely two items that must be configured on a router in order for multicast to even begin working. These items include enabling multicast routing and then enabling Protocol Independent Multicast (PIM) on the interfaces that will carry multicast traffic.

The following sections describe the multicast settings that can be made on a multicast-enabled router (and switches). The first two sections describe required configuration, whereas the configuration described in the remaining sections is optional. At the end of the configuration section, a summary of possible configuration tasks will be listed.

Enabling IP Multicast Routing

First, multicast routing must be enabled on the router. This step is very straightforward, but without it, multicast will not work. Let's look at a configuration of a router that does not have multicast enabled:

```
Current configuration:
!
version 12.0
service timestamps debug uptime
service timestamps log uptime
no service password-encryption
!
hostname RouterA
!
```

```
aaa new-model
aaa authentication login default tacacs+ line
aaa authentication login oldstyle line
aaa accounting exec default start-stop tacacs+
enable secret 5 $1$G7Dq$em.LpM4Huem9uqjZDHLe4.
!
!
!
ip subnet-zero
ip telnet source-interface FastEthernet3/0
```

Notice that there is no multicast information running on this machine. If we were to try to execute a multicast-related command, we wouldn't get any information returned. For example, look at what happens when the **show ip mroute** command is issued:

```
RouterA#sho ip mroute
IP Multicast Routing Table
Flags: D - Dense, S - Sparse, C - Connected, L - Local,
P - Pruned R - RP-bit set, F - Register flag,
 T - SPT-bit set,J - Join SPT, M - MSDP created entry,X -
Proxy Join Timer Running
        A - Advertised via MSDP
Timers: Uptime/Expires
Interface state: Interface, Next-Hop or VCD, State/Mode

RouterA#
```

The syntax for the command is **ip multicast-routing** and an example of the execution follows:

```
RouterA#conf t
Enter configuration commands, one per line.  End with CNTL/Z.
RouterA(config)#ip multicast-routing
RouterA(config)#^Z
RouterA#
```

This enables the multicast on the router. Notice that it was executed while in the global configuration mode. However, the router still cannot exchange multicast information with any neighbors because none of the interfaces have been enabled. This step is next.

Enabling PIM on an Interface

Protocol Independent Multicast (PIM) is one of the required elements for multicast configuration. It enables IGMP on the router and allows it to receive and forward traffic on the specified interface. PIM must be enabled on every interface that is to participate in the multicast network.

PIM interface configuration has many options. Take a look at the available options in IOS 12.0(10)S1, shown in Table 10.1. Most of these options are for advanced multicast configuration that won't be addressed in detail here. The ones that will be discussed here are `dense-mode`, `sparse-mode`, and `sparse-dense-mode`.

TABLE 10.1 IP PIM Configuration Options

IP PIM Options	Description
bsr-border	Specifies border of PIM domain
dense-mode	Enables PIM dense mode operation
nbma-mode	Specifies use of Non-Broadcast Multi-Access (NBMA) mode on interface
neighbor-filter	Specifies PIM peering filter
query-interval	Specifies PIM router query interval
sparse-dense-mode	Enables PIM sparse-dense mode operation
sparse-mode	Enables PIM sparse mode operation
version	Displays PIM version

IP PIM Dense Mode

Dense mode was discussed in Chapter 9. PIM dense mode functions by using the source root shared tree. It also assumes that all PIM neighbors have active multicast members directly connected, and therefore, it initially forwards multicast group data out all PIM-enabled interfaces.

The syntax for this command is very simple, ip pim dense-mode. An example of placing an interface in PIM dense mode follows:

```
RouterA#conf t
Enter configuration commands, one per line.  End with CNTL/Z.
RouterA(config)#interface FastEthernet3/0
RouterA(config-if)#ip pim dense-mode
RouterA(config-if)#^Z
RouterA#
```

This is what the interface configuration looks like now:

```
!
interface FastEthernet3/0
 ip address 172.16.21.4 255.255.255.0
 no ip directed-broadcast
 ip pim dense-mode
!
```

IP PIM Sparse Mode

Sparse mode was described to use shared root source tree distribution and relies on the knowledge of an RP. If an RP cannot be found, the router is unable to forward multicast information, strictly because it does not know where the source of the multicast traffic should come from. If it can't determine where the traffic is supposed to be coming from, the Reverse Path Forwarding (RPF) check will fail and no interfaces will be added to the multicast forwarding table.

Configuration of PIM sparse mode is just as simple as it was for IP dense mode. The command that needs to be used to enable IP PIM sparse mode is ip pim sparse-mode. Sparse mode PIM will also activate IGMP on the interface, allowing the interface to listen for IGMP membership reports. Here is an example of enabling IP PIM sparse mode multicast on an interface:

```
RouterA#conf t
Enter configuration commands, one per line.  End with CNTL/Z.
RouterA(config)#interface FastEthernet3/0
RouterA(config-if)#ip pim sparse-mode
RouterA(config-if)#^Z
RouterA#
```

Here is a look at the interface configuration after the execution shown above:

```
!
interface FastEthernet3/0
 ip address 172.16.21.4 255.255.255.0
 no ip directed-broadcast
 ip pim sparse-mode
!
```

IP PIM Sparse-Dense Mode

The name of this command gives an indication of the functionality it provides. Due to the increasing use of multicast and the variety of applications available today, it is best to configure an interface to be able to use both sparse mode and dense mode. With the previous commands, the interface was assigned the operating mode, and the interface could not change between modes depending on the need at the time.

PIM sparse-dense mode configuration now allows the interface to use whichever forwarding method is needed by the application or multicast group. The interface uses the multicast group notation to decide which mode it needs to operate in. If the interface sees something with the notation (S, G), it will operate in dense mode. If the interface sees notation similar to (*, G), the interface will operate in sparse mode.

An added benefit of implementing sparse-dense mode on the interfaces is the elimination of the need to hard-configure the RP at every leaf router. The Auto-RP information is sent out across the network using dense mode forwarding.

IP PIM sparse-dense mode is enabled using `ip pim sparse-dense-mode` on the interface command line. Here is an example:

```
RouterA#conf t
Enter configuration commands, one per line.  End with CNTL/Z.
RouterA(config)#interface FastEthernet3/0
RouterA(config-if)#ip pim sparse-dense-mode
RouterA(config-if)#^Z
RouterA#
```

Again, here is what the interface looks like once the preceding lines have been entered:

```
!
interface FastEthernet3/0
 ip address 172.16.21.4 255.255.255.0
 no ip directed-broadcast
 ip pim sparse-dense-mode
!
```

In summary, when using the sparse-dense mode configuration on an interface, you need to understand that there are three criteria that will activate the interface and place it into the multicast forwarding table. The first criterion applies to either sparse or dense mode; the others will cause the interface to operate specifically for sparse or dense mode. Look at Table 10.2 for the details.

TABLE 10.2 Interface Activation Criteria for Sparse-Dense Mode Interfaces

Criteria	Mode of Operation
Directly connected group members or DVMRP neighbors	Sparse and dense
Non-pruned PIM neighbors	Dense
Join request received	Sparse

Configuring a Rendezvous Point

If you are using PIM-DM throughout the multicast network, configuring a rendezvous point is an optional task. There are two ways of configuring a rendezvous point for a router. Notice that we did not say, "configuring a router *to be*" a rendezvous point. You can manually specify the IP address of the RP on a router, or you can enable Auto-RP.

Because multiple RPs may exist in a multicast network, the *Auto-RP* function aids by distributing the RP information across a multicast network. Different multicast groups may use different RPs, so this feature keeps track of which groups are using which RP. It will also fine-tune the leaf router's RP by choosing the RP nearest to the leaf. If you don't like to use static routes in a unicast network, you probably don't want to statically configure multicast RPs either.

Because there are two ways of configuring rendezvous points, we will describe both in the following subsections.

Manual RP Configuration

The syntax for the manual RP configuration command is very simple, `ip pim rp-address` *ip-address* `[group-access-list-number] [override]`. The *ip-address* is the IP address of the router that is the RP. The access list number is for a standard IP access list (1–99) or an expanded range from 1300 to 1999. These lists are used to define which multicast groups can or cannot use this RP. If no access list is specified, all multicast groups will use the configured RP. Finally, the override option can be used to override any RP information that may be learned via an Auto-RP update. The static RP takes precedence over any Auto-RP-learned RP. Here is a sample configuration for manual RP configuration:

```
RouterA#conf t
Enter configuration commands, one per line.  End with CNTL/Z.
RouterA(config)#ip pim rp-address 172.16.1.253 50 override
RouterA(config)#^Z
RouterA#
```

Here is a look at the router after the execution. Notice that the command is a global command. Following the global configuration, you will see access-list 50. The list allows only groups within the range of 224.0.0.0 to 224.255.255.255 to use 172.16.1.253 as the RP. Other groups will need

Auto-RP information or another statically configured RP in order to work properly:

```
!
no ip classless
ip route 0.0.0.0 0.0.0.0 172.16.22.2
ip pim rp-address 172.16.1.253 50 override
!
access-list 50 permit 224.0.0.0 0.255.255.255
access-list 50 deny    any
!
```

Auto-RP Configuration

There are also two procedures that can be used to enable Auto-RP; which one you use depends on the state of your multicast network. If you are beginning a new deployment, it isn't necessary to create a default RP. If you are modifying an existing multicast network, you will need to designate a default RP router in the network.

Here is a list of configuration tasks that must be completed to successfully implement Auto-RP in a multicast network:

- Designate a default RP (only when modifying an existing multicast network).
- Advertise each RP and the multicast groups associated with the RP.
- Enable an RP Mapping Agent.

As you can see the list is short and simple. Now that you know what has to be done, let's discuss each step individually.

Designate a Default RP

This step is somewhat tricky, not so much because the configuration is tricky, but because of the decision regarding when to execute the step. The only time you need to designate a default RP is when you are running sparse mode only on any of your interfaces in an existing multicast network. If you are using sparse-dense mode, as suggested, you will not need to execute this step.

This step is executed as described in "Manual RP Configuration" earlier in this chapter. The default RP becomes the statically mapped RP on all of the leaf routers. The default RP should serve all global multicast groups. That is all that has to be done.

Advertise RP Group Assignments

From each RP, a statement needs to be added that assigns and advertises multicast groups to that RP. The multicast groups are then advertised so the RP Mapping Agent can keep track of which RP hosts which multicast groups and resolve conflicts when necessary.

The syntax for the command is ip pim send-rp-announce *type number* scope *ttl* group-list *access-list-number*. The command is entered under the global configuration interface. The first two options are *type* and *number*, which are the interface type and number that indicate the RP IP address. *Scope* defines the boundary of the RP advertisement by using a high TTL value that will be effectively blocked by interfaces with the TTL threshold set. The *group-list* uses the specified access list to determine which multicast group ranges the RP is allowed to announce.

Here is an example of the command as well as a valid access list:

```
RouterA#conf t
Enter configuration commands, one per line.  End with CNTL/Z.
RouterA(config)#access-list 5 permit 224.0.0.0 0.0.255.255
RouterA(config)#$ip pim send-rp-announce fastethernet4/0 scope 230 group-list 5
RouterA(config)#^Z
RouterA#

RouterA#wr t
. . .
!
ip pim send-rp-announce FastEthernet4/0 scope 230 group-list 5
!
access-list 5 permit 224.0.0.0 0.0.255.255
!
. . .
```

Configure the RP Mapping Agent

This router is in charge of learning all of the rendezvous point routers in the network along with the multicast group assignments that each RP advertises. The Mapping Agent will then tell all the routers within the multicast network which RP should be used for their source.

This is done with the `ip pim send-rp-discovery scope ttl` command. As you can see, this command is similar to the command in the preceding section. The scope defines the TTL value for the discovery. After the TTL is reached, the discovery packets are dropped. Here is an example:

```
RouterA#conf t
Enter configuration commands, one per line.  End with CNTL/Z.
RouterA(config)#ip pim send-rp-discovery scope 23
RouterA(config)#^Z
RouterA#
```

In this example, you can see that the TTL value was set to 23. This means that after 23 hops, the discovery has expired. This command is the command that actually assigns to the router the role of RP Mapping Agent.

This concludes the configuration tasks for configuring a rendezvous point in a multicast network. Keep in mind that the RP Mapping Agent can be an RP, although it doesn't have to be. The Mapping Agent's role is to learn of all of the deployed rendezvous points throughout the network and then advertise which groups are available via the closest RP for all multicast-enabled routers in the network.

Configuring TTL

Time to Live (TTL) threshold configuration is done to limit the boundary of scope of the IP multicast network. As you learned in Chapter 9, limiting the scope of a multicast network is based on the TTL value in the multicast packet. Because this command is used to create a boundary, it must be executed on each border interface.

The default value for the TTL threshold is zero. The value can be changed with the `ip multicast ttl-threshold ttl` command. The syntax is straightforward and the *ttl* value that is used is up to the discretion of the network administrator. The range of valid values for this option is between

0 and 255. However, the value should be high enough to stop multicast packets from exiting the interface. Here is an example:

```
RouterA#conf t
Enter configuration commands, one per line.  End with CNTL/Z.
RouterA(config)#interface FastEthernet0/0
RouterA(config-if)#ip multicast ttl-threshold 230
RouterA(config-if)#^Z
RouterA#
```

```
!
interface FastEthernet0/0
 ip address 172.16.5.1 255.255.255.0
 no ip directed-broadcast
 ip multicast ttl-threshold 230
 no ip route-cache
 no ip mroute-cache
 full-duplex
!
```

Joining a Multicast Group

Once the main configuration is done on the router to enable multicast, PIM, rendezvous points, and RP Mapping Agents, the only other major task is allowing hosts to join multicast groups.

Within Cisco IOS, the network administrator has the opportunity to verify functionality and connectivity before users use the multicast system and applications. You can configure a router to join any number of IP multicast groups and, thus, verify functionality.

This is achieved through the ip igmp join-group *group-address* command. The *group-address* is the multicast address of the group you want the router to join. An example follows:

```
RouterA(config)#interface FastEthernet4/0
RouterA(config-if)#ip igmp join-group 224.2.127.254
RouterA(config-if)#^Z
RouterA#
```

This tells the router to become a member of the 224.2.127.254 multicast group. Joining a group facilitates troubleshooting multicast connectivity issues as well.

Troubleshooting IP Multicast Connectivity

Multicast can be a very difficult protocol to troubleshoot. There are, however, a few basic tools (mostly show commands) that can provide you with enough information to verify that connectivity is active or whether other steps, such as debugging, are needed to troubleshoot the problem.

If you do need to debug a multicast-enabled interface, you must first disable the multicast fast switching on the interface. This is done so that the debug messages can be logged. The command to disable fast switching is no ip mroute-cache. The normal unicast fast (or other forms of) switching may be left enabled.

You are familiar with the troubleshooting tools for unicast connectivity, Ping and traceroute. Well, these tools are also available for troubleshooting multicast connectivity. There is one minor difference, though: multicast requires a special version of traceroute, called mtrace or "multicast-traceroute."

Ping

Once a device on the network becomes a member of a group, it can be identified by its layer 3 multicast address as well as the layer 2 MAC address. Because the device has an active address on its interface, it can respond to ICMP request packets. Here is an example:

```
RouterA#ping
Protocol [ip]:
Target IP address: 224.2.143.55
Repeat count [1]: 5
Datagram size [100]:
Timeout in seconds [2]:
Extended commands [n]:
Sweep range of sizes [n]:
Type escape sequence to abort.
Sending 5, 100-byte ICMP Echos to 224.2.143.55, timeout is 2 seconds:
.!!!!
RouterA#
```

This tool can be used to verify connectivity among RPs or other multicast routers.

Mtrace

Cisco also provides a multicast traceroute tool. The multicast version of traceroute is somewhat different than the unicast version. The complete syntax for *mtrace* is mtrace *source* [*destination*] [*group*]. The *source* is the unicast IP address for the source of the multicast group. The *destination* is used when following the forwarding path established by the source or shared tree distribution toward a unicast destination. The *group* option is used to establish the tree for the specified group. If no destination or group options are specified, the mtrace will work from the incoming multicast interfaces back toward the multicast source. Here are a few samples of the command and its output:

```
RouterB#mtrace 198.32.163.74
Type escape sequence to abort.
Mtrace from 198.32.163.74 to 172.16.25.9 via RPF
From source (blaster.oregon-gigapop.net) to destination (?)
Querying full reverse path...
  0  172.16.25.9
 -1  172.16.25.9 PIM/MBGP  [198.32.163.0/24]
 -2  172.16.25.10 PIM/MBGP  [198.32.163.0/24]
 -3  ogig-den.oregon-gigapop.net (198.32.163.13) [AS 4600] PIM
[198.32.163.64/26]
 -4  0car-0gw.oregon-gigapop.net (198.32.163.26) [AS 4600] PIM
[198.32.163.64/26]
 -5  blaster.oregon-gigapop.net (198.32.163.74)
RouterB#

RouterB#mtrace 198.32.163.74 224.2.243.55
Type escape sequence to abort.
Mtrace from 198.32.163.74 to 172.16.25.9 via group
224.2.243.55
From source (blaster.oregon-gigapop.net) to destination (?)
Querying full reverse path...
  0  172.16.25.9
 -1  172.16.25.9 PIM/MBGP Reached RP/Core [198.32.163.0/24]
```

```
-2  172.16.25.10 PIM/MBGP Reached RP/Core [198.32.163.0/24]
-3  ogig-den.oregon-gigapop.net (198.32.163.13) [AS 4600] PIM
Reached RP/Core [198.32.163.64/26]
-4  Ocar-Ogw.oregon-gigapop.net (198.32.163.26) [AS 4600] PIM
[198.32.163.64/26]
RouterB#
```

As you can see, the outputs differ very little, but it is important to see how the paths are established. From the first sample output, no group or destination was specified, so the router strictly used RPF to calculate the path from the source to the router. In the other output, a group address was specified. This caused the router to specifically use the existing forwarding tree for group 224.2.243.55 to get back to the router.

These tools can be useful to determine connectivity as well as effectiveness of placement of RPs and multicast sources. There are other show commands that can aid you as well, but they are not related to the topic of this chapter.

Changing the IGMP Version

There are several settings that can be tweaked in the router to enhance or change performance. The majority of them are beyond the scope of this chapter. However, we will discuss one important feature, changing the IGMP version.

It is important that you understand and know how to perform this change because of the compatibility issues between IGMP versions, as discussed in Chapter 9.

To put it simply, the IGMP version that runs on the hosts must also run on the router. Cisco routers use IGMPv2 by default and do not auto-detect the IGMP version the host is using. The command to change from IGMPv2 to IGMPv1, or vice versa, is ip igmp version (2 | 1). Because the IGMP version needs to match only on the subnet, the command must be entered on the interface that connects to the subnet that houses the IGMPv1 hosts. The other interfaces on the router can remain on IGMPv2.

Enabling CGMP

CGMP must be used when hosts connect to a router via a Catalyst switch. As we discussed in Chapter 9, Catalysts run CGMP so they can manage multicast membership reports from the router accordingly and so they can manage multicast ports on the switch. The router is the device that listens for the

IGMP membership report; it then tells the switch, via CGMP, which port needs to be activated. CGMP must be activated on both the router and the switch.

CGMP Router Configuration

The router configuration syntax is very simple. It must be applied to the interface connected to the Catalyst switch. The command is `ip cgmp [proxy]`. The *proxy* option is used for routers that are not CGMP capable. It allows them to use the proxy router for CGMP. Here is a sample configuration:

```
RouterA#conf t
Enter configuration commands, one per line.  End with CNTL/Z.
RouterA(config)#interface FastEthernet4/0
RouterA(config-if)#ip cgmp
RouterA(config-if)#^Z
RouterA#


!
interface FastEthernet4/0
 ip address 172.16.10.1 255.255.255.0
 no ip directed-broadcast
 ip pim sparse-dense-mode
 no ip route-cache
 ip igmp join-group 224.2.127.254
 ip cgmp
!
```

Catalyst Switch Configuration

The Catalyst syntax is just as simple, if not more so, as the syntax for the router configuration. By default, CGMP is turned off on the switch. If you want multicast to work properly, you must enable CGMP on the switch. This is done by using the syntax `set cgmp enable`. Here is a sample:

```
switch1> (enable) set cgmp enable
CGMP support for IP multicast enabled.
```

```
switch1> (enable)
switch1> (enable) show cgmp statistics
CGMP enabled

CGMP statistics for vlan 1:
valid rx pkts received           6
invalid rx pkts received         0
valid cgmp joins received        6
valid cgmp leaves received       0
valid igmp leaves received       0
valid igmp queries received      0
igmp gs queries transmitted      0
igmp leaves transmitted          0
failures to add GDA to EARL      0
topology notifications received  0
number of packets dropped        0
switch1> (enable)
```

Once CGMP is enabled, you can look at statistics using the `show cgmp statistics` command. This is all that is needed to enable CGMP on the switch so that it can communicate with the router.

Summary

This chapter has been dedicated to the syntax and method of IP multicast configuration in Cisco routers and switches. Several points were discussed about the importance of planning the IP multicast deployment.

In addition to learning the commands for rendezvous points and hosts, you learned a few troubleshooting commands that will aid you in verifying that the multicast network has full functionality.

Key Terms

Before you take the exam, be sure you're familiar with the following terms:

Auto-RP

mtrace

PIM sparse-dense mode

Protocol Independent Multicast (PIM)

rendezvous points (RPs)

Commands Used in This Chapter

There are no access layer switches used in this chapter, so the commands are based on a distribution layer switch.

Command	Meaning
`ip multicast-routing`	Enables IP multicast forwarding on the router.
`ip pim dense-mode`	Enables PIM dense mode operation on the interface.
`ip pim sparse-mode`	Enables PIM sparse mode operation on the interface.
`ip pim sparse-dense-mode`	Enables PIM sparse-dense mode operation on the interface.
`ip pim rp-address` *ip-address* `[group-access-list-number] [override]`	Manually configures an RP address on a multicast router.
`ip pim send-rp-announce` *type number* `scope` *ttl* `group-list` *access-list-number*	Assigns specific multicast group addresses to an RP. The RP can only announce multicast groups that are permitted by the specified access list.
`ip pim send-rp-discovery scope` *ttl*	Configures RP Mapping Agent and allows the router to discover all RPs and group assignments.
`ip multicast ttl-threshold` *ttl*	Applied to all border interfaces to enforce the scope or boundary of the IP multicast network.

Command	Meaning
ip igmp join-group *group-address*	Makes the router become an active member of the specified multicast group.
ping	Used for testing reachability.
mtrace	Displays the forwarding path based on group membership or the RPF.
ip igmp version (*2* | *1*)	Applied to the interface and used to change the version of IGMP used on that interface.
ip cgmp [*proxy*]	Enables CGMP on the specified interface on routers.
set cgmp enable	Used on Catalyst switches to enable CGMP.

Written Lab

Complete this lab by writing out the answers to the following questions.

1. Write the command that enables multicast routing on a router.

2. Write the commands that will enable PIM SM on interface FastEthernet4/0.

3. Write the configuration commands that will enable PIM DM on interface FastEthernet3/0.

4. Write the configuration for enabling PIM sparse-dense mode on interface FastEthernet0/0.

5. Write the command that will show you the multicast route table.

6. Manually configure a router to be an RP using the IP address of 172.16.25.3 and apply access list number 30.

7. Write the command that is used when implementing Auto-RP so that the RP will announce only specific multicast groups. Use access list number 10 and interface FastEthernet 4/0. Use a TTL value of 220.

8. Write the command that enables an RP Mapping Agent. Use a TTL value of 32.

9. Apply a command that sets a TTL threshold of 235 on interface FastEthernet 2/0.

10. Write the commands that will enable CGMP on a router for interface FastEthernet 3/0, and then write the command that will enable CGMP on a switch.

Hands-On Lab

Refer to Figure 10.1 as the diagram for this lab. The objective of this lab is to configure an IP multicast network from scratch. You will implement Auto-RP, PIM sparse-dense mode, and CGMP on all routers and switches. You will not have to configure host applications in this lab. Assume that Routers C and D have multicast sources attached to them.

FIGURE 10.1 Configuring an IP multicast network

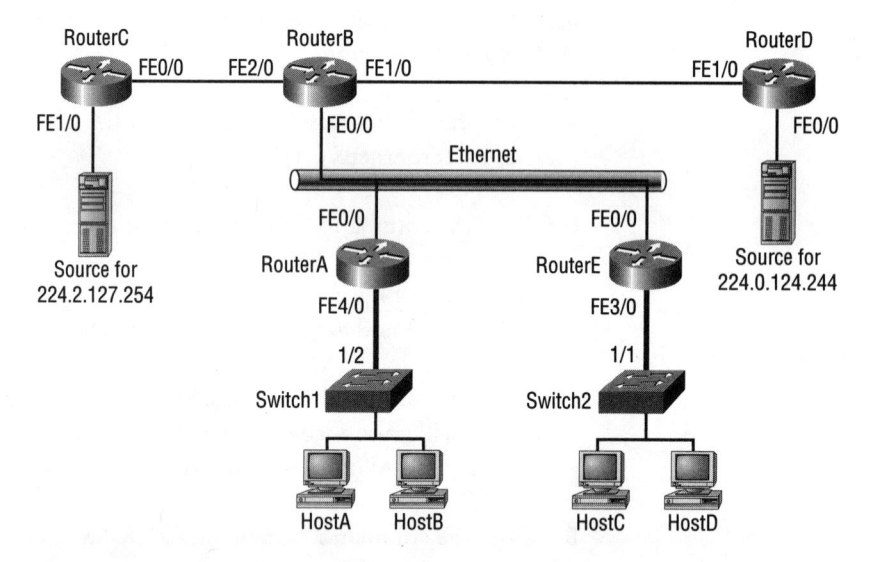

1. Because you are starting from scratch, the first step is to enable multicast on all routers.

```
RouterA#conf t
Enter configuration commands, one per line.  End with CNTL/Z.
RouterA(config)#ip multicast-routing
RouterA(config)#^Z
RouterA#

RouterB#conf t
Enter configuration commands, one per line.  End with CNTL/Z.
RouterB(config)#ip multicast-routing
```

```
RouterB(config)#^Z
RouterB#


RouterC#conf t
Enter configuration commands, one per line.  End with CNTL/Z.
RouterC(config)#ip multicast-routing
RouterC(config)#^Z
RouterC#


RouterD#conf t
Enter configuration commands, one per line.  End with CNTL/Z.
RouterD(config)#ip multicast-routing
RouterD(config)#^Z
RouterD#


RouterE#conf t
Enter configuration commands, one per line.  End with CNTL/Z.
RouterE(config)#ip multicast-routing
RouterE(config)#^Z
RouterE#
```

2. Now, enable PIM sparse-dense mode on all shown connected interfaces.

```
RouterA#conf t
Enter configuration commands, one per line.  End with CNTL/Z.
RouterA(config)#interface FastEthernet4/0
RouterA(config-if)#ip pim sparse-dense-mode
RouterA(config-if)#interface fastethernet0/0
RouterA(config-if)#ip pim sparse-dense-mode
RouterA(config-if)#^Z
RouterA#


RouterE#conf t
Enter configuration commands, one per line.  End with CNTL/Z.
RouterE(config)#interface fastethernet3/0
RouterE(config-if)#ip pim sparse-dense-mode
```

```
RouterE(config-if)#interface fastethernet0/0
RouterE(config-if)#ip pim sparse-dense-mode
RouterE(config-if)#^Z
RouterE#

RouterB#conf t
Enter configuration commands, one per line.  End with CNTL/Z.
RouterB(config)#interface fastethernet0/0
RouterB(config-if)#ip pim sparse-dense-mode
RouterB(config-if)#interface fastethernet1/0
RouterB(config-if)#ip pim sparse-dense-mode
RouterB(config-if)#interface fastethernet2/0
RouterB(config-if)#ip pim sparse-dense-mode
RouterB(config-if)#^Z
RouterB#

RouterC#conf t
Enter configuration commands, one per line.  End with CNTL/Z.
RouterC(config)#interface fastethernet0/0
RouterC(config-if)#ip pim sparse-dense-mode
RouterC(config-if)#interface fastethernet1/0
RouterC(config-if)#ip pim sparse-dense-mode
RouterC(config-if)#^Z
RouterC#

RouterD#conf t
Enter configuration commands, one per line.  End with CNTL/Z.
RouterD(config)#interface fastethernet0/0
RouterD(config-if)#ip pim sparse-dense-mode
RouterD(config-if)#interface fastethernet1/0
RouterD(config-if)#ip pim sparse-dense-mode
RouterD(config-if)#^Z
RouterD#
```

3. Enable CGMP on all router interfaces and switches.

```
RouterA#conf t
Enter configuration commands, one per line.  End with CNTL/Z.
RouterA(config)#interface fastethernet0/0
RouterA(config-if)#ip cgmp
RouterA(config-if)#interface fastethernet4/0
RouterA(config-if)#ip cgmp
RouterA(config-if)#^Z
RouterA#

RouterE#conf t
Enter configuration commands, one per line.  End with CNTL/Z.
RouterE(config)#interface fastethernet0/0
RouterE(config-if)#ip cgmp
RouterE(config-if)#interface fastethernet3/0
RouterE(config-if)#ip cgmp
RouterE(config-if)#^Z
RouterE#

RouterB#conf t
Enter configuration commands, one per line.  End with CNTL/Z.
RouterB(config)#interface fastethernet0/0
RouterB(config-if)#ip cgmp
RouterB(config-if)#interface fastethernet1/0
RouterB(config-if)#ip cgmp
RouterB(config-if)#interface fastethernet2/0
RouterB(config-if)#ip cgmp
RouterB(config-if)#^Z
RouterB#

RouterC#conf t
Enter configuration commands, one per line.  End with CNTL/Z.
RouterC(config)#interface fastethernet0/0
RouterC(config-if)#ip cgmp
RouterC(config-if)#interface fastethernet1/0
RouterC(config-if)#ip cgmp
RouterC(config-if)#^Z
RouterC#
```

```
RouterD#conf t
Enter configuration commands, one per line.  End with CNTL/Z.
RouterD(config)#interface fastethernet0/0
RouterD(config-if)#ip cgmp
RouterD(config-if)#interface fastethernet1/0
RouterD(config-if)#ip cgmp
RouterD(config-if)#^Z
RouterD#

switch1> (enable) set cgmp enable
CGMP support for IP multicast enabled.
switch1> (enable)
switch2> (enable) set cgmp enable
CGMP support for IP multicast enabled.
```

4. Assign multicast group 224.2.127.254 to RouterC via access list 5. This assignment will only allow RouterC to advertise that group. Assign a TTL value of 12. Then assign group 224.0.124.244 to RouterD via access list 6.

```
RouterC#conf t
Enter configuration commands, one per line.  End with CNTL/Z.
RouterC(config)#access-list 5 permit 224.2.127.254 0.0.0.0
RouterC(config)#$ip pim send-rp-announce fastethernet1/0 scope 12 group-list 5
RouterC(config)#^Z
RouterC#

RouterD#conf t
Enter configuration commands, one per line.  End with CNTL/Z.
RouterD(config)#access-list 6 permit 224.0.124.244 0.0.0.0
RouterD(config)#$ip pim send-rp-announce fastethernet1/0 scope 12 group-list 6
RouterD(config)#^Z
RouterD#
```

5. Now configure RouterB to be the RP Mapping Agent. Use a scope of 12.

```
RouterB#conf t
Enter configuration commands, one per line.  End with CNTL/Z.
RouterB(config)#ip pim send-rp-discovery scope 12
RouterB(config)#^Z
RouterB#
```

Review Questions

1. Which of the following commands are necessary in order for multicast to work. (Choose all that apply.)

   A. `ip mroute cache`

   B. `ip pim <sparse-mode | dense-mode | sparse-dense-mode>`

   C. `ip cgmp`

   D. `ip multicast-routing`

2. What are the valid ranges for access lists when an RP address is manually configured? (Choose all that apply.)

   A. 1–100

   B. 1–99

   C. 100–199

   D. 800–899

   E. 1300–1999

3. What three configuration tasks are necessary to enable multicast Auto-RP?

   A. IP multicast routing

   B. Assign the default RP (for existing multicast networks)

   C. Assign the RP Mapping Agent

   D. Advertise RP/group associations

4. What do the options *type* and *number* mean in the command `ip pim send-rp-announce` *type number* `scope` *ttl* `group-list` *access-list-number*? (Choose all that apply.)

   A. PIM mode

   B. IGMP

   C. RP unicast IP address

   D. Interface

   E. Interface number

5. What does the following command accomplish?
   ```
   RouterA#conf t
   Enter configuration commands, one per line.  End with CNTL/Z.
   RouterA(config)#ip multicast-routing
   RouterA(config)#^Z
   RouterA#
   ```

   A. It enables the multicast forwarding process on the router.

   B. It allows IP multicast routing protocols to be configured on the router.

   C. It is defining the RP for the network.

   D. It is a multicast route source tree.

6. Which of the following multicast route notations indicate dense mode?

   A. (*, G)

   B. (G, *)

   C. (S, G)

   D. (G, S)

7. Which of the following multicast route notations indicates the operation of sparse mode?

   A. (*, G)

   B. (G, *)

   C. (S, G)

   D. (G, S)

8. What are the primary functions of RP Mapping Agents? (Choose all that apply.)

   A. Mapping unicast addresses of all RP routers in a multicast network

   B. Sourcing multicast traffic

   C. Resolving multicast group/RP conflicts

   D. Providing member topologies to the RP routers in the network

9. Which of the following is a method of limiting the scope of a multicast network?

   A. Passive interface applied to border interfaces

   B. Distribution lists within an IGP like EIGRP or OSPF

   C. TTL threshold setting on border interfaces

   D. RPF settings within the RP routers

10. Which of the following are valid reasons for configuring a router to be a member?

    A. To allow multicast forwarding

    B. To allow the RP to be a source for the specified group

    C. To allow source root tree forwarding

    D. To allow troubleshooting and verification of multicast functionality

11. Which are tools that can be used to troubleshoot multicast connectivity? (Choose all that apply.)

    A. Ping

    B. `show ip mroute`

    C. traceroute

    D. mtrace

12. What are two methods mtrace utilizes to establish the path between the source and router?

    A. SRT

    B. RPF

    C. Multicast group

    D. PIM

13. From which direction is the mtrace established?

    A. From the default RP of the multicast network to the source

    B. From the source to the RP

    C. From the source to the router interface

    D. From the router interface to the source

14. Where is it necessary to run IGMPv1?

    A. Entire multicast network

    B. All members of a group whose source is IGMPv1

    C. All interfaces on the router

    D. The interface or subnet whose hosts use IGMPv1

15. Which device answers IGMP requests?

   A. Hub

   B. ATM switch

   C. Switch

   D. Router

16. What command is used to manually configure a router to be an RP?

   A. `ip multicast RP <ip-address>`

   B. `ip pim RP <ip-address>`

   C. `ip pim rp-address <ip-address>`

   D. `ip igmp rp-address <ip-address>`

17. Which of the following criteria will activate an interface that is configured to use dense mode? (Choose all that apply.)

   A. Directly connected hosts

   B. Directly connected PIM routers

   C. Router configured as a border router

   D. When the interface receives a prune statement from a directly connected PIM router

18. Which of the following criteria will activate an interface in sparse mode? (Choose all that apply.)

   A. A sparse mode interface is always active.

   B. A directly connected DVMRP neighbor.

   C. An explicit join request on that interface.

   D. A prune request is received on the interface.

19. Which criteria will activate an interface in sparse mode when the interface is configured to use sparse-dense mode? (Choose all that apply.)

    A. Directly connected DVMRP neighbor.

    B. Explicit join request.

    C. Any PIM-configured interface is made active

    D. The interface has directly connected hosts.

20. Which of the following will activate an interface in dense mode if it is configured for sparse-dense mode operation? (Choose all that apply.)

    A. Non-pruned PIM interface

    B. Directly connected hosts

    C. DVMRP neighbor on that interface

    D. An explicit join request

Answers to Written Lab

1. `ip multicast-routing`

2. `conf t`
   `interface fastethernet4/0`
   `ip pim sparse-mode`

3. `conf t`
   `interface fastethernet3/0`
   `ip pim dense-mode`

4. `conf t`
   `interface fastethernet0/0`
   `ip pim sparse-dense-mode`

5. `show ip mroute`

6. `ip pim rp-address 172.16.25.3 30`

7. `ip pim send-rp-announce fast ethernet 4/0 scope 220 group-list 10`

8. `ip pim send-rp-discovery scope 32`

9. `conf t`
   `interface fastethernet2/0`
   `ip multicast ttl-threshold 235`

10. `conf t`
    `interface fastethernet3/0`
    `ip cgmp`

    `set cgmp enable`

Answers to Review Questions

1. **B, D.** These two commands must be entered for multicast forwarding to work. The `ip mroute cache` command enhances performance but is not necessary. CGMP is necessary only when hosts are connected to a router via a Catalyst switch.

2. **B, E.** 1–100 is an invalid range; the range has to be 1–99. 100–199 is used for extended access lists and 800–899 is used for IPX. 1300–1999 is an expanded range.

3. **B, C, D.** IP multicast routing is not part of the Auto-RP configuration.

4. **D, E.** *Type* means interface type, and *number* means the interface number.

5. **A.** The command enables the multicast process on the router, therefore permitting multicast packets to be forwarded.

6. **C.** (S, G) and (*, G) are the only valid notations. (S, G) indicates a source root tree distribution. Dense mode uses source root trees.

7. **A.** (S, G) and (*, G) are the only valid notations. (*, G) indicates a shared root tree distribution. Sparse mode uses shared root trees.

8. **A, C.** RP Mapping Agents keep track of all RP routers in the network via their unicast address. They then provide the nearest RP for the multicast groups it sources to all leaf routers in the multicast network.

9. **C.** The correct way to limit the scope of the multicast network is to configure TTL thresholds for external or border interfaces. RPF is used strictly for reverse path lookup.

10. **D.** By subscribing to a multicast group, the router can execute certain commands to troubleshoot and verify multicast connectivity.

11. A, B, D. Traceroute is used for unicast connectivity; mtrace, however, is used for multicast connectivity.

12. B, C. As shown in the examples in Chapter 10, the traceroute path can be established via RPF information or via multicast group forwarding information.

13. C. From the examples given in Chapter 10, you can see that the path is established from the source toward the multicast router interface.

14. D. The only interfaces that need to be made compatible with IGMPv1 are the interfaces that have hosts that are directly connected and use IGMPv1.

15. D. Routers are the devices that respond to IGMP membership records. Switches process CGMP from the routers. Hubs have no intelligence whatsoever.

16. C. The correct syntax is provided by answer C. The other answers are simply not correct.

17. A, B. Hosts activate the interface through membership reports. PIM interfaces automatically receive multicast forwarding until a prune request is received.

18. B, C. For a sparse mode interface to be active, there must be either a directly connected host or a DVMRP neighbor or a join request must be made. Sparse mode interfaces are inactive otherwise.

19. A, B, D. A PIM-configured interface is considered active only when in dense mode.

20. A, B, C. Join requests are used only in sparse mode operation.

Chapter 11

Access Policies

THE CCNP EXAM OBJECTIVES COVERED IN THIS CHAPTER INCLUDE THE FOLLOWING:

- ✓ Defining access policies
- ✓ Applying access policies to the access layer
- ✓ Applying access policies to the distribution layer
- ✓ Managing network devices
- ✓ Setting Cisco device passwords
- ✓ Configuring privilege levels
- ✓ Configuring banners
- ✓ Limiting VTY access
- ✓ Limiting HTTP access
- ✓ Managing the MAC address table
- ✓ Configuring port security
- ✓ Describing and configuring access lists
- ✓ Configuring route filtering

In this chapter, we'll show you how to identify the important components when you're designing and implementing access policies. How users access the network directly affects how you build your network and what policies you implement.

Access policies start at the physical equipment and extend throughout the entire internetwork. In its IOS, Cisco provides different security options that you can run on a switch or router to help implement access policy security.

Definition of an Access Policy

To document a standard implementation for user access, a company or corporation creates policies. Those policies should include access policies, which describe how users access the network and even how to stop unwanted connections into the network.

Before any access control is implemented on a network, a standard access policy must be created. It would be difficult for all companies to use a standard access policy because networks and business requirements vary widely between companies. However, you should keep in mind some basic standards when designing your access policies.

The following list includes some of the most common access policy standards:

- Physical security to the network equipment
- VLAN management and port security
- Password implementation
- Control of access to the enterprise network

- Documentation of the type of traffic allowed from the switch blocks through the distribution layer to the core layer
- Route filtering (access lists)

When designing your access policy, remember the big picture: access policies are meant to secure the corporate network and prevent unwanted and unneeded traffic from entering it or slowing it down. Network administrators should implement access policies based on a set of defined traffic standards as well as provide a level of security to campus network devices.

Applying Policies to the Hierarchical Model

Throughout this book, when discussing different aspects of network design, we have included a discussion of the Cisco three-layer hierarchical model. A discussion of network policies is no exception. Each layer in the Cisco hierarchical model can have a different access policy because each layer can be responsible for a different task. However, only the access layer and the distribution layer are typically used for implementing policies.

Access Layer

As you already know, the access layer is where users gain access to the network. You need to create security without hindering the company's business requirements. You can provide security at the access layer with port security on layer 2 switches and passwords on all devices in the internetwork.

Distribution Layer

The distribution layer is where routing occurs (that is, where layer 3 devices are present). At this layer, you create routing policies, which will ensure that only traffic that is necessary makes it to the core layer or is switched to another access layer. Because the distribution layer is also responsible for advertising routing information to the core layer, the routing policy can include route filtering with access lists and routing filters.

Core Layer

The idea of the core layer is to pass data as quickly as possible, so typically, no access policies would apply here. Any policy implemented at the core will only slow down data traversing the core. The distribution layer is responsible for preventing unwanted traffic from entering the core layer.

Managing Network Devices

It is important to be able to manage all your network devices. The first thing most administrators perform on their networking equipment is to set the passwords. This is probably a good thing to do right away. However, it is not the only thing you need to do. If all you set is the passwords, you are overlooking some of the other needed security items. This section will discuss the typical security that can be provided on a Cisco internetwork.

You should create a plan for the following:

- Physical security
- Passwords
- Privilege levels
- Banners
- Limiting Telnet and HTTP access

Physical Security

One of the first things you need to document when you're creating an access policy to describe network security is how to create physical security.

Physically accessing equipment is the easiest way to gain access into a campus internetwork. It takes less than a minute to break into any Cisco router or switch if physical access to the device is granted. If you cannot get physical access to a Cisco router or switch, it is impossible to break into it unless you can guess the passwords.

If someone has physical access to your network equipment, they can have almost complete control over it. Most devices have a backdoor for getting in without a password. Creating a security policy doesn't help if you don't create physical security as well. The following are some possible solutions for physical security access policies:

- Create a configuration and control policy for each type of device. For each site and remote branch, have a security plan that details how the links will be secured.

- Design and implement server rooms and network closets that have locks—or even badge entry. Make sure the proper ventilation and power is installed, as well as UPS systems.

- Control direct access to network equipment. Creating and locking server and network rooms is only the beginning of your access policy. You need to buy and install locking racks that stop unauthorized users or administrators from gaining direct access to hardware.

- Secure network links by providing the same type of security for the wiring and network closets that you provide for the physical devices.

Passwords

Passwords are probably the most important aspect of security on your network. Change your passwords frequently and make sure they are not easy-to-decipher passwords such as your wife's or husband's name or even the name of one of your kids. Family names are typically used as passwords because they are easy to remember. However, people trying to break into your network or a piece of equipment know this as well.

Because there are many different ways to access and configure Cisco routers, passwords need to be set on all possible access points. To do this, you must know what they are. Remember, there are really only two ways to enter a Cisco router or switch:

- *Out-of-band management* includes the console and auxiliary ports. Set passwords on both of these physical ports. By default, no passwords are set and anyone can connect and manage the devices. "Out-of-band" comes from "managing the device out of the network."

- *In-band management* includes Telnet, TFTP servers, and Network Management Stations (NMSs). These access points do not allow access by default, but passwords should still be applied. "In-band" comes from "managing the device from within the network."

Setting Router Passwords

There are five types of passwords used to secure your Cisco routers. The first two set your enable password, which is used to secure privileged mode. This will prompt a user for a password when the command `enable` is used. The other three are used to configure a password when user mode is accessed through the console port, the auxiliary port, or via Telnet.

> **Note:** You should already be aware of how to set passwords on Cisco routers and switches and use the information presented in this section as a review.

Enable Passwords

Enable passwords are very important because they stop users from gaining access to privileged mode, where they can view and change the configuration of the device. You set the enable passwords from global configuration mode:

```
Router(config)#enable ?
  last-resort  Define enable action if no TACACS servers respond
  password     Assign the privileged level password
  secret       Assign the privileged level secret
  use-tacacs   Use TACACS to check enable passwords
```

The commands are as follows:

last-resort Used if you set up authentication through a tacacs server and the server is not available. This will allow the administrator to still enter the router. However, it is not used if the tacacs server is working.

password Sets the enable password on older, pre-10.3 systems. Not used if an enable secret is set.

secret The newer, encrypted password. Overrides the enable password if set.

use-tacacs Tells the router to authenticate through a tacacs server. This is convenient if you have dozens or even hundreds of routers. How would you like to change the password on 200 routers? With the tacacs server, you need to change the password only once.

Here is an example of how to set the enable secret password:

```
Router(config)#enable secret todd
Router(config)#enable password todd
The enable password you have chosen is the same as your
enable secret. This is not recommended.  Re-enter the
enable password.
```

If you try to set the enable secret and enable passwords to be the same, the router will give you a nice, polite warning the first time, but if you type the same password again, it will be accepted. However, now neither password will work. If you don't have older legacy routers, don't bother to use the enable password.

Usermode passwords are assigned by using the `line` command:

```
Router(config)#line ?
  <0-4>    First Line number
  aux      Auxiliary line
  console  Primary terminal line
  vty      Virtual terminal
```

The commands are as follows:

aux   Sets the usermode password for the auxiliary port. This is typically used for configuring a modem on the router, but it can be used as a console as well.

console   Sets a console usermode password.

vty   Sets a Telnet password on the router. If the password is not set, then by default, Telnet cannot be used.

To configure the usermode passwords, you configure the line you want and use either the `login` or `no login` command to tell the router to prompt for authentication.

Auxiliary Password

To configure the auxiliary password, go to global configuration mode and type **line aux ?**. Notice that you only get a choice of 0–0 because there is only one port:

```
Router#config t
Enter configuration commands, one per line.  End with CNTL/Z.
Router(config)#line aux ?
  <0-0>   First Line number
Router(config)#line aux 0
Router(config-line)#login
Router(config-line)#password todd
```

It is important to remember the login command or the auxiliary port won't prompt for authentication.

Console Password

To set the console password, use the command line console 0. However, notice that when we tried to type line console 0 ? from the aux line configuration, we got an error. You can still type line console 0 and it will be accepted, but the help screens don't work from that prompt. We typed exit to get back one level:

```
Router(config-line)#line console ?
% Unrecognized command
Router(config-line)#exit
Router(config)#line console ?
  <0-0>  First Line number
Router(config)#line console 0
Router(config-line)#login
Router(config-line)#password todd1
```

Because there is only one console port, we can choose only line console 0.

Telnet Password

To set the usermode password for Telnet access into the router, use the line vty command. Routers that are not running the Enterprise edition of the Cisco IOS default to five VTY lines, 0 through 4. However, if you have the Enterprise edition, you will have significantly more. The routers we're using for this book have 198 (0–197). The best way to find out how many lines you have is to use the question mark:

```
Router(config-line)#line vty 0 ?
<1-197>Last Line Number
<cr>
Router(config-line)#line vty 0 197
Router(config-line)#login
Router(config-line)#password todd2
```

If you try to telnet into a router that does not have a VTY password set, you will receive an error stating that the connection is refused because the password is not set. You can tell the router to allow Telnet connections without a password by using the `no login` command:

```
Router(config-line)#line vty 0 197
Router(config-line)#no login
```

After your routers are configured with an IP address, you can use the Telnet program to configure and check them instead of having to use a console cable. You can use the Telnet program by typing **telnet** from any command prompt (DOS or Cisco).

The Login Option

In the preceding examples, we used the `login` command to indicate to the router where to find the login information that tells it to prompt for authentication. For example, the `login` command was used in the console, auxiliary, and VTY lines. The system then automatically uses the line as a login and will prompt for the password set under that particular line.

However, there are other options you can use that are more specific:

`login` Indicates where to find the user information.

`login local` Indicates that the information will be found locally in the username statement (the username statement will be described shortly).

`login authentication` Used in conjunction with the `login tacacs` command to indicate that the login information is contained on a centralized authentication server.

`login tacacs` Used in conjunction with the `login authentication` command to indicate that the login information is contained on a centralized authentication server. Using a centralized server makes it easier to maintain a large number of users and devices.

Cisco recommends that you require your users to log in to the system with a username and password instead of just handing out the enable secret password to all administrators. Using this method allows you to keep track of administrators and what changes they have made on a device.

To set up usernames, use the `username` command. Here is an example:

```
Username todd password console1
```

Setting the usernames won't do any good until you set the `login local` command on a line. If you want users to be prompted for a username on certain lines, make sure you set the `login local` command on those lines. Do not set the `login local` and then forget to set the usernames and passwords or you will be locked out of your router! The only way to recover is to reload or reboot the router, and this will work only if you didn't save the new configuration. You will have to perform a password recovery technique if you did save the configuration.

Here is an example of setting the `login local` on the console and Telnet lines:

```
Line con 0
Login local
Line vty 0 4
Login local
Exit
```

Session Time-Outs

It is important to not leave open Telnet or console sessions running when you are not at your workstation. It is very easy to forget to log out, so setting the time-outs will provide an additional level of security for an unattended console.

For an IOS-based router, use the **exec-timeout** command under the **line** command. The **exec-timeout 0 0** sets the time-out for the console EXEC session to zero, or to never time out. To set the line to time out after 10 minutes, use **exec-timeout 10**.

Here is an example of how to configure the **exec-timeout** command on the console and telnet lines:

```
Router(config)#line con 0
Router(config-line)#exec-timeout ?
  <0-35791>  Timeout in minutes
Router(config-line)#exec-timeout 0 ?
  <0-2147483>  Timeout in seconds
  <cr>
Router(config-line)#line vty 0 4
Router(config-line)#exec-timeout 10
```

Encrypting Your Passwords

Only the enable secret password is encrypted by default. You need to manually configure the usermode and enable passwords.

Notice that you can see all the passwords except the enable secret when performing a `show running-config` on a router:

```
Router#sh run
[output cut]
!
enable secret 5 $1$rFbM$8.aXocHg6yHrM/zzeNkAT.
enable password todd1
!
[output cut]
line con 0
 password todd1
 login
line aux 0
 password todd
 login
line vty 0 4
 password todd2
 login
line vty 5 197
 password todd2
 login
!
end

Router#
```

To manually encrypt your passwords, use the `service password-encryption` command. Here is an example of how to perform manual password encryption:

```
Router#config t
Enter configuration commands, one per line. End with CNTL/Z.
```

```
Router(config)#service password-encryption
Router(config)#enable password todd
Router(config)#line vty 0 197
Router(config-line)#login
Router(config-line)#password todd2
Router(config-line)#line con 0
Router(config-line)#login
Router(config-line)#password todd1
Router(config-line)#line aux 0
Router(config-line)#login
Router(config-line)#password todd
Router(config-line)#exit
Router(config)#no service password-encryption
Router(config)#^Z
```

By typing the show running-config command, you can see that the enable password and the line passwords are all encrypted:

```
Router#sh run
Building configuration...

[output cut]
!
enable secret 5 $1$rFbM$8.aXocHg6yHrM/zzeNkAT.
enable password 7 0835434A0D
!
[output cut]
!
line con 0
 password 7 111D160113
 login
line aux 0
 password 7 071B2E484A
 login
line vty 0 4
 password 7 0835434A0D
 login
```

```
line vty 5 197
 password 7 09463724B
 login
!
end
```

Router#

Setting Passwords on a CLI-Based switch

To configure the usermode and enable mode passwords on a CLI-based switch, enter enable mode by using the `enable` command and then enter global configuration mode by using the `config t` command.

Once you are in global configuration mode, you can set the usermode and enable mode passwords by using the `enable password` command. The switch's output below shows the configuration of both the usermode and enable mode passwords:

```
(config)#enable password ?
  level  Set exec level password
(config)#enable password level ?
  <1-15>  Level number
```

To enter the usermode password, use level number 1. To enter the enable mode password, use level mode 15. Remember, the password must be at least four characters but not longer than eight characters.

Usermode Password

The switch output below shows the usermode password being set and denied because it is more than eight characters:

```
(config)#enable password level 1 toddlammle
Error: Invalid password length.
Password must be between 4 and 8 characters
```

Enable Password

The following output is an example of how to set both the usermode and enable mode passwords on a CLI-based switch:

```
(config)#enable password level 1 todd
(config)#enable password level 15 todd1
```

```
(config)#exit
#exit
CLI session with the switch is now closed.
Press any key to continue.
```

At this point, you can press Enter and test your passwords. You will be prompted for a usermode password after you press K and then an enable mode password after you type **enable**. Remember that the enable secret password always supercedes an enable password. On a CLI-based switch, use the enable secret command, just as you would with any router:

```
(config)#enable secret sanfran
```

You can use a show running-config to see the current configuration on the switch:

```
#sh run
Building configuration...
Current configuration:

enable secret 5 $1$FMFQ$wFVYVLYn2aXscfB3J95.w.
enable password level 1 "TODD"
enable password level 15 "TODD1"
```

Notice that the enable mode passwords are not encrypted by default, but the enable secret is. This is the same password configuration technique that you will find on a router. The passwords are not case sensitive.

You can set the session time-out on a CLI-based switch with the time-out command under the line console:

```
(config)#line console
(config)#time-out 300
```

The time-out command is set in seconds (300 seconds is 5 minutes).

Setting Passwords on a Set-Based Switch

To configure the usermode and privilege mode passwords on a set-based switch, use the command set password for the usermode password and the command set enablepass for the enable password.

Usermode Password

To set the usermode password, use the command set password, then press Enter:

```
Console> en
Enter password:
Console> (enable) set password [press enter]
Enter old password:
Enter new password:
Retype new password:
Password changed.
```

When you see the "Enter old password" prompt, you can leave it blank and press Enter if you don't have a password set. The output for the "Enter new password" prompt doesn't show on the console screen. If you want to clear the usermode (login) password, type in the old password and then just press Enter when you're asked for a new password.

Enable Password

To set the enable password, use the command set enablepass, then press Enter:

```
Console> (enable) set enablepass
Enter old password:
Enter new password:
Retype new password:
Password changed.
Console> (enable)
```

You can type **exit** at this point to log out of the switch completely, which will allow you to test your new passwords. You can set the session time-out on the set-based switch by using the set logout command:

```
Console> (enable) set logout 5
```

The set logout 5 command will log out an open session not used for 5 minutes.

Privileged Levels

By default, all Cisco devices have two privilege levels: user mode and privilege mode. If you have a large network with many administrators, you should set usernames and passwords for each administrator. This will allow you to monitor each administrator and the changes they make to any device.

This becomes a problem when each administrator has different duties; they should not all have the same amount of access to Cisco devices. By setting additional privilege levels, you can effectively provide each user with the ability to perform certain commands without giving them the opportunity to modify the configuration or even perform a debug on a device. The privilege mode, by default, allows a user to perform all commands, view and change the configuration, and run debugging commands. You probably would not want all administrators to have full privilege mode capabilities.

There are 16 different levels of privilege that can be set, 0–15. By default, user mode is level 1 and the highest privilege mode is 15. Level 0 is used to set up a very limited subset of commands for a specific user or line.

To set up privilege modes, use the `privilege` global configuration command:

```
Router(config)#privilege ?
  alps-ascu              ALPS ASCU configuration mode
  alps-circuit           ALPS circuit configuration mode
  atmsig_e164_table_mode ATMSIG E164 Table
  configure              Global configuration mode
  controller             Controller configuration mode
  crypto-map             Crypto map config mode
  crypto-transform       Crypto transform config mode
  dhcp                   DHCP pool configuration mode
  exec                   Exec mode
  flow-cache             Flow aggregation cache config mode
  interface              Interface configuration mode
  interface-dlci         Frame Relay dlci configuration mode
  ipenacl                IP named extended access-list config-
                         uration mode
  ipsnacl                IP named simple access-list config-
                         uration mode
  ipx-router             IPX router configuration mode
```

ipxenacl	IPX named extended access-list configuration mode
ipxsapnacl	IPX named SAP access-list configuration mode
ipxsnacl	IPX named standard access-list configuration mode
ipxsumnacl	IPX named Summary access-list configuration mode
lane	ATM Lan Emulation Lecs Configuration Table
line	Line configuration mode
map-class	Map class configuration mode
map-list	Map list configuration mode
null-interface	Null interface configuration mode
route-map	Route map config mode
router	Router configuration mode
rtr	RTR Entry Configuration
subscriber-policy	Subscriber policy configuration mode
vc-class	VC class configuration mode
voiceport	Voice configuration mode
voipdialpeer	Dial Peer configuration mode
vpdn-group	VPDN group configuration mode

There are a lot of commands that can be used with the **privilege** command, which allows for very granular control. Here is a list of some of the most commonly used privilege mode commands:

configure Allows global configuration mode

controller Allows controller configuration on interfaces

exec Allows entrance to exec mode

interface Allows interface configuration

ipx-router Allows changes to the IPX routing protocols

line Allows changes to the line commands

map-class Allows changes and configuration of map-class

map-list Allows entrance to map-list

route-map Allows entrance to route map configuration mode

router Allows changes to routing protocols

To configure privileges, you configure an enable password for each level and then assign commands that each level can perform. For Cisco IOS devices, use the following command to set the level passwords:

```
Enable password level level password
```

Then set the `privilege` command as follows using the list of most commonly used privilege mode commands as valid modes:

```
Privilege mode level level command
```

Here is an example of how to set a password for a level 5 user, then enable that user to execute the `ping` command, which is a level 15 command:

```
Router(config)#enable password level 5 todd
Router(config)#privilege exec level 5 ping
Router(config)#^Z
```

Type the command **show privilege** to see the current privilege:

```
Router#sh priv
Current privilege level is 15
Router#
```

You can then have the user log in with the `enable 5` command, which will prompt the user for the level 5 enable password:

```
Router>ena 5
Password:
```

Finally, you can type **show privilege** to see the new privilege level:

```
Router#sh priv
Current privilege level is 5
Router#
```

Banners

You can set a banner on a Cisco router so that when either a user logs in to the router or an administrator telnets into it, for example, the banner will give them information that you want them to have. Another reason for having a banner is to add a security notice to users dialing in to your internetwork. There are four different banners available:

```
Router(config)#banner ?
  LINE     c banner-text c, where 'c' is a delimiting character
  exec     Set EXEC process creation banner
  incoming Set incoming terminal line banner
  login    Set login banner
  motd     Set Message of the Day banner
```

The Message of the Day is the most used and gives a message to every person dialing in or connecting to the router via Telnet, auxiliary port, or console port:

```
Router(config)#banner motd ?
  LINE  c banner-text c, where 'c' is a delimiting character
Router(config)#banner motd #
Enter TEXT message.  End with the character '#'.
$ized to be in Acme.com network, then you must disconnect
immediately.
```

> **NOTE** The router wrapped the text above and inserted a dollar sign ($) to let the administrator know this. The complete message will be used, however, as shown in the output that follows.

```
#
Router(config)#^Z
Router#
00:25:12: %SYS-5-CONFIG_I: Configured from console by console
Router#exit
```

```
Router con0 is now available

Press RETURN to get started.

If you are not authorized to be in Acme.com network, then
you must disconnect immediately.

Router>
```

The above MOTD banner tells anyone connecting to the router that they either must be authorized or must disconnect. It's important that you understand the delimiting character. You can use any character you want, and it is used to tell the router where the end of the message is. So you can't use the delimiting character in the message itself. Also note that at the end of the message, you should press Return, then the delimiting character, then Return again. If you don't do that, the message will still work, but if you have multiple banners, for example, they will be combined as one message and put on one line.

These are the other banners:

Exec banner   You can configure a line-activation (exec) banner to be displayed when an EXEC process (such as a line-activation or incoming connection to a VTY line) is created.

Incoming banner   You can configure a banner to be displayed on terminals connected to reverse Telnet lines. This banner is useful for providing instructions to users who use reverse Telnet.

Login banner   You can configure a login banner to be displayed on all connected terminals. This banner is displayed after the MOTD banner but before the login prompts. The login banner cannot be disabled on a per-line basis. To globally disable the login banner, you must delete the login banner with the `no banner login` command.

Limiting VTY Access

You will have a difficult time trying to stop users from telnetting into a router because any active port on a router is fair game for VTY access. However, you can use a standard IP access list to control access by placing the access list on the VTY lines themselves.

> **Note:** Access lists are in discussed in detail later in this chapter.

To place an access list on a VTY line, follow these steps:

1. Create a standard IP access list that permits only the host or hosts you want to be able to telnet into the routers to do so.

2. Apply the access list to the VTY line with the `access-class` command.

Here is an example of allowing only host 172.16.10.3 to telnet into a router:

```
RouterA(config)#access-list 50 permit 172.16.10.3
RouterA(config)#line vty 0 4
RouterA(config-line)#access-class 50 in
```

Because of the implied deny any at the end of the list, the access list stops any host from telnetting into the router except the host 172.16.10.3.

Controlling HTTP Access

HTTP can be used to gain access to a router or switch and both view and change the configuration of the device. Because any active interface can be used to allow access via HTTP, you can limit access by placing an access list under the HTTP server command.

To turn on HTTP access, use the `ip http server` command. By default, the enable secret password is used to gain access. When you set up usernames and passwords, each user can be prompted for passwords when trying to access the device via a network browser. You can use the `ip access-class` command to add an access list to the HTTP server running on the device. Here is an example of setting up a user with HTTP access from their host 172.16.10.1:

```
Router#config t
Router(config)#username tlammle password cisco
Router(config)#ip http server
Router(config)#access-list 10 permit host 172.16.10.1
Router(config)#ip http access-class 10
```

```
Router(config)#ip http authentication ?
  enable  Use enable passwords
  local   Use local username and passwords
  tacacs  Use tacacs to authorize user

Router(config)#ip http authentication local
Router(config)#
```

User tlammle can now use a network browser to log in and manage a Cisco device.

Password security for HTTP access is similar to password security for console and Telnet access. The following commands can be used for login authentication:

enable Indicates that the enable password should be used. This is the default if nothing is specified.

local Indicates that the local user database is used for authentication.

tacacs Indicates that a tacacs server is used for authentication.

Access Layer Policy

The access layer is where users gain access to the internetwork. If you want total security, you can unplug their workstations from the switch, but that's not usually possible. You need to both allow users to gain access to corporate services and secure your internetwork. Not an easy task. The biggest threat is users going into a network closet and just plugging into an access layer switch. Always lock the closet in which the network equipment is located.

However, by managing the MAC address table, you can manage port security on access layer switches, which allows you to protect your internetwork from a user plugging a device into the switch.

Managing the MAC Address Table

Do you remember how bridges and switches filter a network? They use MAC (hardware) addresses burned into a host's network interface card

(NIC) to make forwarding decisions. The switches create a MAC table that includes dynamic, permanent, and static addresses. This filter table is created when hosts send a frame and the switch learns the source MAC address and from which segment and port it was received.

The switch keeps adding into the MAC filter table new MAC addresses that are sent on the network. As hosts are added or removed, the switch dynamically updates the MAC filter table. If a device is removed, or if it is not connected to the switch for a period of time, the switch will age out the entry.

You can see the switch's filter table by using the command show mac-address-table. The following output shows the information received when using the show mac-address-table command:

```
Todd1900EN#sh mac-address-table
Number of permanent addresses : 0
Number of restricted static addresses : 0
Number of dynamic addresses : 4

Address           Dest Interface    Type       Source Interface List
-----------------------------------------------------------------
00A0.246E.0FA8    Ethernet 0/2      Dynamic    All
0000.8147.4E11    Ethernet 0/5      Dynamic    All
0000.8610.C16F    Ethernet 0/1      Dynamic    All
00A0.2448.60A5    Ethernet 0/4      Dynamic    All
```

The addresses in the table above are from the four hosts connected to a 1900 switch. They are all *dynamic entries*, which means the switch looked at the source address of a frame as it entered the switch interface and placed that address in the filter table. Notice that we have hosts in interfaces 1, 2, 4, and 5.

Administrators can specifically assign permanent addresses to a switch port. These addresses are never aged out. You can do this to provide security to a port, which means that unless you specifically configure a hardware address to a switch port, the hardware address won't work. Administrators can also create static entries in the switch; these entries actually create a path for a source hardware address. This can be really restrictive, and you need to be careful when setting static entries because you can basically shut your switch down if you do not plan the configuration carefully.

Configuring Port Security

Another form of security on an access layer switch is *port security*. Port security is a way of stopping users from plugging a hub into their jack in their office or cubicle and adding a bunch of hosts without your knowledge. By default, 132 hardware addresses can be allowed on a single switch interface. To change this, use the interface command `port secure max-mac-count`.

On a set-based switch, the command is `set port security` *mod/port* `enable` *mac_address*.

The following switch output shows the command `port secure max-mac-count` being set on a CLI-based switch, interface 0/2, to allow only one entry:

```
Todd1900EN#config t
Enter configuration commands, one per line.  End with CNTL/Z
Todd1900EN(config)#int e0/2
Todd1900EN(config-if)#port secure ?
  max-mac-count  Maximum number of addresses allowed on the port
  <cr>

Todd1900EN(config-if)#port secure max-mac-count ?
  <1-132>  Maximum mac address count for this secure port

Todd1900EN(config-if)#port secure max-mac-count 1
```

The secured port or ports you create can use either static or sticky-learned hardware addresses. If the hardware addresses on a secured port are not statically assigned, the port sticky learns the source address of incoming frames and automatically assigns them as permanent addresses. *Sticky-learn* is a term Cisco uses to refer to a port dynamically finding a source hardware address and creating a permanent entry in the MAC filter table.

Distribution Layer Policy

The distribution layer is the place to implement most of your policies for the network. Here, you can exercise considerable flexibility in defining network operation. There are several items that generally should be taken care of at the distribution layer:

- Implementation of tools such as access lists, packet filtering, and queuing
- Implementation of security and network policies, including address translation and firewalls
- Redistribution between routing protocols, including static routing
- Routing between VLANs and other workgroup support functions
- Broadcast and multicast domain definition

Things to avoid at the distribution layer are limited to those functions that exclusively belong to one of the other layers. The best access polices assure that the distribution layer does not send excessive data to the core layers or other switch blocks. Access control at the distribution layer falls into several different categories:

- Filtering traffic between VLANs and to the core layer. Typically, this is provided by an access list.
- Filtering routing protocol updates to the core block. This is provided by *distribution lists*, which are another form of access lists but are specific for routing protocols.

Access Lists

Most of the access policies are implemented at the distribution layer with some type of access list. Access lists are essentially lists of conditions that control access. They're powerful tools that control access both to and from network segments. They can filter unwanted packets and be used to implement security policies. With the right combination of access lists, network managers will be armed with the power to enforce nearly any access policy they can invent.

> **Note:** This is only an overview of access lists. For a detailed explanation, please see *CCNA: Cisco Certified Network Associate Study Guide*, by Todd Lammle (Sybex, 2000), and *CCNP: Routing Study Guide*, by Todd Lammle and Sean Odom (Sybex, 2000).

The IP and IPX access lists work similarly—they're both packet filters that packets are compared with, categorized by, and acted upon. Once the lists are built, they can be applied to either inbound or outbound traffic on any interface. Applying an access list will then cause the router to analyze every packet crossing that interface in the specified direction and take action accordingly.

There are a few important rules a packet follows when it's being compared with an access list:

- It's always compared with each line of the access list in sequential order; that is, it'll always start with line 1, then go to line 2, then line 3, and so on.

- It's compared with lines of the access list only until a match is made. Once the packet matches a line of the access list, it's acted upon, and no further comparisons take place.

- There is an implicit "deny" at the end of each access list—this means that if a packet doesn't match up to any lines in the access list, it'll be discarded.

Each of these rules has some powerful implications when IP and IPX packets are filtered with access lists.

There are two types of access lists used with IP and IPX that we will discuss here:

Standard access lists These use only the source IP address in an IP packet to filter the network. This basically permits or denies an entire suite of protocols. IPX standards can filter on both source and destination IPX addresses. IP standard access lists use numbers 1–99 and IPX standard access lists use numbers 800–899.

Extended access lists These check for both source and destination IP addresses, the protocol field in the Network layer header, and the port number at the Transport layer header. IPX extended access lists use the source and destination IPX addresses, the Network layer protocol field, and socket numbers in the Transport layer header. IP extended access lists use numbers 100–199 and IPX extended access lists use numbers 900–999.

Once you create an access list, you apply it to an interface with either an inbound or outbound list:

Inbound access lists Packets are processed through the access list before being routed to the outbound interface.

Outbound access lists Packets are routed to the outbound interface and then processed through the access list.

There are also some guidelines that should be followed when you're creating and implementing access lists on a router:

- You can assign only one access list per interface, per protocol, or per direction. This means that if you are creating IP access lists, you can have only one inbound access list and one outbound access list per interface.

- Organize your access lists so that the more specific tests are at the top.

- When a new test statement is added to the access list, it will be placed at the bottom of the list.

- You cannot remove one line from an access list. If you try to, you will remove the entire list. It is best to copy the access list to a text editor before trying to edit the list. The only exception is when you're using named access lists.

- Unless your access list ends with a `permit any` command, all packets will be discarded if they do not meet any of the list's tests. Every list should have at least one permit statement, or you might as well shut the interface down.

- Create access lists and then apply them to an interface. Any access list applied to an interface without an access-list present will not filter traffic.

- Access lists are designed to filter traffic going through the router. They will not filter traffic originating from the router.

- Place IP standard access lists as close to the destination as possible.

- Place IP extended access lists as close to the source as possible.

Wildcards

Wildcards are used with access list configuration and summarization and with Open Shortest Path First (OSPF) configuration. Although applying wildcards looks more difficult than it really is, it is important to understand how.

Wildcards are used with access lists to specify a specific host, network, or part of a network. To understand wildcards, you need to understand block sizes. Block sizes are used to specify a range of addresses. There are different block sizes available, including 64, 32, 16, 8, and 4.

When you need to specify a range of addresses, you choose the block size closest to your needs. For example, if you need to specify 34 networks, you need a block size of 64. If you want to specify 18 hosts, you need a block size of 32. If you specify only 2 networks, then a block size of 4 would work.

Wildcards are used with the host or network address to tell the router a range of available addresses to filter. To specify a specific host, the address would look like this:

    172.16.30.5 0.0.0.0

The four zeros represent each octet of the address. Whenever a zero is presented, it means that octet in the address must match exactly. To specify that an octet can be any value, the value of 255 is used. As an example, here is how a full subnet is specified with a wildcard:

    172.16.30.0 0.0.0.255

This tells the router to match up the first three octets exactly, but the fourth octet can be any value.

Now, that was the easy part. What if you want to specify only a small range of subnets? This is where the block sizes come in. You have to specify the range of values in a block size. In other words, you can't choose to specify 20 networks. You can specify only the exact amount as the block size value. For example, the range would have to be either 16 or 32, but not 20.

Let's say that you want to block access to a part of a network, the part that's in the range from 172.16.8.0 through 172.16.15.0. That is a block size of 8. Your network number would be 172.16.8.0, and the wildcard would be 0.0.7.255. Whoa! What is that? The 7.255 is what the router uses to determine the block size. The network and wildcard tell the router to start at 172.16.8.0 and go up a block size of eight addresses to network 172.16.15.0.

It is actually easier than it looks. We could certainly go through the binary math for you, but actually, all you have to do is remember that the wildcard is always one number less than the block size. So, in our example, the wildcard would be 7 because our block size is 8. If you used a block size of 16, the wildcard would be 15. Easy, huh?

Here are some examples to help you really understand it.

The following example tells the router to match the first three octets exactly but that the fourth octet can be anything:

```
RouterA(config)#access-list 10 deny 172.16.10.0 0.0.0.255
```

The next example tells the router to match the first two octets and that the last two octets can be any value:

```
RouterA(config)#access-list 10 deny 172.16.0.0 0.0.255.255
```

Try to figure out this next line:

```
RouterA(config)#access-list 10 deny 172.16.16.0 0.0.3.255
```

The above configuration tells the router to start at network 172.16.16.0 and use a block size of 4. The range would then be 172.16.16.0 through 172.16.19.0.

The example below shows an access list starting at 172.16.16.0 and going up a block size of 8 to 172.16.23.0:

```
RouterA(config)#access-list 10 deny 172.16.16.0 0.0.7.255
```

The next example starts at network 172.16.32.0 and goes up a block size of 32 to 172.16.63.0:

```
RouterA(config)#access-list 10 deny 172.16.32.0 0.0.31.255
```

This last example starts at network 172.16.64.0 and goes up a block size of 64 to 172.16.127.0:

```
RouterA(config)#access-list 10 deny 172.16.64.0 0.0.63.255
```

Here are two more things to keep in mind when you're working with block sizes and wildcards:

- Each block size must start at 0. For example, you can't say that you want a block size of 8 and start at 12. You must use 0–7, 8–15, 16–23, and so on. For a block size of 32, the ranges are 0–31, 32–63, 64–95, and so on.

- Using the command **any** is the same thing as writing out the wildcard 0.0.0.0 255.255.255.255.

Route Filtering

The distribute route command can be used to limit the number of networks advertised by permitting advertisements only to those specified. Distribution lists are applied from within a routing protocol to manipulate which route updates are sent and accepted on the specified interface. All that's necessary for networks in which the edge routers rely only on the default route is to advertise a few choice networks to them. Reducing the advertised routes conserves bandwidth and reduces the load on the edge router.

Controlling the routing table of the core block reduces the routing table size on the core and can also stop users from accessing networks that you don't advertise unless you specifically provide them with a static route.

You can also use access lists to manipulate route advertisements. As an example of this, look at the route table in the router output below before any changes are made in the EIGRP session:

```
Router_C#show ip route
Codes: C - connected, S - static, I - IGRP, R - RIP, M -    [output cut]
Gateway of last resort is not set

     172.16.0.0/16 is variably subnetted, 4 subnets, 3 masks
C       172.16.40.4/30 is directly connected, Serial0
D       172.16.30.0/24 [90/2195456] via 172.16.40.5          , 00:42:51,
        Serial0
D       172.16.20.4/30 [90/2681856] via 172.16.40.5          , 02:33:25,
        Serial0
D       172.16.0.0/16 is a summary, 03:03:56, Null0
Router_C#
```

This information shows that there are three routes learned via EIGRP and one route that's directly connected. Next, we'll filter out the route for the 172.16.30.0 network:

```
Router_C#conf t
Enter configuration commands, one per line.  End with CNTL/Z.
```

```
Router_C(config)#access-list 30 deny 172.16.30.0 0.0.0.255
Router_C(config)#access-list 30 permit any
Router_C(config)#router eigrp 100
Router_C(config-router)#distribute-list 30 in serial0
Router_C(config-router)#^Z
Router_C#
```

After applying access list 30 via the distribute-list command, we executed another show ip route on the router. Here is the result:

```
Router_C#show ip route
Codes: C - connected, S - static, I - IGRP, R - RIP, M -    [output cut]
Gateway of last resort is not set

     172.16.0.0/16 is variably subnetted, 3 subnets, 2 masks
C       172.16.40.4/30 is directly connected, Serial0
D       172.16.20.4/30 [90/2681856] via 172.16.40.5,         00:00:02,
        Serial0
D       172.16.0.0/16 is a summary, 00:00:02, Null0
Router_C#
```

You can see that the 172.16.30.0 network is no longer in the routing table. This is how the distribute-list command works.

Summary

This chapter covered the different aspects of designing and implementing access polices on your internetwork. It is important to create for your network access policies that start at physical security and extend through the entire internetwork.

In this chapter, we covered the following:

- Defining and applying access policies at the access layer and distribution layer

- Managing network devices by setting passwords, using privilege levels and banners, and limiting VTY and HTTP access

- Managing the MAC address table by configuring port security

- Providing an overview of access lists and route filtering

Key Terms

Before you take the exam, be sure you're familiar with the following terms:

distribution lists

in-band management

out-of-band management

Commands Used in This Chapter

The following list includes the commands used in this chapter:

Command	Meaning
`enable secret`	Configures the enable secret password on a CLI device
`enable password`	Configures the enable password on a CLI device
`set password`	Configures the usermode password on a set-based device
`set enablepass`	Configures the enable password on a set-based device
`line console`	Configures the usermode console password on a CLI device
`line vty`	Configures the usermode Telnet password on a CLI device
`line aux`	Configures the usermode aux password on a CLI device
`login local`	Configures a line to set authentication locally
`username`	Configures a username and password for a local login
`exec-timeout`	Changes the time-out of a CLI-based device console

Command	Meaning
service password-encryption	Encrypts the usermode and enable password on a CLI-based device
no service password-encryption	Disables password encryption
time-out	Changes the time-out of a set-based device console
privilege *mode*	Configures privilege modes on a CLI-based device
banner	Configures banners on a CLI-based device
access-class	Configures an access list on the VTY lines
ip http access-class	Configures an access list for HTTP security
ip http authentication local	Configures authentication for username and password when using HTTP to configure a device
sh mac-address-table	Views the MAC filter table on a CLI-based switch
port-secure mac-mac-count	Configures port security on a CLI-based switch
distribute-list	Configures an access list for use on a routing table

Written Lab

1. Port security is typically an access policy at which layer?

2. Access lists are typically used for an access policy at which layer?

3. What command applies an access list to a routing table?

4. What command applies an access list to a VTY line?

5. What command applies an access list to an HTTP server running on a router?

6. What is the standard IP access list number range?

7. Where would you place extended access lists in the network?

8. How do you set port security on a set-based switch?

9. If you wanted to set usernames and passwords for the console port, which command must you set under the `line console 0` command?

10. What are the four types of banners you can set on a Cisco router?

Review Questions

1. What is the range of subnets filtered with the 172.16.32.0 0.0.31.255 wildcard?

   A. 0–31

   B. 32–63

   C. 1–254

   D. 0–31

2. What is the range of subnets filtered with the 192.168.10.64 0.0.0.63 wildcard?

   A. 0–63

   B. 64–127

   C. 0–127

   D. 1–254

3. Standard IP access lists use what parameter to filter a network?

   A. Source IP address

   B. Destination IP address

   C. Source and destination IP addresses

   D. Port numbers

4. Extended IP access lists use what parameters to filter a network? (Choose all that apply.)

   A. Source IP address

   B. Destination IP address

   C. Source and destination IP addresses

   D. Port numbers

5. Where should standard access lists be placed in the network?

    A. Closest to the source

    B. Closest to the destination

    C. On a server

    D. On a switch

6. Where should extended access lists be placed in the network?

    A. Closest to the source

    B. Closest to the destination

    C. On a server

    D. On a switch

7. What is the number range of IP standard access lists?

    A. 1–99

    B. 100–199

    C. 800–899

    D. 900–999

8. What is the number range of IP extended access lists?

    A. 1–99

    B. 100–199

    C. 800–899

    D. 900–999

9. Which of the following is a form of security at the access layer?

    A. Layer 2 switches

    B. Layer 3 switches

    C. Port security

    D. Access lists

10. What command do you use to add an access list to a VTY line?

    A. `access-class`

    B. `access-group`

    C. `vty access-list`

    D. `http access-list`

11. What command do you use to add an access list to an HTTP server running on a router?

    A. `access-class`

    B. `access-group`

    C. `vty access-list`

    D. `http access-list`

12. Which of the following are examples of out-of-band management? (Choose all that apply.)

    A. Console port

    B. Telnet port

    C. Auxiliary port

    D. NMS station

13. Which of the following is an example of in-band management? (Choose all that apply.)

    A. Console port

    B. Telnet port

    C. Auxiliary port

    D. NMS station

14. What command will stop console messages from writing over the command you are trying to type in?

    A. no logging

    B. logging

    C. logging asynchronous

    D. logging synchronous

15. What command will allow users to telnet into a router and not be prompted with a usermode password?

    A. login

    B. no login

    C. You can by default, so no command is needed.

    D. no password

16. What command will set your console to time out after only one second?

    A. timeout 1 0

    B. timeout 0 1

    C. exec-timeout 1 0

    D. exec-timeout 0 1

17. How do you set only your Telnet line 1 to a password of bob?

    A. line vty 0 1
       Login
       Password bob

    B. line vty 0 4
       Login
       Password bob

    C. line vty 1
       Login
       Password bob

    D. line vty 1
       Password bob
       Login

18. How do you set the password for the auxiliary port?

   A. `line aux 1`

   B. `line aux 0`

   C. `line aux 0 4`

   D. `line aux port`

19. Which of the following commands will encrypt your Telnet password on a Cisco router?

   A. `Line telnet 0, encryption on, password todd`

   B. `Line vty 0, password encryption, password todd`

   C. `Service password encryption, line vty 0 4, password todd`

   D. `Password encryption, line vty 0 4, password todd`

20. Which of the following is true about the enable passwords? (Choose all that apply.)

   A. The enable password is encrypted by default.

   B. The enable secret is encrypted by default.

   C. The enable-encrypted password should be set first.

   D. The enable password supercedes the enable secret.

   E. The enable secret password supercedes the enable password.

   F. The enable-encrypted password supercedes all other passwords.

Answers to Written Lab

1. Access layer
2. Distribution layer
3. `distribute list`
4. `access-class` *number in/out*
5. `ip http access-class` *number*
6. 1–99
7. Closest to the source
8. `set port security` *mod/port* `enable` *mac_address.*
9. `login local`
10. Login, exec, incoming, and MOTD

Answers to Review Questions

1. **B.** Wildcards are used to specify a range of subnets. 31 is a wildcard used to filter a block size of 32. The IP address subnet starts at 32 and uses a block size of 32, so the subnets filtered are 32–63.

2. **B.** Wildcards are used to specify a range of subnets. 63 is a wildcard used to filter a block size of 64. The IP address subnet starts at 64 and uses a block size of 64, so the subnets filtered are 64–127.

3. **A.** Standard IP access lists use only source IP addresses to filter a network.

4. **C, D.** Extended IP access lists use source and destination IP addresses, the protocol field in the Network layer header, and the port number in the TCP header.

5. **B.** Standard access lists should be placed closest to the destination and extended access lists should be placed closest to the source.

6. **A.** Standard access lists should be placed closest to the destination and extended access lists should be placed closest to the source.

7. **A.** Standard IP access lists are numbered 1–99.

8. **B.** Extended IP access lists are numbered 100–199.

9. **C.** Adding switches by themselves provides no security. Access lists are applied at the distribution layer. Port security at the access layer stops users from attaching into any port on a switch.

10. **A.** Use the `access-class` *number in/out* command to set an access list on a VTY line.

11. **A.** Use the `ip http access-class` *number* command to set an access list on an HTTP server.

12. **A, C.** Console and auxiliary ports are out of the network and considered out-of-band.

13. **B, D.** VTY lines and NMS stations can manage devices through the network and are considered in-band.

14. **D.** This is a helpful command. The `logging synchronous` under the `line console 0` configuration stops console messages from overwriting the command you are typing.

15. **B.** The command `no login` under the `line vty` command sets the VTY ports to not prompt for authentication.

16. **D.** The `exec-timeout` command sets the console time-out in minutes and seconds.

17. **C.** The command `line vty 0 4` configures all VTY ports. `Line vty 1` will configure only VTY 1. `Login` tells the VTY ports to authenticate, although that command is on by default for Cisco router VTY ports. The last command is `password bob`.

18. **B.** You can gain access to the auxiliary port by using the `line auxiliary 0` command. There is only one auxiliary port, so it is always aux 0.

19. **C.** To encrypt your usermode and enable passwords, use the global configuration command `service password encryption` before setting your passwords.

20. **B, E.** There is no enable-encrypted password. The enable secret is encrypted by default and supercedes the enable password.

Appendix A

Practice Exam

1. Which of the following is true regarding PAgP? (Choose all that apply.)

    A. Only statically assigned VLAN ports can be used to form a bundle.

    B. Dynamically assigned VLAN ports can be used to form a bundle.

    C. Dynamically and statically assigned VLAN ports can be used together to form a bundle.

    D. Ports using different duplex types can be used to form a bundle.

2. What command is valid for configuring a VTP domain name and setting the VTP mode to server on a 5000 server?

    A. `set domain globanet, vtp domain server`

    B. `set domain globalnet server`

    C. `set vtp domain Globalnet mode server`

    D. `set server vtp domain globalnet`

3. You have two routers configured for HSRP. You notice that they alternate as active router. You enable standby debugging and discover the following:
    SB1:Ethernet0 Hello out 10.1.0.2 Speak pri 160 hel 30 hol 100 ip 10.1.0.200
    SB1:Ethernet0 Hello in 10.1.0.1 Active pri 100 hel 3 hol 10 ip 10.1.0.200
    What is the cause of this problem?

    A. Bad priority values.

    B. Wrong IP address.

    C. Cannot determine.

    D. SB1 is an illegal value.

    E. Mismatched timers.

4. Layer 2 switching provides what function?

   A. Logical filtering

   B. Breaking up of broadcast domains

   C. Breaking up of collision domains

   D. Source and destination port address filtering

5. Which of the following configuration commands disable MLS on a router? (Choose all that apply.)

   A. `no ip routing`

   B. `no mls rp ip`

   C. `set mls disable`

   D. `ip security`

6. What is the number range of IP standard access lists?

   A. 1–99

   B. 100–199

   C. 800–899

   D. 900–999

7. What commands will display a virtual MAC address of a VLAN on an internal route processor? (Choose all that apply.)

   A. `show virtual address`

   B. `show vlan #`

   C. `show inter vlan #`

   D. `show run`

8. What two criteria can MLS filters be based on?

    A. Protocol field in Network layer header

    B. Port source/destination numbers in Transport layer header

    C. Digital encapsulation methods

    D. Hexadecimal number used in sockets

9. When does a router interface need to be configured with VTP information?

    A. When it is connected to an ISL trunk

    B. When it is uses 802.1q encapsulation

    C. When it is connected to a VTP server

    D. When it is connected to a VTP client

10. An interface has been configured to use PIM sparse-dense mode. Which of the following criteria force the interface to operate in dense mode? (Choose all that apply.)

    A. DVMRP neighbors that are directly connected.

    B. Non-pruned PIM neighbors.

    C. Join request received by a host.

    D. The interface is connected to a Catalyst 5000 series switch.

11. What command will show you the IP configuration on a 5000 series switch?

    A. `sh ip config`

    B. `sh ip`

    C. `sh int config`

    D. `sh int`

12. Which of the following describe trunked links?

   A. They can carry multiple VLANs.

   B. Switches remove any VLAN information from the frame before it is sent to an access link device.

   C. Access link devices cannot communicate with devices outside of their VLAN unless the packet is routed through a router.

   D. Trunked links are used to transport VLANs between devices and can be configured to transport all VLANs or just a few

13. Which is the correct multicast MAC address if it's mapped from the multicast IP address 227.120.1.32?

   A. 01-00-5e-78-01-20

   B. 01-00-5e-14-01-20

   C. 01-00-5e-14-01-32

   D. 01-00-5e-78-01-32

14. Root bridges are allowed how many designated ports?

   A. 10

   B. 1

   C. 1 for each switch

   D. 20

   E. As many as the root bridge has ports

15. Multi-Layer Switching (MLS) filters on what criteria? (Choose all that apply.)

   A. Media access methods

   B. Preamble field in a frame

   C. MAC source/destination address in a Data Link frame

   D. IP source/destination address in Network layer header

16. An administrator configures router Charlie and router Delta for HSRP. Charlie is given a priority of 200 and Delta is given a priority of 100. After rebooting Charlie, the administrator finds that Delta is the active router. What is the most likely cause?

    A. This is normal because Delta has a lower priority.

    B. Charlie needs a higher priority.

    C. Bad timer values.

    D. Charlie is not configured to preempt.

17. Which command would you use to specify the multicast groups advertised by an RP? The access list being used is access-list 25. The RP's address is 172.16.25.1.

    A. `ip pim rp-address 172.16.25.1 25 override`

    B. `rp-address 172.16.25.1 25 override`

    C. `ip rp-address 172.16.25.1 25 override`

    D. `ip multicast rp-address 172.16.25.1 25 override`

18. What command will show you the IP configuration on a 1900 switch?

    A. `sh ip config`

    B. `sh ip`

    C. `sh int config`

    D. `sh int`

19. How many VLANs are supported on the 1900 switch?

    A. 1,005

    B. 10

    C. 512

    D. 64

20. Choose the correct method for enabling CGMP on a router.

   A. Global configuration: `ip cgmp`

   B. Interface configuration: `ip cgmp`

   C. Global configuration: `pim ip cgmp`

   D. Interface configuration: `pim ip cgmp`

21. Which of the following commands will allow you to verify the MLS configuration on a switch?

   A. `show ip mls`

   B. `show mls rp ip`

   C. `show mls ip`

   D. `show mls rp`

22. What command is valid for setting an IP address on a 5000 series switch?

   A. `ip address 172.16.10.17 mask 255.255.255.0`

   B. `ip address 172.16.10.17 255.255.255.0`

   C. `set int sc0 172.16.10.17 255.255.255.0`

   D. `set int sl0 172.17.10.10 255.255.255.0`

23. Standard IP access lists use what parameter to filter a network?

   A. Source IP address

   B. Destination IP address

   C. Source and destination IP addresses

   D. Port numbers

24. Which of the following is true about layer 3 switching? (Choose all that apply.)

   A. Can update SNMP mangers with MIB information

   B. Runs layer 3 checksums (on header only)

   C. Provides port address filtering

   D. Determines paths based on logical addressing

   E. Processes and responds to any option information

   F. Provides application-specific port addressing

   G. Security

25. Which of the following commands will show you the virtual MAC address of an interface and the BIA?

   A. show virtual address

   B. show vlan #

   C. show inter vlan #

   D. show run

26. Which is the correct multicast MAC address if it's mapped from the multicast IP address 239.2.2.127?

   A. 00-01-53-02-02-7f

   B. 00-01-5e-02-02-7e

   C. 01-00-53-02-02-7e

   D. 01-00-5e-02-02-7f

27. Which of the following is true regarding trunk link configuration?

   A. All switches are trunked by default unless set differently.

   B. When you configure a trunk link for VLANs 1–5, the switch automatically configures VLANs 1–1005 instead.

   C. When you configure a trunk link for VLANs 1–5, the switch automatically configures VLANs 1–500 instead.

   D. Trunked links can run on any 10, 100, or 1000Mbps link

28. What does the command `spantree priority 16` do?

   A. Changes the port priority on an IOS-based switch

   B. Changes the port priority on a set-based switch

   C. Changes the bridge ID priority on an IOS-based switch

   D. Changes the bridge ID priority on a set-based switch

29. Which of the following is valid syntax for assigning the TTL threshold value to an interface?

   A. `multicast ttl threshold` *ttl*

   B. `ip multicast ttl threshold` *ttl*

   C. `ip multicast ttl-threshold` *ttl*

   D. `ip pim ttl-threshold` *ttl*

30. Switches announce their bridge ID to other switches using what?

   A. IP routing

   B. STP

   C. With routing updates during the four STP states of a switch

   D. Bridge Protocol Data Units

   E. Broadcasts during convergence times

31. How do you set ISL on a subinterface to use VLAN 6?

   A. `RSM(config)#encap isl vlan3`

   B. `RSM(config)#encap vlan3 isl`

   C. `RSM(config-if)#encap isl 6`

   D. `RSM(config-if)encap 3 isl`

32. Which is the correct multicast MAC address if it's mapped from the multicast IP address 225.220.52.25?

   A. 01-00-5e-7f-52-25

   B. 01-00-5e-5c-52-25

   C. 01-00-5e-5c-34-19

   D. 01-00-5e-14-34-19

33. The benefits of layer 3 switching include _____ . (Choose all that apply.)

   A. Hardware-based packet forwarding

   B. High-performance packet switching

   C. Port address filtering

   D. High-speed scalability

   E. Layer 3 checksums

   F. Low latency

34. What is the range of subnets filtered with the 192.168.10.16 0.0.0.15 wildcard?

   A. 0–16

   B. 0–31

   C. 16–31

   D. 1–254

35. Which of the following are true regarding access links? (Choose all that apply.)

   A. They can carry multiple VLANs.

   B. Switches remove any VLAN information from the frame before it is sent to an access link device.

   C. Access link devices cannot communicate with devices outside of their VLAN unless the packet is routed through a router.

   D. Access links are used to transport VLANs between devices and can be configured to transport all VLANs or just a few.

36. Which three of the following are disadvantages to running Proxy ARP?

   A. A lot of broadcast traffic

   B. Must wait for the ARP cache to time out in the event of failure

   C. Allows for redundant default gateways on a LAN

   D. No control over which router is primary and secondary

37. What commands should you used to set the IP address and default gateway on a 1900 switch? (Choose all that apply.)

   A. `ip address 172.16.10.16 255.255.255.0`

   B. `ip default-gateway 172.16.10.1`

   C. `ip address 172.16.10.1 mask 255.255.255.0`

   D. `default-gateway 172.16.10.10`

38. What is the purpose of the fast aging time setting on switches?

   A. To allow cache entries to be created more rapidly

   B. To remove unused cache entries

   C. To remove partial cache entries

   D. To remove aged cache entries

39. Extended IP access lists use what parameters to filter a network? (Choose all that apply.)

   A. Source IP address

   B. Destination IP address

   C. Source and destination IP addresses

   D. Port numbers

40. Which of the following statements describes access links?

   A. They can carry multiple VLANs.

   B. Access links are used to transport VLANs between devices and can be configured to transport all VLANs or just a few.

   C. They can be used only with FastEthernet or Gigabit Ethernet.

   D. Access links are links that are part of only one VLAN and referred to as the native VLAN of the port.

41. What is true regarding passwords on a Catalyst 5000 switch? (Choose all that apply.)

   A. They must be a minimum of eight characters.

   B. They are case sensitive.

   C. The passwords cannot be less than four characters or more than eight.

   D. They are not case sensitive.

42. Which is the correct multicast MAC address if it's mapped from the multicast IP address 225.225.110.110?

   A. 01-00-5e-61-52.25

   B. 01-00-5e-61-6e-6e

   C. 01-00-5e-61-61-61

   D. 01-00-5e-6e-61-61

43. Where should extended access lists be placed in the network?

   A. Closest to the source

   B. Closest to the destination

   C. On a server

   D. On a switch

44. Which three of the following are valid LAN switch types?

   A. Cut-through

   B. Store-and-forward

   C. FragmentCheck

   D. FragmentFree

45. Which is the correct multicast MAC address if it's mapped from the multicast IP address 239.192.220.2?

   A. 01-00-5e-40-dc-02

   B. 01-00-5e-5c-dc-02

   C. 01-00-5e-dc-dc-02

   D. 01-00-5e-40-de-02

46. Where should standard access lists be placed in the network?

   A. Closest to the source

   B. Closest to the destination

   C. On a server

   D. On a switch

47. Once switches communicate to the root bridge, how is the root port of the bridge determined?

   A. The switch determines the highest cost of a link to the root bridge.

   B. The switch determines the lowest cost of a link to the root bridge.

   C. By sending and receiving BPDUs between switches. The fastest BPDU transfer rate on an interface becomes the root port.

   D. The root bridge will broadcast the bridge ID, and the receiving bridge will determine what interface this broadcast was received on and make this interface the root port.

48. You run WINIPCFG on a Windows 95 machine and discover that the machine's IP address is the same as its default gateway. Another administrator tells you that this is correct. Which of the following is likely?

A. The segment uses Proxy ARP.

B. The segment uses HSRP.

C. The client is configured incorrectly.

D. The client has static routes.

E. The machine will not function.

49. What is VLAN 0's responsibility?

A. Nothing, it doesn't exist.

B. Managing the backplane of the switch.

C. Providing support for the communication between an RSM and the Catalyst 5000 switch.

D. VLAN 0 is a default VLAN that allows the administrator to manage the network.

50. Which of the following are layer 2 problems associated with bridging technologies with redundant links and solved by STP? (Choose all that apply.)

A. Faster convergence times.

B. Broadcast storms.

C. Multiple frame copies.

D. IP routing will cause flapping on a serial link.

E. Network loops.

51. What happens if a link failure occurs in an EtherChannel bundle?

A. The EARL informs the ASIC.

B. The SAMBA informs the EBC.

C. The EARL informs the EBC.

D. The EBC informs the EARL.

52. What technology was originally designed to assign dial-in clients addresses that belong to the local LAN segment?

   A. Dial Backup

   B. HSRP

   C. VRRP

   D. ICMP Redirects

   E. Proxy ARP

53. Which of the following criteria identify a packet as an enable packet? (Choose all that apply.)

   A. The source MAC address is from an MLS-RP.

   B. The destination MAC address is to an MLS-RP.

   C. The destination IP address is to an MLS-RP.

   D. The destination IP address matches the destination IP address of the candidate packet.

54. You want a bridge to become the root bridge. You check the configuration and find the bridge priority is 32768. What does this mean?

   A. The bridge is already a root bridge.

   B. The bridge will never be a root bridge.

   C. The priority is the default. The bridge ID will be used to determine the root bridge in the network.

   D. The priority is high and the bridge will never be the root bridge in a network.

   E. The bridge priority is low and the bridge will be elected root bridge of the network the next time a BPDU is used.

55. Trunk ports are used for which of the following configurations?

    A. When you need to connect users to a switch port

    B. When you need to connect an external router to a switch and provide ISL routing

    C. When you need to connect several individual router interfaces to several separate VLANs

    D. When connecting FastEthernet links between routers

56. When setting the VLAN port priority, what are the available values you can use?

    A. 0–63

    B. 1–64

    C. 0–255

    D. 1–1005

Answers to Practice Exam

1. **A.** PAgP bundled ports must all be configured the same, including the duplex and speed. Also, dynamic VLANs will not work, so VLANs must be statically assigned or they must all be trunked ports. See Chapter 5 for more information.

2. **C.** You can set the VTP domain and mode with one command: `set vtp domain name mode mode`. For more information, see Chapter 3.

3. **E.** 10.1.0.2 has the highest priority, but it is sending out updates only once every 30 seconds. This allows the other router to become the active router after 3 seconds, but then it is dropped every 30 seconds when a hello is received from the router with a higher priority. See Chapter 8 for more information.

4. **C.** Layer 2 switches break up only collision domains, not broadcast domains. See Chapter 1 for more information.

5. **A, B, D.** When IP routing is disabled, all MLS is subsequently disabled; the same happens when enabling IP security configurations. To turn MLS off the proper way, the command `no mls rp ip` is used. See Chapter 7 for more information.

6. **A.** Standard IP access lists are numbered 1–99. See Chapter 11 for more information.

7. **C. D.** The command `show interface vlan #` and the `show running-config` command will display the virtual hardware address of an interface if set. See Chapter 6 for more information.

8. **A, B.** Multi-layer switching provides filtering of layer 2, 3, and 4. This means that MLS can filter on hardware addresses, logical addresses, and port and socket numbers. See Chapter 1 for more information.

9. **C, D.** ISL and 802.1q are encapsulations used for VLAN assignment. Routers connected to VTP servers or clients must be configured properly. See Chapter 7 for more information.

10. **A, B.** Join requests cause the interface to operate in PIM sparse mode. If a Catalyst is connected, the interface must be configured to use CGMP. See Chapter 10 for more information.

11. **D.** The command to see the IP configuration on a 5000 series switch is `show int`. See Chapter 2 for more information.

12. **A, D.** Trunked links are used to send information about multiple VLANs down one link. Access links carry information about only one VLAN. For more information, see Chapter 3.

13. **A.** This is a straightforward conversion. There are no bits that are lost in the mapping. See Chapter 9 for more information.

14. **E.** Only one root bridge can be used in any network, and this root bridge will always forward from every port. By default, all interfaces on a bridge are designated ports. See Chapter 4 for more information.

15. **C, D.** Multi-layer switching provides filtering of layer 2, 3, and 4. This means that MLS can filter on hardware addresses, logical addresses, and port and socket numbers. See Chapter 1 for more information.

16. **D.** In order for a coup to occur, the router must be configured to pre-empt. See Chapter 8 for more information.

17. **A.** All of these answers utilize the correct IP address and access-list number. However, the command uses the `ip pim` options. See Chapter 10 for more information.

18. **B.** The command `show ip` will display the configured IP configuration of a 1900 switch. See Chapter 2 for more information.

19. **A.** The 1900 switch can support up to 1,005 VLANs but only up to 64 STP instances. See Chapter 5 for more information.

20. **B.** CGMP must be entered on selected interfaces. PIM does not enable CGMP, therefore, the `pim ip cgmp` command is not valid. See Chapter 10 for more information.

21. **C.** The `show mls rp ip` command is used on routers. The syntax is incorrect in the other options. See Chapter 7 for more information.

22. C. To set the IP address on a 5000 series switch, use the command `set int sc0 ip address mask`. See Chapter 2 for more information.

23. A. Standard IP access lists use only source IP addresses to filter a network. See Chapter 11 for more information.

24. A, B, D, E, G. Port addressing at the Transport layer provides virtual circuit identification and application-specific port addressing. Neither of these functions can be used with layer 3 switches. See Chapter 1 for more information.

25. C. The command `show interface vlan #` will show both the virtual MAC address if set and the burned-in address (BIA) of the VLAN interface. See Chapter 6 for more information.

26. D. The MAC prefix is 01-00-5e, and the second octet's hex value is 02, as well as the third's. The fourth octet has a hex value of 7f. See Chapter 9 for more information.

27. B. When a trunked link is configured, the trunked link will automatically send information for all VLANs down this link. You must remove unwanted VLANs from a trunked link by hand. For more information, see Chapter 3.

28. A. On an IOS-based switch, a 1900 for example, use the `spantree priority 16` from interface configuration to change the port priority. See Chapter 5 for more information.

29. C. TTL is controlled by the IP header in the multicast packet. The correct syntax requires a hyphen between `ttl` and `threshold`. See Chapter 10 for more information.

30. D. The bridge ID is sent via a multicast frame inside a Bridge Protocol Data Unit (BPDU) update. See Chapter 4 for more information.

31. C. The subinterface command `encapsulation type vlan` is used to set the VLAN ID and encapsulation method on a subinterface. See Chapter 6 for more information.

32. C. The MAC prefix is 01-00-5e. The second octet can use only the first 7 bits, excluding the bit value of 128. This gives a binary value of 101100, which converts to hex as 5c. The hex values for the last two octets are 34 and 19 respectively. See Chapter 9 for more information.

33. A, B, D, E, F. Layer 3 switching provides everything except filtering by Transport layer (layer 4) port addressing. See Chapter 1 for more information.

34. C. Wildcards are used to specify a range of subnets. 15 is a wildcard used to filter a block size of 16. The IP address subnet starts at 16 and uses a block size of 16, so the subnets filtered are 16–31. See Chapter 11 for more information.

35. B, C. Trunked links are used to send information about multiple VLANs down one link. Access links carry information about only one VLAN. Packets from one VLAN must go through a router to communicate with another VLAN. For more information, see Chapter 3.

36. A, B, D. Proxy ARP is broadcast intensive and can cause a lot of overhead on a router. The ARP cache on a host must time out before it will broadcast an ARP looking for another MAC address of a remote host. Also, you cannot control which router is running and answering the ARPs. See Chapter 8 for more information on Proxy ARP.

37. A, B. The command `ip address address` and `ip default-gateway address` are used to set the IP address information on a 1900 switch. See Chapter 2 for more information.

38. B. When flows are very short, this timer causes the cache entry to be flushed before the normal aging time. Partial entries are flushed by a different mechanism. Aged entries are handled by the normal aging timer. See Chapter 7 for more information.

39. C, D. Extended IP access lists use source and destination IP addresses, the protocol field in the Network layer header, and the port number in the TCP header. See Chapter 11 for more information.

40. D. Trunked links are used to send information about multiple VLANs down one link. Access links carry information about only one VLAN. For more information, see Chapter 3.

41. C, D. The passwords must be at least four characters, and they are not case sensitive. See Chapter 2 for more information.

42. B. By doing the math you'll see that 225 less 128 equals 97, which is 61 converted to hex. See Chapter 9 for more information.

43. A. Standard access lists should be placed closest to the destination and extended access lists should be placed closest to the source. See Chapter 11 for more information.

44. A, B, D. The cut-through LAN switch method only reads the destination hardware address of a frame; the FragmentFree reads the first 64 bytes of each frame to make sure there is no fragmentation. Store-and-forward reads the whole frame, plus runs a CRC on each frame. See Chapter 4 for more information.

45. A. The correct answer is found by subtracting 128 from 192, then converting it to hex, which is 40. See Chapter 9 for more information.

46. B. Standard access lists should be placed closest to the destination and extended access lists should be placed closest to the source. See Chapter 11 for more information.

47. B. Root ports are determined by using the cost of a link to the root bridge. The lowest cost wins. See Chapter 4 for more information.

48. A. A machine with its default gateway set to its own IP address will ARP for every address. See Chapter 8 for more information.

49. C. VLAN 0, which cannot be accessed by an administrator, is used to provide support for the communication between the RSM and the Catalyst 5000 switch. See Chapter 6 for more information.

50. B, C. Network loops, broadcast storms, and multiple frame copies are typically found in a network that has multiple links to remote locations without some type of loop avoidance scheme. See Chapter 4 for more information.

51. D. Should one link in the bundle fail, the Ethernet Bundle Controller (EBC) informs the Enhanced Address Recognition Logic (EARL) ASIC of the failure, and the EARL in turn ages out all addresses learned on that link. See Chapter 5 for more information.

52. E. Proxy ARP has been around for a while and worked well over the years. However, as networks have grown, it has been found that Proxy ARP does not scale well. See Chapter 8 for more information on Proxy ARP.

53. A, D.   The XTAG value for the candidate and enable packet must also match. The destination MAC address is used to identify candidate packets. If the destination IP were that of the MLS-RP, the packet would not need to be switched. See Chapter 7 for more information.

54. C.   The default priorities on all switches are 32768. Because this bridge is set to the default of 32768, the bridge ID will be used to determine the root bridge. See Chapter 4 for more information.

55. B.   A switch port must be configured with a trunking protocol to run ISL inter-VLAN communication to a single router interface. See Chapter 6 for more information.

56. A.   A priority from 0 to 63 can be set for each VLAN. See Chapter 5 for more information.

Appendix B

Commands Used in This Book

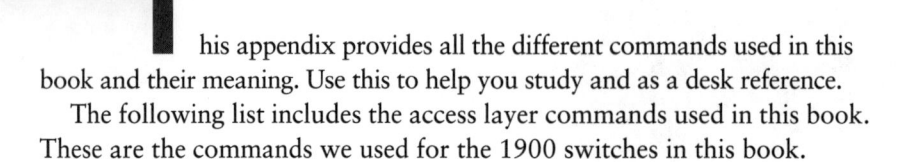

This appendix provides all the different commands used in this book and their meaning. Use this to help you study and as a desk reference.

The following list includes the access layer commands used in this book. These are the commands we used for the 1900 switches in this book.

Command	Meaning	Chapter
banner	Configures banners on a CLI-based device	Chapter 11
Ctrl+Shift+6, then x	Used as an escape sequence	Chapter 2
duplex	Sets the duplex of an interface, with half- or full-duplex	Chapter 2
enable password	Configures the enable password on a CLI device	Chapter 11
enable password level	Sets the usermode (level 1) and the enable password (level 15) of the switch	Chapter 2
enable secret	Configures the enable secret password on a CLI device	Chapter 11
hostname	Assigns a name to the Catalyst 1900 or 2800 series switch	Chapter 2

Command	Meaning	Chapter
`interface`	Used to select an interface	Chapter 3
`interface ethernet module/port`	Used to identify or set parameters on an interface on the 1900 or 2820 switch	Chapter 2
`interface fastethernet module/port`	Displays or changes parameters on the two available FastEthernet interfaces	Chapter 2
`ip address`	Assigns an IP address to the 1900 or 2820 switch	Chapter 2
`no spantree`	Turns off spanning tree for a VLAN	Chapter 4
`no trunk-vlan`	Removes VLANs from a trunked link	Chapter 3
`port-channel mode`	Enables an EtherChannel bundle	Chapter 5
`port-secure mac-mac-count`	Configures port security on a CLI-based switch	Chapter 11
`privilege` *mode*	Configures privilege modes on a CLI-based device	Chapter 11
`sh mac-address-table`	Views the MAC filter table on a CLI-based switch	Chapter 11
`show run`	Displays the running-config of the 1900 and 2820 switch	Chapter 2
`show spantree`	Used to view spanning tree information on a VLAN	Chapters 4, 5

Command	Meaning	Chapter
`show uplink-fast`	Shows the UplinkFast parameters	Chapter 5
`show uplink-fast statistics`	Shows the UplinkFast statistics	Chapter 5
`show vtp`	Shows the switches' VTP configuration	Chapter 3
`shutdown`	Disables a particular interface	Chapter 2
`spantree`	Turns on spanning tree for a VLAN	Chapter 4
`spantree cost`	Configures a cost for an interface	Chapter 5
`spantree priority`	Configures the priority for an interface	Chapter 5
`spantree start-forwarding`	Enables PortFast on an interface	Chapter 5
`trunk`	Turns trunking on or off of interface fa0/26 and fa0/27	Chapter 3
`uplink-fast`	Turns on UplinkFast for the switch	Chapter 5
`vlan`	Sets VLAN information	Chapter 3
`vlan-membership`	Sets an interface to a VLAN	Chapter 3
`vtp mode`	Changes the VTP mode to server, transparent, or client	Chapter 3
`vtp name`	Configures the VTP domain name	Chapter 3
`vtp password`	Sets an optional vtp password	Chapter 3

Commands Used in This Book

The following list includes commands used for configuring the distribution layer switch. These commands were used on the 5000 series switch in this book.

Command	Meaning	Chapter
`clear mls entry destination` *ip-addr-spec* `source` *ip-addr-spec* `flow` *protocol src_port dst_port* `[all]`	Allows all MLS entries to be cleared in addition to allowing specific entries to be terminated.	Chapter 7
`clear trunk`	Clears VLANs from a trunked port.	Chapter 3
Ctrl+C	Used as a break sequence.	Chapter 2
Ctrl+Shift+6, then x	Used as an escape sequence.	Chapter 2
`how spantree uplinkfast`	Shows the UplinkFast parameters and statistics.	Chapter 5
`interface vlan`	Enables interface configuration mode for the specified VLAN interface.	Chapter 6
`ip cgmp [`*proxy*`]`	Enables CGMP on the specified interface on routers.	Chapter 10
`ip igmp join-group` *group-address*	Makes the router become an active member of the specified multicast group.	Chapter 10
`ip igmp version (2 | 1)`	Applied to the interface and used to change the version of IGMP used on that interface.	Chapter 10
`ip multicast ttl-threshold` *ttl*	Applied to all border interfaces to enforce the scope or boundary of the IP multicast network.	Chapter 10

Command	Meaning	Chapter
`ip multicast-routing`	Enables IP multicast forwarding on the router.	Chapter 10
`ip pim dense-mode`	Enables PIM dense mode operation on the interface.	Chapter 10
`ip pim rp-address` *ip-address* `[group-access-list-number] [override]`	Manually configures an RP address on a multicast router.	Chapter 10
`ip pim send-rp-announce` *type number* `scope` *ttl* `group-list` *access-list-number*	Assigns specific multicast group addresses to an RP. The RP can then only announce that it knows multicast groups permitted by the access list specified.	Chapter 10
`ip pim send-rp-discovery scope` *ttl*	Configures RP Mapping Agent and allows the router to discover all RPs and group assignments.	Chapter 10
`ip pim sparse-dense-mode`	Enables PIM sparse-dense mode operation on the interface.	Chapter 10
`ip pim sparse-mode`	Enables PIM sparse mode operation on the interface.	Chapter 10
`mac-address`	Sets a specific MAC address on an interface.	Chapter 6
`mls rp ip`	Enables MLS on an external router, both global and interface specific.	Chapter 7
`mls rp management-interface`	Assigns the interface to the MLS-RP. This allows MLSP updates to use this interface.	Chapter

Command	Meaning	Chapter
`mls rp vlan-id [vlan-id-number]`	Assigns the interface the proper VLAN number.	Chapter 7
`mls rp vtp-domain [domain-name]`	Assigns the interface to the VTP domain.	Chapter 7
`mtrace`	Displays the forwarding path based on group membership or the RPF.	
`ping`	Used for testing reachability.	Chapter 10
`session`	Connects the CLI to a session on a route processor module.	Chapter 6
`set cgmp enable`	Used on Catalyst switches to enable CGMP.	Chapter 10
`set enablepass`	Configures the enable password on a set-based device.	Chapters 2, 11
`set interface sco`	Assigns an IP address to the management interface of the set-based switch.	Chapter 2
`set ip route`	Configures a default route on a set-based switch.	Chapter 6
`set mls agingtime agingtime`	Sets the MLS agingtime value to the specified value.	Chapter 7
`set mls agingtime fast fastagingtime pkt-threshold`	Allows the fast agingtime and packet threshold to be set.	Chapter 7
`set mls enable`	Enables MLS on Catalyst switches. For most switches, this is set to on by default.	Chapter 7

Command	Meaning	Chapter
`set password`	Configures the usermode password on a set-based device.	Chapters 2, 11
`set port channel`	Creates an EtherChannel bundle.	Chapter 5
`set port duplex`	Sets the duplex of a port.	Chapter 2
`set port speed`	Sets the speed of a port.	Chapter 2
`set prompt`	Assigns a name to the Catalyst switch.	Chapter 2
`set spantree`	Turns spanning tree off or on for a VLAN.	Chapter 4
`set spantree backbonefast`	Enables BackboneFast for a switch.	Chapter 5
`set spantree fwddelay`	Changes the forward delay time on a switch.	Chapter 5
`set spantree hello`	Changes the BPDU hello time on a switch.	Chapter 5
`set spantree maxage`	Sets how long a BPDU that is received will stay valid until another BPDU is received.	Chapter 5
`set spantree portcost`	Sets the STP port cost.	Chapter 5
`set spantree portfast`	Enables PortFast on a port.	Chapter 5
`set spantree portpri`	Sets the STP port priority.	Chapter 5
`set spantree portvlanpri`	Configures links to forward only certain VLANs.	Chapter 5

Commands Used in This Book

Command	Meaning	Chapter
`set spantree root`	Makes a set-based switch a root bridge.	Chapter 5
`set spantree uplinkfast`	Enables UplinkFast on a port.	Chapter 5
`set trunk`	Configures trunking on a port.	Chapter 3
`set vlan`	Creates a VLAN and also assigns a port to a VLAN.	Chapter 3
`set vtp domain`	Sets the VTP domain name.	Chapter 3
`set vtp mode`	Sets the VTP mode of the switch.	Chapter 3
`set vtp passwd`	Sets the optional VTP password.	Chapter 3
`sh port capabilities`	Shows the configuration of individual ports.	Chapter 5
`show config`	Shows the configuration of the 5000 series switch.	Chapters 2, 6
`show mls`	Shows MLS information on a switch.	Chapter 7
`show mls entry`	Provides MLS entry data on the MLS-SE.	Chapter 7
`show mls rp`	Provides global MLS information.	Chapter 7
`show mls rp interface`	Provides interface-specific MLS information.	Chapter 7
`show mls rp vtp-domain`	Provides MLS information for the VTP domain.	Chapter 7

Command	Meaning	Chapter
`show module`	Shows the module and numbers of cards in the switch.	Chapter 6
`show port channel`	Shows the status of an EtherChannel bundle.	Chapter 5
`show spantree`	Shows the state of the STP per VLAN.	Chapters 4, 5
`show vlan`	Shows the configured VLANs.	Chapter 3
`show vtp domain`	Shows the VTP domain configurations.	Chapter 3
`show vtp domain`	Provides VTP domain information on the switch.	Chapter 7
`time-out`	Changes the time-out of a set-based device console.	Chapter 11

The following list includes commands used on routers.

Commands	Meaning	Chapter
`access-class`	Configures an access list on the VTY lines	Chapter 11
`debug standby`	Allows you to monitor and verify the HSRP group	Chapter 8
`distribute-list`	Configures an access list for use on a routing table	Chapter 11
`exec-timeout`	Changes the time-out of a CLI-based device console	Chapter 11

Commands	Meaning	Chapter
`ip http access-class`	Configures an access list for HTTP security	Chapter 11
`ip http authentication local`	Configures authentication for username and password when using HTTP to configure a device	Chapter 11
`ip proxy-arp`	Enables the interface for Proxy ARP (on by default)	Chapter 8
`line aux`	Configures the usermode aux password on a CLI device	Chapter 11
`line console`	Configures the usermode console password on a CLI device	Chapter 11
`line vty`	Configures the usermode Telnet password on a CLI device	Chapter 11
`login local`	Configures a line to set authentication locally	Chapter 11
`no ip proxy-arp`	Disables Proxy ARP on an interface	Chapter 8
`no service password-encryption`	Disables password encryption	Chapter 11
`service password-encryption`	Encrypts the usermode and enable password on a CLI-based device	Chapter 11
`show ip arp`	Shows the IP addresses that have been resolved to a hardware address	Chapter 8

Commands	Meaning	Chapter
`show ip interface ethernet 0`	Shows the IP configuration of Ethernet 0, including whether Proxy ARP is configured and if access lists are set on the interface	Chapter 8
`show standby`	Shows the HSRP configuration of an interface	Chapter 8
`standby`	Sets an interface to be part of an HSRP group	Chapter 8
`standby 1 authentication`	Does not provide authentication, only checks that correct information is received	Chapter 8
`standby 1 preempt`	Sets the interface to force an election if a router joins the HSRP group with a higher priority than the other routers in the group	Chapter 8
`standby 1 priority`	Sets the priority of HSRP on an interface	Chapter 8
`standby 1 track serial 0 50`	Tells HSRP to monitor a connected serial link that is not running HSRP	Chapter 8
`username`	Configures a username and password for a local login	Chapter 11

Appendix C

Internet Multicast Addresses

Certain Class D IP networks in the range of 224.0.0.0 through 239.255.255.255 are used for host extensions for IP multicasting as specified in the Request for Comments (RFC) 1112 standard created by the Internet Engineering Task Force (IETF). The well-known addresses are assigned and maintained by the Internet Address Number Authority (IANA). RFC 1112 specifies the extensions required of a host implementation of the Internet Protocol (IP) to support multicasting.

There are a lot of abbreviations and acronyms used in this appendix. The most important found in the well-known addresses are listed here:

DVMRP   Distance Vector Multicast Routing Protocol

DHCP   Dynamic Host Configuration Protocol

OSPF   Open Shortest Path First

RIP   Routing Information Protocol

RP   Route processor

PIM   Protocol Independent Multicast

This appendix will describe the multicast addresses, the purpose of each address, and the RFC or contact acronym.

> **WARNING** These addresses are subject to change. If you cannot find an address listed here that appears to be assigned, refer to the following location: `ftp://ftp.isi.edu/in-notes/iana/assignments/`.

TABLE C.1 Multicast Addresses

Address	Purpose	Reference/Contact Acronym
224.0.0.0	Base Address (Reserved)	RFC1112/JBP
224.0.0.1	All Systems on this Subnet	RFC1112/JBP
224.0.0.2	All Routers on this Subnet	JBP
224.0.0.3	Unassigned	JBP
224.0.0.4	DVMRP Routers	RFC1075/JBP
224.0.0.5	OSPFIGP All Routers	RFC2328/JXM1
224.0.0.6	OSPFIGP Designated Routers	RFC2328/JXM1
224.0.0.7	ST Routers	RFC1190/KS14
224.0.0.8	ST Hosts	RFC1190/KS14
224.0.0.9	RIP2 Routers	RFC1723/GSM11
224.0.0.10	IGRP Routers	Farinacci
224.0.0.11	Mobile-Agents	Bill Simpson
224.0.0.12	DHCP Server / Relay Agent	RFC1884
224.0.0.13	All PIM Routers	Farinacci
224.0.0.14	RSVP-ENCAPSULATION	Braden
224.0.0.15	All-cbt-routers	Ballardie
224.0.0.16	Designated-sbm	Baker
224.0.0.17	All-sbms	Baker
224.0.0.18	VRRP	Hinden
224.0.0.19	IP All L1Iss	Przygienda

TABLE C.1 Multicast Addresses *(continued)*

Address	Purpose	Reference/Contact Acronym
224.0.0.20	IP All L2Iss	Przygienda
224.0.0.21	IP All Intermediate Systems	Przygienda
224.0.0.22	IGMP	Deering
224.0.0.23	GLOBECAST-ID	Scannell
224.0.0.24	Unassigned	JBP
224.0.0.25	Router-to-Switch	Wu
224.0.0.26	Unassigned	JBP
224.0.0.27	Al MPP	Martinicky
224.0.0.28	ETC Control	Zmudzinski
224.0.0.251	mDNS	Cheshire
224.0.1.0	VMTP Managers Group	RFC1045/DRC3
224.0.1.1	NTP Network Time Protocol	RFC1119/DLM1
224.0.1.2	SGI-Dogfight	AXC
224.0.1.3	Rwhod	SXD
224.0.1.4	VNP	DRC3
224.0.1.5	Artificial Horizons-Aviator	XF
224.0.1.6	NSS-Name Service Server	XS2
224.0.1.7	AUDIONEWS-Audio News Multicast	XF2
224.0.1.8	SUN NIS+ Information Service	XM3
224.0.1.9	MTP Multicast Transport Protocol	SXA

TABLE C.1 Multicast Addresses *(continued)*

Address	Purpose	Reference/Contact Acronym
224.0.1.10	IETF-1-LOW-AUDIO	SC3
224.0.1.11	IETF-1-AUDIO	SC3
224.0.1.12	IETF-1-VIDEO	SC3
224.0.1.13	IETF-2-LOW-AUDIO	SC3
224.0.1.14	IETF-2-AUDIO	SC3
224.0.1.15	IETF-2-VIDEO	SC3
224.0.1.16	MUSIC-SERVICE	Guido Van Rossum
224.0.1.17	SEANET-TELEMETRY	Andrew Maffei
224.0.1.18	SEANET-IMAGE	Andrew Maffei
224.0.1.19	MLOADD	Braden
224.0.1.20	Any private experiment	JBP
224.0.1.21	DVMRP on MOSPF	John Moy
224.0.1.22	SVRLOC	Veizades
224.0.1.23	XINGTV	Gordon
224.0.1.24	Microsoft-DS	arnoldm@microsoft.com
224.0.1.25	NBC-PRO	bloomer@birch.crd.ge.com
224.0.1.26	NBC-PFN	bloomer@birch.crd.ge.com
224.0.1.31	Ampr-info	Janssen
224.0.1.32	Mtrace	Casner

TABLE C.1 Multicast Addresses *(continued)*

Address	Purpose	Reference/Contact Acronym
224.0.1.33	RSVP-encap-1	Braden
224.0.1.34	RSVP-encap-2	Braden
224.0.1.35	SVRLOC-DA	Veizades
224.0.1.36	RLN-server	Kean
224.0.1.37	Proshare-mc	Lewis
224.0.1.38	Dantz	Yackle
224.0.1.39	Cisco-rp-announce	Farinacci
224.0.1.40	Cisco-rp-discovery	Farinacci
224.0.1.41	Gatekeeper	Toga
224.0.1.42	Iberiagames	Marocho
224.0.1.43	NWN-Discovery	Zwemmer
224.0.1.44	NWN-Adaptor	Zwemmer
224.0.1.45	ISMA-1	Dunne
224.0.1.46	ISMA-2	Dunne
224.0.1.47	Telerate	Peng
224.0.1.48	Ciena	Rodbell
224.0.1.49	DCAP-servers	RFC2114
224.0.1.50	DCAP-clients	RFC2114
224.0.1.51	MCNTP-directory	Rupp
224.0.1.52	MBONE-VCR-directory	Holfelder

TABLE C.1 Multicast Addresses *(continued)*

Address	Purpose	Reference/Contact Acronym
224.0.1.53	Heartbeat	Mamakos
224.0.1.54	Sun-mc-grp	DeMoney
224.0.1.55	Extended-sys	Poole
224.0.1.56	Pdrncs	Wissenbach
224.0.1.57	TNS-adv-multi	Albin
224.0.1.58	Vcals-dmu	Shindoh
224.0.1.59	Zuba	Jackson
224.0.1.60	Hp-device-disc	Albright
224.0.1.61	TMS-production	Gilani
224.0.1.62	Sunscalar	Gibson
224.0.1.63	MMTP-poll	Costales
224.0.1.64	Compaq-peer	Volpe
224.0.1.65	IAPP	Meier
224.0.1.66	Multihasc-com	Brockbank
224.0.1.67	Serv-Discovery	Honton
224.0.1.68	Mdhcpdisover	RFC2730
224.0.1.69	MMP-bundle-Discovery1	Malkin
224.0.1.70	MMP-bundle-Discovery2	Malkin
224.0.1.71	XYPOINT DGPS Data Feed	Green
224.0.1.72	GilatSkySurfer	Gal

TABLE C.1 Multicast Addresses *(continued)*

Address	Purpose	Reference/Contact Acronym
224.0.1.73	SharesLive	Rowatt
224.0.1.74	NorthernData	Sheers
224.0.1.75	SIP	Schulzrinne
224.0.1.76	IAPP	Moelard
224.0.1.77	AGENTVIEW	Iyer
224.0.1.78	Tibco Multicast1	Shum
224.0.1.79	Tibco Multicast2	Shum
224.0.1.80	MSP	Caves
224.0.1.81	OTT (One-way Trip Time)	Schwartz
224.0.1.82	TRACKTICKER	Novick
224.0.1.83	DTN-mc	Gaddie
224.0.1.84	Jini-announcement	Scheifler
224.0.1.85	Jini-request	Scheifler
224.0.1.86	SDE-Discovery	Aronson
224.0.1.87	DirecPC-SI	Dillon
224.0.1.88	B1Rmonitor	Purkiss
224.0.1.89	3Com-AMP3 dRMON	Banthia
224.0.1.90	ImFtmSvc	Bhatti
224.0.1.91	NQDS4	Flynn
224.0.1.92	NQDS5	Flynn

TABLE C.1 Multicast Addresses *(continued)*

Address	Purpose	Reference/Contact Acronym
224.0.1.93	NQDS6	Flynn
224.0.1.94	NLVL12	Flynn
224.0.1.95	NTDS1	Flynn
224.0.1.96	NTDS2	Flynn
224.0.1.97	NODSA	Flynn
224.0.1.98	NODSB	Flynn
224.0.1.99	NODSC	Flynn
224.0.1.100	NODSD	Flynn
224.0.1.101	NQDS4R	Flynn
224.0.1.102	NQDS5R	Flynn
224.0.1.103	NQDS6R	Flynn
224.0.1.104	NLVL12R	Flynn
224.0.1.105	NTDS1R	Flynn
224.0.1.106	NTDS2R	Flynn
224.0.1.107	NODSAR	Flynn
224.0.1.108	NODSBR	Flynn
224.0.1.109	NODSCR	Flynn
224.0.1.110	NODSDR	Flynn
224.0.1.111	MRM	Wei

TABLE C.1 Multicast Addresses *(continued)*

Address	Purpose	Reference/Contact Acronym
224.0.1.112	TVE-FILE	Blackketter
224.0.1.113	TVE-ANNOUNCE	Blackketter
224.0.1.114	Mac Srv Loc	Woodcock
224.0.1.115	Simple Multicast	Crowcroft
224.0.1.116	SpectraLinkGW	Hamilton
224.0.1.117	Dieboldmcast	Marsh
224.0.1.118	Tivoli Systems	Gabriel
224.0.1.119	PQ-Lic-mcast	Sledge
224.0.1.120	HYPERFEED	Kreutzjans
224.0.1.121	Pipesplatform	Dissett
224.0.1.122	LiebDevMgmg-DM	Velten
224.0.1.123	TRIBALVOICE	Thompson
224.0.1.124	UDLR-DTCP	Cipiere
224.0.1.125	PolyCom Relay1	Coutiere
224.0.1.126	Infront Multi1	Lindeman
224.0.1.127	XRX DEVICE DISC	Wang
224.0.1.128	CNN	Lynch
224.0.1.129	PTP-primary	Eidson
224.0.1.130	PTP-alternate1	Eidson

TABLE C.1 Multicast Addresses *(continued)*

Address	Purpose	Reference/Contact Acronym
224.0.1.131	PTP-alternate2	Eidson
224.0.1.132	PTP-alternate3	Eidson
224.0.1.133	ProCast	Revzen
224.0.1.134	3Com Discp	White
224.0.1.135	CS-Multicasting	Stanev
224.0.1.136	TS-MC-1	Sveistrup
224.0.1.137	Make Source	Daga
224.0.1.138	Teleborsa	Strazzera
224.0.1.139	SUMAConfig	Wallach
224.0.1.140	Unassigned	
224.0.1.141	DHCP-SERVERS	Hall
224.0.1.142	CN Router-LL	Armitage
224.0.1.143	EMWIN	Querubin
224.0.1.144	Alchemy Cluster	O'Rourke
224.0.1.145	Satcast One	Nevell
224.0.1.146	Satcast Two	Nevell
224.0.1.147	Satcast Three	Nevell
224.0.1.148	Intline	Sliwinski
224.0.1.149	8x8 Multicast	Roper

TABLE C.1 Multicast Addresses *(continued)*

Address	Purpose	Reference/Contact Acronym
224.0.1.150	Unassigned	JBP
224.0.1.166	Marratech-cc	Parnes
224.0.1.167	EMS-InterDev	Lyda
224.0.1.168	ltb301	Rueskamp
224.0.2.1	"RWHO" Group (BSD) (unofficial)	JBP
224.0.2.2	SUN RPC PMAPPROC_CALLIT	BXE1
224.2.127.254	SAPv1 Announcements	SC3
224.2.127.255	SAPv0 Announcements	SC3

TABLE C.2 The Multicast Group Assignments for Class D IP Addresses

Multicast Address	Group Assigned	Contact
224.0.0.0-224.0.0.255	Routing Protocols	
224.0.1.27-224.0.1.30	Lmsc-Calren-1 to 4	Uang
224.0.1.151-224.0.1.165	Intline 1 to15	Sliwinski
224.0.1.169-224.0.1.255	Unassigned	JBP
224.0.2.064-224.0.2.095	SIAC MDD Service	Tse
224.0.2.096-224.0.2.127	CoolCast	Ballister
224.0.2.128-224.0.2.191	WOZ-Garage	Marquardt
224.0.2.192-224.0.2.255	SIAC MDD Market Service	Lamberg

TABLE C.2 The Multicast Group Assignments for Class D IP Addresses *(continued)*

Multicast Address	Group Assigned	Contact
224.0.3.000-224.0.3.255	RFE Generic Service	DXS3
224.0.4.000-224.0.4.255	RFE Individual Conferences	DXS3
224.0.5.000-224.0.5.127	CDPD Groups	Bob Brenner
224.0.5.128-224.0.5.191	SIAC Market Service	Cho
224.0.5.192-224.0.5.255	Unassigned	IANA
224.0.6.000-224.0.6.127	Cornell ISIS Project	Tim Clark
224.0.6.128-224.0.6.255	Unassigned	IANA
224.0.7.000-224.0.7.255	Where-Are-You	Simpson
224.0.8.000-224.0.8.255	INTV	Tynan
224.0.9.000-224.0.9.255	Invisible Worlds	Malamud
224.0.10.000-224.0.10.255	DLSw Groups	Lee
224.0.11.000-224.0.11.255	NCC.NET Audio	Rubin
224.0.12.000-224.0.12.063	Microsoft and MSNBC	Blank
224.0.13.000-224.0.13.255	UUNET PIPEX Net News	Barber
224.0.14.000-224.0.14.255	NLANR	Wessels
224.0.15.000-224.0.15.255	Hewlett Packard	Van Der Meulen
224.0.16.000-224.0.16.255	XingNet	Uusitalo
224.0.17.000-224.0.17.031	Mercantile & Commodity Exchange	Gilani

TABLE C.2 The Multicast Group Assignments for Class D IP Addresses *(continued)*

Multicast Address	Group Assigned	Contact
224.0.17.032-224.0.17.063	NDQMD1	Nelson
224.0.17.064-224.0.17.127	ODN-DTV	Hodges
224.0.18.000-224.0.18.255	Dow Jones	Peng
224.0.19.000-224.0.19.063	Walt Disney Company	Watson
224.0.19.064-224.0.19.095	Cal Multicast	Moran
224.0.19.096-224.0.19.127	SIAC Market Service	Roy
224.0.19.128-224.0.19.191	IIG Multicast	Carr
224.0.19.192-224.0.19.207	Metropol	Crawford
224.0.19.208-224.0.19.239	Xenoscience, Inc.	Timm
224.0.19.240-224.0.19.255	HYPERFEED	Felix
224.0.20.000-224.0.20.063	MS-IP/TV	Wong
224.0.20.064-224.0.20.127	Reliable Network Solutions	Vogels
224.0.20.128-224.0.20.143	TRACKTICKER Group	Novick
224.0.20.144-224.0.20.207	CNR Rebroadcast MCA	Sautter
224.0.21.000-224.0.21.127	Talarian MCAST	Mendal
224.0.22.000-224.0.22.255	WORLD MCAST	Stewart
224.0.252.000-224.0.252.255	Domain Scoped Group	Fenner
224.0.253.000-224.0.253.255	Report Group	Fenner

TABLE C.2 The Multicast Group Assignments for Class D IP Addresses *(continued)*

Multicast Address	Group Assigned	Contact
224.0.254.000-224.0.254.255	Query Group	Fenner
224.0.255.000-224.0.255.255	Border Routers	Fenner
224.1.0.0-224.1.255.255	ST Multicast Groups	RFC1190/KS14
224.2.0.0-224.2.127.253	Multimedia Conference Calls	SC3
224.2.128.0-224.2.255.255	SAP Dynamic Assignments	SC3
224.252.0.0-224.255.255.255	DIS transient groups	Joel Snyder
225.0.0.0-225.255.255.255	MALLOC	Handley
232.0.0.0-232.255.255.255	VMTP transient groups	DRC3
233.0.0.0-233.255.255.255	Static Allocations	Meyer2
239.000.000.000-239.255.255.255	Administratively Scoped	IANA/RFC2365
239.000.000.000-239.063.255.255	Reserved	IANA
239.064.000.000-239.127.255.255	Reserved	IANA
239.128.000.000-239.191.255.255	Reserved	IANA
239.192.000.000-239.251.255.255	Organization-Local Scope	Meyer/RFC2365

TABLE C.2 The Multicast Group Assignments for Class D IP Addresses *(continued)*

Multicast Address	Group Assigned	Contact
239.252.000.000- 239.252.255.255	Site-Local Scope	Meyer/ RFC2365
239.253.000.000- 239.253.255.255	Site-Local Scope	Meyer/ RFC2365
239.254.000.000- 239.254.255.255	Site-Local Scope	Meyer/ RFC2365
239.255.000.000- 239.255.255.255	Site-Local Scope	Meyer/ RFC2365

TABLE C.3 Multicast RFCs

Reference RFC	RFC Title
RFC1045	VMTP: Versatile Message Transaction Protocol Specification
RFC1075	Distance Vector Multicast Routing Protocol
RFC1112	Host Extensions for IP Multicasting
RFC1119	Network Time Protocol (Version 1), Specification and Implementation
RFC1190	Experimental Internet Stream Protocol, Version 2 (ST-II)
RFC2328	OSPF Version 2
RFC1723	RIP Version 2: Carrying Additional Information
RFC1884	IP Version 6 Addressing Architecture
RFC2114	Data Link Switching Client Access Protocol

TABLE C.3 Multicast RFCs *(continued)*

Reference RFC	RFC Title
RFC2365	Administratively Scoped IP Multicast
RFC2730	Multicast Address Dynamic Client Allocation Protocol (MADCAP)

TABLE C.4 Contact Name and Address for the Assigned Multicast Addresses

Contact Acronym	Contact Name	E-Mail Address
Albin	Jerome Albin	albin@taec.enet.dec.com
Albright	Shivaun Albright	shivaun_albright@hp.com
Armitage	Ian Armitage	ian@coactive.com
Aronson	Peter Aronson	paronson@esri.com
AXC	Andrew Cherenson	arc@SGI.COM
Baker	Fred Baker	fred@cisco.com
Ballardie	Tony Ballardie	a.ballardie@cs.ucl.ac.uk
Ballister	Tom Ballister	tballister@starguidedigital.com
Banthia	Prakash Banthia	prakash_banthia@3com.com
Barber	Tony Barber	tonyb@pipex.com
Bhatti	Zia Bhatti	zia@netright.com
Blackketter	Dean Blackketter	dean@corp.webtv.net
Blank	Tom Blank	tomblank@microsoft.com

TABLE C.4 Contact Name and Address for the Assigned Multicast Addresses *(continued)*

Contact Acronym	Contact Name	E-Mail Address
Braden	Bob Braden	braden@isi.edu
Bob Brenner	No Contact Information	
Brockbank	Darcy Brockbank	darcy@hasc.com
BXE1	Brendan Eic	brendan@illyria.wpd.sgi.com
BXF	Bruce Factor	ahi!bigapple!bruce@uunet.UU.NET
BXS2	Bill Schilit	schilit@parc.xerox.com
Carr	Wayne Carr	Wayne_Carr@ccm.intel.com
Casner	Steve Casner	casner@isi.edu
Caves	Evan Caves	evan@acc.com
Cheshire	Stuart Cheshire	cheshire@apple.com
Chiang	Steve Chiang	schiang@cisco.com
Cho	Joan Cho	jcho@siac.com
Cipiere	Patrick Cipiere	Patrick.Cipiere@sophia.inria.fr
Costales	Bryan Costales	bcx@infobeat.com
Crawford	James Crawford	jcrawford@metropol.net
Crowcroft	Jon Crowcroft	jon@hocus.cs.ucl.ac.uk
CXM3	Chuck McManis	cmcmanis@sun.com

TABLE C.4 Contact Name and Address for the Assigned Multicast Addresses *(continued)*

Contact Acronym	Contact Name	E-Mail Address
Tim Clark	No Contact Information	
Daga	Anthony Daga	anthony@mksrc.com
Deering	Steve Deering	deering@cisco.com
DeMoney	Michael DeMoney	demoney@eng.sun.com
Dillon	Doug Dillon	dillon@hns.com.
Dissett	Daniel Dissett	ddissett@peerlogic.com
DLM1	David Mills	Mills@huey.udel.edu
DRC3	Dave Cheriton	cheriton@dsg.stanford.edu
Dunne	Stephen Dunne	sdun@isma.co.uk
DXS3	Daniel Steinber	daniel.steinberg@eng.sun.com
Eidson	John Eidson	eidson@hpl.hp.com
Fenner	Bill Fenner	fenner@parc.xerox.com
Farinacci	Dino Farinacci	dino@cisco.com
Felix	Ken Felix	kfelix@pcquote.com
Flynn	Edward Flynn	flynne@nasdaq.com
Gabriel	Jon Gabriel	grabriel@tivoli.com
Gaddie	Bob Gaddie	bobg@dtn.com
Gal	Yossi Gal	yossi@gilat.com

TABLE C.4 Contact Name and Address for the Assigned Multicast Addresses *(continued)*

Contact Acronym	Contact Name	E-Mail Address
Gibson	Terry Gibson	terry.gibson@sun.com
Gilani	Asad Gilani	agilani@nymex.com
GSM11	Gary S. Malkin	gmalkin@xylogics.com
Goland	Yaron Goland	yarong@microsoft.com
Gordon	Howard Gordon	hgordon@xingtech.com
Green	Cliff Green	cgreen@xypoint.com
Guttman	Erik Guttman	erik.guttman@eng.sun.com
Hall	Eric Hall	ehall@ntrg.com
Hamilton	Mark Hamilton	mah@spectralink.com
Handley	Mark Handley	mjh@ISI.EDU
Hinden	Bob Hinden	hinden@Ipsilon.com
Hodges	Richard Hodges	rh@source.net
Holfelder	Wieland Holdfelder	whd@pi4.informatik.uni-mannheim.de
Honton	Chas Honton	chas@secant.com
IANA	IANA	iana@iana.org
Iyer	Ram Iyer	ram@aaccorp.com
Jackson	Dan Jackson	jdan@us.ibm.com
Janssen	Rob Janssen	rob@pe1ch1.ampr.org
JBP	Jon Postel	postel@isi.edu

TABLE C.4 Contact Name and Address for the Assigned Multicast Addresses *(continued)*

Contact Acronym	Contact Name	E-Mail Address
JXM1	Jim Miner	miner@star.com
Kean	Brian Kean	bkean@dca.com
Kreutzjans	Michael Kreutzjans	mike@pcquote.com
KS14	Karen Seo	kseo@bbn.com
Lamberg	Mike Lamberg	mlamberg@siac.com
Lee	Choon Lee	cwl@nsd.3com.com
Lewis	Mark Lewis	Mark_Lewis@ccm.jf.intel.com
Lindeman	Morten Lindeman	Morten.Lindeman@os.telia.no
Lyda	Stephen T. Lyda	slyda@emsg.com
Lynch	Joel Lynch	joel.lynch@cnn.com
Malamud	Carl Malamud	carl@invisible.net
Andrew Maffei	No Contact Information	
Malkin	Gary Scott Malkin	gmalkin@baynetworks.com
Mamakos	Louis Mamakos	louie@uu.net
Manning	Bill Manning	bmanning@isi.edu
Marocho	Jose Luis Marocho	73374.313@compuserve.com
Marquardt	Douglas Marquardt	dmarquar@woz.org
Marsh	Gene Marsh	MarshM@diebold.com

TABLE C.4 Contact Name and Address for the Assigned Multicast Addresses *(continued)*

Contact Acronym	Contact Name	E-Mail Address
Martinicky	Brian Martinicky	Brian_Martinicky@automationintelligence.com
Meier	Bob Meier	meierb@norand.com
Mendal	Geoff Mendal	mendal@talarian.com
Meyer	David Meyer	meyer@ns.uoregon.edu
Meyer2	David Meyer	dmm@cisco.com
Moelard	Henri Moelard	hmoelard@wcnd.nl.lucent.com
Moran	Ed Moran	admin@cruzjazz.com
John Moy	John Moy	jmoy@casc.com
MXF2	Martin Forssen	maf@dtek.chalmers.se
Nelson	Gunnar Nelson	nelsong@nasd.com
Nevell	Julian Nevell	jnevell@vbs.bt.co.uk
Novick	Alan Novick	anovick@tdc.com
O'Rourke	Stacey O'Rourke	stacey@network-alchemy.com
Parnes	Peter Parnes	peppar@marratech.com
Peng	Wenjie Peng	wpeng@tts.telerate.com
Poole	David Poole	davep@extendsys.com
Przygienda	Tony Przygienda	prz@siara.com
Purkiss	Ed Purkiss	epurkiss@wdmacodi.com
Querubin	Antonio Querubin	tony@lava.net

TABLE C.4 Contact Name and Address for the Assigned Multicast Addresses *(continued)*

Contact Acronym	Contact Name	E-Mail Address
Revzen	Shai Revzen	shrevz@nmcfast.com
Rodbell	Mike Rodbell	mrodbell@ciena.com
Roper	Mike Roper	mroper@8x8.com
Guido Van Rossum	No Contact Information	
Rowatt	Shane Rowatt	shane.rowatt@star.com.au
Roy	George Roy	owens@appliedtheory.com
Rubin	David Rubin	drubin@ncc.net
Rupp	Heiko Rupp	hwr@xlink.net
Rueskamp	Bodo Rueskamp	br@itchigo.com
Sautter	Robert Sautter	rsautter@acdnj.itt.com
SC3	Steve Casner	casner@precept.com
Scannell	Piers Scannell	piers@globecastne.com
Scheifler	Bob Scheifler	bob.scheifler@sun.com
Schwartz	Beverly Schwartz	bschwart@bbn.com
Shindoh	Masato Shindoh	j111456@yamato.ibm.co.jp
Shum	Raymond Shum	rshum@ms.com
Simpson	Bill Simpson	bill.simpson@um.cc.umich.edu
Sledge	Bob Sledge	bob@pqsystems.com

TABLE C.4 Contact Name and Address for the Assigned Multicast Addresses *(continued)*

Contact Acronym	Contact Name	E-Mail Address
Sliwinski	Robert Sliwinski	sliwinre@mail1st.com
Stanev	Nedelcho Stanev	nstanev@csoft.bg
Stewart	Ian Stewart	iandbige@yahoo.com
Strazzera	Paolo Strazzera	p.strazzera@telematica.it
Sveistrup	Darrell Sveistrup	darrells@truesolutions.net
SXA	Susie Armstrong	armstrong.wbst128@xerox.com
SXD	Steve Deering	deering@parc.xerox.com
Thaler	Dave Thaler	dthaler@microsoft.com
Thompson	Nigel Thompson	nigelt@tribal.com
Timm	Mary Timm	mary@xenoscience.com
Tynan	Dermot Tynan	dtynan@claddagh.ie
Toga	Jim Toga	jtoga@ibeam.jf.intel.com
Tse	Geordie Tse	gtse@siac.com
Uang	Yea Uang	uang@force.decnet.lockheed.com
Uusitalo	Mika Uusitalo	msu@xingtech.com
Van Der Muelen	Ron van der Muelen	ronv@lsid.hp.com
Veizades	John Veizades	veizades@tgv.com
Velten	Mike Velten	mike_velten@liebert.com

TABLE C.4 Contact Name and Address for the Assigned Multicast Addresses *(continued)*

Contact Acronym	Contact Name	E-Mail Address
Vogels	Werner Vogels	vogels@rnets.com
Volpe	Victor Volpe	vvolpe@smtp.microcom.com
Wallach	Walter Wallach	walt@sumatech.com
Wang	Michael Wang	michael.wang@usa.xerox.com
Watson	Scott Watson	scott@disney.com
Wei	Liming Wei	lwei@cisco.com
Wessels	Duane Wessels	wessels@nlanr.net
White	Peter White	peter_white@3com.com
Wissenbach	Paul Wissenbach	paulwi@vnd.tek.com
Wong	Tony Wong	wongt@ms.com
Woodcock	Bill Woodcock	woody@zocalo.net
Wu	Ishan Wu	iwu@cisco.com
Yackle	Dotty Yackle	ditty_yackle@dantz.com
Zwemmer	Arnoud Zwemmer	arnoud@nwn.nl
Zmudzinski	Krystof Zmudzinski	kzmudzinski@etcconnect.com

Glossary

A&B bit signaling Used in T1 transmission facilities and sometimes called "24th channel signaling." Each of the 24 T1 subchannels in this procedure uses one bit of every sixth frame to send supervisory signaling information.

AAA Authentication, authorization, and accounting. A Cisco description of the processes that are required to provide a remote access security solution. Each is implemented separately, but each can rely on the others for functionality.

AAL ATM Adaptation Layer: A service-dependent sublayer of the data link layer, which accepts data from other applications and brings it to the ATM layer in 48-byte ATM payload segments. CS and SAR are the two sublayers that form AALs. Currently, the four types of AAL recommended by the ITU-T are AAL1, AAL2, AAL3/4, and AAL5. AALs are differentiated by the source-destination timing they use, whether they are CBR or VBR, and whether they are used for connection-oriented or connectionless mode data transmission. *See also: AAL1, AAL2, AAL3/4, AAL5, ATM,* and *ATM layer.*

AAL1 ATM Adaptation Layer 1: One of four AALs recommended by the ITU-T, it is used for connection-oriented, time-sensitive services that need constant bit rates, such as isochronous traffic and uncompressed video. *See also: AAL.*

AAL2 ATM Adaptation Layer 2: One of four AALs recommended by the ITU-T, it is used for connection-oriented services that support a variable bit rate, such as voice traffic. *See also: AAL.*

AAL3/4 ATM Adaptation Layer 3/4: One of four AALs (a product of two initially distinct layers) recommended by the ITU-T, supporting both connectionless and connection-oriented links. Its primary use is in sending SMDS packets over ATM networks. *See also: AAL.*

AAL5 ATM Adaptation Layer 5: One of four AALs recommended by the ITU-T, it is used to support connection-oriented VBR services primarily to transfer classical IP over ATM and LANE traffic. This least complex of the AAL recommendations uses SEAL, offering lower bandwidth costs and simpler processing requirements but also providing reduced bandwidth and error-recovery capacities. *See also: AAL.*

AARP AppleTalk Address Resolution Protocol: The protocol in an AppleTalk stack that maps data-link addresses to network addresses.

AARP probe packets Packets sent by the AARP to determine whether a given node ID is being used by another node in a nonextended AppleTalk network. If the node ID is not in use, the sending node appropriates that node's ID. If the node ID is in use, the sending node will select a different ID and then send out more AARP probe packets. *See also: AARP.*

ABM Asynchronous Balanced Mode: When two stations can initiate a transmission, ABM is an HDLC (or one of its derived protocols) communication technology that supports peer-oriented, point-to-point communications between both stations.

ABR Area Border Router: An OSPF router that is located on the border of one or more OSPF areas. ABRs are used to connect OSPF areas to the OSPF backbone area.

access control Used by Cisco routers to control packets as they pass through a router. Access lists are created and then applied to router interfaces to accomplish this.

access layer One of the layers in Cisco's three-layer hierarchical model. The access layer provides users with access to the internetwork.

access link Is a link used with switches and is only part of one Virtual LAN (VLAN). Trunk links carry information from multiple VLANs.

access list A set of test conditions kept by routers that determines "interesting traffic" to and from the router for various services on the network.

access method The manner in which network devices approach gaining access to the network itself.

access rate Defines the bandwidth rate of the circuit. For example, the access rate of a T1 circuit is 1.544Mbps. In Frame Relay and other technologies, there may be a fractional T1 connection—256Kbps, for example—however, the access rate and clock rate is still 1.544Mbps.

access server Also known as a "network access server," it is a communications process connecting asynchronous devices to a LAN or WAN through network and terminal emulation software, providing synchronous or asynchronous routing of supported protocols.

acknowledgment Verification sent from one network device to another signifying that an event has occurred. May be abbreviated as ACK. *Contrast with: NAK.*

accounting One of the three components in AAA. Accounting provides auditing and logging functionalities to the security model.

ACR allowed cell rate: A designation defined by the ATM Forum for managing ATM traffic. Dynamically controlled using congestion control measures, the ACR varies between the minimum cell rate (MCR) and the peak cell rate (PCR). *See also: MCR* and *PCR.*

active monitor The mechanism used to manage a Token Ring. The network node with the highest MAC address on the ring becomes the active monitor and is responsible for management tasks such as preventing loops and ensuring that tokens are not lost.

address learning Used with transparent bridges to learn the hardware addresses of all devices on an internetwork. The switch then filters the network with the known hardware (MAC) addresses.

address mapping By translating network addresses from one format to another, this methodology permits different protocols to operate interchangeably.

address mask A bit combination descriptor identifying which portion of an address refers to the network or subnet and which part refers to the host. Sometimes simply called the mask. *See also: subnet mask.*

address resolution The process used for resolving differences between computer addressing schemes. Address resolution typically defines a method for tracing network layer (Layer 3) addresses to data-link layer (Layer 2) addresses. *See also: address mapping.*

adjacency The relationship made between defined neighboring routers and end nodes, using a common media segment, to exchange routing information.

administrative distance A number between 0 and 225 that expresses the value of trustworthiness of a routing information source. The lower the number, the higher the integrity rating.

administrative weight A value designated by a network administrator to rate the preference given to a network link. It is one of four link metrics exchanged by PTSPs to test ATM network resource availability.

ADSU ATM Data Service Unit: The terminal adapter used to connect to an ATM network through an HSSI-compatible mechanism. *See also: DSU.*

advertising The process whereby routing or service updates are transmitted at given intervals, allowing other routers on the network to maintain a record of viable routes.

AEP AppleTalk Echo Protocol: A test for connectivity between two AppleTalk nodes where one node sends a packet to another and receives an echo, or copy, in response.

AFI Authority and Format Identifier: The part of an NSAP ATM address that delineates the type and format of the IDI section of an ATM address.

AFP AppleTalk Filing Protocol: A presentation-layer protocol, supporting AppleShare and Mac OS File Sharing, that permits users to share files and applications on a server.

AIP ATM Interface Processor: Supporting AAL3/4 and AAL5, this interface for Cisco 7000 series routers minimizes performance bottlenecks at the UNI. *See also: AAL3/4* and *AAL5.*

algorithm A set of rules or process used to solve a problem. In networking, algorithms are typically used for finding the best route for traffic from a source to its destination.

alignment error An error occurring in Ethernet networks, in which a received frame has extra bits; that is, a number not divisible by eight. Alignment errors are generally the result of frame damage caused by collisions.

all-routes explorer packet An explorer packet that can move across an entire SRB network, tracing all possible paths to a given destination. Also known as an all-rings explorer packet. *See also: explorer packet, local explorer packet,* and *spanning explorer packet.*

AM Amplitude Modulation: A modulation method that represents information by varying the amplitude of the carrier signal. *See also: modulation.*

AMI Alternate Mark Inversion: A line-code type on T1 and E1 circuits that shows zeros as "01" during each bit cell, and ones as "11" or "00," alternately, during each bit cell. The sending device must maintain ones density in AMI but not independently of the data stream. Also known as binary-coded, alternate mark inversion. *Contrast with: B8ZS. See also: ones density.*

amplitude An analog or digital waveform's highest value.

analog Analog signaling is a technique to carry voice and data over copper and wireless media. When analog signals are transmitted over wires or through the air, the transmission conveys information through a variation of some type of signal amplitude, frequency and phase.

analog connection Provides signaling via an infinitely variable waveform. This differs from a digital connection, in which a definite waveform is used to define values. Traditional phone service is an analog connection.

analog transmission Signal messaging whereby information is represented by various combinations of signal amplitude, frequency, and phase.

ANSI American National Standards Institute: The organization of corporate, government, and other volunteer members that coordinates standards-related activities, approves U.S. national standards, and develops U.S. positions in international standards organizations. ANSI assists in the creation of international and U.S. standards in disciplines such as communications, networking, and a variety of technical fields. It publishes over 13,000 standards, for engineered products and technologies ranging from screw threads to networking protocols. ANSI is a member of the IEC and ISO.

anycast An ATM address that can be shared by more than one end system, allowing requests to be routed to a node that provides a particular service.

AppleTalk Currently in two versions, the group of communication protocols designed by Apple Computer for use in Macintosh environments. The earlier Phase 1 protocols supports one physical network with only one network number that resides in one zone. The later Phase 2 protocols support more than one logical network on a single physical network, allowing networks to exist in more than one zone. *See also: zone.*

application layer Layer 7 of the OSI reference network model, supplying services to application procedures (such as electronic mail or file transfer) that are outside the OSI model. This layer chooses and determines the availability of communicating partners along with the resources necessary to make the connection, coordinates partnering applications, and forms a consensus on procedures for controlling data integrity and error recovery.

ARA AppleTalk Remote Access: A protocol for Macintosh users establishing their access to resources and data from a remote AppleTalk location.

area A logical, rather than physical, set of segments (based on either CLNS, DECnet, or OSPF) along with their attached devices. Areas are commonly connected to others using routers to create a single autonomous system. *See also: autonomous system.*

ARM Asynchronous Response Mode: An HDLC communication mode using one primary station and at least one additional station, in which transmission can be initiated from either the primary or one of the secondary units.

ARP Address Resolution Protocol: Defined in RFC 826, the protocol that traces IP addresses to MAC addresses. *See also: RARP.*

ASBR Autonomous System Boundary Router: An area border router placed between an OSPF autonomous system and a non-OSPF network that operates both OSPF and an additional routing protocol, such as RIP. ASBRs must be located in a non-stub OSPF area. *See also: ABR, non-stub area,* and *OSPF.*

ASCII American Standard Code for Information Interchange: An 8-bit code for representing characters, consisting of seven data bits plus one parity bit.

ASICs Application-Specific Integrated Circuits: Used in layer 2 switches to make filtering decisions. The ASIC looks in the filter table of MAC addresses and determines which port the destination hardware address of a received hardware address is destined for. The frame will be allowed to traverse only that one segment. If the hardware address is unknown, the frame is forwarded out all ports.

ASN.1 Abstract Syntax Notation One: An OSI language used to describe types of data that is independent of computer structures and depicting methods. Described by ISO International Standard 8824.

ASP AppleTalk Session Protocol: A protocol employing ATP to establish, maintain, and tear down sessions, as well as sequence requests. *See also: ATP.*

AST Automatic Spanning Tree: A function that supplies one path for spanning explorer frames traveling from one node in the network to another, supporting the automatic resolution of spanning trees in SRB networks. AST is based on the IEEE 802.1 standard. *See also: IEEE 802.1* and *SRB.*

asynchronous connection Defines the start and stop of each octet. As a result, each byte in asynchronous connections requires two bytes of overhead. Synchronous connections use a synchronous clock to mark the start and stop of each character.

asynchronous dial-up Asynchronous dial-up is interchangeable with analog dial-up. Both terms refer to traditional modem-based connections.

asynchronous transmission Digital signals sent without precise timing, usually with different frequencies and phase relationships. Asynchronous transmissions generally enclose individual characters in control bits (called start and stop bits) that show the beginning and end of each character. *Contrast with: isochronous transmission* and *synchronous transmission.*

ATCP AppleTalk Control Program: The protocol for establishing and configuring AppleTalk over PPP, defined in RFC 1378. *See also: PPP.*

ATDM Asynchronous Time-Division Multiplexing: A technique for sending information, it differs from normal TDM in that the time slots are assigned when necessary rather than preassigned to certain transmitters. *Contrast with: FDM, statistical multiplexing,* and *TDM.*

ATG Address Translation Gateway: The mechanism within Cisco DECnet routing software that enables routers to route multiple, independent DECnet networks and to establish a user-designated address translation for chosen nodes between networks.

ATM Asynchronous Transfer Mode: The international standard, identified by fixed-length 53-byte cells, for transmitting cells in multiple service systems, such as voice, video, or data. Transit delays are reduced because the fixed-length cells permit processing to occur in the hardware. ATM is designed to maximize the benefits of high-speed transmission media, such as SONET, E3, and T3.

ATM ARP server A device that supplies logical subnets running classical IP over ATM with address-resolution services.

ATM endpoint The initiating or terminating connection in an ATM network. ATM endpoints include servers, workstations, ATM-to-LAN switches, and ATM routers.

ATM Forum The international organization founded jointly by Northern Telecom, Sprint, Cisco Systems, and NET/ADAPTIVE in 1991 to develop and promote standards-based implementation agreements for ATM technology. The ATM Forum broadens official standards developed by ANSI and ITU-T and creates implementation agreements before official standards are published.

ATM layer A sublayer of the data link layer in an ATM network that is service independent. To create standard 53-byte ATM cells, the ATM layer receives 48-byte segments from the AAL and attaches a 5-byte header to each. These cells are then sent to the physical layer for transmission across the physical medium. *See also: AAL.*

ATMM ATM Management: A procedure that runs on ATM switches, managing rate enforcement and VCI translation. *See also: ATM.*

ATM user-user connection A connection made by the ATM layer to supply communication between at least two ATM service users, such as ATMM processes. These communications can be uni- or bidirectional, using one or two VCCs, respectively. *See also: ATM layer* and *ATMM.*

ATP AppleTalk Transaction Protocol: A transport-level protocol that enables reliable transactions between two sockets, where one requests the other to perform a given task and to report the results. ATP fastens the request and response together, assuring a loss-free exchange of request-response pairs.

attenuation   In communication, weakening or loss of signal energy, typically caused by distance.

AURP   AppleTalk Update-based Routing Protocol: A technique for encapsulating AppleTalk traffic in the header of a foreign protocol that allows the connection of at least two noncontiguous AppleTalk internetworks through a foreign network (such as TCP/IP) to create an AppleTalk WAN. The connection made is called an AURP tunnel. By exchanging routing information between exterior routers, the AURP maintains routing tables for the complete AppleTalk WAN. *See also: AURP tunnel.*

AURP tunnel   A connection made in an AURP WAN that acts as a single, virtual link between AppleTalk internetworks separated physically by a foreign network such as a TCP/IP network. *See also: AURP.*

authentication   The first component in the AAA model. Users are typically authenticated via a username and password, which are used to uniquely identify them.

authority zone   A portion of the domain-name tree associated with DNS for which one name server is the authority. *See also: DNS.*

authorization   The act of permitting access to a resource based on authentication information in the AAA model.

auto duplex   A setting on layer 1 and 2 devices that sets the duplex of a switch or hub port automatically.

automatic call reconnect   A function that enables automatic call rerouting away from a failed trunk line.

autonomous confederation   A collection of self-governed systems that depend more on their own network accessibility and routing information than on information received from other systems or groups.

autonomous switching   The ability of Cisco routers to process packets more quickly by using the ciscoBus to switch packets independently of the system processor.

autonomous system (AS)   A group of networks under mutual administration that share the same routing methodology. Autonomous systems are subdivided by areas and must be assigned an individual 16-bit number by the IANA. *See also: area.*

autoreconfiguration A procedure executed by nodes within the failure domain of a Token Ring, wherein nodes automatically perform diagnostics, trying to reconfigure the network around failed areas.

Auto-RP An IOS feature that allows multicast-enabled routers to detect RP and forward the summary information to other routers and hosts.

auxiliary port The console port on the back of Cisco routers that allows you to dial the router and make console configuration settings.

AVVID Architecture for Voice, Video and Integrated Data: This is a Cisco marketing term to group their convergence efforts. Convergence is the integration of historically distinct services into a single service.

B8ZS Binary 8-Zero Substitution: A line-code type, interpreted at the remote end of the connection, that uses a special code substitution whenever eight consecutive zeros are transmitted over the link on T1 and E1 circuits. This technique assures ones density independent of the data stream. Also known as bipolar 8-zero substitution. *Contrast with: AMI. See also: ones density.*

backbone The basic portion of the network that provides the primary path for traffic sent to and initiated from other networks.

back end A node or software program supplying services to a front end. *See also: server.*

bandwidth The gap between the highest and lowest frequencies employed by network signals. More commonly, it refers to the rated throughput capacity of a network protocol or medium.

BoD Bandwidth on Demand: This function allows an additional B channel to be used to increase the amount of bandwidth available for a particular connection.

baseband A feature of a network technology that uses only one carrier frequency, for example Ethernet. Also named "narrowband." *Compare with: broadband.*

Basic Management Setup Used with Cisco routers when in setup mode. Only provides enough management and configuration to get the router working so someone can telnet into the router and configure it.

baud   Synonymous with bits per second (bps), if each signal element represents one bit. It is a unit of signaling speed equivalent to the number of separate signal elements transmitted per second.

B channel   Bearer channel: A full-duplex, 64Kbps channel in ISDN that transmits user data. *Compare with: D channel, E channel,* and *H channel.*

beacon   An FDDI device or Token Ring frame that points to a serious problem with the ring, such as a broken cable. The beacon frame carries the address of the station thought to be down. *See also: failure domain.*

bearer service   Used by service providers to provide DS0 service to ISDN customers. A DS0 is one 64k channel. An ISDN bearer service provides either two DS0s, called two bearer channels, for a Basic Rate Interface (BRI), or 24 DS0s, called a Primary Rate Interface (PRI).

BECN   Backward Explicit Congestion Notification: BECN is the bit set by a Frame Relay network in frames moving away from frames headed into a congested path. A DTE that receives frames with the BECN may ask higher-level protocols to take necessary flow control measures. *Compare with: FECN.*

BGP4   BGP Version 4: Version 4 of the interdomain routing protocol most commonly used on the Internet. BGP4 supports CIDR and uses route-counting mechanisms to decrease the size of routing tables. *See also: CIDR.*

bidirectional shared tree   A method of shared tree multicast forwarding. This method allows group members to receive data from the source or the RP, whichever is closer. *See also: RP (rendezvous point).*

binary   A two-character numbering method that uses ones and zeros. The binary numbering system underlies all digital representation of information.

BIP   Bit Interleaved Parity: A method used in ATM to monitor errors on a link, sending a check bit or word in the link overhead for the previous block or frame. This allows bit errors in transmissions to be found and delivered as maintenance information.

BISDN   Broadband ISDN: ITU-T standards created to manage high-bandwidth technologies such as video. BISDN presently employs ATM technology along SONET-based transmission circuits, supplying data rates between 155Mbps and 622Mbps and beyond. Contrast with N-ISDN. *See also: BRI, ISDN,* and *PRI.*

bit-oriented protocol   Regardless of frame content, the class of data-link layer communication protocols that transmits frames. Bit-oriented protocols, as compared with byte-oriented, supply more efficient and trustworthy, full-duplex operation. *Compare with: byte-oriented protocol.*

Boot ROM   Used in routers to put the router into bootstrap mode. Bootstrap mode then boots the device with an operating system. The ROM can also hold a small Cisco IOS.

border gateway   A router that facilitates communication with routers in different autonomous systems.

border router   Typically defined within Open Shortest Path First (OSPF) as a router that connected an area to the backbone area. However, a border router can be a router that connects a company to the Internet as well. *See also: OSPF.*

BPDU   Bridge Protocol Data Unit: A Spanning Tree Protocol initializing packet that is sent at definable intervals for the purpose of exchanging information among bridges in networks.

BRI   Basic Rate Interface: The ISDN interface that facilitates circuit-switched communication between video, data, and voice; it is made up of two B channels (64Kbps each) and one D channel (16Kbps). *Compare with: PRI. See also: BISDN.*

bridge   A device for connecting two segments of a network and transmitting packets between them. Both segments must use identical protocols to communicate. Bridges function at the data link layer, Layer 2 of the OSI reference model. The purpose of a bridge is to filter, send, or flood any incoming frame, based on the MAC address of that particular frame.

bridge ID   Used to find and elect the root bridge in a layer 2 switched internetwork. The bridge ID is a combination of the bridge priority and base MAC address.

bridging   A layer 2 process to block or forward frames based on MAC layer addresses. Bridges are lower speed, lower port density switches.

broadband A transmission methodology for multiplexing several independent signals onto one cable. In telecommunications, broadband is classified as any channel with bandwidth greater than 4kHz (typical voice grade). In LAN terminology, it is classified as a coaxial cable on which analog signaling is employed. Also known as wideband. *Contrast with: baseband.*

broadcast A data frame or packet that is transmitted to every node on the local network segment (as defined by the broadcast domain). Broadcasts are known by their broadcast address, which is a destination network and host address with all the bits turned on. Also called "local broadcast." *Compare with: directed broadcast.*

broadcast domain A group of devices receiving broadcast frames initiating from any device within the group. Because they do not forward broadcast frames, broadcast domains are generally surrounded by routers.

broadcast storm An undesired event on the network caused by the simultaneous transmission of any number of broadcasts across the network segment. Such an occurrence can overwhelm network bandwidth, resulting in time-outs.

brute force attack A brute force attack bombards the resource with attempted connections until successful. In the most common brute force attack, different passwords are repeatedly tried until a match that is then used to compromise the network is found.

buffer A storage area dedicated to handling data while in transit. Buffers are used to receive/store sporadic deliveries of data bursts, usually received from faster devices, compensating for the variations in processing speed. Incoming information is stored until everything is received prior to sending data on. Also known as an information buffer.

bursting Some technologies, including ATM and Frame Relay, are considered burstable. This means that user data can exceed the bandwidth normally reserved for the connection; however, this can not exceed the port speed. An example of this would be a 128Kbps Frame Relay CIR on a T1—depending on the vendor, it may be possible to send more than 128Kbps for a short time.

bus topology   A linear LAN architecture in which transmissions from various stations on the network are reproduced over the length of the medium and are accepted by all other stations. *Compare with: ring* and *star.*

bus   Any physical path, typically wires or copper, through which a digital signal can be used to send data from one part of a computer to another.

BUS   broadcast and unknown servers: In LAN emulation, the hardware or software responsible for resolving all broadcasts and packets with unknown (unregistered) addresses into the point-to-point virtual circuits required by ATM. *See also: LANE, LEC, LECS,* and *LES.*

BX.25   AT&T's use of X.25. *See also: X.25.*

bypass mode   An FDDI and Token Ring network operation that deletes an interface.

bypass relay   A device that enables a particular interface in the Token Ring to be closed down and effectively taken off the ring.

byte-oriented protocol   Any type of data-link communication protocol that, in order to mark the boundaries of frames, uses a specific character from the user character set. These protocols have generally been superseded by bit-oriented protocols. *Compare with: bit-oriented protocol.*

cable modem   A cable modem is not actually an analog device, like an asynchronous modem, but rather a customer access device for linking to a broadband cable network. These devices are typically bridges that have a COAX connection to link to the cable network and a 10BaseT Ethernet connection to link to the user's PC.

cable range   In an extended AppleTalk network, the range of numbers allotted for use by existing nodes on the network. The value of the cable range can be anywhere from a single to a sequence of several touching network numbers. Node addresses are determined by their cable range value.

CAC   Connection Admission Control: The sequence of actions executed by every ATM switch while connection setup is performed in order to determine if a request for connection is violating the guarantees of QoS for established connections. Also, CAC is used to route a connection request through an ATM network.

call admission control   A device for managing traffic in ATM networks, determining the possibility of a path containing adequate bandwidth for a requested VCC.

call priority   In circuit-switched systems, the defining priority given to each originating port; it specifies in which order calls will be reconnected. Additionally, call priority identifies which calls are allowed during a bandwidth reservation.

call set-up time   The length of time necessary to effect a switched call between DTE devices.

candidate packets   Packets identified by the MLS-SE as having the potential for establishing a flow cache. This determination is made based on the destination MAC (DMAC) address. The DMAC address must be a MAC addresses associated with a known MLS-RP. *See also: MLS-SE, MLS-SE,* and *MLS-RP.*

CBR   Constant Bit Rate: An ATM Forum QoS class created for use in ATM networks. CBR is used for connections that rely on precision clocking to guarantee trustworthy delivery. *Compare with: ABR* and *VBR.*

CD   Carrier Detect: A signal indicating that an interface is active or that a connection generated by a modem has been established.

CDP   Cisco Discovery Protocol: Cisco's proprietary protocol that is used to tell a neighbor Cisco device about the type of hardware, software version, and active interfaces that the Cisco device is using. It uses a SNAP frame between devices and is not routable.

CDVT   Cell Delay Variation Tolerance: A QoS parameter for traffic management in ATM networks specified when a connection is established. The allowable fluctuation levels for data samples taken by the PCR in CBR transmissions are determined by the CDVT. *See also: CBR* and *PCR.*

cell   In ATM networking, the basic unit of data for switching and multiplexing. Cells have a defined length of 53 bytes, including a 5-byte header that identifies the cell's data stream and 48 bytes of payload. *See also: cell relay.*

cell payload scrambling The method by which an ATM switch maintains framing on some medium-speed edge and trunk interfaces (T3 or E3 circuits). Cell payload scrambling rearranges the data portion of a cell to maintain the line synchronization with certain common bit patterns.

cell relay A technology that uses small packets of fixed size, known as cells. Their fixed length enables cells to be processed and switched in hardware at high speeds, making this technology the foundation for ATM and other high-speed network protocols. *See also: cell.*

Centrex A local exchange carrier service, providing local switching that resembles that of an on-site PBX. Centrex has no on-site switching capability. Therefore, all customer connections return to the CO. *See also: CO.*

CER Cell Error Ratio: In ATM the ratio of the number of transmitted cells having errors to the total number of cells sent in a transmission within a certain span of time.

CGMP Cisco Group Management Protocol: A proprietary protocol developed by Cisco. The router uses CGMP to send multicast membership commands to Catalyst switches.

Challenge Used to provide authentication in Challenge Handshake Authentication Protocol (CHAP) as part of the handshake process. This numerically unique query is sent to authenticate the user without sending the password unencrypted across the wire. *See also: CHAP.*

channelized E1 Operating at 2.048Mpbs, an access link that is sectioned into 29 B-channels and one D-channel, supporting DDR, Frame Relay, and X.25. *Compare with: channelized T1.*

channelized T1 Operating at 1.544Mbps, an access link that is sectioned into 23 B-channels and 1 D-channel of 64Kbps each, where individual channels or groups of channels connect to various destinations, supporting DDR, Frame Relay, and X.25. *Compare with: channelized E1.*

CHAP Challenge Handshake Authentication Protocol: Supported on lines using PPP encapsulation, it is a security feature that identifies the remote end, helping keep out unauthorized users. After CHAP is performed, the router or access server determines whether a given user is permitted access. It is a newer, more secure protocol than PAP. *Compare with: PAP.*

character mode connections Character mode connections are typically terminated at the access server and include Telnet and console connections.

checksum A test for ensuring the integrity of sent data. It is a number calculated from a series of values taken through a sequence of mathematical functions, typically placed at the end of the data from which it is calculated, and then recalculated at the receiving end for verification. *Compare with: CRC.*

choke packet When congestion exists, it is a packet sent to inform a transmitter that it should decrease its sending rate.

CIDR Classless Interdomain Routing: A method supported by classless routing protocols, such as OSPF and BGP4, based on the concept of ignoring the IP class of address, permitting route aggregation and VLSM that enable routers to combine routes in order to minimize the routing information that needs to be conveyed by the primary routers. It allows a group of IP networks to appear to other networks as a unified, larger entity. In CIDR, IP addresses and their subnet masks are written as four dotted octets, followed by a forward slash and the numbering of masking bits (a form of subnet notation shorthand). *See also: BGP4.*

CIP Channel Interface Processor: A channel attachment interface for use in Cisco 7000 series routers that connects a host mainframe to a control unit. This device eliminates the need for an FBP to attach channels.

CIR Committed Information Rate: Averaged over a minimum span of time and measured in bps, a Frame Relay network's agreed-upon minimum rate of transferring information.

circuit switching Used with dial-up networks such as PPP and ISDN. Passes data, but needs to set up the connection first—just like making a phone call.

Cisco FRAD Cisco Frame-Relay Access Device: A Cisco product that supports Cisco IPS Frame Relay SNA services, connecting SDLC devices to Frame Relay without requiring an existing LAN. May be upgraded to a fully functioning multiprotocol router. Can activate conversion from SDLC to Ethernet and Token Ring, but does not support attached LANs. *See also: FRAD.*

CiscoFusion Cisco's name for the internetworking architecture under which its Cisco IOS operates. It is designed to "fuse" together the capabilities of its disparate collection of acquired routers and switches.

Cisco IOS software Cisco Internet Operating System software. The kernel of the Cisco line of routers and switches that supplies shared functionality, scalability, and security for all products under its CiscoFusion architecture. *See also: CiscoFusion.*

CiscoView GUI-based management software for Cisco networking devices, enabling dynamic status, statistics, and comprehensive configuration information. Displays a physical view of the Cisco device chassis and provides device-monitoring functions and fundamental troubleshooting capabilities. May be integrated with a number of SNMP-based network management platforms.

Class A network Part of the Internet Protocol hierarchical addressing scheme. Class A networks have only 8 bits for defining networks and 24 bits for defining hosts on each network.

Class B network Part of the Internet Protocol hierarchical addressing scheme. Class B networks have 16 bits for defining networks and 16 bits for defining hosts on each network.

Class C network Part of the Internet Protocol hierarchical addressing scheme. Class C networks have 24 bits for defining networks and only 8 bits for defining hosts on each network.

classical IP over ATM Defined in RFC 1577, the specification for running IP over ATM that maximizes ATM features. Also known as CIA.

classless routing Routing that sends subnet mask information in the routing updates. Classless routing allows Variable-Length Subnet Mask (VLSM) and supernetting. Routing protocols that support classless routing are RIP version 2, EIGRP, and OSPF.

CLI Command Line Interface: Allows you to configure Cisco routers and switches with maximum flexibility.

clocking   Used in synchronous connections to provide a marker for the start and end of data bytes. This is similar to the beat of a drum with a speaker talking only when the drum is silent.

CLP   Cell Loss Priority: The area in the ATM cell header that determines the likelihood of a cell being dropped during network congestion. Cells with CLP = 0 are considered insured traffic and are not apt to be dropped. Cells with CLP = 1 are considered best-effort traffic that may be dropped during congested episodes, delivering more resources to handle insured traffic.

CLR   Cell Loss Ratio: The ratio of discarded cells to successfully delivered cells in ATM. CLR can be designated a QoS parameter when establishing a connection.

CO   Central Office: The local telephone company office where all loops in a certain area connect and where circuit switching of subscriber lines occurs.

collapsed backbone   A nondistributed backbone where all network segments are connected to each other through an internetworking device. A collapsed backbone can be a virtual network segment at work in a device such as a router, hub, or switch.

collapsed core   A collapsed core is defined as one switch performing both core and distribution layer functions. Typically found in a small network, the functions of the core and distribution layer are still distinct.

collision   The effect of two nodes sending transmissions simultaneously in Ethernet. When they meet on the physical media, the frames from each node collide and are damaged. *See also: collision domain.*

collision domain   The network area in Ethernet over which frames that have collided will spread. Collisions are propagated by hubs and repeaters, but not by LAN switches, routers, or bridges. *See also: collision.*

composite metric   Used with routing protocols, such as IGRP and EIGRP, that use more than one metric to find the best path to a remote network. IGRP and EIGRP both use bandwidth and delay of the line by default. However, Maximum Transmission Unit (MTU), load, and reliability of a link can be used as well.

compression A technique to send more data across a link than would be normally permitted by representing repetitious strings of data with a single marker.

configuration register A 16-bit configurable value stored in hardware or software that determines how Cisco routers function during initialization. In hardware, the bit position is set using a jumper. In software, it is set by specifying specific bit patterns used to set startup options, configured using a hexadecimal value with configuration commands.

congestion Traffic that exceeds the network's ability to handle it.

congestion avoidance To minimize delays, the method an ATM network uses to control traffic entering the system. Lower-priority traffic is discarded at the edge of the network when indicators signal it cannot be delivered, thus using resources efficiently.

congestion collapse The situation that results from the retransmission of packets in ATM networks where little or no traffic successfully arrives at destination points. It usually happens in networks made of switches with ineffective or inadequate buffering capabilities combined with poor packet discard or ABR congestion feedback mechanisms.

connection ID Identifications given to each Telnet session into a router. The `show sessions` command will give you the connections a local router will have to a remote router. The `show users` command will show the connection IDs of users telnetted into your local router.

connectionless Data transfer that occurs without the creating of a virtual circuit. No overhead, best-effort delivery, not reliable. *Contrast with: connection-oriented. See also: virtual circuit.*

connection-oriented Data transfer method that sets up a virtual circuit before any data is transferred. Uses acknowledgments and flow control for reliable data transfer. *Contrast with: connectionless. See also: virtual circuit.*

console port Typically an RJ-45 port on a Cisco router and switch that allows Command-Line Interface capability.

contention media Media access method that is a baseband media; that is, first come, first served. Ethernet is an example of a contention media access.

control direct VCC One of three control connections defined by Phase I LAN Emulation; a bi-directional virtual control connection (VCC) established in ATM by an LEC to an LES. *See also: control distribute VCC.*

control distribute VCC One of three control connections defined by Phase 1 LAN Emulation; a unidirectional virtual control connection (VCC) set up in ATM from an LES to an LEC. Usually, the VCC is a point-to-multipoint connection. *See also: control direct VCC.*

convergence The process required for all routers in an internetwork to update their routing tables and create a consistent view of the network, using the best possible paths. No user data is passed during a convergence time.

core block If you have two or more switch blocks, the Cisco rule of thumb states you need a core block. No routing is performed at the core, only transferring of data. It is a pass-through for the switch block, the server block, and the Internet. The core is responsible for transferring data to and from the switch blocks as quickly as possible. You can build a fast core with a frame, packet, or cell (ATM) network technology.

core layer Top layer in the Cisco three-layer hierarchical model, which helps you design, build, and maintain Cisco hierarchical networks. The core layer passes packets quickly to distribution-layer devices only. No packet filtering should take place at this layer.

cost Also known as path cost, an arbitrary value, based on hop count, bandwidth, or other calculation, that is typically assigned by a network administrator and used by the routing protocol to compare different routes through an internetwork. Routing protocols use cost values to select the best path to a certain destination: the lowest cost identifies the best path. Also known as path cost. *See also: routing metric.*

count to infinity A problem occurring in routing algorithms that are slow to converge where routers keep increasing the hop count to particular networks. To avoid this problem, various solutions have been implemented into each of the different routing protocols. Some of those solutions include defining a maximum hop count (defining infinity), route poising, poison reverse, and split horizon.

CPCS Common Part Convergence Sublayer: One of two AAL sublayers that is service-dependent, it is further segmented into the CS and SAR sublayers. The CPCS prepares data for transmission across the ATM network; it creates the 48-byte payload cells that are sent to the ATM layer. *See also: AAL and ATM layer.*

CPE Customer Premises Equipment: Items such as telephones, modems, and terminals installed at customer locations and connected to the telephone company network.

crankback In ATM, a correction technique used when a node somewhere on a chosen path cannot accept a connection setup request, blocking the request. The path is rolled back to an intermediate node, which then uses GCAC to attempt to find an alternate path to the final destination.

CRC Cyclical Redundancy Check: A methodology that detects errors, whereby the frame recipient makes a calculation by dividing frame contents with a prime binary divisor and compares the remainder to a value stored in the frame by the sending node. *Contrast with: checksum.*

CSMA/CD Carrier Sense Multiple Access Collision Detect: A technology defined by the Ethernet IEEE 802.3 committee. Each device senses the cable for a digital signal before transmitting. Also, CSMA/CD allows all devices on the network to share the same cable, but one at a time. If two devices transmit at the same time, a frame collision will occur and a jamming pattern will be sent; the devices will stop transmitting, wait a predetermined amount of time, and then try to transmit again.

CST Common Spanning Tree: The IEEE uses what is called Common Spanning Tree (CST), which is defined with IEEE 802.1q. The IEEE 802.1q defines one spanning tree instance for all VLANs.

CSU Channel Service Unit: A digital mechanism that connects end-user equipment to the local digital telephone loop. Frequently referred to along with the data service unit as CSU/DSU. *See also: DSU.*

CTD Cell Transfer Delay: For a given connection in ATM, the time period between a cell exit event at the source user-network interface (UNI) and the corresponding cell entry event at the destination. The CTD between these points is the sum of the total inter-ATM transmission delay and the total ATM processing delay.

custom queuing Used by Cisco router IOS to provide a queuing method to slower serial links. Custom queuing allows an administrator to configure the type of traffic that will have priority over the link.

cut-through frame switching A frame-switching technique that flows data through a switch so that the leading edge exits the switch at the output port before the packet finishes entering the input port. Frames will be read, processed, and forwarded by devices that use cut-through switching as soon as the destination address of the frame is confirmed and the outgoing port is identified.

data compression *See: compression.*

data direct VCC A bidirectional point-to-point virtual control connection (VCC) set up between two LECs in ATM and one of three data connections defined by Phase 1 LAN Emulation. Because data direct VCCs do not guarantee QoS, they are generally reserved for UBR and ABR connections. *Compare with: control distribute VCC and control direct VCC.*

data encapsulation The process in which the information in a protocol is wrapped, or contained, in the data section of another protocol. In the OSI reference model, each layer encapsulates the layer immediately above it as the data flows down the protocol stack.

data frame Protocol Data Unit encapsulation at the Data Link layer of the OSI reference model. Encapsulates packets from the Network layer and prepares the data for transmission on a network medium.

datagram A logical collection of information transmitted as a network layer unit over a medium without a previously established virtual circuit. IP datagrams have become the primary information unit of the Internet. At various layers of the OSI reference model, the terms *cell, frame, message, packet,* and *segment* also define these logical information groupings.

data link control layer Layer 2 of the SNA architectural model, it is responsible for the transmission of data over a given physical link and compares somewhat to the data link layer of the OSI model.

data link layer Layer 2 of the OSI reference model, it ensures the trustworthy transmission of data across a physical link and is primarily concerned with physical addressing, line discipline, network topology, error notification, ordered delivery of frames, and flow control. The IEEE has further segmented this layer into the MAC sublayer and the LLC sublayer. Also known as the link layer. Can be compared somewhat to the data link control layer of the SNA model. *See also: application layer, LLC, MAC, network layer, physical layer, presentation layer, session layer,* and *transport layer.*

DCC   Data Country Code: Developed by the ATM Forum, one of two ATM address formats designed for use by private networks. *Compare with: ICD.*

DCE   data communications equipment (as defined by the EIA) or data circuit-terminating equipment (as defined by the ITU-T): The mechanisms and links of a communications network that make up the network portion of the user-to-network interface, such as modems. The DCE supplies the physical connection to the network, forwards traffic, and provides a clocking signal to synchronize data transmission between DTE and DCE devices. *Compare with: DTE.*

D channel   1) Data channel: A full-duplex, 16Kbps (BRI) or 64Kbps (PRI) ISDN channel. *Compare with: B channel, E channel,* and *H channel.* 2) In SNA, anything that provides a connection between the processor and main storage with any peripherals.

DDP   Datagram Delivery Protocol: Used in the AppleTalk suite of protocols as a connectionless protocol that is responsible for sending datagrams through an internetwork.

DDR   dial-on-demand routing: A technique that allows a router to automatically initiate and end a circuit-switched session per the requirements of the sending station. By mimicking keepalives, the router fools the end station into treating the session as active. DDR permits routing over ISDN or telephone lines via a modem or external ISDN terminal adapter.

DE   Discard Eligibility: Used in Frame Relay networks to tell a switch that a frame can be discarded if the switch is too busy. The DE is a field in the frame that is turned on by transmitting routers if the Committed Information Rate (CIR) is oversubscribed or set to 0.

DE bit   The DE bit marks a frame as discard eligible on a Frame Relay network. If a serial link is congested and the Frame Relay network has passed the Committed Information Rate (CIR), then the DE bit will always be on.

default route   The static routing table entry used to direct frames whose next hop is not spelled out in the dynamic routing table.

delay   The time elapsed between a sender's initiation of a transaction and the first response they receive. Also, the time needed to move a packet from its source to its destination over a path. *See also: latency.*

demarc   The demarcation point between the customer premises equipment (CPE) and the telco's carrier equipment.

demodulation   A series of steps that return a modulated signal to its original form. When receiving, a modem demodulates an analog signal to its original digital form (and, conversely, modulates the digital data it sends into an analog signal). *See also: modulation.*

demultiplexing   The process of converting a single multiplex signal, comprising more than one input stream, back into separate output streams. *See also: multiplexing.*

denial-of-service attack   A denial-of-service attack, or DoS, blocks access to a network resource by saturating the device with attacking data. Typically, this is targeted against the link (particularly lower bandwidth links) or the server. DDoS attacks, or distributed denial-of-service attacks, make use of multiple originating attacking resources to saturate a more capable resource.

designated bridge   In the process of forwarding a frame from a segment to the route bridge, the bridge with the lowest path cost.

designated port   Used with the Spanning Tree Protocol (STP) to designate forwarding ports. If there are multiple links to the same network, STP will shut a port down to stop network loops.

designated router   An OSPF router that creates LSAs for a multiaccess network and is required to perform other special tasks in OSPF operations. Multiaccess OSPF networks that maintain a minimum of two attached routers identify one router that is chosen by the OSPF Hello protocol, which makes possible a decrease in the number of adjacencies necessary on a multiaccess network. This in turn reduces the quantity of routing protocol traffic and the physical size of the database.

destination address The address for the network devices that will receive a packet.

dial backup Dial backup connections are typically used to provide redundancy to Frame Relay connections. The backup link is activated over an analog modem.

digital A digital waveform is one where distinct ones and zeros provide the data representation. *See also: analog.*

directed broadcast A data frame or packet that is transmitted to a specific group of nodes on a remote network segment. Directed broadcasts are known by their broadcast address, which is a destination subnet address with all the bits turned on.

discovery mode Also known as dynamic configuration, this technique is used by an AppleTalk interface to gain information from a working node about an attached network. The information is subsequently used by the interface for self-configuration.

distance-vector routing algorithm In order to find the shortest path, this group of routing algorithms repeats on the number of hops in a given route, requiring each router to send its complete routing table with each update, but only to its neighbors. Routing algorithms of this type tend to generate loops, but they are fundamentally simpler than their link-state counterparts. *See also: link-state routing algorithm and SPF.*

distribution layer Middle layer of the Cisco three-layer hierarchical model, which helps you design, install, and maintain Cisco hierarchical networks. The distribution layer is the point where access layer devices connect. Routing is performed at this layer.

distribution lists Access list used to filter incoming and outgoing route table entries on a router.

DLCI Data-Link Connection Identifier: Used to identify virtual circuits in a Frame Relay network.

DNS Domain Name System: Used to resolve host names to IP addresses.

DSAP Destination Service Access Point: The service access point of a network node, specified in the destination field of a packet. *See also: SSAP and SAP.*

DSL Digital Subscriber Line: DSL technologies are used to provide broadband services over a single copper pair, typically to residential customers. Most vendors are providing DSL services at up to 6Mbps downstream, but the technology can support 52Mbps service.

DSR Data Set Ready: When a DCE is powered up and ready to run, this EIA/TIA-232 interface circuit is also engaged.

DSU Data Service Unit: This device is used to adapt the physical interface on a data terminal equipment (DTE) mechanism to a transmission facility such as T1 or E1 and is also responsible for signal timing. It is commonly grouped with the channel service unit and referred to as the CSU/DSU. *See also: CSU.*

DTE data terminal equipment: Any device located at the user end of a user-network interface serving as a destination, a source, or both. DTE includes devices such as multiplexers, protocol translators, and computers. The connection to a data network is made through data channel equipment (DCE) such as a modem, using the clocking signals generated by that device. *See also: DCE.*

DTR data terminal ready: An activated EIA/TIA-232 circuit communicating to the DCE the state of preparedness of the DTE to transmit or receive data.

DUAL Diffusing Update Algorithm: Used in Enhanced IGRP, this convergence algorithm provides loop-free operation throughout an entire route's computation. DUAL grants routers involved in a topology revision the ability to synchronize simultaneously, while routers unaffected by this change are not involved. *See also: Enhanced IGRP.*

DVMRP Distance Vector Multicast Routing Protocol: Based primarily on the Routing Information Protocol (RIP), this Internet gateway protocol implements a common, condensed-mode IP multicast scheme, using IGMP to transfer routing datagrams between its neighbors. *See also: IGMP.*

DXI Data Exchange Interface: Described in RFC 1482, DXI defines the effectiveness of a network device such as a router, bridge, or hub to act as an FEP to an ATM network by using a special DSU that accomplishes packet encapsulation.

dynamic entries Used in layer 2 and 3 devices to create a table of either hardware addresses or logical addresses dynamically.

dynamic routing Also known as adaptive routing, this technique automatically adapts to traffic or physical network revisions.

dynamic VLAN An administrator will create an entry in a special server with the hardware addresses of all devices on the internetwork. The server will then assign dynamically used VLANs.

E1 Generally used in Europe, a wide-area digital transmission scheme carrying data at 2.048Mbps. E1 transmission lines are available for lease from common carriers for private use.

E.164 1) Evolved from standard telephone numbering system, the standard recommended by ITU-T for international telecommunication numbering, particularly in ISDN, SMDS, and BISDN. 2) Label of field in an ATM address containing numbers in E.164 format.

E channel Echo channel: A 64Kbps ISDN control channel used for circuit switching. Specific description of this channel can be found in the 1984 ITU-T ISDN specification, but was dropped from the 1988 version. *See also: B, D,* and *H channels.*

edge device A device that enables packets to be forwarded between legacy interfaces (such as Ethernet and Token Ring) and ATM interfaces based on information in the data link and network layers. An edge device does not take part in the running of any network layer routing protocol; it merely uses the route description protocol in order to get the forwarding information required.

EEPROM Electronically Erasable Programmable Read-Only Memory: Programmed after their manufacture, these nonvolatile memory chips can be erased if necessary using electric power and reprogrammed. *See also: EPROM, PROM.*

EFCI Explicit Forward Congestion Indication: A congestion feedback mode permitted by ABR service in an ATM network. The EFCI may be set by any network element that is in a state of immediate or certain congestion. The destination end-system is able to carry out a protocol that adjusts and lowers the cell rate of the connection based on value of the EFCI. *See also: ABR.*

80/20 rule The 80/20 rule means that 80 percent of the users' traffic should remain on the local network segment and only 20 percent or less should cross the routers or bridges to the other network segments

EIGRP *See: Enhanced IGRP.*

EIP Ethernet Interface Processor: A Cisco 7000 series router interface processor card, supplying 10Mbps AUI ports to support Ethernet Version 1 and Ethernet Version 2 or IEEE 802.3 interfaces with a high-speed data path to other interface processors.

ELAN Emulated LAN: An ATM network configured using a client/server model in order to emulate either an Ethernet or Token Ring LAN. Multiple ELANs can exist at the same time on a single ATM network and are made up of an LAN emulation client (LEC), an LAN Emulation Server (LES), a Broadcast and Unknown Server (BUS), and an LAN Emulation Configuration Server (LECS). ELANs are defined by the LANE specification. *See also: LANE, LEC, LECS, and LES.*

ELAP EtherTalk Link Access Protocol: In an EtherTalk network, the link-access protocol constructed above the standard Ethernet data link layer.

enable packets Packets that complete the flow cache. Once the MLS-SE determines that the packet meets enable criteria, such as source MAC (SMAC) address and destination IP, the flow cache is established and subsequent packets are layer 3 switched. *See also: MLS-SE, MLS-RP.*

encapsulation The technique used by layered protocols in which a layer adds header information to the protocol data unit (PDU) from the layer above. As an example, in Internet terminology, a packet would contain a header from the physical layer, followed by a header from the network layer (IP), followed by a header from the transport layer (TCP), followed by the application protocol data.

encryption The conversion of information into a scrambled form that effectively disguises it to prevent unauthorized access. Every encryption scheme uses some well-defined algorithm, which is reversed at the receiving end by an opposite algorithm in a process known as decryption.

end-to-end VLANs VLANs that span the switch-fabric from end to end; all switches in end-to-end VLANs understand about all configured VLANs. End-to-end VLANs are configured to allow membership based on function, project, department, and so on.

Enhanced IGRP   Enhanced Interior Gateway Routing Protocol: An advanced routing protocol created by Cisco, combining the advantages of link-state and distance-vector protocols. Enhanced IGRP has superior convergence attributes, including high operating efficiency. *See also: IGP, OSPF,* and *RIP.*

enterprise network   A privately owned and operated network that joins most major locations in a large company or organization.

enterprise services   Defined as services provided to all users on the internetwork. Layer 3 switches or routers are required in this scenario because the services must be close to the core and would probably be based in their own subnet. Examples of these services include Internet access, e-mail, and possibly videoconferencing. If the servers that host these enterprise services were placed close to the backbone, all users would have the same distance to them, but this also means that all users' data would have to cross the backbone to get to these services.

EPROM   Erasable Programmable Read-Only Memory: Programmed after their manufacture, these nonvolatile memory chips can be erased if necessary using high-power light and reprogrammed. *See also: EEPROM, PROM.*

error correction   Error correction uses a checksum to detect bit errors in the data stream.

ESF   Extended Superframe: Made up of 24 frames with 192 bits each, with the 193rd bit providing other functions including timing. This is an enhanced version of SF. *See also: SF.*

Ethernet   A baseband LAN specification created by the Xerox Corporation and then improved through joint efforts of Xerox, Digital Equipment Corporation, and Intel. Ethernet is similar to the IEEE 802.3 series standard and, using CSMA/CD, operates over various types of cables at 10Mbps. *Also called: DIX (Digital/Intel/Xerox) Ethernet. See also: 10BaseT, FastEthernet,* and *IEEE.*

EtherTalk   A data-link product from Apple Computer that permits AppleTalk networks to be connected by Ethernet.

excess rate   In ATM networking, traffic exceeding a connection's insured rate. The excess rate is the maximum rate less the insured rate. Depending on the availability of network resources, excess traffic can be discarded during congestion episodes. *Compare with: maximum rate.*

expansion The procedure of directing compressed data through an algorithm, restoring information to its original size.

expedited delivery An option that can be specified by one protocol layer, communicating either with other layers or with the identical protocol layer in a different network device, requiring that identified data be processed faster.

explorer packet An SNA packet transmitted by a source Token Ring device to find the path through a source-route-bridged network.

extended IP access list IP access list that filters the network by logical address, protocol field in the Network layer header, and even the port field in the Transport layer header.

extended IPX access list IPX access list that filters the network by logical IPX address, protocol field in the Network layer header, or even socket number in the Transport layer header.

Extended Setup Used in setup mode to configure the router with more detail than Basic Setup mode. Allows multiple-protocol support and interface configuration.

external route processor A router that is external to the switch. An external layer 3 routing device can be used to provide routing between VLANs.

failure domain The region in which a failure has occurred in a Token Ring. When a station gains information that a serious problem, such as a cable break, has occurred with the network, it sends a beacon frame that includes the station reporting the failure, its NAUN, and everything between. This defines the failure domain. Beaconing then initiates the procedure known as autoreconfiguration. *See also: autoreconfiguration* and *beacon.*

fallback In ATM networks, this mechanism is used for scouting a path if it isn't possible to locate one using customary methods. The device relaxes requirements for certain characteristics, such as delay, in an attempt to find a path that meets a certain set of the most important requirements.

Fast EtherChannel   Fast EtherChannel uses load distribution to share the links called a bundle, which is a group of links managed by the Fast Ether-Channel process. Should one link in the bundle fail, the Ethernet Bundle Controller (EBC) informs the Enhanced Address Recognition Logic (EARL) ASIC of the failure, and the EARL in turn ages out all addresses learned on that link. The EBC and the EARL use hardware to recalculate the source and destination address pair on a different link.

FastEthernet   Any Ethernet specification with a speed of 100Mbps. FastEthernet is 10 times faster than 10BaseT, while retaining qualities like MAC mechanisms, MTU, and frame format. These similarities make it possible for existing 10BaseT applications and management tools to be used on FastEthernet networks. FastEthernet is based on an extension of IEEE 802.3 specification (IEEE 802.3u). *Compare with: Ethernet. See also: 100BaseT, 100BaseTX,* and *IEEE.*

fast switching   A Cisco feature that uses a route cache to speed packet switching through a router. *Contrast with: process switching.*

FDM   Frequency-Division Multiplexing: A technique that permits information from several channels to be assigned bandwidth on one wire based on frequency. *See also: TDM, ATDM,* and *statistical multiplexing.*

FDDI   Fiber Distributed Data Interface: A LAN standard, defined by ANSI X3T9.5 that can run at speeds up to 200Mbps and uses token-passing media access on fiber-optic cable. For redundancy, FDDI can use a dual-ring architecture.

FECN   Forward Explicit Congestion Notification: A bit set by a Frame Relay network that informs the DTE receptor that congestion was encountered along the path from source to destination. A device receiving frames with the FECN bit set can ask higher-priority protocols to take flow-control action as needed. *See also: BECN.*

FEIP   FastEthernet Interface Processor: An interface processor employed on Cisco 7000 series routers, supporting up to two 100Mbps 100BaseT ports.

firewall   A barrier purposefully erected between any connected public networks and a private network, made up of a router or access server or several routers or access servers, that uses access lists and other methods to ensure the security of the private network.

Flash Electronically Erasable Programmable Read-Only Memory (EEPROM). Used to hold the Cisco IOS in a router by default.

flash memory Developed by Intel and licensed to other semiconductor manufacturers, it is nonvolatile storage that can be erased electronically and reprogrammed, physically located on an EEPROM chip. Flash memory permits software images to be stored, booted, and rewritten as needed. Cisco routers and switches use flash memory to hold the IOS by default. *See also: EPROM, EEPROM.*

flat network Network that is one large collision domain and one large broadcast domain.

flooding When traffic is received on an interface, it is then transmitted to every interface connected to that device with the exception of the interface from which the traffic originated. This technique can be used for traffic transfer by bridges and switches throughout the network.

flow A shortcut or MLS cache entry that is defined by the packet properties. Packets with identical properties belong to the same flow. *See also: MLS.*

flow control A methodology used to ensure that receiving units are not overwhelmed with data from sending devices. Pacing, as it is called in IBM networks, means that when buffers at a receiving unit are full, a message is transmitted to the sending unit to temporarily halt transmissions until all the data in the receiving buffer has been processed and the buffer is again ready for action.

FRAD Frame Relay Access Device: Any device affording a connection between a LAN and a Frame Relay WAN. *See also: Cisco FRAD, FRAS.*

fragment Any portion of a larger packet that has been intentionally segmented into smaller pieces. A packet fragment does not necessarily indicate an error and can be intentional. *See also: fragmentation.*

fragmentation The process of intentionally segmenting a packet into smaller pieces when sending data over an intermediate network medium that cannot support the larger packet size.

FragmentFree   LAN switch type that reads into the data section of a frame to make sure fragmentation did not occur. Sometimes called modified cut-through.

frame   A logical unit of information sent by the data link layer over a transmission medium. The term often refers to the header and trailer, employed for synchronization and error control, that surround the data contained in the unit.

Frame Relay   A more efficient replacement of the X.25 protocol (an unrelated packet relay technology that guarantees data delivery). Frame Relay is an industry-standard, shared-access, best-effort, switched data-link layer encapsulation that services multiple virtual circuits and protocols between connected mechanisms.

Frame Relay bridging   Defined in RFC 1490, this bridging method uses the identical spanning–tree algorithm as other bridging operations but permits packets to be encapsulated for transmission across a Frame Relay network.

Frame Relay switching   When a router at a service provider provides packet switching for Frame Relay packets.

frame tagging   VLANs can span multiple connected switches, which Cisco calls a switch-fabric. Switches within this switch-fabric must keep track of frames as they are received on the switch ports, and they must keep track of the VLAN they belong to as the frames traverse this switch-fabric. Frame tagging performs this function. Switches can then direct frames to the appropriate port.

framing   Encapsulation at the Data Link layer of the OSI model. It is called framing because the packet is encapsulated with both a header and a trailer.

FRAS   Frame Relay Access Support: A feature of Cisco IOS software that enables SDLC, Ethernet, Token Ring, and Frame Relay-attached IBM devices to be linked with other IBM mechanisms on a Frame Relay network. *See also: FRAD.*

frequency   The number of cycles of an alternating current signal per time unit, measured in hertz (cycles per second).

FSIP Fast Serial Interface Processor: The Cisco 7000 routers' default serial interface processor, it provides four or eight high-speed serial ports.

FTP File Transfer Protocol: The TCP/IP protocol used for transmitting files between network nodes, it supports a broad range of file types and is defined in RFC 959. *See also: TFTP.*

full duplex The capacity to transmit information between a sending station and a receiving unit at the same time. *See also: half duplex.*

full mesh A type of network topology where every node has either a physical or a virtual circuit linking it to every other network node. A full mesh supplies a great deal of redundancy but is typically reserved for network backbones because of its expense. *See also: partial mesh.*

Gigabit EtherChannel *See Fast EtherChannel.*

Gigabit Ethernet 1000Mbps version of the IEEE 802.3. FastEthernet offers a speed increase of 10 times that of the 10BaseT Ethernet specification while preserving qualities such as frame format, MAC, mechanisms and MTU.

GNS Get Nearest Server: On an IPX network, a request packet sent by a customer for determining the location of the nearest active server of a given type. An IPX network client launches a GNS request to get either a direct answer from a connected server or a response from a router disclosing the location of the service on the internetwork to the GNS. GNS is part of IPX and SAP. *See also: IPX* and *SAP.*

grafting A process that activates an interface that has been deactivated by the pruning process. It is initiated by an IGMP membership report sent to the router.

GRE Generic Routing Encapsulation: A tunneling protocol created by Cisco with the capacity for encapsulating a wide variety of protocol packet types inside IP tunnels, thereby generating a virtual point-to-point connection to Cisco routers across an IP network at remote points. IP tunneling using GRE permits network expansion across a single-protocol backbone environment by linking multiprotocol subnetworks in a single-protocol backbone environment.

Group of Four Used by Cisco Local Management Interface on Frame Relay networks to manage the permanent virtual circuits (PVCs). *See also: PVC.*

guard band The unused frequency area found between two communications channels, furnishing the space necessary to avoid interference between the two.

half duplex The capacity to transfer data in only one direction at a time between a sending unit and receiving unit. *See also: full duplex.*

handshake Any series of transmissions exchanged between two or more devices on a network to ensure synchronized operations.

H channel High-speed channel: A full-duplex, ISDN primary rate channel operating at a speed of 384Kbps. *See also: B, D,* and *E channels.*

HDLC High-Level Data Link Control: Using frame characters, including checksums, HDLC designates a method for data encapsulation on synchronous serial links and is the default encapsulation for Cisco routers. HDLC is a bit-oriented synchronous data-link layer protocol created by ISO and derived from SDLC. However, most HDLC vendor implementations (including Cisco's) are proprietary. *See also: SDLC.*

helper address The unicast address specified, which instructs the Cisco router to change the client's local broadcast request for a service into a directed unicast to the server.

hierarchical addressing Any addressing plan employing a logical chain of commands to determine location. IP addresses are made up of a hierarchy of network numbers, subnet numbers, and host numbers to direct packets to the appropriate destination.

hierarchical network A multi-segment network configuration providing only one path through intermediate segments between source segments and destination segments.

hierarchy *See: hierarchical network.*

HIP HSSI Interface Processor: An interface processor used on Cisco 7000 series routers, providing one HSSI port that supports connections to ATM, SMDS, Frame Relay, or private lines at speeds up to T3 or E3.

holddown The state a route is placed in so that routers can neither advertise the route nor accept advertisements about it for a defined time period. Holddown is used to surface bad information about a route from all routers in the network. A route is generally placed in holddown when one of its links fails.

hop The movement of a packet between any two network nodes. *See also: hop count.*

hop count A routing metric that calculates the distance between a source and a destination. RIP employs hop count as its sole metric. *See also: hop* and *RIP.*

host address Logical address configured by an administrator or server on a device. Logically identifies this device on an internetwork.

HSCI High-Speed Communication Interface: Developed by Cisco, a single-port interface that provides full-duplex synchronous serial communications capability at speeds up to 52Mbps.

HSRP Hot Standby Router Protocol: A protocol that provides high network availability and provides nearly instantaneous hardware fail-over without administrator intervention. It generates a Hot Standby router group, including a lead router that lends its services to any packet being transferred to the Hot Standby address. If the lead router fails, it will be replaced by any of the other routers—the standby routers—that monitor it.

HSSI High-Speed Serial Interface: A network standard physical connector for high-speed serial linking over a WAN at speeds of up to 52Mbps.

hubs Physical-layer devices that are really just multiple port repeaters. When an electronic digital signal is received on a port, the signal is reamplified or regenerated and forwarded out all segments except the segment from which the signal was received.

ICD International Code Designator: Adapted from the subnetwork model of addressing, this assigns the mapping of network layer addresses to ATM addresses. HSSI is one of two ATM formats for addressing created by the ATM Forum to be utilized with private networks. *See also: DCC.*

ICMP Internet Control Message Protocol: Documented in RFC 792, it is a network layer Internet protocol for the purpose of reporting errors and providing information pertinent to IP packet procedures.

IEEE Institute of Electrical and Electronics Engineers: A professional organization that, among other activities, defines standards in a number of fields within computing and electronics, including networking and communications. IEEE standards are the predominant LAN standards used today throughout the industry. Many protocols are commonly known by the reference number of the corresponding IEEE standard.

IEEE 802.1 The IEEE committee specification that defines the bridging group. The specification for STP (Spanning Tree Protocol) is IEEE 802.1d. The STP uses SPA (spanning-tree algorithm) to find and prevent network loops in bridged networks. The specification for VLAN trunking is IEEE 802.1q.

IEEE 802.3 The IEEE committee specification that defines the Ethernet group, specifically the original 10Mbps standard. Ethernet is a LAN protocol that specifies physical layer and MAC sublayer media access. IEEE 802.3 uses CSMA/CD to provide access for many devices on the same network. FastEthernet is defined as 802.3u, and Gigabit Ethernet is defined as 802.3q. *See also: CSMA/CD.*

IEEE 802.5 IEEE committee that defines Token Ring media access.

IGMP Internet Group Management Protocol: Employed by IP hosts, the protocol that reports their multicast group memberships to an adjacent multicast router. The first version, IGMPv1, allows hosts to subscribe to or join specified multicast groups. Enhancements were made to IGMPv2 to facilitate a host-initiated leave process.

IGMP Join process The process by which hosts may join a multicast session outside of the Membership Query interval.

IGMP Leave process IGMPv1 does not have a formal leave process; a period of three query intervals must pass with no host confirmation before the interface is deactivated. IGMPv2 does allow the host to initiate the leave process immediately.

IGMP Query process The router uses IGMP to query hosts for Membership Reports, thus managing multicast on its interfaces.

IGP Interior Gateway Protocol: Any protocol used by the Internet to exchange routing data within an independent system. Examples include RIP, IGRP, and OSPF.

ILMI Integrated (or Interim) Local Management Interface. A specification created by the ATM Forum, designated for the incorporation of network-management capability into the ATM UNI. Integrated Local Management Interface cells provide for automatic configuration between ATM systems. In LAN emulation, ILMI can provide sufficient information for the ATM end station to find an LECS. In addition, ILMI provides the ATM NSAP (Network Service Access Point) prefix information to the end station.

in-band management In-band management is the management of a network device "through" the network. Examples include using Simple Network Management Protocol (SNMP) or Telnet directly via the local LAN. *Compare with: out-of-band management.*

in-band signaling Configuration of a router from within the network. Examples are Telnet, Simple Network Management Protocol (SNMP), or a Network Management Station (NMS).

insured burst In an ATM network, it is the largest, temporarily permitted data burst exceeding the insured rate on a PVC and not tagged by the traffic policing function for being dropped if network congestion occurs. This insured burst is designated in bytes or cells.

interarea routing Routing between two or more logical areas. *Contrast with: intra-area routing. See also: area.*

interface processor Any of several processor modules used with Cisco 7000 series routers. *See also: AIP, CIP, EIP, FEIP, HIP, MIP, and TRIP.*

internal route processors Route Switch Modules (RSM) and Route Switch Feature Cards (RSFC) are called internal route processors because the processing of layer 3 packets is internal to a switch.

Internet The global "network of networks," whose popularity has exploded in the last few years. Originally a tool for collaborative academic research, it has become a medium for exchanging and distributing information of all kinds. The Internet's need to link disparate computer platforms and technologies has led to the development of uniform protocols and standards that have also found widespread use within corporate LANs. *See also: TCP/IP* and *MBONE*.

internet Before the rise in the use of the Internet, this lowercase form was shorthand for "internetwork" in the generic sense. Now rarely used. *See also: internetwork*.

Internet protocol Any protocol belonging to the TCP/IP protocol stack. *See also: TCP/IP*.

internetwork Any group of private networks interconnected by routers and other mechanisms, typically operating as a single entity.

internetworking Broadly, anything associated with the general task of linking networks to each other. The term encompasses technologies, procedures, and products. When you connect networks to a router, you are creating an internetwork.

inter-VLAN routing Cisco has created the proprietary protocol Inter-Switch Link (ISL) to allow routing between VLANs with only one Ethernet interface. To run ISL, you need to have two VLAN-capable FastEthernet or Gigabit Ethernet devices like a Cisco 5000 switch and a 7000 series router.

intra-area routing Routing that occurs within a logical area. *Contrast with: interarea routing*.

intruder detection Intruder detection systems operate by monitoring the data flow for characteristics consistent with security threats. In this manner, an intruder can be monitored or blocked from access. One trigger for an intruder detection system is multiple ping packets from a single resource in a brief period of time.

Inverse ARP Inverse Address Resolution Protocol: A technique by which dynamic mappings are constructed in a network, allowing a device such as a router to locate the logical network address and associate it with a permanent virtual circuit (PVC). Commonly used in Frame Relay to determine the far-end node's TCP/IP address by sending the Inverse ARP request to the local DLCI.

IP Internet Protocol: Defined in RFC 791, it is a network layer protocol that is part of the TCP/IP stack and allows connectionless service. IP furnishes an array of features for addressing, type-of-service specification, fragmentation and reassembly, and security.

IP address Often called an Internet address, this is an address uniquely identifying any device (host) on the Internet (or any TCP/IP network). Each address consists of four octets (32 bits), represented as decimal numbers separated by periods (a format known as "dotted-decimal"). Every address is made up of a network number, an optional subnetwork number, and a host number. The network and subnetwork numbers together are used for routing, while the host number addresses an individual host within the network or subnetwork. The network and subnetwork information is extracted from the IP address using the subnet mask. There are five classes of IP addresses (A–E), which allocate different numbers of bits to the network, subnetwork, and host portions of the address. *See also: CIDR, IP,* and *subnet mask*.

IPCP IP Control Program: The protocol used to establish and configure IP over PPP. *See also: IP* and *PPP*.

IP multicast A technique for routing that enables IP traffic to be reproduced from one source to several endpoints or from multiple sources to many destinations. Instead of transmitting only one packet to each individual point of destination, one packet is sent to a multicast group specified by only one IP endpoint address for the group.

IPX Internetwork Packet Exchange: Network layer protocol (Layer 3) used in Novell NetWare networks for transferring information from servers to workstations. Similar to IP and XNS.

IPXCP IPX Control Program: The protocol used to establish and configure IPX over PPP. *See also: IPX* and *PPP*.

IPX spoofing Provides IPX RIP/SAP traffic without requiring a connection to the opposing network. This allows a per-minute tariffed link, such as ISDN or analog phone, to support IPX without requiring the link to remain active.

IPXWAN Protocol used for new WAN links to provide and negotiate line options on the link using IPX. After the link is up and the options have been agreed upon by the two end-to-end links, normal IPX transmission begins.

IRDP ICMP Router Discovery Protocol: Allows hosts to use the Internet Control Message Protocol (ICMP) to find a new path when the primary router becomes unavailable. IRDP is an extension to the ICMP protocol and not a dynamic routing protocol. This ICMP extension allows routers to advertise default routes to end stations.

ISDN Integrated Services Digital Network: Offered as a service by telephone companies, a communication protocol that allows telephone networks to carry data, voice, and other digital traffic. *See also: BISDN, BRI,* and *PRI*.

ISL routing Inter-Switch Link routing is a Cisco proprietary method of frame tagging in a switched internetwork. Frame tagging is a way to identify the VLAN membership of a frame as it traverses a switched internetwork.

isochronous transmission Asynchronous data transfer over a synchronous data link, requiring a constant bit rate for reliable transport. *Compare with: asynchronous transmission* and *synchronous transmission*.

ITU-T International Telecommunication Union Telecommunication Standardization Sector: This is a group of engineers that develops worldwide standards for telecommunications technologies.

LAN local area network: Broadly, any network linking two or more computers and related devices within a limited geographical area (up to a few kilometers). LANs are typically high-speed, low-error networks within a company. Cabling and signaling at the physical and data link layers of the OSI are dictated by LAN standards. Ethernet, FDDI, and Token Ring are among the most popular LAN technologies. *Compare with: MAN.*

LANE LAN emulation: The technology that allows an ATM network to operate as a LAN backbone. To do so, the ATM network is required to provide multicast and broadcast support, address mapping (MAC-to-ATM), SVC management, in addition to an operable packet format. Additionally, LANE defines Ethernet and Token Ring ELANs. *See also: ELAN.*

LAN switch A high-speed, multiple-interface transparent bridging mechanism, transmitting packets between segments of data links, usually referred to specifically as an Ethernet switch. LAN switches transfer traffic based on MAC addresses. Multilayer switches are a type of high-speed, special-purpose, hardware-based router. *See also: multilayer switch* and *store-and-forward packet switching.*

LAPB Link Accessed Procedure, Balanced: A bit-oriented data-link layer protocol that is part of the X.25 stack and has its origin in SDLC. *See also: SDLC* and *X.25.*

LAPD Link Access Procedure on the D channel. The ISDN data-link layer protocol used specifically for the D channel and defined by ITU-T Recommendations Q.920 and Q.921. LAPD evolved from LAPB and is created to comply with the signaling requirements of ISDN basic access.

latency Broadly, the time it takes a data packet to get from one location to another. In specific networking contexts, it can mean either 1) the time elapsed (delay) between the execution of a request for access to a network by a device and the time the mechanism actually is permitted transmission, or 2) the time elapsed between when a mechanism receives a frame and the time that frame is forwarded out of the destination port.

layer 2 switching Layer 2 switching is hardware based, which means it uses the MAC address from the hosts' NIC cards to filter the network. Switches use Application-Specific Integrated Circuits (ASICs) to build and maintain filter tables. It is OK to think of a layer 2 switch as a multiport bridge

layer 3 switch *See: multilayer switch.*

layered architecture Industry standard way of creating applications to work on a network. Layered architecture allows the application developer to make changes in only one layer instead of the whole program.

LCP Link Control Protocol: The protocol designed to establish, configure, and test data link connections for use by PPP. *See also: PPP.*

leaky bucket An analogy for the basic cell rate algorithm (GCRA) used in ATM networks for checking the conformance of cell flows from a user or network. The bucket's "hole" is understood to be the prolonged rate at which cells can be accommodated, and the "depth" is the tolerance for cell bursts over a certain time period.

learning bridge A bridge that transparently builds a dynamic database of MAC addresses and the interfaces associated with each address. Transparent bridges help to reduce traffic congestion on the network.

LE ARP LAN Emulation Address Resolution Protocol: The protocol providing the ATM address that corresponds to a MAC address.

leased lines Permanent connections between two points leased from the telephone companies.

LEC LAN Emulation Client: Software providing the emulation of the link layer interface that allows the operation and communication of all higher-level protocols and applications to continue. The LEC client runs in all ATM devices, which include hosts, servers, bridges, and routers. The LANE client is responsible for address resolution, data transfer, address caching, interfacing to the emulated LAN, and driver support for higher-level services. *See also: ELAN* and *LES.*

LECS LAN Emulation Configuration Server: An important part of emulated LAN services, providing the configuration data that is furnished upon request from the LES. These services include address registration for Integrated Local Management Interface (ILMI) support, configuration support for the LES addresses and their corresponding emulated LAN identifiers, and an interface to the emulated LAN. *See also: LES* and *ELAN.*

LES LAN Emulation Server: The central LANE component that provides the initial configuration data for each connecting LEC. The LES typically is located on either an ATM-integrated router or a switch. Responsibilities of the LES include configuration and support for the LEC, address registration for the LEC, database storage and response concerning ATM addresses, and interfacing to the emulated LAN *See also: ELAN, LEC,* and *LECS.*

link compression *See: compression.*

link-state routing algorithm A routing algorithm that allows each router to broadcast or multicast information regarding the cost of reaching all its neighbors to every node in the internetwork. Link-state algorithms provide a consistent view of the network and are therefore not vulnerable to routing loops. However, this is achieved at the cost of somewhat greater difficulty in computation and more widespread traffic (compared with distance-vector routing algorithms). *See also: distance-vector routing algorithm.*

LLAP LocalTalk Link Access Protocol: In a LocalTalk environment, the data link-level protocol that manages node-to-node delivery of data. This protocol provides node addressing and management of bus access, and it also controls data sending and receiving to assure packet length and integrity.

LLC Logical Link Control: Defined by the IEEE, the higher of two data-link layer sublayers. LLC is responsible for error detection (but not correction), flow control, framing, and software-sublayer addressing. The predominant LLC protocol, IEEE 802.2, defines both connectionless and connection-oriented operations. *See also: data link layer* and *MAC.*

LMI An enhancement to the original Frame Relay specification. Among the features it provides are a keepalive mechanism, a multicast mechanism, global addressing, and a status mechanism.

LNNI LAN Emulation Network-to-Network Interface: In the Phase 2 LANE specification, an interface that supports communication between the server components within one ELAN.

local explorer packet In a Token Ring SRB network, a packet generated by an end system to find a host linked to the local ring. If no local host can be found, the end system will produce one of two solutions: a spanning explorer packet or an all-routes explorer packet.

local loop Connection from a demarcation point to the closest switching office.

local services Users trying to get to network services that are located on the same subnet or network are defined as local services. Users do not cross layer 3 devices and the network services are in the same broadcast domain as the users. This type of traffic never crosses the backbone.

LocalTalk Utilizing CSMA/CD, in addition to supporting data transmission at speeds of 230.4Kbps, LocalTalk is Apple Computer's proprietary baseband protocol, operating at the data link and physical layers of the OSI reference model.

local VLANs Local VLANs are configured by geographic location; these locations can be a building or just a closet in a building, depending on switch size. Geographically configured VLANs are designed around the fact that the business or corporation is using centralized resources, like a server farm.

loop avoidance   If multiple connections between switches are created for redundancy, network loops can occur. STP is used to stop network loops and allow redundancy.

LSA   link-state advertisement: Contained inside of link-state packets (LSPs), these advertisements are usually multicast packets, containing information about neighbors and path costs, that are employed by link-state protocols. Receiving routers use LSAs to maintain their link-state databases and, ultimately, routing tables.

LUNI   LAN Emulation User-to-Network Interface: Defining the interface between the LAN Emulation Client (LEC) and the LAN Emulation Server, LUNI is the ATM Forum's standard for LAN Emulation on ATM networks. *See also: LES* and *LECS.*

LZW algorithm   A data compression process named for its inventors, Lempel, Ziv, and Welch. The algorithm works by finding longer and longer strings of data to compress with shorter representations.

MAC   Media Access Control: The lower sublayer in the data link layer, it is responsible for hardware addressing, media access, and error detection of frames. *See also: data link layer* and *LLC.*

MAC address   A data-link layer hardware address that every port or device needs in order to connect to a LAN segment. These addresses are used by various devices in the network for accurate location of logical addresses. MAC addresses are defined by the IEEE standard and their length is six characters, typically using the burned-in address (BIA) of the local LAN interface. Variously called hardware address, physical address, burned-in address, or MAC-layer address.

MacIP   In AppleTalk, the network layer protocol encapsulating IP packets in Datagram Delivery Protocol (DDP) packets. MacIP also supplies substitute ARP services.

MAN   metropolitan area network: Any network that encompasses a metropolitan area; that is, an area typically larger than a LAN but smaller than a WAN. *See also: LAN.*

Manchester encoding   A method for digital coding in which a mid-bit–time transition is employed for clocking, and a 1 (one) is denoted by a high voltage level during the first half of the bit time. This scheme is used by Ethernet and IEEE 802.3.

maximum burst   Specified in bytes or cells, the largest burst of information exceeding the insured rate that will be permitted on an ATM permanent virtual connection for a short time and will not be dropped even if it goes over the specified maximum rate. *Compare with: insured burst. See also: maximum rate.*

maximum rate   The maximum permitted data throughput on a particular virtual circuit, equal to the total of insured and uninsured traffic from the traffic source. Should traffic congestion occur, uninsured information may be deleted from the path. Measured in bits or cells per second, the maximum rate represents the highest throughput of data the virtual circuit is ever able to deliver and cannot exceed the media rate. *Compare with: excess rate. See also: maximum burst.*

MBS   Maximum Burst Size: In an ATM signaling message, this metric, coded as a number of cells, is used to convey the burst tolerance.

MBONE   multicast backbone: The multicast backbone of the Internet, it is a virtual multicast network made up of multicast LANs, including point-to-point tunnels interconnecting them.

MCDV   Maximum Cell Delay Variation: The maximum two-point CDV objective across a link or node for the identified service category in an ATM network. The MCDV is one of four link metrics that are exchanged using PTSPs to verify the available resources of an ATM network. Only one MCDV value is assigned to each traffic class.

MCLR   Maximum Cell Loss Ratio: The maximum ratio of cells in an ATM network that fail to transit a link or node compared with the total number of cells that arrive at the link or node. MCDV is one of four link metrics that are exchanged using PTSPs to verify the available resources of an ATM network. The MCLR applies to cells in VBR and CBR traffic classes whose CLP bit is set to zero. *See also: CBR, CLP, and VBR.*

MCR Minimum Cell Rate: A parameter determined by the ATM Forum for traffic management of the ATM networks. MCR is specifically defined for ABR transmissions and specifies the minimum value for the allowed cell rate (ACR). *See also: ACR* and *PCR.*

MCTD Maximum Cell Transfer Delay: In an ATM network, the total of the maximum cell delay variation and the fixed delay across the link or node. MCTD is one of four link metrics that are exchanged using PNNI topology state packets to verify the available resources of an ATM network. There is one MCTD value assigned to each traffic class. *See also: MCDV.*

MIB Management Information Base: Used with SNMP management software to gather information from remote devices. The management station can poll the remote device for information, or the MIB running on the remote station can be programmed to send information on a regular basis.

MIP Multichannel Interface Processor: The resident interface processor on Cisco 7000 series routers, providing up to two channelized T1 or E1 connections by serial cables connected to a CSU. The two controllers are capable of providing 24 T1 or 30 E1 channel groups, with each group being introduced to the system as a serial interface that can be configured individually.

mips millions of instructions per second: A measure of processor speed.

MLP Multilink PPP: A technique used to split, recombine, and sequence datagrams across numerous logical data links.

MLS Multi-Layer Switching: Switching normally takes place at layer 2. When layer 3 information is allowed to be cached, layer 2 devices have the capability of rewriting and forwarding frames based on the layer 3 information.

MLSP Multilayer Switching Protocol: A protocol that runs on the router and allows it to communicate to the MLS-SE regarding topology or security changes.

MLS-RP Multilayer Switching Route Processor: An MLS-capable router or an RSM (Route Switch Module) installed in the switch. *See also: RSM, MLS.*

MLS-SE Multilayer Switching Switching Engine: An MLS-capable switch (a 5000 with an NFFC or a 6000 with an MSFC and PFC). *See also: MLS, NFFC, MSFC, PFC.*

MMP Multichassis Multilink PPP: A protocol that supplies MLP support across multiple routers and access servers. MMP enables several routers and access servers to work as a single, large dial-up pool with one network address and ISDN access number. MMP successfully supports packet fragmenting and reassembly when the user connection is split between two physical access devices.

modem modulator-demodulator: A device that converts digital signals to analog and vice-versa so that digital information can be transmitted over analog communication facilities, such as voice-grade telephone lines. This is achieved by converting digital signals at the source to analog for transmission and reconverting the analog signals back into digital form at the destination. *See also: modulation* and *demodulation.*

modemcap database Stores modem initialization strings on the router for use in auto-detection and configuration.

modem eliminator A mechanism that makes possible a connection between two DTE devices without modems by simulating the commands and physical signaling required.

modulation The process of modifying some characteristic of an electrical signal, such as amplitude (AM) or frequency (FM), in order to represent digital or analog information. *See also: AM.*

MOSPF Multicast OSPF: An extension of the OSPF unicast protocol that enables IP multicast routing within the domain. *See also: OSPF.*

MP bonding MultiPoint bonding: A process of linking two or more physical connections into a single logical channel. This may use two or more analog lines and two or more modems, for example.

MPOA Multiprotocol over ATM: An effort by the ATM Forum to standardize how existing and future network-layer protocols such as IP, Ipv6, AppleTalk, and IPX run over an ATM network with directly attached hosts, routers, and multilayer LAN switches.

MSFC Multilayer Switch Feature Card: A route processor (parallel to an RSM, or Route Switch Module) that is installed as a daughter card on Cisco Catalyst 6000 series switches. *See also: RSM.*

mtrace (multicast traceroute) Used to establish the SPT for a specified multicast group.

MTU maximum transmission unit: The largest packet size, measured in bytes, that an interface can handle.

multicast Broadly, any communication between a single sender and multiple receivers. Unlike broadcast messages, which are sent to all addresses on a network, multicast messages are sent to a defined subset of the network addresses; this subset has a group multicast address, which is specified in the packet's destination address field. *See also: broadcast, directed broadcast.*

multicast address A single address that points to more than one device on the network by specifying a special non-existent MAC address specified in that particular multicast protocol. Identical to group address. *See also: multicast.*

multicast group A group set up to receive messages from a source. These groups can be established based on Frame Relay or IP in the TCP/IP protocol suite, as well as other networks.

multicast send VCC A two-directional point-to-point virtual control connection (VCC) arranged by an LEC to a BUS, it is one of the three types of informational link specified by phase 1 LANE. *See also: control distribute VCC* and *control direct VCC.*

multilayer switch A highly specialized, high-speed, hardware-based type of LAN router, the device filters and forwards packets based on their Layer 2 MAC addresses and Layer 3 network addresses. It's possible that even Layer 4 can be read. Sometimes called a Layer 3 switch. *See also: LAN switch.*

multilayer switching Multilayer switching combines layer 2, 3, and 4 switching technology and provides very high-speed scalability with low latency. This is provided by huge filter tables based on the criteria designed by the network administrator.

multiplexing The process of converting several logical signals into a single physical signal for transmission across one physical channel. *Contrast with: demultiplexing.*

NAK negative acknowledgment: A response sent from a receiver, telling the sender that the information was not received or contained errors. *Compare with: acknowledgment.*

NAT Network Address Translation: An algorithm instrumental in minimizing the requirement for globally unique IP addresses, permitting an organization whose addresses are not all globally unique to connect to the Internet, regardless, by translating those addresses into globally routable address space.

NBP Name Binding Protocol: In AppleTalk, the transport-level protocol that interprets a socket client's name, entered as a character string, into the corresponding DDP address. NBP gives AppleTalk protocols the capacity to discern user-defined zones and names of mechanisms by showing and keeping translation tables that map names to their corresponding socket addresses.

NCP Network Control Protocol: A protocol at the Logical Link Control sublayer of the Data Link layer used in the PPP stack. It is used to allow multiple Network layer protocols to run over a nonproprietary HDLC serial encapsulation.

neighboring routers Two routers in OSPF that have interfaces to a common network. On networks with multiaccess, these neighboring routers are dynamically discovered using the Hello protocol of OSPF.

NetBEUI NetBIOS Extended User Interface: An improved version of the NetBIOS protocol used in a number of network operating systems including LAN Manager, Windows NT, LAN Server, and Windows for Workgroups, implementing the OSI LLC2 protocol. NetBEUI formalizes the transport frame not standardized in NetBIOS and adds more functions. *See also: OSI.*

NetBIOS Network Basic Input/Output System: The API employed by applications residing on an IBM LAN to ask for services, such as session termination or information transfer, from lower-level network processes.

NetView A mainframe network product from IBM, used for monitoring SNA (Systems Network Architecture) networks. It runs as a VTAM (Virtual Telecommunications Access Method) application.

NetWare A widely used NOS created by Novell, providing a number of distributed network services and remote file access.

network address Used with the logical network addresses to identify the network segment in an internetwork. Logical addresses are hierarchical in nature and have at least two parts: network and host. An example of a hierarchical address is 172.16.10.5, where 172.16 is the network and 10.5 is the host address.

network layer In the OSI reference model, it is Layer 3—the layer in which routing is implemented, enabling connections and path selection between two end systems. *See also: application layer, data link layer, physical layer, presentation layer, session layer,* and *transport layer.*

NFFC NetFlow Feature Card: A module installed on Cisco Catalyst 5000 series switches. It is capable of examining each frame's IP header as well as the Ethernet header. This in turn allows the NFFC to create flows.

NFS Network File System: One of the protocols in Sun Microsystems' widely used file system protocol suite, allowing remote file access across a network. The name is loosely used to refer to the entire Sun protocol suite, which also includes RPC, XDR (External Data Representation), and other protocols.

NHRP Next Hop Resolution Protocol: In a nonbroadcast multiaccess (NBMA) network, the protocol employed by routers in order to dynamically locate MAC addresses of various hosts and routers. It enables systems to communicate directly without requiring an intermediate hop, thus facilitating increased performance in ATM, Frame Relay, X.25, and SMDS systems.

NHS Next Hop Server: Defined by the NHRP protocol, this server maintains the next-hop resolution cache tables, listing IP-to-ATM address maps of related nodes and nodes that can be reached through routers served by the NHS.

NIC network interface card: An electronic circuit board placed in a computer. The NIC provides network communication to a LAN.

NLSP NetWare Link Services Protocol: Novell's link-state routing protocol, based on the IS-IS model.

NMP Network Management Processor: A Catalyst 5000 switch processor module used to control and monitor the switch.

node address Used to identify a specific device in an internetwork. Can be a hardware address, which is burned into the network interface card or a logical network address, which an administrator or server assigns to the node.

nondesignated port The Spanning Tree Protocol tells a port on a layer 2 switch to stop transmitting and creating a network loop. Only designated ports can send frames.

non-stub area In OSPF, a resource-consuming area carrying a default route, intra-area routes, interarea routes, static routes, and external routes. Non-stub areas are the only areas that can have virtual links configured across them and exclusively contain an anonymous system boundary router (ASBR). *Compare with: stub area. See also: ASBR* and *OSPF.*

NRZ Nonreturn to Zero: One of several encoding schemes for transmitting digital data. NRZ signals sustain constant levels of voltage with no signal shifting (no return to zero-voltage level) during a bit interval. If there is a series of bits with the same value (1 or 0), there will be no state change. The signal is not self-clocking. *See also: NRZI.*

NRZI Nonreturn to Zero Inverted: One of several encoding schemes for transmitting digital data. A transition in voltage level (either from high to low or vice-versa) at the beginning of a bit interval is interpreted as a value of 1; the absence of a transition is interpreted as a 0. Thus, the voltage assigned to each value is continually inverted. NRZI signals are not self-clocking. *See also: NRZ.*

NT1 network termination 1: Is an ISDN designation to devices that understand ISDN standards.

NT2 network termination 2: Is an ISDN designation to devices that do not understand ISDN standards. To use a NT2, you must use a terminal adapter (TA).

NVRAM Non-Volatile RAM: Random-access memory that keeps its contents intact while power is turned off.

OC Optical Carrier: A series of physical protocols, designated as OC-1, OC-2, OC-3, and so on, for SONET optical signal transmissions. OC signal levels place STS frames on a multimode fiber-optic line at various speeds, of which 51.84Mbps is the lowest (OC-1). Each subsequent protocol runs at a speed divisible by 51.84. *See also: SONET.*

octet Base-8 numbering system used to identify a section of a dotted decimal IP address. Also referred to as a byte.

100BaseT Based on the IEEE 802.3u standard, 100BaseT is the FastEthernet specification of 100Mbps baseband that uses UTP wiring. 100BaseT sends link pulses (containing more information than those used in 10BaseT) over the network when no traffic is present. *See also: 10BaseT, FastEthernet,* and *IEEE 802.3.*

100BaseTX Based on the IEEE 802.3u standard, 100BaseTX is the 100Mbps baseband FastEthernet specification that uses two pairs of UTP or STP wiring. The first pair of wires receives data; the second pair sends data. To ensure correct signal timing, a 100BaseTX segment cannot be longer than 100 meters.

ones density Also known as pulse density, this is a method of signal clocking. The CSU/DSU retrieves the clocking information from data that passes through it. For this scheme to work, the data needs to be encoded to contain at least one binary 1 for each eight bits transmitted. *See also: CSU* and *DSU.*

one-time challenge tokens Used to provide a single use password. This prevents replay attacks and snooping; however, it also requires the user to have a device that provides the token. This physical component of the security model works to prevent hackers from guessing or obtaining the user's password.

OSI Open Systems Interconnection: International standardization program designed by ISO and ITU-T for the development of data networking standards that make multivendor equipment interoperability a reality.

OSI reference model Open Systems Interconnection reference model: A conceptual model defined by the International Organization for Standardization (ISO), describing how any combination of devices can be connected for the purpose of communication. The OSI model divides the task into seven functional layers, forming a hierarchy with the applications at the top and the physical medium at the bottom, and it defines the functions each layer must provide. *See also: application layer, data link layer, network layer, physical layer, presentation layer, session layer,* and *transport layer.*

OSPF Open Shortest Path First: A link-state, hierarchical IGP routing algorithm derived from an earlier version of the IS-IS protocol, whose features include multipath routing, load balancing, and least-cost routing. OSPF is the suggested successor to RIP in the Internet environment. *See also: Enhanced IGRP, IGP,* and *IP.*

OUI Organizationally Unique Identifier: Is assigned by the IEEE to an organization that makes network interface cards. The organization then puts this OUI on each and every card they manufacture. The OUI is 3 bytes (24 bits) long. The manufacturer then adds a 3-byte identifier to uniquely identify the host on an internetwork. The total length of the address is 48 bits (6 bytes) and is called a hardware address or MAC address.

out-of-band management Management "outside" of the network's physical channels. For example, using a console connection not directly interfaced through the local LAN or WAN or a dial-in modem. *Compare to: in-band management.*

out-of-band signaling Within a network, any transmission that uses physical channels or frequencies separate from those ordinarily used for data transfer. For example, the initial configuration of a Cisco Catalyst switch requires an out-of-band connection via a console port.

packet In data communications, the basic logical unit of information transferred. A packet consists of a certain number of data bytes, wrapped or encapsulated in headers and/or trailers that contain information about where the packet came from, where it's going, and so on. The various protocols involved in sending a transmission add their own layers of header information, which the corresponding protocols in receiving devices then interpret.

packet mode connections   Packet mode connections are typically passed through the router or remote access device. This includes Point-to-Point Protocol (PPP) sessions.

packet switch   A physical device that makes it possible for a communication channel to share several connections, its functions include finding the most efficient transmission path for packets.

packet switching   A networking technology based on the transmission of data in packets. Dividing a continuous stream of data into small units—packets—enables data from multiple devices on a network to share the same communication channel simultaneously but also requires the use of precise routing information.

PAD   Packet assembler and disassembler: Used to buffer incoming data that is coming in faster than the receiving device can handle it. Typically, only used in X.25 networks.

PAP   Password Authentication Protocol: In Point-to-Point Protocol (PPP) networks, a method of validating connection requests. The requesting (remote) device must send an authentication request, containing a password and ID, to the local router when attempting to connect. Unlike the more secure CHAP (Challenge Handshake Authentication Protocol), PAP sends the password unencrypted and does not attempt to verify whether the user is authorized to access the requested resource; it merely identifies the remote end. *See also: CHAP.*

parity checking   A method of error-checking in data transmissions. An extra bit (the parity bit) is added to each character or data word so that the sum of the bits will be either an odd number (in odd parity) or an even number (even parity).

partial mesh   A type of network topology in which some network nodes form a full mesh (where every node has either a physical or a virtual circuit linking it to every other network node), but others are attached to only one or two nodes in the network. A typical use of partial-mesh topology is in peripheral networks linked to a fully meshed backbone. *See also: full mesh.*

PAT   Port Address Translation: This process allows a single IP address to represent multiple resources by altering the source TCP or UDP port number.

payload compression Reduces the number of bytes required to accurately represent the original data stream. Header compression is also possible. *See also: compression.*

PCR Peak Cell Rate: As defined by the ATM Forum, the parameter specifying, in cells per second, the maximum rate at which a source may transmit.

PDN Public Data Network: Generally for a fee, a PDN offers the public access to computer communication network operated by private concerns or government agencies. Small organizations can take advantage of PDNs, aiding them creating WANs without investing in long-distance equipment and circuitry.

PDU Protocol Data Unit: The name of the processes at each layer of the OSI model. PDUs at the transport layer are called segments; PDUs at the network layer are called packets or datagrams; and PDUs at the data link layer are called frames. The physical layer uses bits.

PFC Policy Feature Card: The PFC can be paralleled with the NFFC used in Catalyst 5000 switches. It is a device that is capable of examining IP and Ethernet headers in order to establish flow caches.

PGP Pretty Good Privacy: A popular public-key/private-key encryption application offering protected transfer of files and messages.

physical layer The lowest layer—Layer 1—in the OSI reference model, it is responsible for converting data packets from the data link layer (Layer 2) into electrical signals. Physical-layer protocols and standards define, for example, the type of cable and connectors to be used, including their pin assignments and the encoding scheme for signaling 0 and 1 values. *See also: application layer, data link layer, network layer, presentation layer, session layer,* and *transport layer.*

PIM Protocol Independent Multicast: A multicast protocol that handles the IGMP requests as well as requests for multicast data forwarding.

PIM DM Protocol Independent Multicast dense mode: PIM DM utilizes the unicast route table and relies on the source root distribution architecture for multicast data forwarding.

PIM SM   Protocol Independent Multicast sparse mode: PIM SM utilizes the unicast route table and relies on the shared root distribution architecture for multicast data forwarding.

PIM sparse-dense mode   An interface configuration that allows the interface to choose the method of PIM operation.

ping   packet Internet groper: A Unix-based Internet diagnostic tool, consisting of a message sent to test the accessibility of a particular device on the IP network. The acronym (from which the "full name" was formed) reflects the underlying metaphor of submarine sonar. Just as the sonar operator sends out a signal and waits to hear it echo ("ping") back from a submerged object, the network user can ping another node on the network and wait to see if it responds.

pleisochronous   Nearly synchronous, except that clocking comes from an outside source instead of being embedded within the signal as in synchronous transmissions.

PLP   Packet Level Protocol: Occasionally called X.25 Level 3 or X.25 Protocol, a network-layer protocol that is part of the X.25 stack.

PNNI   Private Network-Network Interface: An ATM Forum specification for offering topology data used for the calculation of paths through the network, among switches and groups of switches. It is based on well-known link-state routing procedures and allows for automatic configuration in networks whose addressing scheme is determined by the topology.

point-to-multipoint connection   In ATM, a communication path going only one way, connecting a single system at the starting point, called the "root node," to systems at multiple points of destination, called "leaves." *See also: point-to-point connection.*

point-to-point connection   In ATM, a channel of communication that can be directed either one way or two ways between two ATM end systems. *See also: point-to-multipoint connection.*

poison reverse updates   These update messages are transmitted by a router back to the originator (thus ignoring the split-horizon rule) after route poisoning has occurred. Typically used with DV routing protocols in order to overcome large routing loops and offer explicit information when a subnet or network is not accessible (instead of merely suggesting that the network is unreachable by not including it in updates). *See also: route poisoning.*

polling The procedure of orderly inquiry, used by a primary network mechanism, to determine if secondary devices have data to transmit. A message is sent to each secondary, granting the secondary the right to transmit.

POP 1) Point Of Presence: The physical location where an interexchange carrier has placed equipment to interconnect with a local exchange carrier. 2) Post Office Protocol (currently at version 3): A protocol used by client e-mail applications for recovery of mail from a mail server.

port density Port density reflects the capacity of the remote access device regarding the termination of interfaces. For example, the port density of an access server that serves four T1 circuits is 96 analog lines (non ISDN PRI).

port security Used with layer 2 switches to provide some security. Not typically used in production because it is difficult to manage. Allows only certain frames to traverse administrator-assigned segments.

POTS Plain Old Telephone Service: This refers to the traditional analog phone service that is found in most installations.

PPP Point-to-Point Protocol: The protocol most commonly used for dial-up Internet access, superseding the earlier SLIP. Its features include address notification, authentication via CHAP or PAP, support for multiple protocols, and link monitoring. PPP has two layers: the Link Control Protocol (LCP) establishes, configures, and tests a link; and then any of various Network Control Programs (NCPs) transport traffic for a specific protocol suite, such as IPX. *See also: CHAP, PAP,* and *SLIP.*

PPP callback The point-to-point protocol supports callback to a predetermined number to augment security.

Predictor A compression technique supported by Cisco. *See also: compression.*

presentation layer Layer 6 of the OSI reference model, it defines how data is formatted, presented, encoded, and converted for use by software at the application layer. *See also: application layer, data link layer, network layer, physical layer, session layer,* and *transport layer.*

PRI Primary Rate Interface: A type of ISDN connection between a PBX and a long-distance carrier, which is made up of a single 64Kbps D channel in addition to 23 (T1) or 30 (E1) B channels. *See also: ISDN.*

priority queuing A routing function in which frames temporarily placed in an interface output queue are assigned priorities based on traits such as packet size or type of interface.

process switching As a packet arrives on a router to be forwarded, it's copied to the router's process buffer, and the router performs a lookup on the Layer 3 address. Using the route table, an exit interface is associated with the destination address. The processor forwards the packet with the added new information to the exit interface, while the router initializes the fast-switching cache. Subsequent packets bound for the same destination address follow the same path as the first packet.

PROM programmable read-only memory: ROM that is programmable only once, using special equipment. *Compare with: EPROM.*

propagation delay The time it takes data to traverse a network from its source to its destination.

protocol In networking, the specification of a set of rules for a particular type of communication. The term is also used to refer to the software that implements a protocol.

protocol stack A collection of related protocols.

Proxy ARP Proxy Address Resolution Protocol: Used to allow redundancy in case of a failure with the configured default gateway on a host. Proxy ARP is a variation of the ARP protocol in which an intermediate device, such as a router, sends an ARP response on behalf of an end node to the requesting host.

pruning The act of trimming down the Shortest Path Tree. This deactivates interfaces that do not have group participants.

PSE Packet Switch Exchange: The X.25 term for a switch.

PSN packet-switched network: Any network that uses packet-switching technology. Also known as packet-switched data network (PSDN). *See also: packet switching.*

PSTN   Public Switched Telephone Network: Colloquially referred to as "plain old telephone service" (POTS). A term that describes the assortment of telephone networks and services available globally.

PVC   permanent virtual circuit: In a Frame-Relay network, a logical connection, defined in software, that is maintained permanently. *Compare with:* SVC. *See also: virtual circuit.*

PVP   permanent virtual path: A virtual path made up of PVCs. *See also: PVC.*

PVP tunneling   permanent virtual path tunneling: A technique that links two private ATM networks across a public network using a virtual path; wherein the public network transparently trunks the complete collection of virtual channels in the virtual path between the two private networks.

PVST   Per-VLAN Spanning Tree: A Cisco proprietary implementation of STP. PVST uses ISL and runs a separate instance of STP for each and every VLAN.

PVST+   Per-VLAN Spanning Tree+: Allows CST information to be passed into PVST.

QoS   Quality of Service: A set of metrics used to measure the quality of transmission and service availability of any given transmission system.

queue   Broadly, any list of elements arranged in an orderly fashion and ready for processing, such as a line of people waiting to enter a movie theater. In routing, it refers to a backlog of information packets waiting in line to be transmitted over a router interface.

queuing   A quality of service process that allows packets to be forwarded from the router based on administratively defined parameters. This may be used for time-sensitive protocols, such as SNA.

R reference point   Used with ISDN networks to identify the connection between an NT1 and an S/T device. The S/T device converts the 4-wire network to the two-wire ISDN standard network.

RADIUS   Remote Access Dial-in User Service: A protocol that is used to communicate between the remote access device and an authentication server. Sometimes an authentication server running RADIUS will be called a RADIUS server.

RAM random access memory: Used by all computers to store information. Cisco routers use RAM to store packet buffers and routing tables, along with the hardware addresses cache.

RARP Reverse Address Resolution Protocol: The protocol within the TCP/IP stack that maps MAC addresses to IP addresses. *See also: ARP.*

rate queue A value, assigned to one or more virtual circuits, that specifies the speed at which an individual virtual circuit will transmit data to the remote end. Every rate queue identifies a segment of the total bandwidth available on an ATM link. The sum of all rate queues should not exceed the total available bandwidth.

RCP Remote Copy Protocol: A protocol for copying files to or from a file system that resides on a remote server on a network, using TCP to guarantee reliable data delivery.

redistribution Command used in Cisco routers to inject the paths found from one type of routing protocol into another type of routing protocol. For example, networks found by RIP can be inserted into an IGRP network.

redundancy In internetworking, the duplication of connections, devices, or services that can be used as a backup in the event that the primary connections, devices, or services fail.

reference point Used to define an area in an ISDN network. Providers used these reference points to find problems in the ISDN network.

reliability The measure of the quality of a connection. It is one of the metrics that can be used to make routing decisions.

reload An event or command that causes Cisco routers to reboot.

remote access A generic term that defines connectivity to distant resources using one of many technologies, as appropriate.

remote services Remote services are defined as network services close to users but not on the same network or subnet as the users. The users would have to cross a layer 3 device to communicate with the network services, but they might not have to cross the backbone.

reverse Telnet Maps a Telnet port to a physical port on the router or access device. This allows the administrator to connect to a modem or other device attached to the port.

RFC Request for Comments: RFCs are used to present and define standards in the networking industry.

RIF Routing Information Field: In source-route bridging, a header field that defines the path direction of the frame or token. If the Route Information Indicator (RII) bit is not set, the RIF is read from source to destination (left to right). If the RII bit is set, the RIF is read from the destination back to the source, so the RIF is read right to left. It is defined as part of the Token Ring frame header for source-routed frames, which contains path information.

ring Two or more stations connected in a logical circular topology. In this topology, which is the basis for Token Ring, FDDI, and CDDI, information is transferred from station to station in sequence.

ring topology A network logical topology comprising a series of repeaters that form one closed loop by connecting unidirectional transmission links. Individual stations on the network are connected to the network at a repeater. Physically, ring topologies are generally organized in a closed-loop star. *Compare with: bus topology* and *star topology.*

RIP Routing Information Protocol: The most commonly used interior gateway protocol in the Internet. RIP employs hop count as a routing metric. *See also: Enhanced IGRP, IGP, OSPF,* and *hop count.*

RIP version 2 Newer, updated version of Routing Information Protocol (RIP). Allows VLSM. *See also: VLSM.*

RJ connector registered jack connector: Is used with twisted-pair wiring to connect the copper wire to network interface cards, switches, and hubs.

robbed bit signaling Used in Primary Rate Interface clocking mechanisms.

ROM read-only memory: Chip used in computers to help boot the device. Cisco routers use a ROM chip to load the bootstrap, which runs a power-on self test, and then find and load the IOS in flash memory by default.

root bridge   Used with the Spanning Tree Protocol to stop network loops from occurring. The root bridge is elected by having the lowest bridge ID. The bridge ID is determined by the priority (32,768 by default on all bridges and switches) and the main hardware address of the device. The root bridge determines which of the neighboring layer 2 devices' interfaces become the designated and nondesignated ports.

routed protocol   Routed protocols (such as IP and IPX) are used to transmit user data through an internetwork. By contrast, routing protocols (such as RIP, IGRP, and OSPF) are used to update routing tables between routers.

route poisoning   Used by various DV routing protocols in order to overcome large routing loops and offer explicit information about when a subnet or network is not accessible (instead of merely suggesting that the network is unreachable by not including it in updates). Typically, this is accomplished by setting the hop count to one more than maximum. *See also: poison reverse updates.*

route summarization   In various routing protocols, such as OSPF, EIGRP, and IS-IS, the consolidation of publicized subnetwork addresses so that a single summary route is advertised to other areas by an area border router.

router   A network-layer mechanism, either software or hardware, using one or more metrics to decide on the best path to use for transmission of network traffic. Sending packets between networks by routers is based on the information provided on network layers. Historically, this device has sometimes been called a gateway.

router on a stick   A term that identifies a single router interface connected to a single distribution layer switch port. The router is an external router that provides trunking protocol capabilities for routing between multiple VLANs. *See also: RSM, MSFC.*

routing   The process of forwarding logically addressed packets from their local subnetwork toward their ultimate destination. In large networks, the numerous intermediary destinations a packet might travel before reaching its destination can make routing very complex.

routing domain   Any collection of end systems and intermediate systems that operate under an identical set of administrative rules. Every routing domain contains one or several areas, all individually given a certain area address.

routing metric   Any value that is used by routing algorithms to determine whether one route is superior to another. Metrics include such information as bandwidth, delay, hop count, path cost, load, MTU, reliability, and communication cost. Only the best possible routes are stored in the routing table, while all other information may be stored in link-state or topological databases. *See also: cost.*

routing protocol   Any protocol that defines algorithms to be used for updating routing tables between routers. Examples include IGRP, RIP, and OSPF.

routing table   A table kept in a router or other internetworking mechanism that maintains a record of only the best possible routes to certain network destinations and the metrics associated with those routes.

RP   1) rendezvous point: A router that acts as the multicast source in a multicast network. Primarily in a shared tree distribution. 2) Route Processor: Also known as a supervisory processor, a module on Cisco 7000 series routers that holds the CPU, system software, and most of the memory components used in the router.

RSFC   Route Switch Feature Card: Used to provide routing between VLANs. The RSFC is a daughter card for the Supervisor engine II G and Supervisor III G cards. The RSFC is a fully functioning router running the Cisco IOS.

RSM   Route Switch Module: A route processor that is inserted into the chassis of a Cisco Catalyst 5000 series switch. The RSM is configured exactly like an external router.

RSP   Route/Switch Processor: A processor module combining the functions of RP and SP used in Cisco 7500 series routers. *See also: RP and SP.*

RTS   Request To Send: An EIA/TIA-232 control signal requesting permission to transmit data on a communication line.

S reference point ISDN reference point that works with a T reference point to convert a 4-wire ISDN network to the 2-wire ISDN network needed to communicate with the ISDN switches at the network provider.

sampling rate The rate at which samples of a specific waveform amplitude are collected within a specified period of time.

SAP 1) Service Access Point: A field specified by IEEE 802.2 that is part of an address specification. 2) Service Advertising Protocol: The Novell NetWare protocol that supplies a way to inform network clients of resources and services availability on network, using routers and servers. *See also: IPX.*

SCR Sustainable Cell Rate: An ATM Forum parameter used for traffic management, it is the long-term average cell rate for VBR connections that can be transmitted.

scripts A script predefines commands that should be issued in sequence, typically to complete a connection or accomplish a repetitive task.

SDLC Synchronous Data Link Control: A protocol used in SNA data-link layer communications. SDLC is a bit-oriented, full-duplex serial protocol that is the basis for several similar protocols, including HDLC and LAPB. *See also: HDLC* and *LAPB.*

security policy Document that defines the business requirements and processes that are to be used to protect corporate data. A security policy might be as generic as "no file transfers allowed" to very specific, such as "FTP puts allowed only to server X."

security server A centralized device that authenticates access requests, typically via a protocol such as TACACS+ or RADIUS. *See also: TACACS+, RADIUS.*

seed router In an AppleTalk network, the router that is equipped with the network number or cable range in its port descriptor. The seed router specifies the network number or cable range for other routers in that network section and answers to configuration requests from nonseed routers on its connected AppleTalk network, permitting those routers to affirm or modify their configurations accordingly. Every AppleTalk network needs at least one seed router physically connected to each network segment.

server Hardware and software that provide network services to clients.

set-based Set-based routers and switches use the `set` command to configure devices. Cisco is moving away from set-based commands and is using the Command-Line Interface (CLI) on all new devices.

session layer Layer 5 of the OSI reference model, responsible for creating, managing, and terminating sessions between applications and overseeing data exchange between presentation layer entities. *See also: application layer, data link layer, network layer, physical layer, presentation layer,* and *transport layer.*

setup mode Mode that a router will enter if no configuration is found in nonvolatile RAM when the router boots. Allows the administrator to configure a router step-by-step. Not as robust or flexible as the Command-Line Interface.

SF super frame: A super frame (also called a D4 frame) consists of 12 frames with 192 bits each, and the 193rd bit providing other functions including error checking. SF is frequently used on T1 circuits. A newer version of the technology is Extended Super Frame (ESF), which uses 24 frames. *See also: ESF.*

shared trees A method of multicast data forwarding. Shared trees use an architecture in which multiple sources share a common rendezvous point.

signaling packet An informational packet created by an ATM-connected mechanism that wants to establish connection with another such mechanism. The packet contains the QoS parameters needed for connection and the ATM NSAP address of the endpoint. The endpoint responds with a message of acceptance if it is able to support the desired QoS, and the connection is established. *See also: QoS.*

silicon switching A type of high-speed switching used in Cisco 7000 series routers, based on the use of a separate processor (the Silicon Switch Processor, or SSP). *See also: SSE.*

simplex The mode at which data or a digital signal is transmitted. Simplex is a way of transmitting in only one direction. Half duplex transmits in two directions but only one direction at a time. Full duplex transmits both directions simultaneously.

sliding window The method of flow control used by TCP, as well as several data-link layer protocols. This method places a buffer between the receiving application and the network data flow. The "window" available for accepting data is the size of the buffer minus the amount of data already there. This window increases in size as the application reads data from it and decreases as new data is sent. The receiver sends the transmitter announcements of the current window size, and it may stop accepting data until the window increases above a certain threshold.

SLIP Serial Line Internet Protocol: An industry standard serial encapsulation for point-to-point connections that supports only a single routed protocol, TCP/IP. SLIP is the predecessor to PPP. *See also: PPP.*

SMDS Switched Multimegabit Data Service: A packet-switched, datagram-based WAN networking technology offered by telephone companies that provides high speed.

SMTP Simple Mail Transfer Protocol: A protocol used on the Internet to provide electronic mail services.

SNA System Network Architecture: A complex, feature-rich, network architecture similar to the OSI reference model but with several variations; created by IBM in the 1970s and essentially composed of seven layers.

SNAP Subnetwork Access Protocol: SNAP is a frame used in Ethernet, Token Ring, and FDDI LANs. Data transfer, connection management, and QoS selection are three primary functions executed by the SNAP frame.

snapshot routing Snapshot routing takes a point-in-time capture of a dynamic routing table and maintains it even when the remote connection goes down. This allows the use of a dynamic routing protocol without requiring the link to remain active, which might incur per-minute usage charges.

socket 1) A software structure that operates within a network device as a destination point for communications. 2) In AppleTalk networks, an entity at a specific location within a node; AppleTalk sockets are conceptually similar to TCP/IP ports.

SOHO small office, home office: A contemporary term for remote users.

SONET Synchronous Optical Network: The ANSI standard for synchronous transmission on fiber-optic media, developed at Bell Labs. It specifies a base signal rate of 51.84Mbps and a set of multiples of that rate, known as Optical Carrier levels, up to 2.5Gbps.

source trees A method of multicast data forwarding. Source trees use the architecture of the source of the multicast traffic as the root of the tree.

SP Switch Processor: Also known as a ciscoBus controller, it is a Cisco 7000 series processor module acting as governing agent for all CxBus activities.

span A full-duplex digital transmission line connecting two facilities.

SPAN Switched Port Analyzer: A feature of the Catalyst 5000 switch, offering freedom to manipulate within a switched Ethernet environment by extending the monitoring ability of the existing network analyzers into the environment. At one switched segment, the SPAN mirrors traffic onto a predetermined SPAN port, while a network analyzer connected to the SPAN port is able to monitor traffic from any other Catalyst switched port.

spanning explorer packet Sometimes called limited-route or single-route explorer packet, it pursues a statically configured spanning tree when searching for paths in a source-route bridging network. *See also: all-routes explorer packet, explorer packet,* and *local explorer packet.*

spanning tree A subset of a network topology, within which no loops exist. When bridges are interconnected into a loop, the bridge, or switch, cannot identify a frame that has been forwarded previously, so there is no mechanism for removing a frame as it passes the interface numerous times. Without a method of removing these frames, the bridges continuously forward them—consuming bandwidth and adding overhead to the network. Spanning trees prune the network to provide only one path for any packet. *See also: Spanning Tree Protocol* and *spanning tree algorithm.*

spanning-tree algorithm (STA) An algorithm that creates a spanning tree using the Spanning Tree Protocol (STP). *See also: spanning tree* and *Spanning Tree Protocol.*

Spanning Tree Protocol (STP) The bridge protocol (IEEE 802.1d) that enables a learning bridge to dynamically avoid loops in the network topology by creating a spanning tree using the spanning-tree algorithm.

Spanning-tree frames called bridge protocol data units (BPDUs) are sent and received by all switches in the network at regular intervals. The switches participating in the spanning tree don't forward the frames; instead, they're processed to determine the spanning-tree topology itself. Cisco Catalyst series switches use STP 802.1d to perform this function. *See also: BPDU, learning bridge, MAC address, spanning tree,* and *spanning-tree algorithm.*

SPF Shortest Path First algorithm: A routing algorithm used to decide on the shortest-path spanning tree. Sometimes called Dijkstra's algorithm and frequently used in link-state routing algorithms. *See also: link-state routing algorithm.*

SPID Service Profile Identifier: A number assigned by service providers or local telephone companies and assigned by administrators to a BRI port. SPIDs are used to determine subscription services of a device connected via ISDN. ISDN devices use SPID when accessing the telephone company switch that initializes the link to a service provider.

split horizon Useful for preventing routing loops, a type of distance-vector routing rule where information about routes is prevented from leaving the router interface through which that information was received.

spoofing 1) In dial-on-demand routing (DDR), where a circuit-switched link is taken down to save toll charges when there is no traffic to be sent, spoofing is a scheme used by routers that causes a host to treat an interface as if it were functioning and supporting a session. The router pretends to send "spoof" replies to keepalive messages from the host in an effort to convince the host that the session is up and running. *See also: DDR.* 2) The illegal act of sending a packet labeled with a false address, in order to deceive network security mechanisms such as filters and access lists.

spooler A management application that processes requests submitted to it for execution in a sequential fashion from a queue. A good example is a print spooler.

SPX Sequenced Packet Exchange: A Novell NetWare transport protocol that augments the datagram service provided by network layer (Layer 3) protocols, it was derived from the Switch-to-Switch Protocol of the XNS protocol suite.

SQE Signal Quality Error: In an Ethernet network, a message sent from a transceiver to an attached machine that the collision-detection circuitry is working.

SRB Source-Route Bridging: Created by IBM, the bridging method used in Token-Ring networks. The source determines the entire route to a destination before sending the data and includes that information in route information fields (RIF) within each packet. *Contrast with: transparent bridging.*

SRT source-route transparent bridging: A bridging scheme developed by IBM, merging source-route and transparent bridging. SRT takes advantage of both technologies in one device, fulfilling the needs of all end nodes. Translation between bridging protocols is not necessary. *Compare with: SR/TLB.*

SR/TLB source-route translational bridging: A bridging method that allows source-route stations to communicate with transparent bridge stations aided by an intermediate bridge that translates between the two bridge protocols. Used for bridging between Token Ring and Ethernet. *Compare with: SRT.*

SSAP Source Service Access Point: The SAP of the network node identified in the Source field of the packet. *See also: DSAP and SAP.*

SSE Silicon Switching Engine: The software component of Cisco's silicon switching technology, hard-coded into the Silicon Switch Processor (SSP). Silicon switching is available only on the Cisco 7000 with an SSP. Silicon-switched packets are compared to the silicon-switching cache on the SSE. The SSP is a dedicated switch processor that offloads the switching process from the route processor, providing a fast-switching solution, but packets must still traverse the backplane of the router to get to the SSP and then back to the exit interface.

SS-7 signaling Signaling System 7: The current standard for telecommunications switching control signaling. This is an out-of-band signaling that establishes circuits and provides billing information.

Stac A compression method developed by Stacker Corporation for use over serial links.

standard IP access list   IP access list that uses only the source IP addresses to filter a network.

standard IPX access list   IPX access list that uses only the source and destination IPX address to filter a network.

star topology   A LAN physical topology with endpoints on the network converging at a common central switch (known as a hub) using point-to-point links. A logical ring topology can be configured as a physical star topology using a unidirectional closed-loop star rather than point-to-point links. That is, connections within the hub are arranged in an internal ring. *See also: bus topology* and *ring topology.*

startup range   If an AppleTalk node does not have a number saved from the last time it was booted, then the node selects from the range of values from 65280 to 65534.

state transitions   Digital signaling scheme that reads the "state" of the digital signal in the middle of the bit cell. If it is five volts, the cell is read as a one. If the state of the digital signal is zero volts, the bit cell is read as a zero.

static route   A route whose information is purposefully entered into the routing table and takes priority over those chosen by dynamic routing protocols.

static VLANs   Static VLANs are manually configured port-by-port. This is the method typically used in production networks.

statistical multiplexing   Multiplexing in general is a technique that allows data from multiple logical channels to be sent across a single physical channel. Statistical multiplexing dynamically assigns bandwidth only to input channels that are active, optimizing available bandwidth so that more devices can be connected than with other multiplexing techniques. Also known as statistical time-division multiplexing or stat mux.

STM-1   Synchronous Transport Module Level 1. In the European SDH standard, one of many formats identifying the frame structure for the 155.52Mbps lines that are used to carry ATM cells.

store-and-forward packet switching A technique in which the switch first copies each packet into its buffer and performs a cyclical redundancy check (CRC). If the packet is error-free, the switch then looks up the destination address in its filter table, determines the appropriate exit port, and sends the packet.

STP 1) Shielded Twisted Pair: A two-pair wiring scheme, used in many network implementations, that has a layer of shielded insulation to reduce EMI. 2) Spanning Tree Protocol.

stub area An OSPF area carrying a default route, intra-area routes, and interarea routes, but no external routes. Configuration of virtual links cannot be achieved across a stub area, and stub areas are not allowed to contain an ASBR. *See also: non-stub area, ASBR,* and *OSPF.*

stub network A network having only one connection to a router.

STUN Serial Tunnel: A technology used to connect an HDLC link to an SDLC link over a serial link.

subarea A portion of an SNA network made up of a subarea node and its attached links and peripheral nodes.

subarea node An SNA communications host or controller that handles entire network addresses.

subchannel A frequency-based subdivision that creates a separate broadband communications channel.

subinterface One of many virtual interfaces available on a single physical interface.

subnet *See: subnetwork.*

subnet address The portion of an IP address that is specifically identified by the subnet mask as the subnetwork. *See also: IP address, subnetwork,* and *subnet mask.*

subnet mask Also simply known as mask, a 32-bit address mask used in IP to identify the bits of an IP address that are used for the subnet address. Using a mask, the router does not need to examine all 32 bits, only those selected by the mask. *See also: address mask* and *IP address.*

subnetwork   1) Any network that is part of a larger IP network and is identified by a subnet address. A network administrator segments a network into subnetworks in order to provide a hierarchical, multilevel routing structure, and at the same time protect the subnetwork from the addressing complexity of networks that are attached. Also known as a subnet. *See also: IP address, subnet mask,* and *subnet address.* 2) In OSI networks, the term specifically refers to a collection of ESs and ISs controlled by only one administrative domain, using a solitary network connection protocol.

SVC   switched virtual circuit: A dynamically established virtual circuit, created on demand and dissolved as soon as transmission is over and the circuit is no longer needed. In ATM terminology, it is referred to as a switched virtual connection. *See also: PVC.*

switch   1) In networking, a device responsible for multiple functions such as filtering, flooding, and sending frames. It works using the destination address of individual frames. Switches operate at the data link layer of the OSI model. 2) Broadly, any electronic/mechanical device allowing connections to be established as needed and terminated if no longer necessary.

switch block   The switch block is a combination of layer 3 switches and layer 3 routers. The layer 2 switches connect users in the wiring closet into the access layer and provide 10 or 100Mbps dedicated connections. 1900/2820 and 2900 Catalyst switches can be used in the switch block.

switched Ethernet   Device that switches Ethernet frames between segments by filtering on hardware addresses.

switched LAN   Any LAN implemented using LAN switches. *See also: LAN switch.*

switch-fabric   The central functional block of any switch design; responsible for buffering and routing the incoming data to the appropriate output ports.

synchronous transmission   Signals transmitted digitally with precision clocking. These signals have identical frequencies and contain individual characters encapsulated in control bits (called start/stop bits) that designate the beginning and ending of each character. *See also: asynchronous transmission* and *isochronous transmission.*

T reference point   Used with an S reference point to change a 4-wire ISDN network to a 2-wire ISDN network.

T1   Digital WAN that uses 24 DS0s at 64K each to create a bandwidth of 1.536Mbps, minus clocking overhead, providing 1.544Mbps of usable bandwidth.

T3   Digital WAN that can provide bandwidth of 44.763Mbps.

TACACS+   Terminal Access Control Access Control System: An enhanced version of TACACS, this protocol is similar to RADIUS. *See also: RADIUS.*

tag switching   Based on the concept of label swapping, where packets or cells are designated to defined-length labels that control the manner in which data is to be sent, tag switching is a high-performance technology used for forwarding packets. It incorporates data-link layer (Layer 2) switching and network layer (Layer 3) routing and supplies scalable, high-speed switching in the network core.

tagged traffic   ATM cells with their cell loss priority (CLP) bit set to 1. Also referred to as discard-eligible (DE) traffic. Tagged traffic can be eliminated in order to ensure trouble-free delivery of higher priority traffic, if the network is congested. *See also: CLP.*

TCP   Transmission Control Protocol: A connection-oriented protocol that is defined at the transport layer of the OSI reference model. Provides reliable delivery of data.

TCP header compression   A compression process that compresses only the TCP header information, which is typically repetitive. This would not compress the user data. *See also: compression.*

TCP/IP   Transmission Control Protocol/Internet Protocol. The suite of protocols underlying the Internet. TCP and IP are the most widely known protocols in that suite. *See also: IP* and *TCP.*

TDM   time division multiplexing: A technique for assigning bandwidth on a single wire, based on preassigned time slots, to data from several channels. Bandwidth is allotted to each channel regardless of a station's ability to send data. *See also: ATDM, FDM,* and *multiplexing.*

TE terminal equipment: Any peripheral device that is ISDN-compatible and attached to a network, such as a telephone or computer. TE1s are devices that are ISDN-ready and understand ISDN signaling techniques. TE2s are devices that are not ISDN-ready and do not understand ISDN signaling techniques. A terminal adapter must be used with a TE2.

TE1 A device with a four-wire, twisted-pair digital interface is referred to as terminal equipment type 1. Most modern ISDN devices are of this type.

TE2 Devices known as terminal equipment type 2 do not understand ISDN signaling techniques, and a terminal adapter must be used to convert the signaling.

telco A common abbreviation for the telephone company.

Telnet The standard terminal emulation protocol within the TCP/IP protocol stack. Method of remote terminal connection, enabling users to log in on remote networks and use those resources as if they were locally connected. Telnet is defined in RFC 854.

10BaseT Part of the original IEEE 802.3 standard, 10BaseT is the Ethernet specification of 10Mbps baseband that uses two pairs of twisted-pair, Category 3, 4, or 5 cabling—using one pair to send data and the other to receive. 10BaseT has a distance limit of about 100 meters per segment. *See also: Ethernet* and *IEEE 802.3*.

terminal adapter A hardware interface between a computer without a native ISDN interface and an ISDN line. In effect, a device to connect a standard async interface to a non-native ISDN device, emulating a modem.

terminal emulation The use of software, installed on a PC or LAN server, that allows the PC to function as if it were a "dumb" terminal directly attached to a particular type of mainframe.

TFTP Conceptually, a stripped-down version of FTP, it's the protocol of choice if you know exactly what you want and where it's to be found. TFTP doesn't provide the abundance of functions that FTP does. In particular, it has no directory browsing abilities; it can do nothing but send and receive files.

Thicknet   Also called 10Base5. Bus network that uses a thick cable and runs Ethernet up to 500 meters.

Thinnet   Also called 10Base2. Bus network that uses a thin coax cable and runs Ethernet media access up to 185 meters.

token   A frame containing only control information. Possessing this control information gives a network device permission to transmit data onto the network. *See also: token passing.*

token bus   LAN architecture that is the basis for the IEEE 802.4 LAN specification and employs token passing access over a bus topology. *See also: IEEE.*

token passing   A method used by network devices to access the physical medium in a systematic way based on possession of a small frame called a token. *See also: token.*

Token Ring   IBM's token-passing LAN technology. It runs at 4Mbps or 16Mbps over a ring topology. Defined formally by IEEE 802.5. *See also: ring topology* and *token passing.*

toll network   WAN network that uses the Public Switched Telephone Network (PSTN) to send packets.

trace   IP command used to trace the path a packet takes through an internetwork.

traffic shaping   Used on Frame Relay networks to provide priorities of data.

transparent bridging   The bridging scheme used in Ethernet and IEEE 802.3 networks, it passes frames along one hop at a time, using bridging information stored in tables that associate end-node MAC addresses within bridge ports. This type of bridging is considered transparent because the source node does not know it has been bridged, because the destination frames are sent directly to the end node. *Contrast with: SRB.*

transport layer   Layer 4 of the OSI reference model, used for reliable communication between end nodes over the network. The transport layer provides mechanisms used for establishing, maintaining, and terminating virtual circuits, transport fault detection and recovery, and controlling the flow of information. *See also: application layer, data link layer, network layer, physical layer, presentation layer,* and *session layer.*

TRIP Token Ring Interface Processor: A high-speed interface processor used on Cisco 7000 series routers. The TRIP provides two or four ports for interconnection with IEEE 802.5 and IBM media with ports set to speeds of either 4Mbps or 16Mbps set independently of each other.

trunk link Link used between switches and from some servers to the switches. Trunk links carry information about many VLANs. Access links are used to connect host devices to a switch and carry only VLAN information that the device is a member of.

TTL Time To Live: A field in an IP header, indicating the length of time a packet is valid.

TUD Trunk Up-Down: A protocol used in ATM networks for the monitoring of trunks. Should a trunk miss a given number of test messages being sent by ATM switches to ensure trunk line quality, TUD declares the trunk down. When a trunk reverses direction and comes back up, TUD recognizes that the trunk is up and returns the trunk to service.

tunneling A method of avoiding protocol restrictions by wrapping packets from one protocol in another protocol's packet and transmitting this encapsulated packet over a network that supports the wrapper protocol. *See also: encapsulation.*

20/80 rule This rule means that 20 percent of what the user performs on the network is local, whereas up to 80 percent crosses the network segmentation points to get to network services.

UART The Universal Asynchronous Receiver/Transmitter: A chip that governs asynchronous communications. Its primary function is to buffer incoming data, but it also buffers outbound bits.

U reference point Reference point between a TE1 and an ISDN network. The U reference point understands ISDN signaling techniques and uses a 2-wire connection.

UDP User Datagram Protocol: A connectionless transport layer protocol in the TCP/IP protocol stack that simply allows datagrams to be exchanged without acknowledgements or delivery guarantees, requiring other protocols to handle error processing and retransmission. UDP is defined in RFC 768.

unicast   Used for direct host-to-host communication. Communication is directed to only one destination and is originated only from one source.

unidirectional shared tree   A method of shared tree multicast forwarding. This method allows only multicast data to be forwarded from the RP.

unnumbered frames   HDLC frames used for control-management purposes, such as link startup and shutdown or mode specification.

UTP   unshielded twisted-pair: Copper wiring used in small-to-large networks to connect host devices to hubs and switches. Also used to connect switch to switch or hub to hub.

VBR   Variable Bit Rate: A QoS class, as defined by the ATM Forum, for use in ATM networks that is subdivided into real time (RT) class and non-real time (NRT) class. RT is employed when connections have a fixed-time relationship between samples. Conversely, NRT is employed when connections do not have a fixed-time relationship between samples, but still need an assured QoS.

VCC   Virtual Channel Connection: A logical circuit that is created by VCLs. VCCs carry data between two endpoints in an ATM network. Sometimes called a virtual circuit connection.

VIP   1) Versatile Interface Processor: An interface card for Cisco 7000 and 7500 series routers, providing multilayer switching and running the Cisco IOS software. The most recent version of VIP is VIP2. 2) Virtual IP: A function making it possible for logically separated switched IP workgroups to run Virtual Networking Services across the switch ports of a Catalyst 5000.

virtual circuit   Abbreviated VC, a logical circuit devised to assure reliable communication between two devices on a network. Defined by a virtual path connection (VPC)/virtual path identifier (VCI) pair, a virtual circuit can be permanent (PVC) or switched (SVC). Virtual circuits are used in Frame Relay and X.25. Known as virtual channel in ATM. *See also: PVC* and *SVC*.

virtual ring   In an SRB network, a logical connection between physical rings, either local or remote.

VLAN Virtual LAN: A group of devices on one or more logically segmented LANs (configured by use of management software), enabling devices to communicate as if attached to the same physical medium, when they are actually located on numerous different LAN segments. VLANs are based on logical instead of physical connections and thus are tremendously flexible.

VLSM variable-length subnet mask: Helps optimize available address space and specify a different subnet mask for the same network number on various subnets. Also commonly referred to as "subnetting a subnet."

VPN virtual private network: A method of encrypting point-to-point logical connections across a public network, such as the Internet. This allows secure communications across a public network.

VTP VLAN Trunk Protocol: Used to update switches in a switch-fabric about VLANs configured on a VTP server. VTP devices can be a VTP server, client, or transparent device. Servers update clients. Transparent devices are only local devices and do not share information with VTP clients. VTPs send VLAN information down trunked links only.

VTP pruning VLAN Trunk Protocol is used to communicate VLAN information between switches in the same VTP domain. VTP pruning stops VLAN update information from being sent down trunked links if the updates are not needed.

WAN wide area network: A designation used to connect LANs together across a DCE (data communications equipment) network. Typically, a WAN is a leased line or dial-up connection across a PSTN network. Examples of WAN protocols include Frame Relay, PPP, ISDN, and HDLC.

weighted fair queuing Default queuing method on serial links on all Cisco routers.

wildcard Used with access-list, supernetting, and OSPF configurations. Wildcards are designations used to identify a range of subnets.

windowing Flow-control method used with TCP at the Transport layer of the OSI model.

WinSock Windows Socket Interface: A software interface that makes it possible for an assortment of applications to use and share an Internet connection. The WinSock software consists of a Dynamic Link Library (DLL) with supporting programs such as a dialer program that initiates the connection.

workgroup switching A switching method that supplies high-speed (100Mbps) transparent bridging between Ethernet networks as well as high-speed translational bridging between Ethernet and CDDI or FDDI.

X.25 An ITU-T packet-relay standard that defines communication between DTE and DCE network devices. X.25 uses a reliable data-link layer protocol called LAPB. X.25 also uses PLP at the network layer. X.25 has mostly been replaced by Frame Relay.

X.25 protocol First packet-switching network, but now mostly used in Europe. Replaced in U.S. by Frame Relay.

XTAG A locally significant numerical value assigned by the MLS-SE to each MLS-RP in the layer 2 network. *See also: MLS-SE, MLS-RP.*

ZIP Zone Information Protocol: A session-layer protocol used by Apple-Talk to map network numbers to zone names. NBP uses ZIP in the determination of networks containing nodes that belong to a zone. *See also: ZIP storm* and *zone.*

ZIP storm A broadcast storm occurring when a router running AppleTalk reproduces or transmits a route for which there is no corresponding zone name at the time of execution. The route is then forwarded by other routers downstream, thus causing a ZIP storm. *See also: broadcast storm* and *ZIP.*

zone A logical grouping of network devices in AppleTalk. *See also: ZIP.*

Index

Note to the Reader: Throughout this index **boldfaced** page numbers indicate primary discussions of a topic. *Italicized* page numbers indicate illustrations.

NUMBERS

100BaseT, 55, **579**
100BaseTX, **579**
10Base T
    comparing with FastEthernet and Gigabit Ethernet, 60–61
    definition of, **601**
    distance and, 56
    using at Access Layer, 55
10Base T/UTP, 54
10Base2/Thinnet, 54
10Base5/Thicknet, 54
20/80 rule, 8
    definition of, **603**
    network design and, 10
    overview of, 8–9
80/20 rule, 7
    definition of, **554**
    overview of, 6–7

A

A&B bit signaling, **526**
AAA, **526**
AAL (ATM Adaptation Layer), **526**
AARP (AppleTalk Address Resolution Protocol), **527**
ABM (Asynchronous Balanced Mode), **527**
ABR (Area Border Router), 369, **527**
Abstract Syntax Notation One (ASN.1), **532**
access control lists (ACLs)
    definition of, **527**
    MLS-RP configuration and, 283
access layer
    10Base T and, 55
    access policies and, 425, 444–446
    Cisco hierarchy and, 24–25
    configuration of, 86
    configuring switches for, 86–89
    definition of, **527**
    MAC addresses and, 444–445
    port security and, 446
    switches at, 25
access layer commands. *See* commands, Catalyst 1900
access links
    definition of, **527**
    overview of, 113
access lists
    definition of, **527**
    distribution layer and, 447–449
    guidelines for, 449
access methods, **527**
access policies, 424–464
    access layer and, 444–446
        MAC addresses and, 444–445
        port security and, 446
    banners and, 441–442
    commands for, 454–455
    distribution layer and, 447–452
        access lists and, 447–449
        wildcards and, 450–452
    HTTP access and, 443–444
    key terms for, 454
    overview of, 424–425
    passwords and, 427–437
        CLI-based switches and, 435–436
        encryption and, 433–435
        login option and, 431–432
        router passwords and, 427–431
        session time-outs and, 432
        set-based switches and, 436–437
    physical security and, 426–427
    privilege levels and, 438–440
    review, answers, 463–464
    review, questions, 457–461
    route filtering and, 452–453
    VTY access and, 442–443

access rate, 527
access servers, 527
accounting, 528
acknowledgement (ACK), 528
ACLs. *See* access control lists (ACLs)
ACR (allowed cell rate), 528
active monitor, 528
active router, 317
address learning, *152*
    definition of, 528
    layer 2 switches and, 151, 152–153
address mapping, 528
address resolution, 528
Address Resolution Protocol (ARP)
    broadcast communication and, 343
    definition of, 531
    finding MAC addresses with, 316
Address Translation Gateway (ATG), 532
adjacency, 528
administrative distance, 528
administrative weight, 529
ADSU (ATM Data Service Unit), 529
advertisements
    definition of, 529
    RP and, 396–397
    VTP and, *124, 125*
AEP (AppleTalk Echo Protocol), 529
AFI (Authority and Format Identifier), 529
AFP (AppleTalk Filing Protocol), 529
AIP (ATM Interface Processor), 529
algorithms
    definition of, 529
    distance-vector routing algorithm, 551
    DUAL algorithm, 552
    link-state routing algorithm, 569
    LZW algorithm, 571
    SPF algorithm, 595
    STA algorithm, 594
    STP and, 157
alignment errors, 529
all-routes explorer packet, 529
allowed cell rate (ACR), 528
Alternate Market Inversion (AMI), 530
AM (Amplitude Modulation), 529
American National Standards Institute (ANSI), 530
American Standard Code for Information Interchange (ASCII), 531
AMI (Alternate Market Inversion), 530

amplitude, 530
Amplitude Modulation (AM), 529
analog, 530
ANSI (American National Standards Institute), 530
anycast, 530
AppleTalk, 530
AppleTalk Address Resolution (AARP), 527
AppleTalk Control Program (ATCP), 532
AppleTalk Echo Protocol (AEP), 529
AppleTalk Filing Protocol (AFP), 529
AppleTalk Remote Access (ARA), 531
AppleTalk Session Protocol (ASP), 532
AppleTalk Transaction Protocol (ATP), 533
AppleTalk Update-based Routing Protocol (AURP), 534
application layer, 531
Application-Specific Integrated Circuits (ASICs)
    definition of, 531
    filter tables and, 150
ARA (AppleTalk Remote Access), 531
Architecture for Voice, Video and Integrated Data (AVVID), 535
area, 531
Area Border Router (ABR), 369, 527
ARM (Asynchronous Response Mode), 531
ARP. *See* Address Resolution Protocol (ARP)
ASB (Asynchronous Balanced Mode), 527
ASBR (Autonomous System Boundary Router), 531
ASCII (American Standard Code for Information Interchange), 531
ASICs. *See* Application-Specific Integrated Circuits (ASICs)
ASN.1 (Abstract Syntax Notation One), 532
ASP (AppleTalk Session Protocol), 532
assessment test, xxiv–liii
    answers, xlviii–liii
    questions, xxiv–xlvii
AST (Automatic Spawning Tree), 532
AS. *See* autonomous system (AS)
Asynchronous Balanced Mode (ASB), 527
asynchronous connections, 532
asynchronous dial-up, 532
Asynchronous Response Mode (ARM), 531
Asynchronous Time-Division Multiplexing (ATDM), 532
Asynchronous Transfer Mode (ATM), 533
asynchronous transmission, 532
ATCP (AppleTalk Control Program), 532

ATDM (Asynchronous Time-Division
    Multiplexing), 532
ATG (Address Translation Gateway), 532
ATM ARP server, 533
ATM (Asynchronous Transfer Mode), 533
ATM Data Service Unit (ADSU), 529
ATM endpoint, 533
ATM Forum, 533
ATM Interface Processor (AIP), 529
ATM layer, 533
ATM user-user connection, 533
ATMM (ATM Management), 533
ATP (AppleTalk Transaction Protocol, 533
attenuation, 534
AURP (AppleTalk Update-based Routing
    Protocol), 534
AURP tunnel, 534
authentication, 534
Authority and Format Identifier (AFI), 529
authority zones, 534
authorization, 534
auto duplex, 534
auto-negotiation, 58
Auto-RP, 535
automatic call reconnection, 534
Automatic Spawning Tree (AST), 532
autonomous confederation, 534
autonomous switching, 534
autonomous system (AS)
    definition of, 534
    MOSPF and, 369
Autonomous System Boundary Router (ASBR), 531
autoreconfiguration, 535
auxiliary password, 429–430
auxiliary ports, 535
AVVID (Architecture for Voice, Video and
    Integrated Data), 535

B

B channel, 536
B8ZS (Binary 8-Zero Substitution), 535
back end, 535
backbone, 535

BackboneFast, 209–210
    configuring and verifying, 209–210
    overview of, 209
Backward Explicit Congestion Notification
    (BECN), 536
bandwidth
    contention media and, 52
    definition of, 535
    demands on, 340
    performance problems and, 5
Bandwidth on Demand (BoD), 535
banners, 441–442
baseband, 535
Basic Management Setup, 535
Basic Rate Interface (BRI), 537
baud, 536
beacon, 536
bearer service, 536
BECN (Backward Explicit Congestion
    Notification), 536
BGP$, 536
bidirectional shared trees
    definition of, 536
    distribution with, 362–363, *363*
binary, 536
Binary 8-Zero Substitution (B8ZS), 535
BISDN (Broadband ISDN), 536
Bit Interleaved Parity (BIP), 536
bit-oriented protocol, 537
blocking, 160
BoD (Bandwidth on Demand), 535
books. *See* reference books
Boot ROM, 537
border gateways, 537
border routers, 537
Boston Software, exam preparation questions, xxxii
BPDUs. *See* Bridge Protocol Data Units (BPDUs)
BRI (Basic Rate Interface), 537
bridge ID, 158, 537
Bridge Protocol Data Units (BPDUs)
    definition of, 537
    STP and, 158–159
bridges
    compared with switches, 151
    definition of, 537
bridging, 537
broadband, 538
Broadband ISDN (BISDN), 536

broadcast and unknown servers (BUS), 539
broadcast communication, 342
    definition of, 538
    forward/filter decisions and, 154
    networks and, 340
    overview of, 342–343
    performance problems and, 6
broadcast control, 101–102
broadcast domains
    definition of, 538
    routers and, 226
broadcast storms
    definition of, 538
    loop avoidance and, *155*
broadcast traffic, 312
brute force attacks, 538
buffers, 538
bursting, 538
bus, 539
BUS (broadcast and unknown servers), 539
bus topology, 539
BX.25, 539
bypass mode, 539
bypass relay, 539
byte-oriented protocol, 539

C

cable media, 52–55
    IEEE 802 project and, 53–54
    overview of, 52–53
    switch block connections and, 62–64
        connecting to console port, 62–63
        connecting to Ethernet port, 63
        startup and, 63–64
    switched Ethernet and, 54–55
cable modems, 539
cable range, 539
CAC (Connection Admission Control), 539
cache, MLS cache, 270–275
    displaying entries, 287
    making entries, 288
    removing entries, 288
call admission control, 540

call priority, 540
call set-up time, 540
CAM (Content Addressable Memory), 358
campus networks
    Cisco products for, 25–27
        access layer switches and, 25
        core layer switches, 26–27, 26–27
        distribution layer switches, 26
    elements of, 27–35
        core blocks, 29–32
        layer 2 backbones, 32–34
        layer 3 backbones, 34–35
        switch blocks, 28
    hierarchical model for, 20–25
        access layer of, 24–25
        core layer of, 23
        distribution layer of, 23–24
        overview of, 20–22
    history of, 4–9
        20/80 rule, 8–9
        80/20 rule, 6–7
        bandwidth and, 5
        broadcast and multicast and, 6
        collisions and, 4–5
    key terms for, 36
    new model for, 10–12
        features of, 10–11
        network services and, 10–11
    overview of, 2–4
    review, answers, 48–50
    review, questions, 39–47
    switching technologies for, 12–20
        layer 2 switching, 15–17
        layer 3 switching, 18–19
        layer 4 switching, 19
        multi-layer switching, 19–20
        OSI model and, 12–15
        routing and, 17
candidate packets, 271
    definition of, 540
    identifying, 270–272
Canonical Format Indicator (CFI), 116
Carrier Detect (CD), 540
Carrier Sense Multiple Access/Collision Detection (CSMA/CD)
    10BaseT and, 55
    definition of, 547
    FastEthernet and, 56

Catalyst 1900
   clearing VLANs from trunk links, 119
   configuring trunk ports for, 119
   enabling/disabling spanning tree on, 165–166
   erasing configuration of, 81
   FragmentFree switching and, 163–164
   inter-VLAN routing and, 242–244
   interface for, 73–74
   setting descriptions, 75–76
   setting hostname, 69
   setting IP information, 71–72
   setting passwords, 66–68
   setting port speed and duplex, 77–78
   startup and, 64
   static VLANs and, 109–112
   verifying IP connectivity, 79
   VTP configuration for, 131
Catalyst 5000
   clearing VLANs from trunk links, 119
   configuring trunk ports for, 117–118
   enabling/disabling spanning tree on, 166–168
   erasing configuration of, 80–81
   inter-VLAN routing and, 244–247
   interface for, 72–73
   NFFC and, 266
   RSM and, 234–235
   setting descriptions, 75
   setting hostname, 68–69
   setting IP information, 70–71
   setting passwords, 65–65
   setting port speed and duplex, 76–77
   startup and, 63–64
   static VLANs and, 108–109
   verifying IP connectivity, 79
   VTP configuration for, 130–131
Catalyst 6000, 266
CBR (Constant Bit Rate), **540**
CBT. *See* Core Base Trees (CBT)
CCDA (Cisco Certified Design Associate), xxv–xxvi
CCDP (Cisco Certified Design Professional), xxxvi
CCIE (Cisco Certified Internetwork Expert), xix, xxiii–xxv
   requirements for, xxiii–xxiv
   skills needed for, xxiv–xxv
CCNA: Cisco Certified Network and Associate Study Guide, xviii
CCNA (Cisco Certified Network Associate), xx
CCNA Virtual Lab e-trainer, xxxii–xxxiii

CCNP (Cisco Certified Network Professional)
   exams required for, xxii–xxiii
   overview of, xx–xxiii
   skills needed for, xxi–xxii
CCNP: Remote Access Study Guide, xxii
CCNP: Support Study Guide, xxii
CD, accompanying book, xxxi–xxxiii
   Boston Software exam preparation, xxxii
   CCNA Virtual Lab e-trainer, xxxii–xxxiii
   EdgeTest, xxxi
   electronic flashcards, xxxi–xxxii
   PDF reference books, xxxii
CD (Carrier Detect), **540**
CDP (Cisco Discovery Protocol), **540**
CDVT (Cell Delay Variation Tolerance), **540**
cell, **540**
Cell Delay Variation Tolerance (CDVT), **540**
Cell Error Ratio (CER), **541**
Cell Loss Priority (CLP), **544**
Cell Loss Ratio (CLR), **544**
cell payload scrambling, **541**
cell relay, **541**
Cell Transfer Delay (CTD), **547**
Central Office)CO), **544**
Centrex, **541**
CER (Cell Error Ratio), **541**
certification programs
   CCDA, xxv–xxvi
   CCDP 2.0, xxxvi
   CCIE, xviii, xxiii–xxv
   CCNA 2.0, xx
   CCNP 2.0, xx–xxiii
CFI (Canonical Format Indicator), 116
CGMP. *See* Cisco Group Management Protocol (CGMP)
Challenge, **541**
Challenge Handshake Authentication Protocol (CHAP), **541**
Channel Interface Processor (CIP), **542**
Channel Service Unit (CSU), **547**
channelized E1, **541**
channelized T1, **541**
CHAP (Challenge Handshake Authentication Protocol), **541**
character mode connections, **542**
checksum, **542**
choke packets, **542**
CID (Cisco Internetwork Design), xxiii

CIDR (Classless Interdomain Routing), **542**
CIP (Channel Interface Processor), **542**
CIR (Committed Information Rate), **542**
circuit switching, **542**
Cisco
    Catalyst products, 25–27
        access layer switches, 25
        core layer switches, 26–27
        distribution layer switches, 26
    history of, xviii–xx
    IOS software, xix, 61–62, 543
Cisco Certified Design Associate (CCDA), xxv–xxvi
Cisco Certified Design Professional (CCDP), xxxvi
Cisco Certified Internetwork Expert (CCIE), xix,
    xxiii–xxv
    requirements for, xxiii–xxiv
    skills needed for, xxiv–xxv
Cisco Certified Network Associate (CCNA) 2.0, xx
Cisco Certified Network Professional (CCNP) 2.0
    exams required for, xxii–xxiii
    overview of, xx–xxiii
    skills needed for, xxi–xxii
Cisco Discovery Protocol (CDP), **540**
Cisco Frame-Relay Access Device
    (Cisco FRAD), **542**
Cisco Group Management Protocol (CGMP),
    357–358
    CGMP join, *357*, 357–358
    definition of, **541**
    enabling, 386, 402–404
    host management and, 358
    IP multicast and, 389
Cisco hierarchical model, 20–25, *21*, *22*
    access layer, 24–25
    applying policies to, 425
    core layer, 23
    distribution layer, 23–24
    lab for, 37–38
    overview of, 20–22
Cisco Internetwork Design (CID), xxiii
CiscoFusion, **543**
CiscoView, **543**
Class A networks, **543**
Class B networks, **543**
Class C networks, **543**
Class D IP addresses, 500, 510–514
classical IP over ATM, **543**
Classless Interdomain Routing (CIDR), **542**

classless routing, **543**
CLI-based switches, 435–436
client mode, VTP, 123
clocking, **544**
CLP (Cell Loss Priority), **544**
CLR (Cell Loss Ratio), **544**
CO (Central Office), **544**
collapsed backbone
    definition of, **544**
    VLANs and, 103–105
collapsed core, *30*
    definition of, **544**
    overview of, 30–31
collision domains
    definition of, **544**
    layer 2 switches and, 226
collisions
    definition of, **544**
    performance problems and, 4–5
commands, Catalyst 1900
    banner, 441, 455, 488
    Ctrl+Shift+6 then x, 488
    duplex, 73, 77, 83, 488
    enable password, 435, 454, 488
    enable password level, 67, 83, 488
    enable secret, 436, 454, 488
    hostname, 69, 83, 488
    interface, 134, 489
    interface ethernet module/port, 73, 83, 489
    interface fastethernet module/port, 74, 83, 489
    ip address, 71, 83, 489
    no spantree, 169, 489
    no trunk-vlan, 119, 134, 489
    port-channel mode, 203, 211, 489
    port-secure mac-mac-count, 446, 455, 489
    privilege mode, 438, 439–440, 455, 489
    sh mac-address-table, 445, 455, 489
    show run, 76, 83, 489
    show spantree, 166–168, 169, 192, 194, 197,
        204, 211, 489
    show trunk, 120–121, 134
    show uplink-fast, 208, 211, 490
    show uplink-fast statistics, 208, 211, 490
    show vtp, 130–131, 134, 490
    shutdown, 73, 83, 490
    spantree, 165, 169, 490
    spantree priority, 196, 211, 490
    spantree start-forwarding, 206, 211, 490

spantreecost, 192, 211
trunk, 490
uplink-fast, 208, 211, 490
vlan, 108, 134, 490
vlan-membership, 111, 134, 490
vtp mode, 129, 134, 490
vtp name, 129, 134, 490
vtp password, 129, 134, 490
commands, Catalyst 5000
   clear mls entry destination, 288, 292, 491
   clear trunk, 119, 134, 491
   interface vlan, 235, 239, 491
   ip cgmp [proxy], 403, 406, 491
   ip igmp join-group group-address, 399, 406
   ip igmp version (2|1), 402, 406, 491
   ip multicast-routing, 390, 405, 492
   ip multicast ttl-threshold ttl, 398, 405, 491
   ip pim dense-mode, 392, 405, 492
   ip pim rp-address, 492
   ip pim rp-address ip-address, 395, 405
   ip pim send-rp-announce, 397, 405, 492
   ip pim send-rp-discovery scope ttl, 398, 405, 492
   ip pim sparse-dense-mode, 394, 405, 492
   ip pim sparse-mode, 393, 405, 492
   mac-address, 237, 239, 492
   mls rp ip, 276, 291, 492
   mls rp management-interface, 280, 292, 492
   mls rp vlan-id, 279, 292, 493
   mls rp vtp-domain, 278, 292, 493
   mtrace, 401, 406, 493
   ping, 400, 406, 493
   session, 233, 239, 493
   set cgmp enable, 403, 406, 493
   set enablepass, 65–66, 84, 436, 437, 454, 493
   set interface sc0, 70, 84, 493
   set ip route, 238, 239, 493
   set mls agingtime, 285, 292, 493
   set mls agingtime fast, 286, 292, 493
   set mls enable, 284, 291, 493
   set password, 65–66, 84, 436, 454, 494
   set port channel, 200, 203, 211, 494
   set port duplex, 77, 84, 494
   set port speed, 76, 84, 494
   set prompt, 68–69, 83, 494
   set spantree, 165, 169, 494
   set spantree backbonefast, 187, 209, 212, 494
   set spantree fwddelay, 187, 212, 494
   set spantree hello, 187, 212, 494
   set spantree maxage, 187, 212, 494
   set spantree portcost, 191, 211, 494
   set spantree portfast, 187, 205, 212, 494
   set spantree portpri, 193–194, 211, 494
   set spantree portvlanpri, 195, 211, 494
   set spantree root, 187, 189, 211, 495
   set spantree uplinkfast, 187, 207, 212, 495
   set trunk, 117, 134, 495
   set vlan, 108–109, 134, 495
   set vtp domain, 128–129, 134, 495
   set vtp mode, 129, 134, 495
   set vtp password, 128, 134, 495
   sh port capabilities, 495
   show config, 73, 84, 236, 239, 495
   show mls, 269, 291, 495
   show mls entry, 284, 287, 292, 495
   show mls rp, 281, 292, 495
   show mls rp interface, 281, 292, 495
   show mls rp vtp-domain, 281, 292, 495
   show module, 232–233, 239, 496
   show port capability, 201, 212
   show port channel, 203, 204, 212, 496
   show spantree, 166–168, 169, 189–190, 195–196, 211, 496
   show spantree uplinkfast, 208, 212, 491
   show vlan, 110, 111–112, 134, 496
   show vtp domain, 130, 134, 277–278, 291, 496
   time-out, 437, 455, 496
commands, used on routers
   access-class, 443, 455, 496
   debug standby, 321, 322, 323, 496
   distribute-list, 452, 455, 496
   exec-timeout, 432, 454, 496
   ip http access-class, 443, 455, 497
   ip http authentication local, 455, 497
   ip proxy-arp, 310, 322, 497
   line aux, 429, 454, 497
   line console, 429, 454, 497
   line vty, 429, 454, 497
   login local, 432, 454, 497
   no ip proxy-arp, 310, 322, 497
   no service password-encryption, 455, 497
   service password-encryption, 433, 455, 497
   show ip arp, 316, 322, 497
   show ip interface ethernet 0, 309, 322, 498
   show standby, 315, 321, 322, 498
   standby, 320, 322, 498
   standby 1 authentication, 320, 323, 498

standby 1 preempt, 320, 323, 498
standby 1 priority, 320, 322, 498
standby 1 track serial 0 50, 318, 323, 498
username, 431–432, 454, 498
Committed Information Rate (CIR), **542**
Common Part Convergence Sublayer (CPCS), 547
Common Spanning Tree (CST)
    advantages/disadvantages of, 184
    definition of, **183**, 547
    IEEE 802.1q and, 182
composite metrics, **544**
compression, **545**
configuration register, **545**
congestion, **545**
congestion avoidance, **545**
congestion collapse, **545**
Connection Admission Control (CAC), **539**
connection ID, **545**
connection-oriented, **545**
connectionless, **545**
console password, 430
console port, **545**
Constant Bit Rate (CBR), **540**
Content Addressable Memory (CAM), 358
contention media, 52, **545**
control direct VCC, **546**
control distribute VCC, **546**
convergence
    definition of, **546**
    fast convergence and, 10, 34
    STP and, 161–162
Core Base Trees (CBT)
    data distribution with, 373
    overview of, 373–374
core blocks, 29, 29–32
    collapsed core and, *30*, 30–31
    core size and, 32
    definition of, 27, **546**
    dual core and, 31–32
    Gigabit Ethernet and, 60
    overview of, 29–30
core layer
    applying policies at, 425
    Cisco hierarchy and, 23
    definition of, **546**
    switches at, 26–27
costs, **546**
count to infinity, **546**

coup, 317
CPCS (Common Part Convergence Sublayer), **547**
CPE (Customer Premises Equipment), **547**
crankback, **547**
CRC. *See* cyclic redundancy checks (CRCs)
CSMA/CD (Carrier Sense Multiple Access/Collision Detection). *See* Carrier Sense Multiple Access/Collision Detection (CSMA/CD)
CST. *See* Common Spanning Tree (CST)
CSU (Channel Service Unit), **547**
CTD (Cell Transfer Delay), **547**
custom queuing, **548**
Customer Premises Equipment (CPE), **547**
cut-through frame switching
    definition of, **548**
    LAN switch methods, 163–164
cyclic redundancy checks (CRCs)
    definition of, **547**
    store-and-forward switching and, 163, 164

D

D channel, **549**
data communications equipment (DCE), **549**
data compression. *See* compression
Data Country Code (DCC), **549**
data direct VCC, **548**
data encapsulation, *14*
    definition of, **548**
    OSI model and, 13–15
Data Exchange Interface (DXI), **552**
data frames, **548**
Data Link and Medium Access Control (DLMAC), 53
Data-Link Connection Identifier (DLCI), **551**
data link control layer, **548**
data link layer, **548**–**549**
Data Service Unit (DSU), **552**
Data Set Ready (DSR), **552**
data terminal equipment (DTE), **552**
Datagram Delivery Protocol (DDP), **549**
datagrams, **548**
DCC (Data Country Code), **549**
DCE (data communications equipment), **549**

DCN (Designing Cisco Networks) exam, xxv
DDP (Datagram Delivery Protocol), 549
DDR (dial-on-demand routing), 549
DE bit, 549
DE (Discard Eligibility), 549
debug, MLS, 282
default route, 550
delay, 550
demarc, 550
demodulation, 550
demultiplexing, 550. *See also* multiplexing
denial-of-service attack, 550
designated bridges, 550
designated ports
    definition of, 550
    root bridges and, 157
    selecting, 159–160
designated routers, 550
Designing Cisco Networks (DCN), xxv
destination address, 551
Destination Service Access Point (DSAP), 551
deterministic failover, 10
deterministic paths, 10
dial backup, 551
dial-on-demand routing (DDR), 549
Diffusing Update Algorithm (DUAL), 552
digital, 551. *See also* analog
Digital, Intel, Xerox (DIX), 53
Digital Subscriber Line (DSL), 552
directed broadcast, 551
Discard Eligibility (DE), 549
discovery mode, 551
DISL (Dynamic ISL), 116
Distance Vector Multicast Routing Protocol
    (DVMRP), 367
    definition of, 552
    overview of, 366–367
    preparing for IP multicast and, 387
distance-vector routing algorithm, 551
distribution layer
    access lists and, 447–449
    access policies and, 425, 447–452
    Cisco hierarchy and, 23–24
    configuration of, 86
    configuring switches for, 86–89
    definition of, 551
    switches at, 26
    wildcards and, 450–452

distribution layer commands. *See* commands,
    Catalyst 5000
distribution lists, 447, 551
distribution trees, 359–363
    shared trees and, 361–363
    source tree and, 359–361
DIX (Digital, Intel, Xerox), 53
DLCI (Data-Link Connection Identifier), 551
DLMAC (Data Link and Medium Access
    Control), 53
Domain Name System (DNS), 551
DSAP (Destination Service Access Point), 551
DSL (Digital Subscriber Line), 552
DSR (Data Set Ready), 552
DSU (Data Service Unit), 552
DTE (data terminal equipment), 552
DTP (Dynamic Trucking Protocol), 116
dual core blocks, *31*, 31–32
DUAL (Diffusing Update Algorithm), 552
duplex
    Catalyst 1900, 77–78
    Catalyst 5000, 76–77
    full-duplex Ethernet, 57–58
DVMRP. *See* Distance Vector Multicast Routing
    Protocol (DVMRP)
DXI (Data Exchange Interface), 552
dynamic entries
    definition of, 553
    MAC addresses and, 445
Dynamic ISL (DISL), 116
dynamic routing
    definition of, 553
    fault-tolerant routing and, 306, 312
Dynamic Trucking Protocol (DTP), 116
dynamic VLANs
    definition of, 553
    overview of, 107–108

E

E channel, 553
E1, 553
E.164, 553
EARL (Enhanced Address Recognition Logic), 199

EBC (Ethernet Bundle Controller), 199
edge devices, 553
EdgeTest, xxxi
EEPROM (Electronically Erasable Programmable Read-Only Memory), 553
EFCI (Explicit Forward Congestion Indication), 553
EIGRP (Enhanced EIGRP), 555
EIP (Ethernet Interface Processor), 554
ELAN (Emulated LAN), 554
ELAP(EtherTalk Link Access Protocol), 554
electronic flashcards, xxxi–xxxii
Electronically Erasable Programmable Read-Only Memory (EEPROM), 553
Emulated LAN (ELAN), 554
enable packets, 272
    definition of, 554
    identifying, 272–274
enable password
    CLI-based switches and, 435–436
    overview of, 428–429
    set-based switches and, 437
encapsulation, 554
encryption
    definition of, 554
    passwords and, 433–435
end-to-end VLANs
    definition of, 554
    VLAN boundaries and, 106
Enhanced Address Recognition Logic (EARL), 199
Enhanced EIGRP (EIGRP), 555
enterprise networks, 555
enterprise services
    definition of, 555
    network services and, 11
Erasable Programmable Read-Only Memory (EPROM), 555
error correction, 555
ESF (Extended Superframe), 555
Ether Talk, 555
EtherChannel, 199–204
    configuring, 200–204
    FastEtherChannel and, 199–200
    guidelines for, 200
Ethernet, 555
Ethernet Bundle Controller (EBC), 199
Ethernet Interface Processor (EIP), 554
Ethernet media
    10Base T, 55–56
    FastEthernet, 56–58
    Gigabit Ethernet, 59–61

Ethernet_II, 54
EtherTalk Link Access Protocol (ELAP), 554
exams
    assessment test, xxiv–liii
        answers, xlviii–liii
        questions, xxiv–xlvii
    CCIE Routing and Switching, xxiv
    CCNA, xviii
    CCNP
        Remote Access exam (640-505), xxii
        Routing exam (640-503), xxii
        Support exam (640-506), xxii
        Switching exam (640-504), xviii, xxii, xxviii–xxix, xxxi
    Cisco Internetwork Design (640-025), xxiii
    Designing Cisco Networks (640-441), xxv
    Foundation R/S exam (640-509), xxiii
    locations for taking, xxviii
    practice exam, 465–486
        answers, 481–486
        questions, 465–480
    study methods for, xxx–xxxi
    tips for taking, xviii–xxix
excess rate, 555
exec banners, 442
expansion, 556
expedited delivery, 556
Explicit Forward Congestion Indication (EFCI)), 553
explorer packets, 556
extended access lists, 448
extended IP access lists, 556
extended IPX access lists, 556
Extended Setup, 556
Extended Superframe (ESF), 556
external route processors. *See also* routers
    configuring, 230–232
    definition of, **226**, 556
    enabling MLS and, 276–277

F

failure domains, 556
fallback, 556
Fast EtherChannel, 557
Fast Serial Interface Processor (FSIP), 560
fast switching, 557

FastEthernet, 56–59
    auto-negotiation and, 58
    comparing with 10BaseT and Gigabit Ethernet, 60–61
    definition of, 557
    distance and, 58–59
    full-duplex Ethernet and, 57–58
    inter-VLAN routing and, 230
    MII and, 57
    specifications for, 56–57, 82
    using at all layers, 56
FastEthernet Interface Processor (FEIP), 557
fault-tolerant routing, 307–313. *See also* Hot Standby Routing Protocol (HSRP)
    commands for, 322–323
    dynamic routing protocols and, 312
    IRDP and, 313
    key terms for, 322
    labs for, 324–330, *325*
    overview of, 306
    Proxy ARP and
        advantages/disadvantages of, 312
        disabling on Cisco routers, 310–312
        enabling on Cisco routers, 309–310
        implementing with routers, 308–309
        origins of, 307–308
FDDI. *See* Fiber Distributed Data Interface (FDDI)
FDM (Frequency-Division Multiplexing), 557
FECN (Forward Explicit Congestion Notification), 557
FEIP (FastEthernet Interface Processor), 557
Fiber Distributed Data Interface (FDDI)
    definition of, 557
    fault tolerance in, 306
File Transfer Protocol (FTP), 560
filter tables, 150
filtering
    bridges and switches and, 151
    forward/filter decisions and, 153
firewalls, 557
Flash, 558
flash memory, 558
flat networks, *101*, 558
flooding
    definition of, 558
    PIM DM and, 369–370
flow, 558
flow control, 558

Forward Explicit Congestion Notification (FECN), 557
forwarding
    layer 2 switches and, 153–154
    STP states and, 160
Foundation R/S exam (640-509), xxiii
FRAD (Frame Relay Access Device), 558
fragmentation, 558
FragmentFree
    definition of, 559
    LAN switch methods and, 163–164
fragments, 558
frame identification. *See* frame tagging
frame modification, 273–274, *274*
Frame Relay, 559
Frame Relay Access Device (FRAD), 558
Frame Relay Access Support (FRAS), 559
Frame Relay bridging, 559
Frame Relay switching, 559
frame tagging
    definition of, 559
    VLAN identification and, 113
frames
    definition of, 559
    frame modification and, 273–274
    LAN switching modes and, *163*
    multiple copies of, 155–156, *156*
framing, 559
FRAS (Frame Relay Access Support), 559
frequency, 559
Frequency-Division Multiplexing (FDM), 557
FSIP (Fast Serial Interface Processor), 560
FTP (File Transfer Protocol), 560
full duplex
    definition of, 560
    FastEthernet and, 57–58
full mesh, 560

G

gateways, 237–238
GDA (Group Destination Address), 357
Generic Routing Encapsulation (GRE), 560
Get Nearest Server (GNS), 560

Gigabit EtherChannel, 199. *See also* Fast EtherChannel
Gigabit Ethernet, 59–61
    comparing with 10BaseT and FastEthernet, 60–61
    definition of, **560**
    inter-VLAN routing and, 230
    protocol architecture for, 60
    time slots and, 61
    using in switch, core, and server blocks, 59–60
Gigabit Media Independent Interface (GMII), 60
global configuration mode
    setting passwords from, 428
    setting usermode and enable mode passwords from, 435
GMII (Gigabit Media Independent Interface), 60
GNS (Get Nearest Server), **560**
grafting
    definition of, **560**
    PIM DM and, 372
GRE (Generic Routing Encapsulation), **560**
Group Destination Address (GDA), 357
Group of Four, **561**
Group-Specific Query, IGMPv2, 355–356
groups
    joining, 399–402
    multicast communication and, 351–352
guard band, **561**

H

H channel, **561**
half duplex, **561**
handshake, **561**
HDLC (High-Level Data Link Control), **561**
helper addresses, **561**
hierarchical addressing, **561**
hierarchical model, Cisco. *See* Cisco hierarchical model
hierarchical networks, **561**
High-Level Data Link Control (HDLC), **561**
High Level Interface (HILI), 53
High-Speed Communication Interface (HSCI), **562**
High-Speed Serial Interface (HSSI), **562**

HILI (High Level Interface), 53
HIP (HSSI Interface Processor), **561**
holddown, **562**
hop, **562**
hop count, **562**
host addresses, **562**
host names
    Catalyst 1900, 69
    Catalyst 5000, 68–69
host-to-host communication, 341
Hot Standby Routing Protocol (HSRP), 313–321
    configuring, *315*, 315–319
        active router properties and, 317
        HSRP tracking and, 318–319
    definition of, **562**
    fault tolerance in, 306
    multiple destinations and, *319*, 319–320
    multiple groups and, *320*, 320–321
    overview of, 313–314
    review, answers, 337–338
    review, questions, 331–335
    router states and, 314
HSCI (High-Speed Communication Interface), **562**
HSRP. *See* Hot Standby Routing Protocol (HSRP)
HSSI (High-Speed Serial Interface), **562**
HSSI Interface Processor (HIP), **561**
HTTP access, 443–444
hubs, **562**

I

IANA (Internet Address Name Authority), 346, 500
ICD (International Code Designator), **562**
ICMP. *See* Internet Control Message Protocol (ICMP)
ICMP Router Discovery Protocol (IRDP)
    definition of, **567**
    fault tolerant routing and, 306, 313
IEEE (Institute of Electrical and Electronics Engineers)
    802 project of, 53
    802.1, **563**
    802.10 (FDDI), 114
    802.1d, 157

802.1q
  CST and, 182
  overview of, 114
  VLAN identification and, 115–116
802.3
  cabling standards and, 54
  definition of, 563
802.3z, 60
802.5, 563
  comparing IEEE STP with Cisco STP, 182–185
  definition of, 563
IETF (Internet Engineering Task Force), 500
IGMP. See Internet Group Management Protocol (IGMP)
IGMP Join process, 354, 354, 563
IGMP Leave process, 356, 356, 563
IGMP Query process, 352–354, 353, 564
IGP (Interior Gateway Protocol), 564
ILMI (Integrated Local Management Interface), 564
in-band management, 427, 564
in-band signaling, 564
inbound access lists, 449
Installing and Maintain Cisco Routers (IMCR), course, xxiii
Institute of Electrical and Electronics Engineers. See IEEE (Institute of Electrical and Electronics Engineers)
insured burst, 564
Integrated (or Interim) Local Management Interface (ILMI), 564
Integrated Services Digital Network (ISDN), 567
Inter-Switch Link Protocol (ISL)
  definition of, 567
  inter-VLAN routing, external configuration, 230–232
  inter-VLAN routing, internal configuration, 232–238
    assigning MAC addresses to VLAN interfaces, 237
    defining default gateways, 237–238
    route processors and, 232–235
    RSM and, 235–237
  overview of, 114
  VLAN identification and, 114–115
inter-VLAN routing. See virtual LANs (VLANs), routing between
interarea routing, 564
interface processors, 564

Interior Gateway Protocol (IGP), 564
internal route processors
  configuring, 232–238
  definition of, 229, 564
International Code Designator (ICD), 562
International Telecommunication Union Telecommunication Standardization Sector (ITU-T), 567
Internet, 564–565
internet, 565
Internet Address Name Authority (IANA), 346, 500
Internet Control Message Protocol (ICMP)
  definition of, 563
  fault tolerance in, 306
  IRDP and, 313
Internet Engineering Task Force (IETF), 500
Internet Group Management Protocol (IGMP)
  changing versions of, 402
  definition of, 563
  IP multicast and, 389
Internet Group Management Protocol Version 1 (IGMPv1), 352–355
  changing, 402
  processes of, 352
    IGMP Join, 354, 354
    IGMP Leave, 355
    IGMP Query, 352–354, 353
Internet Group Management Protocol Version 2 (IGMPv2), 355–356
  changing, 402
  processes of
    IGMP Leave, 356, 356
    IGMP Query, 355–356
Internet multicast address. See multicast addresses
Internet protocol, 565
Internet Protocol (IP), 566
internetwork, 565
Internetwork Packet Exchange (IPX), 566
internetworking, 565
Internetwork Operating System (IOS). See IOS software
intra-area routing, 565
Intranets, 16
intruder detection, 565
Inverse ARP (Inverse Address Resolution Protocol), 565
IOS based switches, 62
IOS software, xix, 61–62, 543

IP access lists, 448
IP addresses, 566
IP connectivity, verifying
    Catalyst 1900, 79
    Catalyst 5000, 79
    mtrace and, 401–402
    ping and, 400–401
IP Control Program (IPCP), 566
IP information
    Catalyst 1900, 71–72
    Catalyst 5000, 70–71
IP (Internet Protocol), 566
IP multicast, 386–422. *See also* multicast
        communication
    changing IGMP version, 402
    commands for, 405–406
    definition of, 566
    enabling CGMP, 402–404
        router configuration, 403
        switch configuration, 403–404
    enabling IP routing, 389–391, 389–391
    enabling PIM, 391–394, 391–394
        configuration options for, 391
        IP PIM dense mode, 392
        IP PIM sparse-dense mode, 393–394
        IP PIM sparse mode, 392–393
    end-to-end deployment of, 388
    joining multicast groups, 399–402
    key terms for, 404–405
    labs for, 407–413, *408*
    planning for, 387
    rendezvous points and, 395–398
    reserved addresses for, 345–346
    review, answers, 421–422
    review, questions, 414–419
    testing IP connectivity and, 400–402
        mtrace, 401–402
        ping, 400–401
    TTL and, 398–399
IPCP (IP Control Program), 566
IPX access lists, 448
IPX Control Program (IPXCP), 566
IPX (Internetwork Packet Exchange), 566
IPX spoofing, 566
IPXCP (IPX Control Program), 566
IPXWAN, 567
IRDP. *See* ICMP Router Discovery
ISDN (Integrated Services Digital Network), 567

ISL. *See* Inter-Switch Link Protocol (ISL)
isochronous transmission, 567
ITU-T (International Telecommunication Union
        Telecommunication Standardization
        Sector), 567

L

LAN Emulation Address Resolution Protocol (LE
        ARP), 569
LAN Emulation Client (LEC), 569
LAN Emulation Configuration Server (LECS), 569
LAN Emulation (LANE), 114, 567
LAN Emulation Network-to-Network Interface
        (LNNI), 570
LAN Emulation Server (LES), 569
LAN Emulation User-to-Network Interface
        (LUNI), 571
LAN switches
    cut-through method, 163–164
    definition of, 568
    FragmentFree method, 163–164
    store-and-forward method, 163–164
LANs (local area networks)
    connected to routers, *104*
    definition of, 570
LAPB (Link Access Procedure, Balanced), 568
LAPD (Link Access Procedure on the D
        channel), 568
latency, 568
layer 2, 340
layer 2 addresses, 349
layer 2 switches, 15–17
    collision domains and, 226
    definition of, 568
    functions of, 151–156
        address learning, 151, 152–153
        forward/filter decisions and, 151, 153–154
        loop avoidance, 151, 154–156
    limitations of, 16–17
    overview of, 15–16
    scaling, 32–34
layer 3, 340
layer 3 addresses, 349

layer 3 routing, 232
layer 3 switches. *See also* Multi-Layer
    Switching (MLS)
  definition of, 568
  inter-VLAN routing and, 226
  overview of, 18–19
  scaling, 34–35
layer 4 switches, 19
layered architecture, 568
LCP (Link Control Protocol), 568
LE ARP (LAN Emulation Address Resolution
    Protocol), 569
leaky buckets, 568
learning bridges
  definition of, 569
  STP states and, 160
leased lines, 569
LEC (LAN Emulation Client), 569
LECS (LAN Emulation Configuration Server), 569
LES (LAN Emulation Server), 569
Link Access Procedure, Balanced (LAPB), 568
Link Access Procedure on the D channel
    (LAPD), 568
link compression. *See* compression
Link Control Protocol (LCP), 568
link-state advertisements (LSAs), 368, 571
link-state routing algorithm, 569
listening, 160
LLAP (LocalTalk Link Access Protocol), 570
LLC (Logical Link Control), 53, 570
LMI, 570
LNNI (LAN Emulation Network-to-Network
    Interface), 570
load balancing
  layer 3 switches and, 34
  Proxy ARP and, 312
local area networks (LANs). *See* LANs (local area
    networks)
local explorer packets, 570
local loops, 570
local services
  definition of, 570
  network services and, 11
local VLANs
  definition of, 570
  VLAN boundaries and, 106–107
LocalTalk, 570
LocalTalk Link Access Protocol (LLAP), 570

Logical Link Control (LLC), 53, 570
login authentication, 444
login banners, 442
login command options, 431–432
loop avoidance
  definition of, 571
  layer 2 switches and, 151, 154–156
  multiple loops and, 156
  STP and, 157
LSAs (link-state advertisements), 368, 571
LUNI (LAN Emulation User-to-Network
    Interface), 571
LZW algorithm, 571

M

MAC addresses
  address learning and, 152–153
  assigning to VLAN interfaces, 237
  definition of, 571
  MAC address table and, 444–445
MAC (Media Access Control). *See* Media Access
    Control (MAC)
MacIP, 571
mainframe blocks, 27
MAN (metropolitan area networks), 571
Management Information Base (MIB), 573
Manchester encoding, 572
mapping
  IP multicast to Ethernet, 346–350
  RP mapping agent and, 398
MASBR (Multicast Autonomous Border
    Router), 369
maximum burst, 572
Maximum Burst Size (MBS), 572
Maximum Cell Delay Variation (MCDV), 572
Maximum Cell Loss Ratio (MCLR), 572
Maximum Cell Transfer Delay (MCTD), 573
maximum transmission unit (MTU), 575
MBGP (Multicast Border Gateway Protocol), 387
MBONE (multicast backbone), 387, 572
MBS (Maximum Burst Size), 572
MCDV (Maximum Cell Delay Variation), 572
MCLR (Maximum Cell Loss Ratio), 572

MCR (Minimum Cell Rate), **573**
MCTD (Maximum Cell Transfer Delay), **573**
Media Access Control (MAC)
  access layer and, 444–445
  address learning and, 152–153
  ARP and, 316
  assigning MAC addresses to VLAN interfaces, 237
  definition of, **571**
  forward/filter decisions and, 153
  layer 2 switches and, 150
  MAC address table and, 444–445
  multicast communication and, 346–347, 347, 348
  unicast communication and, 341
Media Independent Interface (MII), 57, 60
metropolitan area networks (MAN), **571**
MIB (Management Information Base), **573**
MII (Media Independent Interface), 57, 60
Minimum Cell Rate (MCR), **573**
minimum rate, 572
MIP (Multichannel Interface Processor), **573**
mips, **573**
MLP (Multilink PPP), **573**
MLS. *See* Multi-Layer Switching (MLS)
MLS-RP. *See* Multilayer Switching Route Processor (MLS-RP)
MLS-SE. *See* Multilayer Switching Switching Engine (MLS-SE)
MLSP. *See* Multilayer Switching Protocol (MLSP)
MLSP discovery
  definition of, **267**
  overview of, 268, *268*
MMP (Multichassis Multilink PPP), **574**
modem, **574**
modem eliminator, **574**
modemcap database, **574**
modulation, **574**
MOSPF. *See* Multicast Open Shortest Path First (MOSPF)
MP bonding (MultiPoint bonding), **574**
MPOA (Multiprotocol over ATM), **574**
MSA management, 280
MSFC. *See* Multilayer Switch Feature Card (MSFC)
mtrace (multicast traceroute)
  definition of, **575**
  testing IP multicast connectivity and, 401–402
MTU (maximum transmission unit), **575**

Multi-Layer Switching (MLS), 264–304
  commands for, 291–292
  definition of, **573**
  fundamentals, 264–276
    disabling MLS, 275–276
    MLS cache, 270–275
    MLS procedures, 266–267
    MLS requirements, 266
    MLSP discovery, 268
    router on a stick, *265*
    XTAGs, 269–270
  key terms for, 291
  labs for, 293–295, *294*
  MLS engine configuration, 283–288
    displaying cache entries, 287
    enabling MLS on MLS-SE, 283–288
    making cache entries, 284–286
    removing cache entries, 288
    verifying, 286
  MLS-RP configuration, 276–283
    access lists and, 283
    enabling MLS, 276–277
    interface configuration, 279–280
    MSA management configuration, 280
    verifying, 281–282
    VLAN assignments, 279
    VTP domain assignments, 277–278
  NetFlow Feature Card (NFFC) and, 229
  overview of, 19–20
  review, answers, 302–304
  review, questions, 296–300
  topologies for, 288–290
    multiple switches, one router, 288, *289*
    router on a stick, 288, *289*
    single switch, two routers, 288, **290**
multicast addresses
  contact information for, 515–523
  definition of, **575**
  group assignments for Class D IP Addresses, 510–514
  multicast RFCs and, 514–515
  table of, 501–510
Multicast Autonomous Border Router (MASBR), 369
multicast backbone (MBONE), 387, 572
Multicast Border Gateway Protocol (MBGP), 387
multicast communication, 340–384, **344**
  bridging function of, 340

multicast groups – network devices, managing 623

definition of, **575**
forward/filter decisions and, 154
internetworks and, 350–358
    CGMP and, 357–358
    IGMPv1 and, 352–355
    IGMPv2 and, 355–356
    subscribing and maintaining groups, 351–352
key terms for, 376
multicast addressing and, 345–350
    mapping IP multicast to Ethernet, 346–350
    reserved addresses and, 345–346
network design and, 11
overview of, 343–344
performance problems and, 6
review, answers, 382–384
review, questions, 377–380
routing traffic and, 358–375
    distribution trees and, 359–363
    managing delivery, 363–364
    protocols for, 365–372
    sparse mode protocols for, 372–375
    TTL and, 364–365
multicast groups, **575**
Multicast Open Shortest Path First (MOSPF), 367–369
    definition of, **574**
    inter-area and inter-AS, 368–369
    intra-area, 368
multicast protocols
    overview of, 365–372
    sparse mode protocols, 372–375
multicast send VCC, **575**
Multichannel Interface Processor (MIP), **573**
Multichassis Multilink PPP (MMP), **574**
Multilayer Switch Feature Card (MSFC)
    definition of, **575**
    enabling MLS and, 276
    MLS requirements and, 266
multilayer switches, **575**
multilayer switching, **575**
Multilayer Switching Protocol (MLSP), 229
    definition of, **573**
    MLS components and, 266
    MSA management and, 280
Multilayer Switching Route Processor (MLS-RP)
    access lists and, 283
    definition of, **573**
    enabling MLS, 276–277

    interface configuration, 279–280
    MLS components and, 266
    MSA management configuration, 280
    verifying, 281–282
    VLAN assignments, 279
    VTP domain assignments, 277–278
Multilayer Switching Switching Engine (MLS-SE)
    definition of, **574**
    displaying cache entries, 287
    enabling MLS on, 283–288
    making cache entries, 284–286
        modifying cache aging time, 285
        modifying fast aging time, 285–286
    MLS components and, 266
    removing cache entries, 288
    verifying, 286
Multilink PPP (MLP), **573**
multiple links, 227, 227–228
multiplexing, **576**
MultiPoint (MP) bonding, **574**
Multiprotocol over ATM (MPOA), **574**
multiprotocol support, 11

N

NAK (negative acknowledgement), **576**
Name Binding Protocol (NBP), **576**
NAT (Network Address Translation), **576**
NBP (Name Binding Protocol), **576**
neighboring routers, **576**
NetBEUI, **576**
NetBIOS, **576**
NetFlow Feature Card (NFFC)
    definition of, **577**
    MLS requirements and, 266
    multi-layer switching and, 229
NetView, **577**
NetWare, **577**
NetWare Link Services Protocol (NLSP), **578**
network access servers. *See* access servers
Network Address Translation (NAT), **576**
network addresses, **577**
network devices, managing, 426–444
    banners and, 441–442

HTTP access and, 442–443
  passwords and, 427–437
    Catalyst 1900, 66–68
    Catalyst 5000, 65–65
    CLI-based switches and, 435–436
    encryption and, 433–435
    login option and, 431–432
    router passwords, 427–431
    session time-outs and, 432
    set-based switches and, 436–437
  physical security and, 426–427
  privileged levels and, 438–440
  VTY access and, 442–443
Network File System (NFS), 577
network interface cards (NICs), 445, 577
network layers, 577
Network Management Processor (NMP), 578
Network Management Stations (NMSs), 435
network segmentation, 6
network services
  enterprise services, 11
  local services, 11
  remote services, 11
network termination 1 (NT1), 578
network termination 2 (NT2), 578
networks. *See also* campus networks
  broadcast communication and, 340
  flat networks, *101*
Next Hop Resolution Protocol (NHRP), 577
NFFC. *See* NetFlow Feature Card (NFFC)
NFS (Network File System), 577
NHRP (Next Hop Resolution Protocol), 577
NICs (network interface cards), 445, 577
NLSP (NetWare Link Services Protocol), 578
NMP (Network Management Processor), 578
node addresses, 578
non-stub area, 578
Non-Volatile RAM (NVRAM)
  definition of, 579
  erasing switch configuration and, 80–81
nondesignated ports, 578. *See also* designated ports
Nonreturn to Zero Inverted (NRZI), 578
Nonreturn to Zero (NRZ), 578
NT1 (network termination 1), 578
NT2 (network termination 2), 578
NVRAM (Non-Volatile RAM)
  definition of, 579
  erasing switch configuration and, 80–81

O

OC (Optical Carrier), 579
octet, 579
one-time challenge tokens, 579
ones density, 579
Open Shortest Path First (OSPF)
  definition of, 580
  multicast and, 367
  wildcards and, 450
Open Systems Interconnection (OSI), 13
  data encapsulation and, 13–15
  definition of, 579, 580
  layers and functions of, 12–13
  multicast and, 340
Optical Carrier (OC), 579
Organizationally Unique Identifier (OUI), 580
OSI. *See* Open Systems Interconnection (OSI)
OSPF. *See* Open Shortest Path First (OSPF)
OUI (Organizationally Unique Identifier), 580
out-of-band management, 427, 580
out-of-band signaling, 580
outbound access lists, 449

P

Packet assembler and disassembler (PAD), 581
packet filters, 448
Packet Level Protocol (PLP), 583
packet mode connections, 581
Packet Switch Exchange (PSE), 585
packet-switched network (PSN), 585
packet switches, 581
packet switching, 581
packets. *See also* Protocol Data Units (PDUs)
  candidate packets, 270–272
  definition of, 580
  enable packets, 272–274
  fields in, 265
  layer 3 switching and, 267
  MLS-SE and, 274–275
PAD (Packet assembler and disassembler), 581

PAgP (Port Aggregation Protocol), 204–205
parity checking, **581**
partial mesh, **581**
passwords, 427–437
    Catalyst 1900, 66–68
    Catalyst 5000, 65–65
    CLI-based switches and, 435–436
    encryption and, 433–435
    login option and, 431–432
    router passwords and, 427–431
    session time-outs and, 432
    set-based switches and, 436–437
PAT (port address translation), **581**
path costs. *See* costs
payload compression, **582**. *See also* compression
PCR (Peak Cell Rate), **582**
PDN (Public Data Network), **582**
PDUs. *See* Protocol Data Units (PDUs)
Peak Cell Rate (PCR), **582**
peer problems, 35
Per-VLAN Spanning Tree (PVST)
    advantages/disadvantages of, 183–184
    definition of, **183**, **586**
    spanning tree protocols and, 165
Per-VLAN Spanning Tree+ (PVST+)
    advantages/disadvantages of, 184–185
    definition of, **586**
performance, networks
    20/80 rule, 8–9
    80/20 rule, 6–7
    bandwidth and, 4–5
    broadcasts and multicasts and, 6
    collisions and, 4–5
permanent virtual circuit (PVC), **586**
permanent virtual path (PVP), **586**
PFC. *See* Policy Feature Card (PFC)
PGP (Pretty Good Privacy), **582**
physical layer, **582**
physical security, 426–427
PIM dense mode (PIM DM)
    flooding and, 369–370, *370*
    grafting and, 372, *372*
    IP multicast and, 392
    pruning and, 370–371, *371*
PIM (Protocol Independent Multicast), 369
    definition of, **582**
    IP multicast configuration and, 391

PIM sparse mode (PIM SM), 393–394
    definition of, **583**
    IP multicast and, 392–393
    overview of, 374–375
    pruning and, *375*
ping
    definition of, **583**
    testing connectivity with, 78–79, 400–401
Plain Old Telephone Service (POTS), **584**
pleisochronous, **583**
PLP (Packet Level Protocol), **583**
PNNI (Private Network-Network Interface), **583**
Point Of Presence (POP), **584**
point-to-multipoint connection, **583**
point-to-point communication
    definition of, **583**
    unicast and, 340
Point-to-Point Protocol (PPP), **584**
poison reverse updates, **583**
Policy Feature Card (PFC)
    definition of, **582**
    MLS requirements and, 266
polling, **584**
POP (Point Of Presence), **584**
port address translation (PAT), **581**
Port Aggregation Protocol (PAgP), 204–205
PortFast, 205–206
    configuring, 205–206
    overview of, 205
ports
    bridges and switches, 151
    density, **584**
    security
        access layer and, 446
        definition of, **584**
    speed
        Catalyst 1900, 77–78
        Catalyst 5000, 76–77
    STP and
        selecting designated ports, 159–160
        selecting port states, 160–162
        setting port cost, 191–193
        setting port priority, 193–197
POTS (Plain Old Telephone Service), **584**
PPP callback, **584**
PPP (Point-to-Point Protocol), **584**

practice exam, 465–486. *See* exams, practice exam
   answers, 481–486
   questions, 465–480
Predictor, **584**
presentation layer, **584**
Pretty Good Privacy (PGP), **582**
PRI (Primary Rate Interface), **585**
priority queuing, **585**
Private Network-Network Interface (PNNI), **583**
privilege levels, 438–440
process switching, **585**
programmable read-only memory (PROM), **585**
propagation delays, **585**
Protocol Data Units (PDUs)
   definition of, **582**
   OSI encapsulation and, 14
   unicast and, 341
Protocol Independent Multicast dense (PIM DIM) mode. *See* PIM dense mode (PIM DM)
Protocol Independent Multicast (PIM). *See* PIM (Protocol Independent Multicast)
Protocol Independent Multicast sparse (PIM SM) mode. *See* PIM sparse mode (PIM SM)
protocol stacks, **585**
protocols, **585**
Proxy Address Resolution Protocol (Proxy ARP)
   advantages/disadvantages of, 312
   definition of, **585**
   dial-up connections and, *308*
   disabling on Cisco routers, 310–312
   enabling on Cisco routers, 309–310
   fault tolerance in, 306
   implementing with routers, *308*, 308–309
   origins of, 307–308
pruning
   definition of, **585**
   PIM DM and, 370–371
   PIM SM and, *375*
PSE (Packet Switch Exchange), **585**
PSN (packet-switched network), **585**
PSTN (Public Switched Telephone Network), **586**
Public Data Network (PDN), **582**
Public Switched Telephone Network (PSTN), **586**
PVC (permanent virtual circuit), **586**
PVP (permanent virtual path), **586**
PVP tunneling, **586**
PVST. *See* Per-VLAN Spanning Tree (PVST)
PVST+. *See* Per-VLAN Spanning Tree+ (PVST+)

Q

QoS (Quality of Service), **586**
Quality of Service (QoS), **586**
queues, **586**
queuing, **586**

R

R reference point, **586**
RADIUS (Remote Access Dial-in User Service), **586**
random access memory (RAM), **587**
RARP (Reverse Address Resolution Protocol), **587**
rate queue, **587**
RCP (Remote Copy Protocol), **587**
read-only memory (ROM), **588**
redistribution, **587**
redundancy
   definition of, **182**, **587**
   STP and
      BackboneFast and, 209–210
      EtherChannel and, 199–204
      Port Aggregation Protocol and, 204–205
      PortFast and, 205–206
      UplinkFast and, 206–208
reference books
   CCNA: *Cisco Certified Network and Associate Study Guide*, xviii
   CCNP: *Remote Access Study Guide*, xxii
   CCNP: *Routing Study Guide*, xxii
   CCNP: *Support Study Guide*, xxii
   PDF reference books on CD, xxxii
reference points, **587**
reliability, **587**
reload, **587**
remote access, **587**
Remote Access Dial-in User Service (RADIUS), **586**
Remote Copy Protocol (RCP), **587**
remote services
   definition of, **587**
   network services and, 11

rendezvous points (RPs), 395–398
    auto configuration, 396–398
        advertising RP group assignments, 396–397
        default RPs, 396–397
        RP mapping agent and, 398
    definition of, 590
    IP multicast networks and, 386
    manual configuration, 395–396
    placement of, 387
Request for Comments. See RFCs (Request for Comments)
Request To Stand (RTS), 590
reserved addresses, 345–346
Reverse Address Resolution (RARP), 587
Reverse Path Forwarding (RPF), 363–364, 392
reversed Telnet, 588
revision number, VTP, 126
RFCs (Request for Comments)
    definition of, 588
    multicast addresses and, 514–515
RIF (Routing Information Field), 588
ring, 588
ring topology, 588
RIP (Routing Information Protocol), 588
RIP version 2, 588
RJ connector, 588
robbed bit signaling, 588
ROM (read-only memory), 588
root bridges
    configuring, 186–191
    determining, 186
    overview of, 157
    STP and, 158–159
route bridges, 589
route filtering, 452–453
route poisoning, 589
route summarization, 589
Route Switch Feature Card (RSFC)
    definition of, 590
    layer 3 routing with, 232
    RSMs and, 229
Route Switch Modules (RSMs), 229–230
    broadcasts and, 102
    configuring, 232–235
    creating VLANs on, 235–237
    definition of, 590
    internal route processors and, 226, 229
        layer 3 routing with, 232
        MLS and, 265
Route/Switch Processor (RSP), 590
routed protocols, 589
router passwords, 427–431
    auxiliary password, 429–430
    console password, 430
    enable password, 428–429
    Telnet password, 430–431
routers. See also external route processors
    broadcast domains and, 226
    compared with switches, 105
    definition of, 589
    inter-VLAN routing and, 232–235
    LANs connected to, *104*
    multiple links and, *227*
routers on a stick, 265, *288*, *289*, 589
routing
    definition of, 589
    overview of, 17
routing domains, 590
Routing Information Field (RIF), 588
Routing Information Protocol (RIP), 588
routing metrics, 590
routing protocols, 590
routing tables, 590
RP mapping agent, 398
RPF (Reverse Path Forwarding), 363–364, 392
RPs. See rendezvous points (RPs)
RSFC. See Route Switch Feature Card (RSFC)
RSMs. See Route Switch Modules (RSMs)
RSP (Route/Switch Processor), 590
RTS (Request To Stand), 590

S

S reference point, 591
sampling rate, 591
SAP (Service Access Point), 591
SAP (Service Advertising Protocol), 591
scalability
    network infrastructure, 10
    VLANs and, 103
SCR (Sustainable Cell Rate), 591

scripts, **591**
SDLC (Synchronous Data Link Control), **591**
security. *See also* passwords
    physical security, 426–427
    policies, **591**
    servers, **591**
    VLANs and, 102–103
seed routers, **591**
Sequence Packet Exchange (SPX), **595**
Serial Tunnel (STUN), **598**
server blocks
    definition of, 27
    Gigabit Ethernet and, 60
Server farms, 16
server mode, VTP, 123
servers, **592**
Service Access Point (SAP), **591**
Service Advertising Protocol (SAP), **591**
Service Profile Identifier (SPID), **595**
session layer, **592**
session time-outs, 432
set-based, 62, 436–437, **592**
setup mode, **592**
SF (super frame), **592**
shared trees
    definition of, **592**
    distribution with, 361–363, *362*
Shortest Path First (SPF) algorithm, **595**
Signal Quality Error (SQE), **596**
signaling packets, **592**
Signaling System 7 (SS-7), **596**
silicon switching, **592**
Silicon Switching Engine (SSE), **596**
Simple Mail Transfer Protocol (SMTP), **593**
simplex, **592**
sliding windows, **593**
SLIP (Serial Line Internet Protocol), **593**
small office, home office (SOHO), **593**
SMDS (Switched Multimegabit Data Service), **593**
SMTP (Simple Mail Transfer Protocol), **593**
SNA (System Network Architecture), **593**
SNAP (Subnetwork Access Protocol), **593**
snapshot routing, **593**
sockets, **593**
SOHO (small office, home office), **593**
SONET (Synchronous Optical Network), **594**
Source-Route Bridging (SRB), **596**
source-route translational bridging (SR/TLB), **596**

source-route transparent bridging (SRT), **596**
Source Service Access Point (SSAP), **596**
source trees
    definition of, **594**
    distribution with, 359–361, *361*
SP (Switch Processor), **594**
span, **594**
SPAN (Switched Port Analyzer), **594**
spanning explorer packet, **594**
spanning-tree algorithm (STA), **594**
Spanning Tree Protocol (STP), 156–168
    Cisco vs. IEEE versions, 182–185
        Common Spanning Tree (CST), 184
        Per-VLAN Spanning Tree (PVST), 183–184
        Per-VLAN Spanning Tree+ (PVST+), 184–185
    commands for, 169, 211–212
    configuring, 165–168
    default timers for, *161*
    definition of, **594–595**, **598**
    example using, 162–163
    key terms for, 210
    labs for, 213–216
    layer 2 backbone and, *33*, 33–34
    link costs and, 160
    overview of, 156–157
    port states and, 160–162
    redundant links and, 199–210
        BackboneFast and, 209–210
        EtherChannel and, 199–204
        Port Aggregation Protocol and, 204–205
        PortFast and, 205–206
        UplinkFast and, 206–208
    review, answers, 223–224
    review, questions, 171–176, 178–179, 217–221
    scaling for large networks, 185–199
        configuring root bridge, 186–191
        determining root bridge, 186
        setting port cost, 191–193
        setting port priority, 193–197
        setting timers, 197–199
    selecting designated ports, 159–160
    selecting root bridges, 158–159
spanning trees
    bridges and switches and, 151
    definition of, **594**
    operations of, *157*
    per-VLAN operation, 165

sparse mode protocols
   CBT, 373–374
   PIM SM, 374–375
sparse-dense mode interfaces. *See* PIM sparse mode (PIM SM)
SPF (Shortest Path First) algorithm, **595**
SPID (Service Profile Identifier), **595**
split horizon, **595**
spoofing, **595**
spooler, **595**
SPX (Sequence Packet Exchange), **595**
SQE (Signal Quality Error), **596**
SR/TLB (source-route translational bridging), **596**
SRB (Source-Route Bridging), **596**
SRT (source-route transparent bridging), **596**
SS-7 signaling (Signaling System 7), **596**
SSAP (Source Service Access Point), **596**
SSE (Silicon Switching Engine), **596**
STA (spanning-tree algorithm) (STA), **594**
Stac, **596**
standard access lists, 448
standard IP access list, **597**
standard IPX access list, **597**
star topology, **597**
startup range, **597**
state transitions, **597**
static routes, **597**
static VLANs
   configuring, 108–112
      Catalyst 1900, 108–109
      Catalyst 5000, 108–109
   definition of, **597**
   overview of, 107
statistical multiplexing, **597**
sticky-learn, **446**
STM-1 (Synchronous Transport Module Level 1), **597**
store-and-forward packet switching
   definition of, **598**
   LAN switch methods, 163–164
STP. *See* Spanning Tree Protocol (STP)
stub area, **598**
stub network, **598**
STUN (Serial Tunnel), **598**
subarea, **598**
subarea node, **598**
subchannel, **598**
subinterface, **598**

subnet, **598**
subnet addresses, **598**
subnet masks, **598**
subnetwork, **599**
Subnetwork Access Protocol (SNAP), **593**
super frame (SF), **592**
Sustainable Cell Rate (SCR), **591**
SVC (switched virtual circuit), **599**
switch blocks
   cabling, 62–64
      connecting to console port, 62–63
      connecting to Ethernet port, 63
      switch startup and, 63–64
   definition of, **27**, **599**
   Gigabit Ethernet and, 59
   overview of, 28
   review, answers, 96–98
   review, questions, 90–95
   size of, 28
   VLANs and, 105–112
      configuring static VLANs, 108–112
      defining VLAN boundaries, 106–107
      VLAN memberships, 107–108
switch-fabric, **112**, **599**
switch interfaces
   Catalyst 1900
      interface descriptions and, 75–76
      port access and, 73–74
   Catalyst 5000
      interface descriptions and, 75
      port access and, 72–73
Switch Processor (SP), **594**
switch topologies
   multiple switches, one router, 288, *289*
   router on a stick, 288, *289*
   single switch, two routers, 288, **290**
switched Ethernet
   definition of, **599**
   overview of, 54–55
switched LAN, **599**
Switched Multimegabit Data Service (SMDS), **593**
Switched Port Analyzer (SPAN), **594**
switched virtual circuit (SVC), **599**
switches
   Catalyst 1900
      erasing configuration, 81
      interface for, 73–74
      setting descriptions for, 75–76

setting hostname, 69
setting IP information, 71–72
setting passwords, 66–68
setting port speed and duplex, 77–78
verifying IP connectivity, 79
  Catalyst 5000
    erasing configuration, 80–81
    interface for, 72–73
    setting descriptions for, 75
    setting hostname, 68–69
    setting IP information, 70–71
    setting passwords, 65–65
    setting port speed and duplex, 76–77
    verifying IP connectivity, 79
  compared with bridges, 151
  compared with routers, 105
  definition of, **599**
  removing physical boundaries with, *104*
switching technologies, 12–20
  lab for, 36–37
  layer 2 switching, 15–17
  layer 3 switching, 18–19
  layer 4 switching, 19
  multi-layer switching, 19–20
  OSI model and, 12–15
  routing and, 17
Synchronous Data Link Control (SDLC), **591**
Synchronous Optical Network (SONET), **594**
synchronous transmission, **599**
Synchronous Transport Module Level 1 (STM-1), **597**
System Network Architecture (SNA), **593**

T

T reference point, **600**
T1, **600**
T3, **600**
TACACS+, **600**
Tag Protocol Identifier (TPID), 116
tag switching, **600**
tagged traffic, **600**
TCP header compression, **600**

TCP/IP (Transmission Control Protocol/Internet Protocol), **600**
TCP (Transmission Control Protocol), **600**
TDM (time division multiplexing), **600**
TE (terminal equipment), **601**
TE1, **601**
TE2, **601**
telco, **601**
Telnet, **601**
  setting Telnet passwords, 429, 430–431
  testing IP connectivity and, 78–79
terminal adapter, **601**
terminal emulation, **601**
terminal equipment (TE), **601**
tests. *See* exams
TFTP, **601**
Thicknet, **602**
Thinnet, **602**
time division multiplexing (TDM), **600**
time slots, 61
Time To Live (TTL)
  configuring for IP multicast, 398–399
  configuring thresholds for, 386
  definition of, **603**
  multicast traffic and, 364–365
  threshold utilization and, *365*
timers, STP, 197–199
token, **602**
token bus, **602**
token passing, **602**
Token Ring, **602**
Token Ring Interface Processor (TRIP), **603**
toll network, **602**
TPID (Tag Protocol Identifier), 116
trace, **602**
traceroute, 78–79
traffic shaping, **602**
Transmission Control Protocol/Internet Protocol (TCP/IP), **600**
Transmission Control Protocol (TCP), **600**
transparent bridging, **602**
transparent mode, VTP, 123
transport layer, **602**
TRIP (Token Ring Interface Processor), **603**
trunk links
  clearing VLANs from, 119
  definition of, **603**
  inter-VLAN routing and, 228, 228–229

overview of, 113
verifying, 120–121
Trunk Up-Down (TUD), **603**
trunking, 116–121
    clearing VLANs from trunk lines, 119
    configuring trunk ports, 117–118
    verifying trunk links, 120–121
TTL. *See* Time To Live (TTL)
TUD (Trunk Up-Down), **603**
tunneling, **603**

U

U reference point, **603**
UART (Universal Asynchronous Receiver/Transmitter), **603**
unicast communication, *342*
    definition of, **604**
    overview of, 341–342
    point-to-point communication and, 340
Unicast Source Address (USA), 357
unidirectional shared tree
    definition of, **604**
    distribution with, 362
Universal Asynchronous Receiver/Transmitter (UART), **603**
unnumbered frames, **604**
unshielded twisted pair (UTP), **604**
UplinkFast, 206–208
    configuring, 207–208
    overview of, 206–207
USA (Unicast Source Address), 357
User Datagram Protocol (UDP), **603**
usermode passwords
    assigning with line command, 429
    CLI-based switches and, 435
    set-based switches and, 437
UTP (unshielded twisted pair), **604**

V

Variable Bit Rate (VBR), **604**
VCC (Virtual Channel Connection), **604**
Versatile Interface Processor (VIP), **604**
VID (VLAN ID), 116
Virtual Channel Connection (VCC), **604**
virtual circuits, **604**
Virtual IP (VIP), **604**
virtual LANs (VLANs), 9, 100–148
    benefits of, 100–105
        broadcast control, 101–102
        collapsed backbone and, 103–105
        flexibility and scalability, 103
        security, 102–103
    broadcast problems and, 6
    controlling traffic patterns with, 9
    definition of, **605**
    identifying, 112–116
        802.1q and, 115–116
        frame tagging and, 113
        Inter-Switch Link Protocol and, 114–115
    inter-VLAN communication and, *241*
    key terms for, 133
    labs for, 135–139
    MLS-RP configuration and, 279
    review, answers, 147–148
    review, questions, 140–145
    scaling switch blocks for, 105–112
        configuring static VLANs, 108–112
        defining VLAN boundaries, 106–107
        VLAN memberships, 107–108
    trunking, 116–121
        clearing VLANs from trunk lines, 119
        configuring trunk ports, 117–118
        verifying trunk links, 120–121
    VTP and, 121–133
        adding switches to VTP domains, 131–132
        advertisements and, 123–125
        configuring, 126–131
        modes of operation of, 122–123
        pruning and, 132–133
        revision number for, 126
virtual LANs (VLANs), routing between, 226–262
    definition of, **565**
    ISL external and, 230–232

ISL internal and, 232–238
    assigning MAC addresses, 237
    defining default gateways, 237–238
    route processors and, 232–235
    RSM and, 235–237
key terms for, 238
labs for, 240–253
    external inter-VLAN routing, 241–252
    internal inter-VLAN routing, 252–253
options for, 226–230
    multiple links, 227–228
    route switch modules, 229–230
    single trunk link, 228–229
review, answers, 261–262
review, questions, 254–259
virtual ring, 604
Virtual Router Redundancy Protocol (VRRP), 306
VLAN ID (VID), 116
VLAN Management Policy Server (VMPS), 108
VLAN Trunk Protocol (VTP), 121–133, 121–133
    adding to VTP domains, 131–132
    advertisements and, 123–125, *124*, *125*
    configuring, 126–131
        Catalyst 1900, 131
        Catalyst 5000, 130–131
        domain, 128–129
        verifying configuration, 130
        version type, 127–128
        VTP mode, 129–130
    definition of, 605
    MLS-RP configuration and, 277–278
    modes of operation, *122*, 122–123
    revision number for, *126*
    VTP pruning and
        definition of, **132**, 605
        enabling, 132–133
VLANs. *See* virtual LANs (VLANs)
VLSM (variable-length subnet mask), 605
VMPS (VLAN Management Policy Server), 108
VPN (virtual private network), 605
VRRP (Virtual Router Redundancy Protocol), 306
VTP. *See* VLAN Trunk Protocol (VTP)
VTY access, 442–443. *See also* telnet

W

WAN blocks, **27**
WAN (wide area network), 605
weighted fair queuing, 605
wildcards
    definition of, 605
    distribution layer and, 450–452
windowing, 605
WinSock (Windows Sockets Interface), 606
workgroup switching, 606

X

X.25, 606
XTAGs
    definition of, 606
    unique identifiers of, 269–270

Z

ZIP storms, 606
zone, 606
Zone Information Protocol (ZIP), 606

SYBEX™ INTRODUCES

Mastering™ Cisco® Routers

Mastering™ Cisco® Routers
Chris Brenton
ISBN 0-7821-2643-X
708pp • $49.99

Designed for administrators and students who need to get up to speed quickly with Cisco routers

- Learn how to administer, configure, and manage Cisco routers
- Install, configure, and manage the Cisco Internetworking Operating System
- Implement secure and reliable virtual private networking

SYBEX®
www.sybex.com

SYBEX e-trainer™: Premium Value at an Affordable Price!

Virtual Test Centers™
simulated testing environment
from Sybex®

MCSE: Windows 2000 Professional Virtual Test Center
0-7821-3000-3 • US $49.99

A+ Virtual Test Center
0-7821-3006-2 • US $49.99

Network+ Virtual Test Center
0-7821-3007-0 • US $49.99

Java Virtual Test Center — Q2, 2001
0-7821-3008-9 • US $49.99

OCP: Oracle8i DBA Virtual Test Center — Q2, 2001
0-7821-3009-7 • US $89.99

CCNA Virtual Test Center
0-7821-3005-4 • US $49.99

Virtual Test Center

- Hundreds of challenging exam questions
- Supports drag-and-drop and hot-spot question formats (where appropriate)
- Computer adaptive testing capabilities
- Reporting features to help identify weak areas
- Detailed explanations & study references for all questions

STUDY — Study Guides / Virtual Trainers™

PRACTICE — Virtual Labs™ / Virtual Test Centers™

REVIEW — Exam Notes™

Also Available:

MCSE: Windows® 2000 Server Virtual Test Center
ISBN 0-7821-3001-1 • US $49.99

MCSE: Windows 2000 Network Infrastructure Administration Virtual Test Center
ISBN 0-7821-3002-X • US $49.99

MCSE: Windows 2000 Directory Services Administration Virtual Test Center
ISBN 0-7821-3003-8 • US $49.99

MCSE: Windows 2000 Core Requirements Virtual Test Center
ISBN 0-7821-3004-6 • US $149.96 • Covers 4 core MCSE exams!

For a complete list of Virtual Test Centers, visit **certification.sybex.com**.

Sybex—The Leader in Certification

SYBEX

The Best CCNP Switching Book/CD Package on

Get ready for Cisco's CCNP Switching exam with the most comprehensive and challenging sample tests anywhere!

The Sybex EdgeTests feature:

- Chapter-by-chapter exam coverage of all the review questions from the book
- Random tests that simulate the exam format from Cisco
- A bonus exam available only on the CD

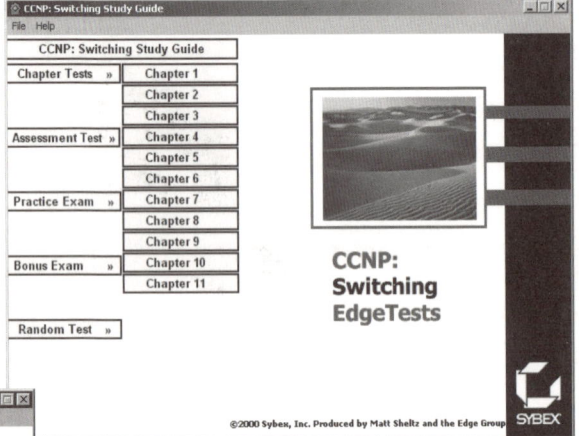

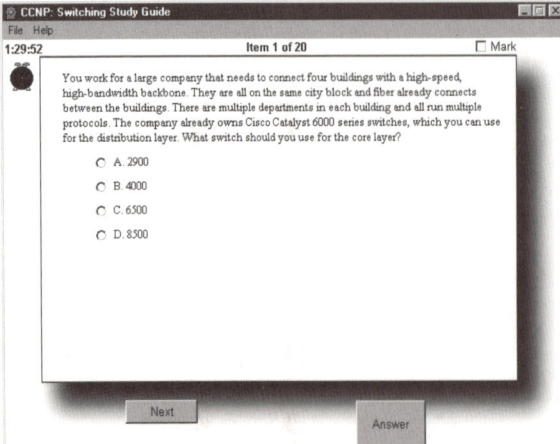

Use the Electronic Flashcards to jog your memory and prep last-minute for the exam!

- Reinforce your understanding of key CCNP Switching exam concepts with more than 200 hardcore flashcard-style questions.

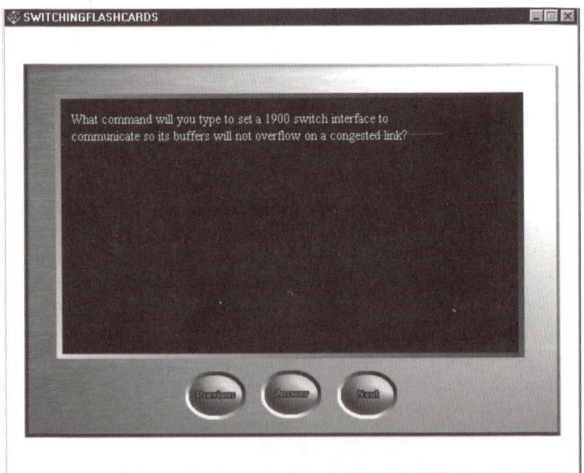

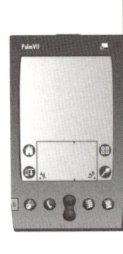

Electronic Flashcards now available for your Palm device as well!

- Download the Flashcards to your Palm device and go on the road. Now you can study for the CCNP Switching exam anywhere, any time.